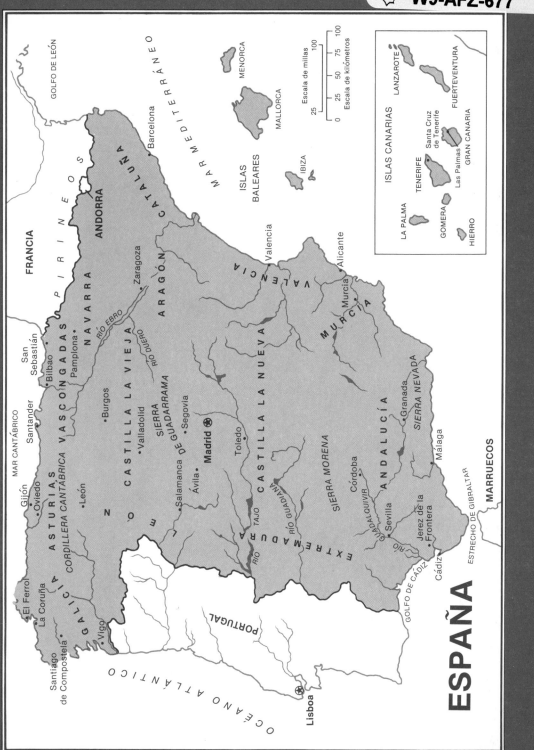

ESPAÑA

FRANCIA

GOLFO DE LEÓN

MAR MEDITERRÁNEO

MENORCA

MALLORCA

ISLAS BALEARES

IBIZA

Escala de millas
Escala de kilómetros

ISLAS CANARIAS

LANZAROTE

FUERTEVENTURA

Santa Cruz de Tenerife

TENERIFE

GRAN CANARIA

Las Palmas

LA PALMA

GOMERA

HIERRO

Barcelona

CATALUÑA

ANDORRA

P I R I N E O S

NAVARRA

Zaragoza

ARAGÓN

RÍO EBRO

RÍO DUERO

VALENCIA

Valencia

Alicante

Murcia

MURCIA

SIERRA NEVADA

Granada

Málaga

ANDALUCÍA

SIERRA MORENA

Córdoba

Sevilla

Jerez de la Frontera

RÍO GUADALQUIVIR

GUADIANA

RÍO

Cádiz

GOLFO DE CÁDIZ

ESTRECHO DE GIBRALTAR

MARRUECOS

San Sebastián

Bilbao

Pamplona

Burgos

VASCONGADAS

CORDILLERA CANTÁBRICA

MAR CANTÁBRICO

Santander

Gijón

Oviedo

ASTURIAS

León

Valladolid

CASTILLA LA VIEJA

SIERRA DE GUADARRAMA

Segovia

Madrid

Toledo

Salamanca

Ávila

CASTILLA LA NUEVA

RÍO TAJO

EXTREMADURA

GALICIA

El Ferrol

La Coruña

Santiago de Compostela

Vigo

OCÉANO ATLÁNTICO

PORTUGAL

Lisboa

¿HABLA ESPAÑOL?

AN INTRODUCTORY COURSE

◆

FOURTH EDITION

¿HABLA ESPAÑOL?

AN INTRODUCTORY COURSE

◆

FOURTH EDITION

TERESA MÉNDEZ-FAITH,
St. Anselm College

BEVERLY MAYNE KIENZLE,
Harvard University

With contributions by Deana M. Smalley

Harcourt Brace Jovanovich College Publishers
Fort Worth   Philadelphia   San Diego
New York   Orlando   Austin   San Antonio
Toronto   Montreal   London   Sydney   Tokyo

¿HABLA ESPAÑOL?

AN INTRODUCTORY COURSE

♦

FOURTH EDITION

Publisher **Vincent Duggan**
Associate Publisher **Marilyn Pérez-Abreu**
Developmental Editor **Kathleen DiNuzzo Ossip**
Project Editor **Julia Price**
Senior Project Manager **Françoise Leffler**
Design Supervisor **Kathie Vaccaro**
Production Manager **Priscilla Taguer**
Text and Cover Design **Grafica**
Cover Art **Richard Taddei**
Illustrations **Axelle Fortier**
Photo Research **Rona Tuccillo**
Compositor **Waldman Graphics**

Photo credits appear on page xviii.

Library of Congress Cataloging-in-Publication Data

Méndez-Faith, Teresa.
 ¿Habla español? : an introductory course / Teresa Méndez-Faith,
 Beverly Mayne Kienzle ; with contributions by Deana M. Smalley.—
 4th ed.
      p.   cm.
   English and Spanish.
   Includes index.
   ISBN 0-03-014158-3
   1. Spanish language—Textbooks for foreign speakers—English.
 I Kienzle, Beverly Mayne.   II. Smalley, Deana M.   III. Title.
 PC4129.E5M46 1989
 468.2'421—dc19   88-28237
                    CIP

**Harcourt Brace Jovanovich, Inc. would like to thank Edward David Allen,
Professor of Education at The Ohio State University, for his guidance and
inspiration over the life of *¿Habla español?* and for his valuable work on
previous editions.**

ISBN 0-03-013918-X

Printed in the United States of America

1 2 3 039 9 8 7 6 5

Harcourt Brace Jovanovich, Inc.
The Dryden Press
Saunders College Publishing

PREFACIO

This fourth edition of *¿Habla español? An Introductory Course,* a widely used program for first-year college Spanish, has been carefully revised in response to a comprehensive survey of users and the advice and suggestions of reviewers. As in previous editions, it presents the basic grammar of Spanish, introduces the culture of the contemporary Hispanic world, and provides for the development of listening, speaking, reading, and writing skills with a range of communicative activities for the classroom.

Changes to the Fourth Edition

1. The book has been shortened throughout so that it may be more easily completed in one academic year (two semesters or three quarters). Chapter 20 contains grammar points that are for recognition only; the future and conditional perfect and the passive are also presented for recognition only.

2. A section called **Funciones y actividades,** which features two or more language functions with explanations, examples, and activities, has been added to each chapter. The chapters therefore integrate a grammatical syllabus with a notional-functional one. Some examples of language functions covered are: beginning or ending conversations, agreeing or disagreeing, accepting or declining invitations, and expressing sympathy. Notional-functional material is integrated into the chapter and discussed and summarized at the beginning of the **Funciones y actividades** sections. These all-new sections contain a variety of activities integrating the grammar, vocabulary, and language of the chapter. Many are interactive, to be done in pairs or small groups, including role-plays.

3. The sequence of grammatical structures has been revised. Commands and the present progressive have been moved forward so that they are now covered in the first half of the book; the preterit is also presented earlier.

4. The amount of vocabulary has been decreased considerably, with more emphasis on high-frequency vocabulary words.

5. Many of the dialogues have been reworked to simplify them and/or make them more interesting. They are translated through Chapter 8.

6. The exercises have been revised to include new contextualized activities; some of the simpler drills, such as substitution exercises, have been eliminated.

7. Some of the grammatical explanations have been revised.

8. Cultural notes have been shortened and/or simplified.

9. Study hints have been condensed and occur in the first ten chapters only.

10. Pronunciation activities now occur only in the **Capítulo preliminar** of the text, although there will be pronunciation exercises in the laboratory manual and on tape.

11. The interchapter **lecturas** have been updated and in some cases rewritten.

12. Many of the photographs and drawings are new.

Organization

The fourth edition consists of a preliminary lesson and twenty chapters, with nine illustrated readings. The preliminary lesson emphasizes pronunciation and presents useful expressions, numbers 0-99, **hay, estar** and subject pronouns, negation, and a discussion of cognates. Each of the following twenty chapters focuses on a theme and a particular Hispanic country or one of the Hispanic communities of the United States and follows this sequence:

1. An illustrated presentation of thematic vocabulary with exercises.

2. Three to five grammar topics, each introduced by a mini-dialogue showing the structure in a natural context. The mini-dialogues are translated through Chapter 8, but beginning with Chapter 9 they are glossed with English definitions of words not previously presented. Grammar explanations are clear, concise, and thoroughly illustrated with example sentences. A broad spectrum of activities follows, from controlled to open-ended. Exercise instructions are in Spanish beginning with Chapter 12. Personalized questions, interviews, and small-group activities at the end of each grammar exercise section encourage students to internalize the structure and take a step toward genuine communication.

3. In the first ten chapters, a section of study hints suggests ways that students may improve the efficiency of their learning and acquire communication strategies.

4. A long dialogue followed by comprehension questions uses the new structures of the chapter to present further insight into Hispanic life; cultural notes in English describe customs and points of interest.

5. The section **Funciones y actividades** presents language functions and practices them with activities.

6. A list of active vocabulary concludes the chapter. The list begins with cognates that have been introduced at least twice in the chapter; these words are not defined as students are encouraged to recognize them. Other cognates may be used in the chapter, but if they are used only once they are not included in the active vocabulary list. Following the cognates section are verbs, thematic vocabulary, **Otras palabras y frases**, **Expresiones útiles** (which include those expressions from the **Funciones y actividades** sections that are practiced within the chapter), and, in some chapters, **Cognados falsos**, or false cognates.

The dialogues, example sentences, contextualized exercises, and communicative activities in a chapter all focus on the chapter's theme, country or region, and vocabulary, leading to a highly integrated, memorable language experience. Optional **lecturas** following every second chapter survey cultural and historical matters spanning the entire Hispanic world.

At the back of the text are appendices detailing Spanish rules of syllabication, accentuation, and capitalization; verb tables; Spanish-English and English-Spanish end vocabularies; a glossary of grammatical terms; and an index to the grammar and functions of the text. Entries in the Spanish-English end vocabulary include the number of the chapter or **lectura** where the word first occurs.

Supplementary Materials

1. *Workbook/lab manual.* In this fourth edition, the workbook and the laboratory manual have been combined. The workbook section provides writing practice and additional opportunities to use the vocabulary and grammatical structures introduced in class. Also included are four **Repasos**, which review key grammar points and provide self-test sections for students. The laboratory manual section, coordinated with the tape program, includes all exercise instructions and other necessary written or visual material related to the listening tasks.

2. *Laboratory tape program and tapescript.* The cassettes are available at no cost to institutions adopting the text. A complete tapescript for use by the laboratory director and by classroom instructors is available on request from Holt, Rinehart and Winston. The tape for each chapter includes a pronunciation section, one or more mini-dialogues or some other listening comprehension passage with exercises, new structural and vocabulary exercises, and a dictation or other written activity. The listening comprehension tasks involved are appropriate in level of difficulty for the chapters in which they appear, but instructors may want to recycle them subsequently in the course for extra listening practice and review.

3. *Testing Program.* The testing program to accompany this fourth edition provides an end-of-chapter test for the **Capítulo preliminar** and for each of the twenty regular chapters, as well as a cumulative final exam. Each test is divided into written and listening sections and evaluates student mastery of chapter vocabulary and grammar and reading, listening, and writing skills.

4. *Instructor's Annotated Edition.* This edition of the textbook includes numerous marginal annotations throughout, presenting practical suggestions, additional grammatical and vocabulary observations, and supplementary oral exercises.

5. *Software.* Study Disk™ software to accompany *¿Habla español?,* available in Apple and IBM versions, provides extra practice with the grammar and vocabulary of each chapter. The three-disk set includes more than 2300 items in the forms of drills, tests, and games for one or two students.

6. *Video.* Two proficiency-based videocassettes highlight real-life language and situations. Each of the 20 units includes a short dialogue dealing with a survival situation, a **minidrama,** and an unscripted, authentic cultural segment. A Viewer's Manual and a complete script are also available.

7. *Situation Cards.* A set of 144 *Situation Cards for Oral Proficiency* enable instructors to simulate the ACTFL proficiency interview. The cards focus on the functional situations presented in the **Funciones y actividades** section of the text, and an accompanying booklet provides suggestions for evaluating speaking ability.

8. *Overhead Transparencies.* Fifty full-color overhead transparency acetates may be used for teaching vocabulary or encouraging student description and discussion.

Acknowledgments

The authors would like to thank the following people from Holt, Rinehart and Winston for their help on this fourth edition: Marilyn Pérez-Abreu for initiating the project and for her guidance; Kathy Ossip for her excellent editing and review of the manuscript; Julia Price for so capably steering the manuscript through production, and Suzanne Shetler for a thorough copyediting. Thanks also to Ray Faith for his careful and painstaking work on the computerized end vocabularies. We are also grateful to the artist, Axelle Fortier, and to the following reviewers, whose comments, both favorable and critical, were instrumental in the development of this edition:

Victor Arizpe, *Texas A&M University;* Ed Colhoun, *Simon Fraser University;* Janis Cox, *Longview Community College;* Susana Durán, *Gulf Coast Community College;* Roger Fernández, *Los Angeles City College;* David A. Foltz, *Principia College;* David Foster, *Arizona State University;* Phyllis Golding, *Queens College;* John Gutiérrez, *University of Virginia, Charlottesville;* Steven Hutchinson, *University of Wisconsin, Madison;* Carlos Jerez-Farrán, *University of Notre Dame;* Américo López-Rodríguez, *Golden West College;* Jan Macian, *University of Missouri, Columbus;* Carlos E. Martín, *Central Washington University;* Gerald Petersen, *University of Nevada, Reno;* Stanley Rose, *University of Montana, Missoula;* Louise Rozwell, *Monroe Community College;* Jana Sandarg, *Augusta College;* Ruth Smith, *Northeast Louisiana University;* Cheryl Strand, *University of Washington, Seattle;* Judith Strozer, *University of Washington, Seattle;* Donna Wilson, *Highline Community College.*

PHOTO CREDITS

ÍNDICE GENERAL

¿HABLA ESPAÑOL?

AN
INTRODUCTORY
COURSE

◆

FOURTH EDITION

Estudiantes en una sala
de clase de la Universi-
dad Nacional Autónoma
de México (UNAM)

EN LA SALA DE CLASE

This preliminary chapter will help you start speaking Spanish. Learning to pronounce Spanish should be your first objective; listen carefully to your instructor and mimic what you hear. You probably will be able to guess the meaning of most words; you can look up the rest in the list at the end of the chapter or at the back of the book. This chapter is organized as follows:

Funciones

- Greetings
- Useful expressions

Vocabulario. In this introductory chapter you will talk about the classroom.

Gramática. You will discuss and use:

1. The pronunciation of vowels and diphthongs
2. The pronunciation of consonants and the rules for word stress
3. The cardinal numbers 0–99, and the expression **hay** (*there is, there are*)
4. The verb **estar** (*to be*) and subject pronouns
5. The formation of negative sentences

As you make your way through this introductory chapter, think pronunciation; hear the music of Spanish speech. Spanish speakers the world over welcome any sincere attempt to speak their language. If you try to pronounce as well as you can, they will see that your heart is in the right place, an assumption that is vital to the success of communication in any language.

LAS PRESENTACIONES (INTRODUCTIONS)

Buenos días. Me llamo
Elvira García. ¿Cómo se
llama usted, señorita?

Me llamo
Elena Ramírez.

Mucho gusto, señorita.
Igualmente, señora
García.

Y usted, señor,
¿Cómo se llama?

Me llamo
Miguel Guzmán.

Buenos días,
señor Guzmán.

PREGUNTAS *(QUESTIONS)*

In Spanish, **preguntas**, or *questions,* begin with an inverted question mark that
signals that a question will follow (**¿Cómo se llama?**). Similarly, Spanish
exclamations begin with an inverted exclamation point: **¡Salud!** *(Cheers!)* The
following **preguntas** are based on the dialogue of introductions you have just read
between **la profesora**, **la señorita**, and **el señor**. Answer them, using the cues in
parentheses.

   1. ¿Cómo se llama la profesora? (**Se llama Elvira...**)   2. ¿Cómo se llama la
señorita? (**Se llama Elena...**)   3. ¿Cómo se llama el señor? (**Se llama Miguel...**)   4. ¿Se llama Elena Ramírez la señorita? (**Sí, se llama...**)   5. ¿Cómo
se llama usted? (**Me llamo...**)

Diálogo.   In pairs, read the following dialogue aloud. One of you should take the
role of **Joaquín**, the other the role of **Francisca**.

   JOAQUÍN   Buenos días. Me llamo Joaquín Mendoza. ¿Cómo se llama
             usted, señorita?

FRANCISCA   Me llamo Francisca Contreras.
JOAQUÍN   Mucho gusto, Francisca.
FRANCISCA   Igualmente, Joaquín.

Now recreate the conversation, substituting your own names for those of **Joaquín** and **Francisca**.

En la Universidad Simón Bolívar, Caracas, Venezuela:
—Mucho gusto.
—Igualmente.

I.   Pronunciación: las vocales (vowels); los diptongos

A. Las vocales.   Spanish has five simple vowels, represented in writing by the letters **a, e, i** (or **y**), **o,** and **u.** Their pronunciation is short, clear, and tense. In the following examples the stressed syllables appear in bold type.

a   Similar in sound to the *a* in the English word *father,* but more open, tense, and short.
           Ana, pa**pá**, ma**má**, Cata**li**na, ba**na**na, A**de**la
e   Similar in sound to the *e* in the English word *met.*
           E**le**na, **Pe**pe, Te**re**sa, ele**fan**te, Fede**ri**co
i (y) Pronounced like the *i* in the English word *police.*
           y, di**fí**cil, sí, Cris**ti**na, cafete**rí**a, Mi**guel**, Isa**bel**
o   Similar in sound to the *o* in the English words *cord* and *cold.*
           no, An**to**nio, ofi**ci**na, hospi**tal**, **Pa**co, Teo**do**ro, doc**tor**
u   Pronounced like the *oo* in the English words *cool* and *fool* (never the sound of *oo* in *book* or of *u* in *cute* or *university*).
           Ra**úl**, **Úr**sula, **Cu**ba, univer**sal**, oc**tu**bre, universi**dad**

B. Los diptongos.   Nearly every stressed vowel in English is pronounced as a diphthong, a gliding from one vowel position to another. Spanish vowels, pronounced in isolation, are never diphthongs, but when two of them occur side by side, partial fusions sometimes result, and a diphthong is produced. Of the five Spanish vowels, **i** and **u** are classified as weak; **a, e,** and **o** are strong. Two strong vowels next to each other remain as two separate sounds, or syllables: **real (re-al), Laos (La-os).** Two weak vowels, or a weak plus a strong vowel, form a diphthong, a single syllable with a glide from one sound to the other. Listen to the following examples, and repeat each one.

ia	Patricia, Alicia, Santiago, gracias	ui (uy)	Luis, muy, ruina
ua	Juan, Eduardo, cuatro, Guatemala	ai (ay)	hay, aire, bailan, Jaime
ie	Gabriel, Diego, diez, cierto	au	Paula, auto, Aurelio, restaurante
ue	Consuelo, Manuel, bueno, pues		
io	Mario, radio, adiós, Antonio	ei (ey)	rey, seis, treinta, veinte
uo	antiguo, cuota	eu	feudal, Europa, Eugenio
iu	triunfo, ciudad, veintiuno	oi (oy)	hoy, soy, estoico

EJERCICIOS

A. Repetición y práctica.   Listen and repeat the following words after your instructor. Try to imitate his/her pronunciation as well as you can.

1. Catalina 3. café 5. repita 7. octubre 9. especial
2. Felipe 4. televisión 6. pasaporte 8. clase 10. oficina

B. Pronunciación.   Say the following words after your instructor, focusing your attention on the sounds of the vowels and diphthongs.

1. laboratorio 3. Ruiz 5. béisbol 7. restaurante 9. puerta
2. Ecuador 4. Europa 6. escritorio 8. auto 10. Luisa

Study Hint: Getting Organized

¡Felicitaciones! You've decided to learn Spanish. A second language helps you meet people, enriches your travels, prepares you for a profession, and broadens your perspective on your own culture and those of others. Here are a few suggestions to help you organize the work you'll need to do inside and outside the classroom.

1. Be sure to have all the supplies your instructor recommends—textbook, workbook, notebook, cassettes, and so on.

2. Familiarize yourself with your textbook—the table of contents, the index, the appendices, the vocabulary lists, and the organization of each chapter.

3. Study every day, first reviewing previous lessons and then learning the current material.

4. Work with a classmate or a friend to review vocabulary or to practice speaking and reading aloud. For speaking practice, try to find a native speaker of Spanish or an advanced Spanish student.

II. Pronunciación: consonantes; reglas de acentuación *(rules for word stress)* y enlace *(linking)* de frases

EL PROFESOR	Buenas tardes, estudiantes.
LA CLASE	Buenas tardes, profesor.
EL PROFESOR	Repitan, por favor: la ventana.
LA CLASE	La ventana.
EL PROFESOR	¿Qué es esto?
LA CLASE	Es la ventana.
EL PROFESOR	Y..., ¿qué es esto?
LA CLASE	Es el libro.
EL PROFESOR	¡Muy bien!
CARLOS	Perdón, profesor, ¿cómo se dice *wall* en español?
EL PROFESOR	¿Clase?
LA CLASE	Se dice «pared».
EL PROFESOR	¡Excelente!

EJERCICIOS

A. ¿Qué es esto? (*What is this?*)   In Spanish, tell what each of the following items is.

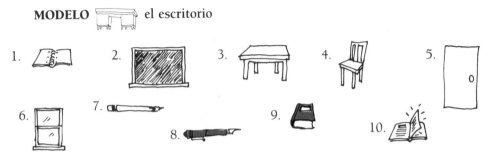

MODELO el escritorio

1. 2. 3. 4. 5.

6. 7. 8. 9. 10.

B. Y..., ¿qué es esto? (*And . . . what is this?*)   Working in pairs, one classmate points out an object and the other answers.

¿Qué hay (*What is there*) en la sala de clase?

MODELO TOMÁS ¿Qué es esto?
JULIA Es el libro.
TOMÁS Y... ¿ qué es esto?
JULIA Es la silla.

A. Las consonantes.   Many consonants are pronounced similarly in Spanish and English. Others are pronounced very differently.

b,v In Spanish, the letters **b** and **v** are pronounced in precisely the same way. At the beginning of a word, both sound much like an English *b*, whereas in the middle of a word they sound somewhere between *b* and *v* in English.
Bogotá, Valencia, Verónica, **b**urro, ventana, Eva, Sebastián

c,z In Spanish America, the letters **c** (before **e** and **i**) and **z** are pronounced like an English *s*.*

Alicia, Galicia, Cecilia, Zaragoza, La **Paz**, pizarra, lápiz

A **c** before **a, o, u,** or any consonant other than **h** is pronounced like a *k*.

inca, coca, costa, Cuzco, secreto, clase

ch The combination of **c** and **h, ch** is a separate Spanish letter, with its own section in word lists and dictionaries. It is pronounced like the *ch* in the English words *change, check, chip.*

chocolate, Chile, cha-cha-**chá**

d The letter **d** has two sounds. At the beginning of a word or after an **n** or **l**, it is somewhat like *d* in English, but softer, with the tongue touching the upper front teeth.

día, Diego, Miran**da**, Matil**de**

In all other positions, it is similar to *th* in the English word *then.*

Felici**dad**, E**duar**do, Ri**car**do, pa**red**, estu**dian**te

g,j The **g** before **i** or **e**, and the **j**, are both pronounced approximately like an English *h.*

Jorge, Jose**fi**na, geolo**gía**, Ja**lis**co, re**gión**, **pá**gina, e**jem**plo

g The **g** before **a, o,** or **u** is pronounced approximately like the English *g* in *gate.* In the combinations **gue** and **gui** the **u** is not pronounced, and the **g** has the same sound as the English *g.*

a**mi**go, a**mi**ga, Gus**ta**vo, Mi**guel**, gui**ta**rra

In the combinations **gua** and **guo**, the **u** is pronounced like a *w* in English.

an**ti**guo, Guate**ma**la

h Spanish **h** is silent.

La Ha**ba**na, Hon**du**ras, Her**nán**dez, ho**tel**, **Hu**go, **Hil**da

ll The **ll** is a separate Spanish letter, with its own section in word lists and dictionaries. Although there are some regional variations in pronunciation, in most Spanish-speaking countries its sound is much like that of *y* in the English word *yes.*

llama, Va**lle**jo, Se**vi**lla, Mu**ri**llo, **si**lla

ñ The sound of **ñ** is roughly equivalent to the sound of *ny* in the English word *canyon.*

se**ñor**, ca**ñón**, espa**ñol**

q A **q** is always followed in Spanish by a silent **u**; the **qu** combination represents the sound of *k* in English.

Quito, En**ri**que

r The letter **r** is used to represent two different sounds. At the beginning of a word or after **l, n,** or **s**, it has the same sound as **rr** (see below). Elsewhere, it represents an **r** sound so soft that it is close to the British pronunciation of *very* or the *tt* in the American English words *kitty* and *Betty.*

Pa**tri**cia, El**vi**ra, tor**ti**lla, Pi**lar**, profe**sor**

rr The letter sequence **rr**, while not a separate letter, and alphabetized in Spanish as in English, represents a special trilled sound, like a Scottish burr or a child imitating the sound of a motor. The same sound is

---

*In most parts of Spain a **c** before **e** or **i**, a **z** before **a, e, i, o,** or **u**, and a final **z** are pronounced like *th* in the English word *thin*. This is a characteristic feature of the peninsular accent.

represented by a single **r,** not **rr,** at the beginning of a word or after **l, n,** or **s.**

    error, ho**rr**or, ho**rr**ible, te**rr**ible
    Rosa, **Ri**ta, Robe**r**to, **ra**dio
    En**r**ique, Israel, alrede**dor** *(around)*

Listen to the difference between **perro** *(dog)* and **pero** *(but).*

    perro, **pe**ro

x   The letter **x** represents several different sounds in Spanish. Before a consonant, it is often pronounced like an English *s,* although some Latin Americans pronounce it like the English *x.*

    exte**rior,** **tex**to

Before a vowel, it is like the English *gs.*

    e**xa**men, exis**ten**cia

In many words **x** used to have the sound of the Spanish **j.** In most of these words the spelling has been changed, but a few words can be spelled either with an **x** or a **j:** **Mé**xico (**Mé**jico), Qui**xo**te (Qui**jo**te).

Don't forget that **ch** and **ll** are separate Spanish letters. When you are searching in a dictionary or vocabulary list for a word beginning with either letter, remember that they follow **c** and **l,** respectively.

clase   coco   chocolate   libro   Lupe   llama

The same principle of alphabetization holds when the letter occurs in the middle of a word.

lección   lectura *(reading)*   leche *(milk)*   silogismo   silueta   silla

B. El alfabeto

a	a	**f**	efe	**l**	ele	**p**	pe	**u**	u
b	be, be larga	**g**	ge	**ll**	elle	**q**	cu	**v**	ve, ve corta
c	ce	**h**	hache	**m**	eme	**r**	ere	**w**	doble ve
ch	che	**i**	i	**n**	ene	**rr**	erre	**x**	equis
d	de	**j**	jota	**ñ**	eñe	**s**	ese	**y**	i griega
e	e	**k**	ka	**o**	o	**t**	te	**z**	zeta

C. Reglas de acentuación.

A few short rules describe the way most Spanish word are accentuated, or stressed.

1. Most words ending in a vowel, **-n,** or **-s** are stressed on the next-to-last syllable.

cla-ses, **co**-mo, re-**pi**-tan, his-**to**-ria, **bue**-nos, e-le-**fan**-te

2. Most words ending in a consonant other than **-n** or **-s** are stressed on the last syllable.

es-pa-**ñol,** fa-**vor,** Mu-**ñoz,** se-**ñor,** us-**ted,** pre-li-mi-**nar**

3. Words that are stressed in any other way have a written accent on the vowel of the syllable that is stressed.

ca-**fé,** a-**quí, nú**-me-ro, in-**glés, lá**-piz, a-**diós**

4. Written accent marks are also used to mark the difference between pairs of words spelled the same, and also on all question words.

el *the* él *he,* si *if* sí *yes,* como *as* ¿cómo? *how?*

D. El enlace. Linking—the running together of words—occurs in every spoken language. In American English, *Do you want an orange?* becomes approximately "D'ya wan' a norange?" Anyone who attempts to speak English only as it is written is sure to sound like a computerized toy. Linking in Spanish is influenced by the following considerations.

1. The final vowel of a word links with the initial vowel of the next word.

Mi amiga se llama Amalia.	*My friend's name is Amalia.*
Ella estudia inglés.	*She studies English.*
La señorita Rivas ama a Andrés.	*Miss Rivas loves Andrés.*

2. Two identical consonants are pronounced as one.

el loco	*the crazy one*
los señores	*the gentlemen*

3. A final consonant usually links with the initial vowel of the next word.

Es estudiante.	*He's a student.*
Son excelentes.	*They are excellent.*

EJERCICIOS

A. ¿Cómo se llama usted? Ask a classmate his or her name. Your classmate will give it, then spell it out using Spanish letter names.

> **MODELO** ¿Cómo se llama usted?
> **Me llamo Juan Garza, jota-u-a-ene ge-a-ere-zeta-a.**

En la cafetería de la Universidad de las Américas, Cholula, México

B. ¿Cómo se escribe? Say each word, then say how it's spelled (**se escribe**) using Spanish letter names.

1. ventana	3. escritorio	5. página	7. cuaderno	9. puerta
2. pizarra	4. lápiz	6. pared	8. se llama	10. silla

C. Dictado (*Dictation*).   In pairs, ask each other to spell these words. One partner takes 1 through 4 and the other takes 5 through 8. The partner who is writing should do so with the textbook closed.

1. español   3. escritorio   5. ventana   7. estudiante
2. mesa   4. pared   6. cuaderno   8. Eduardo

D. Práctica.   Read each word and say which vowel is stressed.

1. señorita   3. lápiz   5. horrible   7. ejemplo   9. pregunta
2. tiza   4. familia   6. hospital   8. Guillermo   10. papel

E. ¿Acentos? (*Accent marks?*)   Listen carefully as your instructor reads each word and note which syllable is stressed. If the word is stressed as either of the two rules would lead you to expect, no accent mark is needed. But if the word is an exception to the rules, an accent mark must be written. Name the vowel that receives the mark.

1. Francisco   3. capitulo   5. Ramon   7. auto   9. ingles
2. television   4. laboratorio   6. adios   8. Hernandez   10. Madrid

III. Los números 0–99; hay

A. Cardinal numbers 0–99

0 cero			
1 uno (un, una)	11 once	21 veintiuno (-ún, -una)	31 treinta y uno (un, una)
2 dos	12 doce	22 veintidós	32 treinta y dos
3 tres	13 trece	23 veintitrés	33 treinta y tres
4 cuatro	14 catorce	24 veinticuatro	*etc.*
5 cinco	15 quince	25 veinticinco	40 cuarenta
6 seis	16 dieciséis	26 veintiséis	50 cincuenta
7 siete	17 diecisiete	27 veintisiete	60 sesenta
8 ocho	18 dieciocho	28 veintiocho	70 setenta
9 nueve	19 diecinueve	29 veintinueve	80 ochenta
10 diez	20 veinte	30 treinta	90 noventa

Notice the accents in **dieciséis, veintidós, veintitrés,** and **veintiséis,** all of which end in **-s.** The compound **veintiún** also takes an accent. **Uno** becomes **un** before a masculine noun and **una** before a feminine noun. (The concept of gender will be taken up in the next chapter; for the rest of this chapter, use **una** before words that end in **-a,** like **mesa** or **silla,** and use **un** before words that end in **-o** or **-or,** like **escritorio** or **profesor.** The form **uno** is used when counting: 0, 1, 2, 3, etc.)

B. Hay is the impersonal form of **haber;** it means *there is* or *there are* and can be used with singular or plural nouns. You will learn how to form plural nouns in the next chapter. For now, notice that nouns ending in vowels are made plural by adding **-s** and nouns ending in consonants are made plural by adding **-es.**

Hay treinta y una sillas en la sala de clase.	*There are thirty-one chairs in the classroom.*
Hay siete días en una semana.	*There are seven days in a week.*
Hay un hotel en la avenida Balboa.	*There is a hotel on Balboa Avenue.*
Hay veintiún libros en la mesa.	*There are twenty-one books on the table.*

EJERCICIOS

A. Cero, uno, dos, tres...   Count to thirty, each student taking a turn. Then count to fifty by twos, by fives, and by tens.

B. Números y más (*more*) números...   Read each of the following expressions.

1. 11 profesores	3. 52 señoras	5. 33 ventanas	7. 90 universidades
2. 80 libros	4. 1 hotel	6. 45 estudiantes	8. 65 páginas

C. Libros y más libros...   Imagine that you are in a bookstore in downtown Madrid and a clerk is quoting the prices (in **pesetas,** the monetary unit of Spain) of various books to you. Read aloud the lowest price in each group of three.

1. treinta y tres pesetas
   cincuenta pesetas
   cuarenta pesetas
2. noventa y dos pesetas
   setenta pesetas
   sesenta y cinco pesetas
3. setenta pesetas
   ochenta pesetas
   sesenta pesetas

4. veintiocho pesetas
   cincuenta y una pesetas
   treinta y cuatro pesetas
5. ochenta y siete pesetas
   treinta y seis pesetas
   cuarenta y nueve pesetas

D. ¿Verdadero o falso? (*True or false?*)   If the statement is true, say **verdadero.** If it is false, say **falso** and restate it, giving the correct answer.

> **MODELO**   Hay tres estudiantes en la clase.
> **No, hay veintiún estudiantes en la clase.**

1. Hay cinco profesores en la clase.
2. Hay quince sillas en la clase.
3. Hay una pizarra en la pared.
4. Hay veinticuatro horas *(hours)* en un día.
5. Hay tres ventanas y cuatro puertas en la clase.
6. Hay doctores en un hospital.
7. Hay pasaportes en una farmacia.
8. Hay nueve días en octubre.

Study Hint: Recognizing Cognates (1)

Cognates are words that are similar in spelling and meaning in two languages. Spanish and English share a very large number.

A. Sometimes the words are identical in the two languages.
chocolate, final, capital, doctor, horrible, hospital

B. Sometimes the words differ only in minor or easily predictable ways.
1. Except for **cc, rr, ll,** and **nn,** doubled consonants are never used in Spanish.
pasaporte *passport*   clase *class*
profesor *professor*
2. No word in Spanish can begin with **s-** plus a consonant. English words that begin that way often have cognates beginning with **es-**.
especial *special*   español *Spanish*
estudiante *student*   estupendo *stupendous, great*
3. The endings **-ción** and **-sión** in Spanish correspond to the English endings *-tion* or *-sion*.
imaginación, nación, televisión, negación

4. The Spanish ending **-dad** corresponds to the English ending *-ty*.
actividad, realidad, universidad
5. The Spanish endings **-ente** and **-ante** generally correspond to the English endings *-ent* and *-ant*.
presidente, restaurante, importante
6. The Spanish ending **-mente** generally corresponds to the English ending *-ly*.
finalmente, rápidamente

C. Sometimes words in the two languages are spelled alike but have come to mean something very different. Such pairs are called *false cognates*.
asistir   *to attend (class, etc.)*
atender   *to assist, attend to (someone)*
éxito   *success*
suceso   *event, happening*

Despite the hazards posed by false cognates, the existence of so many cognates in Spanish and English is a great resource to the language learner. Look for cognates in every new sentence and text you encounter.

EJERCICIOS

A. Repita.   Listen, look, then repeat the following cognates, using your best Spanish pronunciation.

1. hospital   3. clase   5. pasaporte   7. octubre   9. excelente
2. televisión   4. ejemplo   6. universidad   8. capital   10. estudiante

B. En clase (*In class*).   Each of the following classroom expressions in Spanish contains at least one cognate. You don't need to memorize these expressions, but you should be able to understand them when your instructor uses them. Match the Spanish expressions with their English equivalents.

1. Repitan, por favor.
2. No comprendo.
3. Contesten en español.
4. Abran el libro en la página 10.
5. Muy bien. Excelente.
6. Por ejemplo,...
7. ¡Usen su imaginación!

a. I don't understand (comprehend).
b. Open your books to page 10.
c. Very good. Excellent.
d. Use your imagination!
e. Answer in Spanish.
f. Repeat, please.
g. For example, . . .

IV.   *Estar* y los pronombres sujetos

Una parada de autobús (*bus stop*) en Madrid, España

En un autobús

SR. HERNÁNDEZ	Hola, María. ¿Cómo *estás*?
MARÍA	*Estoy* muy bien, señor Hernández, gracias.
SR. HERNÁNDEZ	¿Y qué tal el resto de la familia...?, ¿*están* todos bien?
MARÍA	Sí, todos *están* muy bien. Y *ustedes,* ¿cómo *están*?
SR. HERNÁNDEZ	*Nosotros* también *estamos* bien, gracias.
MARÍA	¡Qué suerte! Adiós, señor Hernández.
SR. HERNÁNDEZ	Adiós, María.

1. ¿Cómo está María? Y la familia de María, ¿está bien también?   2. ¿Están María y el señor Hernández en la clase de español? ¿y usted?   3. ¿Cómo está la familia del señor Hernández?   4. ¿Cómo está usted ahora? ¿y la familia de usted?

On a bus.   MR. HERNÁNDEZ: Hi, María. How are you? MARÍA: I'm very well, Mr. Hernández. Thank you. MR. HERNÁNDEZ: And how's the rest of the family . . .?, is everybody OK? MARÍA: Yes, everybody is very well. And how are all of you? MR. HERNÁNDEZ: We are also fine, thanks. MARÍA: How great! Good-bye, Mr. Hernández. MR. HERNÁNDEZ: Good-bye, María.

A. **Estar** *(to be)* is an infinitive verb form. It is conjugated by removing the **-ar** ending and adding other endings to the **est-** stem.

estar

	Singular			Plural	
yo*	**estoy**	*I am*	nosotros(-as)	**estamos**	*we are*
tú	**estás**	*you are*	vosotros(-as)	**estáis**	*you are*
él		*he is*	ellos		
ella	**está**	*she is*	ellas	**están**	*they are*
usted		*you are*	ustedes		*you are*

B. Subject pronouns are used far less frequently in Spanish than in English, since in Spanish the verb endings indicate the subject of the sentence. Subject pronouns are used in Spanish mainly to avoid confusion or for emphasis.

Estoy bien.	*I'm fine.* (statement of fact)
Yo estoy bien.	*I'm fine.* (emphatic)
Él está aquí. (Ella está aquí.)	*He is here. (She is here.)* (clarification)

C. There are several ways to say *you* in Spanish. The familiar singular form, **tú,** is used in speaking to friends, young children, and family members. It corresponds roughly to "first-name basis" in English. Students usually address each other with the **tú** form. The **usted** form is used in more formal situations, such as with older people, people you do not know, or people in authority. Students usually address their teacher with the **usted** form. If you are in a situation where you are unsure which form to use, it is usually better to use the **usted** form unless the native speaker requests otherwise.

D. In most parts of Spain the plural of **tú** is **vosotros** (masculine) and **vosotras** (feminine). In Latin America, **ustedes** is used as the plural of both **tú** and **usted.**

E. **Usted** and **ustedes** are frequently abbreviated in written Spanish, as **Ud.** and **Uds.** or **Vd.** and **Vds.**

¿Ud. está con Manuel?	*You are with Manuel?*
¿Vds. están bien?	*You are fine?*

F. The subject pronouns **él, ella, nosotros, nosotras, vosotros, vosotras, ellos,** and **ellas** show gender, either masculine or feminine. In speaking about two or more males, or a mixture of males and females, the masculine forms **nosotros, vosotros,** and **ellos** are used. The feminine forms **nosotras, vosotras,** and **ellas** are used only to refer to two or more females.

Ellos (Juan y José) están en Madrid.	*They (Juan and José) are in Madrid.*
Ellos (Juan y María) están en clase.	*They (Juan and María) are in class.*
Ellas (Rita y Teresa) están en México.	*They (Rita and Teresa) are in Mexico.*
Nosotros (Elena, Ricardo y yo) estamos en casa.	*We (Elena, Ricardo, and I) are at home.*

*Notice that **yo,** the first-person singular subject pronoun, is not capitalized.

EJERCICIOS

A. Los pronombres (*Pronouns*).   Read each of the following phrases and then provide the corresponding subject pronouns.

> **MODELOS**   Sara y Pepe   **ellos**
>
> tú y Marta   **ustedes** (or **vosotros[-as]**, in Spain)

1. Josefina
2. Carlos
3. Carmen y Beatriz
4. Eduardo y yo
5. Elena y yo
6. Víctor y el señor Gómez
7. Amalia, Alicia, Ana y Arturo
8. tú y Marta
9. tú y yo
10. la señorita Alfonsín

B. ¿Tú, usted o ustedes?   Your best friend is going to Argentina to visit some friends and relatives, and you are helping him or her review conversational Spanish. Remind your friend which subject pronoun should be used when speaking to each of the following persons.

> **MODELOS**   Pepe   **tú**
>
> el señor   **usted**
>
> la señora Ruiz y Susana   **ustedes**

1. el profesor
2. Juanita
3. tú y Juanita
4. el señor y la señora Méndez
5. la señorita Pérez
6. los estudiantes
7. el doctor
8. Juan Manuel

C. La señora Ramos.   Mrs. Ramos always likes to know where everyone is and how they are. Answer her questions in the affirmative and use subject pronouns, as in the example.

> **MODELO**   ¿Eva está en Guatemala?
> **Sí, ella está en Guatemala.**

1. ¿Susana y Jorge están en Madrid?
2. ¿Pedro está en Los Ángeles?
3. ¿Alberto y Elena están aquí?
4. ¿Usted y Ricardo están bien?
5. ¿Eva y Luisa están con Marta?
6. ¿Tú y Alicia están bien?
7. ¿La señora López está en Barcelona?
8. ¿Ustedes están en casa?

D. Imaginación y lógica.   Make complete sentences, combining each of the subjects on the left with an appropriate ending on the right.

> **MODELO**   **Papá y yo estamos en casa.**

usted	están en México
vosotros	estoy bien
papá y yo	está en San Francisco
Cecilia y mamá	estás aquí
tú	estamos en casa
yo	está con Pablo
la familia de Teresa	estáis en España

V. La negación

To make a sentence negative, place **no** before the verb.

Irene está bien.

Rosa *no* está bien.

Me llamo Roberto.

No me llamo Roberto.
Me llamo Manuel.

Hay dos libros en la mesa.

No hay dos libros
en la silla.

EJERCICIO

¿Sí o no?   Answer **sí** if the statement is correct and **no** if it is not.

> **MODELOS**   *English* se dice «inglés» en español.
> **Sí, *English* se dice «inglés» en español.**
>
> Barcelona está en México.
> **No, Barcelona no está en México.**

1. Nosotros estamos en el hospital.
2. El profesor (la profesora) se llama Pablo Picasso.
3. Nicaragua está en América Central.
4. San Francisco está en Maine.
5. *Chair* se dice «mesa» en español.
6. Usted se llama Albert Einstein.
7. Nosotros estamos en casa.
8. *Paper* se dice «papel» en español.
9. La pizarra está en la mesa.
10. España está en Europa.

Funciones y *actividades*

GREETINGS

In Spanish, as in English, there are many ways to say the same thing, some more formal than others and some appropriate only to very specific circumstances. In the **Funciones y actividades** sections, you will see different ways to express some common language functions, or uses—in this case, greetings. What do you say to someone to open a conversation? That depends on the circumstances.

1. With a friend or in an informal situation:

Hola, Miguel. ¿Cómo estás?	*Hi, Miguel. How are you?*
Hola. ¿Qué tal?	*Hi. How's it going?*

¿Qué tal? has many uses and meanings. Basically, it just means *How are things?* But combined with other words, it has other meanings; for instance, **¿Qué tal la familia?** *How is the family?* or **¿Qué tal si estudiamos más...?** *What if (What would you say if) we study more . . . ?*

2. With a stranger or in a more formal situation:

Buenos días. ¿Cómo está usted?	*Good morning (good day). How are you?*
Yo me llamo... ¿Cómo se llama usted?	*My name is . . . What is your name?*
Buenas tardes.	*Good afternoon. (until about sunset)*
Buenas noches.	*Good night. (after sunset; used mainly upon retiring)*

3. You meet another student or your roommate for the first time:

Hola. Me llamo...	*Hi. My name is . . .*

And what do you say in response to the question **¿Cómo está(s)?** Here are some possible answers.

Muy bien, gracias.	*Very well, thanks.*	Bien.	*Good.*
No muy bien.	*Not too well.*	Más o menos.	*So-so. (literally, "More or less.")*
Así así.	*So-so.*	Mal.	*Bad.*

When meeting someone for the first time, you can say:

Mucho gusto.	*Glad to meet you.*

There are several ways to respond to this. Any of the following answers would be appropriate:

Igualmente.	*Likewise. (Glad to meet you too.)*
Encantado(-a).	*I am delighted (to meet you).*
El gusto es mío.	*The pleasure is mine.*

USEFUL EXPRESSIONS

The following are useful expressions that could come in handy in various situations.

—Adiós. *Good-bye.*
—Hasta luego.
  See you later.

—Por favor. *Please.*
—Tengo una pregunta...
  I have a question . . .

—Con permiso.
  Excuse me.
—Cómo no. *Certainly.*

—Perdón. *Sorry;*
  I beg your pardon.

—No comprendo.
  I don't understand.

—¡Felicitaciones!
  Congratulations!
—Gracias. *Thanks.*

—Muchas gracias. *Thanks very much.*

—De nada. *You're welcome.*

Now do the following activities, using the expressions you have just learned.

A. Mini-dramas. With a partner, create short conversations for the following situations.

1. You are meeting someone for the first time. Greet the person and introduce yourself in Spanish. Ask his or her name and, when he or she answers, say, "Glad to meet you."
2. You meet a friend on the street. Say hello and ask how things are going. Your friend responds, "So-so." You ask, "How's the family?" He or she replies that they are well. Both of you say good-bye.

B. Una expresión apropiada. Tell what the people in each drawing might be saying in Spanish. Use any of the expressions or sentences from the previous pages, if appropriate.

MODELO

—**Mucho gusto.**
—**Igualmente.**

1.   2.   3.

Me llamo Señora Gómez.

4.   5.   6.

C. Respuestas *(Answers).* What replies might you give to the following statements?

MODELO ¡Hola, Teresa! ¿Qué tal?
           Muy bien, gracias, Susana. ¿Y tú?

1. Adiós.
2. Muchas gracias.
3. Mucho gusto.
4. ¡Hola!
5. ¿Cómo se llama el profesor (la profesora)?
6. Buenos días.
7. ¡Felicitaciones!
8. Hasta luego.

VOCABULARIO ACTIVO

*Cognados Cognates

el auto	especial	el hospital	el pasaporte
la capital	el, la estudiante	la imaginación	el profesor, la profesora
la clase	excelente	el laboratorio	el restaurante
el doctor, la doctora	falso	el modelo	la televisión
el ejemplo	la familia	el número	la universidad
el ejercicio	horrible	octubre	

La sala de clase The classroom

el capítulo	chapter
el cuaderno	notebook, workbook
el escritorio	desk
el español	Spanish
el inglés	English
el lápiz	pencil
el libro	book
la mesa	table
la página	page
el papel	paper
la pared	wall
la pizarra	chalkboard
la pluma	pen
la pregunta	question
la puerta	door
la silla	chair
la tiza	chalk
la ventana	window

Otras palabras y frases Other words and phrases

el amigo, la amiga	friend
aquí (or acá)	here
bien	well, OK
la casa	house, home
en casa	at home
¿Cómo se dice...?	How do you say . . .?
con	with
el día	day
en	in, on; at
estar	to be
estar bien (mal, así así)	to be well (unwell, so-so)
hay	there is, there are
muy	very
no	no, not

la peseta	peseta, monetary unit of Spain
¿Qué es esto?	What is this?
el señor	man, gentleman, Mr., Sir
la señora	woman, lady, Mrs., Ma'am
la señorita	young lady, Miss
sí	yes
un, una	a, an; one
verdadero	true
y	and

Expresiones útiles Useful expressions

Adiós.	Good-bye.
Buenas tardes.	Good afternoon.
Buenos días.	Good morning. Hello.
¿Cómo está(s)?	How are you?
¿Cómo se llama usted?	What is your name?
Gracias.	Thanks. Thank you.
Hola.	Hello. Hi.
Igualmente.	Likewise.
Me llamo...	My name is . . .
Mucho gusto.	Glad to meet you.
Muy bien.	Very well.
Perdón.	Pardon me.
Por favor.	Please.
¿Qué tal?	How are you doing? How is it going?

Don't forget: Cardinal numbers 0–99, page 10
Subject pronouns, page 14

*In the vocabulary lists in this text, definite articles (**el, la, los, las**) are given with all nouns to indicate gender.

Tres generaciones de una familia hispana

LA FAMILIA

Funciones

- Asking for information
- Using the telephone
- Ending a conversation

Vocabulario. In this chapter you will talk about family relationships.

Gramática. You will discuss and use:

1. The present tense of **ser**, a second verb corresponding to *to be*
2. Correct word order and intonation in Spanish sentences
3. The present tense of regular verbs that end in **-ar**
4. The gender and number of nouns and articles
5. The contractions **al** and **del**

Cultura. The dialogues take place in Madrid, the capital of Spain, and Barcelona, another important Spanish city.

LA FAMILIA DE JUAN

Las Personas

hombre	*man*
mujer	*woman*
niño	*boy*
niña	*girl*
papá	*dad, papa*
mamá	*mom, mamma*
parientes	*relatives*

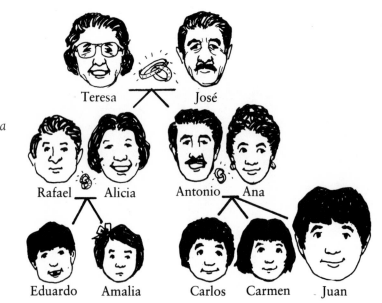

Teresa y José

esposos	*spouses* (esposo *husband*, esposa *wife*)
padres	*parents* (padre *father*, madre *mother*)
abuelos	*grandparents* (abuelo *grandfather*, abuela *grandmother*)
suegros	*mother- and father-in-law* (suegro *father-in-law*, suegra *mother-in-law*)

Ana y Rafael

cuñados	*sister- and brother-in-law* (cuñado *brother-in-law*, cuñada *sister-in-law*)
tíos	*aunt and uncle* (tío *uncle*, tía *aunt*)

Juan y Amalia

hijos	*children* (hijo *son*, hija *daughter*)
nietos	*grandchildren* (nieto *grandson*, nieta *granddaughter*)
sobrinos	*nephews and nieces* (sobrino *nephew*, sobrina *niece*)
hermanos	*brothers and sisters* (hermano *brother*, hermana *sister*)
primos	*cousins* (primo *male cousin*, prima *female cousin*)

Los parientes.   Supply the correct answer.

> **MODELO**   ¿La esposa de Rafael?   **Alicia**

1. ¿Los hijos de Rafael y Alicia?
2. ¿Los primos de Carlos?
3. ¿Los abuelos de Amalia?
4. ¿La hermana de Juan?
5. ¿El esposo de Ana?

El árbol genealógico (*The family tree*).   Look at Juan's family tree and explain who each person is by choosing the correct term from the list.

> **MODELO**   hermana, hija, madre, tía
>> **Alicia es** (*is*) **la hermana de Antonio y la tía de Carmen.**

Mujeres y niñas.   abuela, esposa, hermana, hija, madre, prima, tía

1. Carmen es la _____ de Juan y la _____ de Ana y Antonio.
2. Teresa es la _____ de Alicia y la _____ de Carlos.
3. Ana es la _____ de Eduardo y la _____ de Antonio.
4. Amalia es la _____ de Rafael y la _____ de Juan.

Hombres y niños.   abuelo, esposo, hermano, hijo, padre, primo, tío

5. José es el _____ de Antonio y Alicia y el _____ de Carlos y Carmen.
6. Antonio es el _____ de Teresa y el _____ de Amalia.
7. Juan es el _____ de Carmen y Carlos y el _____ de Eduardo y Amalia.
8. Rafael es el _____ de Alicia y el _____ de Eduardo.

Mi árbol genealógico.   Draw your own family tree and explain who each person is with the vocabulary you have just learned.

Preguntas

1. Ana y Antonio son (*are*) los padres de Juan. ¿Cómo se llama el padre de Amalia? ¿y la madre?   2. Teresa es la esposa de José. ¿Cómo se llama el esposo de Alicia?   3. ¿Cómo se llaman los primos de Carmen?   4. ¿Cómo se llama la madre de Antonio y Alicia?   5. Eduardo y Amalia son los hijos de Rafael y Alicia. ¿Cómo se llaman los hijos de Ana y Antonio?   6. Ana y Antonio son los tíos de Eduardo y Amalia. ¿Cómo se llaman los tíos de Carlos, Carmen y Juan?

I. El presente de indicativo del verbo *ser*

Un café en la Plaza Mayor, Madrid

En un café, en Madrid

PEDRITO	Ustedes no *son* de aquí..., ¿verdad?
SR. LARKIN	No, la doctora Silva y yo *somos* de los Estados Unidos. Yo *soy* de Tejas.
PEDRITO	Usted habla muy bien el español.
SR. LARKIN	Gracias, *eres* muy amable.
PEDRITO	Y usted, doctora Silva, ¿*es* también de Tejas?
DRA. SILVA	No, *soy* de California, Pedrito.
PEDRITO	¡De California! De allí también *son* Superman y el ratón Mickey, ¿no...?

1. Pedrito, el señor Larkin y la doctora Silva están en Madrid, ¿no? 2. El señor Larkin no es de Madrid, ¿verdad? 3. ¿Habla español el señor Larkin? ¿y la doctora Silva? 4. La doctora Silva es de California, ¿no? Y Pedrito, ¿es de California también? 5. Según (*According to*) Pedrito, ¿quiénes (*who*) son también de California? 6. ¿De dónde (*where*) es usted?

In a café in Madrid. PEDRITO: You are not from here . . . , right? MR. LARKIN: Dr. Silva and I are from the United States. I'm from Texas. PEDRITO: You speak Spanish very well. MR. LARKIN: Thanks, you're very kind. PEDRITO: And you, Dr. Silva, are you also from Texas? DR. SILVA: No, I'm from California, Pedrito. PEDRITO: From California! Superman and Mickey Mouse are from there also, right . . .?

Ser, another verb meaning *to be,* is highly irregular; its forms must be memorized. (The differences between **ser** and **estar** will be discussed in Chapter 2.)

ser   to be

yo	**soy**	nosotros(-as)	**somos**
tú	**eres**	vosotros(-as)	**sois**
usted, él, ella	**es**	ustedes, ellos(-as)	**son**

Soy yo.	*It's I.*
Tú eres muy amable.	*You're very kind.*
Susana es la hermana de Camilo.	*Susana is Camilo's sister.*
Nosotros no somos de España.	*We are not from Spain.*
Ricardo es profesor de español.	*Ricardo is a Spanish teacher (professor, instructor).*
Él es italiano.	*He is an Italian.*

Note that after forms of **ser** the indefinite article is not used with a profession or nationality unless it is modified by an adjective, as you will see on page 66.

EJERCICIOS

A. A que eres de Chile... (*I'll bet you're from Chile*).   Professor Benítez is a specialist in regional accents. Every time she hears someone speak, she guesses where the speaker is from. Make statements as she would, following the model.

MODELO José / España **José es de España, ¿no?**

1. el doctor Parodi / Argentina
2. los señores García / Cuba
3. Teresa / Paraguay
4. la señorita / Colombia
5. usted / Puerto Rico
6. los amigos de Susana / Chile
7. el profesor / Uruguay
8. ustedes / México

B. ¿Verdadero o falso? If the statement is true, say **verdadero.** If it is false, say **no** or **falso** and restate it to make it correct.

1. Madrid es la capital de Bolivia.
2. Yo no soy Michael Jackson.
3. Julio Iglesias es de España.
4. Ustedes no son estudiantes.
5. Jane Fonda es tu prima.
6. Nosotros somos doctores.
7. Yo soy estudiante de español.
8. Ronald Reagan no es el presidente de los Estados Unidos.
9. *Don Quijote de la Mancha* es un libro muy interesante.
10. Usted es pariente de Madonna.

C. ¿Quién soy? (*Who am I?*) Tell a group of three or four classmates several things about yourself.

MODELOS Soy Sandy. Soy estudiante de español. Soy de California... ¿y tú...?

Soy Ricardo. No soy de aquí. Soy de Montreal. También soy estudiante de español. ¿y tú...?

II. El orden de las palabras y la entonación

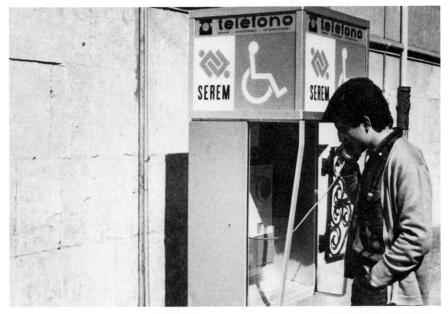

—¡Hola!,
¿está Pablo en casa?

En el teléfono

LUISA   Hola.

CAMILO   Hola, ¿está Pablo en casa?

LUISA   No..., pero ¿quién habla?

CAMILO   Habla Camilo...

LUISA   ¿Camilo Espínola, el amigo argentino?

CAMILO   Sí, soy Camilo. Y usted es Ana, ¿verdad?

LUISA   No, no soy Ana. Me llamo Luisa.

CAMILO   ¡Ah, la hermana de Pablo! Mucho gusto, Luisa.

LUISA   Igualmente, Camilo... Pablo está en la universidad.

CAMILO   ¡Qué lástima! Pero gracias por la información, Luisa, y ¡hasta luego!

LUISA   Hasta pronto, Camilo, y buenas noches.

---

1. ¿Está Pablo en casa?   2. ¿Está Pablo en la universidad?   3. Está Camilo con Ana?   4. La señorita se llama Ana, ¿verdad?   5. Luisa está en casa, ¿no?

On the telephone. LUISA: Hello. CAMILO: Hello, is Pablo home? LUISA: No . . ., but who is this? CAMILO: This is Camilo speaking. LUISA: Camilo Espínola, the Argentinean friend? CAMILO: Yes, I am Camilo. And you're Ana, right? LUISA: No, I'm not Ana. My name is Luisa. CAMILO: Ah, Pablo's sister! Glad to meet you, Luisa. LUISA: Likewise, Camilo . . . Pablo is at the university. CAMILO: What a pity! But thanks for the information, Luisa, and see you later! LUISA: See you soon, Camilo, and good night.

Changes in the order of words within a sentence, changes in sentence intonation, and the addition of particles and tags to the sentence can all affect sentence meaning.

A. As seen in the previous chapter, a common way to make a Spanish sentence negative is to place the word **no** in front of the verb.

Mamá está aquí.	*Mom is here.*
Papá no está aquí.	*Dad isn't here.*

B. *Yes/no* questions are questions that can be answered with a simple **sí** or **no**. A simple way to pose such questions is to make a statement but with the voice rising toward the end of the sentence.

Habla español.	*You speak Spanish.*
¿Habla español?	*Do you speak Spanish?*
Artemio y Luisa están aquí.	*Artemio and Luisa are here.*
¿Artemio y Luisa están aquí?	*Artemio and Luisa are here?*

Another way to ask *yes/no* questions is to put the subject after the verb. If the subject is a noun, it sometimes goes at the end of the question.

¿Es Madrid la capital de España?	*Is Madrid the capital of Spain?*
¿Se llama Luis el primo de María?	*Is Luis the name of María's cousin?*
¿Está enfermo Pablo?	*Is Pablo sick?*

In negative questions the word **no** precedes the verb.

¿Alfonso no está en Madrid? ⎫
¿No está Alfonso en Madrid? ⎬ *Isn't Alfonso in Madrid?*
¿No está en Madrid Alfonso? ⎭

C. A statement can be made into a question by adding a "confirmation tag" at the end to ask a person to confirm or deny the information just stated. Three common tags in Spanish are **¿de acuerdo?**, **¿verdad?**, and **¿no?** (The tag **¿no?** is never used after a negative sentence.)

Usted se llama Rodolfo, ¿verdad?	*Your name is Rodolfo, right?*
Los estudiantes están aquí, ¿no?	*The students are here, aren't they?*
Pablo no está en casa hoy, ¿verdad?	*Pablo is not home today, is he?*
Abran los libros, ¿de acuerdo?	*Open your books, OK?*

Notice that **¿de acuerdo?** is used when some kind of action is proposed.

EJERCICIOS

A. ¿Cómo? (*What?*)   You can't believe that you heard correctly. Ask questions in three ways to obtain confirmation of the information.

> **MODELO**   El profesor se llama Antonio García.
> **¿El profesor se llama Antonio García?**
> **¿Se llama Antonio García el profesor?**
> **¿Se llama el profesor Antonio García?**

1. Papá está en casa.
2. Alfredo está bien.
3. Ellos son doctores.
4. El señor no se llama Raúl García.
5. Valencia está en España.

B. La información.   You are preparing for a test and are a little unsure about the following information. Ask for confirmation by adding **¿no?** or **¿verdad?**, as appropriate.

> **MODELO**   Santa Mónica está en Los Ángeles.
> **Santa Mónica está en Los Ángeles, ¿verdad?**

1. Veintiséis y quince son cuarenta y uno.
2. Ávila está en España.
3. El libro se llama *¿Habla español?*.
4. No hay ocho ventanas en la clase.
5. La Plaza de España está en Madrid.
6. La mamá de Clara se llama Victoria.

III. El presente de indicativo de los verbos terminados en -*ar*

Estudiantes y profesores de la Universidad de Madrid

En la Universidad de Madrid

TERESA   Tú *estudias* sociología, ¿verdad?

MARIO   Sí, ahora *estudiamos* la familia italiana. Por eso *busco* un libro sobre Italia.

TERESA   ¡Qué interesante! ¿*Hablan* ustedes también de la cultura italiana en general?

MARIO   Sí, el esposo de la profesora Ortega, un italiano de Milán, *enseña* una clase de cultura.

TERESA   ¡Estupendo! *Deseo* viajar a Italia en octubre y *necesito* mucha información. ¿*Visito* la clase mañana?

MARIO   ¡Cómo no! Bueno, entonces nos vemos mañana, ¿de acuerdo?

TERESA   De acuerdo. Y ¡hasta mañana!

---

1. ¿Están en Acapulco Teresa y Mario?   2. ¿Qué (*What*) estudia Mario? ¿Y qué estudia él ahora?   3. ¿Busca Mario un libro sobre México o sobre Italia?   4. ¿Es italiana la profesora Ortega? ¿y el esposo de ella?   5. ¿Qué enseña el esposo de la profesora Ortega?   6. ¿Desea visitar España Teresa? ¿Viaja ella en octubre?   7. Y usted, ¿desea viajar a Italia también? (¿a México? ¿a España? ¿a...?)

At the University of Madrid.   TERESA: You're studying sociology, right? MARIO: Yes, now we're studying the Italian family. That is why I'm looking for a book on Italy. TERESA: How interesting! Do you also talk about Italian culture in general? MARIO: Yes, Professor Ortega's husband, an Italian from Milan, teaches a class on culture. TERESA: Wonderful! I want to travel to Italy in October and I need a lot of information. Shall I visit the class tomorrow? MARIO: Sure. Well, then we'll see each other tomorrow, OK? TERESA: OK. And see you tomorrow (literally, "And till tomorrow!")

A. Spanish infinitives all end in **-ar, -er,** or **-ir. Hablar** *(to speak)* is a regular **-ar** verb—all its forms follow a regular pattern. To produce the present-tense forms of **hablar** or any other regular **-ar** verb, drop the infinitive ending **-ar** and add the present-tense endings **-o, -as, -a, -amos, -áis,** and **-an.**

hablar to speak, to talk			
yo	**hablo**	nosotros(-as)	**hablamos**
tú	**hablas**	vosotros(-as)	**habláis**
usted, él, ella	**habla**	ustedes, ellos(-as)	**hablan**

¿Hablas español?   *Do you speak Spanish?*

The "shoe," formed by the verbs in color, is a reminder that the four forms in it are stressed on the stem syllable **ha-.** In the other two forms, stress falls on an ending syllable: **-bla-, -bláis.** The shifting of stress between stem and ending is an important feature of nearly every Spanish verb.

B. Other common regular **-ar** verbs are:

bailar	*to dance*
buscar	*to look for*
contestar	*to answer*
desear	*to want*
enseñar	*to teach, to show*
estudiar	*to study*
llamar	*to call*
llegar	*to arrive*
llevar	*to carry, to take*
mirar	*to look at, to watch*
necesitar	*to need*
pasar	*to pass; to spend (time)*
preguntar	*to ask*
regresar	*to return*
tomar	*to take, to drink*
trabajar	*to work*
viajar	*to travel*

Anahí pregunta: «¿Qué es esto?»   *Anahí asks: "¿What's this?"*
Graciela y Miguel desean estudiar   *Graciela and Miguel wish to study*
   español.   *   Spanish.*
¿Enriqueta? Viaja a Toledo hoy.   *Enriqueta? She's traveling to Toledo*
     *   today.*

Llegamos a casa mañana.   *We are arriving home tomorrow.*

Note that verbs of motion, such as **viajar** and **llegar,** require the preposition **a** before a noun that indicates a destination, but not otherwise: **Viaja a Toledo,** but **Viaja con Susana.**

C. The present tense in Spanish corresponds to several structures in English.

Tomo café.
$\left\{\begin{array}{l}\textit{I drink coffee.} \\ \textit{I do drink coffee.} \\ \textit{I'm drinking coffee.}\end{array}\right.$

¿Estudias italiano?
$\left\{\begin{array}{l}\textit{Do you study Italian?} \\ \textit{Are you studying Italian?}\end{array}\right.$

D. Present-tense verbs usually describe actions as if they were happening in the present time. But the present tense may also be used to imply that an action will take place in the immediate future.

Lola lleva el libro ahora.   *Lola's taking (will take) the book now.*

Estudian con nosotros.   *They're studying (will study) with us.*

EJERCICIOS

A. Nosotros dos.   Francisco frequently forgets to include his twin brother Alejandro in his plans. Take the part of Alejandro and correct Francisco's statements.

MODELO   Llevo los libros a la universidad.
Llevamos los libros a la universidad.

1. Necesito un cuaderno.
2. Llevo el cuaderno.
3. Busco la clase de español.
4. Llego a la clase de español.
5. Contesto las preguntas de la profesora.
6. Estudio la cultura de España.
7. Pregunto «¿Qué tal la familia?».
8. Regreso a casa ahora.

B. Imaginación y lógica.   Take one word or phrase from as many columns as possible to form original sentences. Be sure to use the correct form of the verb in the second column. Use the phrases as many times as you wish.

MODELOS   **Las estudiantes toman café.**

Las estudiantes desean viajar a México.

Las estudiantes				
Yo no	enseñ-			
El profesor	bail-	o		
Nosotros	lleg-	as		español bien.
El presidente	viaj-	a		a México.
Los abuelos no	habl-	amos		café.
Papá y mamá	tom-	an	viajar	el papel.
Tú	necesit-		hablar	bien.
	dese-		tomar	los libros y los cuadernos.
			regresar	a la clase mañana.
			mirar	televisión.

C. Día de fiesta (*Holiday*).   Today is a holiday and school is closed. Give affirmative answers to these questions.

MODELO   Miro televisión. ¿y Roberto?
Roberto mira televisión también.

1. Trabajo en casa. ¿y los hijos de Carmen?
2. Bailo mucho. ¿y usted?
3. Tomo café con la tía Lolita. ¿y el profesor Vega?
4. Visito a los abuelos. ¿y tú?
5. Estudio el Capítulo 1. ¿y ellos?

D. En acción.   Describe to a classmate what the following people are doing.

MODELO   El profesor y los estudiantes...
El profesor enseña y los estudiantes trabajan en la clase.

1. La estudiante...

2. Los señores García...

3. Roberto...

4. Él...

5. Los amigos...

6. El niño...

E. Traducción (*Translation*).   Give the Spanish equivalent of the following sentences.

1. We want to travel to Spain.
2. Tomás and Marisol are looking for the book.
3. Do you speak Spanish, Martín?
4. Doesn't Clara drink coffee?
5. The González family is in Madrid.
6. They are asking "What is the girl's name?"

Entrevista (*Interview*)

Interview a classmate using the following questions. Possible affirmative answers are given on the right. The person asking the questions may want to glance at the answers. The person answering the questions should have his or her book closed.

1. ¿Estudias en casa?   Sí, estudio en casa.
2. ¿Deseas hablar español bien?   Sí, deseo hablar español bien.
3. ¿Llevas los libros a clase?   Sí, llevo los libros a clase.
4. ¿Trabaja bien la clase?   Sí, la clase trabaja bien.
5. ¿Bailas bien?   Sí, bailo bien.
6. ¿Tomas café?   Sí, tomo café.
7. ¿Viajas mucho?   Sí, viajo mucho.
8. ¿Deseas viajar a España?   Sí, deseo viajar a España.

IV. Género y número de sustantivos y artículos

El aeropuerto de Madrid

En el aeropuerto

AGENTE   Buenos días. *Los pasaportes,* por favor.
RAMÓN   *Un momento...* aquí están.
ISABEL   Ramón, ¿Dónde está *la cámara...?* ¿Y *los regalos* para *las hijas* de Juan?
RAMÓN   ¡Dios mío! *La cámara* está en *el avión...* ¡y *los regalos* también están allí...!

---

1. ¿Necesita los pasaportes el agente?   2. ¿Lleva los pasaportes Ramón?
3. ¿Qué busca Isabel?   4. ¿Está la cámara en el avión? ¿y los regalos...?
5. Isabel y Ramón, ¿están en el avión o en el aeropuerto?

At the airport.   AGENT: Good morning. Passports, please. RAMÓN: Just a moment . . . here they are. ISABEL: Ramón, where are the camera and the presents for Juan's daughters? RAMÓN: Good grief! The camera is on the plane . . . and the gifts are also there . . .!

A. In Spanish all nouns are either masculine or feminine. Articles in Spanish are also either masculine or feminine, to reflect the gender of the noun they modify. The definite article has four forms:

	Singular		Plural	
Masculine	**el** regalo	*the gift*	**los** regalos	*the gifts*
Feminine	**la** cámara	*the camera*	**las** cámaras	*the cameras*

B. The indefinite article in Spanish also has four forms:

	Singular		Plural	
Masculine	**un** primo	*a cousin*	**unos** primos	*some (a few) cousins*
Feminine	**una** familia	*a family*	**unas** familias	*some (a few) families*

Notice that **unos (unas)** can mean *some* or *a few.*

C. Most Spanish nouns ending in **-o** in the singular are masculine. Most nouns ending in **-a** in the singular are feminine.

el aeropuerto	*the airport*	la farmacia	*the drugstore, pharmacy*
el abuelo	*the grandfather*	la abuela	*the grandmother*

Two common exceptions are **el día** *(the day)* and **la mano** *(the hand).*

D. Most nouns ending in **-ma, -pa,** or **-ta** that have a cognate in English are masculine. (These words entered both the Spanish and English languages from Greek.)

el drama	el mapa	el problema
el sistema	el poeta	

E. With nouns that do not end in **-o** or **-a** in the singular, it can be helpful to learn the definite article when you learn the noun. Notice that most nouns ending in **-dad** and **-ión** are feminine. (**El avión** is an exception.)

el hotel	*the hotel*	la verdad	*the truth*
el inglés	*English*	la región	*the region*
el viaje	*the trip*	la ciudad	*the city*
		la capital	*capital (city)*

F. The gender of many nouns that refer to people can be changed by changing the noun ending and the article.

el primo	*the (male) cousin*	la prima	*the (female) cousin*
el señor	*the man*	la señora	*the woman, lady*
un hijo	*a son*	una hija	*a daughter*
un amigo	*a (male) friend*	una amiga	*a (female) friend*

However, for some nouns the ending does not change, and so the gender of the person the noun refers to is shown by the gender of the article.

un turista	*a (male) tourist*	una turista	*a (female) tourist*
un artista	*a (male) artist*	una artista	*a (female) artist*
un agente	*a (male) agent*	una agente	*a (female) agent*

G. The plural of most nouns ending in a vowel is formed by adding **-s: libro, libros; mesa, mesas; viaje, viajes.** The plural of most nouns ending in a consonant is formed by adding **-es: hotel, hoteles; ciudad, ciudades; región, regiones.*** A final **z** must be changed to **c** before adding **-es: lápiz, lápices.** The masculine plural of nouns referring to people may include both genders.

el niño	*the boy*
el señor González	*Mr. González*
el tío	*the uncle*
los niños	*the boys* or *the boys and girls*
los señores González	*Mr. and Mrs. González*
los tíos	*the aunt and uncle*

H. The definite article is used with titles such as **señor, señora, señorita, doctor(a),** or **profesor(a)** when you are talking or asking about an individual.

Un artista habla con el señor Martínez.	*An artist is talking to Mr. Martínez.*
El doctor García necesita unas semanas de vacaciones.†	*Dr. García needs a few weeks of vacation.*

But the definite article is not used with titles when you are speaking to the person directly.

Buenos días, señor Martínez.	*Good day, Mr. Martínez.*
¿Cómo está usted, doctor García?	*How are you, Dr. García?*

EJERCICIOS

A. Preguntas y respuestas (*Questions and answers*).   With a classmate, create questions and answers by replacing the nouns with the cues suggested.

> **MODELO**   Estudiante 1:   **¿Están aquí** los turistas?
> Estudiante 2:   **No, los turistas están en** la ciudad.

	Estudiante 1	Estudiante 2
1.	pasaportes	hotel
2.	aviones	aeropuerto
3.	estudiantes	clase

---

*Notice that there is no accent mark on **regiones**, since the emphasis falls naturally on the next-to-the-last syllable.

†*Vacation* (singular) in English is always expressed by **vacaciones** (plural) in Spanish.

4. profesores   universidad
5. mamá y papá   casa
6. agentes   museo

MODELO   Estudiante 1:   **¿Buscas** un lápiz?
             Estudiante 2:   **No, busco** una pluma.

	Estudiante 1	Estudiante 2
1.	farmacia	hotel
2.	cuaderno	libro
3.	regalo	cámara
4.	papel	pizarra
5.	teléfono	restaurante
6.	tiza	mapa

B. **¿Qué necesitan...?**   Marta and the Garcías have a list of things they need. Tell what they need, following the model.

MODELO   silla
             Marta necesita una silla. Los García necesitan unas sillas.

1. cuaderno   5. libro
2. lápiz   6. mesa
3. pluma   7. cámara
4. papel   8. semana de vacaciones

C. **Formación de frases.**   Make up sentences using the following words. Provide the definite articles, as in the model.

MODELO   abuelo de Pablo / hablar / con / señorita González
             El abuelo de Pablo habla con la señorita González.

1. niño / buscar / regalo
2. doctor / viajar / a / ciudad
3. estudiantes / hablar / con / profesor
4. mamá de Ana / llevar / pasaportes
5. tú / estudiar / capítulos
6. nosotros / mirar / pizarra
7. primo de Juan / llegar / a / capital
8. turistas / estar / en / hotel

D. **Traducción.**   Give the Spanish equivalent of the following sentences.

1. Mr. Gómez is looking at the notebook.
2. Dr. García, how is the boy?
3. Mrs. Rodríguez is spending three days in Barcelona with a friend.
4. How are you, Miss Vega?
5. She travels to the city with the family.
6. Professor Martínez wants to speak with the students.

V. Las contracciones *al* y *del*

España atrae (*attracts*) a muchos turistas.

En la Plaza de la Universidad, en Barcelona

UN TURISTA   Por favor, señor, ¿dónde está «La casa de la paella»? ¿Está cerca o lejos de aquí?

UN SEÑOR   Está muy cerca. Es un restaurante muy bueno. Mire, está allí a la izquierda, *al* lado *del* Hotel Continental.

---

1. ¿Busca un restaurante mexicano el turista?   2. ¿Está cerca el restaurante?
3. ¿Está al lado del hospital o al lado del hotel?

At Plaza de la Universidad, in Barcelona.   A TOURIST: Excuse me, sir. Where is "The House of the Paella"? Is it near or far from here? A GENTLEMAN: It's very near. It's a very good restaurant. Look, it's there on the left, beside the Continental Hotel.

$$a + el = al$$
$$de + el = del$$

The definite article **el** contracts with **a** to form **al** and with **de** to form **del**. The other articles do not contract.

Los señores Méndez llegan al teatro (a la ciudad, a los Estados Unidos).
Mr. and Mrs. Méndez arrive at the theater (at the city, in the United States).

Estamos lejos del museo (de la universidad, de los hoteles).
We're far from the museum (from the university, from the hotels).

El hotel está a la derecha de la farmacia (del hospital, del restaurante).
The hotel is to the right of the pharmacy (of the hospital, of the restaurant).

EJERCICIOS

A. ¿Verdadero o falso?   Look at the map of South America inside the front cover. Then react to the following statements with **verdadero** or **falso**. If the statement is false, correct it.

1. Ecuador está al norte del Perú.
2. Uruguay está al sur del Brasil.
3. El Salvador está en Sudamérica.
4. La Argentina está al oeste de Chile.
5. Venezuela está lejos del Paraguay.
6. Colombia está cerca del Uruguay.

B. Imaginación y lógica.   Form sentences for each group of words, using them in the order given.

MODELO   hotel / izquierda / aeropuerto
El hotel está a la izquierda del aeropuerto.

1. restaurante / lado / universidad
2. hospital / izquierda / farmacia
3. universidad / cerca / teatro
4. museo / derecha / agencia
5. aeropuerto / lejos / ciudad

Preguntas

1. ¿Desea usted viajar a la ciudad de México? ¿al Perú? ¿a Europa...?   2. ¿Lleva usted un pasaporte cuando viaja al Canadá? ¿a la Argentina? ¿a Tejas? ¿a Nueva York?   3. En la clase de español, ¿está usted cerca o lejos de la puerta? ¿Quién está a la derecha de usted? ¿y a la izquierda?   4. ¿Está la universidad lejos o cerca del aeropuerto? ¿de un restaurante argentino?

Study Hint: Learning Vocabulary

To learn new vocabulary, say words aloud and try to put them into context by using them in a sentence. Review vocabulary frequently. The following ideas might help you review more efficiently:

1. When you can't remember the meaning of a word you know you've seen before, place a pencil dot by it in the vocabulary list. Then study even more frequently the words you've marked.

2. There are many cognates in Spanish and English: pairs of words that are similar in spelling and meaning. Each chapter vocabulary (the **Vocabulario ac-** tivo section) in this book starts with a list of the cognates used in that particular chapter. Study carefully their differences in spelling.

3. Some words—greetings and everyday expressions, for example—are better learned in phrases than individually. Other words can be learned in groups—pairs of synonyms (words of similar meaning) or antonyms (words of opposite meaning); and clusters of words in grammatical categories, like conjunctions (*and, or, nor, but, because,* etc.).

La Puerta del Sol

Janet and her cousin Susan have just arrived in Madrid from los Estados Unidos. *They are in* La Puerta del Sol, *an important square in the heart of the old part of the city.*

JANET   Perdón, señor, deseamos visitar el Museo del Prado.[1] ¿Qué autobús° tomamos?

SEÑOR RUIZ   ¡Qué lástima!° Hoy los museos están cerrados°...

SUSAN   Pues, entonces mañana°. ¿Visitamos la casa del presidente de España hoy, Janet?

SEÑOR RUIZ   Perdón. En España el jefe de estado° es el rey°.

SUSAN   Entonces, ¿qué tipo de gobierno° hay en España?

SEÑOR RUIZ   Hay una monarquía.

JANET   Ah, sí, y el rey se llama Juan Carlos, ¿verdad?

SEÑOR RUIZ   Exactamente, y la esposa del rey se llama Sofía. Hoy están en Toledo[2] porque° hay una celebración importante.

JANET   En la monarquía aquí en España, ¿hay también un parlamento?[3]

SEÑOR RUIZ   Sí, hay un parlamento y también hay un presidente del gobierno.

SUSAN   ¿Usted trabaja en Madrid, señor?

SEÑOR RUIZ   No, yo no trabajo en Madrid, señorita. Trabajo en la Universidad de Salamanca.[4] Soy profesor. Enseño filosofía.

JANET   ¡Qué interesante!° A propósito,° nosotras deseamos visitar la ciudad de Salamanca.

SUSAN   Yo necesito comprar° un mapa de España. También deseo comprar libros en español... ¿Hay una librería° cerca?

SEÑOR RUIZ   Sí, aquí muy cerca hay una librería importante. Yo también deseo comprar un texto°. ¿Caminamos° a la librería ahora?

SUSAN   Pues..., ¿caminamos, Janet?

JANET   Bueno, de acuerdo°.

---

el autobús *bus*   ¡Qué lástima! *What a shame!*   cerrados *closed*   Pues, entonces mañana *Well, then, tomorrow*   el jefe de estado *chief of state*   el rey *king*   ¿qué tipo de gobierno...? *what type of government?*   porque *because*   ¡Qué interesante! *How interesting!*   a propósito *by the way*   comprar *to buy*   la librería *bookstore* el texto *text, textbook*   caminar *to walk*   de acuerdo *OK*

PREGUNTAS

1. ¿Qué museo desean visitar Janet y Susan?   2. ¿Están cerrados hoy los museos? 3. ¿Hay rey en España? ¿Hay presidente?   4. ¿Qué tipo de gobierno hay en España?   5. ¿Cómo se llama el rey de España? ¿Cómo se llama la esposa del rey? 6. ¿Hay un parlamento en España?   7. ¿Trabaja en Madrid el señor Ruiz? ¿En qué universidad trabaja? ¿Qué enseña?   8. ¿Qué necesita Janet? ¿Qué desea comprar el señor Ruiz?   9. Hay una monarquía en los Estados Unidos? ¿Qué hay? 10. ¿Cómo se llama el presidente (la presidenta) de los Estados Unidos? ¿Y cómo se llama la esposa (el esposo) del presidente (de la presidenta)...?

NOTAS CULTURALES

1. **El Museo del Prado** is an art museum in Madrid that houses the world's richest and most comprehensive collection of Spanish painting. The most important works of Velázquez are there, as well as major works by El Greco and Goya. The Prado also contains an impressive selection of other schools of European painting, especially Italian and Flemish art.

2. The city of Toledo lies 67 kilometers (42 miles) southwest of Madrid. It is considered one of Spain's most historically and architecturally important cities.

3. The Spanish parliament, called **las Cortes**, is the national legislative body of the country. **Las Cortes** has two chambers, **el Senado** and **la Cámara de Diputados.** Spain is divided into seventeen autonomous regions, divisions that correspond to historic provinces plus a separate region for metropolitan Madrid. All of the autonomous regions have representatives in **las Cortes.**

4. **La Universidad de Salamanca,** located in the city of Salamanca in western Spain, is one of Spain's leading universities. From its founding in 1218 until the end of the sixteenth century, the university was a leading center of learning in Europe, ranking with the universities of Paris and Oxford.

Funciones y *actividades*

In this chapter, you have seen examples of some important language functions, or uses. Here is a summary and some additional information about these functions of language:

ASKING FOR INFORMATION

To ask for information, you can use confirmation tags or interrogative words, as you have seen in this chapter.

Confirmation tags:

¿de acuerdo?   ¿verdad?   ¿no?

Remember that **¿no?** is not used after a negative sentence and that **¿de acuerdo?** is used when some kind of action is proposed. In Spanish, just as in English, these tags can be used when you simply want to confirm an answer (that you think you know) or when you do not know the answer to your question. Remember too that the most common way of asking *yes/no* questions is to invert the normal order of subject and verb:

¿Viaja usted a Italia mañana?
¿Son ustedes estudiantes de español?

So far you have learned **¿cómo?** *(how?)* and **¿qué?** *(what?)*, two frequently used interrogative words:

¿Qué es esto?
¿Cómo se llama usted?
¿Cómo se dice *pencil (mother, city, etc.)* en español?

You will learn a few more interrogative words in the next chapter.

USING THE TELEPHONE

In the conversation at the beginning of Section II, Luisa answers the telephone by saying **Hola.** In Mexico and Central America, however, people are likely to say **Bueno,** and in some areas you may hear **Aló.** In Spain you might hear **Dígame** (*literally,* "tell me"). Notice that she asks who is calling by saying **¿Quién habla?,** but she might also ask **¿De parte de quién?** *(On behalf of whom?).* With either question, you may say **Habla** and then your name—for example, **Habla Luis** (*This is Luis, literally,* "Luis speaking").

ENDING A CONVERSATION

Adiós.	*Good-bye.*
Hasta luego.	*See you later.*
Hasta pronto.	*See you soon.*
Bueno, nos vemos.	(*literally,* "Well, we'll see each other [soon].")
Hasta mañana.	*See you tomorrow.*

Feliz fin de semana.	*Have a good weekend* (*literally,* "Happy end of the week.")

There are other ways to say *good-bye*, but the above are the most common. In the southern part of South America, where there has been a lot of Italian influence, people often just say **¡Chau!**

Now do the following activities using the expressions you have just learned.

A. ¿Qué dicen? (*What are they saying?*) Tell what the people in the following drawings are probably saying.

1.   2.   3.

B. ¿Formal o informal? Tell which expressions are formal and which are informal. (Formal language almost always involves longer sentences then informal language.)

1. Nosotros estamos bien, gracias. Y usted, ¿cómo está, señorita?
2. Bien, gracias. ¿y tú?
3. Hola, Roberto. ¿Qué tal?
4. ¿Cómo está usted, doña Carmen?
5. Feliz fin de semana, señor Ortiz.
6. ¿Adónde vas, Julio?

C. La familia. Complete these sentences about your family.

1. Mamá y papá están ahora en...
2. Mi (*my*) hermano(-a) se llama... Estudia en la escuela secundaria (la universidad de) (*high school, the university of ...*)...
3. Mi abuelo(-a) viaja a...
4. Mi familia pasa las vacaciones en...

D. ¡Rápido! Select someone to be **la víctima**. Using questions from this chapter or from the **Capítulo preliminar**, the rest of the class will ask questions as rapidly as possible, and the victim will answer as many as he or she can. New victims should be selected from those who are slow to ask questions. In case you cannot think of any questions, here are some to use as starters.

1. ¿Hablas español? ¿italiano?   2. En la clase de español, ¿necesitas estudiar mucho?   3. ¿Viajas mucho?   4. ¿Deseas viajar a España?   5. ¿Cómo se dice *window* en español? ¿y *door*?   6. ¿Cómo se llaman los hijos de los tíos de una persona?   7. ¿Está el profesor en casa?   8. ¿Cómo estás?   9. ¿Trabajas en la cafetería?   10. ¿Regresas a clase mañana?

E. Mini-dramas. In small groups, create conversations for the following situations.

1. You call up your friend Silvia. Her mother, Mrs. García, answers the phone. She asks who is calling. You tell her your name, and she tells you that Silvia is not home right now. You ask how Silvia is, and she says that she is fine. Silvia is at the university but will be back soon. You tell Mrs. García that you plan to go by her house in a few minutes and (using a confirmation tag) find out if that's OK. She says yes, and you say you'll see her soon. You both say good-bye.
2. You and a friend are in a café in Madrid. You talk for a while, then your friend suggests visiting the **Museo del Prado**. You ask someone who is sitting at a table next to you if the museum is near or far from there. He/She answers, "It is very far, and it is probably closed (**probablemente cerrado**) today." "What a pity!" («**¡Qué lástima!**»), you reply. Then you thank him/her for the information. As an alternative, your friend suggests, "What if («**¿Qué tal si...?**») we visit the city of Toledo today?" You say, "OK, but we need a car. We'll take Uncle Jorge's car . . ." Your friend answers "OK," and you both leave the café.

VOCABULARIO ACTIVO

Cognados

el aeropuerto	la cámara	italiano	el presidente, la presidenta
el, la agente	en general	el mapa	el problema
argentino	la farmacia	el museo	el teatro
el, la artista	el hotel	la persona	el teléfono
el café	la información	la plaza	el, la turista

Verbos — Verbs

bailar	to dance
buscar (qu)	to look for
contestar	to answer
desear	to want, to wish
enseñar	to teach; to show
estudiar	to study
hablar	to talk; to speak
llamar	to call
llegar (gu)	to arrive
llevar	to carry; to take (along); to wear
mirar	to look (at); to watch
necesitar	to need
pasar	to pass; to spend (time)
preguntar	to ask
regresar	to return, to go back
ser	to be
tomar	to take; to drink
trabajar	to work
viajar	to travel
visitar	to visit

La familia

la abuela	grandmother
el abuelo	grandfather
la esposa	wife
el esposo	husband
la hermana	sister
el hermano	brother
la hija	daughter
el hijo	son
la madre	mother
la mamá	mom, mamma
la niña	girl, child
el niño	boy, child
el padre	father
los padres	parents; fathers
el papá	dad, papa
los parientes	relatives
el primo, la prima	cousin
los señores	Mr. and Mrs.
la tía	aunt
el tío	uncle

Otras palabras y frases

a	to
ahora	now
a la derecha	to the right
a la izquierda	to the left
al (a + el)	to the; at the
al lado (de)	next (to), beside
allí (or allá)	there
el avión	airplane
Bueno	Good; OK; Well
cerca (de)	near (to), nearby
la ciudad	city
de	of; from; about; made of
del (de + el)	from the; of the
¿Dónde?	Where?
enfermo	sick
los Estados Unidos	United States
el este	east
el hombre	man
hoy	today
lejos (de)	far (from)
mañana	tomorrow
la mujer	woman
mucho	a lot, (very) much
el norte	north
o	or
el oeste	west
pero	but
pronto	soon
¿qué?	what?
el regalo	gift
la semana	week
el sur	south
también	also

la traducción	*translation*
las vacaciones	*vacation*
la verdad	*truth*
el viaje	*trip*

Expresiones útiles

Bueno, nos vemos.	*Well, I'll be seeing you (literally, "Well, we'll see each other [soon]").*
¿De acuerdo?	*OK? Do you agree?*
Hasta luego.	*See you later.*
Hasta mañana.	*See you tomorrow.*
Hasta pronto.	*See you soon.*
Hola. ¿Quién habla?	*Hello. Who is this?*
¿No?	*Right? True?*
¿Verdad?	*Right? True?*

Don't forget: Definite and indefinite articles, page 33.

CAPÍTULO
DOS

Vista de Buenos
Aires, Argentina

DESCRIPCIONES

Funciones

- Making descriptions (1)

- Expressing admiration

- Describing locations

Vocabulario.   In this chapter you will describe people, places, and things.

Gramática.   You will discuss and use:

1. The present tense of regular **-er** and **-ir** verbs
2. Interrogative words
3. The prepósitions **a** and **de**, and the personal **a**
4. Adjectives and ordinal numbers
5. **ser** versus **estar**—when to use each verb

Cultura.   The dialogues take place in Buenos Aires, the capital of Argentina.

Esteban es... argentino, sociable, sensible *(sensitive)*.
Está en un restaurante con Pedro, Luis y Alicia.

Maricruz es... joven *(young)*, idealista, optimista.
Está en (la) clase. Está contenta.
Los estudiantes están contentos también.

Marta es... realista, responsable, inteligente.
Está en la universidad.

El museo es... importante, grande *(large)*, interesante.
Está en la ciudad.

Antónimos *(Antonyms).*   Give the opposite of each word.

1. realista
2. insociable
3. irresponsable
4. pesimista
5. aburrido *(boring)*
6. pequeño *(small)*
7. insensible
8. descontento
9. estúpido
10. viejo *(old)*

Preguntas

1. ¿Es optimista Esteban? ¿Maricruz? ¿Marta?   2. ¿Es usted optimista?   3. ¿Es sociable Marta? ¿Maricruz? ¿Esteban?   4. ¿Es usted sociable?   5. ¿Están contentos los estudiantes?   6. ¿Está contenta Maricruz?   7. ¿Están ustedes contentos?   8. ¿Está Maricruz en (la) clase o en un restaurante?   9. ¿Están ustedes en (la) clase?   10. ¿Está la universidad Cornell en una ciudad grande o pequeña? ¿y Harvard? ¿y la universidad de ustedes?   11. ¿Cómo es el profesor o la profesora? *(What is he or she like?)*   12. ¿Cómo son los estudiantes? (¿inteligentes y responsables? ¿jóvenes o viejos? ¿sociables o insociables?)   13. ¿Qué adjetivo(s) asocia usted *(do you associate)* con Michael Jackson? ¿con Bob Hope?   14. ¿Qué personas asocia usted con estos *(these)* adjetivos: descortés, idealista, popular, pesimista, intelectual?   15. ¿Qué adjetivo(s) asocia usted con su *(your)* restaurante favorito? ¿con su automóvil ideal? ¿con su libro de español?

I. El presente de indicativo de los verbos terminados en -*er* y en -*ir*

Luisa y Juan
estudian en la
biblioteca.

En la biblioteca de la Universidad Nacional, en Buenos Aires

JUAN *Lees* y *escribes* mucho, Luisa. ¿Qué *lees* ahora?

LUISA *Leo* un libro de filosofía y tomo notas porque necesito escribir una composición.

JUAN ¿Cómo? No *comprendo*. *Vivimos* en el siglo veinte. *Debemos* leer libros prácticos.

LUISA Pero Juan, también *debemos* estudiar filosofía. En la filosofía *descubrimos* «la verdad en la vida y la vida en la verdad».

JUAN *Creo* que los filósofos desean descubrir la verdad, pero tú *debes* descubrir la vida y vivir en la realidad..., ¿*comprendes*?

---

1. ¿Lee mucho Luisa? ¿Qué lee ahora?   2. ¿Qué escribe Luisa ahora?   3. ¿Qué cree Juan que debemos leer?   4. Según (*According to*) Luisa, ¿qué descubrimos en la filosofía?   5. ¿Está Ud. de acuerdo (*Do you agree*) con Juan? ¿y con Luisa? ¿Qué cree usted?

In the library at the National University, in Buenos Aires. JUAN: You're reading and writing a lot, Luisa. What are you reading now? LUISA: I'm reading a philosophy book and taking notes because I need to write a composition. JUAN: What? I don't understand. We're living in the twentieth century. We ought to read practical books. LUISA: But Juan, we must also study philosophy. In philosophy we discover "the truth in life and life in the truth." (This is a well-known phrase of the Spanish philosopher Miguel de Unamuno.) JUAN: I think that philosophers want to discover the truth, but you ought to discover life and live in reality. . . . Do you understand?

A. To form the present tense of a regular verb whose infinitive ends in **-er,** drop the infinitive ending **-er** and add the endings **-o, -es, -e, -emos, -éis,** and **-en.**

comer to eat

yo	**como**	nosotros(-as)	**comemos**
tú	**comes**	vosotros(-as)	**coméis**
usted, él, ella	**come**	ustedes, ellos, ellas	**comen**

¿Qué comes? Como unos
 sandwiches.
Marcelo come muchos sandwiches.

*What are you eating? I'm eating
 some sandwiches.*
Marcelo eats a lot of sandwiches.

The four forms printed in color are stressed on the stem syllable **co-;** the other two forms are stressed on an ending syllable **(-me[mos], -méis).**

B. Here are some other regular **-er** verbs.

aprender	*to learn*	deber	*to owe; should, ought to*
			(+ infinitive)
comprender	*to understand*	leer	*to read*
correr	*to run*	responder	*to respond*
creer (que)	*to think or believe (that)*	vender	*to sell*

Laura y yo creemos que la clase es
 aburrida.
Debo leer un libro de filosofía hoy
 pero no está en la biblioteca.
Venden libros en español en la
 librería del centro.
Esteban corre a la oficina de
 correos.

Laura and I think the class is boring.

*I should read a philosophy book
 today, but it's not in the library.*
*They sell books in Spanish in the
 downtown bookstore.*
Esteban runs to the post office.

C. To form the present tense of a regular verb whose infinitive ends in **-ir,** drop the infinitive ending **-ir** and add the endings **-o, -es, -e, -imos, -ís,** and **-en.**

vivir to live

yo	**vivo**	nosotros(-as)	**vivimos**
tú	**vives**	vosotros(-as)	**vivís**
usted, él, ella	**vive**	ustedes, ellos, ellas	**viven**

¿Viven ustedes en la calle Suárez?
No, vivimos en la calle Cabrillo.

Do you live on Suárez Street?
No, we live on Cabrillo Street.

The **-ir** verb endings are the same as the **-er** verb endings except in the **nosotros** and **vosotros** forms, the two forms stressed on a syllable that shows the conjugation ending.

D. Other common regular **-ir** verbs are:

abrir	*to open*	describir	*to describe*	recibir	*to receive, get*
decidir	*to decide*	escribir	*to write*		

¿Abres la ventana?	*Are you opening the window?*
Escribe un libro. Describe Buenos Aires.	*She's writing a book. It describes Buenos Aires.*
¿Reciben ustedes muchos regalos de la Argentina?	*Do you receive many gifts from Argentina?*
Escribimos cartas a la familia.	*We write letters to the family.*

EJERCICIOS

A. Actividades. Professor Benítez describes the activities of students in her class, but she always forgets a few people. Correct her, following the model.

MODELO Adela escribe muchos ejercicios. (Roberto y Juan)
Roberto y Juan también escriben muchos ejercicios.

1. Rolando aprende inglés. (Elena, yo, Mario y yo, ellas)
2. Ustedes escriben dos páginas. (nosotros, ellos, yo, Luis)
3. Tú abres la ventana. (los otros estudiantes, yo, Ramón, nosotros)

B. Imaginación y lógica. Assemble sentences from the three columns to tell what people do or do not do.

MODELOS **Los estudiantes corren a la clase.**

Usted no vive en el centro, ¿verdad?

Los estudiantes	leer	las preguntas
Yo	creer	sandwiches, ¿no?
Mi amiga y yo	correr	el libro todos los días
Usted	abrir	en el presidente
La profesora de inglés	comer	en el centro, ¿verdad?
Muchas personas	aprender	en la calle, ¿verdad?
Tú	vivir	a la clase
		las puertas
		en la biblioteca, ¿no?

C. En acción. Say what these people seem to be doing.

1. Las mujeres...

2. El señor García...

3. Juana...

4. Los estudiantes...   5. El niño...   6. La estudiante..

D. ¡Rápido!   Select someone to be **la víctima**. To be fair about it, you may want to draw cards (**robar cartas**). Everyone else will ask the lucky winner the following questions, in rapid succession, and the **víctima** will give complete-sentence answers to as many as he or she can. After a minute or two, select someone else for the same treatment.

1. ¿Corres a las clases?   2. ¿Lees libros prácticos?   3. ¿Estudias filosofía? 4. ¿Aprendemos mucho en la clase de español?   5. ¿Debes estudiar mucho? 6. ¿Comprendes el libro de español? (¿de filosofía? ¿de inglés?   7. ¿Abres la ventana? ¿Abres la puerta?   8. ¿Qué venden en la librería?   9. ¿Recibes muchas cartas?   10. ¿Escribes muchas cartas? ¿Qué describes en las cartas? 11. ¿Vives cerca o lejos de la universidad? ¿cerca o lejos de la oficina de correos?   12. ¿Comes en casa o en la cafetería de la universidad?

II. Las palabras interrogativas

Bariloche, con su lago Nahuel Huapi, es un centro turístico de la Argentina.

En la biblioteca de la Universidad de Buenos Aires

PEDRO   *¿Por qué* miras el mapa de la Argentina, Cindy?
CINDY   Porque deseo viajar.
PEDRO   *¿Adónde* deseas viajar? ¿Y *con quién?*
CINDY   Deseo visitar Bariloche con Sofía, una amiga italiana, pero, ¡creo que
        está muy lejos!
PEDRO   *¿Cuándo* viajan ustedes?
CINDY   Hoy. Llegamos a Bariloche mañana.
PEDRO   ¿Y *cómo* viajan ustedes...? ¿En avión?
CINDY   Sí, en avión.
PEDRO   Pues, ¡feliz viaje! Y hasta pronto.
CINDY   Hasta pronto. Chau, Pedrito.

---

1. ¿Qué mira Cindy? ¿Por qué?   2. ¿Con quién viaja Cindy?   3. ¿Adónde viajan
ellas?   4. ¿Cuándo llegan a Bariloche?   5. ¿Cómo viajan Cindy y Sofía?

In the library at the University of Buenos Aires.   PEDRO: Why are you looking at the map of Argentina,
Cindy? CINDY: Because I want to travel. PEDRO: Where do you want to travel? And with whom?
CINDY: I want to visit Bariloche with Sofía, an Italian friend, but I think it's very far away! PEDRO:
When are you traveling? CINDY: Today. We arrive in Bariloche tomorrow. PEDRO: And how are you
traveling . . .? By plane? CINDY: Yes, by plane. PEDRO: Well, (have a) good trip! See you soon. CINDY:
See you soon. Bye, Pedrito.

A. Information questions, unlike the *yes/no* questions discussed in Chapter 1,
invite the listener to respond with specific information. Such questions usually
begin with a question word. Some common question words are:

¿adónde?	*(to) where?*	¿dónde?	*where?*
¿cómo?	*how?*	¿por qué?	*why?*
¿cuál? ¿cuáles?	*which?*	¿qué?	*what?*
¿cuándo?	*when?*	¿quién? ¿quiénes?	*who?*
¿cuánto(-a,-os,-as)?	*how much? how many?*		

Notice that question words always have a written accent.

B. The question word is usually followed directly by a verb. The speaker's voice
falls at the end of the question.

¿Qué buscan los hermanos?	*What are the brothers looking for?*
¿Por qué viajas a los Andes?	*Why are you traveling to the Andes?*
¿Cómo regresas a Buenos Aires?	*How are you returning to Buenos Aires?*
¿Cuándo llegas a la ciudad?	*When do you arrive in the city?*
¿Dónde está el hospital?	*Where is the hospital?*
¿Adónde viajan los turistas?	*Where are the tourists traveling to?*
¿Cuántos estudiantes hay aquí?	*How many students are there here?*
¿Quién debe hablar ahora?	*Who ought to speak now?*
¿Cuál es el avión a Lima?	*Which is the plane to Lima?*

C. ¿Por qué?, meaning *why?*, is written as two words. Contrast it with **porque,** meaning *because,* written as one word and with no accent mark.

¿Por qué no regresas a Mendoza?	*Why don't you return to Mendoza?*
Porque trabajo aquí en Buenos Aires.	*Because I work here in Buenos Aires.*

D. ¿Dónde? asks about the location of a person, place, or thing. The word combines with the preposition **a** to ask where someone or something is going: **¿adónde?;** and with **de** to ask where someone or something is coming from: **¿de dónde?**.

¿Adónde viaja Sofía?	*Where's Sofía traveling to?*
¿De dónde regresan ellos?	*Where are they returning from?*

E. ¿Quién(es)?, like other pronouns, is often used with prepositions, but does not combine with them as one word.

¿Quién es la profesora aquí?	*Who is the professor here?*
¿A quién hablas?	*To whom are you speaking?*
¿Con quién(es) estudias?	*With whom are you studying?*
¿De quién es el libro?	*Whose book is it?*

F. ¿Qué? and **¿cuál(es)?** mean *what?* or *which?*

1. ¿Qué?, the word most often used, has just one form. It asks for a definition, an identification, or an explanation. **¿Qué?** usually means *what?*

¿Qué es esto? Es una computadora.	*What is this? It's a computer.*
¿Qué es la filosofía? Pues, no estoy seguro.	*What is philosophy? Well, I'm not sure.*
¿Qué deseas? Deseo viajar.	*What do you want? I want to travel.*
¿Qué ciudad deseas visitar? Bariloche.	*What city do you want to visit? Bariloche.*

2. ¿Cuál(es)? is used when the questioner asks for a selection from a list of possibilities. **¿Cuál(es)?** usually means *which?*

¿Cuál es el avión a Mendoza?	*Which is the plane to Mendoza?*
¿Cuáles llegan mañana?	*Which ones arrive tomorrow?*

G. ¿Cuánto(-a, -os, -as)? (*how much? how many?*), used as an adjective and as a pronoun, agrees in gender and number with the noun it describes or to which it refers.

¿Cuántos libros hay?	*How many books are there?*
¿Cuántas (computadoras) venden?	*How many (computers) are they selling?*

H. Words like **donde** (*where*), **cuando** (*when*), and **como** (*like, as*) are often *used as adverbial conjunctions, in which case no accent is written.*

Donde vives hay muchos museos, ¿verdad?	*There are a lot of museums where you live, right?*

Siempre están allí cuando llego.	*They're always there when I arrive.*
Juan es estudiante, pero habla como profesor.	*Juan is a student, but he speaks like a professor.*

But when such words reflect an embedded question, they are regarded as question words, and an accent is written on them to identify them as such. (You don't need to make this distinction in your own writing at this point, however.)

Preguntan { dónde hay un restaurante italiano.
cómo se dice *book* en español.
cuándo llegamos allí.

They're asking { *where there is an Italian restaurant.*
how "book" is said in Spanish.
when we arrive there.

EJERCICIOS

A. Una pregunta...   Using the question word indicated, ask questions to elicit the answers shown.

MODELO   ¿Qué?
Pablo busca el laboratorio.
¿Qué busca Pablo?

1. ¿Qué?
   a. Cindy y Sofía visitan Bariloche.
   b. Pablo estudia español.
   c. Paco necesita información.
2. ¿Con quién? ¿Con quiénes?
   a. Pedro habla con Cindy.
   b. Cindy está con Sofía.
   c. El profesor trabaja con los estudiantes.
3. ¿Quién? ¿Quiénes?
   a. Sofía y Teresa visitan Venezuela.
   b. Teresa desea visitar Tucumán.
   c. Clara y Pedro están en Buenos Aires.
4. ¿Dónde? ¿Adónde?
   a. La catedral está lejos de la escuela.
   b. María y Elena viajan a Tucumán.
   c. El restaurante está cerca de la plaza.
5. ¿Cuándo? ¿Cómo?
   a. Pedro regresa mañana a la universidad.
   b. Cindy y Sofía viajan en avión.
   c. La amiga de Cindy se llama Sofía.
6. ¿Por qué?
   a. Carmen no está aquí porque está en Rosario.
   b. Cindy mira el mapa porque desea viajar.
   c. Pedro busca un cuaderno porque necesita estudiar.

7. ¿Cuánto(-a, -os, -as)?
   a. Teresa desea visitar cinco plazas interesantes.
   b. Hay quince estudiantes en la clase de Pedro.
   c. Hay seis ciudades importantes en la Argentina.

B. Una charla (*A conversation*). Complete the following dialogue with the appropriate question words.

MIGUEL   Hola, Pedro, (1) ¿_____ estás?

PEDRO   No muy bien, Miguel. (2) ¿_____ es la clase de español?

MIGUEL   Mañana. (3) ¿_____ no estás muy bien?

PEDRO   Pues, porque estoy enfermo. (4) ¿_____ capítulos necesitamos estudiar?

MIGUEL   Ocho. ¿Deseas estudiar con nosotros?

PEDRO   ¿Con (5) _____ estudias?

MIGUEL   Con Teresa y Adela.

PEDRO   (6) ¿_____ desean estudiar hoy?

MIGUEL   Hoy deseamos estudiar la Argentina y el Paraguay.

PEDRO   El Paraguay... (7) ¿_____ está el Paraguay?

MIGUEL   Está cerca de la Argentina, al norte.

PEDRO   Y, (8) ¿_____ se llama la capital del Paraguay?

MIGUEL   Asunción. Pedro, tú necesitas estudiar mucho.

Entrevista

Ask a classmate the following questions. Then report the information to the class.

1. ¿Adónde deseas viajar, a la Argentina o al Perú?   2. ¿Deseas viajar en avión? ¿Por qué?   3. ¿Qué ciudad deseas visitar: San Francisco o Los Ángeles?   4. ¿Qué estudias? (¿matemáticas? ¿inglés? ¿filosofía?)   5. ¿Dónde estudias, en la biblioteca o en casa?   6. ¿Cuándo necesitas estudiar, hoy o mañana?

III. Las preposiciones a y de; a personal

En un típico restaurante argentino, Buenos Aires

En un restaurante de Buenos Aires

JULIA   Buenos días, Oscar.

OSCAR   Buenos días, Julia. ¿A quién buscas hoy? ¿Necesitas a Roberto...?

JULIA   No, busco a Elena, la hermana de Ramón.

OSCAR   ¡Ah! Elena, la estudiante de Uruguay. Ella está con una prima y visitan el norte argentino.

JULIA   ¿Y regresan pronto?

OSCAR   Creo que sí. Elena debe regresar porque trabaja aquí mañana.

---

1. ¿A quién busca Julia?   2. ¿Quién es Elena?   3. ¿Con quién está Elena? ¿Qué visitan?   4. ¿Por qué debe regresar Elena mañana?

In a restaurant in Buenos Aires. JULIA: Hello, Oscar. OSCAR: Hello, Julia. Who are you looking for today? Do you need Roberto . . .? JULIA: No, I'm looking for Elena, Ramon's sister. OSCAR: Ah! Elena, the student from Uruguay. She's with a cousin and they're visiting northern Argentina. JULIA: Are they coming back soon? OSCAR: I think so. Elena has to come back because she works here tomorrow.

A. **A** and **de**. Generally, **a** means *to,* and **de** means *from* or *of.*

Ella viaja a Bariloche.	*She's traveling to Bariloche.*
Regresan de Córdoba.	*They're returning from Córdoba.*

Other English equivalents are possible in specific contexts. Sometimes no equivalent word at all is used in English.

La hermana de Benigno está aquí.	*Benigno's sister is here.*
Carmen está de vacaciones.	*Carmen is on vacation.*

1. Use **en**, not **a**, to express location.

Ellos están en casa.	*They are at home.*
Nosotros estamos en el restaurante.	*We are at the restaurant.*

2. **De** is used to indicate possession (like an apostrophe in English), place of origin, and material out of which something is made.

Usted es de la Argentina, ¿verdad?	*You're from Argentina, right?*
El libro es de la profesora, ¿no?	*The book is the professor's, isn't it?*
El cuaderno es de papel.	*The notebook is made of paper.*

3. **De** is used as part of certain prepositions.

La catedral está cerca de la oficina de correos.	*The cathedral is near the post office.*
Los apartamentos no están lejos de la plaza.	*The apartments are not far from the plaza.*
El hospital está enfrente de la escuela.	*The hospital is opposite the school.*

4. Remember that when **a** or **de** precedes the definite article **el**, the preposition and the article contract: **al, del. A** and **de** do not contract with the other articles: **la, los, las.** There are no other contractions in Spanish.

Germán llega al museo.	*Germán arrives at the museum.*
Adelita viaja a la ciudad.	*Adelita travels to the city.*
Hay un restaurante dentro del hotel.	*There's a restaurant inside the hotel.*
La avenida está lejos de la universidad.	*The avenue is far from the university.*

5. **A** and **de** do not contract with the **El** that is capitalized as part of a name, or with the pronoun **él.**

Enrique viaja al Perú.*	*Enrique travels to Peru.*
Enriqueta viaja a El Salvador.†	*Enriqueta travels to El Salvador.*
Son de él.	*They're his.*

B. The personal **a.**

El señor mira *a* la señorita.

El señor mira los precios.

Elena busca *al* niño.

Elena busca el Hotel Nacional en el mapa.

---

*The **el** in **el Perú** is not capitalized and is sometimes omitted altogether.
†The **El** in **El Salvador** is capitalized; it is never omitted.

1. In Spanish, direct objects that refer to specific, known persons must be preceded by **a**. (In the sentence *I see Jim, Jim* is the direct object.) This is called the personal **a**.

Victoriano mira a la doctora.	*Victoriano looks at the doctor.*
Nacha llama a un amigo.	*Nacha calls a friend.*
La tía Pilar visita a los Navarro.	*Aunt Pilar is visiting the Navarros.*
But: Roberto mira la pizarra.	*Roberto is looking at the chalkboard.* (The direct object is a thing: no **a**)

2. The personal **a** is omitted in most uses of the verb **tener** *(to have).**

Tengo una hermana.   *I have a sister.*

EJERCICIOS

A. *¿A o de?*   Complete the sentences using the model below and adding words as necessary.

> **MODELO**   Es el lápiz... (la profesora).   **Es el lápiz de la profesora.**

1. Miro... (las amigas, el señor, los libros, los estudiantes, Carmen, el restaurante, el niño).
2. Es la computadora... (la señora, el profesor, los primos de Raúl, el laboratorio de lenguas, las amigas de Armando).
3. El restaurante está lejos... (el teatro, la catedral, los museos, el hospital).
4. Miguel vive cerca... (la universidad, los teatros, el centro, las librerías).

B. **Un detective.**   Alfonso is an amateur detective. Tell what (or whom) he's looking for, using the cues.

> **MODELO**   el hotel / los turistas
> **Alfonso busca el hotel y también busca a los turistas.**

1. La casa de Luis / Luis
2. el pasaporte / unos regalos
3. el señor Méndez / un restaurante
4. los abuelos / el pasaporte
5. las cámaras / las primas
6. los estudiantes / el profesor Ruiz

C. Traducción.   Give the Spanish equivalents of the following sentences.

1. Juan looks at Adela.   2. I want to visit Mr. Flores.   3. They are looking for an Italian restaurant.   4. The doctor is calling the parents now.

Preguntas

1. ¿Visita usted a unos amigos hoy? ¿al (a la) profesor(a) de español?   2. ¿Llama usted mucho a los amigos? ¿a un(a) amigo(-a) en particular? ¿A quién desea usted

---

*Tener *(to have)* will be introduced in Chapter 3.

llamar hoy? ¿mañana?   3. ¿Mira usted televisión? ¿Mira usted a veces (*sometimes*) al presidente en la televisión?   4. ¿Necesita usted a veces a los profesores? ¿al (a la) profesor(a) de español?   5. Cuando usted está de vacaciones, ¿qué visita? (¿museos? ¿teatros? ¿otras ciudades?) ¿A quién(es) visita? (¿a amigos? ¿a la familia? ¿a otras personas?)

IV. Los adjetivos y los números ordinales

El famoso obelisco domina la vista de la Avenida 9 de Julio en Buenos Aires.

En la Avenida 9 de Julio, una avenida importante de Buenos Aires

ISABEL ¡Hola, Clara! ¿Qué tal...? ¿Estás *contenta* en el hotel...?

CLARA Sí, y también estoy muy *cómoda*. Mi habitación está en el *décimo* piso...y ¡hay una vista *linda* de la ciudad!

ISABEL ¡Qué suerte! Las *primeras* impresiones son muy *importantes*. Creo que es tu *primer* viaje a Buenos Aires, ¿no?

CLARA Sí... pero es la *tercera* visita de Robert.

ISABEL ¿Robert...? ¿tu amigo *norteamericano*...?

CLARA Sí... Él y yo buscamos un *buen* restaurante *argentino*.

ISABEL Pues, cerca del Congreso está «La casa *argentina*». Es un restaurante *agradable* y los precios no son *altos*.

CLARA ¿Preparan comida *típica* allí?

ISABEL Sí, preparan *muchos* platos *excelentes* y también hay allí vinos *argentinos* que son *deliciosos*.

CLARA ¿Es *grande* el restaurante?

ISABEL No, es *pequeño* pero muy *cómodo*...¡y *romántico*!

1. ¿Está contenta Clara en el hotel?   2. ¿También visita Buenos Aires un amigo de Clara?   3. ¿Dónde está «La casa argentina»? ¿Cómo son los precios allí? 4. ¿Qué preparan en el restaurante?   5. ¿Es «La casa argentina» un restaurante grande? ¿Cómo es?

On Avenida 9 de Julio, an important avenue in Buenos Aires.   ISABEL: Hi, Clara! How's everything? Are you happy in the hotel? CLARA: Yes, and I'm very comfortable, too. My room is on the tenth floor . . . and there's a pretty view of the city! ISABEL: How lucky! First impressions are always important. I think this is your first trip to Buenos Aires, isn't it? CLARA: Yes, but it's Robert's third visit. ISABEL: Robert? Your North American friend? CLARA: Yes. He and I are looking for a good Argentine restaurant. ISABEL: Well, near the Congress is "The Argentine House." It's a pleasant restaurant and the prices are not high. CLARA: Do they prepare typical food there? ISABEL: Yes, they prepare many excellent dishes and there are also Argentine wines there that are delicious. CLARA: Is the restaurant large? ISABEL: No, it's small, but very comfortable . . . and romantic!

A. Agreement of adjectives

1. In Spanish, adjectives must agree in number and in gender with the nouns they modify. The most common singular endings for adjectives are **-o** *(masculine)* and **-a** *(feminine)*.

un doctor simpático	*a nice doctor*
una doctora simpática	*a nice doctor*
un estudiante argentino	*an Argentine student*
una estudiante argentina	*an Argentine student*
un museo mexicano	*a Mexican museum*
una universidad mexicana	*a Mexican university*
un vino delicioso	*a delicious wine*
una comida deliciosa	*a delicious meal*
un chico hispano	*an Hispanic boy*
una chica hispana	*an Hispanic girl*

2. Adjectives of nationality that end in consonants, and adjectives that end in **-dor,** are made feminine by adding **-a.**

un turista inglés*	*an English tourist*
una turista inglesa	*an English tourist*
un chico trabajador	*a hardworking guy*
una chica trabajadora	*a hardworking girl*
un muchacho alemán	*a German boy*
una muchacha alemana	*a German girl*

3. With very few exceptions, adjectives that don't end in **-o(-a)** or **-dor** have the same forms in the masculine and the feminine.

un examen difícil	*a difficult exam*
una pregunta difícil	*a difficult question*

*Remember that the written accent on the last syllable of the masculine form will not be necessary after you change the adjective to the feminine. Note also that adjectives of nationality are not capitalized.

el señor optimista	*the optimistic gentleman*
la señora optimista	*the optimistic lady*
un restaurante agradable	*a pleasant restaurant*
una persona agradable	*a pleasant person*

4. To form the plural of an adjective that ends in a vowel, add **-s.** To form the plural of an adjective that ends in a consonant, add **-es.**

las ciudades grandes	*the big cities*
unos exámenes difíciles	*some difficult exams*
los turistas corteses	*the polite tourists*
unas preguntas fáciles	*some easy questions*

B. Position of adjectives

1. Most adjectives are descriptive—that is, they specify size, shape, color, type, nationality, and so forth. Descriptive adjectives usually follow the nouns they modify.

un hombre hispano	*an Hispanic man*
una persona pesimista	*a pessimistic person*
unos señores amables	*some nice gentlemen*
la chica española	*the Spanish girl*
unos niños descorteses	*some impolite children*

2. However, adjectives that specify quantity usually precede the nouns they modify.

dos páginas	*two pages*
muchos regalos	*many presents*

3. Bueno(-a) and **malo(-a)** may be placed before or after a noun.

una buena comida	*a good meal*	una mala clase	*a bad class*
una comida buena		una clase mala	

C. Shortening of adjectives

1. Before a masculine singular noun, **bueno** is shortened to **buen** and **malo** to **mal.**

un buen restaurante	*a good restaurant*
un mal día	*a bad day*

2. Grande becomes **gran** before a singular noun of either gender; it normally means *great* when it precedes a noun and *large* when it follows a noun.

un gran libro	*a great book*
un libro grande	*a big book*
una gran ciudad	*a great city*
una ciudad grande	*a large city*

EJERCICIOS

A. Las invitadas (*The guests*).   Ana's friends are giving her a surprise party (for females only). Who will be the guests? Follow the model to find out.

> **MODELO**   una prima (bueno y trabajador)
> **una prima buena y trabajadora**

1. una estudiante (español)
2. una profesora (mexicano)
3. una muchacha (argentino)
4. una mujer (hispano típico)
5. una gran amiga (norteamericano)
6. una chica (inteligente y responsable)
7. una doctora (amable y simpático)
8. una tía (idealista y agradable)

B. Adjetivos correspondientes.   Complete each sentence with the adjectives in parentheses that could modify the person or thing indicated.

> **MODELO**   Estudio en una universidad (buena, grande, chileno, deliciosa)
> **Estudio en una universidad buena y grande.**

1. Preparan una comida (sociable, hispana, optimista, típica).
2. Trabajan en un restaurante (grande, argentina, elegante, trabajador, agradable).
3. Aquí hay hoteles (típicos, pequeños, contentos, cómodos).
4. Hablan con una turista (italiana, inglés, sensible, cortés, simpática, joven).
5. Buscamos una avenida (amable, típica, elegante, sociable, pesimista).

C. Una familia interesante.   The Padillas are an interesting and unusual family. None of the children takes after the parents. In fact, they are the exact opposites! Tell what each of them is like, following the models.

> **MODELOS**   El señor Padilla es sociable.
> **Los hijos son insociables.**
>
> La señora Padilla es cortés.
> **Las hijas son descorteses.**

1. El señor Padilla es sensible.
2. La señora Padilla es idealista.
3. El señor Padilla es viejo.
4. La señora Padilla es interesante.
5. El señor Padilla es optimista.

D. El amigo (La amiga) ideal.   Según usted, ¿cómo es el amigo (la amiga) ideal? Describe the ideal friend. Refer to the **Vocabulario activo** for help.

Preguntas

1. ¿Viaja usted mucho? ¿Adónde viaja cuando está de vacaciones? ¿Viaja con otros(-as) chicos(-as)?   2. ¿Hay buenos restaurantes argentinos aquí? ¿mexicanos? ¿italianos? ¿españoles? ¿Dónde? ¿Son altos los precios allí?   3. ¿Prepara usted comida típica norteamericana? ¿argentina? ¿mexicana?   4. ¿Cómo es la comida de la cafetería de la universidad? ¿buena o mala? ¿horrible o deliciosa?

5. ¿Cómo son los estudiantes de la universidad? ¿inteligentes? ¿responsables? ¿buenos? ¿malos? ¿trabajadores? ¿simpáticos?   6. ¿Cómo es la clase de español? ¿fácil o difícil? ¿interesante o aburrida? ¿grande o pequeña?

D. Ordinal numbers

1. The ordinal numbers *first* to *tenth* in Spanish are:

primero	*first*	sexto	*sixth*
segundo	*second*	séptimo	*seventh*
tercero	*third*	octavo	*eighth*
cuarto	*fourth*	noveno	*ninth*
quinto	*fifth*	décimo	*tenth*

2. Ordinal numbers are used to order or place in sequence and agree in number and gender with the nouns they modify. They are usually placed before the noun.*

Voy a viajar en segunda clase.	*I'm going to travel second class.*
Los primeros días de octubre son muy bonitos.	*The first days of October are very pretty.*
Es la décima pregunta.	*It's the tenth question.*

3. The final **-o** of **primero** and **tercero** is dropped before a masculine singular noun.

Tomo el tercer examen del semestre.	*I'm taking the third exam of the semester.*
Es el primer auto que venden.	*It's the first car they're selling.*

But before feminine and plural nouns, the ending is not dropped.

Ella es la tercera estudiante en llegar.	*She is the third student to arrive.*

4. For ordinal numbers higher than *tenth,* the cardinal numbers are normally substituted. They follow the noun.

Vivimos en la Avenida Once.	*We live on Eleventh Avenue.*
Vivimos en la Calle 34.	*We live on 34th Street.*
Estamos en el siglo veinte.	*We're in the twentieth century.*

EJERCICIOS

A. **El profesor distraído** (*The absent-minded professor*).   Professor Rodríguez is absent-minded and asks the class many simple questions. Answer his questions, following the model.

> **MODELO**   ¿Es hoy el primer día de clase o el segundo? (2^0)
> **Hoy es el segundo día de clase.**

---

*Ordinal numbers are abbreviated by writing the ending as a superscript after a number: **el 4° libro, la 3ª clase, los 1ᵒˢ días, el 1ᵉʳ examen.**

1. ¿En qué avenida está la librería de la universidad? (5ª, 9ª, 1ª, 7ª, 2ª)
2. ¿Qué capítulo estudiamos hoy? (1⁰, 8⁰, 4⁰, 3⁰, 10⁰)
3. ¿En qué siglo vivimos? (19, 20, 21)

B. ¿En qué piso están? Tell where these people are, according to the drawing.

MODELO ¿Está Roberto en la planta baja (*ground floor*)?
No, él escribe ejercicios en el octavo piso.

¿Dónde trabaja el señor Pérez? Trabaja (1) _____. Y Rosa, ¿dónde vive? Vive (2) _____. ¿El doctor Echeverría está con Rosa? No, está (3) _____.

La abuela invita al niño a comer en el restaurante. Comen (4) _____. Pobre Rafael está enfermo. Está (5) _____. ¿Y los hijos del señor Espinosa? Estudian (6) _____.

Tres turistas italianos buscan un apartamento (7) _____. Pero, aquí cerca hay personas que bailan, ¿no? Sí, son unos estudiantes que bailan (8) _____. Están de vacaciones.

V. *Ser vs. estar*

La Calle Florida,
Buenos Aires

En la Calle Florida, una calle elegante en el centro de Buenos Aires

ROBERTO Por favor, señor. ¿Dónde *está* la catedral?
DARÍO *Está* en la Plaza de Mayo.
ROBERTO ¿*Es* una iglesia antigua?
DARÍO Sí, *es* antigua,... pero no muy antigua. No *es* de estilo colonial.
Usted no *es* de aquí, ¿verdad?
ROBERTO No, *soy* turista. *Estoy* con unos amigos. *Somos* de Córdoba. *Estamos*
perdidos.
DARÍO Pues, la catedral no *está* lejos. *Es* fácil llegar allí. *Es* muy linda y *está*
cerca de un parque grande.
ROBERTO Muchas gracias, señor.
DARÍO De nada, señor. Adiós.

---

1. ¿Dónde está Roberto? 2. ¿Está la catedral en la Calle Florida? 3. ¿Cómo
es la catedral? 4. ¿Quién es Roberto? ¿Con quiénes está él? 5. ¿De dónde son
Roberto y los amigos de él?

On Calle Florida, an elegant street in the center of Buenos Aires. ROBERTO: Please, sir, where is the
cathedral? DARÍO: It's in the Plaza de Mayo. ROBERTO: Is it an old church? DARÍO: Yes, it's old, but
not very old. It's not in the colonial style. You're not from here, are you? ROBERTO: No, I'm a tourist.
I'm with some friends. We're from Córdoba. We're lost. DARÍO: Well, the cathedral is not far away.
It's easy to get there. It's very pretty and it's near a large park. ROBERTO: Thank you very much, sir.
DARÍO: You're welcome, sir. Good-bye.

A. Ser and **estar** both mean *to be.* **Ser** is used:

1. To link the subject to a noun (or to an adjective used as a noun).

Silvia es italiana.	*Silvia is (an) Italian.*
Somos turistas.	*We are tourists.*
José Luis no es comunista.	*José Luis is not a communist.*
El señor García es profesor.*	*Mr. García is a professor.*

2. With **de** to indicate place of origin, what something is made of, or possession— who owns it.

Soy de la Argentina.	*I'm from Argentina.*
Las páginas son de papel.	*The pages are made of paper.*
El cuaderno es de Ricardo.	*The notebook is Ricardo's.*

3. To indicate where an event takes place.

El concierto es en el Teatro Colón.	*The concert is at the Teatro Colón.*
La fiesta es en el hotel.	*The party is at the hotel.*

4. With equations or arithmetic.

Dos más dos son cuatro.	*Two plus two are four.*
Ocho menos siete es uno.	*Eight minus seven is one.*

5. With adjectives to express qualities or characteristics that are considered normal for the subject.

Teresa es alta.	*Teresa is tall.*
Los argentinos son amables.	*Argentines are nice.*

B. Estar is used:

1. To indicate location or position.

El hotel está cerca de la Avenida Colón.	*The hotel is near Avenida Colón.*
Estamos enfrente de la biblioteca.	*We are in front of the library.*
La oficina de correos está a la izquierda, ¿verdad?	*The post office is on the left, isn't it?*
No, está a la derecha.	*No, it's on the right.*

2. With adjectives to indicate the condition of a person or thing at a particular time, often the result of a change.

¿Cómo estás? Estoy bien, gracias.	*How are you? I'm fine, thank you.*
¿Por qué estás triste, Adela?	*Why are you sad, Adela?*
No estoy aburrido en la clase de español.	*I'm not bored in Spanish class.*

---

*When **ser** links the subject to a singular noun (or adjective used as a noun) indicating profession, nationality, religion, or political affiliation, the indefinite article is not used unless the noun is modified by an adjective or adjective phrase.

EJERCICIOS

A. Imaginación y lógica. Write original sentences, affirmative or negative, using items from each of the three columns.

MODELOS   **Los primos de Juan no están en la Argentina.**

La tía de Elena es italiana.

Diego		de Buenos Aires
La fiesta		en Bariloche
La profesora		norteamericano(-a, -os, -as)
Nosotros	ser	en la clase de español
Tú	estar	triste(s)
Elena y Marta		contento(-a, -os, -as)
Los muchachos		aburrido(-a, -os, -as)
Usted		inteligente
Yo		simpático(-a, -os, -as)
El profesor		perdido(-a, -os, -as)
		en un hotel grande

B. En las nubes (*In the clouds*).   When Rubén daydreams, he misses half of what is said. He asks questions to confirm what he thinks he's heard. Answer his questions, following the models.

MODELOS   ¿Los viajes? ¿interesantes?
Sí, los viajes son interesantes.

¿Tomás? ¿en clase?
Sí, Tomás está en clase.

1. ¿Ricardo? ¿en Bogotá?
2. ¿Los López? ¿de vacaciones?
3. ¿La universidad? ¿grande?
4. ¿Los abuelos? ¿bien?
5. ¿Nosotros? ¿estudiantes?
6. ¿Yo? ¿de Nueva York?
7. ¿Marta? ¿perdida?
8. ¿El libro? ¿de papel especial?
9. ¿Tú? ¿aburrido hoy?
10. ¿El concierto? ¿Teatro Nacional?

C. Las vacaciones de mis padres. Complete the following paragraph using the appropriate forms of **ser** and **estar**.

Ahora yo (1) _____ en la clase de español. Pepito (2) _____ en casa porque no (3) _____ bien. Él y yo (4) _____ hermanos pero no (5) _____ con mamá y papá ahora. Ellos (6) _____ en Buenos Aires. Ellos (7) _____ en un hotel grande. Mamá (8) _____ muy feliz allí. La ciudad (9) _____ bonita y el hotel (10) _____ de estilo colonial. Se llama el Hotel Continental y (11) _____ cerca de la oficina de correos. Papá y mamá (12) _____ de vacaciones. No (13) _____ aburridos en Buenos Aires. (14) _____ unas vacaciones interesantes, ¿verdad?

D. Traducción. Translate the following passage into Spanish.

Magda is in Buenos Aires. She's not Argentine; she's from Colombia. She's in a hotel. She's very comfortable because the hotel is very modern. The hotel is to the right of the post office. Magda is happy because she's visiting Buenos Aires and it is a pretty city. She wants to visit San Miguel de Tucumán tomorrow.

Preguntas

1. ¿Es usted argentino(-a)? ¿norteamericano(-a)? 2. ¿De dónde es usted? 3. ¿Cómo es usted? ¿bueno(-a)? ¿inteligente? ¿amable? ¿sensible? 4. ¿Dónde está la universidad? ¿cerca o lejos de la ciudad? 5. ¿Cómo está usted hoy? ¿y la familia? 6. ¿Está lindo el día? 7. ¿Son trabajadores los profesores y los estudiantes aquí? 8. ¿Cuál es el capítulo que estudiamos ahora: el primero o el segundo? 9. ¿Cuántas personas hay en la clase? ¿Cuántas están aquí hoy? 10. ¿Dónde están los estudiantes que no están aquí?

Study Hint: Studying Verbs

Spanish verbs have many endings. Here are some hints on how to study them:

1. Make charts on flashcards, especially for irregular verbs like **ser** and **estar**, but also for model regular verbs. Use charts to help memorize the endings.

2. Practice the forms by writing them in sentences. Make up questions, too. Think of *yes/no* and information questions.

3. Practice with a partner, taking turns asking and answering. Don't limit yourself to questions directed to "you" and vary the vocabulary. If you study alone, ask yourself the questions by reading aloud or recording them.

Here is an example based on the verb **trabajar. Yo trabajo en la cafetería de estudiantes. Elena trabaja en el hospital. Nosotros trabajamos mucho, ¿no? Muchos estudiantes trabajan en la universidad. ¿Dónde trabajas tú?**

Un gaucho en la pampa
argentina

EN BUENOS AIRES, EL PARÍS DE SUDAMÉRICA

En un autobús°. Los señores Brinsdon son turistas ingleses y están de vacaciones en Buenos Aires. Buscan el Museo de Historia Natural.[1]

SEÑOR BRINSDON	¡Dios mío!° El tráfico está horrible y el aire está contaminado°.
SEÑORA BRINSDON	Es el precio del progreso. Pero los porteños[2] son amables y la ciudad es bonita, ¿no?
SEÑOR BRINSDON	Sí, pero es muy grande. Estamos perdidos... ¿Cómo llegamos al museo?
SEÑORA BRINSDON	¿Por qué no preguntamos?
SEÑOR BRINSDON	Buena idea. *(Habla con una pasajera°.)* Por favor... ¿Dónde está el Museo de Historia Natural?
LA PASAJERA	Está lejos. Ustedes no son de aquí, ¿verdad?
SEÑORA BRINSDON	No, somos ingleses.
LA PASAJERA	¡Ah!, son de Inglaterra°. Pues... bienvenidos° al París de Sudamérica. ¿Por qué desean visitar el museo?
SEÑORA BRINSDON	Para ver las exposiciones sobre los animales[3] típicos del país°, sobre° la cultura de los indios y sobre...
LA PASAJERA	Un momento, por favor. Me llamo Alicia Discotto[4] y soy agente de viajes°. Por casualidad° estamos enfrente de la Agencia de Viajes Discotto. ¿Por qué no bajamos°?
SEÑOR BRINSDON	¿Para visitar el museo?
LA PASAJERA	No. Pero es posible visitar una estancia° moderna, ver° a los gauchos[5] y...
SEÑORA BRINSDON	Gracias, señora. Otro día,° quizás°. Hoy deseamos visitar el famoso Museo de Historia Natural.
LA PASAJERA	Bueno, adiós... ¡Y buena suerte°!

La señora Discotto baja del autobús. Los señores Brinsdon no bajan.

SEÑORA BRINSDON	Todavía° estamos perdidos. ¿Por qué no preguntas?
SEÑOR BRINSDON	Buena idea. *(A un pasajero)* Por favor... ¿dónde está el Museo de Historia Natural?
EL PASAJERO	Está lejos. Ustedes no son de aquí, ¿verdad?...

el autobús *bus* ¡Dios mío! *Good heavens!* contaminado *polluted* la pasajera *passenger* Inglaterra *England* bienvenidos *welcome* el país *country* sobre *on* agente de viajes *travel agent* por casualidad *by chance* bajar *to get down; get off (a bus)* la estancia *ranch* ver *to see* otro día *another day* quizás *perhaps* ¡buena suerte! *good luck!* todavía *still*

PREGUNTAS

1. ¿Dónde están los señores Brinsdon? 2. ¿De dónde son ellos? 3. ¿Qué buscan? 4. ¿Cómo se llama la pasajera? 5. ¿Qué museo desean visitar los señores Brinsdon? ¿Por qué? 6. ¿Llegan al museo los señores Brinsdon? 7. ¿Visita usted museos con frecuencia *(frequently)*?

NOTAS CULTURALES

1. The **Museo de Historia Natural**, known also as the **Museo de la Plata**, is in the city of La Plata, about 40 miles from Buenos Aires. It is a famous museum of natural history, science, anthropology, and ethnology.
2. **Porteño** (literally, *port dweller*) is the usual term for someone who lives in Buenos Aires, Argentina's capital and main port on the **Río de la Plata. Porteños** call their city the "Paris of South America."
3. Because of the variety of its terrain, Argentina has a number of unusual animals, like the **jaguar**; the **cóndor**, the largest bird of flight; and the **carpincho**, the largest living rodent, which sometimes attains a weight of 100 pounds and in some parts of South America is hunted by the natives for food.
4. If you think the name Discotto sounds more Italian than Spanish, you are correct. A large number of Argentineans are of Italian descent. The British, French, and Germans have also contributed to Argentina's population. Many Europeans settled in Argentina during the country's economic expansion during the second half of the nineteenth century.
5. The **gaucho**, or Argentine cowboy, is now more a legendary figure than a real one. In the early 1800s thousands of these men led a nomadic life on the **pampas** (*dry grasslands*), living off the wild herds of cattle and horses that had descended from those of the Spanish conquistadors. The word is also used for the descendants of the original **gauchos** who now work as ranchhands on the large **estancias** (*Argentine ranches*) and preserve some of the old traditions.

Funciones y *actividades*

In this chapter you have seen examples of some important language functions, or uses. Here is a summary and some additional information about these functions of language.

MAKING DESCRIPTIONS (1)

You've seen how to use adjectives with both **ser** and **estar**. Consult the **Vocabulario activo** for a complete list of adjectives from this chapter.

EXPRESSING ADMIRATION

A common way to express admiration is with an exclamation containing an adjective. To form exclamations, you can use the word **¡Qué...!** + an adjective. The adjective should agree in gender and number with the noun it describes.

¡Qué interesante! (el libro)	*How interesting!* (describing the book)
¡Qué lindas! (las niñas)	*How pretty!* (describing the girls)

You can also use **¡Qué...!** + a noun,
¡Qué...! + an adjective + a noun,
or **¡Qué...!** + noun + **más** + adjective.

¡Qué suerte!	*How lucky!*
¡Qué linda casa!	*What a pretty house!*
¡Qué señora más simpática!	*What a nice lady!*
¡Qué chicos más trabajadores!	*What hardworking young people!*

DESCRIBING LOCATIONS

Here are some prepositions of place or position that you have seen so far in this book.

a la derecha	*on, to the right*
a la izquierda	*on, to the left*
al lado de	*beside, next to*
cerca de	*near*
enfrente de	*in front of, opposite*
lejos de	*far from*

Now do the following activities, using the expressions you have just learned.

A. Descripciones. Use ¡**Qué**... + adjective!, ¡**Qué**... + noun!, ¡**Qué**... + adjective + noun! or ¡**Qué**... + noun + **más** + adjective! to describe these pictures. You may want to choose from these adjectives: **alto**, **bajo** *(short)*, **grande**, **pequeño**, **elegante**, **interesante**, **difícil**, **viejo**, **joven**. For other possibilities, refer to the **Vocabulario activo** in this chapter.

MODELO

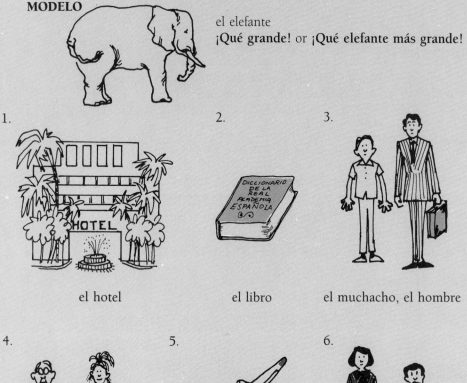

el elefante
¡**Qué grande!** or ¡**Qué elefante más grande!**

1.   2.   3.

el hotel   el libro   el muchacho, el hombre

4.   5.   6.

la abuela, la muchacha   el avión   la mujer, el hombre

B. Poema. In small groups write a short poem about someone you know. Use the following guidelines.

Line 1: name of person(s)   La profesora Valdés
Line 2: two adjectives that describe the person(s)   simpática, inteligente
Line 3: a place you associate with the person(s)   en la clase
Line 4: other adjectives   amable y cortés

C. En la plaza. Describe the picture, using prepositions and answering the
question, **¿Dónde está...?**, for the following things.

   MODELO   la escuela
   La escuela está cerca de los apartamentos Gloria.

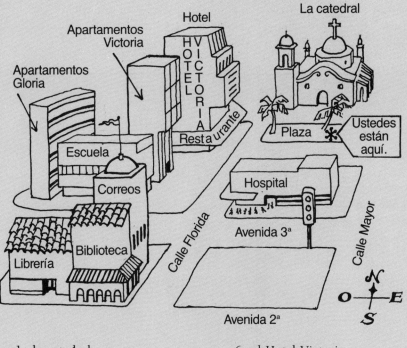

1. la catedral
2. el hospital
3. la escuela
4. la oficina de correos
5. los apartamentos Victoria

6. el Hotel Victoria
7. el restaurante
8. la librería
9. la biblioteca
10. ustedes (*Where are you?*)

D. Mini-dramas.   Role-play the following situations.

1. Your boyfriend or girlfriend has called you the following things during a
fight: irresponsible, impolite, insensitive, and so on. A friend calls you,
and you describe the conversation: _____ **dice que yo soy...**(_____
says that I am . . .). Your friend tells you that these things aren't true—
you're not really irresponsible, impolite, insensitive, and so on.

2. You and a friend are on a bus in Buenos Aires. "What a pretty city!"
your friend says. You ask a passenger where the **Teatro Colón** is and if it
is far. The passenger replies, "No, it's nearby." You have a short
conversation with the passenger, who asks who you are, where you are
from, and so forth. The passenger compliments you on your Spanish,
and you say, "Thank you, you're very nice." "The **Teatro Colón** is there
on the left," says the passenger. You say good-bye and get off.

VOCABULARIO ACTIVO

Cognados

el apartamento	concierto	hispano	mexicano	realista
la avenida	contento	idealista	norteamericano	responsable
la cafetería	delicioso	importante	optimista	el sandwich
la catedral	elegante	insociable	pesimista	sociable
colonial	el estilo	inteligente	práctico	típico
la computadora	la filosofía	interesante		

Verbos

abrir	to open
aprender	to learn
comer	to eat
comprender	to understand, comprehend
correr	to run
creer (que)	to believe, think (that)
deber	ought to, should, must + infinitive
describir	to describe
descubrir	to discover
escribir	to write
leer	to read
recibir	to receive
responder	to answer, respond
vender	to sell
vivir	to live

Adjetivos

aburrido	bored, boring
agradable	pleasant
alto	high; tall
amable	kind, nice, pleasant
bonito	pretty
bueno	good
cómodo	comfortable
cortés	polite
descortés	impolite
difícil	difficult
fácil	easy
feliz	happy
grande	large; great
joven	young
lindo	pretty
malo	bad
mucho	much; many, a lot of
pequeño	small
perdido	lost
sensible	sensitive
simpático	nice

trabajador	hardworking
triste	sad
viejo	old

Otras palabras y frases

la biblioteca	library
la calle	street
la carta	letter
el centro	downtown; center
la comida	food; meal
la chica	girl
el chico	boy
la escuela	school
estar de acuerdo	to agree, to be in agreement (with)
estar de vacaciones	to be on vacation
la habitación	room
la librería	bookstore
la muchacha	girl
el muchacho	boy
la oficina de correos	post office
el piso	floor
porque	because
el precio	price
Pues,...	Well, . . .
Según (Ana, José, etcétera)	According to (Ana, José, etc.)
el siglo	century
la vida	life
el vino	wine

Expresiones útiles

dentro (de)	inside, within
enfrente (de)	in front of, opposite
más	plus; more

> Don't forget: Interrogative words, pages 52–54
> Ordinal numbers, page 63

Hay veinte millones de habitantes en la Ciudad de México. Es la ciudad más grande del mundo. ¿Qué más puede Ud. decir de la ciudad?

Ávila es una pequeña ciudad en España. La muralla *(wall)* alrededor de la ciudad se construyó en el siglo XI. ¿Cómo es diferente Ávila de una ciudad norteamericana?

Los países del Caribe, Centroamérica y algunas partes de Sudamérica tienen un clima tropical. Aquí se ve una selva *(forest)* tropical en Costa Rica. ¿Qué problemas presenta una zona tropical a los habitantes?

La economía de México depende mucho del turismo. En las costas del país hay centenares de bellas playas como las de Cancún. ¿Qué otros países hispanos atraen muchos turistas? ¿Por qué?

En los Andes del Perú, los indios usan las llamas como bestias de carga *(beasts of burden)* porque pueden travesar las montañas fácilmente. ¿Cómo es el clima de esta región? ¿Hay una región similar en los EEUU?

Los gauchos viven en las pampas de la Argentina donde cuidan *(take care of)* el ganado *(cattle)*. Describa el gaucho. ¿Cómo se compara con el «cowboy»?

Los indios de México y de Guatemala son famosos por sus telas hechas a mano *(fabrics made by hand)*. ¿Qué hacen con las telas?

En algunos países hispanoamericanos más de cincuenta por ciento de la gente trabaja en la agricultura. ¿Qué cultiva el hombre en esta foto? ¿Qué otros productos se cultivan en el mundo hispánico?

Los mercados al aire libre son muy populares en los pueblos. ¿Qué venden estos indios en el mercado?

Muchos méxicoamericanos viven en California y otras partes del suroeste de nuestro país. ¿Qué muestra esta pintura mural de su cultura?

El Paseo del Río es muy famoso en San Antonio, Tejas. Se puede dar un paseo en barco o caminar por allí. Durante los días festivos, se presentan espectáculos hispanos como éste. ¿Cómo se celebran los días festivos en su comunidad?

En la ciudad de Nueva York, los puertorriqueños celebran sus orígenes cada año con un desfile (parade) por la Quinta Avenida. ¿Cuáles son los desfiles más populares de este país?

LECTURA I

El mundo° hispánico

world

¿Desea usted hablar español y pasar unas semanas estupendas? Bueno, un viaje a tierras° hispánicas es una idea excelente. Siempre° es posible viajar con la imaginación, ¿no...?

lands, countries
always

Primero llegamos a México, al sur de los Estados Unidos. En el centro hay una meseta° donde está la capital, Ciudad de México, una ciudad grande,

plateau

Ciudad de México, capital del país

moderna, con muchos parques° y museos. En los pueblos° hallamos° tradiciones antiguas°, comidas regionales deliciosas ¡y mucha hospitalidad!

parks towns
we find
ancient

¿Visitamos ahora el Caribe°? En tres de las islas° del Caribe la gente° habla español: los cubanos en Cuba, los puertorriqueños en Puerto Rico y los dominicanos en la República Dominicana.

The Caribbean
islands
people

San Juan, Puerto Rico

Al sur de México está América Central. Es una región tropical con muchas montañas° y volcanes activos. En seis de las pequeñas repúblicas (Guatemala, El Salvador, Honduras, Nicaragua, Costa Rica y Panamá), la gente habla español. En Belice hablan inglés.

mountains

La Plaza de Mayo, plaza colonial de Buenos Aires, Argentina

Llegamos luego° a los nueve países° hispanos de América del Sur: al norte, Venezuela, Colombia y (el) Ecuador; en el centro, (el) Perú, Bolivia y (el) Paraguay; y al sur, Chile, (la) Argentina y (el) Uruguay. (El) Brasil y las Guayanas no son países hispanos.

then countries

Sudamérica (América del Sur) es un mundo de contrastes geográficos donde es posible visitar ruinas de civilizaciones muy antiguas y también ciudades muy modernas y cosmopolitas.

La Costa del Sol, España

Finalmente, cruzamos° el Océano Atlántico y llegamos a España°, un país   we cross Spain
de regiones muy diferentes. En la costa del Mediterráneo, el clima° es ideal.   climate
La capital, Madrid, está en la meseta central donde las temperaturas son
extremas. Andalucía, al sur, es famosa por sus° ciudades históricas y su   **por...** for its
música.

Y ahora, ¿cuál de los países del mundo hispánico desea usted visitar?

PREGUNTAS

1. ¿Cómo es la capital de México? ¿Qué hallamos en los pueblos?   2. ¿Cuáles
son las tres islas del Caribe donde la gente habla español?   3. ¿Cuántas repúblicas
hispanas forman América Central?   4. ¿En América del Sur, qué países hispanos
están al norte? ¿en el centro? ¿y al sur?   5. ¿Qué países de América del Sur no
son hispanos?   6. ¿Qué es posible visitar en Sudamérica?   7. ¿Por qué es famosa
Andalucía?

Breve repaso de geografía (*Brief geography review*).   Complete the following
sentences with words and phrases from the reading.

    MODELO   Cruzamos el _____ _____ y visitamos _____.
              Cruzamos el Océano Atlántico y visitamos España.

1. Un viaje a tierras _____ es una idea _____.
2. La capital de México _____ Ciudad de México y _____ en una
   meseta.
3. En los pueblos mexicanos hallamos comidas _____ _____.
4. América Central _____ una región con volcanes _____.
5. Sudamérica _____ un mundo de contrastes _____.
6. Madrid _____ en la meseta central de España.
7. En la costa del Mediterráneo, el clima es _____.

La biblioteca de la
UNAM, Ciudad de
México

ESTUDIOS UNIVERSITARIOS

Vocabulario. In this chapter, you will talk about university studies.

Gramática. You will discuss and use:

1. The present tense of **tener**
2. Idiomatic expressions with **tener**
3. Demonstrative adjectives and pronouns
4. The present participle and the present progressive tense
5. Cardinal numbers from 100 to 1,000,000 and their multiples

Cultura. The dialogues take place in Veracruz and Mexico City, the capital of Mexico.

Funciones

- Using numbers
- Expressing incomprehension

En la librería universitaria. In the university bookstore, students from the Universidad Nacional Autónoma de México (UNAM) are looking for books. Say what field each is studying.

> **MODELO** Consuelo busca libros sobre (*about*) las civilizaciones de
> Sudamérica.
> **Consuelo estudia antropología.**

> LIBRERÍA UNIVERSITARIA
>
> | | |
> |---|---|
> | Antropología | Física |
> | Arquitectura | Historia |
> | Biología | Ingeniería |
> | Ciencias de | Literatura |
> | computación | Matemáticas |
> | Ciencias naturales | Medicina |
> | Ciencias políticas | Psicología |
> | Ciencias sociales | Química |
> | Filosofía | Sociología |

1. Lola busca libros con muchas ecuaciones ($24x + 6y = 150$).
2. Sofía busca libros de Cervantes y de Shakespeare.
3. Chepa busca libros de Freud.
4. Maruja busca libros sobre los gobiernos (*governments*) de Sudamérica.
5. Manuel busca libros sobre la estructura del átomo.
6. Rosalía busca libros sobre los animales y las plantas.

Asociaciones. Match these famous people with their fields.

> **MODELO** Albert Einstein ____g.____ física

1. Miguel de Cervantes   a. filosofía
2. Albert Einstein   b. música
3. Wolfgang Mozart   c. antropología
4. Sócrates   d. literatura
5. Sigmund Freud   e. arquitectura
6. Frank Lloyd Wright   f. psicología
7. Joyce Brothers   g. física
8. Marie Curie
9. Margaret Mead

Preguntas

1. ¿Qué estudia usted?   2. ¿Cree usted que la química (la física, el español, la historia, la medicina...) es aburrida(-o) o interesante? ¿Es fácil o difícil?   3. ¿Qué debe estudiar usted si desea ser doctor(a)? (¿ingeniero[-a]? ¿biólogo[-a]? ¿psicó-

logo[-a]?)   4. Ahora muchas personas estudian ciencias de computación, ¿verdad? ¿Y usted también estudia ciencias de computación?   5. ¿Desea estudiar las civilizaciones de México? (¿la civilización española? ¿la historia de Sudamérica?)   6. ¿Lee usted libros de ciencias? (¿de ciencias naturales? ¿de literatura? ¿de música? ¿de matemáticas? ¿de sociología? ¿de ingeniería? ¿de ciencias políticas?)

I. El presente de indicativo de *tener*

En una librería hay libros para todos.

En una librería cerca de la UNAM

BÁRBARA	¿*Tienes* tiempo de asistir a la conferencia esta tarde?
DORA	No, no *tengo* tiempo, Bárbara. Roberto y yo *tenemos* otros planes para hoy: caminar por el parque, visitar el Museo de Antropología...
BÁRBARA	¿Y el examen de historia que *tienen* mañana?
DORA	No *tiene* importancia. Además, en el museo aprendo mucho, especialmente cuando estoy allí con Roberto.
BÁRBARA	Comprendo... La escuela de la vida, ¿no?

1. ¿Tiene tiempo Dora de asistir a la conferencia?   2. ¿Qué planes tienen Dora y Roberto?   3. ¿Cree Dora que el examen tiene importancia? ¿Por qué?   4. ¿En qué escuela aprende Dora?

In a bookstore near UNAM.   BÁRBARA: Do you have time to attend the lecture this afternoon? DORA: No, I don't have time, Bárbara. Roberto and I have other plans for today: walking in the park, visiting the Museum of Anthropology . . . BÁRBARA: And the history exam you have tomorrow? DORA: It's not important (has no importance). Besides, I learn a lot in the museum, especially when I'm there with Roberto. BÁRBARA: I understand . . . The school of life, right?

The verb **tener** is irregular.

tener to have

tengo	tenemos
tienes	tenéis
tiene	tienen

Notice that the **yo** form ends in **-go.** The three forms stressed on the stem change their stem vowel from **e** to **ie.**

No tengo mucho tiempo.	*I don't have much time.*
¿Tenemos tiempo de comer?	*Do we have time to eat?*
¿Qué tienes allí? —Muchas cosas.	*What do you have there?—Lots of things.*
Arnaldo tiene otros planes para hoy.	*Arnaldo has other plans for today.*
Los señores Salazar tienen muchos libros sobre la medicina azteca.	*Mr. and Mrs. Salazar have a lot of books about Aztec medicine.*

EJERCICIOS

A. ¿Tienen planes? Tell about everyone's plans for today and tomorrow, following the model.

MODELO Ellos tienen exámenes hoy. (tú)
Tú no tienes exámenes hoy.

1. Roberto tiene planes interesantes para mañana. (tú, los turistas, nosotros)
2. No tengo tiempo hoy. (ellas, nosotros, Dora, los estudiantes)
3. Tenemos una fiesta mañana. (los amigos de Ana, Armando, yo, Elena y Juan, usted, tú)

B. Imaginación y lógica. Create ten sentences using the following sentence elements. Use each subject pronoun twice.

		un examen de sociología hoy
		una amiga estupenda
él	tenemos	un libro de historia española
yo	tienen	una casa muy grande
ustedes	tiene	tiempo de llamar a Susana
tú	tengo	dos clases de psicología
nosotros	tienes	muchas ideas aburridas
		abuelos mexicanos
		una hermana doctora
		los libros de Gloria

C. Una charla (*A chat*). Complete the dialogue with the correct forms of **tener.**

DELIA Ernesto, ¿(1) _____ (tú) tiempo de visitar al tío Pedro?
ERNESTO Sí, mamá. (2) _____ tiempo. Y Conchita y yo (3) _____ un libro para él.

DELIA   Pero Conchita (4) _____ un examen hoy, ¿no?

ERNESTO   ¡Sí! Además, creo que ella (5) _____ otros planes.
El problema es que necesito unos pesos. ¿(6) _____ (tú) unos pesos para el taxi?

Preguntas

1. ¿Tiene la universidad una biblioteca buena?   2. ¿Tienen programas en español aquí en la televisión?   3. ¿Tiene usted una clase de francés? (¿de matemáticas? ¿de biología? ¿de literatura?) ¿Son fáciles o difíciles?   4. ¿Tiene usted amigos(-as) mexicanos(-as)? (¿argentinos[-as]? ¿españoles[-as]?)   5. ¿Tenemos muchos estudiantes trabajadores en la clase? ¿en esta universidad?   6. ¿Tiene usted una familia grande o pequeña? ¿Cuántos hermanos tiene usted?   7. ¿Tiene usted muchos libros? ¿y muchos libros de español?

II. Expresiones idiomáticas con *tener*

La plaza central de Veracruz

En casa de la familia Lorenzo en Veracruz. Carlos, un estudiante mexicano, y John, un estudiante norteamericano, hablan con la señora Lorenzo.

CARLOS   Mamá, *tenemos ganas de* viajar a la playa.

SRA. LORENZO   ¿Cómo? ¿A la playa? Pero tú y John *tienen que* estudiar, ¿no? Y también *tienen que* comer pronto.

CARLOS   Pero no *tenemos hambre.* Y hoy yo no *tengo que* trabajar mucho para las clases de mañana.

JOHN   Además, *tenemos calor.* Dicen que las playas de Veracruz son muy agradables.

SRA. LORENZO   Pues, muchachos, yo *tengo dolor de cabeza*. Uds. viajan a la playa y yo tomo dos aspirinas, ¿de acuerdo?

1. ¿Adónde tienen ganas de viajar Carlos y John?   2. ¿Por qué no desean comer? 3. ¿Tiene que trabajar mucho Carlos para las clases de mañana?   4. ¿Tiene calor John?   5. ¿Qué problema tiene la señora Lorenzo?

At the home of the Lorenzo family in Veracruz. Carlos, a Mexican student, and John, an American student, are talking with Mrs. Lorenzo. CARLOS: *Mom, we feel like traveling to the beach.* SEÑORA LORENZO: *What? To the beach? But you and John have to study, don't you? And you also have to eat soon.* CARLOS: *But we're not hungry. And today I don't have to work much for tomorrow's classes.* JOHN: *Besides, we're hot. They say that the beaches in Veracruz are very pleasant.* SEÑORA LORENZO: *Well, boys, I have a headache. You travel to the beach and I'll take two aspirins. OK?*

A. Many expressions in Spanish use the verb **tener.** For example:

tener...años	*to be . . . years old*
tener ganas de + infinitive	*to feel like (doing something)*
tener prisa	*to be in a hurry*
tener que + infinitive	*to have to (do something)*

¿Cuántos años tiene Marisa?	*How old is Marisa?*
Marisa tiene 29 años.	*Marisa is 29.*
Tengo ganas de visitar Puebla.	*I feel like going to Puebla.*
Cuando estamos de vacaciones, no tenemos prisa.	*When we're on vacation, we're not in a hurry.*
Tienes que trabajar.	*You've got to work.*

B. The construction **tener** + noun often corresponds to English *to be* + adjective.

tener		to be	
	calor		*warm, hot*
	frío		*cold*
	hambre		*hungry*
	sed		*thirsty*
	celos		*jealous*
	cuidado		*careful*
	éxito		*successful*
	miedo		*afraid*
	razón		*right* (**no tener razón =** *to be wrong, mistaken*)
	sueño		*sleepy*
	suerte		*lucky*

Tenemos calor. Viajamos a la playa.	*We're warm. We are traveling to the beach.*
Cristóbal no tiene miedo de viajar a Cuba.	*Cristóbal isn't afraid to travel to Cuba.*
El Sr. Padilla no tiene razón.	*Mr. Padilla is mistaken.*

C. In other instances **tener** is equivalent to *to have,* but note that the indefinite article is not used in Spanish in these cases.*

tener dolor de cabeza	*to have a headache*
tener dolor de estómago	*to have a stomachache*
tener fiebre	*to have a fever*

D. To express ideas similar to English *very,* a form of the adjective **mucho,** agreeing with the noun, is used with **tener.** Notice that **calor** and **dolor** are masculine nouns, and **fiebre, hambre, razón, sed,** and **suerte** are feminine.

José María tiene muchos años.	*José María is very old.*
Tengo muchas ganas de ir.	*I feel very much like going.*
Delia tiene mucha prisa.	*Delia's in a big hurry.*
Cuando Ramón tiene mucho calor, bebe muchos refrescos.	*When Ramón is very warm, he drinks lots of cold drinks.*
Cuando Elena cruza la calle, tiene mucho cuidado.	*When Elena crosses the street, she's very careful.*
Marcos tiene mucha fiebre.	*Marcos has a high fever.*
Pues, su padre tiene mucha razón.	*Well, your father is very right.*

EJERCICIOS

A. Asociaciones.   Which **tener** expression do you associate with the following?

> **MODELO**   Cuando cruzo una calle o avenida...   **tener cuidado**

1. Cuando leo «Veracruz es la capital de México»...
2. Cuando viajo al desierto...
3. Cuando recibo cinco mil pesos...
4. Cuando tomo una aspirina...
5. Cuando deseo comer...
6. Cuando corro mucho...
7. Cuando recibo una A en un examen...
8. Cuando deseo tomar una Coca-Cola...
9. Cuando deseo viajar a la playa...
10. Cuando necesito estar en un hospital...

B. Fuera de control *(Out of control).*   **El profesor Galdós** feels that his students are doing exactly as they please today. Answer the questions for his students, using an expression with **tener.**

> **MODELO**   ¿Por qué abres la ventana, Miguel?
> **Porque tengo calor.**

1. ¿Por qué comes ahora, Susana?
2. ¿Por qué toma una Coca-Cola Edgar?
3. ¿Por qué toman aspirinas Marta y Roberto?
4. ¿Por qué no estudian ustedes?
5. ¿Por qué cree Jorge que Guadalajara es la capital de México?

---

*Tener is sometimes used in informal speech to ask the time: **¿Qué hora tienes?** *What time do you have?* The standard expressions for telling time are presented in Chapter 5.

C. En acción. Describe the following pictures, using a **tener** expression for each.

MODELO   El señor Gutiérrez tiene prisa.

1.   2.   3.

4.   5.   6.

Preguntas

1. ¿Tiene usted frío hoy? ¿calor?   2. ¿Tiene usted hambre? ¿sed?   3. ¿Cuántos años tiene usted?   4. «Nueva York es la capital de los Estados Unidos.» ¿Tengo razón o no? ¿Cómo se llama la capital de los Estados Unidos?   5. ¿Tiene ganas de viajar? ¿Adónde? ¿Por qué?   6. En general, ¿qué desea beber cuando tiene sed?   7. ¿Tiene usted cuidado cuando cruza una avenida o una calle?   8. En general, ¿tiene usted miedo de viajar en avión? ¿de recibir una F en español? (¿en física? ¿en historia? ¿en química?)   9. En general, ¿tiene usted sueño en la clase de español (¿de biología? ¿de inglés? ¿de matemáticas?)

III.   Los adjetivos y pronombres demostrativos

El Estadio Olímpico
de la UNAM

**El profesor Movitz de la Universidad de Michigan visita
la Universidad Nacional Autónoma de México.**

PROFESOR MOVITZ	Y *aquel* edificio, ¿qué es?
PROFESORA LÓPEZ	¿*Aquél* que tiene el mural estupendo? Es el estadio de *esta* universidad. *Ese* mural es de Diego Rivera.
PROFESOR MOVITZ	¡Ah, sí! El famoso pintor mexicano. En Michigan tenemos un mural interesante de Rivera. Está en el Museo Metropolitano de Arte de Detroit.
PROFESORA LÓPEZ	¡Sí, tiene razón! Pero creo que después de *estas* dos horas en la UNAM, ¡usted debe tener mucha sed! ¿Tiene ganas de tomar un refresco, un té o un café?
PROFESOR MOVITZ	Pues..., ¡*ésa* es una buena idea!
PROFESORA LÓPEZ	En *aquella* cafetería que está al lado de la librería tienen una gran variedad de refrescos...
PROFESOR MOVITZ	Entonces, ¿por qué no caminamos en *esa* dirección?

---

1. ¿Qué edificio mira el profesor Movitz?   2. ¿Quién es Diego Rivera?
3. ¿Tiene sed el profesor Movitz?   4. ¿Tiene la cafetería muchos refrescos?

Professor Movitz of the University of Michigan is visiting the National Autonomous University of Mexico. PROFESSOR MOVITZ: And that building, what is it? PROFESSOR LÓPEZ: That one over there that has the great (stupendous) mural . . .? It's the stadium of this university. That mural (a mural done in mosaics) is by Diego Rivera. PROFESSOR MOVITZ: Oh, yes! The famous Mexican painter. We have an interesting mural by Rivera in Michigan. It's in the Metropolitan Art Museum in Detroit. PROFESSOR LÓPEZ: Yes, you're right. But I think that after these two hours in UNAM, you must be very thirsty. Do you feel like having a cold drink, some tea, or coffee . . .? PROFESSOR MOVITZ: Well . . . , that's a good idea! PROFESSOR LÓPEZ: In that cafeteria next to the bookstore they have a large variety of cold drinks . . . PROFESSOR MOVITZ: Well, why don't we walk in that direction?

A. Demonstrative adjectives

1. Demonstrative adjectives are used to point out a particular person or object. They precede the nouns they modify and agree with them in gender and number.

Demonstrative Adjectives			
	Singular	**Plural**	
Masculine	**este** *this*	**estos** *these*	
Feminine	**esta**	**estas**	
Masculine	**ese** *that*	**esos** *those*	
Feminine	**esa**	**esas**	
Masculine	**aquel** *that (over there)*	**aquellos** *those (over there)*	
Feminine	**aquella**	**aquellas**	

¿Comes en esta cafetería?   *Do you eat in this cafeteria?*
Este edificio es muy alto.   *This building is very high.*

¿Ese programa? Es aburrido.	*That program? It's boring.*
Esos chicos son bajos.	*Those boys are short.*
Esas señoritas son mexicanas.	*Those young ladies are Mexican.*
Llevo aquel diccionario, por favor.	*I'll take that dictionary, please.*
Aquella estudiante no es hispana.	*That student (over there) isn't Hispanic.*

2. Both **ese** and **aquel** correspond to *that* in English. **Ese** may be used in most contexts. **Aquel,** which refers to something far away from the speaker, is used less frequently in Spanish America than in Spain.

B. Demonstrative pronouns

1. Demonstrative pronouns in Spanish have the same form as demonstrative adjectives, except that the pronouns have written accents. They agree in gender and number with the noun they replace.

¿Éste? Es un libro de historia.	*This? It's a history book.*
¿Éstos? Son calendarios.	*These? They're calendars.*
¿Ése? Es un estudiante mexicano.	*That one? He's a Mexican student.*
¿Quiénes son aquellas chicas?	*Who are those girls?*
¿Aquéllas? Son amigas de Carmen.	*Those? They're friends of Carmen.*

2. A demonstrative pronoun is used when the noun is not present.

Adjective Noun		**Pronoun**
Busco	este	libro.	Busco	éste.
I'm looking for this book.		*I'm looking for this one.*

3. Spanish also has three neuter pronouns that refer to statements, ideas, or something that has not yet been identified: **esto** *this,* **eso** *that,* and—in Spain— **aquello** *that* (distant). They have no plural forms and do not take a written accent.

¿Qué aprendemos de todo esto?	*What do we learn from all this?*
¿Qué es eso?	*What's that (thing, situation, etc.)?*
¿Qué es esto? Es un calendario.	*What's this? It's a calendar.*
Todo aquello tiene lugar lejos de aquí.	*All that takes place far from here.*

EJERCICIOS

A. Preguntas y respuestas. Answer each question with one word, as in the model, pointing with your finger to the object as you respond.

MODELO ¿Cuál es el libro de usted? **Éste.**

1. ¿Cuáles son los papeles de la profesora (del profesor)?
2. ¿Cuáles son los libros de español que usamos este semestre?
3. ¿Cuál(es) es (son) la(s) pizarra(s) de la clase?
4. ¿Cuál es la silla de usted?
5. ¿Cuál es el escritorio de la profesora (del profesor)?

B. La transformación.   Switch the subject of each sentence from feminine to masculine and make related changes.

> **MODELO**   Aquellas profesoras son buenas.
> **Aquellos profesores son buenos.**

1. Esta mujer es muy trabajadora.
2. Esa niña es muy buena.
3. Esas señoras son de Puebla.
4. Aquella señora es estudiante.
5. Estas mexicanas son amables.
6. Esas turistas ingleses están en Veracruz.

C. Imaginación y lógica.   Create sentences, using words from each column and making the necessary changes.

los chicos			cafetería
yo			restaurantes
ella			casa
usted			mesas
Juan y yo	comer en	este	museos
tú	hablar con	ese	librería
Diego y Clara	tener ganas de visitar	aquel	estadio moderno
los turistas			profesora
			señores mexicanos

D. ¿Cómo son ellos?   Using adjectives from the list given below or others you know, describe your classmates. Use demonstrative adjectives and pronouns to indicate whom you are describing.

> **alto, bajo, simpático, inteligente, feliz, joven, viejo, responsable, sensible, trabajador, triste, bonito**

> **MODELOS**   Ese señor es bajo pero esta señorita es alta.
>
> Esas señoras son trabajadoras.

Preguntas

1. ¿Cómo es esta ciudad?   2. ¿Hay un hotel bueno en esta ciudad? ¿Cómo se llama?   3. ¿Es moderno ese hotel?   4. ¿Hay un hospital en esta ciudad? ¿Cómo se llama?   5. ¿Cómo es ese hospital?   6. ¿Hay otras universidades en esta ciudad? ¿Hay muchas? ¿Cómo se llaman?   7. Y esta universidad, ¿es grande o pequeña?   8. ¿Hay restaurantes estupendos en esta ciudad? ¿Cómo se llaman?   9. ¿Son altos los precios en esos restaurantes?   10. ¿Escribe usted muchas composiciones este semestre?

IV. El gerundio y el presente progresivo

Las pirámides de
Teotihuacán, an-
tigua ciudad azteca

Gloria y Manuel hablan por teléfono.

GLORIA — Tengo dolor de cabeza porque *estoy estudiando* para un examen de
ciencias de computación, pero no *estoy aprendiendo* mucho. ¡Esto es
muy aburrido, Manuel! ¿No tienes ganas de visitar las pirámides de
Teotihuacán...?

MANUEL — Pues, en este momento, toda la familia *está comiendo* y *mirando* un
partido de fútbol en televisión.

GLORIA — Pero, ¡una visita a Teotihuacán es más interesante! ¿Qué aprendes
mirando un partido de fútbol...? En las pirámides tienes toda una
lección de historia.

MANUEL — Tienes razón, Gloria. Ahora mismo paso por allí.

1. ¿Qué está estudiando Gloria?   2. ¿Cómo está?   3. ¿Qué tiene ganas de visitar?   4. ¿Qué está mirando la familia de Manuel?   5. ¿Aprende Manuel mirando
un partido de fútbol?

Gloria speaks to Manuel on the telephone. GLORIA: I have a headache because I'm studying for a
computer science exam, but I'm not learning much. This is very boring, Manuel! Don't you feel
like visiting the pyramids at Teotihuacán? MANUEL: Well, right now (at this moment), the whole
family is eating and watching a soccer match on television. GLORIA: But a visit to Teotihuacán is
more interesting. What do you learn by watching a soccer match . . . ? You have a whole history
lesson in the pyramids. MANUEL: You're right, Gloria. I'm coming by there right now.

A. Present participles in English end in *-ing*. In Spanish, present participles are formed by adding **-ando** to the infinitive stem of **-ar** verbs and **-iendo** to the infinitive stem of most **-er** and **-ir** verbs.

hablar, hablando	*speaking*
comer, comiendo	*eating*
vivir, viviendo	*living*

Hablando de Teotihuacán, las pirámides son antiguas y muy interesantes.	*(Since we are) speaking of Teotihuacán, the pyramids are ancient and very interesting.*

B. Present participles of verbs whose stem ends in a vowel take the ending **-yendo** rather than **-iendo.**

creer, creyendo	*believing*
leer, leyendo	*reading*

The present participle of **ir** is **yendo.**

C. A present participle is combined with a present-tense form of **estar** to form the present progressive. The present progressive is used to emphasize that an action is going on at the moment.

México está progresando mucho.	*Mexico is progressing a lot.*
Ahora mismo estoy comiendo.	*I'm eating right now.*
Este año la familia Wong está viviendo en Cuernavaca.	*This year the Wong family is living in Cuernavaca.*

D. In Spanish the present progressive is used much less frequently than in English. The simple present tense in Spanish is used to describe ongoing actions and can be translated with an English progressive form.

¿Qué escribes en estos días?	*What are you writing these days?*
Escribo un libro sobre el calendario azteca.	*I'm writing a book on the Aztec calendar.*

The present progressive emphasizes the immediacy of an action and the fact that it is occurring at that very moment.

Ahora estoy trabajando en el segundo capítulo del libro.	*Now I'm working on the second chapter of the book.*
En este momento mis hermanas están llegando a México.	*Right now my sisters are arriving in Mexico.*

EJERCICIOS

A. **En este momento...**   Marta and Juan are discussing what they and their friends are doing right now. Form sentences following the model.

> **MODELO**   Ahora Roberto está hablando con Juanita. ¿Y Gloria? (escribir una composición)
> **Ahora Gloria está escribiendo una composición.**

1. En este momento Miguel está corriendo. ¿Y María? (tomar café)
2. Ahora mismo Enrique está leyendo. ¿Y José? (bailar en una discoteca)
3. Ahora Pepe y Luis están viajando en avión. ¿Y Raúl y Ana? (vivir en Puebla)
4. Ahora mismo Eduardo y Catalina están estudiando. ¿Y nosotros? (hablar)

B. Hablando de México.   Following the model, say what is going on at the present time in Mexico.

MODELO   México progresa mucho.
En este momento, México está progresando mucho.

1. Los amigos de Juana viven en la capital.
2. Carlos Fuentes escribe un libro.
3. Los estudiantes viajan a Cuernavaca.
4. Venden muchas cosas bonitas.
5. Los turistas visitan el Museo Nacional de Arqueología.
6. Los mexicanos comen en restaurantes buenos.
7. Descubren otras pirámides.

Preguntas

1. ¿Está usted estudiando ahora?   2. ¿Están mirando televisión los amigos?
3. ¿Está usted comiendo en este momento? ¿pensando? ¿contestando preguntas?
¿abriendo regalos?   4. ¿Aprenden ustedes mucho escuchando la radio? ¿escuchando al profesor o a la profesora de español? ¿mirando televisión? ¿leyendo un libro de historia? ¿escribiendo composiciones? ¿estudiando para los exámenes?

V. Los números cardinales 100 a 1.000.000

Coatlicue, diosa
(*goddess*) azteca de
la Tierra y la
Muerte

En la Librería Porrúa en la Calle San Juan de Letrán

RAMOS	Buenas tardes, señorita. Necesito un libro sobre los aztecas.
SRTA. CASTILLO	Tenemos muchos... Por ejemplo, aquí tiene éste, *Historia del calendario azteca.* ¿Es usted estudiante?
RAMOS	Sí. ¿Y el precio, por favor?
SRTA. CASTILLO	*Mil-trescientos-cincuenta-pesos.*
RAMOS	Más despacio, por favor.
SRTA. CASTILLO	*Mil trescientos cincuenta* pesos.
RAMOS	¡Es el año de la inflación! ¿Y aquél que está allá?
SRTA. CASTILLO	*¿El reverso de la conquista?* Ése cuesta *novecientos treinta* pesos, señor.
RAMOS	Bueno, gracias. No tengo mucho dinero. Aquí los libros son muy caros... Tengo que buscar el libro que necesito en la biblioteca.

1. ¿Dónde está el estudiante?   2. ¿Qué necesita el estudiante?   3. ¿Tienen allí libros sobre los aztecas?   4. Por ejemplo, ¿qué libros tienen? ¿Cómo se llaman? 5. ¿Compra un libro el estudiante? ¿Por qué?   6. Según el estudiante, ¿son caros los libros en esa librería?   7. Por ejemplo, ¿qué precio tiene el primer libro? ¿y el segundo libro?   8. Según el estudiante, ¿qué tiene que hacer él?

In the **Porrúa** Bookstore on **San Juan de Letrán** Street   RAMOS: Good afternoon, Miss. I need a book on the Aztecs. SEÑORITA CASTILLO: We have many (of them) . . . For example, here you have this one, *History of the Aztec Calendar.* Are you a student? RAMOS: Yes. And the price, please? SEÑORITA CASTILLO: One-thousand-three-hundred-fifty-pesos. RAMOS: More slowly, please. SEÑORITA CASTILLO: One thousand three hundred fifty pesos. RAMOS: This is the year of inflation! And that one over there? SEÑORITA CASTILLO: *The Other Side of the Conquest?* That one costs nine hundred thirty pesos, Sir. RAMOS: Well, no thank you. I don't have much money. Books are very expensive here. . . . I'll have to look in the library for the book I need.

100	cien(to)	200	doscientos(-as)	900	novecientos(-as)
101	ciento uno(-a)	201	doscientos uno(-a)	1000	mil
102	ciento dos	300	trescientos(-as)	1001	mil uno(-a)
111	ciento once	400	cuatrocientos(-as)	1010	mil diez
120	ciento veinte	500	quinientos(-as)	1100	mil cien(to)
121	ciento veintiuno(-a)	600	seiscientos(-as)	1101	mil ciento uno(-a)
130	ciento treinta	700	setecientos(-as)	1200	mil doscientos(-as)
131	ciento treinta y uno(-a)	800	ochocientos(-as)	1.000.000	un millón (de)

A. **Cien** is used before a number larger than itself (**mil** and **millón),** before a noun, and in counting (**noventa y nueve, cien, ciento uno...**). **Ciento** is used before a smaller number. It does not have a feminine singular form.

ciento nueve calles	*109 streets*
ciento cincuenta niñas	*150 girls*
cien mil habitantes	*100,000 inhabitants*

B. The hundreds from 200 to 900 do agree in gender with the nouns they modify.

doscientos ocho niños	*208 boys*
doscientas ocho niñas	*208 girls*
setecientas cuatro calles	*704 streets*

C. Uno becomes **un** before a masculine noun, **una** before a feminine noun.

trescientas una escuelas	*301 schools*
ciento ochenta y un libros	*181 books*

D. The word **y** is used between tens and units but not between hundreds and tens or between hundreds and units.

treinta y uno	*31*
ciento veinte	*120*
ciento uno	*101*

E. Mil is used to express the number 1,000.

mil novecientos ochenta y nueve	*1989*
mil sesenta y seis	*1066*
dos mil uno	*2001*
cuarenta mil treinta y tres	*40,033*
doscientos mil cuatrocientos veintiuno	*200,421*
But: miles de estudiantes	*thousands of students*

F. Un millón *(one million)* is followed by **de** before a noun. The plural is **millones.**

Ella desea ganar un millón de dólares.	*She wants to win one million dollars.*
Ahora él tiene tres millones de pesos.	*Now he has three million pesos.*

G. In writing numerals and decimals, Spanish and English follow opposite practices in the use of the period and the comma.

Spanish	**English**
1.000.000	1,000,000
13,6	13.6

EJERCICIOS

A. El dictado *(Dictation).* Take turns reading the following sequences of numbers with a classmate and jotting them down. Then check to see that the numbers as written are correct.

1. 1; 100; 1.000; 1.000.000
2. 3; 13; 33; 333; 333.333
3. 6; 16; 66; 1.666; 66.000
4. 5; 15; 55; 500; 1.500; 500.000; 5.000.000
5. 7; 77; 700; 1776; 17.000; 70.000; 70.000.000

B. Los datos y las cifras *(Facts and figures).* Looking for a clue to tomorrow's lottery, Sr. Roque de la Huerta circled the following numbers in his copy of *Excelsior,* one of Mexico's great newspapers. Read the items to the class.

1. 1985
2. la página 161
3. 555.000 personas
4. 120.000 estudiantes
5. 201 señoras

6. 100 pesos
7. 179 hoteles modernos
8. 999 turistas nerviosas
9. precio: $1.000.000 (pesos)
10. 30.125 espectadores *(spectators)*

C. El examen de historia. One person will read the events listed, and another will select the correct date for each event from the choices given. Check the dates at the bottom of the page if you're not sure.

MODELO Cristóbal Colón llega a las Américas.
1492 (mil cuatrocientos noventa y dos)

1. Los norteamericanos escriben la Declaración de Independencia.
2. Miguel de Cervantes escribe *Don Quijote.*
3. México tiene una revolución.
4. Ronald Reagan es presidente de los Estados Unidos.
5. John F. Kennedy es el presidente norteamericano.

a. 1980
b. 1910
c. 1960
ch. 1776
d. 1969
e. 1605
f. 1492

Preguntas

1. ¿Más o menos *(more or less)* cuántas personas viven en esta ciudad? 2. ¿Cuántos estudiantes hay en esta universidad? ¿en esta clase? 3. ¿Qué precio tiene un Mercedes Benz? 4. ¿Más o menos cuántas personas viven en la ciudad de Nueva York? ¿en California? 5. ¿Aproximadamente *(Approximately)* cuánto gana *(earns)* un profesor o una profesora? 6. Si hay 1500 pesos en un dólar, ¿cuántos pesos hay en $10? ¿en $100? 7. ¿Cuántos son quinientos y quinientos cinco? 8. ¿Qué precio debe tener una casa pequeña en esta ciudad?

Study Hint: Utilizing Study Time

Learning a second language requires daily practice and review. Here are some hints on how to budget your study time:

1. Always review before you begin studying new material.

2. Make use of short periods of time as well as longer ones. Don't postpone studying until you have one or two hours. Even fifteen minutes of studying verbs or vocabulary can refresh your memory.

3. Personalize your study of Spanish, imagining what you would say in Spanish in various situations at the university, at home, or with a Spanish-speaking friend. Try talking or just thinking to yourself in Spanish as often as possible, not just when you are preparing for class or studying for a test.

---

1. ch. 1776   2. e. 1605   3. b. 1910   4. a. 1980   5. c. 1960

La Piedra del Sol está en el Museo
Nacional de Antropología de la capital
mexicana.

MÉXICO: EL MUSEO NACIONAL DE ANTROPOLOGÍA

*Martha, una joven neoyorquina°, estudiante de antropología, está en el
Museo Nacional de Antropología de la Ciudad de México[1] con Felipe,
un amigo mexicano.*

FELIPE   ¿Todavía° crees que los buenos museos están todos en Nueva
York?

MARTHA   Bueno...allá tenemos unos treinta y cinco o cuarenta. Pero éste...
¡Qué estupendo! Es una maravilla°. Hay arquitectos que vienen° a
México sólo° para visitar este museo.

FELIPE   Sí, eso es verdad, y también vienen antropólogos o estudiantes de
antropología como tú. Aquí es posible aprender mucho sobre las
civilizaciones indígenas° del pasado°.

MARTHA   ¿Estudian ustedes la historia de los aztecas y de los mayas en la
universidad?

FELIPE   ¡Claro!° Mi hermana es profesora de historia y tiene muchos estudiantes en una clase de civilización azteca. Ellos van en excursiones regulares a lugares históricos. Por ejemplo, hoy visitan las
pirámides de Teotihuacán.[2]

MARTHA   ¿Cómo? Más despacio, por favor. ¿Las pirámides de qué?

FELIPE   De Teotihuacán, una antigua ciudad azteca que está cerca de aquí.

MARTHA   ¡Ah, sí! Tengo fotografías de Teotihuacán en uno de mis libros,
pero es difícil pronunciar el nombre de ese lugar. Yo deseo visitar
esas pirámides, pero hoy debo explorar este museo.

Entran a otra sala.°

MARTHA   ¡Hombre!° Aquél debe ser el famoso calendario azteca.[3] ¡Qué im-
presionante°!

FELIPE   Y es un calendario bastante° exacto. El año azteca tiene dieciocho meses° de veinte días... y cinco días extras.

MARTHA   Ahora que hablas del tiempo, es hora de° comer, ¿no?

FELIPE   Sí, y dentro del museo hay una cafetería excelente.

MARTHA   Creo que debemos comer tortillas[4] en honor de Cinteotl, el dios° del maíz°.

FELIPE   Para neoyorquina, tú sabes° mucho.

MARTHA   Gracias. Todos los neoyorquinos somos inteligentes.

FELIPE   ¡Y modestos!

---

neoyorquina *New Yorker, from New York*   todavía *still*   la maravilla *marvel, wonder*   vienen *come*   sólo *only*   indígenas *native, indigenous*   el pasado *the past*   ¡Claro! *Of course!*   Entran a otra sala. *They go into another room.*   ¡Hombre! *Wow!*   impresionante *impressive*   bastante *rather, very*   meses *months*   es hora de... *it's time to . . .*   el dios *god*   el maíz *corn*   sabes *you know*

PREGUNTAS

1. ¿Dónde están los dos amigos?   2. ¿Quién cree que todos los buenos museos están en Nueva York?   3. ¿Quiénes vienen a México para visitar el Museo Nacional de Antropología? ¿Por qué?   4. ¿Qué estudian Felipe y los otros estudiantes mexicanos en la universidad?   5. ¿Es profesora de arquitectura la hermana de Felipe?   6. ¿Qué visitan hoy los estudiantes de esa profesora?   7. ¿Es bastante exacto el calendario azteca?   8. ¿Cuántos meses tiene el calendario azteca? 9. ¿Quién es Cinteotl?   10. ¿Dónde comen los dos amigos?   11. ¿Come usted tortillas? ¿Y toma usted tequila? ¿Kahlúa?

NOTAS CULTURALES

1. The National Museum of Anthropology in Mexico City is an immense building with a huge suspended roof and central patio. It houses exhibits from all over the world, but most contain artifacts from the many Indian peoples that have successively inhabited various regions of Mexico.

2. **Teotihuacán**, which means "city of the gods" or "where men become gods," dates from the first century A.D. Located 33 miles north of Mexico City, it covers 8 square miles and contained dwelling places, plazas, temples, and palaces of priests and nobles. The Pyramid of the Moon, at the north end, and the great Pyramid of the Sun, at the east end, are its most impressive features.

3. The Aztec calendar stone, or **Piedra del Sol**, is a gigantic carved stone from the sixteenth century. The Aztec year consisted of eighteen months, each with twenty days. Five extra days, considered unlucky and dangerous, followed. During this time, the Aztecs stayed close to home and behaved cautiously for fear that an accident would set a bad pattern for the entire year ahead.

4. Tortillas are flat corn pancakes, sometimes eaten with fillings, but more often eaten plain like bread. Corn has been a staple of the Mexican diet for as long as history and mythology record.

Funciones y *actividades*

In this chapter you have seen examples of some important language functions, or uses. Here is a summary and some additional information about some of these functions of language.

USING NUMBERS

You have practiced using numbers for dates, counting, and stating prices. When you travel to a Spanish-speaking country, you'll need to use numbers for many reasons. Here are some important questions and statements that involve numbers.

¿Cuánto cuesta(n)?	*How much does it (do they) cost?*
¿Cuánto cuesta esa computadora?	*How much is that computer?*
¿Cuánto cuestan esos libros de historia azteca?	*How much do those books on Aztec history cost?*
Éste cuesta 9.500 pesos.	*This one costs 9,500 pesos.*
Ése cuesta 10.000 pesos.	*That one costs 10,000 pesos.*
En total, cuestan 19.500 pesos.	*They cost a total of 19,500 pesos.*
¿Cuál es el número de teléfono...?	*What is the telephone number . . . ?*
¿Cúal es el número de teléfono del Hotel Continental?	*What is the telephone number of the Continental Hotel?*
Es 5-18-07-00.	*It's 5-18-07-00.*
¿Cuál es su número de teléfono?	*What is your telephone number?*
Es 5-63-60-66.	*It's 5-63-60-66.*

Telephone numbers, especially the last four, are often expressed in pairs.

Necesito cambiar un cheque de viajeros de 50 dólares.	*I need to change a $50 traveler's check.*
¿Cuál es el número de su pasaporte?	*What is the number of your passport?*
Es 060027583.	*It's 060027583.*

EXPRESSING INCOMPREHENSION

Even in your native language, you probably find that you frequently have to stop someone who is speaking and ask him or her to clarify or explain something, repeat part of a sentence, slow down, and so on. In a foreign language, it's even more important to learn how to stop a speaker and ask for clarification. Here are some ways to express that you just aren't following and need some help.

¿Cómo?	*What?*	¿Perdón?	*Pardon me?*
No comprendo.	*I don't understand.*	¿Qué?	*What? (very informal)*
¿Mande?	*What? (Mexico)*		

¿Cómo? is used to ask the speaker to repeat; **¿Qué?** will usually elicit a specific answer to the question *What?* If you want the speaker to repeat, you can say:

Otra vez, por favor.	*Again, please.*	**Repita, por favor.**	*Repeat, please.*

If you want him or her to slow down, you can say:

Más despacio, por favor.   *Slower, please.*

If you miss part of a statement or question, you can use a question word to ask just for the part you missed.

¿Pero dónde (cuándo, por qué, etcétera)...?

When you have a general idea of what the speaker is saying but just want to confirm that you understand, you may want to use the confirmation tags: **¿(no es) verdad?** and **¿no?**.

María estudia química, ¿verdad?

Now do the following activities, using the expressions you have just learned.

A. Un momento, por favor. You don't understand what someone is saying to you when you hear the following sentences. Interrupt the speaker and ask for clarification.

> **MODELO**   El avión de Caracas llega en tres horas.
> **¿Cómo? ¿Cuándo llega el avión?**

1. Roberto estudia ciencias sociales y matemáticas en la Universidad de Salamanca.
2. La señora Otavalo vive en Chiquinquirá, pero ahora está en Bucaramanga.
3. El señor Montenegro tiene sesenta y seis años. La señora Montenegro tiene sesenta y dos años. Ellos tienen una fiesta mañana.
4. ¿El número de teléfono del señor Barrios? 62-84-51.
5. Aquelestudiantesellamaosvaldo. Creoqueesmuysimpático. (Said rapidly)

B. Mini-dramas. Role-play the following situations.

1. You are in the Porrúa Bookstore in Mexico City. You want to buy a book on Aztec history. You ask the price. The sales clerk answers: 13,600 pesos. You say that you need to change a $10 traveler's check. (In 1987 there were 1360 pesos in one dollar.) She asks you three questions: 1. the telephone number of your hotel; 2. your room number; and 3. your passport number. You answer the questions. She says thank you and cashes the check. You say thank you and good-bye.
2. You're at the doctor's office. The doctor asks how old you are. You reply. She asks why you are there, and you reply that you have a headache and that you're sleepy. She tells you that you don't have a fever, but that you should take two aspirins and call tomorrow.
3. You are in the National Museum of Anthropology in Mexico City. Someone comes up to you and asks where the famous Aztec calendar stone is. You don't understand at first and ask for clarification. She explains, but you say you don't know. (**No sé.**) Then you ask where the museum's cafeteria is. She tells you but you don't understand at first, so you ask her to say it more slowly. You thank her and say good-bye.

VOCABULARIO ACTIVO

Cognados

la aspirina	el dólar	mexicano	la pirámide
azteca	el estadio	moderno	el plan
el calendario	estupendo	el momento	el programa
la civilización	el examen	el mural	progresar
la composición	la importancia	la música	el semestre

Verbos y expresiones con *tener*

beber	*to drink*
cruzar	*to cross, go across*
ganar	*to earn; win*
tener	*to have*
tener calor	*to be warm, hot*
tener cuidado	*to be careful*
tener fiebre	*to have a fever*
tener frío	*to be cold*
tener ganas	*to want to, feel like (doing something)*
tener hambre	*to be hungry*
tener miedo	*to be afraid*
tener prisa	*to be in a hurry*
tener que + infinitive	*to have to . . .*
tener razón	*to be right*
tener sed	*to be thirsty*
tener sueño	*to be sleepy*
tener suerte	*to be lucky*
tener dolor de cabeza	*to have a headache*
tener dolor de estómago	*to have a stomachache*

Estudios universitarios (University studies)

la antropología	*anthropology*
la arqueología	*arqueology*
la arquitectura	*arquitecture*
la biología	*biology*
la ciencia	*science*
las ciencias de computación	*computer science*
las ciencias naturales	*natural sciences*
las ciencias políticas	*political science*
las ciencias sociales	*social science*
la física	*physics*
la historia	*history*
la ingeniería	*engineering*
la literatura	*literature*
las matemáticas	*mathematics*
la medicina	*medicine*
la música	*music*
la psicología	*psychology*

la química	*chemistry*
la sociología	*sociology*

Otras palabras y frases

ahora mismo	*right now*
el año	*year*
bajo	*short*
caro	*expensive*
cien(to)	*(one) hundred*
la cosa	*thing*
cuando	*when (conjunction)*
el edificio	*building*
menos	*less*
mil	*(one) thousand*
el millón	*million*
para	*for, in order to*
el partido de fútbol	*soccer game*
el peso	*peso, currency of Mexico*
el refresco	*soft drink; refreshment*
la playa	*beach*
por ejemplo	*for example*
el tiempo	*time*
todo	*(a) whole, (an) entire*

Expresiones útiles

¿Cómo?	*What? Pardon me.*
Más despacio, por favor.	*More slowly, please.*

Cognados falsos

asistir a	*to attend*
la conferencia	*lecture; sometimes conference*

Don't forget: Demonstrative adjectives and pronouns, pages 86–87
Cardinal numbers from 100 to 1,000,000, pages 92–93

El Lago de los
Incas en los Andes
chilenos

LAS ESTACIONES Y EL TIEMPO

Vocabulario. In this chapter, you will talk about the weather, the seasons, and the calendar.

Gramática. You will discuss and use:

1. The present tense of **hacer**, a verb with the general meaning of *to make* or *to do,* and weather expressions using this verb and others
2. The present tense of **ir** *(to go)* and the **ir a** + *infinitive* construction, which corresponds to *to be going to (do something)*
3. Direct object pronouns
4. The days of the week and dates

Cultura. The dialogues take place in Chile.

Funciones

- Making small talk
- Giving a warning
- Expressing gratitude

¿QUÉ TIEMPO HACE HOY?

Hace (muy) buen tiempo.

Hace (muy) mal tiempo.
Llueve (mucho).*

Hace (mucho) frío.
Nieva en las montañas.*
Hay (mucha) nieve.

Hace (mucho) calor y
(mucho) sol en la playa.

Hace (mucho) viento.

Está nublado (hay nubes).

Hay niebla.

Hace fresco.

Preguntas

Create questions to which the following would be possible answers.

    MODELO   Hace mucho calor hoy.
                ¿Qué tiempo hace hoy? or **¿Hace mucho calor hoy?**

1. Hace buen tiempo aquí.
2. Hace mucho frío en el sur de Chile.
3. Hace calor al norte, cerca de la playa (cerca del mar).
4. Hace viento cerca del mar.
5. Siempre llueve (*It always rains*) en el sur.

---

*__Nieva__ and **llueve** are forms of verbs that will be discussed in detail in Chapters 5 and 6.

LAS ESTACIONES DEL AÑO*

el invierno   el verano   la primavera   el otoño

En muchos países tropicales, hay dos estaciones: la estación de lluvias y la estación seca.

In many tropical countries, there are two seasons: the rainy season and the dry season.

LOS MESES DEL AÑO‡

enero	abril	julio	octubre
febrero	mayo	agosto	noviembre
marzo	junio	septiembre	diciembre

Preguntas

1. ¿Hace frío hoy? ¿calor?   2. ¿Hace frío en la clase? ¿calor?   3. ¿Qué tiempo hace aquí en el invierno? ¿en la primavera?   4. ¿Qué tiempo hace en los Andes? ¿en el Sáhara?   5. ¿En qué estación hace mucho sol aquí? ¿mucho viento? 6. ¿En qué meses hace frío? ¿calor?   7. ¿Cuáles son los meses de verano aquí? 8. Según usted, ¿qué mes del año es muy lindo? ¿Qué mes es terrible? ¿Por qué? 9. ¿En qué estación estamos ahora?   10. ¿En qué meses llueve aquí? ¿y cuándo nieva?

¿Verdadero o falso?   Si es falso, ¿por qué?

1. Aquí hace frío en el verano.   2. Hace mucho viento cerca del mar.   3. Ahora hace buen tiempo en Alaska.   4. En mayo aquí estamos en verano.   5. En el invierno hay mucha niebla aquí.   6. Aquí siempre llueve en el otoño.   7. Ahora hace frío en Chile.   8. Aquí no nieva en el invierno.   9. Hace calor en Siberia.

---

*The seasons are reversed in the southern hemisphere, so that when it is winter in North America it is summer in countries like Chile and Argentina.

‡Note that seasons and months are not capitalized in Spanish.

I. El presente de indicativo del verbo *hacer*; expresiones de tiempo

¿Qué tiempo hace
en Viña del Mar,
Chile?

En una universidad en Santiago de Chile

HUGO   ¿Qué *haces,* Tomás?
TOMÁS   *Hago* la maleta. Viajo con Edmundo esta tarde a Viña del Mar.
        Hacemos el viaje en tren.
HUGO   Pues, ¡tienen suerte! *Hace buen tiempo, no hace mucho calor* y creo que
        hoy *no llueve.*
TOMÁS   Realmente, ¡es un día estupendo!

1. ¿Qué hace Tomás?   2. ¿Con quién viaja?   3. ¿Cómo viajan?   4. ¿Qué
tiempo hace?   5. ¿Viaja usted en tren de vez en cuando *(from time to time)*?

At a university in Santiago, Chile.   HUGO: What are you doing, Tomás? TOMÁS: I'm packing (literally,
"making" or "doing") my suitcase. I'm traveling this afternoon with Edmundo to Viña del Mar (a
Chilean resort). We're making the trip by train. HUGO: Well, you're lucky! It's nice weather, it's not
hot, and I think it won't rain today. TOMÁS: Really, it's a great day!

A. **Hacer** is regular in the present tense except for the **yo** form, **hago.**

hacer to do, to make

hago	hacemos
haces	hacéis
hace	hacen

Hago un viaje en tren todos los veranos.	I take a trip by train every summer.
¿Haces la maleta? Cuidado con el regalo para Esteban.	Are you packing your suitcase? Be careful with the present for Esteban.
¿Qué haces? Hago la comida.	What are you doing? I'm making dinner (the food).
¿Qué hacen ustedes en el invierno? Esquiamos en las montañas.	What do you do in winter? We ski in the mountains.
Ramón hace ejercicios y Anita estudia la lección de alemán.	Ramón is doing exercises and Anita is studying the German lesson.

Notice the idioms **hacer un viaje, hacer la maleta,** and **hacer ejercicios.**

B. The third-person singular form **hace** is used with certain nouns to make statements about the weather, as you saw at the beginning of this chapter.

Hace frío y viento allí en el invierno.	It's cold and windy there in the winter.
Siempre hace buen tiempo en la primavera.	It's always nice weather in the spring.
Hace sol en el campo pero hace fresco en la playa.	It's sunny in the country but it's cool at the beach.
Allí hace calor.	It's hot there.

Note that **caliente** is used to mean *hot* when not referring to weather or to people (or animals):

La comida está caliente.	The food is hot.

C. Because **frío, viento, calor,** and **sol** are nouns, the word **mucho** (not **muy**) is used to express *very.*

Hace mucho frío (viento, calor, sol).	It's very cold (windy, warm, sunny).

D. Here are some weather expressions that do not use **hace.**

Hay niebla y nubes en la costa.	There are fog and clouds on the coast.
Está nublado.	It's cloudy.
Nieva y llueve de vez en cuando aquí.	It snows and rains from time to time here.

EJERCICIOS

A. ¿Qué hacemos?   Tell what everyone is making or doing.

MODELO   mamá y papá / un viaje a Valparaíso
Mamá y papá hacen un viaje a Valparaíso.

1. yo / la maleta
2. Juan y Julia / la comida
3. usted / un viaje en tren
4. el hijo de Rafael / un avión de papel
5. nosotros / ejercicios

B. ¿Qué haces, Paco?   Jorge is trying to find someone to go to the movies with him. Complete his questions to Paco using the appropriate form of **hacer.**

JORGE   ¿Qué _____ Pedro hoy?
PACO   Estudia para un examen.
JORGE   ¿Qué _____ tú?
PACO   Lola y yo deseamos visitar un museo.
JORGE   ¿Qué _____ Juan y Sonia?
PACO   Ellos desean hablar con unos amigos chilenos.
JORGE   ¿Qué _____ Ana?
PACO   Visita a unos tíos.
JORGE   Y, ¿qué _____ yo?
PACO   ¿Por qué no estudias la lección de alemán?

C. La traducción.   Give the Spanish equivalent of the following sentences.

1. It's very windy in the fall.
2. The weather is nice in the spring.
3. It's hot in the country.
4. Why does it snow a lot in the mountains?
5. What's the weather like today?
6. It's cloudy at the beach.

Preguntas

1. ¿Qué tiempo hace ahora?   2. ¿Hace usted la comida hoy?   3. ¿Hace usted muchos viajes? ¿Adónde?   4. ¿Hace viajes en tren? ¿en avión? ¿en auto? 5. Cuando hace la maleta, ¿lleva muchas cosas? ¿Lleva una maleta grande o pequeña? ¿Por qué?   6. ¿Hace usted ejercicios?

II. El presente del verbo *ir*; *ir a* + infinitivo

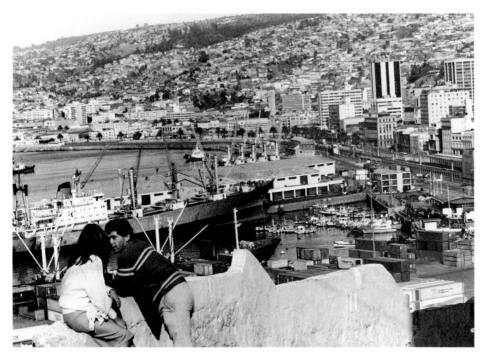

Valparaíso, puerto
principal de Chile

En una calle de Concepción: Un reportero habla con la gente.

EL REPORTERO	*¿Va a ir* usted de vacaciones este verano, señor?
RAMÓN	Sí, *voy* a Viña del Mar. *Voy a pasar* las vacaciones en la playa.
EL REPORTERO	¿Y usted, señora?
GLORIA	*Voy a* Santiago con una amiga. *Vamos a ir* de compras.
EL REPORTERO	¿Y tú, niño? *¿Vas a ir* de vacaciones este verano?
PEDRITO	Sí, señor. *Voy a ir* al paraíso con la familia. *Vamos a visitar* a los ángeles. ¿Verdad, papá?
RAFAEL	No, no *vamos* al paraíso, hijo; *vamos* a Valparaíso.

---

1. ¿Adónde va Ramón de vacaciones?   2. ¿Qué va a hacer Gloria?   3. ¿Adónde va la familia de Pedrito?

On a street in Concepción: A reporter is talking to people. REPORTER: Are you going to go on vacation this summer, sir? RAMÓN: Yes, I'm going to Viña del Mar. I'm going to spend my vacation at the beach. REPORTER: And you, ma'am? GLORIA: I'm going to Santiago with a friend. We're going to go shopping. REPORTER: And you, little boy? Are you going to go on vacation this summer? PEDRITO: Yes, sir. I'm going to Paradise with my family. We're going to visit the angels. Right, Dad? RAFAEL: No, we're not going to Paradise, son; we're going to Valparaíso.

A. The verb **ir** is irregular in the present tense.

ir to go

voy	vamos
vas	vais
va	van

B. Like other verbs of motion, **ir** is usually followed by the preposition **a** before a destination.

Pedrito va a Valparaíso.	*Pedrito is going to Valparaíso.*
En Viña del Mar todo el mundo va a la playa.	*In Viña del Mar everyone goes to the beach.*

C. The verb **ir** is also followed by the preposition **a** before an infinitive. The **ir a** + *infinitive* construction expresses an action or event that is going to take place in the near future.

Voy a pasar otra semana en el campo.	*I'm going to spend another week in the country.*
Van a ser unas vacaciones excelentes.	*It's going to be an excellent vacation.*

D. Vamos a + *infinitive* can mean *we're going to do something* or *let's do something.*

Vamos a visitar Valparaíso.	*Let's visit Valparaíso. (We're going to visit Valparaíso.)*

E. The expression **ir de compras** means *to go shopping. To go on vacation* is **ir de vacaciones. Ir de campamento** is *to go camping.*

Vamos de compras mañana, ¿de acuerdo?	*Let's go shopping tomorrow, OK?*
¿Adónde van de vacaciones?	*Where are you going on vacation?*
Vamos de campamento en las montañas.	*We're going camping in the mountains.*

EJERCICIOS

A. ¿Adónde vamos? Everyone is leaving for vacation. Say what they are doing by completing the sentences with the correct form of **ir**.

1. Felipe y Manuel _____ a ir a Santiago; van a visitar museos y teatros.
2. Raquel _____ a Viña del Mar y _____ a leer muchos libros.
3. Yo _____ a visitar a los abuelos y _____ a pasar unos días en la playa.
4. Tú _____ a ir al campo y allí _____ a visitar a unos tíos.
5. Sara _____ a hacer un viaje y _____ a ir de campamento en las montañas.

B. Tarde o temprano (*Sooner or later*). Luis always procrastinates. Answer the questions for Luis, following the model.

MODELO ¿Trabajas ahora? **No, pero voy a trabajar mañana.**

1. ¿Haces ejercicios ahora?
2. ¿Lees el Capítulo 4 hoy?
3. ¿Vas a la biblioteca ahora?
4. ¿Llamas a la familia ahora?
5. ¿Visitas al tío hoy?

C. ¿Qué van a hacer? Complete the following sentences with the appropriate form of **ir** and any additional information needed to tell what is going to happen.

MODELO Este verano el profesor...
Este verano el profesor va a estar en casa.

1. Mañana yo...
2. Hoy los estudiantes...
3. Hoy hace buen tiempo. Mañana...
4. En diciembre todos los estudiantes...
5. Este verano yo...

D. Una encuesta (*A survey*). Find out how your classmates will spend their vacations and report back to the class.

1. ¿Quiénes van al mar?
2. ¿Quiénes van a las montañas?
3. ¿Quiénes van de campamento?
4. ¿Quiénes van a esquiar?
5. ¿Quiénes van a asistir a la universidad?
6. ¿Quiénes van a trabajar?
7. ¿Quiénes van a viajar?
8. ¿Quiénes van a visitar a los amigos?
9. ¿Quiénes van a regresar a casa?

Preguntas

1. ¿Adónde va usted de vacaciones este año?
2. ¿Va a trabajar o va a viajar en el verano?
3. ¿Va usted mucho a las montañas? ¿Va de campamento allí? ¿Esquían allí en el invierno?
4. ¿Va mucho a la biblioteca?
5. ¿Qué va a hacer usted esta tarde?
6. ¿Va a trabajar? ¿Dónde?
7. ¿Va a visitar a unos amigos hoy?
8. ¿Va a comer esta noche en un restaurante o en casa?

III. Pronombres de complemento directo

Hay mucha nieve en los Andes.

Julio y Rosa van de campamento en los Andes.

JULIO	¿Dónde está la radio?
ROSA	Aquí *la* tienes.
JULIO	¿Y el televisor?
ROSA	Está en el auto.
JULIO	Voy a buscar*lo* ahora. ¿*Me* esperas?
ROSA	Sí, *te* espero aquí.
	Julio regresa.
JULIO	El televisor *lo* tengo, pero ¿dónde están las baterías?
ROSA	¿No *las* tienes allí?
JULIO	No.
ROSA	¡Qué terrible! ¿Qué hacemos ahora?

1. ¿Dónde están Julio y Rosa? ¿Qué hacen?   2. ¿Qué busca Julio? ¿Dónde está?
3. ¿Qué otra cosa necesitan?   4. ¿Va usted de campamento de vez en cuando?
¿Lleva muchas cosas?

Julio and Rosa are camping in the Andes. JULIO: Where's the radio? ROSA: Here it is (Here you have it). JULIO: And the television? ROSA: It's in the car. JULIO: I'm going to get it now. Will you wait for me? ROSA: Yes, I'll wait for you here. *Julio returns.* JULIO: I have the television, but where are the batteries? ROSA: Don't you have them there? JULIO: No. ROSA: How terrible! What shall we do now?

A. In Chapter 3 you saw that the direct object in a sentence indicates the person or thing that receives the action of the verb directly. In the sentence *I see Jim*, *Jim* is the direct object. A direct object pronoun is a pronoun that replaces a direct object noun. In the sentence *I see him*, *him* is the direct object pronoun.

Direct Object Pronouns	
Singular	*Plural*
me *me*	**nos** *us*
te *you* **(tú)**	**os** *you* **(vosotros, vosotras)**
lo *him, it, you* **(usted)**	**los** *them, you* **(ustedes)**
la *her, it, you* **(usted)**	**las** *them, you* **(ustedes)**

B. **Lo** and **la** are the direct object pronouns that correspond to the subject pronouns **él, ella,** and **usted. Lo** is used to refer to a person or thing of masculine gender, and **la** is used to refer to a person or thing of feminine gender. **Lo** is also used to refer to actions or situations.*

¿El cuaderno? No lo tengo.	*The notebook? I don't have it.*
¿La otra lección? La leemos ahora.	*The other lesson? We are reading it now.*
¡No lo creo!	*I don't believe it!*

C. **Los** and **las** are the direct object pronouns that correspond to the subject pronouns **ellos, ellas,** and **ustedes. Los** is used to refer to people or things of masculine gender, and **las** is used to refer to people or things of feminine gender. **Los** is used to refer to groups of mixed gender.

¿Esos museos? Los voy a visitar mañana.	*Those museums? I'm going to visit them tomorrow.*
¿Las maletas? Las llevamos con nosotros.	*The suitcases? We're taking them with us.*
¿Esa casa y ese apartamento? Los vendemos.	*That house and that apartment? We're selling them.*

D. Use **te** when speaking to someone you address as **tú.** Use **lo** when speaking to a man, and **la** when speaking to a woman, whom you address as **usted. Os, los,** and **las** are comparable forms for the plural.

Te llamo mañana, Carlota.	*I'll call you tomorrow, Carlota.*
Adiós, señorita. La llamo mañana.	*Good-bye, miss. I'll call you tomorrow.*

For clarity or politeness, when **lo** or **la** corresponding to **usted** is used before a verb, **a usted** may be added after the verb. **A ustedes** is added when the pronoun is plural.

¿Lo espero a usted, señor?	*Shall I wait for you, sir?*
¿Las espero a ustedes, señoras?	*Shall I wait for you, ladies?*

---

*In Spain, speakers frequently use **le** and **les** to refer to a man or men and **lo** and **los** when the direct object is a thing or idea. This distinction is often not made in Latin America. Depending on one's background, one may say **Le veo** or **Lo veo**; both mean *I see him.*

E. Direct object pronouns are placed directly before a conjugated verb.*

¿Me esperas?	*Will you wait for me?*
¿La bicicleta? José no la tiene.	*The bicycle? José doesn't have it.*
Nos miran ahora.	*They're looking at us now.*

F. Direct object pronouns are placed after an infinitive and are attached to it.

Es imposible describirlos.	*It's impossible to describe them.*
Tienen que buscarlo.	*They have to look for it.*

However, if the infinitive is part of a larger verb construction, the direct object pronoun can either be attached to the infinitive, as above, or placed in front of the entire verb construction. In spoken Spanish, the latter position is more common. For practical purposes, both structures convey the same meaning.

¿El programa de televisión? Lo voy a mirar ahora. (Voy a mirarlo ahora.)	*The television program? I'm going to watch it now.*
¿La otra ventana? La tenemos que abrir. (Tenemos que abrirla.)	*The other window? We have to open it.*

G. Direct object pronouns can either precede a construction with the present progressive or follow the present participle and be attached to it.

¿El programa? Estoy mirándolo ahora. Lo estoy mirando ahora.	*The program? I'm watching it now.*

Note that an accent is required over the present participle when a pronoun is attached: **mirándolo.** This preserves the stressed syllable of the participle.

EJERCICIOS

A. Imaginación y lógica.   Create sentences by combining elements from each of the columns.

	a Pablo		
	a los señores Alba		lo
No llamo	a las chicas	porque	la visito mañana.
	a Margarita		los
	a don Carlos		las

B. En breve (*In short*).   Shorten the sentences, replacing the noun object with the corresponding direct object pronoun.

MODELO   Felipe lee el libro de español.   **Felipe lo lee.**

1. Elvira hace la comida.
2. Paco busca a los niños.

---

*A conjugated verb form is one with an ending that indicates tense, person, and number. The infinitive form is a nonconjugated form.

3. Susana espera a Pablo y Felipe.
4. ¿Vamos a comprar ese auto?
5. Eduardo, voy a vender esta bicicleta.
6. No necesitamos esas mesas.
7. Abuela llama a los parientes en Viña del Mar.
8. Aurelio, ¿por qué no abres las ventanas?

C. Al revés (*Backwards*).   Edit the conversation, changing the position of the pronouns in italics.

MODELO   ¿Cuándo lo vamos a visitar?
¿Cuándo vamos a visitarlo?

RAFA   Esos refrescos son muy buenos. ¿Por qué *los* vas a comprar?
HUGO   Porque Susana *nos* va a visitar.
RAFA   ¿Quién *la* va a invitar (*invite*)?
HUGO   Yo. *La* voy a llamar ahora.
RAFA   ¿Tienes su (*her*) número de teléfono?
HUGO   *Lo* voy a buscar.
RAFA   ¿Cuándo vas a hacer la comida?
HUGO   ¿Yo? No, amigo. ¡Tú *la* vas a hacer!

D. Entrevista.   Ask someone the following questions. The other person should answer using a direct object pronoun. (Fibs are permitted!)

MODELO   ¿Deseas mirar el programa?
Sí, lo deseo mirar, or **No, no lo deseo mirar.**

1. ¿Tomas el café de la cafetería?
2. ¿Visitas a la doctora mañana?
3. ¿Compras los libros en la universidad?
4. ¿Los llama el profesor a ustedes?
5. ¿Te necesitan los amigos?
6. ¿Me llamas todos los días?
7. ¿Buscas clases buenas?
8. ¿Lees la información del libro?
9. ¿Te miran los otros estudiantes?
10. ¿Contestas las preguntas del profesor (de la profesora)?

Preguntas

Answer using a direct object pronoun whenever possible.

1. ¿Mira usted televisión?   2. ¿Compra usted café en la cafetería? ¿Come la comida de allí?   3. ¿Va a leer la lección de español hoy? ¿Tiene el libro de español allí?   4. ¿Llama usted mucho a los amigos? ¿Los visita?   5. ¿Desea visitar Chile?

IV. Las fechas

enero
```
D  L  M  M  J  V  S
               1  2
 3  4  5  6  7  8  9
10 11 12 13 14 15 16
17 18 19 20 21 22 23
24 25 26 27 28 29 30
31
```

febrero
```
D  L  M  M  J  V  S
    1  2  3  4  5  6
 7  8  9 10 11 12 13
14 15 16 17 18 19 20
21 22 23 24 25 26 27
28 29
```

marzo
```
D  L  M  M  J  V  S
       1  2  3  4  5
 6  7  8  9 10 11 12
13 14 15 16 17 18 19
20 21 22 23 24 25 26
27 28 29 30 31
```

abril
```
D  L  M  M  J  V  S
               1  2
 3  4  5  6  7  8  9
10 11 12 13 14 15 16
17 18 19 20 21 22 23
24 25 26 27 28 29 30
```

mayo
```
D  L  M  M  J  V  S
 1  2  3  4  5  6  7
 8  9 10 11 12 13 14
15 16 17 18 19 20 21
22 23 24 25 26 27 28
29 30 31
```

junio
```
D  L  M  M  J  V  S
          1  2  3  4
 5  6  7  8  9 10 11
12 13 14 15 16 17 18
19 20 21 22 23 24 25
26 27 28 29 30
```

julio
```
D  L  M  M  J  V  S
               1  2
 3  4  5  6  7  8  9
10 11 12 13 14 15 16
17 18 19 20 21 22 23
24 25 26 27 28 29 30
31
```

agosto
```
D  L  M  M  J  V  S
    1  2  3  4  5  6
 7  8  9 10 11 12 13
14 15 16 17 18 19 20
21 22 23 24 25 26 27
28 29 30 31
```

septiembre
```
D  L  M  M  J  V  S
          1  2  3
 4  5  6  7  8  9 10
11 12 13 14 15 16 17
18 19 20 21 22 23 24
25 26 27 28 29 30
```

octubre
```
D  L  M  M  J  V  S
                   1
 2  3  4  5  6  7  8
 9 10 11 12 13 14 15
16 17 18 19 20 21 22
23 24 25 26 27 28 29
30 31
```

noviembre
```
D  L  M  M  J  V  S
       1  2  3  4  5
 6  7  8  9 10 11 12
13 14 15 16 17 18 19
20 21 22 23 24 25 26
27 28 29 30
```

diciembre
```
D  L  M  M  J  V  S
          1  2  3
 4  5  6  7  8  9 10
11 12 13 14 15 16 17
18 19 20 21 22 23 24
25 26 27 28 29 30 31
```

Un calendario hispano

En una calle de Santiago de Chile

PABLO Ana, ¿cuándo vamos al teatro? ¿El lunes? ¿el martes? ¿el miércoles?

ANA Bueno, es que...

PABLO Vamos *el viernes*, ¿no? Es *el veintisiete de septiembre.*

ANA Pues... *el viernes* tengo que estudiar.

PABLO ¿Y *el veintiocho*? Es *sábado.*

ANA Ese día tengo que trabajar.

PABLO ¿Y *el veintinueve*... o *el treinta*?

ANA *El treinta y uno* está bien.

PABLO ¡Qué bien! Gracias, Ana. ¡Hasta *el treinta y uno*!

ANA ¡Chau, Pablo!

PABLO (*Mira un calendario.*) *El treinta de septiembre, el primero de octubre*...
Pero, ¡Ana! ¡Un momento!

---

1. ¿Adónde desea ir Pablo? 2. ¿Qué tiene que hacer Ana el viernes? ¿el sábado?
3. ¿Van a ir al teatro el treinta y uno? ¿Por qué sí o por qué no?

On a street in Santiago, Chile. PABLO: Ana, when are we going to the theater? Monday? Tuesday? Wednesday? ANA: Well, it's (just) that . . . PABLO: Let's go on Friday, OK? It's the twenty-seventh of September. ANA: Well, on Friday I have to study. PABLO: And the twenty-eighth? It's Saturday. ANA: That day I have to work. PABLO: And the twenty-ninth . . . or the thirtieth? ANA: The thirty-first is fine. PABLO: Great! Thanks, Ana. See you on the thirty-first! ANA: Good-bye, Pablo! PABLO: (*He looks at a calendar.*) The thirtieth of September, the first of October . . . But, Ana, just a minute!

A. The days of the week in Spanish are all masculine. They are not capitalized.

Los días de la semana:

domingo	*Sunday*	miércoles	*Wednesday*	viernes	*Friday*
lunes	*Monday*	jueves	*Thursday*	sábado	*Saturday*
martes	*Tuesday*				

B. The definite article is always used with the days of the week and dates as an equivalent of *on,* when *on* could be used in English.

Elena llega el martes.
Llega el quince de mayo.
Vamos a la playa el domingo.

Elena is arriving (on) Tuesday.
She arrives (on) May 15th.
We're going to the beach (on) Sunday.

C. The definite article is omitted when the day of the week follows a form of the verb **ser.**

Hoy es jueves.

Today is Thursday.

D. Cardinal numbers **(dos, tres, cuatro)** are used to express dates, with one exception: **el primero** *(the first).*

¿Qué fecha es hoy? Es el dos de abril.
¿Cuándo es el cumpleaños de Martín? Es el primero de octubre.

What's today's date? It's the second of April.
When is Martín's birthday? It's the first of October.

E. The plurals of **sábado** and **domingo** are formed by adding **-s: los sábados, los domingos.** The plurals of the other days are formed simply with the use of the plural article **los.**

La gente va al campo los domingos.
Estoy en la universidad los martes y los jueves.

People go to the country on Sundays.
I'm at the university on Tuesdays and Thursdays.

F. When the year is given, **de** is used between the month and the year.

el 31 de diciembre de 1999

the thirty-first of December, 1999

EJERCICIOS

A. **¿Qué fecha es?**   With a classmate, test each other's memory for dates.

MODELO   el Día de San Valentín   **Es el catorce de febrero.**

1. el Día de Año Nuevo *(New Year's Day)*
2. el Día de la Independencia de los Estados Unidos
3. la Navidad *(Christmas)*
4. el cumpleaños de Martin Luther King
5. el cumpleaños de Abraham Lincoln
6. el Día de la Raza *(Columbus Day)*

B. **Días de la semana.**   Complete the sentences.

MODELO   No tengo muchas clases los...
            ...viernes.

1. Si hoy es jueves, mañana es...

2. Vamos a la clase de español los...
3. El primer día de la semana es...
4. El día favorito de muchos niños es...
5. El día favorito de muchos estudiantes es...

C. Los meses.

> Treinta días tiene noviembre,
> con abril, junio y septiembre.
> De veintiocho sólo hay uno;
> los otros, de treinta y uno.

1. ¿Qué meses tienen 30 días?
2. ¿Cuántos meses tienen 31 días? ¿Cuáles son?
3. ¿Qué mes tiene 28 días?
4. En los Estados Unidos, ¿cuáles son los meses de invierno? ¿y en Chile?

Preguntas

1. ¿Qué día es hoy? 2. En general, ¿cuáles son los días en que no hay clase?
3. ¿Qué día hay exámenes en la clase? 4. ¿Cuál es la fecha favorita de usted?
5. ¿Cuándo es el cumpleaños de usted?

Study Hint: Increasing Your Vocabulary

You can increase your Spanish vocabulary in many ways. Either choose vocabulary from this text that you want to focus on or decide on a type of vocabulary (for example, travel phrases or medical expressions) and locate a source for it. Dictionaries, phrase books for travelers, and vocabulary-building books are available in many bookstores.

Some people have found that writing a word a day on their calendars is a good way to acquire vocabulary. Others tape a word to their bathroom mirror and practice it while preparing themselves for the day. You may want to keep a vocabulary notebook with words and phrases you have chosen to learn, along with model sentences.

Words are easier to learn in relation to other words or when linked to something visual than in isolation. Try creating a short "composition" with a group of words; each word then acquires associations in your mind that will help you remember it. Determined students sometimes paste magazine photographs to cardboard and attach appropriate labels in Spanish. Charts, sketches, maps, and other visual aids can be labeled and posted in a location where you can study them frequently.

If you learn one or two words or expressions a day, your progress in the language will be impressive. Work your new vocabulary into classroom activities and compositions, and you'll find that they'll become a dependable part of your active vocabulary.

CHILE, UN PAÍS DE INMIGRANTES

La Avenida O'Higgins, Santiago de Chile

Jessica, una estudiante de Canadá, pasa las vacaciones de verano en Santiago. Visita a unos amigos chilenos. Van en auto.

JESSICA   ¡Huy!° Tengo mucho frío. ¿Siempre hace frío en Santiago?

GABRIELA   No, no siempre. Pero hoy es el primero de julio. Estamos en invierno. ¿Qué tiempo hace ahora en Vancouver?

JESSICA   En Vancouver hace calor. Los domingos todo el mundo va a la playa.

ANDRÉS   ¡Qué gracioso!° En Chile vamos a la playa en diciembre, enero y febrero.

JESSICA   En esos meses tenemos mucha nieve en Canadá. ¿Y ahora esquían ustedes aquí?

GABRIELA   Sí, porque es invierno, Jessica.

JESSICA   ¡Dios mío! Aquí hacen todo al revés°.

ANDRÉS   Aquí somos normales; ustedes hacen todo al revés.

GABRIELA   Creo que vamos a tener lluvia. ¿Por qué no vamos a tomar once?[1]

JESSICA   ¿Once qué?

GABRIELA   Ah, no me comprendes... Es una expresión chilena, Jessica. Tomar té°, pues. Vamos a la Alameda, una avenida que está en el centro.

ANDRÉS   En realidad° se llama Avenida O'Higgins, en honor del héroe° nacional de Chile...[2]

JESSICA   O'Higgins... No lo creo. ¿No es de Irlanda?

GABRIELA   ¡Qué va!° En este país Bernardo O'Higgins es muy famoso; él es líder° de la revolución chilena de 1814 a 1818.

ANDRÉS   Sí, Jessica. En Chile hay gente de origen inglés, español, ale-
          mán... Es un país de inmigrantes, como° Canadá.
JESSICA   Y también es el país de Isabel Allende. El libro *La casa de los
          espíritus* es famoso en Canadá y Estados Unidos.[3] Lo leo ahora.
ANDRÉS   No es posible llevarte a esa casa... pero te vamos a llevar a un
          salón de té° inglés. ¡Té caliente para todos!

¡Huy! *Wow!*	¡Qué gracioso! *How funny!*	al revés *backwards, reversed*	el té *tea*
En realidad *In reality*	en honor del héroe *in honor of the hero*	¡Qué va! *Oh, come on!*	
líder *leader*	como *like, as*	salón de té *tea house*	

PREGUNTAS

1. ¿Dónde pasa Jessica las vacaciones de verano?   2. ¿Qué tiempo hace en Santiago? ¿Es verano allí?   3. ¿Qué tiempo hace en Vancouver?   4. ¿Cuándo van a
la playa en Chile?   5. ¿Qué es la Alameda? ¿Cómo se llama en realidad?
6. ¿Quién es Bernardo O'Higgins?   7. ¿Es Chile un país de inmigrantes? ¿y Canadá?   8. ¿Qué libro lee Jessica? ¿De quién es?   9. ¿Adónde van a llevar a Jessica
Andrés y Gabriela?

NOTAS CULTURALES

1. Chileans and many other Latin Americans pause in the late afternoon for a **merienda**, a snack usually including biscuits and jam, cookies, or pastry accompanied by tea, coffee, or a soft drink. In most countries, at about four or five in the afternoon, people say that it's time to **tomar el té**. In Chile and Argentina, however, one frequently hears the expression **tomar once**. This is said to have derived from a euphemism used by gentlemen in colonial times when they would leave the ladies with their teapots and go out to have a brandy (**aguardiente**). To avoid offending the ladies, the gentlemen would refer to the beverage by the number of letters in the word, eleven.

2. Bernardo O'Higgins is the hero of Chile's war of independence against Spain (1814–1818). His mother was Chilean, his father an Irishman who moved to Spain and was later appointed viceroy of Peru by the Spanish government. (This was a most unusual case in socially rigid, colonial Spanish America.) A brilliant and daring general during the war, O'Higgins served afterwards as the first leader of the government of Chile.

3. Isabel Allende, niece of the deposed president of Chile Salvador Allende, has written several novels that have been popular worldwide. Her book *La casa de los espíritus* (*The House of the Spirits*) is about the history of modern-day Chile, focusing primarily on the era when the democratic government of Salvador Allende was overthrown by the current dictator, General Augusto Pinochet.

Funciones y *actividades*

In this chapter you have seen examples of some important language functions, or uses. Here is a summary and some additional information about these functions of language.

MAKING SMALL TALK

Here are some common phrases to open a casual conversation; as in English, weather is a common topic for small talk.

¡Qué calor (frío, viento, etcétera)!	*How hot (cold, windy, and so on) it is!*
¡Qué buen tiempo!	*What nice weather!*
¡Qué tiempo más estupendo!	*What great weather!*
¿Cree(s) que vamos a tener lluvia (un invierno frío, un verano seco, etcétera)?	*Do you think we're going to have (some) rain (a cold winter, a dry summer, and so on)?*

Here are some expressions unrelated to the weather that can be used to open conversations.

¿Qué estudias tú?	*What are you studying? (to another student)*
¡Qué coincidencia! ¿Usted también va a Santiago (estudia biología, es de los Estados Unidos, etcétera)?	*What a coincidence! You're also going to Santiago (studying biology, from the United States, and so on)?*

GIVING A WARNING

The expression **¡Cuidado!** *(Be careful! Watch out!)* is used to give a warning. **¡Espere(n)!** *(Wait!)* is also used.

EXPRESSING GRATITUDE

Here are some ways to express gratitude:

Gracias. Muchas gracias.	*Thank you. Thank you very much.*
Mil gracias.	*Thank you very much (literally, "a thousand thanks").*
Muy agradecido(-a).	*(I'm) very grateful.*
Usted es (Tú eres) muy amable.	*You're very kind.*

A common response to **Gracias** is **De nada.** *(You're welcome. It's nothing.)*

Now do the following activities, using the expressions you have just learned.

A. ¿Qué dicen? (*What are they saying?*) Tell what the people in the following drawings are probably saying.

B. ¡Rápido! Select someone to be **la víctima**. Using questions from this or preceding chapters, the rest of the class will ask questions as rapidly as possible, and the victim will answer as many as he or she can. New victims should be selected from those who are slow to ask questions. Here are some questions to begin with:

1. ¿Qué día es hoy?   2. ¿Tienes un día favorito? ¿Cuál? ¿Por qué?
3. ¿Adónde vas los domingos? ¿los sábados?   4. ¿Qué tiempo hace hoy?
5. En general, ¿qué haces en el verano? ¿y en el invierno?   6. ¿Cuándo vas de vacaciones? ¿Adónde vas?   7. ¿Qué haces cuando tienes dolor de cabeza?

C. Mini-dramas.   Role-play the following situations.

1. You are waiting for a bus. A person your age is also waiting. You both make small talk about the weather. A car comes by close to the curb. "Watch out!" you say, as water splashes onto the curb. He or she thanks you. You ask where he or she is going and he or she responds, "The museum on O'Higgins Avenue." "What a coincidence!" you say. You are going to the museum also. "The bus is coming (arriving)," says your new friend, and you both get on.
2. You are in a supermarket line. You see a very attractive person of the opposite sex in the line ahead of you. Make small talk about the weather.

VOCABULARIO ACTIVO

Cognados

la bicicleta	chileno	la independencia	la radio	el tren
la coincidencia	favorito	el, la inmigrante	el reportero, la reportera	tropical
la costa	imposible	posible	terrible	

Verbos

comprar	to buy
esperar	to hope; to wait (for)
esquiar	to ski
hacer	to do; to make
hacer buen (mal) tiempo	to be good (bad) weather
hacer calor (frío, fresco, viento, sol)	to be hot (cold, cool, windy, sunny)
hacer la maleta	to pack one's suitcase
hacer un viaje	to take a trip
¿Qué tiempo hace?	What's the weather like?
ir	to go
ir de campamento	to go camping
ir de compras	to go shopping
ir de vacaciones	to go on vacation

Las estaciones y el tiempo

la estación	season (also, station)
la fecha	date
el invierno	winter
Llueve.	It's raining.
la lluvia	rain
el mes	month
la niebla	fog
Hay niebla.	It's foggy.
Nieva.	It's snowing.
la nieve	snow
la nube	cloud
Hay nubes.	It's cloudy.
nublado	cloudy
estar nublado	to be cloudy
el otoño	fall, autumn
la primavera	spring
el sol	sun
hacer sol	to be sunny
el tiempo	weather; time
el verano	summer
el viento	wind

Otras palabras y frases

alemán	German
caliente	hot (not used for weather or people)
el campamento	camp
ir de campamento	to go camping
el campo	country (as opposed to city)
el cumpleaños	birthday
de vez en cuando	from time to time
(el) Dios	God
la gente	people
la lección	lesson
la maleta	suitcase
el mar	sea
el mundo	world
todo el mundo	everyone
otro	other, another
el país	country, nation
realmente	really
seco	dry
siempre	always
sólo adv.	only
el televisor	television set

Expresiones útiles

Cuidado.	Watch out. Be careful.
De nada.	You're welcome. It's nothing.
Mil gracias.	Thanks very much. (literally, "A thousand thanks.")
Muy agradecido(-a)	I'm very grateful.

Don't forget: Direct object pronouns, page 110
Days of the week, page 113
Months of the year, page 102

LECTURA II

La gente

Una española en Barcelona

Pero, ¿es posible? ¿Es española esa chica rubia° de ojos° azules°? Sí, señor.

En Galicia, una región del nordeste de España, la gente es de origen céltico, como los irlandeses° y escoceses°. Tenemos que ir a Andalucía, en el sur, para encontrar° al español de piel° oscura° y de pelo° y ojos negros°.

La gente y la cultura de España, como la geografía, es muy variada°. La historia española explica° esta mezcla° de razas y culturas. Hoy coexisten en el país tipos humanos muy variados y cuatro lenguas° diferentes: el español, la lengua oficial; el gallego, una lengua similar al portugués; el catalán, una lengua romance del nordeste; y el vasco, una lengua antigua° de las provincias del norte.

¿Y si cruzamos el Atlántico? Pues, también descubrimos una gran variedad. En lugares como México, por ejemplo°, la mayor parte° de la gente es mestiza, producto de la mezcla entre indios y españoles. Está muy orgullosa° de esa herencia° india.

blond eyes blue

Irish Scots
find skin dark
hair black

varied

explains mixture

languages

ancient

por... for example mayor... majority
proud heritage

Estudiantes en Oaxaca, México

En otras partes de Hispanoamérica, como en Bolivia y Guatemala, los indios forman la mayor parte de la población° y muchos viven en pequeños pueblos° de las montañas, separados° de la vida moderna de las ciudades.

population
towns sepa-
rated

En países como Argentina, Uruguay y Chile casi° todo el mundo es de origen europeo: español, italiano, francés, inglés, alemán, etcétera. En el Caribe°, la influencia africana es muy importante. Por ejemplo, la mayor parte

almost

Caribbean

Una dominicana en Santo Domingo

de la población de la República Dominicana es mulata (parte negra y parte europea). Y muchos puertorriqueños tienen sangre° india, negra y española. El mundo hispano es, pues, un mundo muy variado.

blood

PREGUNTAS

1. ¿De qué origen es la gente de Galicia? 2. En España la gente y la cultura es muy variada. ¿Qué cosa explica esto? 3. ¿Cuántas lenguas hablan en España? ¿Cuáles son? 4. ¿Dónde forman los indios la mayor parte de la población? 5. ¿De qué origen es la gente de Argentina, Uruguay y Chile? 6. ¿Qué influencia es importante en el Caribe?

¿Verdadero o falso? If the statement is false, give the correct answer.

1. En España no hay gente rubia.
2. El gallego es una lengua similar al francés.
3. En México y Bolivia la mayoría de la gente es mestiza.
4. Los mestizos son el producto de la mezcla entre negros y españoles.
5. Muchos indios de Bolivia y Guatemala viven en pequeños pueblos de las montañas.
6. La mayor parte de la población de la República Dominicana es mulata.

La comunidad
hispana celebra el
Día de Puerto Rico
en Nueva York.

LA CIUDAD Y SUS PROBLEMAS

Funciones

- Telling time
- Expressing sympathy
- Expressing lack of
  sympathy

Vocabulario. In this chapter you will talk about
life in big cities.

Gramática. You will discuss and use:

1. The present tense of verbs that change their stem
   vowel from **e** to **ie** when stressed on the stem
   and of **venir** *(to come),* which has a **yo** form
   (vengo) like that of **tener (tengo)**
2. Possessive adjectives, corresponding to *her, your,
   my,* etc.
3. Indirect object pronouns
4. Expressions for telling time

Cultura. The dialogues take place in the Puerto
Rican community of metropolitan New York.

PROBLEMAS DE HOY

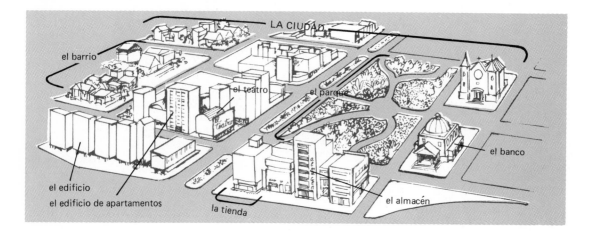

LA CIUDAD

el barrio

el teatro

el parque

el banco

el edificio

el edificio de apartamentos

la tienda

el almacén

la contaminación
(del aire, del agua)*

la pobreza (*poverty*),
el hambre

la inflación

el metro

el autobús

el, la criminal,
el crimen, el robo

---

*The article **la** becomes **el** before feminine nouns beginning with a stressed **a** o **ha: el agua** (*water*). (No change occurs with a modifying adjective or the plural: **El agua está buena, las aguas.**) This book lists such nouns with an *f*: **el agua** *f*.

el policía, la mujer policía*

el tráfico

la discriminación contra
(*against*) las mujeres,
las minorías

el desempleo (*unemployment*),
la huelga (*strike*), las personas
sin (*without*) trabajo

la basura

Problemas urbanos de Nueva York.   New Yorkers face many urban problems.
For each citizen listed on the left, tell which problem listed on the right might
seem the most urgent to him or her. Follow the model.

> **MODELO**   **Una mujer policía cree que el crimen es un problema urgente.**

una mujer que trabaja en una
   oficina
una mujer policía
una madre de seis hijos
una persona sin trabajo
un señor con mucho dinero
   (*money*)
una persona que vive lejos del
   lugar (*place*) donde trabaja
un doctor

el desempleo
la contaminación del aire
la discriminación contra las mujeres
el robo
el crimen
el tráfico
la inflación

---

*la **policía** = *police (force)*

Asociación de ideas.   Match each word on the left with a word on the right that you associate with it.

MODELO   plaza   **parque**

1. plaza
2. calle
3. dinero
4. casa
5. pobreza
6. crimen

a. banco
b. apartamento
c. desempleo
d. robo
e. avenida
f. parque

Preguntas

1. ¿Vive usted en una ciudad grande o pequeña? ¿en una casa o en un apartamento?   2. ¿En qué calle o avenida vive usted?   3. ¿Qué problemas tienen donde usted vive?   4. ¿Qué problemas hay en las grandes ciudades?   5. Según usted, ¿cuál es el problema más importante de Estados Unidos?

I. El presente de indicativo de los verbos con cambio en la raíz e → *ie*; el verbo *venir*

¿Quiere Ud. ver una película en español?

En el Cine Edison de la Avenida Broadway en Nueva York

MARGARITA	En esta ciudad hay muchos cines, pero yo *vengo* aquí todos los viernes.
ANA	Sí, ¡qué suerte vivir cerca de un buen cine! Y tiene películas en español. ...Tengo sed. Margarita, ¿*quieres* una Coca-Cola, un café o...?
MARGARITA	Una Coca-Cola, por favor. ¿Y tú?
ANA	Yo *prefiero* café. ¿*Quieres* esperar aquí?
MARGARITA	*Prefiero* entrar.
	Ellas entran.
MARGARITA	Ana, la película *empieza.* Pero estas señoras hablan y hablan.
ANA	Perdón, señora. ¡Es imposible *entender*!
LA SEÑORA	¿Cómo? ¿Usted no *entiende*? Pero, ¡caramba! ¡Ésta es una conversación privada!

1. ¿Dónde están Ana y Margarita?   2. ¿Qué quiere Margarita: un café o una Coca-Cola?   3. ¿Qué prefiere Ana?   4. ¿Por qué no entienden la película Ana y Margarita?   5. ¿Cómo es la conversación de las señoras?   6. ¿Qué tipo de películas prefiere usted: las cómicas o las dramáticas? ¿Por qué?

At the Edison movie theater on Broadway in New York. MARGARITA: There are a lot of movie theaters in this city, but I come here every Friday. ANA: Yes, how lucky to live near a good theater! And it has movies in Spanish. . . . I'm thirsty. Margarita, do you want a Coca-Cola, coffee, or . . .? MARGARITA: A Coca-Cola, please. And you? ANA: I prefer coffee. Do you want to wait here? MARGARITA: I prefer to go in. *(They go in.)* MARGARITA: Ana, the film is beginning. But these ladies are talking and talking. ANA: Excuse me, ma'am. It's impossible to hear (understand). THE WOMAN: What? You can't hear? But, good grief! This is a private conversation!

A. Certain verbs in Spanish are known as stem-changing verbs. These verbs have regular endings, but show a change in the stem when the stem is stressed. In the following verbs, the **e** of the stem is changed to **ie** in the four forms within the familiar shoe pattern.

pensar to think		**entender** to understand, hear		**preferir** to prefer	
pienso	**pensamos**	entiendo	**entendemos**	prefiero	**preferimos**
piensas	**pensáis**	entiendes	**entendéis**	prefieres	**preferís**
piensa	piensan	entiende	entienden	prefiere	prefieren

B. Here are some other **e** to **ie** stem-changing verbs. Verbs of this type are shown in vocabulary lists with the marker **(ie): cerrar (ie).**

cerrar	*to close*
comenzar (a)	*to begin (to)*

empezar (a)	*to begin (to)*
mentir	*to lie*
nevar	*to snow*
perder	*to lose; to waste*
querer	*to want; to love*
recomendar	*to recommend*
sentir	*to feel*

Comienza } a trabajar. Empieza }	*He begins to work.*
Felipe quiere entrar en el parque.	*Felipe wants to go into the park.*
Preferimos regresar tarde.	*We prefer to return late.*
Siempre pierden dinero y también pierden el tiempo. Y yo pierdo paciencia con ellos.	*They always lose money and they also waste time. And I'm losing patience with them.*
Cierran varias tiendas en la avenida Lexington.	*They're closing several stores on Lexington Avenue.*
Elena no miente.	*Elena's not lying (doesn't lie).*
¿Recomiendan ese restaurante puertorriqueño?	*Do they recommend that Puerto Rican restaurant?*

Sentir is often used with **lo** to mean *to be sorry.*

Lo sentimos, señora. Eso debe ser terrible.	*We're sorry, ma'am. That must be terrible.*

Pensar followed by **de** means *to think of* in the sense of *to have an opinion* of someone or something.

¿Qué piensas del puesto?	*What do you think about the job (position)? (What is your opinion?)*

Pensar followed by **en** means *to think of* or *about.*

Pienso en ella de vez en cuando.	*I think about her from time to time.*

Pensar followed directly by an infinitive means *to intend* or *plan* to do something.

Pienso ayudar a ese niño pobre.	*I plan to help that poor child.*

C. Venir has three of the four usual **e → ie** stem changes plus an irregular **yo** form like that of **tener.**

venir to come

vengo	venimos
vienes	venís
viene	vienen

¿Vienen los señores Suárez hoy?	*Are Mr. and Mrs. Suárez coming today?*

EJERCICIOS

A. **Conversaciones.** Complete the following two conversations. Refer to the stem-changing verb with the same number in the list at the right.

JOSÉ	Yo (1) _____ las clases en septiembre.
LOLA	¿Qué (2) _____ estudiar tú?
JOSÉ	(3) _____ estudiar biología.
LOLA	¿No (4) _____ tomar clases fáciles?
JOSÉ	Yo (5) _____ ser doctor. (6) _____ la paciencia con la literatura y la filosofía.
LOLA	Pues, José, ¿(7) _____ tiempo de ir al cine con los amigos mañana?
JOSÉ	Lo (8) _____ , Lola, pero Paco y yo (9) _____ ir a la biblioteca.

1. empezar
2. pensar
3. pensar
4. preferir
5. querer
6. perder
7. tener
8. sentir
9. pensar

DON CARLOS	La tía Marta y yo (1) _____ regresar a Puerto Rico. Nosotros (2) _____ viajar en noviembre.
PEPE	Pero mamá (3) _____ en diciembre. ¿No (4) _____ ustedes esperar?
DON CARLOS	No, Pepe, nosotros (5) _____ la tienda el primero. (6) _____ a hacer las maletas.
PEPE	Pero, tío, (yo) no (7) _____ . ¿Por qué no (8) _____ (ustedes) la tienda después de Año Nuevo?
DON CARLOS	Es que (nosotros) (9) _____ mucho frío en el invierno.

1. querer
2. pensar
3. venir
4. preferir
5. cerrar
6. empezar
7. entender
8. cerrar
9. tener

B. **Pues, nosotros no.** Take the role of Rodolfo's coworkers Raúl and Blanca and react negatively to his complaints.

MODELO Pienso viajar en marzo.
Pues, nosotros no pensamos viajar en marzo.

1. Prefiero vivir en Puerto Rico.
2. Quiero vivir en San Juan.
3. Pierdo la paciencia con los precios aquí.
4. Pienso mucho en los problemas de esta ciudad.
5. Vengo tarde al trabajo de vez en cuando.
6. Siento mucho frío aquí.
7. Comienzo a tener varios problemas.

C. **Traducción.** Give the Spanish equivalent of the following sentences.

1. Does it snow in Puerto Rico?
2. Don't you think the children lie once in a while? Yes, and I also think they waste a lot of time at the beach.
3. I feel cold. Do you want to go in? Yes. The movie is starting.

D. **Encuesta** (*Survey*).   Divide into groups of three. One person will ask the other two the following questions. Use the **nosotros** form in the answers.

MODELO   ¿Recomiendan ustedes la cafetería de la universidad?
Sí, la recomendamos. or **No, no la recomendamos.**

1. ¿Tienen ustedes muchas oportunidades de hablar español?
2. ¿Prefieren esta clase o una clase de física?
3. ¿Quieren mirar películas en español en esta clase?
4. ¿Entienden las lecciones?
5. ¿Vienen tarde a la clase?
6. ¿Piensan tomar otra clase de español?
7. ¿Mienten de vez en cuando al profesor (a la profesora)?
8. ¿Cierran el libro durante (*during*) un examen?

Preguntas

1. ¿Entiende usted mucho de los problemas de las ciudades grandes? 2. ¿Prefiere usted las ciudades grandes o pequeñas? 3. ¿Nieva mucho en Nueva York? ¿en las montañas de Puerto Rico? 4. ¿Dónde nieva mucho? 5. ¿Piensa usted que hay mucha discriminación contra las mujeres? ¿contra las minorías? 6. ¿Piensa usted que la contaminación es un problema importante? ¿la inflación? ¿la pobreza? 7. ¿Pierde usted mucho tiempo en el tráfico? 8. ¿Prefiere usted ir a la universidad en autobús, tren, auto o bicicleta? 9. ¿Viene usted a clase mañana? 10. ¿Quiere usted vivir en Nueva York? ¿Por que sí o por qué no?

II.   Los adjetivos posesivos

Niños hispanos en
una escuela de
Nueva York

En un parque cerca de una escuela en Nueva York

SR. MORALES ¿Cuándo va a terminar la huelga, profesor?

PROFESOR Mañana quizás... , pero *nuestros* problemas no terminan: mucho trabajo, poco salario, clases de cuarenta niños, etcétera.

SR. MORALES ¡Qué barbaridad! Pues... ¿y cómo va *mi* hijo Ricardo en *sus* estudios?

PROFESOR Pues, no muy bien. Por ejemplo, *su* composición de ayer, sobre los «forty-niners» en California, no tiene mucha información.

SR. MORALES Comprendo, pero es *mi* culpa. En *nuestra* casa hablamos poco de fútbol americano.

---

1. Según el profesor, ¿cuándo va a terminar la huelga?   2. ¿Qué problemas tienen los profesores?   3. ¿Cómo va el hijo del señor Morales en sus estudios?   4. ¿Está bien su composición de ayer?   5. ¿Por qué cree el señor Morales que es su culpa? 6. ¿Cómo va usted en sus estudios? ¿Va a recibir buenas notas (*grades*) en sus exámenes finales?

In a park near a school in New York. MR. MORALES: When is the strike going to end? TEACHER: Tomorrow perhaps . . . , but our problems are not ending: lots of work, low pay, classes of forty children, etc. MR. MORALES: Good grief! Well . . . and how is my son Ricardo doing in his studies? TEACHER: Well, not too well. For example, his composition yesterday, about the "forty-niners" in California, doesn't have much information (in it). MR. MORALES: I understand, but it's my fault. In our house we don't talk much about football.

mi, mis	*my*	**nuestro(-a, -os, -as)**	*our*
tu, tus	*your*	**vuestro(-a, -os, -as)**	*your*
su, sus	*your, his, her*	**su, sus**	*your, their*

A. Possessive adjectives are placed in front of the nouns they modify (the items possessed) and agree with them in number and gender. They do not agree with the possessor.

Mis hermanas viven en San Juan.	*My sisters live in San Juan.*
¿Tu esposa cambia de empleo?	*Is your wife changing jobs?*
¿Cuál es su apellido?	*What's his (her, your, their) last name?*
Entonces, sus clases son interesantes, ¿no?	*Then your (his, her, their) classes are interesting, right?*
Nuestra oficina está cerca del banco.	*Our office is near the bank.*
Nuestros trenes siempre llegan a tiempo.	*Our trains always arrive on time.*

B. Because **su** and **sus** have several potential meanings *(his, her, your, their)*, sometimes for the sake of clarity it is better to use the following construction to show possession:

definite article + noun + **de** $\begin{cases} \text{él} \\ \text{ella} \\ \text{usted} \\ \text{ellos} \\ \text{ellas} \\ \text{ustedes} \end{cases}$

Su madre es doctora.
La madre de ella es doctora. $\Big\}$ Her mother is a doctor.

EJERCICIOS

A.   ¿De quién(es) es (son)?   From the list of items, identify those that go with the key word, as shown in the model.

> **MODELO**   mis: libro, cuadernos, pluma, libros, clases, mamá
> **mis cuadernos, mis libros, mis clases**

1. nuestras: lección, amigas, café, papel, clases, problemas
2. su: estudios, auto, casa, amigos, padre, abuelos
3. tus: padre, hermanos, lecciones, abuela, bicicleta, crimen
4. mi: tío, calle, papeles, gente, apellido, familia
5. nuestro: lección, clase, café, verano, fecha, vacaciones

B.   El abuelo de Ricardo.   Ricardo's grandfather doesn't hear very well, so Ricardo has to repeat everything for him. Answer the grandfather's questions for Ricardo.

> **MODELO**   ABUELO ¿Con quién comemos? ¿Con los hijos de Isabel?
> RICARDO **Sí, comemos con los hijos de Isabel.**
> **Comemos con sus hijos.**

1. ¿De quién es la casa? ¿De Isabel?
2. ¿Quién es María? ¿La hija de Isabel?
3. ¿Adónde vamos? ¿A la oficina del doctor Pérez?
4. ¿Cómo vamos? ¿En el auto de tus padres?
5. ¿Quiénes vienen con nosotros? ¿Los tíos de Luis?

C.   ¿Nosotros?   In pairs, respond to these questions. Use **nuestro(-a, -os, -as)**.

1. ¿Cómo son sus padres? ¿sus hermanos?
2. ¿Cómo es su clase de español? ¿su universidad o escuela? ¿su ciudad?

Entrevista

Interview a classmate to find answers to the following questions.

1. ¿Cuál es tu ciudad favorita? ¿Por qué? ¿Tiene problemas tu ciudad favorita?
2. ¿Cuál es la ciudad favorita de tus padres? ¿Por qué?   3. ¿Cuántas personas hay en tu familia?   4. ¿Cómo se llaman tus hermanos?   5. ¿Dónde trabaja tu padre? ¿Cambia de trabajo mucho? ¿Trabaja tu madre?   6. ¿Qué piensas de nuestra clase?   7. ¿Cuál es tu clase favorita?   8. ¿Cuál es tu estación favorita? ¿Por qué?

III. Los pronombres de complemento indirecto

Hay muchos letreros (*signs*) en español en el metro neoyorquino.

En el metro de Nueva York

FELIPE	Hola, Gonzalo. ¿Qué tal?
GONZALO	Bien. ¿Y tú?
FELIPE	Bastante bien. ¿Adónde vas?
GONZALO	Voy de compras. Tengo que mandar*les* regalos a papá, a mamá y al tío Fernando en Puerto Rico. *Le* voy a comprar un reloj al tío Fernando. Él *me* escribe todas las semanas. Y pienso mandar*les* una radio a mis padres. ¿Adónde vas tú?
FELIPE	Voy al Parque Central. ¡Qué fácil es viajar en metro! El metro es muy rápido, no hay problemas de tráfico y es bastante seguro.
GONZALO	Pero la gente es descortés, y hay muchos robos.
FELIPE	Si tú crees que el metro no es seguro, ¿por qué llevas ese reloj Rolex?
GONZALO	Y si tú crees que es seguro, ¿por qué llevas ese bate de béisbol?

1. ¿Adónde va Gonzalo? ¿Qué va a hacer?   2. ¿Qué le va a comprar a su tío Fernando? ¿Qué les va a comprar a sus padres?   3. ¿Adónde va Felipe?   4. ¿Qué piensa Felipe del metro? ¿Qué piensa Gonzalo del metro?   5. ¿Viajas tú en metro de vez en cuando?

In a New York subway.   FELIPE: Hi, Gonzalo. How are you? GONZALO: Fine. And you? FELIPE: OK. Where are you going? GONZALO: I'm going shopping. I have to send presents to Dad, Mom, and Uncle Fernando in Puerto Rico. I'm going to buy a watch for Uncle Fernando. He writes to me every week. And I'm thinking of sending my parents a radio. Where are you going? FELIPE: I'm going to Central Park. How easy it is to travel by subway! The subway is very fast, there are no problems with traffic, and it's quite safe. GONZALO: But the people are rude, and there are a lot of robberies. FELIPE: If you think the subway's not safe, why are you wearing that Rolex watch? GONZALO: And if you think it's safe, why are you carrying that baseball bat?

A. The indirect object in a sentence indicates the person or thing that receives the action of the verb indirectly. That is, it indicates to or for whom something is done, told, made, etc. In the sentence *I told Carmen the truth*, *Carmen* is the indirect object. (*The truth* is the direct object.) In English, indirect objects often are replaced by prepositional phrases: *I told Carmen the truth, I told the truth to Carmen; I bought Carmen the book, I bought the book for Carmen*. An indirect object pronoun is a pronoun that replaces an indirect object noun: *I bought her the book.*

B. Except for the third-person singular and plural forms, the indirect object pronouns are the same as the direct object pronouns.

Indirect Object Pronouns	
Singular	**Plural**
me *(to, for) me*	**nos** *(to, for) us*
te *(to, for) you (fam)*	**os** *(to, for) you (fam)*
le *(to, for) you, him, her, it*	**les** *(to, for) you, them*

¿Me hablas?	*Are you speaking to me?*
Les quiero escribir sobre el viaje.	*I want to write to them about the trip.*
¿Qué me recomiendan?	*What do they (you, pl) recommend to me?*

C. Indirect object pronouns follow the same rules for placement as direct object pronouns; that is, they precede a conjugated verb or they can come after and be attached to an infinitive or present participle.

No queremos venderte ese libro. ⎫ No te queremos vender ese libro. ⎭	*We don't want to sell you that book.*
Estoy comprándoles esta cámara. ⎫ Les estoy comprando esta cámara. ⎭	*I'm buying them this camera.*

Note that an accent is added to the participle to preserve its stressed syllable: **comprándoles.**

D. Ordinarily it is clear from the context to what or whom the indirect object pronoun refers. Occasionally, however, a prepositional phrase (**a él, a usted,** and the like) is used or is necessary for emphasis or clarity.

Le hablo a $\begin{cases} \text{él.} \\ \text{ella.} \\ \text{usted.} \end{cases}$ Les hablo a $\begin{cases} \text{ellos.} \\ \text{ellas.} \\ \text{ustedes.} \end{cases}$

E. An indirect object pronoun is usually included in a sentence even when the indirect object noun is also expressed. This may seem redundant to English speakers but is considered good Spanish.

Camilo le escribe a Catalina. **(le =**   *Camilo is writing to Catalina.*
  a Catalina)
Les hacemos la comida a los   *We're making the food for the*
  niños. **les = a los niños)**   *children.*

EJERCICIOS

A. Entrevista.   Interview a classmate using the following questions. Possible answers using direct and indirect object pronouns are shown. The person answering should keep the textbook closed.

1. ¿Les escribes a tus padres?   Sí, les escribo.
2. ¿Escribes tus ideas importantes?   No, no las escribo.
3. ¿Les hablas mucho a tus amigos?   Sí, les hablo mucho.
4. ¿Hablas alemán?   No, no lo hablo.
5. ¿Te habla mucho tu padre?   Sí, (él) me habla mucho.
6. ¿Vendes tus libros?   Sí, los vendo.
7. ¿Le hacen los estudiantes muchas   Sí, le hacen muchas preguntas.
   preguntas al profesor o a la
   profesora?
8. ¿Te escriben tus amigos?   No, no me escriben.
9. ¿Quieres mucho a tus hermanos?   Sí, los quiero mucho.
10. ¿Le abres la puerta a tu mamá?   Sí, le abro la puerta.
11. ¿Te mandan dinero tus padres?   Sí, (ellos) me mandan dinero.
12. ¿Les mandas dinero a ellos?   No, no les mando dinero.

B. La construcción.   Make sentences from the words given, using the pattern shown in the model.

MODELO   Silvia / hablar / al doctor
        Silvia le habla.

1. Pepe / leer el libro / a los niños enfermos
2. Yo / hacer / la comida / a Carmencita
3. Tú / hablar / de tus primos / a tus amigos
4. Silvia / vender / la bicicleta / a nosotros
5. Ella / comprar / un regalo / a los tíos

C. El cumpleaños de Miguelito.   Es el cumpleaños de Miguelito. ¿Qué regalos le compran sus parientes?

MODELO   **Su abuelo le compra un televisor.**

Preguntas

1. ¿Les escribe usted a sus parientes? ¿Les escribe mucho o poco?   2. ¿Le habla usted mucho a su mamá?   3. ¿Quién le hace la comida a usted?   4. ¿Les manda usted regalos a sus amigas? ¿a sus amigos? ¿al profesor?

IV. La hora

—Por favor, ¿tienes hora?

En una calle de Brooklyn

UN SEÑOR	Por favor, señora, *¿qué hora es?*
UNA SEÑORA	*Son las tres y media de la tarde.*
UN SEÑOR	¿Sí? Es temprano. ¿Y cómo anda su reloj?
UNA SEÑORA	Pues, como todos: de izquierda a derecha.

1. En el momento de la conversación, ¿qué hora es?   2. ¿Cómo anda el reloj de la señora?   3. ¿Lleva usted reloj? ¿Anda bien?

On a street in Brooklyn. MAN: Please, madam, what time is it? WOMAN: It's three-thirty in the afternoon. MAN: Yes? (Really?) It's early. And how is your watch working (literally, "walking" or "going")? WOMAN: Well, like all of them: from left to right.

¿QUÉ HORA ES?

Es la una y diez.

Es la una y cuarto (y quince).

Es la una y media (y treinta).

Son las dos menos veinte.

Son las dos menos cuarto.

Son las dos en punto.

de la mañana

de la tarde

de la noche

¿A qué hora?

¿A qué hora llega el avión?   Llega a las diez y cuarto de la mañana.

A. To ask what time it is, use **¿Qué hora es?** To ask at what time something happens, use **¿A qué hora...?**

¿Qué hora es?

What time is it?

¿A qué hora termina la clase?

What time does the class end?

B. Notice that from the half hour to the hour, minutes are usually subtracted from the next hour in Spanish.

Son las cuatro menos diez.

It's three-fifty.

C. To identify a time as A.M., use **de la mañana.** To identify a time as P.M., from noon to sunset, use **de la tarde,** and for later hours, **de la noche.**

¡Ay, Dios mío! Ramón llega al aeropuerto a las tres de la mañana.

Oh, my goodness! Ramón is arriving at the airport at 3:00 A.M.

En San Juan vamos al cine a las diez de la noche.

In San Juan we go to the movies at 10:00 P.M.

Tengo una clase de ciencias políticas a las cuatro de la tarde.

I have a political science class at 4:00 P.M.

D. To say that something happened in or during the morning, afternoon, or night, use **por la mañana, tarde,** or **noche.**

Trabajamos por la mañana.

We work in the morning.

Por la tarde ella estudia.

During the afternoon she studies.

No comemos mucho por la noche.

We don't eat a lot at night (in the evening).

EJERCICIOS

A. ¿Qué hora es?   Look at the five clocks below and tell the time in Spanish.

1.

2.

3.

4.    5.

B. **¿A qué hora llega el avión?**   Using the times given below, tell when the plane will arrive.

MODELO   2:30 P.M.
El avión llega a las dos y media de la tarde.

1. 6:30 P.M.
2. 8:45 A.M.
3. 10:15 P.M.
4. 9:30 A.M.
5. 6:45 A.M.
6. 9:00 P.M.

C. **Llegadas y salidas** (*Arrivals and departures*).   Write different times such as 3:00 P.M. or 6:05 A.M. on a sheet of paper and read them to a classmate (as if they were arriving and departing flights). The classmate will write the times down and read them back when the list is complete. **En español, ¡claro!** (*In Spanish, of course!*)

D. **¿Cómo?**   One student makes the following statements. His or her partner asks questions so that the original statement will be repeated.

MODELO   Empiezo a trabajar a las diez de la mañana.
¿A qué hora empiezas a trabajar? or **¿Cuándo empiezas a trabajar?**

1. Los estudiantes entran en la clase a las once.
2. Como en la cafetería a las doce y media.
3. Empiezo a estudiar a las siete todas las noches.
4. El avión llega a las ocho y media.
5. Miro la televisión a las siete.
6. Son las dos y media.

Preguntas

1. ¿Qué hora es ahora?   2. ¿A qué hora llega usted a la universidad?   3. ¿A qué hora empieza la clase de español? ¿Llega usted tarde o temprano? ¿a la hora en punto? ¿A qué hora termina la clase?   4. ¿A qué hora regresa usted a su casa? 5. ¿A qué hora de la noche empieza a estudiar usted?   6. ¿Mira televisión? ¿A qué hora?

Study Hint: Nonverbal Communication

Nonverbal communication, such as gestures, touching, and other aspects of body language, are very important in the communication process.

The amount of space between two people when they talk is known as social distance. Keeping the correct distance—not too far away, so you seem unfriendly, nor too close, so you seem overly familiar—is basic to effective communication. In many Hispanic countries, the distance between speakers is generally less than in the United States and Canada. Try not to back away when people are speaking to you!

Gestures are also very important. While some are nearly universal—wagging a finger to express *no,* for example—others have radically different meanings in different countries. A common gesture meaning *OK* in the United States, made by forming a circle with the thumb and index finger, has a vulgar meaning in some Spanish-speaking countries. How can you learn what gestures mean to a Spanish speaker? A few excellent books have been written on the subject, including Jerald Green's *A Gesture Inventory for the Teaching of Spanish* and Desmond Morris' *Gestures*. But your best bet is to observe Spanish speakers and ask them about any gestures they make that are new to you.

As for touching, the **abrazo** *(hug)* is commonly used by men in Spanish-speaking countries, and women often walk arm in arm along the street. For effective communication, be sensitive to new customs as you continue to sharpen your linguistic skills.

Una agencia de empleos en Nueva York

LOS PUERTORRIQUEÑOS DE NUEVA YORK

La oficina de empleos del edificio municipal de la ciudad de Nueva York

RAFAEL ¡Carlos! ¿Qué haces aquí?

CARLOS Hola, Rafa. Yo trabajo en esta oficina. ¿Y tú?

RAFAEL Pues, vengo a buscar empleo. Pero este formulario°...

CARLOS ¿No lo entiendes? Te ayudo. Empiezas con tu nombre y apellido, Ralph Álvarez. Después...

RAFAEL Pero ése no es mi nombre. Me llamo Rafael Álvarez Balboa.[1]

CARLOS Aquí prefieren los nombres fáciles.

RAFAEL Está bien. Quizás si cambio de nombre, mi suerte° también va a cambiar. Empiezo a pensar que en esta ciudad los americanos tienen todos los buenos empleos.

CARLOS Pero ¡nosotros también somos americanos! Ahora los boricuas no perdemos las oportunidades por problemas de nacionalidad.[2]

RAFAEL Si no las perdemos, entonces ¿por qué no tengo trabajo?

CARLOS Es que hay muchos sin trabajo, Rafa. Pero, bueno, ¿qué tipo de trabajo quieres?

RAFAEL Pues, tengo diploma de guardia de seguridad°.

CARLOS ¿Quieres esperar aquí un momento? Para ese tipo de trabajo, pienso que hay varios puestos vacantes. Le voy a hablar a la secretaria. (...)

CARLOS Tenemos un puesto en Brooklyn y otro en una tienda en Manhattan. ¿Cuál prefieres?

RAFAEL ¿Qué me recomiendas?

CARLOS ¿Por qué no llamas a los dos lugares?

RAFAEL Buena idea. Son las cuatro y cuarto. Debo llamar ahora. Gracias, Carlos.

CARLOS De nada. ¡Y buena suerte!

---

el formulario *form*   la suerte *luck*   guardia de seguridad *security guard*

PREGUNTAS

1. ¿Por qué va Rafael a la oficina de empleos? ¿Qué hace Carlos allí? 2. ¿Entiende Rafael el formulario? ¿Quién lo ayuda? 3. ¿Cree Carlos que en la oficina prefieren nombres difíciles? 4. Según Rafael, ¿quiénes tienen todos los buenos trabajos en Nueva York? 5. ¿Qué cree Rafael que va a pasar si cambia de nombre? 6. Según Carlos, ¿pierden los puertorriqueños muchas oportunidades de trabajo por problemas de nacionalidad? 7. ¿Qué tipo de diploma tiene Rafael? 8. ¿Hay trabajos para guardia de seguridad? 9. ¿Hay mucho desempleo ahora en este país? ¿En qué regiones?

NOTAS CULTURALES

1. Most people of Spanish descent use both their father's and mother's surnames (apellidos), sometimes separating them with y. The father's surname is put first, the mother's surname second. A married woman adds her husband's paternal surname after de and, for most purposes, stops using her mother's maiden name. Study the following family history. **Rosita Gómez Estrada** marries **Felipe Pérez Alarcón** and is now called **Rosita Gómez de Pérez**. Their children are called **Francisco (Paco) Pérez Gómez** and **Margarita Pérez Gómez.**

2. Puerto Ricans in New York commonly refer to themselves as **boricuas**. The term comes from **Boriquén**, the name used by the Taíno Indians who inhabited the island before the arrival of Columbus. Since Puerto Rico is **un estado libre asociado** (U.S. commonwealth), its inhabitants are U.S. citizens, and visas are not required to enter either Puerto Rico or the United States.

Funciones y *actividades*

In this chapter, you have seen examples of some important language functions, or uses. Here is a summary and some additional information about these functions of language.

TELLING TIME

See Section IV for time expressions. Digital watches have changed traditional ways of stating time. Spanish speakers now often say **Son las ocho y cincuenta** instead of the traditional **Son las nueve menos diez.**

EXPRESSING SYMPATHY

Here are some expressions to show that you feel sympathy for someone or understand what he or she is going through.

¡Qué lástima!	*What a shame (pity)!*
¡Qué mala suerte!	*What bad luck!*
¡Qué barbaridad!	*Good grief! (literally, "What barbarity!")*
¡Qué horror!	*How horrible!*
¡Pobrecito(-a)!	*Poor thing!*
Eso debe ser terrible.	*That must be terrible.*
¡Ay, Dios mío!	*Oh, my goodness! (literally, "Oh, my God!")*
¡Caramba!	*Good grief!*

EXPRESSING LACK OF SYMPATHY

Here are some expressions to use when you think someone is creating his or her own bad fortune or "has it coming."

¡Buena lección!	*That's a good lesson for you!*
Es de esperar.	*It's to be expected.*
¿Qué espera(s)?	*What do you expect?*
¿Qué importancia tiene eso?	*What's so important about that?*
¿Y qué?	*So what?*
Es su (tu) culpa. Tiene(s) la culpa.	*It's your fault.*

Now do the following activities, using the expressions you have just learned.

A. Los relojes. Rosita loves her new digital watch. Isaac is proud of his old-fashioned one, which has hands. When one says what time it is, the other replies by confirming the hour, using the opposite style of time-telling. Supply the missing replies.

> **MODELO** ISAAC   Son las tres menos cuarto.
> ROSITA   **Sí, según mi reloj, son las dos y cuarenta y cinco.**

1. Son las ocho menos veinticinco.
2. Es la una y treinta.

3. Son las doce menos diez.
4. Son las once menos cuarto.
5. Son las diez y cincuenta y cinco.
6. Son las ocho y cuarenta y cinco.

B. ¿Siente compasión? Your friend Pedro is always getting into trouble and having problems. Sometimes it's just bad luck, but sometimes he brings trouble on himself. Express sympathy or lack of sympathy with him when you find out each of the following things.

MODELOS   Su mamá está en el hospital.
           ¡Qué mala suerte!

           Va en su Fiat a cien kilómetros por hora. Un policía lo ve
           (*sees him*).
           Tienes la culpa. (Es tu culpa.)

1. Busca empleo, pero siempre llega tarde a las entrevistas.
2. Hay un robo en el edificio donde vive y pierde su bicicleta.
3. Recibe una F en un examen porque no estudia mucho.
4. No está en buenas condiciones físicas porque no come bien y no hace ejercicios.
5. Llega tarde al aeropuerto porque hay mucho tráfico; pierde el avión.
6. Tiene un accidente de automóvil pero es inocente; el otro conductor (*driver*) tiene la culpa.
7. Compra un auto nuevo pero no anda bien.
8. Va a la playa y pierde su cámara.

C. Problemas. Everyone has problems. In small groups, find out at least one problem—large or small—that someone in the group has. Ask your teacher for help in stating it if necessary. Then take turns expressing sympathy (or lack of sympathy) to the person with the problem.

D. ¡Rápido! Select someone to be **la víctima.** Using questions found anywhere in this chapter or earlier ones, the rest of the class will ask questions as rapidly as possible, and the victim will answer as many as he or she can. New victims should be selected from those who are slow to ask questions. Here are some questions to use as starters.

1. ¿Tienes empleo? ¿Buscas empleo? 2. ¿Prefieres vivir en una casa o en un apartmento? ¿Por qué? 3. ¿Prefieres vivir en una ciudad grande, en una ciudad pequeña o en el campo? 4. ¿Es más difícil vivir en una ciudad o en el campo? ¿Por qué? 5. ¿Cuáles son los problemas de la vida urbana? ¿Hay también cosas buenas? 6. ¿Qué problemas hay en el campo? ¿Cuáles son las cosas buenas? 7. ¿Cuáles son las ciudades grandes de su estado? ¿Cuántas personas viven en esas ciudades?

VOCABULARIO ACTIVO

Cognados

el aire	el, la criminal	la nacionalidad	el parque
el americano, la americana	la discriminación	la oficina	puertorriqueño
el banco	la idea	la oportunidad	el tráfico
la conversación	la inflación	la paciencia	urbano
el crimen	la minoría		

Verbos

andar	to walk; to run (as a watch, car)
ayudar	to help
cambiar	to change
cerrar (ie)	to close
comenzar (ie)	to begin
empezar (ie)	to begin, to start
entender (ie)	to understand; to hear
entrar (en)	to enter, come or go in
mandar	to send
mentir (ie)	to lie
nevar (ie)	to snow
pensar (ie)	to think
pensar (+ inf)	to intend, plan (to do something)
pensar de	to think of, have an opinion of
pensar en	to think of, think about
perder (ie)	to lose; to miss (a train, plane, etc.)
perder el tiempo	to waste time
preferir (ie)	to prefer
querer (ie)	to want; to love, like
recomendar (ie)	to recommend
sentir (ie)	to feel; to be sorry
venir (ie)	to come

La ciudad y sus problemas

el autobús	bus
el barrio	neighborhood
la basura	garbage, trash
el cine	movies; movie theater
la contaminación	pollution
el desempleo	unemployment
el empleo	job, employment
el hambre f	hunger
la huelga	strike

el metro	subway
la pobreza	poverty
el policía (la mujer policía)	police officer
la policía	police force
el robo	theft
la tienda	store, shop
el trabajo	work, job

La hora — Time

¿A qué hora?	At what time?
de la mañana	A.M.
de la noche	P.M. (after sunset)
de la tarde	P.M. (noon to sunset)
en punto	on the dot
la una y media	1:30
media: media hora	half an hour
por la mañana	in the morning
por la noche	in the evening, at night (after sunset)
por la tarde	in the afternoon (until sunset)
el reloj	watch; clock
tarde	late
temprano	early

Otras palabras y frases

el agua f	water
el apellido	surname
bastante	enough; rather, quite
contra	against
después (de)	after; later, afterwards, then
el dinero	money
entonces	then; well
llegar tarde	to be late, arrive late
el lugar	place
la mañana	morning

la noche	*evening, night (after sunset)*
el nombre	*name*
nuevo	*new*
la película	*movie, film*
pobre	*poor*
poco	*little; pl few*
el puesto	*position, job*
quizás	*perhaps*
seguro	*safe; sure*
si	*if*
sin	*without*
sobre	*on, about*
la tarde	*afternoon (until sunset)*
varios	*various; several*

Expresiones útiles

¡Ay, Dios mío!	*Oh, my goodness!*
¡Caramba!	*Good grief!*
culpa: Tiene(s) la culpa.	*It's your fault.*
Es su (tu) culpa.	
Eso debe ser terrible.	*That must be terrible.*
¡Qué barbaridad!	*Good grief! (literally, "What barbarity!")*

Don't forget: Possessive adjectives,
pp. 131–132
Indirect object pronouns, p. 134

Una familia méxico-americana almuerza en un parque de San Antonio, Tejas.

COMIDAS Y BEBIDAS

Funciones

- Expressing likes
- Expressing dislikes
- Ordering a meal in a restaurant

Vocabulario. In this chapter you will talk about foods and meals.

Gramática. You will discuss and use:

1. The present tense of verbs that change their stem vowel from **o** to **ue** when the stem vowel is stressed and the verb **jugar** (*to play*)
2. Pronouns that serve as objects of prepositions
3. The present tense of stem-changing **-ir** verbs, **e** to **i**; and the verbs **pedir** versus **preguntar**, which can both mean *to ask*
4. The present tense of **gustar**, a verb used to convey the meaning of *to like*, and other grammatically similar verbs

Cultura. The dialogues take place in Mexican-American communities in California, Texas, Colorado, and New Mexico.

EL DESAYUNO

1. los huevos
2. el jamón
3. el pan
4. la mantequilla
5. la sal
6. la pimienta
7. el café
8. el té
9. la leche
10. el jugo
11. el azúcar
12. los cereales

EL ALMUERZO*

Platos principales

1. la hamburguesa
2. la carne: el bistec
3. el pescado
4. el pollo
5. el cerdo

Otras comidas

1. el arroz
2. la ensalada ⎫
3. la lechuga ⎭ las verduras

4. el maíz
5. el tomate
6. las papas

*__El almuerzo__ is a large midday meal, traditionally the main meal of the day. In modern cities, however, the midday meal is becoming lighter and the evening meal more substantial as work schedules change and commuting home for lunch becomes more difficult.

Bebidas

1. el vino
2. la cerveza
3. el agua mineral
4. el refresco

Las frutas

1. la manzana
2. la naranja
3. los plátanos
4. la piña

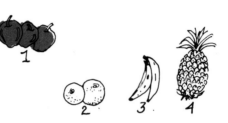

Postres

1. el pastel, la torta
2. el flan (*a kind of custard*)
3. el helado
4. el queso y las frutas

LA CENA

1. la sopa
2. los frijoles
3. el sandwich

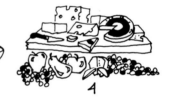

PARA COMER Y TOMAR...

1. el vaso
2. la taza
3. el tenedor
4. el cuchillo
5. la cuchara
6. el plato

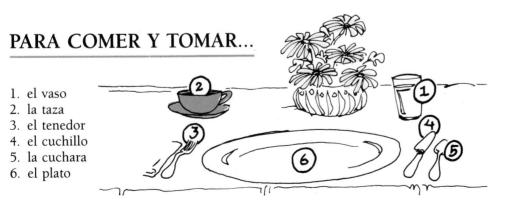

¿Qué come usted?

1. Para el desayuno, ¿qué come usted? ¿Come huevos con jamón, cereales o sólo toma café?   2. ¿Prefiere el café con leche y azúcar?   3. A la hora del almuerzo, ¿qué come usted? ¿una hamburguesa? ¿una ensalada? ¿un postre? 4. ¿A qué hora cena usted (*do you have dinner*)? ¿Qué come en la cena? 5. ¿Come usted mucha carne? ¿mucho pescado? ¿Prefiere café o té? 6. ¿Cuáles son sus frutas favoritas? ¿Qué frutas no come usted?   7. Cuando tiene mucha sed, ¿qué toma? ¿Toma usted mucho café? ¿vino? ¿cerveza? 8. ¿Qué no comen las personas que quieren ser delgadas (*slim*)? ¿helado? ¿ensaladas? ¿pasteles? (¿tortas?) ¿carne? ¿verduras? ¿maíz?

¿Qué es esto?   Cover the vocabulary lists on pages 148 and 149 and name the food items shown in the pictures at the beginning of the chapter. A classmate will listen to you to check your accuracy.

¿Qué tiene?   Match the foods in the left-hand column with the ingredients they contain in the right-hand column.

1. una ensalada   a. azúcar, leche, huevos
2. una sopa   b. carne, papas, verduras
3. una torta   c. lechuga, tomates
4. un sandwich   d. pan, jamón, lechuga, tomate

I. El presente de indicativo de los verbos con cambios en la raíz o → *ue*; el verbo *jugar*

Hay buenos restaurantes mexicanos en la Calle Olvera, Los Ángeles.

En la casa de la familia Ojeda en Los Ángeles*

ALICIA ¿Qué buscas, tío?

CÉSAR *Almuerzo* con el señor Portilla a la una y no *encuentro* el paraguas.

ALICIA Ya no *llueve.* Susana y yo *podemos* llevarte al restaurante. ¿Dónde *almuerzan?*

CÉSAR *Almorzamos* en la calle Olvera. ¿*Recuerdas* el restaurante donde hacen esas enchiladas deliciosas?

ALICIA No, no lo *recuerdo.* Pero lo *puedo* encontrar si tú me *muestras* el camino.

1. ¿Qué busca César? ¿Lo puede encontrar?   2. ¿Por qué no necesita César paraguas?   3. ¿Dónde almuerzan César y el señor Portilla?   4. ¿Recuerda Alicia el restaurante? ¿Cómo lo van a encontrar?   5. ¿Almuerza usted en restaurantes mexicanos de vez en cuando?

At the Ojeda family's house in Los Angeles. ALICIA: What are you looking for, Uncle? CÉSAR: I'm having lunch with Mr. Portilla at one o'clock and I can't find my umbrella. ALICIA: It's not raining any longer. Susana and I can take you to the restaurant. Where are you having lunch? CÉSAR: We're having lunch on Olvera Street. Do you remember the restaurant where they make those delicious enchiladas? ALICIA: No, I don't remember it. But I can find it if you show me the way.

A. Certain Spanish verbs show a stem change from **o** to **ue** when the stem is stressed. This change does not occur in the first- and second-person plural forms because the stress does not fall on the stem.

recordar to remember		**volver** to return		**dormir** to sleep	
recuerdo	recordamos	vuelvo	volvemos	duermo	dormimos
recuerdas	recordáis	vuelves	volvéis	duermes	dormís
recuerda	recuerdan	vuelve	vuelven	duerme	duermen

B. Here are some other **o** to **ue** stem-changing verbs.

almorzar	to have lunch
contar	to count; to count on; to tell
costar	to cost
encontrar	to find
llover	to rain
mostrar	to show
poder	to be able, can
soñar (con)	to dream (about)

*More people of Mexican descent live in Los Angeles than in any city in Mexico except Mexico City and Guadalajara. Olvera Street's authentic Mexican restaurants and shops reflect the Mexican heritage of Los Angeles.

No encuentro el arroz aquí.	*I don't find the rice here.*
Podemos comprar naranjas y manzanas en esta tienda.	*We can buy oranges and apples in this store.*
¿Cuánto cuestan los plátanos?	*How much do the bananas cost?*
Elvira siempre duerme bien en las montañas.	*Elvira always sleeps well in the mountains.*
Sueño con Enrique.	*I dream about Enrique.*
Paco siempre cuenta historias muy interesantes.	*Paco always tells very interesting stories.*

C. Verbs of this type are shown in vocabulary lists with the marker **(ue): recordar (ue).**

D. The verb **jugar** *(to play a game or sport)* is the only verb in Spanish that changes its stem vowel **u** to **ue.**

jugar to play

juego	jugamos
juegas	jugáis
juega	juegan

Before the name of a sport or game, **jugar** is usually followed by the preposition **a.**

Susana juega al tenis hasta las dos.   *Susana plays tennis until 2:00.*

EJERCICIOS

A. ¡Ah... buena idea!   These people have some good ideas about how to spend a lazy Sunday. Tell what you and a friend are going to do.

> **MODELO**   Los muchachos duermen hasta las diez de la mañana.
> **Nosotros también dormimos hasta las diez de la mañana.**

1. Marisol sueña con un buen flan.
2. La familia almuerza en un restaurante.
3. Arturo puede jugar al tenis esta tarde.
4. Luis y Marta juegan en la plaza.
5. El profesor encuentra un programa interesante en la televisión.
6. David y Marisol vuelven tarde del cine.
7. Los niños cuentan los libros que tienen.
8. Teresa duerme todo el día.
9. Roberto le muestra la ciudad a Alicia.
10. Susana recuerda una fiesta en el centro.

B. Conversaciones. Complete the conversations by filling in each blank with the correct form of the stem-changing verb from the list at the right.

1. volver
2. llover
3. poder
4. almorzar
5. costar
6. recordar
7. volver

MAMÁ Rosario, ¿por qué no (1) _____ a la cama (*bed*)?

ROSARIO Porque (2) _____ mucho. No (3) _____ dormir.

* * *

MANUEL Toño y yo vamos al restaurante Santa Fe. (4) _____ con María y Cristina.

PAPÁ ¿Cuánto (5) _____ la comida en ese restaurante?

MANUEL (Yo) no (6) _____ los precios. (Nosotros) (7) _____ a las tres.

Preguntas

1. ¿Cuánto cuesta una buena hamburguesa? ¿un café? ¿un helado?   2. ¿Vuelve usted tarde o temprano de la universidad hoy?   3. ¿Llueve mucho aquí? ¿Dónde llueve mucho?   4. ¿Duerme usted bien, en general? Si toma mucho café o té, ¿puede dormir usted?   5. ¿Vuelven ustedes a clase mañana?   6. ¿Puede contar usted hasta cien en alemán?

Encuesta

Find out the following information from your classmates.

1. ¿Cuántas horas duermen por la noche?   2. ¿Cuántos juegan al tenis?   3. ¿Cuántos almuerzan en la cafetería de la universidad?   4. ¿Cuántos almuerzan en casa?   5. ¿A qué hora almuerzan?   6. ¿Qué almuerzan?   7. ¿Cuántos vuelven tarde a casa?   8. ¿Cuántos sueñan por la noche? ¿Cuántos recuerdan sus sueños (*dreams*)? ¿Con qué o con quién sueñan?

II. Pronombres usados como complemento de preposición

Hay una gran comunidad mexicana en San Antonio, Tejas.

En una tienda en San Antonio, Tejas

MARTÍN   ¡Qué bien hacer las compras *contigo*!
CONSUELO   Igualmente, Martín. Para *mí* también es un placer estar *contigo*.
MARTÍN   ¿Qué llevamos? Tenemos pan, plátanos, chocolate, un pastel...
¿este helado es para *ti*?
CONSUELO   Sí, es para *mí*. ¿Dónde están las cervezas?
MARTÍN   Detrás de *ti*. Ahora necesito comprar agua mineral.
CONSUELO   ¿Agua mineral?
MARTÍN   ¡Claro! Siempre la tengo en casa cuando estoy a dieta.

---

1. ¿Dónde están Martín y Consuelo?   2. ¿Qué compran?   3. ¿Dónde están las cervezas?   4. ¿Qué quiere comprar Martín? ¿Por qué?   5. ¿Quiere usted ser más delgado(-a)? ¿Está a dieta?

In a store in San Antonio, Texas. MARTÍN: How nice it is to do the shopping with you! CONSUELO: Likewise, Martín. For me, too, it's a pleasure to be with you. MARTÍN: What shall we get (take)? We have bread, bananas, chocolate, a cake. . . . Is this ice cream for you? CONSUELO: Yes, it's for me. Where are the beers? MARTÍN: Behind you. Now I need to buy mineral water. CONSUELO: Mineral water? MARTÍN: Of course. I always have it in the house when I'm on a diet.

A. Prepositions show the relationship between a noun or pronoun and other sentence elements. Typical relationships are of place (for example, *on, in front of*), time *(before, after)*, purpose *(for)*, possession *(of)*, and manner *(with)*. The prepositions **a** and **de** were discussed in Chapter 2.

Here is a list of common prepositions in Spanish.

a	to, at	por	for, by, through
acerca de	concerning, about	según	according to
antes de	before	sin	without
cerca de	near	sobre	about, over, on, upon
con	with		
contra	against		
de	of, from		
debajo de	under		
desde	from (a certain time), since		
después de	after		
detrás de	behind		
durante	during		
en	in, on, at		
entre	between		
excepto	except		
hacia	toward		
hasta	until		
lejos de	far from		
para	for, to, in order to		

B. Here are the pronouns used as objects of prepositions in Spanish.

Singular	Plural
mí *me, myself*	**nosotros(-as)** *us, ourselves*
ti *you (fam), yourself*	**vosotros(-as)** *you (fam), yourselves*
usted *you*	**ustedes** *you*
él *him*	**ellos(-as)** *them*
ella *her*	

Notice the accent on **mí** (but not on **ti**). Accents are not written on one-syllable words except to differentiate them from another word with the same spelling. The accent on the pronoun **mí** differentiates it from the possessive adjective **mi.**

C. Prepositional pronouns always follow a preposition. They have the same forms as subject pronouns, except for **mí** and **ti.**

Esta taza es para ella.	*This cup is for her.*
Ella no quiere cenar sin ti.	*She doesn't want to eat dinner without you.*

D. The preposition **con** combines with **mí** to form **conmigo** and with **ti** to form **contigo.**

Siempre puedes contar conmigo.	*You can always count on me.*
La camarera quiere hablar contigo.	*The waitress wants to talk to you.*

E. The subject pronouns **yo** and **tú** are used instead of **mí** and **ti** after the prepositions **entre, excepto,** and **según.**

Entre tú y yo...	*Between you and me. . . .*
Todos almuerzan allí excepto yo.	*Everybody eats lunch there except me.*
Según tú, ¿cuesta mucho cenar en ese restaurante?	*In your opinion, does it cost a lot to eat dinner at that restaurant?*

EJERCICIOS

A. **¡Claro que sí!**   Lola and Héctor have a rather stormy relationship. Take Lola's part and contradict Héctor's statements.

> **MODELO**   No puedo hablar contigo.
> **Claro que puedes hablar conmigo.**

1. No sueño contigo.
2. No necesito estar cerca de ti.
3. No pienso en ti.
4. Hoy no almuerzo contigo.
5. No juego al tenis contigo esta tarde.
6. No puedo contar contigo.

B. La vida de Jorge.   Include the information suggested by the English cues in these sentences about Jorge's activities.

> **MODELO**   (*with me*) Jorge quiere ir a la playa...
> **Jorge quiere ir a la playa conmigo.**

1. (*near her*) Jorge almuerza en el restaurante...
2. (*about you—tú*) Jorge habla mucho...
3. (*for us*) Jorge tiene unos vasos...
4. (*except me*) Todos los amigos de Jorge tienen que trabajar hoy...
5. (*behind me*) Jorge siempre anda...
6. (*of you—tú*) Cuando está en casa, Jorge piensa...
7. (*near her*) Jorge quiere a Melinda. Él vive en un apartamento...
8. (*between you—tú—and me*) Jorge va a andar...

C. Rápido.   Select someone to be **la víctima.** Everybody else will ask the following questions in rapid succession, and **la víctima** will attempt to answer as many as possible. Then someone else should be selected for the same treatment.

1. ¿Cómo se llama la persona que está enfrente de ti?   2. ¿Quién está detrás de ti?   3. ¿Quieres jugar al tenis conmigo esta tarde?   4. ¿Tienes un regalo para mí?   5. Voy a México. ¿Quieres ir conmigo?   6. ¿Crees que todos tienen dinero aquí excepto tú?   7. ¿Quién está entre tú y la puerta?

III. El presente de indicativo de los verbos con cambios de raíz e → *i*; *pedir* vs. *preguntar*

Una calle en el
barrio mexicano de
Denver, Colorado

En una casa en Denver, Colorado

ARTURO	Papá, ¿puedo *pedirte* un favor? Necesito dinero.
SR. FLORES	¿Otra vez me *repites* eso? ¿Por qué no le *preguntas* a tu mamá dónde está su bolso?
ARTURO	Mamá *dice* que no tiene dinero. Y Paco y yo queremos comprar hamburguesas y refrescos.
SR. FLORES	¡Caramba! Los niños de hoy no tienen idea del valor del dólar.
ARTURO	Sí, papá. Tengo muy buena idea de su valor. Por eso te *pido* diez.

1. ¿Qué le pide Arturo a su papá?   2. ¿Qué debe preguntarle Arturo a su mamá? 3. ¿Qué dice la mamá?   4. ¿Qué quieren comprar Arturo y Paco?   5. ¿Qué dice el señor Flores sobre los niños de hoy?   6. ¿Cuántos dólares le pide el niño? 7. ¿Les pide usted dinero a sus padres de vez en cuando?

In a house in Denver, Colorado. ARTURO: Dad, can I ask you a favor? I need money. MR. FLORES: You're repeating that to me again? Why don't you ask your mom where her purse is? ARTURO: Mom says she doesn't have any money. And Paco and I want to buy hamburgers and soft drinks. MR. FLORES: Good grief! The children of today don't have any idea of the value of a dollar. ARTURO: Yes, Dad. I have a good idea of its value. That's why I'm asking you for ten.

A. Certain **-ir** verbs show a stem change from **e** to **i** when the stem syllable is stressed.

pedir to ask for		seguir to continue; to follow		servir to serve	
pido	pedimos	sigo	seguimos	sirvo	servimos
pides	pedís	sigues	seguís	sirves	servís
pide	piden	sigue	siguen	sirve	sirven

Repetir *(to repeat)* is another **e** to **i** stem-changing verb.

Repiten las palabras.	*They repeat the words.*
Pide jugo de naranja.	*He's ordering orange juice.*
Seguimos a los García al restaurante.	*We're following the Garcías to the restaurant.*
El camarero sirve la comida.	*The waiter is serving the meal (food).*

The verb **seguir** can also mean *to take* (a course) in the expression **seguir un curso.**

Sigo cuatro cursos ahora.	*I'm taking four courses now.*

B. Pedir means *to ask for something, to request (someone) to do something.*
Preguntar means *to ask a question.*

Pedimos la cena. / We're ordering (asking for) dinner.
Me piden un favor. / They're asking me for a favor.
¿Por qué no le preguntas a la camarera si sirven vino aquí? / Why don't you ask the waitress if they serve wine here?
Me preguntan dónde está el azúcar. / They ask me where the sugar is.

C. The verb **decir** also shows the **e** to **i** stem change. In addition, its **yo** form, **digo,** is irregular.

decir to say, tell

digo	decimos
dices	decís
dice	dicen

¡Te digo que no! / I'm telling you no!
Siempre decimos la verdad. / We always tell the truth.

EJERCICIOS

A. Ellos no, pero nosotros sí. Say that we do the following things, unlike other people. Follow the model.

MODELO Luis no dice la verdad.
 Pero nosotros sí decimos la verdad.

1. El profesor no sigue un curso de español.
2. Muchos estudiantes no le piden favores al profesor.
3. Ellos no sirven la comida a las seis.
4. Juana no repite los modelos.
5. Los malos estudiantes no dicen que van a estudiar.

B. ¿Cuál es la pregunta? The following are possible answers. For each of them, give a reasonable question, as in the model.

MODELO Seguimos dos cursos.
 Cuántos cursos siguen ustedes?

1. Pido un vino.
2. Mi hermano sirve el desayuno hoy.
3. Sí, repetimos mucho en esta clase.
4. Sigo cursos de inglés y español.
5. Mamá dice que necesitamos frijoles y mantequilla.

C. ¿Pedir o preguntar? Complete the paragraph with the correct forms of **pedir** or **preguntar.**

Ana quiere ir al cine. Les (1) _____ dinero a sus padres. Llama al cine para (2) _____ a qué hora empieza la película. También le (3) _____ a la chica

que trabaja allí si la película es buena. Después, llama a una amiga y le
(4) _____ si quiere ir al cine con ella. Su amiga dice que sí. Entonces Ana le
(5) _____ un favor a su mamá: «¿Puedo usar el auto?» Su mamá le dice:
«¿Por qué no le (6) _____ permiso (*permission*) a tu papá?» Su papá le dice:
«Puedes usar el auto, pero, ¿qué me respondes si te (7) _____ a qué hora
vuelves?» Ana le dice que regresa antes de las once y le (8) _____ las llaves
(*keys*) del auto. Después dice «Gracias, hasta luego» y va a buscar a su amiga.

Preguntas

1. ¿Cuál es su restaurante favorito? ¿Qué platos sirven allí?   2. Cuando usted va
a la cafetería y tiene hambre, ¿qué pide? ¿cuando tiene sed?   3. ¿Les pide muchos
favores a sus amigos? ¿a sus padres? ¿a sus profesores?   4. ¿Qué les pregunta
siempre a sus profesores? ¿Siempre le dicen la verdad? ¿Siempre dicen la verdad
los presidentes? ¿los policías?   5. ¿Qué cursos sigue ahora?   6. ¿Qué cursos
piensa seguir?   7. ¿Qué dice cuando siente compasión por una persona? ¿Qué
dice cuando no entiende una palabra?

IV. *Gustar* y verbos parecidos

¿A Ud. le gustan los chiles rellenos?

En un restaurante en Nuevo México

CAMARERO   ¿Qué desea pedir, señor?
SR. GUTIÉRREZ   Dos platos de chiles rellenos. *Me gustan* mucho los chiles
rellenos. Y picantes—¡a mí *me encanta* la comida picante!
CAMARERO   Sí, señor. (*Unos minutos más tarde, le trae un plato de chiles
rellenos.*) Aquí lo tiene. ¿Qué otra cosa *le falta*?

SR. GUTIÉRREZ   ¿Me puede traer otro plato? Siempre pido un plato de chiles rellenos para mí y otro para mi amigo Antonio. Es un buen amigo, y ahora vive en Chicago. Como a los dos *nos encantan* los platos picantes, especialmente los chiles rellenos, yo siempre pido un plato extra para él y él siempre pide un plato extra para mí. Lo hacemos por razones sentimentales, para recordar el pasado.

CAMARERO   ¡Ah! Sí, señor. Entiendo. Ahora le sirvo otro plato. ¡Buen provecho!

Pasan unas semanas. Otra vez entra el señor Gutiérrez en el restaurante.

CAMARERO   Buenas tardes, señor.

SR. GUTIÉRREZ   Buenas tardes. Un plato de chiles rellenos, por favor.

CAMARERO   ¿Un plato? ¿Es que... ya no vive su amigo?

SR. GUTIÉRREZ   O, él está muy bien. Pero yo... mi doctor me dice que ya no debo comer platos picantes....

---

1. ¿Qué pide el señor Gutiérrez?   2. ¿Al señor Gutiérrez le gusta la comida picante?   3. ¿Qué le sirve el camarero?   4. ¿Por qué siempre pide dos platos de chiles rellenos el señor Gutiérrez?   5. ¿Qué pasa unas semanas después?   6. ¿Cómo está el amigo del señor Gutiérrez? ¿Qué dice el doctor del señor Gutiérrez?   7. ¿A usted le gustan los platos picantes?

In a restaurant in New Mexico. WAITER: What do you want to order, sir? MR. GUTIÉRREZ: Two plates of chiles rellenos (stuffed peppers)—I like chiles rellenos very much. And hot (spicy). I love spicy food! WAITER: Yes, sir. (*A few minutes later, he brings him one plate of chiles rellenos.*) Here you are. What else do you need? (literally, "What other thing are you missing?") MR. GUTIÉRREZ: Please bring me another plate . . . I always order one plate of chiles rellenos for myself and another for my friend Antonio. He's a good friend and now he lives in Chicago. Since both of us love hot food, especially chiles rellenos, I always order an extra plate for him, and he always orders an extra plate for me. We do it for sentimental reasons, to remember the past. WAITER: Oh! OK, sir, I understand. Now I'll serve you another plate. Enjoy your meal! (*A few weeks go by. Mr. Gutiérrez comes into the restaurant again.*) WAITER: Good afternoon, sir. MR. GUTIÉRREZ: Good afternoon. One plate of chiles rellenos, please. WAITER: One plate? Is . . . Is your friend no longer living? MR. GUTIÉRREZ: Oh, he's fine. But as for me, my doctor says I shouldn't eat hot foods (dishes) anymore. . . .

A. Gustar means *to please* or *to be pleasing to*. It is used to express likes and dislikes. The person, thing, or idea that is pleasing (pleases) is the subject of the sentence. The person who is pleased is the indirect object. (In English, the verb *to disgust* functions the same way: *Your attitude disgusts us = We don't like your attitude.*) **Gustar** is usually used in the third-person singular or plural, depending on whether what pleases or displeases is singular or plural.

Me gusta este pan.   *I like this bread. (This bread pleases me.)*

Me gustan estas papas.   *I like these potatoes. (These potatoes please me.)*

¿Te gustan las verduras?	*Do you like vegetables? (Are vegetables pleasing to you?)*
No le gusta la cerveza alemana.	*She doesn't like German beer.*
Nos gustan mucho las piñas.	*We like pineapples a lot.*
Nos gustan.	*We like them.*

B. The prepositional phrase **a** + noun or pronoun is often added for emphasis or clarity. It is usually placed at the beginning of the sentence.

A Fernando le gusta el chocolate.	*Fernando likes chocolate.*
A muchos hispanos les gusta el café con leche.	*Many Hispanic people like coffee with milk.*
A usted le gustan los vinos buenos, ¿no?	*You like good wines, don't you?*

Notice the prepositional phrase **¿a Pepe?** in the following exchange.

Me gusta la sopa.	*I like the soup. (The soup is pleasing to me.)*
¿Y a Pepe?	*And Pepe? (And to Pepe?)*
A Pepe no le gusta.	*Pepe doesn't like it. (To Pepe, it isn't pleasing.)*

C. If what is liked (or what is pleasing) is an action expressed with an infinitive, the third-person singular of **gustar** is used.

No me gusta cocinar, pero sí me gusta comer.	*I don't like to cook, but I do like to eat.*

D. Other verbs that function like **gustar** include:

encantar	*to delight*
faltar	*to be lacking or missing*
importar	*to matter, be important*
interesar	*to interest*
molestar	*to bother*

Me encantan las naranjas.	*I love oranges.*
Me faltan un tenedor y un cuchillo.	*I need a fork and spoon (a fork and spoon are missing or lacking).*
No nos importa el dinero.	*Money doesn't matter to us.*
A sus abuelos les molesta el tráfico.	*The traffic bothers her grandparents.*

EJERCICIOS

A. ¿Qué le molesta a Inés?   Tell what is bothering Inés.

MODELOS   el tiempo
Le molesta el tiempo.

la lluvia y el viento
Le molestan la lluvia y el viento.

1. el tráfico
2. sus hermanos
3. el programa de televisión
4. la contaminación
5. los exámenes

B. ¡Pero no me gusta!   Little Eduardo is very difficult to please. Take his part and give his reasons for not eating what his mother gives him.

MODELO   ¿Por qué no tomas el helado?
No me gusta el helado.

1. ¿Por qué no comes las verduras?
2. ¿Por qué no tomas la leche?
3. ¿Por qué no comes unas frutas?
4. ¿Por qué no tomas ese refresco?
5. ¿Por qué no comes el queso?

C. ¿Qué nos falta...?   Everybody is out to dinner tonight. Why? Because they are all lacking something they need to prepare a meal at home! Tell who needs what.

MODELOS   a Rubén / sal / comida
A Rubén le falta sal para la comida.

a nosotros / frutas / el postre
A nosotros nos faltan frutas para el postre.

1. a Eduardo / lechuga / ensalada
2. a mí / leche / flan
3. a ustedes / papas / ensalada de papas
4. a ti / arroz / arroz con pollo
5. a nosotros / verduras / sopa
6. a los Ruíz / carne / hamburguesa
7. a Marta / sal y pimienta / bistec

D. Opiniones.   Look at the pictures and create sentences about what you think is going on. Use pronouns and the verbs **encantar, gustar, importar, interesar,** and **molestar.** Talk about yourself when appropriate.

MODELO

A ellos les encanta ir a la playa cuando hace sol.

1.

2.

3.

4.

5.

6.

E. ¿Qué les gusta? Ask whether or not your classmates like the following things. Move around the class, jotting down the answers you hear. Then compile the results.

MODELO *la carne*

Usted dice: **¿Te gusta la carne?**

Sara: **Sí, me gusta mucho. (No, no me gusta.)**

Usted escribe: **A Sara le gusta (A Sara no le gusta) la carne.**

1. dormir por la tarde
2. las películas viejas
3. esquiar
4. el agua mineral
5. las naranjas
6. la comida mexicana
7. la ciudad de Los Ángeles
8. viajar a otros países

F. ¡Anda! (*Go on!*) Finish the statement in any appropriate way.

MODELO Al profesor le gusta(n)...

Al profesor le gusta hablar español.

1. No me gusta(n)...
2. A mis padres les encanta(n)...
3. A los estudiantes de hoy les molesta(n)...

4. A mis amigos les interesa(n)...
5. A mí no me importa(n)...
6. A mis hermanos no les interesa(n)...
7. Los sábados me encanta(n)...
8. En la clase de español nos falta(n)...

G. Traducción.   Give the Spanish equivalents of the following sentences.

1. We like beans.
2. I love ice cream.
3. Is the sun bothering you?
4. Money is important to them.
5. Are you (**tú**) interested in mathematics?
6. She needs a cup.

Preguntas

1. ¿Qué cosas le interesan a usted? ¿Qué cosas le encantan?   2. ¿A usted le gusta ir de compras? ¿cocinar? ¿ir al cine? ¿Qué (tres o cuatro) cosas le gusta hacer a usted?   3. ¿Qué (tres o cuatro) cosas le molestan o no le gusta hacer?   4. ¿Qué les molesta mucho a sus padres? ¿a sus profesores? ¿a usted?   5. En su casa, ¿tiene las cosas que necesita para hacer una ensalada? ¿un postre? Si, no, ¿qué le falta?

Study Hint: Reviewing for Exams

You're going to have a Spanish exam? Don't panic. Review the study suggestions on pages 37 and 68.
   1. The first step in studying for exams is to map out what chapters and topics will be covered. Then identify any gaps you may have in your understanding of the material. Use the **repasos** (in the **Cuaderno de ejercicios**) to test your knowledge. Take an extra day or two to review the chapters so you will have plenty of time to ask your instructor for clarification.
   2. Next, look at the **Vocabulario activo** sections of this textbook. Make photocopies and fold the copies so the Spanish expressions appear on one side and the English equivalents appear on the other. Go through the list several times until you know the Spanish words thoroughly. Then give yourself a spelling test. Use the same list, writing the Spanish words on another sheet in response to the English cues, or work with a partner, spelling the items aloud. Try spelling the words into a cassette recorder if you don't have a partner. If you pronounce a Spanish word before spelling it, you may retain it better.
   3. Review verbs next, making sure you can run through all the forms for each one. Use the models in the textbook chapters or in the verb tables at the back of the book. Now you're ready!

PARA
EL
CINCO
DE
MAYO...

Mujer con ropa mexicana
tradicional en un desfile
(parade) del cinco de mayo,
San José

*Unos estudiantes méxico-americanos organizan una celebración para el cinco
de mayo en San José, California.*[1]

ALICIA	Bueno, ¿qué tenemos que hacer?
CRISTINA	Tenemos que encontrar una banda mariachi° y otra de salsa°.
FELIPE	Hay una buena banda mariachi en Berkeley.
CRISTINA	Mi primo José está en una banda de salsa.
ALICIA	Entonces, ¿por qué no invitamos a los dos grupos? ¿Y qué hacemos para comer?
MANUEL	¿Por qué no servimos tacos y enchiladas?
ALICIA	¡Estupenda idea! ¿Podemos contar contigo para hacer las compras°? Necesitamos pollo, carne, lechuga, tomates...
MANUEL	La verdad es que prefiero hacer la comida. No me gusta hacer las compras.
FELIPE	Pues yo las hago. A mí realmente no me gusta cocinar.
ALICIA	Bueno... ¿y qué más?
MANUEL	¿Por qué no invitamos al Teatro Campesino?[2] ¿Qué piensas, Alicia?
ALICIA	¡Me encanta la idea! Si la gente del Teatro Campesino no puede venir, quizás el profesor González puede leer poesía°.

CRISTINA	Sí, quizás... pero ¿quién va a hablar sobre el origen de la celebración?
MANUEL	¿Por qué no invitamos a César Chávez?[3]
ALICIA	De acuerdo, y si él no puede venir, ¿invitamos a un representante de MEChA?[4]
FELIPE	¡Sí, claro! ¿Y qué más nos falta?
CRISTINA	Nos falta reservar el parque. Yo puedo hacer eso.
ALICIA	Bueno, creo que ya es bastante para empezar. ¡Manos a la obra!°

mariachi *Mexican music or musicians, whose music includes guitar and trumpet*   salsa *salsa, Latin music that has elements of jazz, blues, and rock*   hacer las compras *to do the shopping* poesía *poetry*   ¡Manos a la obra! *Let's get to work!*

PREGUNTAS

1. ¿Qué organizan los estudiantes?   2. ¿Qué necesitan encontrar?   3. ¿Qué comida van a servir? ¿Quién va a comprarla?   4. ¿A quién le gusta cocinar? 5. ¿A quién van a invitar los estudiantes? ¿Quién va a hablar sobre el origen de la celebración?   6. ¿Qué más les falta?   7. ¿Celebran el cinco de mayo donde usted vive?

NOTAS CULTURALES

1. May 5th, celebrated by Mexican-Americans as well as Mexicans since the latter part of the nineteenth century, commemorates the defeat of the invading French army on that date at the city of Puebla, Mexico, in 1862 by Mexican forces.

2. The **Teatro Campesino** has earned an international reputation and has inspired many other Mexican-American theater groups. It was founded in 1965 by Luis Valdez to help organize farm workers. Its first plays dealt with the farm workers' strike. They were short, improvisational pieces performed in a mixture of Spanish and English. Later the **Teatro Campesino** broadened its repertoire to include other issues affecting Mexican-Americans.

3. César Chávez founded the National Farm Workers Association (now the United Farm Workers, AFL-CIO). In September of 1965 the union participated in a strike at the Delano, California grape fields. Chávez initiated a five-year table grape boycott and eventually obtained contracts with 26 Delano grape growers. Chávez remains in the forefront of the struggle for farm workers' rights.

4. The **Movimiento Estudiantil Chicano de Aztlán (MEChA)** is a Mexican-American student group that was organized in California in 1969. Members of **MEChA** work on and off campus to achieve educational, cultural, and socioeconomic goals.

Funciones y *actividades*

In this chapter, you have seen examples of some important language functions, or uses. Here is a summary and some additional information about these functions of language.

EXPRESSING LIKES

Me gusta(n)...	*I like . . .*
Me interesa(n)...	*I'm interested in . . .*
Me encanta(n)...	*I love . . .*
...es bonito (interesante, etcétera).	*. . . is pretty (interesting, etc.).*
...está bueno (delicioso, etcétera).	*. . . is good (delicious, etc.; used for foods).*

EXPRESSING DISLIKES

No me gusta(n)...	*I don't like . . .*
No me interesa(n)...	*I'm not interested in . . .*
...es horrible (aburrido, etcétera).	*. . . is horrible (boring, etc.).*
...está frío (muy picante, etcétera).	*. . . is cold (very spicy, etc.).*

ORDERING A MEAL IN A RESTAURANT

Here are some useful expressions for ordering in a restaurant:

¿Qué nos recomienda?	*What do you recommend to us?*
¿Nos puede traer...?	*Can you bring us . . .?*
Nos falta(n)...	*We need . . .*
...está muy delicioso (bueno).	*. . . is very delicious (good).*
La cuenta, por favor.	*The check, please.*

These are some expressions a waiter might use:

¿Qué desea(n) pedir?	*What do you wish (would you like) to order?*
¡Buen provecho!	*Enjoy the meal!*

Now do the activities on the next page, using the expressions you have just learned.

A. **Gustos** (*Likes*).   Working with a classmate, find out five things that he or she likes and five things that he or she dislikes. You might want to start by asking about the following things:

MODELO   ¿Te gusta ir de campamento?
         No, para mí eso es muy aburrido. (Sí, me encanta.)

el chocolate	los tomates	el pescado
ir al doctor	jugar al tenis	esquiar
ir a la playa	ir de compras	la lluvia
la nieve	la cerveza	los postres
los autos Toyota	las películas de... (nombre)	

B. **Entrevista.**   Ask a classmate the following questions. Then report the information to the class.

1. ¿Qué bebidas o comidas te gustan más cuando hace calor? ¿cuando hace frío? ¿cuando no tienes tiempo de cocinar? ¿cuando estás a dieta? ¿cuando estás en un restaurante elegante?
2. ¿Cocinas todas las noches? ¿Qué cocinas cuando tienes invitados (*guests*)?
3. ¿Cuáles son tus postres favoritos?
4. ¿Qué cosas te encantan?

C. **En el restaurante «La Azteca».**   Arrange the dialogue below in order. Then create your own dialogue, based on the menu.

—Pues es la primera vez que estamos aquí. ¿Qué nos recomienda?
—¿Qué tal la comida?
—Nuestro plato favorito es el arroz con pollo, pero las enchiladas y el pescado también están deliciosos.
—Excelente. Volvemos mañana con unos amigos.
—Para mí el arroz con pollo, entonces.
—No, sólo la cuenta, por favor.
—Buenas noches, señores. ¿Qué desean comer?
—A mí me gusta el pescado—el pescado y una ensalada, por favor.
—¿Qué les servimos de postre? ¿Les servimos café?

Restaurante La Azteca

Sopa de verduras	<u>Postres</u>
Ensalada verde	Flan
Coctel de frutas: papaya, plátano, piña	Queso
	Helado
<u>Platos principales</u>	
Arroz con pollo	
Bistec	<u>Bebidas</u>
Enchiladas de pollo	Agua mineral
Tamales (de cerdo)	Vino
Chiles rellenos	Cerveza
Burrito supremo	Café, té

VOCABULARIO ACTIVO

Cognados

los cereales	la dieta: estar a dieta	el favor	principal
el curso	la enchilada	la fruta	el tenis
el chile relleno	la ensalada	la hamburguesa	el tomate
el chocolate	extra	mineral	

Verbos

almorzar (ue, c)	to eat lunch
cocinar	to cook
contar (ue)	to count; to tell (a story)
contar con	to count on
costar (ue)	to cost
decir (i)	to say, tell
dormir (ue)	to sleep
encantar	to delight; to love (with indirect object)
encontrar (ue)	to find
faltar	to be missing or lacking; to need (with indirect object)
gustar	to be pleasing; to like
importar	to matter; to be important
interesar	to interest
invitar	to invite
jugar (ue)	to play (game, sport)
llover (ue)	to rain
mostrar (ue)	to show
pedir (i)	to ask for, order
recordar (ue)	to remember
repetir (i)	to repeat
seguir (i)	to follow
seguir un curso	to take a course
servir (i)	to serve
poder (ue)	to be able, can
soñar (ue) (con)	to dream (about)
volver (ue)	to return, to go back

La comida

el almuerzo	lunch
el arroz	rice
el azúcar	sugar
la bebida	drink
el bistec	steak
la carne	meat
la cena	supper
el cerdo	pork
la cerveza	beer
la cuchara	spoon
el cuchillo	knife
el desayuno	breakfast
el flan	caramel custard
el frijol	bean; kidney bean
el helado	ice cream
el huevo	egg
el jamón	ham
el jugo	juice
la leche	milk
la lechuga	lettuce
el maíz	corn
la mantequilla	butter
la manzana	apple
la naranja	orange
la papa	potato
el pescado	fish
picante	hot, spicy
la pimienta	pepper
la piña	pineapple
el plátano	banana; plantain
el plato	plate; dish
el pollo	chicken
el postre	dessert
el queso	cheese
la sal	salt
la taza	cup
el tenedor	fork
la torta	cake
las verduras	vegetables
el vino	wine

Otras palabras y frases

el camarero, la camarera	*waiter (waitress)*
¡Claro!	*Of course! Sure!*
como	*like, as*
la cuenta	*check, bill*
delgado	*slim*
la historia	*story*
la palabra	*word*
el pasado	*past*
el valor	*value, price*
ya	*already*
ya no	*no longer, any longer*

Expresiones útiles

¡Buen provecho!	*Enjoy your meal!*
¿Nos puede traer...?	*Can you bring us ...?*

Falsos cognados

molestar	*to bother, annoy*
el pan	*bread*
el pastel	*pastry, cake*
la sopa	*soup*
el vaso	*(drinking) glass*

Don't forget: Prepositions, page 154
Prepositional object pronouns, page 155

ESPAÑA

Madrid, la capital de España, tiene muchas plazas y fuentes. El Palacio de Comunicaciones (el correo) está en la Plaza de Cibeles. Describa la foto.

Estos jóvenes son miembros de una tuna. Generalmente son estudiantes universitarios. Caminan por las calles de Madrid dando serenatas. ¿Cómo se visten?

Por toda España se ve la influencia de antiguas civilizaciones en la arquitectura. El famoso acueducto de Segovia es de la época romana pero todavía funciona. ¿Para qué se usa un acueducto?

El Patio de los Leones está en la Alhambra, un antiguo palacio árabe en Granada. ¿Dónde hay influencia de antiguas civilizaciones en los EEUU?

El Escorial es un monasterio y palacio. Fue construido en el siglo XVI por Felipe II. La biblioteca tiene más de cuarenta mil libros raros. Describa el interior de la biblioteca.

En Europa sólo Suiza tiene más montañas que España. ¿Qué hacen estas personas en las montañas?

España es un país marítimo. Por eso el pescado y los mariscos son productos importantes. ¿En qué regiones de los EEUU es importante la pesca?

Barcelona tiene cuatro millones de habitantes y es un centro industrial muy importante. En el Barrio Gótico hay muchos edificios muy antiguos. ¿Qué hacen estas personas en la plaza de la catedral?

La Semana Santa en Sevilla es una ocasión solemne. Para las procesiones la gente lleva pasos *(floats)* y se viste de penitente. Describa esta procesión.

El flamenco es un baile tradicional de los gitanos *(gypsies)*. Durante la Feria de Abril en Sevilla algunas jóvenes llevan el vestido típico y se divierten cantando y bailando. ¿Cuáles son los bailes y la música folklórica de los EEUU?

LECTURA III

Los Hispanos de los Estados Unidos

Unos 18 millones de hispanos viven hoy en los Estados Unidos (sin contar los varios millones de inmigrantes indocumentados°). Hay tres grupos principales: los méxico-americanos (60 por ciento del total), los puertorriqueños y los cubanos.

undocumented

La presencia hispana en el territorio del suroeste° de los Estados Unidos es muy anterior° a la presencia anglosajona°. Nombres de estados como Nevada y Colorado, y de ciudades como San Francisco y Las Vegas, muestran su origen hispano. Con la victoria militar contra México en 1848, los Estados Unidos toman el territorio que hoy forma el suroeste norteamericano. Muchos habitantes° de esta región son descendientes de los primeros colonizadores° españoles; otros son trabajadores° mexicanos que vienen a este país.

southwest
earlier Anglo-
  Saxon

inhabitants
colonists
  workers

La misión San Carlos Borromeo de Carmelo existe desde el siglo XVIII.

La historia de los puertorriqueños en los Estados Unidos empieza con la victoria de los Estados Unidos en la guerra° de 1898 contra España; desde entonces, Puerto Rico es territorio de los Estados Unidos. Hoy los puerto-

war

Una familia
puertorriqueña en
Nueva York

rriqueños son ciudadanos° de los Estados Unidos. En Nueva York viven más puertorriqueños que en San Juan, la capital de Puerto Rico. — citizens

La mayor parte° de los cubanos están aquí como exiliados° políticos del régimen° de Fidel Castro. Hay cubanos en todos los estados, pero la gran — La... Most / exiles regime

La «pequeña Habana» de Miami, Florida

mayoría° vive en Miami, Florida. Allí tienen un barrio muy próspero. La primera gran ola° de inmigrantes cubanos viene en 1959 y la segunda en 1980. — la... great majority / wave

La mayoría de los inmigrantes indocumentados de habla hispana° son de México y Centroamérica, donde hay ahora grandes problemas económicos y políticos. Estos inmigrantes cruzan el río° Bravo (*Rio Grande* en inglés) o entran por los estados del suroeste de los Estados Unidos en busca de una vida mejor° o para escaparse° de la persecución política. — de... Spanish-speaking / river / better escape

PREGUNTAS

1. ¿Cuántos hispanos viven en los Estados Unidos?   2. ¿Cuáles son los tres grupos principales?   3. En el suroeste de los Estados Unidos, ¿es la presencia hispana anterior o posterior a la anglosajona?   4. ¿Qué estados y ciudades con nombres españoles recuerda usted?   5. ¿Cuándo toman los Estados Unidos los territorios que hoy forman el suroeste americano?   6. ¿De quiénes son descendientes muchos habitantes de esos estados?   7. ¿Desde cuándo es Puerto Rico parte del territorio de los Estados Unidos?   8. ¿Por qué entran sin problema los puertorriqueños a los Estados Unidos?   9. ¿Dónde viven muchos cubano-americanos? 10. ¿Por qué vienen ahora muchos centroamericanos a los Estados Unidos?

Entrevista.   Imagine that you are interviewing some Hispanic friends in the United States about their lives here and in the countries they come from. Make a list of questions you would like to ask. Work in a group of three to four students. Each student asks questions of another, who answers on behalf of a group of Hispanics.

> **MODELO**   Entrevistador(a): ¿Son los puertorriqueños ciudadanos de
> *(Interviewer)*   los Estados Unidos?
> Entrevistado(-a): Sí, somos ciudadanos de los Estados
> *(Interviewee)*   Unidos.

Un grupo de
colombianos juegan
al dominó.

DIVERSIONES Y PASATIEMPOS

Funciones

- Making requests
- Offering assistance

Vocabulario.   In this chapter you will talk about what people do in their free time.

Gramática.   You will discuss and use:

1. The present tense of verbs with irregular first-person singular forms (**dar, ofrecer, oír, parecer, poner, salir, traducir, traer,** and **ver**)

2. **Saber** and **conocer**, which can both mean *to know*

3. Two-object pronoun constructions, as in the English *Give it to me.*

4. Command forms directed to people addressed as **usted(es)**

Cultura.   The dialogues take place in Colombia.

DIVERSIONES Y PASATIEMPOS

programar la
computadora

pintar

bailar, ir al baile

ir a ver una obra de
teatro o a escuchar
un concierto

nadar

cocinar

escuchar música
(clásica, rock,
folklórica),
escuchar discos

tocar la guitarra
(el piano, el violín)

ir al cine a ver
una película

jugar a los naipes
(las cartas)

pescar

sacar fotos

cantar canciones
folklóricas

dar paseos

hacer (dar, tener) una fiesta

A. Completen las frases. Choose the correct word to complete each sentence.

1. José (toca, juega) la guitarra.
2. Vamos al (cine, teatro) a ver una película.
3. El tango es (un baile, una canción).
4. Pedro y Julia (tocan, juegan) a los naipes.
5. Queremos escuchar un concierto en el (Cine, Teatro) Rialto.
6. En el verano vamos a la playa a tomar sol y a (nadar, cocinar).
7. Si necesitamos hacer ejercicio (cocinamos, nadamos).

B. Los pasatiempos (*Pastimes*). How much time do you dedicate to each of these activities? Keep score on a separate piece of paper: 5 = a lot, 3 = a little, 0 = none.

MODELOS   dar paseos   **5**

               pescar   **0**

dar paseos	tocar la guitarra, el piano, etcétera
jugar al tenis	nadar
ir al cine	esquiar
cantar	jugar a juegos de mesa (*board games*)
jugar a los naipes	(Monopolio, Trivia, etcétera)
pasar tiempo en las	bailar, ir a bailes
montañas / la playa	hacer fiestas con amigos
sacar fotos	ir al teatro / a conciertos / a museos
leer	comer en restaurantes
cocinar	estudiar español
mirar televisión	escribir cartas
hablar por teléfono	

Análisis

85+   Usted es una persona muy activa. Pasa todo su tiempo en los juegos y las diversiones. ¿Cuándo trabaja? ¿Cuándo duerme?

65–85   Usted tiene una vida muy normal. Pero de vez en cuando trabaja o estudia mucho, ¿verdad?

0–65   ¡Pobre de usted! Tiene una vida muy aburrida, ¿no?

Preguntas

1. ¿Qué hace usted los sábados y domingos? ¿Va al cine? ¿Escucha música? ¿Mira televisión?   2. ¿Qué va a hacer el fin de semana que viene (*next weekend*)? 3. ¿Prefiere usted bailar o escuchar música? ¿Por qué?   4. ¿Toca la guitarra? ¿el piano? ¿el violín?   5. ¿Va mucho al cine? ¿Cómo se llama su película favorita? ¿Prefiere las películas cómicas o las películas que le hacen pensar?   6. ¿Qué hace usted por la noche?   7. ¿Qué pasatiempos les gustan a usted y a sus amigos? 8. ¿Cuál es su pasatiempo favorito? ¿Por qué?   9. ¿Qué le gusta hacer en el verano? ¿en el invierno?   10. ¿Qué diversiones prefiere usted cuando no está con amigos?

I. El presente de verbos con formas irregulares en la primera persona singular (*dar, ofrecer, oír, parecer, poner, salir, traducir, traer y ver*)

Vista del barrio El Prado de Barranquilla, Colombia

En la Universidad del Norte, Barranquilla, Colombia

JACKIE   Marisa, tengo un problema con Juan.

MARISA   ¿Qué pasa? ¿Te puedo ayudar?

JACKIE   Espero que sí. Lo *veo* todos los fines de semana. Me *trae* chocolates, *oye* mis problemas con el español, me *ofrece* su ayuda ¡y también *traduce* mis composiciones del inglés al español! Y yo sólo le *doy* lecciones de inglés.

MARISA   ¡Pero eso me *parece* estupendo! Realmente no *veo* el problema...

JACKIE   Bueno, tienes que *oír* la situación. Todos los días me llama para *ver* si estoy en casa. Dice que no le soy fiel.

MARISA   ¡Qué insolencia!

JACKIE   Quizás yo le *parezco* muy independiente a Juan, pero él me *parece* muy celoso a mí.

MARISA   ¿Por qué no lo llamas todas las noches tú, para *ver* si él está en casa?

JACKIE   No puedo. Si estoy en casa todas las noches, ¿cuándo *salgo* con Jaime o con Miguel?

---

1. ¿Con quién tiene un problema Jackie?   2. ¿Qué hace Juan para Jackie? ¿Por qué la llama todos los días?   3. ¿Cómo es Juan, según Jackie?   4. ¿Qué recomienda Marisa?   5. ¿Qué problema tiene Jackie?   6. ¿Tiene usted un problema similar?

At the University of the North, Barranquilla, Colombia. JACKIE: Marisa, I have a problem with Juan. MARISA: What's the matter? Can I help you? JACKIE: I hope so. I see him every weekend. He brings me chocolates, listens to (hears) my problems with Spanish, offers his help, and he also translates my compositions from English to Spanish! And all I do is (literally, "I only") give him English lessons. MARISA: But that seems great to me! I really don't see the problem. JACKIE: Well, you have to hear the situation. Every day he calls me to see if I'm home. He's says I'm not faithful to him. MARISA: What insolence! JACKIE: Maybe I seem very independent to Juan, but he seems very jealous to me. MARISA: Why don't you call him every night, to see if he's home? JACKIE: I can't. If I'm home every night, when will I go out with Jaime or Miguel?

A. Certain Spanish verbs are regular in all present-tense forms but the **yo** form. One of these verbs is **hacer (hago),** which you have already studied. Others include the following.

dar	**doy**	*I give*
poner	**pongo**	*I put*
salir	**salgo**	*I leave, go out*
traer	**traigo**	*I bring*
ver	**veo**	*I see*

Le doy consejos a Diego.	*I give Diego advice.*
Siempre pongo los naipes aquí.	*I always put the cards here.*
Salgo después de la cena.	*I'm leaving after dinner.*
Traigo los boletos conmigo.	*I'm bringing the tickets with me.*
Veo a Inés pero a Gonzalo no.	*I see Inés but not Gonzalo.*

The verb **dar** is used in a number of idiomatic expressions:

darle hambre (sed, sueño)	*to make (someone) hungry (thirsty, sleepy)*
darle las gracias	*to thank (someone)*
dar un paseo	*to take a walk*

¡Qué hambre me da ese pastel!	*How hungry that pastry (cake) is making me!*
Esa música nos da mucho sueño.	*That music is making us very sleepy.*
Vamos a dar un paseo por la plaza.	*We're going to take a walk around the plaza.*
Los García nos dan las gracias por el baile.	*The Garcías thank us for the dance.*

B. Many three-syllable verbs that end in **-cer** or **-cir** are regular in the present tense except for the **yo** form, which ends in **-zco.** In dictionaries and vocabulary lists, these verbs may be followed by **(zc).**

ofrecer	**ofrezco**	*I offer*
parecer	**parezco**	*I seem, appear, resemble*
traducir	**traduzco**	*I translate*

| Parezco triste hoy, ¿no? | I appear sad today, don't I? |
| Traduzco la poesía francesa. | I translate French poetry. |

The verb **parecer** is often used with indirect object pronouns, like **gustar** and similar verbs, discussed in Chapter 6.

¿Qué te parece esa idea?	How does that idea seem to you? (What do you think about that idea?)
¿Qué te parecen los discos?	How do the records seem to you?
Maravillosos.	Wonderful.

C. The verb **oír** *(to hear)* has a **-g-** in the **yo** form, like **traer** and **decir.** It also has changes in other forms.

oír   to hear

oigo	oímos
oyes	oís
oye	oyen

| Oigo una canción. ¿Quién la canta? | I hear a song. Who's singing it? |

EJERCICIOS

A. Alfonso no, pero yo sí.   Say that you do or are doing the following things, even though Alfonso doesn't.

MODELO   Alfonso no da un paseo hoy.
Pero yo sí doy un paseo hoy.

1. Alfonso no ve a nuestros amigos hoy.
2. Alfonso no sale de vacaciones todos los años.
3. Alfonso no trae una guitarra a la fiesta.
4. Alfonso no pone dinero en el banco.
5. Alfonso no oye la conversación.
6. Alfonso no parece contento ahora.
7. Alfonso no ve películas en español.

B. Complete las frases.   Choosing one of the verbs suggested in parentheses, supply the correct form to complete each sentence.

MODELO   (salir, dar) Nosotros _____ un paseo por la plaza. El paseo nos _____ sueño.
Nosotros damos un paseo por la plaza. El paseo nos da sueño.

1. (traducir, oír) Carmen _____ el libro al español. Y yo lo _____ al francés.
2. (poner, traer) ¿Qué _____ en la mesa Isabel y Carlos? Pues yo _____ los naipes al lado.
3. (traer, oír) (Yo) _____ música. ¿Tú no la _____?

4. (traer, dar) Yo _____ los refrescos conmigo. ¿Qué _____ Alejandro y Lupita?

5. (parecer, ofrecer) ¿Te _____ aburrida (yo)? Vamos al concierto de Julio Iglesias esta noche. ¿Qué te _____ la idea?

6. (salir, ver) No _____ (yo) los boletos. ¿Los _____ tú?

C. Complete la conversación. Complete the following conversation with the verb forms indicated.

CAMARERO	¿(1) _____ (poner: yo) aquí el biftec, señora?
OLGA	Sí, gracias. Y, ¿nos (2) _____ (traer: usted) dos ensaladas, por favor?
CAMARERO	Sí, las (3) _____ (traer: yo) ahora mismo.
OLGA	¿Cuándo (4) _____ (salir: tú) para Medellín?
PILAR	(5) _____ (salir: yo) el viernes.
OLGA	Me (6) _____ (parecer) muy poco tiempo para...
CAMARERO	Perdón, señora. No (7) _____ bien (oír: yo). ¿Les (8) _____ (dar: yo) enchiladas o ensaladas?
OLGA	Ensaladas. Y la cuenta, por favor.

Preguntas

1. ¿A qué hora sale usted de casa?   2. ¿Qué trae a clase?   3. ¿A quién ve todos los días?   4. ¿Pone usted dinero en el banco? Y sus amigos, ¿ponen dinero en el banco?   5. ¿Ve usted las películas nuevas que salen?   6. ¿Le gusta dar paseos? ¿Con quién da paseos?   7. ¿Quién le ofrece ayuda con los estudios? ¿con los problemas? ¿A quién le ofrece ayuda usted?

II. *Saber y conocer*

Esta gente sabe bailar muchos bailes folklóricos colombianos.

En una casa en Barranquilla, Colombia

JACKIE   ¿*Sabes* bailar la cumbia, Juan?

JUAN   Sí, y también *sé* bailar el tango. *Conozco* una buena discoteca adonde podemos ir el viernes. ¿O tú prefieres ir a un concierto?

JACKIE   ¿*Sabes?*... el viernes voy al cine con Jaime Ramírez. ¿Lo *conoces?*

JUAN   Creo que sí. ¿Ese pescado frío y aburrido?

JACKIE   Juan, Jaime es muy simpático. *Conoce* a todo el mundo. Y sólo somos amigos.

JUAN   ¿Simpático? Si sales con él, estás loca.

JACKIE   Ah, Juan, me parece que el loco eres tú, no yo.

JUAN   Tienes razón. ¡Estoy loco por ti!

---

1. ¿Qué sabe hacer Juan?   2. ¿Qué quiere hacer el viernes?   3. ¿Qué va a hacer Jackie el viernes?   4. ¿Qué piensa Juan de Jaime?   5. ¿Qué dice Jackie de Jaime? 6. ¿Por quién o por qué está loco(-a) usted? ¿por los libros? ¿por Michael J. Fox? ¿por Madonna? ¿por el tenis? ¿por...?

In a house in Barranquilla, Colombia. JACKIE: Do you know how to dance the cumbia (traditional Latin dance), Juan? JUAN: Yes, and I can also dance the tango. I know a good discotheque where we can go on Friday. Or do you prefer to go to a concert? JACKIE: You know . . . this Friday I'm going to a movie with Jaime Ramírez. Do you know him? JUAN: I think so. That cold, boring jerk (literally, "fish")? JACKIE: Juan, Jaime is very nice. He knows everyone. And we're just friends. JUAN: Nice? If you go out with him, you're crazy. JACKIE: Juan, it seems to me you're the crazy one, not me! JUAN: You're right. I'm crazy about you!

A. **Saber** and **conocer** have irregular **yo** forms but are regular in the other forms of the present tense.

saber		conocer	
sé	sabemos	conozco	conocemos
sabes	sabéis	conoces	conocéis
sabe	saben	conoce	conocen

B. Both **saber** and **conocer** mean *to know,* but they are not interchangeable. **Saber** means *to know a fact* or *have specific information about something or someone.* Used before an infinitive, **saber** means *to know how to do something.* **Conocer** means *to know* or *be acquainted with a person, place, or thing.* It can also mean *to meet (someone) for the first time.*

Mi hermana sabe nadar bien.   *My sister knows how to swim well.*
No sé mucho de Colombia.   *I don't know much about Colombia.*

Tienes que conocer a Benito.	*You've got to meet Benito.*
Conozco a Claudia pero no sé dónde está.	*I know (am acquainted with) Claudia, but I don't know (have information about) where she is.*
Sé jugar al tenis pero no conozco este club.	*I know how to (I can) play tennis, but I don't know (I'm not familiar with) this club.*

Note that before a direct object that refers to a person or persons, **conocer** is followed by the personal **a.**

C. Sometimes a choice must be made between **saber** *(to know how to)* and **poder** *(to be able to).*

¿Sabes bailar la cumbia?	*Can you (do you know how to) dance the cumbia?*
¿Puedes bailar?	*Can you (are you able to) dance?*

EJERCICIOS

A. Conversaciones.   With a classmate, complete the conversations using appropriate forms of **saber** and **conocer.**

> JOSÉ ¿Tus padres (1) _____ hablar francés?
> EVA No, pero (2) _____ bien París.
>
> JUAN ¿(3) _____ (tú) a Mercedes Sosa?
> ADELA No, pero (4) _____ quién es.
>
> FELIPE ¿(5) _____ ustedes el centro?
> TERESA No, no lo (6) _____.

B. Breves encuentros *(Brief encounters).*   Working with a partner, act out these short conversations.

1. A: Ask if this bus goes to the Museo del Oro.
   B: Say that you don't know because you don't know the city very well.
2. A: Ask if your partner knows Felipe Restrepo.
   B: Say yes and that you know he's in one of your classes.

Preguntas

1. ¿Sabe usted bailar bien? ¿cantar? ¿tocar la guitarra (el piano, el violín)? ¿Qué sabe hacer bien?   2. ¿Qué no sabe hacer ahora pero quiere aprender a hacer?
3. ¿Conoce un buen lugar para bailar? ¿para escuchar música? ¿Dónde?   4. ¿Sabe usted cómo se llama la capital de Colombia? ¿La conoce?   5. ¿Conoce usted la ciudad de Nueva York? ¿Qué ciudades conoce usted bien?   6. ¿Quién sabe qué hora es?   7. ¿Qué quiere saber bien usted?

III. Construcciones con dos pronombres: de complemento indirecto y directo

La Catedral de Sal

Fernando está de visita en Bogotá, Colombia.

FERNANDO   ¿Conoces la Catedral de Sal, Francisco?*
FRANCISCO   Sí, y *te la* quiero mostrar.
FERNANDO   ¿Está cerca de aquí?
FRANCISCO   No muy cerca. Creo que hay un autobús que va allí, pero no recuerdo el número. Podemos preguntár*selo* a un policía. ¿Por qué no vamos allí esta tarde? ¿Tienes tu cámara?
FERNANDO   Sí.
FRANCISCO   ¿*Me la* puedes dar por un momento? Quiero sacarte una foto aquí enfrente de esta iglesia.
FERNANDO   Gracias. ¿Sabes si hay una Catedral de Pimienta también?
FRANCISCO   ¡Ay, ay, ay!

---

*The Salt Cathedral is in a town about 35 miles from Bogotá, in a huge salt mine. Workers erected small altars where they would pray for protection from mine accidents. Eventually a large altar was constructed, carved out of salt rock within walls made of salt. The cathedral holds 8,000 people.

1. ¿Qué quiere mostrarle Francisco a su amigo Fernando?   2. ¿Está cerca?
3. ¿Cómo van a ir allí?   4. ¿Cuándo van a ir?   5. ¿Qué quiere hacer Francisco?
6. ¿Saca usted muchas fotos cuando está de vacaciones?

Fernando is visiting Bogotá, Colombia.   FERNANDO: Are you familiar with the Salt Cathedral, Francisco? FRANCISCO: Yes, and I want to show it to you. FERNANDO: Is it nearby? FRANCISCO: Not very near. I think there's a bus that goes there, but I forget the number. We can ask a policeman. Why don't we go there this afternoon? Do you have your camera? FERNANDO: Yes. FRANCISCO: Can you give it to me for a moment? I want to take a picture of you in front of this church. FERNANDO: Thanks. Do you know if there's a Pepper Cathedral, too? FRANCISCO: Good grief!

A. When an indirect and a direct object pronoun are used in the same sentence, the indirect always precedes the direct object pronoun. The two object pronouns (indirect, direct) precede a conjugated verb directly. They are never separated by another word.

Te doy cinco entradas para el teatro.	*I'm giving you five theater tickets.*
Te las doy.	*I'm giving them to you.*
Pero no te las doy hoy.	*But I'm not giving them to you today.*
Me van a traer unos discos.	*They're going to bring me some records.*
Me los van a traer.	*They're going to bring them to me.*
Ella nos muestra su guitarra nueva.	*She shows us her new guitar.*
Nos la muestra.	*She shows it to us.*

B. When used with an infinitive, the object pronouns (indirect, direct) may either be attached to the infinitive or precede the conjugated verb. Note that when two object pronouns are attached to the infinitive, an accent is required over the last syllable of the infinitive.

Voy a comprarte una entrada.	*I'm going to buy you a ticket.*
Te la voy a comprar. ⎫	
Voy a comprártela. ⎭	*I'm going to buy it for you.*

C. Two object pronouns beginning with the letter *l* cannot occur in a row. If a third-person indirect object pronoun **(le, les)** is used with a third-person direct object pronoun **(lo, la, los, las)**, the indirect object pronoun is replaced by **se.** The various meanings of **se** may be clarified by adding to the sentence: **a él, a ella, a usted, a ellos, a ellas, a ustedes.**

Elena les canta una canción (a ellos).	*Elena is singing them a song.*
Elena se la canta (a ellos).	*Elena is singing it to them.*
El camarero le reserva una mesa (a ella).	*The waiter reserves a table for her.*
El camarero se la reserva (a ella).	*The waiter reserves it for her.*

EJERCICIOS

A. **Lupe la generosa.** Tell what Lupe gives away, and to whom, as suggested by the cues. Then shorten your statement using direct and indirect object pronouns.

> **MODELO** el lápiz / Marisa
> **Lupe le da el lápiz a Marisa. Se lo da.**

1. la guitarra / Miguel	5. el pastel / los niños
2. el dinero / sus hermanos	6. la información / la joven
3. los regalos / Rosa	7. las gracias / la camarera
4. las cartas / usted	8. diez pesos / mamá

B. **¿Qué haces, Ramón?** Ramón is doing many things for many people lately. Tell what he does, following the model.

> **MODELO** dar el disco a su hermano
> **Le da el disco a su hermano.**
> **Se lo da.**

1. traducir la carta para su amigo Hans
2. escribir la composición para su prima
3. leer la historia a su hermana
4. describir la lección de francés a su amiga Ana
5. ofrecer los refrescos a sus primos
6. tocar la canción «Guantanamera» para sus abuelos
7. mandar las cartas para su papá
8. servir el desayuno a su mamá
9. vender su auto por muy poco dinero a su amigo Pablo

C. **Promesas** (*Promises*). Carlos wants to borrow his father's car to take his girlfriend to a party. Answer Carlos' father's questions, as Carlos would.

> **MODELOS** ¿Me vas a pedir el auto mañana?
> **No, no te lo voy a pedir mañana. (No, no voy a pedírtelo.)**
>
> ¿Siempre nos vas a decir la verdad a tu mamá y a mí?
> **Sí, se la voy a decir. (Sí, voy a decírsela.)**

1. ¿Le vas a dar los discos a tu hermana?
2. ¿Les vas a dar vino a tus hermanos?
3. ¿Nos vas a pedir dinero todos los días?
4. ¿Me vas a traer el auto antes de las once?
5. ¿Le vas a dar problemas a tu madre?

D. **Breves encuentros.** With a partner, act out these conversations.

> PEPE I want to buy you a present.
> PEPA Great! And when are you going to buy it for me?
> PEPE Well, I can't tell you that (literally, "it").

PEPA   Are you going to give it to me before (**antes del**) Saturday?
PEPE   No, I can't give it to you before February 14.

LUIS   Why don't you give me the tickets for the play?
LUISA   I can't give them to you because I don't have them. Those tickets
cost a lot, Luis. You and I can go to the movies and have lunch for
the price (**el valor**) of one ticket!
LUIS   Good idea! Can you reserve (**reservar**) a table for us at a restaurant?
LUISA   I'll ask my father to reserve it for us.

Preguntas

1. ¿Les pide usted dinero a sus amigos? ¿Se lo dan?   2. ¿Le dan dinero sus padres
para la universidad?   3. ¿Les manda cartas a sus padres?   4. ¿Sabe usted cantar
«La Bamba»? ¿Nos la canta ahora?   5. ¿Toca un instrumento musical? ¿Está
aprendiendo a tocarlo?   6. ¿Le va a comprar usted un regalo especial a un(-a)
amigo(-a)?   7. ¿Me hace usted un favor? ¿Me abre la puerta (las ventanas)?
8. ¿Les pide consejos a sus amigos? ¿Se los dan? ¿Los sigue usted?

IV. Los mandatos de *usted*, *ustedes*

Vista de Medellín,
Colombia

En una casa en Bogotá

EN LA RADIO   *Asista* a un concierto estupendo de Leonor González Mina este
viernes en el Teatro Colón a las ocho de la noche.* *Escuche* sus
últimas canciones y *vea* a los bailarines del «Ballet de
Colombia». Para más información, *llame*...

*Leonor González Mina is a well-known Colombian folk singer.

MARÍA	Vamos al concierto del viernes, ¿no?	
ESPERANZA	Sí. ¿Quién compra las entradas?	
MARÍA	Felipe y yo vamos a Medellín por unos días. *Compren* ustedes las entradas, ¿de acuerdo?	
ESPERANZA	Con mucho gusto.	
ESTEBAN	¿Dónde los encontramos?	
FELIPE	En la puerta del teatro. *Esperen* allí a las 7:45, ¿de acuerdo?	
ESPERANZA	Sí. No *lleguen* tarde.	
FELIPE	¡Y no *olviden* las entradas!	

1. ¿Quién da un concierto en el Teatro Colón? ¿Cuándo va a ser?   2. ¿Por qué no pueden comprar las entradas Felipe y María?   3. ¿Qué les pide Esperanza a Felipe y a María?   4. ¿Qué les pide Felipe a Esteban y a Esperanza?   5. ¿A usted le gusta ir a conciertos? ¿Qué tipo de música le gusta?

In a house in Bogotá. ON THE RADIO: Attend a wonderful concert by Leonor González Mina this Friday in the Colón Theater at 8:00 P.M. Listen to her latest songs and see the dancers of the "Ballet of Colombia." For more information, call . . . MARÍA: We're going to the concert on Friday, aren't we? ESPERANZA: Yes. Who'll buy the tickets? MARÍA: Felipe and I are going to Medellín for a few days. You buy the tickets, OK? ESPERANZA: With pleasure. ESTEBAN: Where shall we meet you? FELIPE: At the door of the theater. Wait there at 7:45, OK? ESPERANZA: Yes. Don't be (arrive) late. FELIPE: And don't forget the tickets!

A. The command forms of verbs are used to ask or tell people to do things. In Spanish, one set of commands is used with people you normally address as **usted,** and another set with people you address as **tú.**

B. To form the singular formal **(usted)** command of all regular verbs, drop the **-o** ending from the **yo** form of the present tense and add **-e** for **-ar** verbs or **-a** for **-er** and **-ir** verbs. The **ustedes** command is formed by adding **-n** to the singular command forms.

-ar	Compro esta guitarra.	Compre (usted) esta guitarra. Compren (ustedes) estas guitarras.
-er	Como la manzana.	Coma (usted) la manzana. Coman (ustedes) la manzana.
-ir	Escribo la carta.	Escriba (usted) la carta. Escriban (ustedes) la carta.

The pronouns **usted** and **ustedes** are usually omitted, but they are sometimes added after a command to soften it, make it more polite.

C. Commands are made negative by placing **no** before the verb.

No escuche (usted) esa música.   *Don't listen to that music.*
No vendan (ustedes) esos boletos.   *Don't sell those tickets.*

D. If a verb has an irregularity or a stem change in the **yo** form of the present tense, this irregularity or stem change is carried over into the command forms.

No salga ahora.	*Don't leave now.*
Recuerde el número de teléfono.	*Remember the telephone number.*
Tengan cuidado.	*Be careful.*
Duerman un poco.	*Sleep a little (while).*

E. A number of verbs have a spelling change in the **usted** and **ustedes** command forms.

c → qu	buscar	yo busco	busque(n)
g → gu	llegar	yo llego	llegue(n)
z → c	empezar	yo empiezo	empiece(n)

Busquen el último disco de Claudia de Colombia.	*Look for the latest record by Claudia of Colombia.*
Empiece el juego.	*Begin the game.*

F. Here are some irregular **usted** and **ustedes** commands.

ir	vaya, vayan	*estar*	esté, estén
ser	sea, sean	*dar*	dé, den
saber	sepa, sepan		

The accent on **dé** is written to distinguish the word from the preposition **de.**

Vaya de campamento.	*Go camping.*
Sean prácticos.	*Be practical.*
Sepa que programan la computadora hoy.	*Be aware that they're programming the computer today.*
No esté triste.	*Don't be sad.*
No den un paseo ahora.	*Don't take a walk now.*

EJERCICIOS

A. Un viaje a la capital. Anita's daughters are going to Bogotá. Give advice to them as she would, following the models.

MODELO hacer las maletas varios días antes de salir
Hagan las maletas varios días antes de salir.

1. llevar su cámara
2. preguntar el precio de los hoteles
3. visitar la Catedral de Sal
4. ver el Museo Nacional
5. sacar muchas fotos de la ciudad
6. ir al Museo del Oro
7. asistir a una obra de teatro en el Teatro Colón
8. leer unos libros sobre Bogotá

> **MODELO** no llegar tarde al aeropuerto
> **No lleguen tarde al aeropuerto.**

1. no llevar muchas maletas
2. no hablar con la gente en la calle
3. no perder el dinero
4. no cruzar las calles sin mirar
5. no olvidar llamarme
6. no comprar la comida en la calle
7. no salir después de las diez de la noche

B. En la clase de español. Miss Ochoa teaches a Spanish class. Give instructions to her students as she would, following the model.

> **MODELO** señor Smith / estudiar la lección
> **Señor Smith, estudie la lección.**

1. señorita Allen y señor Green / no hablar inglés
2. señorita Brooks / cerrar el libro
3. señor Sims / no comer en la clase
4. todos / pensar en español
5. señor Newman / no llegar tarde
6. señorita Johnson / venir temprano
7. todos / traer sus libros
8. señora LaSalle / repetir la pregunta
9. todos / contestar en español

C. En acción. Describe the drawings, using **usted(es)** commands.

MODELO

Vengan para comer.

D. Ay, ¿qué hago? Give advice to someone who tells you the following things.

MODELO Tengo dolor de cabeza. **Pues, tome unas aspirinas.**

1. Tengo sed.
2. Quiero aprender alemán.
3. Necesito más dinero.
4. Tengo hambre.
5. Estoy aburrido.
6. No me gusta mirar películas en la televisión.
7. No sé dónde está la biblioteca.
8. Quiero ser más delgado.
9. Necesito unas vacaciones.
10. Tengo sueño.

Study Hint: Recognizing Cognates (2)

1. Many words that end in *-y* in English end in **-ia, -ía,** or **-io** in Spanish.

la familia	*family*
la cortesía	*courtesy*
necesario	*necessary*

2. Adjectives ending in *-ous* in English very often end in **-oso(-a)** in Spanish.

generoso(-a)	*generous*
montañoso(-a)	*mountainous*

3. Some words that begin with *s* + consonant in English begin with **es-** in Spanish.

la estación	*station; season*
estudiar	*study*
especial	*special*

4. The Spanish suffix **-ero** indicates profession. It is equivalent to the *-er* suffix in English.

carpintero	*carpenter*
ranchero	*rancher*

5. Some cognates may have a letter added or deleted in Spanish.

presente	*present*
el profesor	*professor*

6. Other cognates may have a slight spelling change.

la foto	*photo*
abril	*April*

7. Some cognates are related via a common root, many times a Latin word. The meaning of the Spanish word is easy to remember if you can think of a related word in English.

Spanish	English	Related Word
el libro	book	library
el baile	dance	ballet
comprender	to understand	comprehend
el cristal	glass	crystal

8. False cognates (sometimes called **amigos falsos,** *false friends*) should be memorized, since they do not have the same meaning in both English and Spanish. If used incorrectly, some can even be embarrassing.

asistir	*to attend*
molestar	*to bother, annoy*
el pastel	*cake, pie, or pastry*
la sopa	*soup*
último	*latest, most recent*
el vaso	*glass*

La ciudad de Bogotá, vista desde Monserrate

BOGOTÁ: CIUDAD DE ESMERALDAS°[1]

John y Susan, turistas de California, visitan a unos amigos colombianos en Bogotá.

SUSAN	¡Qué bueno está el café!
JAIME	Los expertos dicen que el café colombiano es el más suave° del mundo.
SUSAN	Y yo también lo digo.
JULIANA	¿Qué te parece Bogotá, John?
JOHN	Veo que es una ciudad muy moderna. Y la gente es muy amable. Me gusta mucho.
JAIME	¿Adónde quieren ir mañana?
SUSAN	Pues no sé. Queremos conocer la ciudad. ¿Qué nos recomiendan ustedes?
JAIME	Vayan a ver la ciudad desde Monserrate, y después den un paseo por el centro.[2]
JULIANA	Lleven suéter° porque hace fresco por la altitud. Muchas veces° llueve por la tarde.
SUSAN	¡Caramba! Olvidamos el mapa.
JAIME	Nosotros tenemos uno muy bueno y se lo podemos dar.

JOHN	Muchas gracias.
JULIANA	No olviden visitar el Museo del Oro.³ Es una maravilla°. Y si quieren comprar esmeraldas, las venden en una tienda cerca de allí.
JOHN	¿Compramos una esmeralda, Susan?
SUSAN	Sí, ¿por qué no? ¿Me la das a mí o se la llevamos a tu madre...?
JAIME	Vayan a la Quinta de Bolívar también.⁴
JULIANA	Y no olviden el club Noches de Colombia. Allí tocan música muy buena.
JAIME	Bogotá es una ciudad maravillosa para los turistas. También está el Museo de Arte Moderno...
JOHN	¿Conocen ustedes todos esos lugares?
JULIANA	Claro que no. Vivimos aquí.

---

las esmeraldas *emeralds*   suave *smooth, mellow*   el suéter *sweater*   muchas veces *often*   la maravilla *marvel, wonder*

PREGUNTAS

1. ¿Quiénes visitan a unos amigos en Bogotá, Colombia?   2. ¿Qué dicen los expertos del café colombiano?   3. ¿A John le gusta Bogotá?   4. ¿Qué les recomienda Jaime a John y a Susan? ¿Qué se les va a dar?   5. ¿Qué les recomienda Juliana?   6. ¿Qué van a comprar John y Susan?   7. ¿Conocen Jaime y Juliana todos los lugares que recomiendan?   8. ¿Conoce usted todos los lugares turísticos de la ciudad donde usted vive?

NOTAS CULTURALES

1. Emeralds are one of Colombia's great natural resources. Exportation and prices are controlled by the government, and the jewels are sold at very low prices.

2. At the top of Monserrate mountain is a world-famous church and shrine, which can be reached by funicular railroad, cable car, or on foot. There is a magnificent view of the capital, Bogotá, which is at 8,600 feet.

3. One of the world's greatest collections of Indian jewelry is housed in the **Museo del Oro.** The collection traces its beginnings back to two early Indian tribes: the Chibcha and the Quimbay.

4. Simón Bolívar was born in Caracas, Venezuela, in 1783. He led Venezuela's fight for freedom from Spain. In 1817 he captured Caracas, earning the name **El Libertador.** He was also responsible for freeing Ecuador, Colombia, Panama, and Peru and for founding Bolivia, which bears his name. The widely visited home of Simón Bolívar is now a museum of the colonial era. It was given to Bolívar after the Colombian revolution; he lived there from 1826 to 1828.

Funciones y *actividades*

In this chapter, you have seen examples of some important language functions, or uses. Here is a summary and some additional information about these functions of language.

MAKING REQUESTS

Here are some expressions that you can use when you need or want to ask for something:

¿Me hace el favor de + inf...?	Will you do me the favor of . . .?
¿Me puede + inf...?	Can you . . . for me?
¿Me podría dar (pasar, etcétera)... por favor?	Could you give (pass, etc.) me . . . , please?

Podría is a conditional form of **poder** meaning *could*. It is used for **yo, usted, él, and ella.** (You will see other conditional forms in a later chapter.) In a shop, you should first greet the shopkeeper before making a request—it's considered rude not to.

Buenos días. Busco... Necesito...

The words **quiero** and **deseo** are rarely used in requests; these words are very direct and can sound rude or childish. After all, you wouldn't normally begin a polite request in English with *I want* . . . , but rather *I would like* . . . or *Please give me.... I would like* in Spanish is **Quisiera....** (This form is covered in a later chapter, but for now learn to recognize that **Quisiera...** means *I would like. . . .*)

Quisiera un café, por favor.	I would like a (cup of) coffee, please.

OFFERING ASSISTANCE

Here are some ways to offer assistance.

¿En qué puedo servirle?	How can I help you? (Shopkeepers and others use this quite often.)
Le (Te) hago (sirvo, etcétera)... con mucho gusto.	I'll do (serve, etc.) . . . for you with pleasure.
¿Le (Te) puedo + inf... ?	May I . . . (for) you?
Si quiere, podría...	If you like, I could . . .
¿Puedo ayudarlo(la)?	Can I help you?

Now do the following activities, using the expressions you have just learned.

A. ¿Qué dicen?   Tell what the people in the drawings might be saying as they make requests.

1.   2.   3.

4.   5.   6.

B. Conversación.   Arrange the following conversation in order.

—¡Cómo no!... y con mucho gusto, señora.
—Tenemos muchas. ¿Qué tipo de guitarra quisiera?
—Pues, no sé. ¿Qué me recomienda?
—No, va a aprender. ¿Cuánto cuesta ésa?
—Buenos días. ¿En qué puedo servirle, señora?
—Sólo 2.000 pesos.
—Está bien. La llevo.
—Buenos días, señorita. Busco una guitarra para mi hijo.
—¿Necesita alguna otra cosa (*anything else*)? Le podría mostrar libros de música o... .
—A ver. Ésta es muy buena. ¿Ya sabe tocar su hijo?
—No, gracias. Pero, ¿me podría envolver (*wrap*) la guitarra, por favor?

C. Mini-dramas.   Role-play these situations.

1. A friend of yours is having a dinner party. After the meal, you ask if you can help her with the dishes. She says no but asks if you would make the coffee. Of course, you say, you'd be glad to do it. You ask if you should serve it. She thanks you and says she's very grateful for your help.
2. You go into a shop to buy a record. Greet the shopkeeper, who asks if he or she can help you. Ask if he or she has records by (of) Claudia de Colombia. He or she says yes, of course, and offers to show them to you. You ask how much they cost, and the shopkeeper says they are 2000 pesos each. You say you'll take one. The shopkeeper thanks you and you both say good-bye.

D. ¿Qué pasa en la fiesta? Use your imagination to describe in Spanish what is happening at the party with as many details as possible.

E. ¿Qué pasatiempo me gusta más? Divide into groups. One of the groups will think of a favorite activity among those discussed in this chapter. The others will ask questions until they guess what the hobby or pastime is. The following questions may be useful. The person answering the questions should answer only **sí** or **no**.

1. ¿Es un pasatiempo para todos: hombres y mujeres? 2. ¿Hacemos esa actividad afuera (*outside*) o adentro (*inside*)? 3. ¿Hacemos esa actividad con otros? 4. ¿Cuesta dinero hacer esa actividad? ¿Cuesta mucho o poco? 5. ¿Necesitamos cosas especiales—instrumentos musicales, ropa (*clothes*) especial—para hacer esa actividad? 6. ¿Hacemos esa actividad más en el invierno? ¿en el verano? 7. ¿Tenemos que estar en buenas condiciones físicas para esa actividad? 8. ¿Dónde hacemos esa actividad? ¿en casa? ¿en las montañas? 9. ¿Es una actividad que a muchos les gusta? 10. ¿Es una actividad que necesita mucha preparación? 11. ¿Es una actividad que hacen en unos países y no en otros? 12. ¿Es una diversión que hacemos durante el día o por la noche?

VOCABULARIO ACTIVO

Cognados

el club	la discoteca	generoso	el piano	el violín
colombiano	la foto	la guitarra	el tango	la visita: estar de visita

Verbos

cantar	to sing
conocer (zc)	to know, be acquainted with; to meet
dar	to give
darle las gracias	to thank (someone)
darle hambre, sed, sueño	to make (someone) hungry, thirsty, sleepy
dar un paseo	to take a walk, go for a stroll
escuchar	to listen (to)
nadar	to swim
ofrecer (zc)	to offer
oír	to hear
olvidar	to forget
parecer (zc)	to seem, appear
pescar	to fish
pintar	to paint
poner (g)	to put; to place
programar	to program
saber	to know (facts, information); to learn, to find out
saber (+ inf)	to know how (to do something)
sacar fotos	to take pictures
salir (g)	to go out, leave; to come out
tocar (qu)	to touch; to play (musical instrument)
traducir (zc)	to translate
traer (g)	to bring
ver	to see

Diversiones y pasatiempos

el bailarín, la bailarina	dancer
el baile	dance
el boleto	ticket (for an event or transportation)
la canción	song
el conjunto	ensemble

la cumbia	Latin American dance
el disco	record
la diversión	diversion, pastime
la entrada	ticket (for an event)
la fiesta	party; holiday; celebration
el fin de semana	weekend
el juego	game
los naipes	(playing) cards
la obra	work, artistic work
la obra de teatro	play
el pasatiempo	pastime
el paseo	walk, stroll; ride, short trip
la poesía	poetry

Otras palabras y frases

la ayuda	help
celoso	jealous
el consejo	(piece of) advice
los consejos	advice
fiel	faithful
francés	French
el francés	French (language)
loco	crazy
maravilloso	marvelous
más de (+ number)	more than
el oro	gold
el pescado	(slang) jerk (literally, "fish")
¡Qué insolencia!	What insolence!
la semana (el mes) que viene	next week (month)
último	latest, most recent

Expresiones útiles

¿Me hace el favor de...?	Will you do me the favor of...?
¿Me puede + inf...?	Can you ... for me?
¿Puedo ayudarlo(la)?	Can I help you?

CAPÍTULO OCHO

Las Ramblas, Barcelona

LA ROPA, LOS COLORES Y LA RUTINA DIARIA

Vocabulario. In this chapter you will learn to describe clothing and daily activities.

Gramática. You will discuss and use:

1. Reflexive constructions
2. **Tú** commands
3. Commands with object pronouns
4. The preterit of regular verbs

Cultura. The dialogues take place in Barcelona, Spain.

Funciones

● Expressing hesitation

● Making descriptions (2)

LA ROPA

¿Qué lleva Carmen... ?

¿Qué lleva José... ?

¿Qué ropa llevan?   Describe what the people are wearing in the drawings below.

1   2   3   4.   5

¿Qué llevan Carmen y José?   Describe what Carmen or José wear in the following situations. Complete the sentences, eliminating the inappropriate words.

1. Cuando llueve, Carmen lleva... (un impermeable, un pijama, calcetines, un vestido, un paraguas)
2. Cuando va a la playa, José lleva... (un sombrero, sandalias, un abrigo, un traje de baño)
3. Cuando viaja a otro país, Carmen lleva... (sandalias, ropa interior, pantalones, un bolso, un vestido, una camisa)
4. Cuando trabaja en la oficina, José lleva... (medias, calcetines, un traje, una corbata, un traje de baño, zapatos de tenis)
5. Cuando nieva, Carmen lleva... (un suéter de lana, botas, guantes, sandalias, jeans)
6. Cuando duerme, José lleva... (una falda, jeans, un pijama, una corbata)

LOS COLORES

rojo   anaranjado   amarillo   azul   marrón   verde

Violeta   negro   gris   blanco   claro   oscuro

¿DE QUÉ COLOR ES?

1. el sol   2. el árbol   3. la manzana   4. la naranja   5. las uvas

6. el elefante   7. la bandera   8. la bandera de   9. el océano   10. la nieve
de España   los EE.UU.

Preguntas

1. ¿Qué lleva usted hoy? ¿Lleva usted calcetines blancos hoy? ¿pantalones ama-
rillos? ¿zapatos de tenis? ¿una falda?   2. ¿De qué color es la camisa o la blusa
de usted? ¿de verde o azul claro? ¿Y los pantalones o la falda? ¿de azul oscuro o
gris claro?   3. ¿Cuánto cuesta un paraguas? ¿y una corbata?   4. ¿Qué ropa lleva
usted en el otoño? ¿y en el invierno?   5. ¿Qué ropa lleva usted cuando va a las
montañas? ¿y a la playa?   6. ¿Cuál es su color favorito?   7. ¿Qué colores no le
gustan mucho?   8. ¿Qué ropa lleva usted hoy?

I. Verbos reflexivos

La Plaza de
Cataluña, Barcelona

Tres muchachos sudamericanos están en Barcelona.

ANTONIO ¡José! ¿Vas a llevar ese sombrero al centro? ¿Cómo vas a *divertirte* o a conocer a chicas si *te vistes* así?

JOSÉ No voy al centro con ustedes... Voy a *quedarme* en el hotel. Es que no *me divierto* caminando por el centro. Además las chicas de Barcelona no quieren hablar español... ¿Cómo vamos a *divertirnos* si nosotros no sabemos catalán?

PACO Pero José... Es cierto que prefieren hablar catalán...¡pero también hablan español! *Te quejas* demasiado...¿Por qué no vienes con nosotros? No tienes que caminar. Puedes *sentarte* en un café, tomar un refresco, hablar con la gente...

JOSÉ Pues...voy a descansar aquí. Quiero *acostarme* temprano porque mañana debo *levantarme* a las seis.

ANTONIO ¿*Te levantas* a las seis los sábados? ¡A esa hora nosotros pensamos *acostarnos*!

---

1. ¿Qué van a hacer los tres muchachos?   2. ¿Le gusta caminar por el centro a José? ¿Por qué sí o por qué no?   3. Según Paco, ¿prefieren hablar catalán o español las chicas de Barcelona?   4. Si José no quiere caminar por el centro, ¿qué otras cosas puede hacer él? ¿Se queja demasiado José?   5. Finalmente, ¿qué va a hacer José? ¿Por qué?   6. ¿A qué hora piensan acostarse Paco y Antonio? Y usted, ¿a qué hora se levanta los sábados, en general?

Three South American boys are in Barcelona. ANTONIO: José! Are you going to wear that hat downtown? How are you going to have fun or meet girls if you dress like that? JOSÉ: I'm not going downtown with you. I'm going to stay in the hotel. The thing is that I don't have a good time walking downtown. Besides, the girls in Barcelona don't want to speak Spanish . . . How are we going to have fun if we don't know Catalan? (the language of Cataluña) PACO: But José, it's true that they prefer to speak Catalan . . . , but they also speak Spanish! You complain too much . . . Why don't you come with us? You don't have to walk . . . You can sit in a café, have a soft drink, talk with people . . . JOSÉ: Well . . . I'm going to rest here. I want to go to bed early because tomorrow I have to get up at six. ANTONIO: You get up at six on Saturdays? We're planning to go to bed at that time!

A. In a reflexive construction, the action of the verb "reflects" back to the subject of the sentence, as in the sentences *I enjoy myself* or *The child dresses herself* or *He hurt himself.* In Spanish, reflexive constructions require the reflexive pronouns **me, te, se, nos, os,** and **se.** Except for the third person **se** (singular and plural), these forms are the same as the direct and indirect object pronouns. The pronoun **se** attached to an infinitive indicates that the verb is reflexive.

levantarse   to get up

me levanto	nos levantamos
te levantas	os levantáis
se levanta	se levantan

Notice that some Spanish reflexive forms such as **levantarse** are not translated as reflexive constructions in English. Spanish uses the reflexive construction much more frequently than does English.

B. The following verbs are reflexive, with stem changes indicated in parentheses.

acostarse (ue)	*to go to bed*
acostumbrarse (a)	*to get used (to)*
bañarse	*to bathe*
casarse (con)	*to get married (to)*
despertarse (ie)	*to wake up*
divertirse (ie)	*to have a good time; to enjoy oneself*
dormirse (ue)	*to fall asleep*
enfadarse	*to get angry*
enojarse	*to get angry*
irse	*to leave, go away*
lavarse	*to wash (oneself)*
llamarse	*to be named*
mudarse	*to move (change residence)*
ponerse	*to put on*
preocuparse (por)	*to worry (about)*
quedarse	*to remain, to stay*
quejarse (de)	*to complain (about)*
quitarse	*to take off*
sentarse (ie)	*to sit down*
vestirse (i)*	*to get dressed*

C. Reflexive pronouns, like object pronouns, precede conjugated verbs; they follow and are attached to infinitives and present participles.

¿Nos sentamos aquí?	*Shall we sit here?*
Me divierto mucho en las fiestas.	*I have a very good time at parties.*
Te quejas demasiado.	*You complain too much.*
¿Por qué te preocupas?	*Why are you worrying?*
No queremos mudarnos.	*We don't want to move.*
Raúl se va pero yo me quedo.	*Raúl is leaving but I'm staying.*
Hace calor; me voy a quitar el suéter.	*It's hot; I'm going to take off my sweater.*

*Conjugated like **servir** (page 157)

Felipe va a ponerse el abrigo azul.*	Felipe is going to put on his blue coat.
Susana se va a poner el vestido elegante.	Susan is going to put on her elegant dress.
Pero en este momento está poniéndose el pijama.	But right now she's putting on her pajamas.

D. Most Spanish verbs that are used reflexively can also be used nonreflexively. In some cases the use of the reflexive form changes the meaning significantly. Contrast the following pairs of sentences.

Se llama Carmen.	Her name is Carmen.
José llama a Carmen todos los días.	José calls Carmen every day.
Nos acostamos a las nueve.	We go to bed at nine.
Acostamos a los niños entre las ocho y las nueve.	We put the children to bed between eight and nine.
Juana se despierta temprano.	Juana wakes up early.
Juana despierta a sus hijos temprano.	Juana wakes up her children early.
Me lavo todos los días.	I wash (myself) every day.
Lavo el traje marrón todas las semanas.	I wash the brown suit every week.

E. The reflexive pronouns **nos** and **se** may be used with a first- or third-person plural verb, respectively, in order to express a reciprocal reflexive action. This construction corresponds to the English *each other* or *one another*.[†]

Todos se miran.	They're all looking at one another.
Nos vemos de vez en cuando.	We see each other from time to time.

EJERCICIOS

A. A ver. ¿Qué pasa? (*Let's see. What's happening?*)   Form sentences with the words given, adding any additional ones you may need.

>   **MODELOS**   Ana / mudarse / Madrid / abril
>   **Ana se muda a Madrid en abril.**
>
>   ustedes / quejarse / exámenes
>   **Ustedes se quejan de los exámenes.**

---

*Notice that when **ponerse** or **quitarse** is used with articles of clothing, the definite article is used and not the possessive as in English. This will be practiced in Chapter 19.

[†]This construction will be discussed more fully in Chapter 15.

1. Ricardo / ponerse / la camisa blanca y los pantalones negros
2. Ella / enfadarse / con sus amigas
3. Juanita y José / casarse / en junio
4. Abuelita / preocuparse / el viaje
5. Yo / irse / diez / noche
6. jóvenes / divertirse / fiesta
7. Tú / quitarse / el abrigo rojo
8. Nosotros / lavarse / antes de acostarnos
9. Tú y Diana / sentarse / y / estudiar / lección
10. amiga / llamarse / Beatriz Muñoz
11. estudiantes / acostumbrarse / vivir / con sus padres
12. niños / levantarse / siete / y / bañarse / ocho

B. Nuestra rutina diaria (*Our daily routine*).   Lucía is telling Martín about her family's daily routine. Combine elements from all three columns to form logical affirmative or negative sentences, as Lucía would. Use each subject and verb at least once.

mis dos hermanos	levantarse	tarde todas las noches
papá	acostarse	en casa todo el día
nosotros	despertarse	y después toma(n) el desayuno
yo	divertirse	a las once de la noche, ¿no?
mi abuela	quedarse	temprano para no perder el autobús
tú	lavarse	de los problemas del mundo
papá y mamá	irse	aquí porque quiere(n)
tú y David	sentarse	y luego sale(n)
	vestirse	antes de las ocho de la mañana
	quejarse	del tiempo que hace
		y mira(n) televisión

C. Completar las frases.   Complete the sentences with the correct form of the more appropriate verb.

MODELO   Nosotros **vamos** (ir / irse) de compras los sábados.

1. En general, yo _____ (acostar / acostarse) a mi hijo temprano.
2. ¿A qué hora _____ (levantar / levantarse) ustedes?
3. Tú _____ (divertir / divertirse) en las fiestas, ¿no?
4. Nosotros preferimos _____ (quedar / quedarse) en casa esta noche.
5. Jorge _____ (lavar / lavarse) el auto todos los viernes.
6. ¿Cuándo vas a _____ (llamar / llamarse) a Susana?
7. ¿Quién _____ (despertar / despertarse) antes de las siete?
8. Cuando hace frío, yo siempre _____ (poner / ponerse) el abrigo.

D. En acción.   Describe the following pictures, using a reflexive verb for each.

MODELO

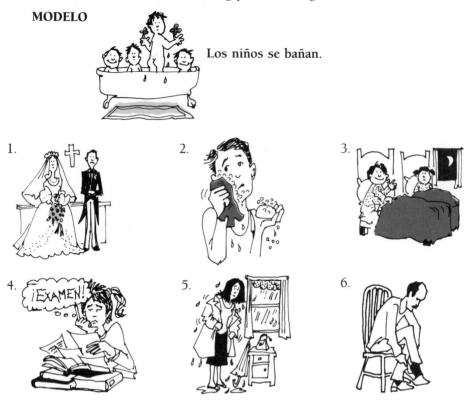

Los niños se bañan.

1.   2.   3.

4.   5.   6.

E. Traducción.   Give the Spanish equivalent of the following sentences.

1. I always get up early.
2. When do you generally go to bed?
3. He calls her every day.
4. We are going to have a good time at the concert tonight.
5. She puts them to bed at eight.
6. My cousin complains about his old red car.
7. I am used to this house.
8. They see one another at work.

Preguntas

With a classmate, take turns asking and answering the following questions.

1. ¿A qué hora se despierta usted? ¿Se levanta en pocos minutos?   2. ¿A qué hora le gusta a usted levantarse? ¿Le gusta levantarse tarde o temprano?   3. ¿Qué se pone usted cuando hace frío? ¿cuando hace calor?   4. ¿Qué se pone usted cuando va a un concierto? ¿a un museo? ¿a sus clases? ¿a la casa de un(a) amigo(-a)?   5. ¿Se enoja usted de vez en cuando? ¿con quién(es)? ¿con sus profesores? ¿Por qué?   6. ¿Se preocupa usted de vez en cuando? ¿Por qué? ¿por dinero? ¿por los exámenes? ¿por su familia? ¿por sus amigos?   7. ¿Va a quedarse usted en casa este fin de semana? ¿y antes de los exámenes finales? ¿y durante las vacaciones?   8. ¿A qué hora se acuesta usted? Y en general, ¿a qué hora se duerme?

II. Los mandatos de *tú*

Un edificio
de Gaudí,
extraordinario
arquitecto moderno

Cerca de la Universidad de Barcelona

FERMÍN Oye, Tito, ¿me puedes decir cómo llegar a la Plaza de Cataluña? Necesito ir a una tienda que está cerca de allí para comprar un paraguas y un impermeable antes de mi viaje a Galicia. Dicen que allí llueve mucho.

TITO A ver... *toma* el autobús aquí y *ve* hasta la Plaza de la Universidad; *baja* del autobús allí, y desde la Plaza, *camina* derecho por la Ronda Universidad. Después, *dobla* a la derecha. ¡Cuidado!, *no dobles* a la izquierda. *Sigue* derecho hasta ver la tienda. Está enfrente de la Plaza.

FERMÍN ¿Crees que llego a tiempo para comprar las cosas hoy? ¿No es fácil perderse?

TITO Depende del tráfico... Pero, *no te preocupes*. Uno de los niños te acompaña. *(Llama a Toño.)* ¡Toño! Ve con el tío Fermín a la Plaza de Cataluña, ¿eh?

TOÑO ¿La plaza de Cataluña? ¡Oh, ya sé! *(Llama a Lisa.)* ¡Lisa! *¡Ven* aquí! *¡Corre!* ¡Vamos a la juguetería con el tío Fermín!

1. ¿Adónde quiere ir Fermín? ¿Por qué?   2. Según las direcciones de Tito, ¿dónde debe bajar del autobús Fermín?   3. ¿Para qué quiere llegar Fermín a la Plaza de Cataluña?   4. ¿Quiénes lo van a acompañar?   5. ¿Adónde cree Toño que van a ir?

Near the University of Barcelona. FERMÍN: Listen, Tito. Can you tell me how to get to the Plaza de Cataluña? I need to go to a store that is near there to buy an umbrella and a raincoat before my trip to Galicia. They say that it rains a lot there. TITO: Let's see. . . . Take the bus here and go to the Plaza de la Universidad; from there, walk straight ahead on Ronda Universidad. Then, turn right. Be careful! Don't turn left. Continue straight until you see the store. It's opposite the Plaza. FERMÍN: Do you think I'll arrive on time to buy the things today? Isn't it easy to get lost? TITO: It depends on the traffic. . . . But, don't worry. One of the children will accompany you. (*He calls Toño.*) Toño! Go with Uncle Fermín to the Plaza de Cataluña, OK? TOÑO: The Plaza de Cataluña? Oh, now I know! (*He calls Lisa.*) Lisa! Come here! Run! Let's go to the toy store with Uncle Fermín!

A. Informal singular (**tú**) affirmative commands for regular verbs are the same as the third-person singular, present-tense form. The pronoun **tú** is usually not used; occasionally it is added for emphasis.

Gloria lleva un impermeable verde.	Gloria is wearing a green raincoat.
Lleva (tú) una falda larga.	Wear a long skirt.
Juan lee el mapa.	Juan is reading the map.
Lee (tú) la novela.	Read the novel.
Julia sube al autobús amarillo* y paga 50 pesetas.	Julia gets on the yellow bus and pays 50 pesetas.
Sube (tú) al autobús anaranjado y paga 50 pesetas.	Get on the orange bus and pay 50 pesetas.
Felipe cruza la calle.	Felipe crosses the street.
Cruza la calle.	Cross the street.

B. Some irregular affirmative **tú** commands are

decir	di	**ir**	ve	**salir**	sal	**tener**	ten
hacer	haz	**poner**	pon	**ser**	sé	**venir**	ven

Irene, di «gracias».	Irene, say "thank you."
Haz la maleta.	Pack the suitcase.
Ve al parque de diversiones.	Go to the amusement park.
Pon el suéter violeta en el auto.	Put the purple sweater in the car.
Sal ahora o no llegas a tiempo.	Leave now or you won't arrive on time.
¡Ten cuidado, José!	Be careful, José!
Ven acá, María.	Come here, María.

C. Negative **tú** commands are formed by adding an **s** to the **usted** commands.

No doble (usted) aquí. No dobles (tú) aquí.	Don't turn here.
No vuelva (usted) tarde. No vuelvas (tú) tarde.	Don't come back late.
No salga (usted) ahora. No salgas (tú) ahora.	Don't leave now.
No vaya (usted) al parque zoológico ahora. No vayas (tú) al parque zoológico ahora.	Don't go to the zoo now.

---

*Subir a with a means of transportation means *to get on*. Subir without the preposition a means *to climb* or *to go up*: Subimos una montaña. Los precios suben.

EJERCICIOS

A. ¡No salgas muy tarde!   Eliana has invited Lelia to come to her house at approximately 8 P.M. Using the phrases below, play the role of Eliana and form affirmative **tú** commands to give Lelia directions on how to get to your house.

> **MODELO**   salir antes de las siete.
> **Sal antes de las siete.**

1. tomar la calle Colón
2. caminar hasta la tienda Alegría
3. doblar a la izquierda
4. ir a la estación de autobuses
5. subir al autobús número 85
6. pagar 60 pesetas
7. leer los nombres de las calles
8. bajar del autobús en la calle de Ibiza
9. seguir por la calle de Mallorca hasta el número 121, que es donde vivo

B. ¡Feliz viaje!   Rubén is planning a trip to Barcelona, but he's very confused after talking to Marisa and Arturo. While Marisa, his girlfriend, tells him to do one thing, Arturo advises him to do just the opposite! Play the roles of both Marisa and Arturo, following the model.

> **MODELO**   buscar un hotel en el centro
> MARISA **Busca un hotel en el centro.**
> ARTURO **No busques un hotel en el centro.**

1. visitar el parque zoológico
2. ir al teatro los fines de semana
3. ver bailes folklóricos catalanes
4. asistir a muchos conciertos
5. comer mucho pescado
6. usar el autobús; no andar mucho
7. hacer un viaje a Tarragona y a Gerona
8. sacar fotos de todos los monumentos

C. Conversación.   Complete the conversation between Carlos and his mother with **tú** commands. Pay attention to Carlos' reactions in order to guess what his mother is suggesting.

CARLOS	Ay, mamá, estoy aburrido.
PILAR	Pues, _____ algo.
CARLOS	¿Qué hago?
PILAR	_____
CARLOS	Pienso estudiar esta noche para las clases de mañana.
PILAR	Pues _____ unas páginas de esa novela.
CARLOS	No me gusta leer novelas.
PILAR	_____ tu cuarto.
CARLOS	No quiero pintar mi cuatro.
PILAR	Entonces _____ una carta a tu tía Julia.
CARLOS	¡Pero, mamá!, sabes que no me gusta escribir cartas...
PILAR	¡Ay!, pues entonces _____ de la casa por unos minutos... Puedes dar un paseo por el parque y decidir.
CARLOS	¡Buena idea! Voy a salir para dar un paseo y decidir qué hacer después.

III. Los mandatos con pronombres complementos

El Paseo Colón con
su monumento,
Barcelona

*En Barcelona, donde los señores Castellón, turistas de Ecuador,
viajan en auto con sus tres hijos.*

PEPE	Papá, tengo hambre. ¿Cuándo vamos a llegar a esa montaña donde está el parque de diversiones? *¡Dímelo,* por favor!
SR. CASTELLÓN	*Déjanos* en paz, Pepe. Y *siéntense,* niños, por favor—vamos a parar. *(Para el auto.)* Silvia, *dame* el mapa y busca una manzana en la bolsa. *Dásela* a Pepe...
SRA. CASTELLÓN	¿Otra vez estamos perdidos? Mejor salgo a preguntar.
PAQUITA	¡Qué bien! ¡Qué bien! ¡Llegamos!
SRA. CASTELLÓN	No, niños. *Quédense* en el auto. *No me sigan...* *(Sale del auto y regresa en unos minutos.)* Dice el señor que hay que volver hasta el monumento a Colón, seguir derecho por el Paseo de Colón* y después doblar a la derecha.
SR. CASTELLÓN	¡Pero no puede ser! Tenemos que doblar a la izquierda allí...
SRA. CASTELLÓN	*Cálmate,* Mario. Ten paciencia.
	Media hora más tarde.
SR. CASTELLÓN	Niños, ¡estamos en el parque de diversiones! ¡Miren! *¡Véanlo* con sus propios ojos! Pero, ¿qué les pasa? *¡Despiértense!* *¡No se duerman* ahora!
LOS NIÑOS	Zzzzzzzzzzz.

*Just off the harbor in Barcelona is the Columbus Monument, an iron column with a bronze statue of Co-
lumbus. The **Paseo de Colón**, a boulevard lined with palms, runs from the Monument along the harbor.

1. ¿Dónde está la familia Castellón?   2. ¿Qué quieren saber los niños?   3. ¿Por qué para el señor Castellón?   4. ¿Qué hace la señora Castellón?   5. Según el señor, ¿qué deben hacer?   6. Cuando llegan al parque de diversiones, ¿qué están haciendo los niños?

In Barcelona, where the Castellón family, tourists from Ecuador, are traveling by car with their three children. PEPE: Papa, I'm hungry. When are we going to arrive at that mountain where the amusement park is? Tell me, please! SR. CASTELLÓN: Leave us in peace, Pepe. And please sit down, children; we're going to stop. *(He stops the car.)* Silvia, give me the map and look for an apple in the bag. Give it to Pepe . . . SRA. CASTELLÓN: Are we lost again? I'd better get out to ask. PAQUITA: Great! Great! We're here! SRA. CASTELLÓN: No, children. Stay in the car. Don't follow me . . . *(She gets out of the car and comes back in a few minutes.)* The gentleman says that we have to go back to the Colón monument, continue straight ahead along the Paseo de Colón, and then turn right. SR. CASTELLÓN: But that can't be! We have to turn left there . . . SRA. CASTELLÓN: Calm yourself, Mario. Be patient. *(A half hour later.)* SR. CASTELLÓN: Children, we're at the amusement park! Look! See for yourselves! But, what's happening to you? Wake up! Don't fall asleep now! THE CHILDREN: Zzzzzzzzzzz.

A. Object and reflexive pronouns are attached to affirmative commands, familiar and formal. The stressed vowel of the command form is still stressed when pronouns are attached. In order to comply with the rules for word stress (p. 8), an accent mark must usually be written over the stressed vowel.

Compra los zapatos. Cómpralos (tú).	*Buy the shoes. Buy them.*
Lee la guía turística. Léela (tú).	*Read the tourist guide. Read it.*
Pónganse los pijamas.	*Put on your pajamas.*
Denle (ustedes) los regalos a tía Carmen.	*Give the gifts to Aunt Carmen.*
Perdónenme (ustedes).	*Pardon (excuse) me.*
Despiértense (ustedes) temprano para salir a tiempo.	*Wake up early in order to leave on time.*

B. Object pronouns precede negative commands, familiar and formal.

No cierres la puerta. No la cierres (tú).	*Don't close the door. Don't close it.*
No te preocupes.	*Don't worry.*
No te pongas una corbata violeta.	*Don't put on a purple tie.*
No saque la foto aquí. No la saque aquí.	*Don't take the photo here. Don't take it here.*
No les digan (ustedes) eso.	*Don't tell them that.*

C. When both a direct object pronoun and an indirect object pronoun are used, the indirect object pronoun precedes the direct object pronoun, just as with statements or questions. Remember that **se** replaces the indirect object pronouns **le** and **les** when they are used with **la, lo, las** or **los.**

Dímelo. No me lo digas (tú).	*Tell me (it). Don't tell me (it).*
Déjenselos.	*Leave them for them (him, her).*
No se los dejen (ustedes).	*Don't leave them for them (him, her).*

EJERCICIOS

A. Búscalos aquí, por favor. You have just arrived home from a long trip and are telling your brother to please look for certain things for you. Follow the model.

> **MODELO** el mapa / el auto
> **Búscalo en el auto, por favor.**

1. las fotos / la maleta grande
2. el paraguas / el auto
3. la corbata azul / aquí
4. el sombrero amarillo / allá
5. los zapatos marrones / la maleta pequeña

B. No lo compre, señora. You are a tourist guide in an open-air market and realize that one of the ladies in your group is about to purchase some overpriced items. Advise her not to buy them. Follow the model.

> **MODELO** una chaqueta de lana
> **No la compre, señora.**

1. unos sombreros violetas
2. un vestido elegante
3. una blusa típica
4. varias maletas pequeñas
5. una guía turística
6. libros y cuadernos
7. una guitarra grande
8. unas sandalias anaranjadas

C. ¡Háganlo ahora! Replace the nouns with object pronouns.

> **MODELO** Escribe la carta, Susana.
> **Escríbela, Susana.**

1. Lee tu lección, Pablo.
2. Compra frutas, Carmela.
3. Abre tu maleta, Marcelo.
4. Lleva esta camisa verde, Miguel.
5. Cuente su dinero, señora.
6. Deje los cheques aquí, señor.
7. Pidan la guía turística, chicos.
8. Pongan los sombreros negros allí, señores.

D. ¡No lo hagan! Replace the nouns with object pronouns.

> **MODELO** No busques los calcetines allí, Teresa.
> **No los busques allí, Teresa.**

1. No traigas los trajes de invierno, Mónica.
2. No hagas esas cosas, Antonio.
3. No ponga el paraguas en la mesa, señorita.
4. ¡No perdonen a esas muchachas, amigos!
5. No comas estos postres, Paco.
6. No lleve ese impermeable anaranjado, señor.
7. No cuenten sus secretos, chicas.
8. No hagan ese viaje, muchachos.
9. No crucen la calle, niños.

E. Órdenes de papá.   Roberto and Carolina's father is away for a few days on a trip. He left a note with a list of things they should do while he's away. Using the reflexive verbs and the names provided, write the commands or suggestions he leaves for them. Use the **tú** or **ustedes** form, as appropriate.

MODELOS   acostarse temprano hoy (Roberto y Carolina)
　　　　　　Acuéstense temprano hoy.

　　　　　　irse al banco mañana (Carolina)
　　　　　　Vete al banco mañana.

1. levantarse a las siete (Roberto)
2. acostarse antes de las doce (Carolina)
3. sentarse a la mesa con Roberto (Carolina)
4. quedarse en casa el jueves (Roberto)
5. irse al cine el viernes (Roberto y Carolina)
6. vestirse bien si van al concierto (Roberto y Carolina)
7. divertirse este fin de semana (Roberto y Carolina)

F. Preguntas y respuestas.   Work with a classmate to answer the following questions.

1. ¿Qué mandatos oye mucho un niño? Dé cuatro o cinco de esos mandatos.
2. ¿Qué mandatos quiere usted darle a un(a) amigo(-a)? Dé cuatro o cinco de esos mandatos.
3. ¿Qué mandatos le hacen sus padres que a usted no le gustan? Dé cuatro o cinco de esos mandatos.
4. ¿Qué clase de mandatos a usted sí le gustan? Dé cuatro o cinco de esos mandatos.

IV. El pretérito de los verbos regulares

Una tienda de ropa
elegante de
Barcelona

En «La Elegancia», una tienda de Barcelona

SRA. RODRÍGUEZ   Buenas tardes, señor. Necesito comprar ropa de invierno...
Mi marido me *llamó* de la oficina para decirme que en dos
días ¡viajamos a Boston...!

DEPENDIENTE   ¡Un viaje a Boston! ¡Qué lindo! ¿Ya *visitó* los Estados Unidos
antes?

SRA. RODRÍGUEZ   Sí, *viajé* a Boston con mi marido el año pasado y no me
gustó... *Llovió* casi todos los días y... ¡*nevó* dos veces!

DEPENDIENTE   Entonces, para la lluvia, señora, usted necesita este
impermeable. Lo tenemos en amarillo claro y en azul oscuro
y vendemos paraguas de muchos colores... rojo, verde, azul
oscuro...

SRA. RODRÍGUEZ   Pero, señor, usted no comprende. Es que... no quiero ir a
Boston... ¡Hace mucho frío allí!

DEPENDIENTE   Para el frío, señora, este abrigo elegante y abrigado...

SRA. RODRÍGUEZ   Pero... el año pasado, no *salí* mucho del hotel.

DEPENDIENTE   Pues... con este abrigo y ese impermeable, señora, ¡usted
puede salir todos los días y visitar todos los sitios históricos
de Boston!

SRA. RODRÍGUEZ   ¡Usted tiene razón! ¡Mil gracias...! Y a propósito, ¿cuánto
cuesta todo esto?

---

1. ¿Por qué necesita comprar ropa de invierno la señora Rodríguez?   2. ¿De dónde
la llamó su marido? ¿Para qué?   3. ¿Adónde viajaron ellos el año pasado? ¿Le gustó
a ella el viaje? ¿Por qué sí o por qué no?   4. ¿Qué le recomienda el dependiente
para la lluvia? ¿Cómo es el abrigo que él le desea vender?   5. Cuando sale de la
tienda, ¿cree usted que está contenta la señora? ¿Por qué?

In "La Elegancia," a Barcelona shop. SRA. RODRÍGUEZ: Good afternoon, sir. I need to buy winter
clothing. . . . My husband called me from the office to tell me that in two days we're traveling to
Boston! DEPENDIENTE: A trip to Boston! How nice! Have you already visited the United States before?
SRA. RODRÍGUEZ: Yes, I traveled to Boston with my husband last year and I didn't like it. . . . It rained
almost every day and . . . it snowed twice! DEPENDIENTE: Then, madam, for the rain you need this
raincoat. We have it in light yellow and dark blue and we sell umbrellas in many colors . . . red,
green, dark blue . . . SRA. RODRÍGUEZ: But, sir, you don't understand. It's that . . . I don't want to go
to Boston. . . . It's very cold there! DEPENDIENTE: For the cold, madam, this elegant and warm
overcoat . . . SRA. RODRÍGUEZ: But . . . last year, I didn't go out of the hotel very much. DEPENDIENTE:
Well . . . with this overcoat and that raincoat, madam, you can go out every day and visit all the
historic sites of Boston. SRA. RODRÍGUEZ: You're right! Thank you very much! By the way, how much
does all this cost?

The preterit is used to relate actions or events that occurred and were completed
at a specific time or within a definite period in the past.

A. The preterit of regular **-ar** verbs is formed by adding the endings **-é, -aste,
-ó, -amos, -asteis, -aron** to the stem.

comprar

compré	compramos
compraste	comprasteis
compró	compraron

Ayer yo me compré unos jeans muy lindos.	*Yesterday I bought myself some very nice jeans.*
Ellos no caminaron por esa avenida.	*They did not walk along that avenue.*

B. The preterit of regular **-er** and **-ir** verbs is formed by adding the endings **-í, -iste, -ió, -imos, -isteis, -ieron** to the stem.

volver		**escribir**	
volví	volvimos	escribí	escribimos
volviste	volvisteis	escribiste	escribisteis
volvió	volvieron	escribió	escribieron

¿No volviste a la tienda la semana pasada?	*Didn't you go back to the store last week?*
Mi tía me escribió desde Mallorca.	*My aunt wrote me from Mallorca.*

C. Notice that, in contrast to present-tense forms, regular preterit forms are stressed on the endings and not the stems: **Llego temprano.** *(I arrive early.)* **Llegó temprano** *(He [she] arrived early.)* Notice also that the **nosotros** forms of **-ar** and **-ir** verbs are the same in the preterit as they are in the present tense.

	Present	*Preterit*
-ar verbs	compramos	compramos
-er verbs	volvemos	volvimos
-ir verbs	escribimos	escribimos

D. A number of verbs have a spelling change in the first person singular of the preterit. Verbs ending in **-gar, -car,** and **-zar** have the following spelling changes, respectively: **g** to **gu, c** to **qu,** and **z** to **c.** These changes are required to preserve the sound of the last syllable of the infinitive.

llegar		**tocar**		**cruzar**	
llegué	llegamos	toqué	tocamos	crucé	cruzamos
llegaste	llegasteis	tocaste	tocasteis	cruzaste	cruzasteis
llegó	llegaron	tocó	tocaron	cruzó	cruzaron

Llegué a las ocho anoche.	*I arrived at eight last night.*
Toqué el piano por dos horas.	*I played the piano for two hours.*
Crucé la calle con cuidado.	*I crossed the street carefully.*

E. Verbs such as **creer** and **leer** show a spelling change in the third person singular and plural: **creyó, creyeron; leyó, leyeron.** This change is made because an *i* between two vowels becomes a *y*. The other preterit forms of these verbs are regular.

Jorge leyó que los edificios del famoso arquitecto Gaudí son muy interesantes.	*Jorge read that the famous architect Gaudi's buildings are very interesting.*
Creyeron su historia. ¿De veras?	*They believed his story. Really?*

F. The verb **nacer** *(to be born)* is used almost exclusively in the preterit.

¿Dónde naciste? Nací en Gerona.	*Where were you born? I was born in Gerona.*

G. The following expressions are often used with the preterit:

anoche	*last night*	ayer	*yesterday*
el año pasado	*last year*	la semana pasada	*last week*

EJERCICIOS

A. Imaginación y lógica. Combine elements from all three columns to form logical affirmative or negative sentences in the past. Use each subject twice.

ese estudiante	asistir	a un partido de fútbol
tú	llegar	a la estación de autobuses
nosotros	buscar	cartas a la familia
yo	salir	ayer después de la clase
mi amiga	mudarse	a un concierto la semana pasada
tú y Luis	escribir	composiciones en español
	comer	el año pasado
		ayer para Barcelona
		a una casa nueva
		zapatos nuevos

B. ¿Otra vez? ¡No lo puedo creer! Mrs. Fernández is talking to her son Nicolás. Respond as Nicolás would, saying that the same things happened yesterday.

> **MODELOS** Hoy tocas el piano.
> **¡Pero ayer toqué el piano también!**
>
> Hoy Ana llega tarde.
> **¡Pero ayer llegó tarde también!**

1. Hoy corro por el parque.
2. Hoy Ana lleva una blusa azul.
3. Hoy te levantas temprano.
4. Hoy escribo cartas.
5. Hoy tú y Ana preparan la cena.
6. Hoy tu papá sale con sus amigos.
7. Hoy comemos después del partido de fútbol.

C. El sábado pasado.   Look at the pictures and describe what the people did last Saturday. A few infinitives are listed by each picture to give you ideas. Give at least two sentences for each picture.

MODELO

cantar, empezar, gustar

El sábado pasado Julio Iglesias cantó en el Teatro Nuevo. Nos gustó mucho el concierto. El concierto empezó a las ocho y terminó a las diez y media.

1.

visitar, llegar, abrir, salir

2.

aprender, perder, ganar, correr

3.

hablar, llamar, trabajar, llevar

4.

cenar, comer, beber, gustar

5.

estudiar, leer, buscar

D. Traducción.   Give the Spanish equivalents of the following sentences.

1. They bought clothing for winter.
2. He called Juanita, but she didn't answer.
3. The tourists returned from Montserrat last night.
4. Did you attend a concert last weekend?
5. We wrote several letters yesterday.
6. I ate dinner late last night.

Preguntas

1. ¿A qué hora cenó usted anoche?   2. ¿Miró televisión?   3. ¿Habló con un(a) amigo(-a) por teléfono?   4. ¿Leyó un libro? ¿Qué libro?   5. ¿Escribió cartas? ¿composiciones?   6. ¿Salió anoche? ¿Visitó a unos amigos?   7. ¿Asistió a un concierto o a un partido de fútbol la semana pasada?   8. ¿A qué hora llegó a clase? ¿A qué hora se levantó hoy?   9. ¿Dónde nació usted? ¿Cuándo?

Study Hint: Listening for Comprehension

Listening is perhaps the most essential language skill. Here are some suggestions for developing your listening skills:

1. Train your ears to recognize key words. Listen frequently to the tapes in your language laboratory and practice taking dictation from them.

2. Talk with your Spanish-speaking friends as often as possible.

3. Look for other opportunities to listen to Spanish—plays, movies, records, radio and television programs. Although the Spanish may be too difficult for you, just relax and listen for key words you do understand. Even listening to the rhythm of the language is helpful.

Una tuna

**Un hombre español y dos mujeres norteamericanas
dan un paseo por las Ramblas de Barcelona.[1]**

HUGO   ¿Nos sentamos aquí?

SHARON Buena idea. Creo que pronto llega la tuna.[2]

PATTY   ¿La tuna? ¿Y qué es eso?

SHARON Pues..., las tunas son estudiantes que salen en grupos para cantar
y tocar la guitarra. Casi° siempre se visten de° negro. Llevan unas
capas° o túnicas° largas.

PATTY   ¡Qué interesante! Gracias por la información, Sharon. Pero, ¿aquel
muchacho los conoce a ustedes?

Llega Omar.

OMAR   ¡Hola, guapas°! ¡Qué vestidos más elegantes!° Voy a sentarme aquí
para poder mirarlas y admirarlas...

HUGO   Ten cuidado, Patty. Omar siempre dice piropos.[3]

PATTY   Entonces, me levanto y me voy. Además, quiero ver tres o cuatro
museos más. Visité el Museo de Arte Moderno y aprendí mucho,
pero también quiero ver el Museo de Arte de Cataluña, la Galería
Dalí, el Museo de Picasso[4] y...

SHARON Omar es inofensivo. Siéntate y quédate con nosotros.

PATTY   Bueno, me quedo, pero no puedo acostumbrarme a los piropos, y

---

Casi *almost*   se visten de *they dress in*   capas *capes*   túnicas *tunics*   guapas
good-looking   ¡Qué vestidos más elegantes!   *What elegant dresses!*

realmente quiero ver más atracciones culturales. Ya asistí a muchos conciertos buenos, visité iglesias... Es que cada día me interesa más la arquitectura. Y hablando de arquitectura, ¿está lejos de aquí el Parque Güell? ¡Me fascina la arquitectura de Gaudí![5]

OMAR   ¡A mí también, guapa! Te acompaño al Parque Güell. Conozco muy bien la ciudad.

PATTY   Gracias, Omar ...Me pregunto si realmente eres inofensivo, como cree Sharon...

OMAR   ¡Claro que sí! ¡Inofensivo como un bebé, muchacha!

PREGUNTAS

1. ¿Dónde están el hombre y las mujeres?   2. ¿Qué es una tuna?   3. ¿Qué llevan los estudiantes de la tuna?   4. ¿Qué dice siempre Omar?   5. ¿Le gustan a Patty los piropos?   6. ¿Cuáles son los museos que quiere visitar Patty?   7. ¿Quién es Gaudí? ¿Le gusta o no a ella la arquitectura de Gaudí?   8. ¿Qué le ofrece Omar a Patty? ¿Conoce él la ciudad?   9. Según Sharon, ¿cómo es Omar? Y según Omar, ¿tiene razón ella? ¿Qué piensa usted?

NOTAS CULTURALES

1. **Las Ramblas**, a wide, tree-lined boulevard beginning near the harbor, changes names (beginning with **Rambla de Santa Mónica** and ending with **Rambla de los Estudios**) as it moves toward the center of the city. A favorite promenade renowned for its charm, **Las Ramblas** has seats beneath the trees along both sides and many stalls where birds and flowers are sold. There are also many cafés along the sidewalks.

2. The **tunas** are groups of students who sing and play guitars and other instruments, usually receiving some donations from bystanders. This tradition goes back to the Middle Ages, when many poor scholars did have to sing for their supper. Nowadays, each school within a university has its own **tuna**. Sometimes the students stroll through the streets at night, dressed in academic gowns, and serenade their girlfriends. Often the girlfriends toss down ribbons for them to wear on their robes.

3. **Piropos** are compliments made by men to women, often to women passing by on the street. Some Spaniards consider it an art to be able to instantly devise a **piropo** appropriate to a particular occasion. This is a time-honored custom and is usually not taken as harmful or offensive.

4. Barcelona has been the residence of the famous modern Spanish artists **Pablo Picasso**, **Salvador Dalí**, and **Joan Miró**. Its museums house their paintings and also many outstanding works of other artists and periods.

5. **Antonio Gaudí** (1852–1926), a Modernist architect, designed a number of unusual buildings in Barcelona including a series of fantastic buildings in the **Parque Güell**, and the **Templo de la Sagrada Familia**, a monumental church, which is still not finished.

Funciones y *actividades*

In this chapter, you've seen examples of some important language functions, or uses. Here is a summary and some additional information about these functions of language.

EXPRESSING HESITATION

There will often be times when you don't have a ready answer for something someone has asked—this happens even in your native language, but it can happen even more frequently when you are speaking a foreign language. Here are some expressions you can use to fill in those moments of conversational hesitation.

A ver.	*Let's see.*	Pues...	*Well . . .*
Es que...	*The thing is that . . . (literally,* "It's that . . .")	Bueno...	*Well . . .*
Buena pregunta.	*Good question.*	Depende de...	*It depends on . . .*

MAKING DESCRIPTIONS (2)

There will be many times when you have to describe something in Spanish, whether you are in a shop, trying to describe what you want to buy or whether you are just trying to explain to someone what something is—especially if you don't know the word for it in Spanish. Here are some ways to ask for a description and to describe something.

¿De qué color es? Es rojo (blanco, etcétera).	*What color is it? It's red (white, etc.).*
¿De qué tamaño es? Es grande (pequeño, el tamaño de un libro...).	*What size is it? It's big (little, the size of a book . . .).*
¿De qué es? Es de madera (plástico, metal...).	*What is it made of? It's made of wood (plastic, metal . . .).*
¿Para qué sirve? Sirve para tocar (leer, escribir...).	*What do you use it for? You use it for playing (reading, writing . . .).*

Relative pronouns—**que** *(that, which)*, **quien** *(who, whom)*—are often helpful when making descriptions.*

No sé su nombre, pero la muchacha de quien hablas es rubia, alta, elegante y habla muy bien el español, ¿no?	*I don't know her name, but the girl of whom you speak is blonde, tall, elegant, and speaks Spanish very well, right?*
El abrigo que él siempre lleva en el invierno es marrón.	*The coat (that) he always wears in winter is brown.*

Now do the following activities, using the expressions you have just learned.

---

*Relative pronouns will be discussed further in Chapter 11.

A. Preguntas.   Ask a classmate the following questions. Your classmate should express hesitation before answering them, using one of the expressions from this chapter.

1. ¿Qué tipo de ropa te pones cuando quieres hacerle una buena impresión a la gente? ¿Qué color de ropa prefieres? ¿Te pones ropa elegante, informal... ?
2. ¿Cuál es tu color favorito? ¿Por qué?
3. ¿Qué color asocias tú con el otoño? ¿con la primavera? ¿con la alegría (*happiness*)?
4. ¿Cuántas horas duermes cada (*every*) noche? Para ti, ¿es fácil o difícil despertarte? ¿Duermes bien en general?

B. ¿Qué es esto?   In small groups, one person will think of the name of an object that he or she can say in Spanish (something that has been presented in this book or in class). The others will take turns asking yes/no questions about the object. The person who guesses the object then takes a turn.

C. Descríbalos.   Imagine that you are in a Spanish-speaking country and you need the following items but don't know the Spanish words. Describe each item using the hints on page 219 and, if necessary, gestures. (The Spanish words are given at the bottom of the page.)

1. pajamas
2. bathing suit
3. blanket
4. clothes hanger
5. hotel or restaurant bill
6. toothpaste
7. credit card
8. spoon

D. Mini-dramas.   Role-play the following situations in Spanish with one of your classmates. Be sure to express hesitation before answering the questions.

1. Your friend wants to know what sort of clothing to wear to a party.
2. A prospective freshman asks you about various aspects of campus and college life.
3. Your friend asks you to recommend a good movie or a good restaurant.
4. Your friend is going out on a blind date and would like some suggestions for topics of conversation or places to go.

1. el pijama   2. el traje de baño   3. la manta o la frazada   4. la percha   5. la cuenta   6. la pasta de dientes   7. la tarjeta de crédito   8. la cuchara

VOCABULARIO ACTIVO

Cognados

la estación	los jeans	la novela	el pijama	las sandalias
la guía turística	el monumento	el parque zoológico	la rutina	el suéter

Verbos

acompañar	to accompany
bajar (de)	to get off, get down from
caminar	to walk
cenar	to have dinner
decidir	to decide
dejar	to leave
doblar	to turn
llevar	to wear
nacer	to be born
pagar	to pay (for)
parar	to stop
subir (a)	to go up, to get into

Verbos reflexivos

acostarse (ue)	to go to bed
acostumbrarse	to get used to
bañarse	to bathe
casarse (con)	to get married (to)
despertarse (ie)	to wake up
divertirse (ie)	to have a good time; to enjoy oneself
dormirse (ue)	to fall asleep
enfadarse	to get angry
enojarse	to get angry
irse	to leave, go away
lavarse	to wash (oneself)
levantarse	to get up
llamarse	to be named
mudarse	to move (change residence)
ponerse	to put on
preocuparse (por)	to worry (about)
quedarse	to remain, to stay
quejarse (de)	to complain
quitarse	to take off
sentarse (ie)	to sit down
vestirse (i)	to get dressed

La ropa Clothes, clothing

el abrigo	overcoat
la blusa	blouse
el bolso	pocketbook, purse
la bota	boot
los calcetines	socks
la camisa	shirt
la corbata	tie
la chaqueta	jacket
la falda	skirt
los guantes	gloves
el impermeable	raincoat
la lana	wool
las medias	stockings
los pantalones	pants
el paraguas	umbrella
la ropa interior	underwear
el sombrero	hat
el traje	suit; outfit
el traje de baño	bathing suit
el vestido	dress
el zapato	shoe
los zapatos de tenis	tennis shoes

Los colores

amarillo	yellow
anaranjado	orange
azul	blue
blanco	white
claro	light
gris	grey
marrón	brown
negro	black
oscuro	dark
rojo	red
verde	green
violeta	purple

Otras palabras y frases

anoche	*last night*
ayer	*yesterday*
la bandera	*flag*
demasiado	*too much* (adv)
largo	*long*
el parque de diversiones	*amusement park*
pasado	*last*
la semana pasada	*last week*
el año pasado	*last year*

Expresiones útiles

A ver.	*Let's see.*
Buena pregunta.	*Good question.*
¿De qué color es...?	*What color is . . .?*
Depende de...	*It depends on . . .*

Don't forget: Reflexive pronouns, page 200

LECTURA IV

La música

En España hay una gran variedad de música y bailes folklóricos. En Cataluña, por ejemplo, bailan la sardana, un baile muy antiguo que refleja° el amor° que la gente siente por su región. En la foto vemos a un grupo de jóvenes catalanes° bailando la sardana delante de° la Catedral de Barcelona. En ge-

reflects/love
young people from Cataluña/ in front of

Catalanes bailando la sardana delante de la Catedral de Barcelona

neral, cada° región de España tiene su baile típico; la gente del lugar lo conoce y se divierte bailándolo, especialmente en las fiestas. Un baile famoso es el flamenco de Andalucía. Es un baile muy sensual, acompañado de° voz, guitarra y castañuelas°. Tradicionalmente, los gitanos° son los maestros° del flamenco.

También es rico y variado° el folklore de Hispanoamérica. Aquí la música

each

accompanied by castanets/ gypsies/ masters

varied

Las guitarras y las palmadas (*clapping*) son parte
del flamenco de Andalucía.

y los bailes reflejan una combinación de elementos indígenas°, españoles y, a veces°, africanos. En general, los instrumentos musicales de cuerda° son de origen español, los de viento de origen indio, y los de percusión de origen africano. Instrumentos típicos hispanoamericanos son, por ejemplo, el arpa paraguaya°, las diferentes flautas° indígenas en la región de los Andes (la quena en el Perú o la zampoña en Bolivia); las guitarras y sus diversas variantes, como el charango° andino° o el guitarrón° de México.

Indian
sometimes/
string

Paraguayan
harp/flutes
guitar made
from shell of
an armadillo/
Andean/large
guitar

Este hombre toca el arpa paraguaya.

El papel° de los trovadores y juglares° en la época medieval corresponde
hoy día a los payadores° de la Argentina y del Uruguay que cantan melodías
tristes sobre la vida solitaria del gaucho y sobre sus desilusiones amorosas.°
En las fiestas, muchas veces los payadores compiten entre ellos, improvisando
canciones (letra° y música) sobre temas° que les da el público.

Vemos en la fotografía a unos bailarines del famoso Ballet Folklórico de
México. Pero la música mexicana no es la única° que busca su inspiración

Los bailarines del Ballet Folklórico de México

en el folklore. Así,° por ejemplo, las melodías tristes de la quena andina o
los sonoros ritmos del Caribe tienen gran influencia en la música actual° de
Hispanoamérica. Hoy día ésta es muy conocida° en todas partes del mundo.
¿Quién no baila o, por lo menos°, conoce ritmos típicos hispanoamericanos
como el tango, la samba, la salsa, la rumba o el merengue... ?

---

role/minstrels

Gaucho singers

*love disappoint-
ments*

lyrics/themes

the only one

Thus

present

well known

at least

PREGUNTAS

1. ¿Cómo se llama el baile típico de Cataluña? ¿Qué refleja?   2. ¿Qué combinación de elementos está presente en la música de Hispanoamérica?   3. ¿Puede nombrar dos o tres instrumentos típicos hispanoamericanos? ¿De dónde son? 4. ¿Dónde hay payadores? ¿Qué hacen?   5. ¿Dónde busca inspiración la música hispanoamericana? Y la música de los Estados Unidos, ¿dónde busca inspiración? 6. ¿Cuáles son algunos (some) de los ritmos típicos de Hispanoamérica? ¿Sabe usted bailar el tango? ¿la salsa? ¿un ritmo hispanoamericano? ¿Cuál... ? 7. ¿Conoce a uno o más cantantes hispanoamericanos?   ¿A quién(es)? 8. ¿Conoce una o más canciones hispanoamericanas? ¿Cuál(es)? ¿Sabe cantarla(s)? ¿tocarla(s) en el piano o en la guitarra? ¿en el guitarrón? ¿en el arpa paraguaya... ?

Posibilidades múltiples.   Complete the sentences below by choosing the letter that corresponds to the correct answer. Follow the model.

> **MODELO**   Los instrumentos de percusión son de origen
> a. indio   ⓑ. africano   c. español

1. El flamenco es un baile que asociamos con
   a. Galicia   b. Andalucía   c. Cataluña
2. Los maestros tradicionales del flamenco son
   a. los gitanos   b. los catalanes   c. los africanos
3. Los instrumentos de cuerda son de origen
   a. indio   b. africano   c. español
4. Y los instrumentos de viento son de origen
   a. indio   b. africano   c. español
5. La quena es un instrumento típico de(l)
   a. Paraguay   b. Perú   c. Ecuador
6. Los payadores cantan melodías sobre la vida de
   a. los gitanos   b. los trovadores   c. los gauchos

Un partido de fútbol muy emocionante entre los *Aztecs* de Los Ángeles y los *Cosmos* de Nueva York

DEPORTES Y DEPORTISTAS

Funciones

- Expressing relief
- Expressing surprise
- Expressing anger

Vocabulario. In this chapter you will talk about sports.

Gramática. You will discuss and use:

1. The preterit of stem-changing verbs
2. The preterit of irregular verbs
3. Special meanings of **saber, conocer, querer,** and **poder** in the preterit

Cultura. The dialogues take place in Miami, New York, Los Angeles, Tampa, and Boston.

DEPORTES

la natación, nadar

el fútbol, jugar (al) fútbol

el tenis, jugar (al) tenis

el correr (el jogging), correr

la corrida de toros

el fútbol americano

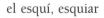

el esquí, esquiar

la pesca, pescar

el patinaje, patinar

el atletismo   el jai alai, la cancha *(court)*   el golf

Asociación de ideas.   Give the first four or five words that come to your mind (nouns, adjectives, verbs, etc.) when you think of the sports listed below.

MODELO   el golf   **calor, aburrido, jugar, pelota, fácil**

1. el jai alai
2. el tenis
3. el fútbol americano
4. el esquí
5. la natación
6. la corrida de toros

La palabra incorrecta.   Choose the word that does not belong and tell why.

1. pelota, raqueta, esquí, abrigo
2. aficionado, piscina, torero, toro
3. llevar, jugar, nadar, esquiar
4. básquetbol, béisbol, pista, fútbol
5. jugador, pequeño, interesante, popular
6. correr, cenar, patinar, pescar

Preguntas

1. En un equipo *(team)* de béisbol hay nueve jugadores. ¿Cuántos jugadores hay en un equipo de fútbol americano? ¿de fútbol? ¿de tenis? ¿de básquetbol?
2. ¿Juega usted al fútbol? ¿al tenis? ¿Qué deportes practica usted?   3. ¿Es usted aficionado(-a) al básquetbol? ¿al béisbol? ¿al fútbol? ¿Le gusta caminar? ¿correr? ¿Dónde y cuándo?   4. ¿Con qué deporte(s) asocia usted a Fernando Valenzuela? ¿a Chris Evert? ¿a Babe Ruth? ¿a Kareem Abdul-Jabbar? ¿a Billie Jean King? ¿a Bill Rogers? ¿a Pelé? ¿a Larry Bird? ¿a Hank Aaron? ¿a Martina Navratilova? ¿a Refrigerator Perry?

I. El pretérito de verbos con cambios en la raíz

Un jugador de
jai alai

En la cafetería de Boston University

EVA   *Sentí* no poder hablar contigo anoche, Alfonso. Te llamé pero no contestaste... ¿*Volviste* tarde?

ALFONSO   Sí, muy tarde. Pasé todo el día° en Connecticut. Visité a mis padres y después asistí a un partido° de jai alai con Elena.

EVA   ¿*Se divirtieron?*

ALFONSO   Sí, mucho. Pedro Ramos y Paco González *jugaron* muy bien.

EVA   ¡Qué bien!° Pero...¿ganaste dinero?

ALFONSO   No, *perdí* treinta dólares, pero Elena ganó cuarenta. Así que° ganamos diez. Hoy me *desperté* a las once. ¡*Dormí* casi° diez horas... !

Pasé...día *I spent the whole day*   partido *game*   ¡Qué bien! *Good! (How nice!)*
Así que *So*   casi *almost*

1. ¿A quién llamó Eva?   2. ¿Contestó él el teléfono?   3. ¿Dónde pasó todo el día Alfonso? ¿Visitó a sus amigos?   4. ¿Asistieron a un partido de béisbol Elena y Alfonso? ¿Se divirtieron ellos?   5. ¿Quiénes jugaron bien?   6. ¿Ganó dinero Alfonso? ¿y Elena?   7. ¿A qué hora se despertó Alfonso? ¿Cuántas horas durmió él?

A. In the preterit, stem-changing is limited to **-ir** verbs. No **-ar** or **-er** verb changes its stem vowel in the preterit.

Infinitive		Present	Preterit
pensar (ie)		piensa	pensó
encontrar (ue)	usted	encuentra	encontró
perder (ie)		pierde	perdió
volver (ue)		vuelve	volvió

Tu equipo ganó ayer, ¿no? Sí, ¡por fin!	*Your team won yesterday, right? Yes, finally!*
La tenista encontró la raqueta en la cancha, cerca de la red.	*The tennis player found the racket in the court, close to the net.*
Ayer perdí el partido y hoy llegué tarde a la carrera de autos.	*Yesterday I lost the match, and today I arrived late at the car race.*

B. All **-ir** verbs that change their stem vowels in the present tense also show a stem-vowel change in the preterit in the third person singular and plural.

1. All **-ir** verbs showing the change **e → ie** or **e → i** in the present show the change **e → i** the third person singular and plural of the preterit.

sentir (ie, i)   **pedir (i, i)**

sentí	sentimos	pedí	pedimos
sentiste	sentisteis	pediste	pedisteis
sintió	**sint**ieron	**pid**ió	**pid**ieron

Other **(ie, i)** verbs like **sentir** include **divertir(se), mentir,** and **preferir**. Other **(i, i)** verbs like **pedir** include **repetir, seguir, servir,** and **vestir(se).**

Alfredo no te mintió. Él siguió cinco cursos el semestre pasado.	*Alfredo didn't lie to you. He took five courses last semester.*

2. Two **-ir** verbs showing the change **o → ue** in the present show the change **o → u** in the third person singular and plural of the preterit.

dormir (ue, u)

dormí	dormimos
dormiste	dormisteis
durmió	**durm**ieron

Morir(se) (to die) is conjugated like **dormir.** No other verbs have this change.

El año pasado murieron tres toreros en las corridas de toros. ¡Qué barbaridad!	*Last year three bullfighters died in the bullfights. How terrible!*
¿Así que dormiste en el estadio? ¡Qué increíble!	*So you slept at the stadium? How amazing!*

EJERCICIOS

A. Imaginación y lógica. Combine elements from all three columns to form logical affirmative or negative sentences using the preterit. Use each subject twice.

MODELOS **Mi amiga no pidió una raqueta de tenis.**

Mi amiga buscó a un jugador del equipo.

		antes de las diez
ese atleta		una raqueta de tenis
tú	pedir	a Raúl en el estadio
nosotros	asistir	café negro
yo	dormir	a un partido fascinante
mi amiga	volver	después del concierto
tú y Luis	encontrar	diez horas anoche
		a una corrida de toros

B. ¿Otra vez? ¡No lo puedo creer! Mrs. Fernández is talking to her son Nicolás. Respond as Nicolás would, saying that the same things happened yesterday.

MODELO Hoy sirves la comida.
¡Pero ayer serví la comida también!

1. Hoy corro por el parque.
2. Hoy vistes a Carlitos.
3. Hoy te acuestas temprano.
4. Hoy tu papá juega al fútbol.
5. Hoy escribo cartas.
6. Hoy tú y Raúl sirven la cena.
7. Hoy tu papá vuelve tarde.
8. Hoy Carlitos se despierta a las diez.
9. Hoy Carlitos duerme contigo.
10. Hoy empiezas tus lecciones antes de la cena.

C. Unas charlas. Supply the correct preterit forms of the verbs indicated in parentheses.

MARTÍN ¿Ya (1) _____ (**vestirse**) a los niños?
BÁRBARA Sí, y ya (2) _____ (**salir**) a jugar con sus amigos.
MARTÍN ¿(3) _____ (**dormir**) bien Conchita?
BÁRBARA Sí, ella y Pablito (4) _____ (**dormir**) unas diez horas anoche.
MARTÍN ¡Qué bien! Creo que ellos (5) _____ (**divertirse**) mucho en casa de los Pérez ayer.

JORGE ¿Dónde (6) _____ (sentarse) tú en el partido anoche?
MIGUEL (7) _____ (sentarse) detrás del equipo Cosmos.
JORGE ¿(8) _____ (seguir) bien el juego?
MIGUEL Sí, lo (9) _____ (entender), pero (10) _____ (dormirse) después de media hora.

D. El sábado pasado. Look at the pictures and describe what the people did last Saturday. Use your imagination. (Several infinitives are listed by each picture to give you ideas.) Give at least two sentences for each picture.

MODELO

Roberto: preferir, jugar, dormir

El sábado pasado Roberto no salió con sus amigos. Él prefirió quedarse en casa y mirar un partido de fútbol por televisión. Según él, los dos equipos jugaron muy bien. Después del partido, él se acostó y durmió unas ocho horas.

1.

El señor Díaz: llamar, hablar, pedir un sandwich, preferir

2.
yo, «los aztecas», «los conquistadores»: asistir, jugar, perder, ganar

3.

Ramón y Ana Luisa: bailar hablar, divertirse, sentirse muy feliz (felices)

4.

Juan, Jaime: despertarse, jugar, correr mucho, acostarse

5.

Susana, Jesús, el violinista: asistir, vestirse, escuchar música, tocar, volver

Preguntas

1. ¿A qué hora se despertó usted esta mañana? 2. ¿Le sirvió el desayuno su mamá? 3. ¿Se vistió usted antes o después de desayunar? 4. ¿A qué hora salió de casa? 5. ¿Se divirtió usted anoche? ¿Cómo se divirtió? 6. ¿A qué hora se acostó anoche? 7. ¿Y durmió bien?

II. El préterito de verbos irregulares

Pedro Guerrero, super-estrella de los *Cardinals* de St. Louis

Una conversación telefónica entre dos amigos cubano-americanos en Los Ángeles

RODOLFO   *Fui* a tu casa el viernes de noche, pero como° no vi luz° en tu ventana volví a casa. ¿Qué *hiciste* esa noche?

JULIO   *Fui* al partido de béisbol. Lolita me *dio* las entradas... Ella y su esposo no *pudieron* ir.

RODOLFO   ¡Qué lástima!° Y el partido ... , ¿*estuvo* bueno?

JULIO   Pedro Guerrero, la super-estrella° de los *Cardinals, hizo* tres carreras°.

RODOLFO   ¡Qué increíble!° ¡Pero *dijeron* en la radio que los *Cardinals* perdieron... !

JULIO   Sí, *tuvieron* mala suerte en la última entrada°. El lanzador° de los *Dodgers* cogió° una pelota casi imposible. Los *Cardinals* perdieron pero ¡*fue* un partido muy emocionante°!

---

como *since*   luz *light*   ¡Qué lástima! *What a shame!*   la super-estrella *superstar* hizo tres carreras *scored three runs*   entrada *inning*   lanzador *pitcher* cogió *caught*   emocionante *exciting*

---

1. ¿Cuándo fue Rodolfo a casa de Julio? ¿Por qué no lo encontró?   2. ¿Quién le dio las entradas a Julio? ¿Por qué?   3. Según Julio, ¿fue aburrido o emocionante el partido? ¿Por qué?   4. ¿Por qué perdieron los Dodgers?

A. Several important verbs in Spanish are irregular in the preterit, in both their stems and endings. These forms do not have written accents.

Infinitive	Preterit Stem	Preterit Endings
hacer	hic-	
querer	quis-	
venir	vin-	-e
		-iste
poder	pud-	-o
poner	pus-	-imos
saber	sup-	-isteis
		-ieron
andar	anduv-	
estar	estuv-	
tener	tuv-	

The endings in the chart are attached to the stems shown. **Hacer** is the only verb with a spelling change; the third-person singular form, **hizo,** must be written with a **z,** not a **c,** to avoid suggesting that the sound of the stem changes. **Haber,** which has the form **hay** in the present, in the preterit has the form **hubo** *(there was, there were).*

Paco hizo una carrera. ¡Cuánto me alegro!	*Paco made a run. How happy I am!*
Gracias a Dios pudimos hablar con los jugadores. ¡Qué alivio!	*Thank goodness we were able to speak to the players. What a relief!*
¿Hubo un accidente aquí? Sí, tuve un pequeño accidente.	*Was there an accident here? Yes, I had a little accident.*
¿Estuviste en el estadio anoche? ¡Qué partido emocionante!, ¿no?	*Were you in the stadium last night? What an exciting game!, right?*
Los aficionados vinieron temprano.	*The fans came early.*

B. Decir and **traer** are also irregular in the preterit, but note that the third-person plural ending after **j** is **-eron,** not **-ieron.**

decir		traer	
dije	dijimos	traje	trajimos
dijiste	dijisteis	trajiste	trajisteis
dijo	di**jeron**	trajo	tra**jeron**

Dijeron que también lo vieron anoche en el bar. ¡Eso es demasiado!	*They said they also saw him last night in the bar. That's too much!*

Ana me trajo una raqueta y tres pelotas nuevas. ¡Qué amable!	*Ana brought me a racket and three new balls. How nice!*

Verbs ending in **-ducir** change **c** to **j** in the preterit, with the **-eron** ending in the third person plural.

conducir to drive

conduje	condujimos
condujiste	condujisteis
condujo	condujeron

Other verbs like **conducir** include **traducir** and **producir.**

¿Y condujiste su coche nuevo sin su permiso? ¡Eso es el colmo!	*And you drove his new car without his permission? That's the last straw!*
Colombia produjo y exportó mucho café el año pasado.	*Colombia produced and exported a lot of coffee last year.*
Un poeta cubano-americano tradujo esos poemas.	*A Cuban-American poet translated those poems.*

C. **Ir** and **ser** have the same forms in the preterit.

ir, ser

fui	fuimos
fuiste	fuisteis
fue	fueron

Fuimos a la piscina a nadar.	*We went to the swimming pool to swim.*
Roberto Clemente fue un gran deportista. Murió en 1972.	*Roberto Clemente was a great athlete. He died in 1972.*

D. **Dar,** an irregular **-ar** verb, requires the **-er, -ir** preterit endings, though without accent marks.

dar

di	dimos
diste	disteis
dio	dieron

Creo que te di el dinero para los esquís, ¿no?	*I believe I gave you the money for the skis, right?*

EJERCICIOS

A. Imaginación y lógica. Using elements from all three columns, form affirmative or negative sentences in the preterit. Use each subject twice.

MODELOS **Mi hermana no quiso jugar al tenis hoy.**

Mi hermana tuvo la oportunidad de asistir a ese partido.

		a nadar, ¿verdad?
usted	querer	en el estadio anoche
nosotros	venir	jugar al tenis hoy
tú y Anita	estar	que correr mucho ayer
yo	poner	las raquetas en el auto
tú	tener	el auto en el garage, ¿no?
mi hermana	ir	con ellos el lunes pasado
		la oportunidad de asistir a ese partido

B. Para escoger y completar. Fill in each blank with the appropriate preterit form of one of the verbs suggested in parentheses. (One verb may fill two blanks in a sentence.)

1. (decir, dar) Carmen me _____ las entradas, y yo se las _____ a mi hermano.
2. (tener que, traer) Martina no _____ la raqueta. El Club Universo _____ prestarle una raqueta nueva.
3. (ser, ir) Anoche Santiago y yo _____ a nadar en la piscina de los Martínez y ustedes _____ al cine, ¿verdad?
4. (conducir, hacer) ¿Quién _____ el auto de Rita? Primero _____ yo y después Rafael.
5. (morir, haber) _____ una tragedia en el barrio anoche. _____ seis personas.
6. (hacer, poder) Nuestro equipo _____ tres carreras pero el otro equipo _____ cinco.

C. ¿Qué hicieron? Complete the sentences with appropriate information. Use verbs in the preterit.

MODELO Anoche mis amigos...
Anoche mis amigos vinieron a cenar a casa y nos divertimos mucho.

1. La semana pasada, el presidente...
2. El año pasado, mi familia y yo...
3. Anoche, mi hermano...
4. Esta mañana, llegué a clase y después...
5. El domingo pasado, mis padres...
6. En 1492, Cristóbal Colón...
7. En 1963, John F. Kennedy...
8. En 1969, los astronautas norteamericanos...

D. La invención. Create statements or questions of your own using the cue words given and verbs in the preterit.

> **MODELOS** pescar ayer
> **Abuelo y yo fuimos a pescar ayer.**
> **¿Por qué no me llevaste contigo a pescar ayer?**

1. tenis el miércoles pasado
2. tres tazas de café esta mañana
3. bailar el sábado pasado
4. partido de fútbol la semana pasada
5. a las seis de la mañana
6. ver una película fascinante
7. un amigo en el partido de béisbol
8. por teléfono ayer

E. ¿Qué voy a escribir en mi diario? Every night you write down the day's events in your journal. Write ten events that happened in your life yesterday.

> **MODELO** **Hoy Marina y yo caminamos mucho. Pasamos toda la tarde en el centro. Primero comimos en un restaurante. Luego, ella me llevó a...**

Entrevista

Interview a classmate, using the following questions and others you may wish to add.

1. ¿Cuál fue el último partido de fútbol (tenis, béisbol) que viste?
2. ¿Adónde fuiste ayer? 3. ¿Qué hiciste durante el fin de semana?
4. ¿Tuviste que estudiar para un examen la semana pasada? 5. ¿Qué trajiste a clase hoy? 6. ¿Dónde pusiste tus cosas—libros, cuadernos, lápices, dinero—cuando te sentaste? 7. ¿Viniste a clase temprano hoy? ¿y ayer? 8. ¿A qué hora llegaste a tu primera clase hoy? ¿y ayer? 9. ¿Te acostaste muy tarde anoche? ¿a qué hora? ¿Y a qué hora te despertaste esta mañana? 10. ¿Miraste televisión anoche? ¿Viste un programa interesante? ¿Qué programa...?

III. Connotaciones especiales del pretérito de *saber, conocer, querer y poder*

Roberto Cabañas (el número 19) de los *Cosmos*

En el estadio de fútbol de Tampa, Florida

MARIO   ¡Qué sorpresa° encontrarte aquí, Jaime...! ¿Qué tal, Susana?

SUSANA   Bien...y veo que ustedes ya se conocen. ¿Cuándo *se conocieron*°...?

JAIME   *Nos conocimos*° en 1986, en la Universidad de Florida. Allí los dos jugamos en el mismo° equipo de fútbol.

SUSANA   ¡Ah, qué interesante! Y hablando de fútbol, ¿oyeron la buena noticia°...? *Supe*° esta mañana que Cabañas* no juega hoy.

JAIME   ¿Por qué no?

SUSANA   No sé...*No pude* enterarme° de los detalles. Me dijo Carlos que Cabañas tiene un problema y *no quiso*° venir a Tampa.

MARIO   Pues, sin él los jugadores del Cosmos *pudieron* vencer° al equipo de Montreal la semana pasada, así que ¡todavía es° muy temprano para cantar victoria°!

¡Qué sorpresa...! *What a surprise...!*   se conocieron *did you meet (each other)*   Nos conocimos *We met*   mismo *same*   noticia *news*   Supe *I found out*   No pude enterarme *I couldn't find out*   no quiso *refused*   pudieron vencer *were able to defeat (succeeded in defeating)*   todavía es *it is still*   cantar victoria *to celebrate (literally, "to sing victory")*

---

1. ¿Cuándo y dónde se conocieron Jaime y Mario? ¿Cómo se conocieron ellos?
2. ¿Qué supo Susana del equipo Cosmos? ¿Pudo enterarse de los detalles?
3. ¿Qué le dijo Carlos a Susana?   4. Según usted, ¿cree Mario que los jugadores del Cosmos pueden vencer al equipo de Tampa sin Cabañas? Comente su respuesta.

The following verbs have special English translations in the preterit: **saber** and **conocer** *(to know)*, **querer** *(to want, wish)*, and **poder** *(to be able, can)*.

Preterit of:	English translation
saber	*to find out*
conocer	*to meet, to make the acquaintance of*
querer *(affirmative)*	*to try to*
querer *(negative)*	*to refuse*
poder *(affirmative)*	*to be able to, to manage to*
poder *(negative)*	*to try, but fail to*

Ellos conocieron a María en la fiesta.	*They met María (for the first time) at the party.*
Recientemente supimos que ganó tu equipo.	*Recently we found out (learned) that your team won.*

---

*Roberto Cabañas, Paraguayan star forward of the New York Cosmos

Marta no quiso casarse.	*Marta refused to get married.*
Quise ir al partido pero no pude.	*I tried to go to the game but could not.*
Juan no pudo encontrar su raqueta.	*Juan could not (tried but failed to) find his racket.*
La semana pasada ella pudo nadar una milla sin parar.	*Last week she was able to (managed to) swim a mile without stopping.*

EJERCICIOS

A. Preguntas y respuestas.   Working with a classmate, create new questions and answers as suggested by the cues.

1. ¿Cuándo supieron (ustedes) la noticia? La supimos ayer. (tú, Oscar, Carmen y Jaime, Salvador y yo)
2. ¿Dónde conociste (tú) a Santiago? Lo conocí en la universidad Cornell. (nosotros, Priscilla y Bartolo, Catalina, yo)
3. ¿Qué no quiso hacer Ana? No quiso ir a ese restaurante. (Julia y yo, Walter y Eric, Howard, tú)
4. ¿Qué no pudo entender Jorge? No pudo entender la conferencia. (Pedro y yo, Juan y Eva, ustedes, Teresa)

B. Traducción.   Give the Spanish equivalent of the following sentences.

1. Raúl tried to skate, but couldn't.
2. Last week we learned about your trip to Florida.
3. She refused to play tennis with him.
4. Marisa and I met at a soccer game.

C. La invención.   Create questions to which the following sentences would be logical answers. Use question words (**qué, dónde, cuándo,** etc.) and the preterit.

MODELOS   En el aeropuerto.
   ¿Dónde estuvieron ayer?

   ¿Dónde se conocieron ustedes?

1. En septiembre de 1986.
2. El verano pasado.
3. En Miami.
4. Café negro.
5. A un partido de béisbol.
6. En un partido de tenis.
7. Porque llovió mucho.
8. Diez dólares.

Preguntas

1. ¿Cuándo conoció usted a su profesor(a) de español? 2. ¿Hubo examen en esta clase la semana pasada? ¿en su clase de matemáticas (física, filosofía, literatura, historia...)? 3. ¿Cuándo supo usted la nota *(grade)* de su último examen? ¿Cómo le fue? 4. ¿Practica usted deportes? ¿Qué deportes? 5. ¿Es usted aficionado al béisbol (básquetbol, fútbol, fútbol americano, vólibol, tenis)? 6. ¿Cuál es su equipo favorito? ¿Ganó su equipo recientemente? ¿Perdió...? 7. ¿Qué hizo usted cuando supo que su equipo ganó (perdió)? 8. En general, ¿qué hace usted cuando está muy contento(-a)? ¿y cuando está muy triste...?

Study Hint: Using a Bilingual Dictionary

A bilingual dictionary can be a tremendous aid to students studying a second language. Used incorrectly, however, it can cause frustration and misunderstandings. Here are some guidelines for using a Spanish/English—English/Spanish dictionary.

1. Familiarize yourself with the format and parts of your dictionary. Pay close attention to the lists of abbreviations and symbols. Understanding your dictionary's format will enable you to select Spanish words more accurately.

2. After you look up a Spanish equivalent for an English word, double-check your choice by looking up the Spanish word in the other half of the dictionary and read its definition in English. You may find the word you chose is not an equivalent at all in the context for which you need it.

3. Remember that Spanish verbs are listed in the infinitive form. You will need to conjugate them properly to fit in your sentence.

4. Adjectives are given in the masculine singular form. Be sure to make them agree in gender and number with the nouns they modify.

5. Think about how the word you are looking up is to be used in the sentence. What part of speech is required? In English, a single word often serves as two different parts of speech—the word *swimming,* for example, may be a noun (the sport) or a verbal form (the present participle of *to swim*). To pick the right equivalent, you have to know how the word will be used.

6. Many English words and phrases do not have exact word-for-word translations in Spanish. Slang and familiar expressions are especially difficult to translate from one language to another. It is usually better to paraphrase the idea of the expression than to give a literal equivalent for each of its words.

7. A final word of caution: don't reach for the dictionary automatically. If you are stumped by a word in a reading passage, try to guess its meaning from the context. If you are writing a composition, try to paraphrase the idea you want to express using words you're already familiar with . . . And good luck with your dictionary!

DESPUÉS DE LA CARRERA

¡El campeón!...Alberto Salazar

En la línea de llegada° del Maratón de Boston, el periodista° Reynaldo Díaz habla con el ganador°, Alberto Salazar[1].

DÍAZ   ¡Felicitaciones, Alberto! Corriste como campeón°.

ALBERTO   Es que practiqué mucho para esta carrera...Pero, ¡qué sorpresa verte aquí, Reynaldo! ¿Cuándo volviste de California...?

DÍAZ   Anoche...¡y sólo regresé para poder verte ganar hoy! Ahora dime—porque estoy aquí como periodista—¿a qué edad° empezaste a correr en los grandes maratones?

ALBERTO   Pues, el primer maratón que gané fue en Nueva York, en 1980. Después volví a ganarlo° en 1981.

DÍAZ   ¡Qué bien! Me dijeron que te encanta pescar, que lees mucho y que te gusta estar solo°. ¿Es verdad todo eso...?

ALBERTO   Sí... El mes pasado lo pasé solo. Fui al campo para prepararme para el maratón. Pesqué, leí y corrí varias millas° por día. Pero también descansé y pensé mucho. Ah!, aquí llega mi esposa, Reynaldo...

Alberto y Molly se abrazan°.

ALBERTO ¿Pudiste ver toda la carrera?

MOLLY Sí..., y ¡cuánto me alegro, Alberto! Estuve un poco nerviosa al final, cuando se cayó° el hombre que estaba° detrás de ti. Pero gracias a Dios no se lastimó°. Fui a verlo. No quiso hablar conmigo...

ALBERTO Es que probablemente fue muy difícil para él. La verdad es que corrió muy bien. Creo que yo gané sólo porque tengo más experiencia que él°. Ahora voy a ver si me quiere hablar a mí...

ALBERTO Nando, corriste muy bien.

FERNANDO Sí, tienes razón. Corrí muy bien pero me caí...y por eso perdí la carrera.

ALBERTO Pues, esta vez llegaste en segundo lugar. ¿No vas a correr en Nueva York?

FERNANDO Claro, y ese maratón, ¡lo voy a ganar yo!

---

línea de llegada *finish line*	periodista *journalist*	ganador *winner*	como
campeón *like a champion*	edad *age*	volví a ganarlo *I won it again*	solo *alone*
millas *miles*	se abrazan *embrace each other*	se cayó *fell down*	estaba *was*	no
se lastimó *didn't hurt himself*	más...él *more experience than he does*		

PREGUNTAS

1. ¿Quién ganó el maratón? Según el periodista, ¿cómo corrió él?   2. En este diálogo, ¿dice Alberto a qué edad empezó él a correr en los grandes maratones? ¿Cómo contesta él la pregunta del periodista?   3. ¿Qué dijo Alberto del Maratón de Nueva York?   4. ¿Qué le dijeron a Díaz sobre los pasatiempos de Alberto? ¿Le dieron buena información? ¿Cómo sabemos eso?   5. ¿Cómo se preparó Alberto para ese maratón?   6. ¿Qué le pasó al corredor que llegó en segundo lugar? 7. Según Fernando, ¿por qué perdió la carrera? Y según él, ¿qué va a pasar en el Maratón de Nueva York?   8. ¿Corrió usted en el Maratón de Boston el año pasado? ¿y en el de Nueva York? ¿Piensa correr en el futuro? ¿Cuándo? ¿Dónde?

NOTA CULTURAL

1. Alberto Salazar, Cuban-born runner who now lives in the United States, was the winner of the New York Marathon in 1980, 1981, and 1982 and of numerous other races.

Funciones y *actividades*

In this chapter, you have seen examples of several important language functions, or uses. Here is a summary and some additional information about these functions of language.

EXPRESSING RELIEF

¡Qué bien!	*Good! (How nice!)*
¡Qué alivio!	*What a relief!*
¡Cuánto me alegro!	*How happy I am!*
¡Qué alegría!	*How wonderful (literally, "What happiness!")*
¡Por fin!	*Finally! (when something good has finally happened)*
Gracias a Dios.	*Thank God. (Thank goodness.)*

EXPRESSING SURPRISE

¡Qué sorpresa!	*What a surprise!*
¡Qué lindo (amable, etcétera)!	*How pretty (kind, etc.)!*
¡Qué increíble!	*How amazing!*

EXPRESSING ANGER

¡Esto (Eso) es el colmo!	*This (That) is the last straw!*
¡Esto (Eso) es demasiado!	*This (That) is too much!*
¡Qué barbaridad!	*Good grief! (How terrible! How absurd!)*

Now do the following activities, using the expressions you have just learned.

A. ¿Qué se dice?   Give an appropriate expression that you could use in each of the following situations.

> **MODELO**   El equipo de béisbol de su universidad perdió todos los partidos que jugó este año.
>   **¡Qué barbaridad!**

1. Supo que su padre tuvo un accidente de auto, pero por suerte ya salió del hospital y está bien.
2. Recibió una A en un examen para el que (*for which*) usted sólo estudió diez minutos.
3. Recibió una F en un examen para el que usted estudió todo el fin de semana.
4. La semana pasada un compañero de clase le pidió un favor. Usted prometió (*promised*) hacérselo ese mismo día pero olvidó... Ayer volvió a ver a su compañero.

5. Fue con un(a) amigo(-a) a cenar a un restaurante; pidieron bistec y vino. Les trajeron un bistec delicioso y un buen vino francés. La cena estuvo excelente pero no supieron el precio hasta que llegó la cuenta... (¿El precio total de la cena...? ¡Cincuenta dólares!)

6. Su mamá lo (la) llamó para contarle que va a visitarlo(la) este fin de semana.

7. Jugó al tenis con la raqueta de su compañero(-a) de cuarto y la perdió. No recuerda dónde la dejó... Su compañero(-a) está muy enojado(-a).

8. Recibió una carta de sus abuelos con un pasaje de avión y dos boletos para asistir al próximo campeonato mundial (*world championship*) de fútbol.

B. Mini-drama. You meet a visitor from a Hispanic country who has just arrived here. The visitor asks you questions about sports that are popular in this country. Perhaps he or she does not know how to play a particular sport, so you attempt to explain the rules. Finally, you and the visitor arrange a time to play the sport. You tell him or her what to wear, what to bring, and where to meet you.

VOCABULARIO ACTIVO

Cognados

el accidente	el detalle	el golf	la raqueta
el básquetbol	el espectador, la espectadora	el jai alai	el vólibol
el béisbol	el esquí	el maratón	
cubano-americano	fascinante	practicar	

Verbos

conducir (zc, j)	to drive
enterarse (de)	to find out (about)
morir(se)(ue, u)	to die
patinar	to skate
producir (zc, j)	to produce
vencer (z)	to defeat

Deportes y deportistas   Sports and athletes

el aficionado, la aficionada	fan, enthusiast
el campeón, la campeona	champion
la cancha	court; (sport) field (e.g., cancha de fútbol)
la corrida de toros	bullfight
el equipo	team
el esquiador, la esquiadora	skier
el fútbol	soccer
el fútbol americano	football
el, la futbolista	football player
el jugador, la jugadora	player
el nadador, la nadadora	swimmer
la natación	swimming
el partido	match, game
el patinaje	skating
la pesca	fishing
la piscina	swimming pool
la pista	track
la red	net
el torero	bullfighter
el toro	bull

Otras palabras y frases

así que	so
casi	almost
divertido	amusing, funny
emocionante	exciting

la luz	light
la milla	mile
la noticia	(piece of) news
por fin	finally
recientemente	recently

Expresiones útiles

¡Cuánto me alegro!	How happy I am!
¡Eso es demasiado!	That is too much!
Gracias a Dios	Thank God. (Thank goodness.)
¡Qué alegría!	How wonderful!
¡Qué alivio!	What a relief!
¡Qué amable!	How nice!
¡Qué barbaridad!	How terrible! (Good grief! How absurd!)
¡Qué bien!	Good! (How nice!)
¡Qué increíble!	How amazing!
¡Qué sorpresa!	What a surprise!

Españoles en bicicleta por las montañas cantábricas de la costa norte de su país.

LA SALUD Y EL CUERPO

Funciones

- Expressing disbelief
- Making comparisons

Vocabulario.   In this chapter you will learn to name the parts of the body and to express various states of health and sickness.

Gramática.   You will discuss and use:

1. Comparisons of equality
2. Comparisons of inequality and the superlative
3. Expressions of obligation
4. Common uses of **por** and **para**

Cultura.   The dialogues take place in Northern Spain.

EL CUERPO HUMANO

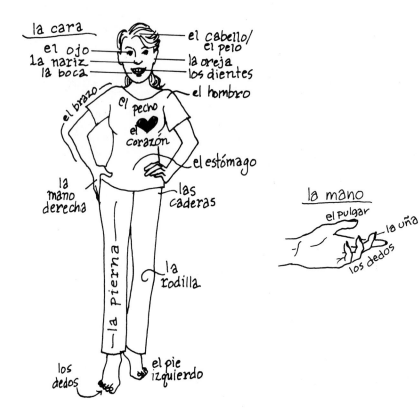

la cara
el ojo
la nariz
la boca
el cabello/ el pelo
la oreja
los dientes
el hombro
el brazo
el pecho
el corazón
el estómago
la mano derecha
las caderas
la pierna
la rodilla
los dedos
el pie izquierdo

la mano
el pulgar
la uña
los dedos

¿QUÉ TENGO, DOCTOR? LOS SÍNTOMAS

Me duele todo el cuerpo, desde la cabeza hasta los pies.

Me duele la espalda. No puedo moverme bien.

Tengo dolor de garganta.

Y también tengo dolor de estómago.

Tengo tos.

Tengo fiebre.

Tengo mareos.

EL DIAGNÓSTICO

Está resfriado(a), nada más.
Tiene resfrío (catarro).
Tiene una buena gripe
(influenza).

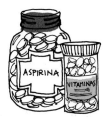

una pastilla,
una píldora

unas cápsulas

la receta
la farmacia
la medicina

una inyección

el termómetro

el laboratorio

¡**Vamos a dibujar!** (*Let's draw!*)   Your instructor will draw a part of a person's body on the blackboard and then hand the chalk to someone else, saying **Dibuje el (la, los, las)**..., por favor. The person chosen will draw what is asked for, and then hand the chalk to someone else, giving a similar command. Continue until the entire body has been drawn. Some body parts you will want to include are:

el brazo (derecho, izquierdo)	el pecho
los ojos	el pelo
las piernas	las manos
los dos pies	la nariz
el corazón	las orejas
la cabeza	la boca

Now add clothing to the figure in the same way. For a man, include: **la camisa, los pantalones, los zapatos.** For a woman, include: **la blusa, la falda, los zapatos.**

Desde la cabeza hasta los pies.   Complete the sentences with the appropriate word from the list in parentheses.

1. Cuando tengo una pregunta, levanto (*I raise*) (los pies, el cuello, los dientes, la mano).
2. Ella tomó mucho vino. Tiene dolor de (espalda, cabeza, hombro, pulgar).
3. Mi amiga lleva a su bebé en (el pelo, la cara, la espalda, el dedo).
4. Cuando estoy resfriado, el médico me pone (una inyección, una cadera, una rodilla).
5. Una aspirina es (una pastilla, un síntoma, una vitamina).
6. Para tener buena salud, tomo (termómetros, vino, catarros, vitaminas).
7. Cuando tenemos tos, nos duele (el brazo, la garganta, el pie izquierdo, la rodilla derecha).
8. Para ver, usamos (el cuello, el pulgar, el estómago, los ojos).

Preguntas

1. ¿Qué parte del cuerpo usamos para hablar? ¿para pensar? ¿para comer? ¿para caminar? ¿para escribir?   2. ¿Hace usted ejercicios físicos? ¿Nada? ¿Anda en bicicleta (*ride a bike*)? ¿Corre? ¿Cuándo? ¿por la mañana? ¿por la tarde?   3. ¿Qué parte del cuerpo usa usted para andar en bicicleta? ¿para nadar? ¿para correr? ¿para jugar al golf?   4. ¿Toma usted vitaminas todos los días? ¿Cuándo tiene usted más energía: por la noche o por la mañana? ¿el sábado por la noche o el lunes por la mañana?   5. En general, ¿le duele la cabeza cuando toma un examen? ¿cuando baila en una discoteca? ¿cuando se levanta los domingos por la mañana? ¿cuando estudia en la biblioteca?   6. ¿Cuándo toma usted aspirinas? ¿y un jarabe para la tos?   7. ¿Qué usamos para saber si tenemos fiebre o no?   8. ¿Qué síntomas tiene una persona que está resfriada? ¿y una persona que tiene gripe?

I. Comparaciones de igualdad

Ávila, antigua
ciudad del norte
de España

Una pareja° venezolana de edad mediana° visita la ciudad de Ávila.

MIGUEL   ¡Esto es increíble!° ¡Hay *tantas*° iglesias aquí en Ávila! ¿Cómo
            sobreviven° después de *tantos* años?

SOLEDAD   Es porque los españoles hacen mucho para conservar° sus edificios
            y monumentos antiguos°. El gobierno° los protege° y es difícil
            destruirlos° sin sufrir castigos severos°...

MIGUEL   ¿De veras?° Y esa muralla°, ¿es *tan* antigua *como* el resto de la
            ciudad? ¿Cuándo la construyeron°?

SOLEDAD   A ver...No me acuerdo. Es que estoy resfriada y me duele la cabeza.

MIGUEL   Pues...necesitas descansar para curarte° pronto. Vamos al hotel.
            ¡Parece que nosotros no nos conservamos *tan* bien *como*° los
            edificios y monumentos españoles!

---

pareja *couple*   **de edad mediana** *middle-aged*   **¡Esto es increíble!** *This is incredible!*
tantas *so many*   **sobreviven** *survive, last*   **conservar** *preserve*   **antiguo** *old*   **El
gobierno** *The government*   **protege** *protects*   **destruir** *to destroy*   **sufrir castigos
severos** *undergoing stiff penalties*   **¿De veras?** *Really?*   **muralla** *wall, fortification*
construyeron *build*   **curarte** *to get well*   **tan bien como** *as well as*

---

1. ¿Cómo sobreviven tantas iglesias en Ávila?   2. ¿Es fácil destruir un edificio
antiguo en España? ¿Por qué?   3. ¿Recuerda Soledad mucho de la historia española? ¿Por qué?   4. ¿Se conservan bien Soledad y Miguel?

A. Comparisons of equality are formed by using **tan** before an adverb or adjective and **como** following it.

Las playas de La Coruña no son tan bonitas como la playa de San Sebastián.

The beaches of La Coruña aren't as pretty as the beach of San Sebastián.

A Juan no le va tan bien como a Carlos.

Juan isn't doing as well as Carlos.

¡No puede ser! Él es tan inteligente como Carlos.

It can't be! He is as intelligent as Carlos.

Mi madre no se curó tan rápidamente como esperamos.

My mother wasn't cured as quickly as we had hoped.

B. **Tan** can also mean *so.*

¡La enfermera es tan simpática!

The nurse is so nice!

C. **Tanto(-a, -os, -as)** is used before a noun. **Tanto como** after a verb means *as much as.* **Tanto** by itself means *so much.*

Este año Jaime no tuvo tantas enfermedades como el año pasado.

This year Jaime didn't have as many illnesses as last year.

Yo no me enfermo tanto como mi hermana.

I don't get sick as much as my sister.

¡Ay, me duele tanto el brazo!

Oh, my arm hurts so much!

La inyección me dolió mucho.

The injection hurt a lot.

EJERCICIOS

A. Comparaciones.   Compare yourself to other people, following the model.

MODELO   Manuel estudia tanto como yo. (hablar)
Manuel habla tanto como yo.

1. Gloria come tanto como yo. (trabajar, enfermarse, hacer ejercicios, correr, dormir)
2. Rubén es tan inteligente como yo. (Luisa, tus amigos, esa chica, tú, Tito y Mercedes)
3. Alejandra tiene tanta ropa como yo. (novelas, cuentos, dinero, dolores, problemas)

B. ¡Se parecen tanto!   María y Marta are very much alike. Compare them, following the models.

MODELOS   inteligente   **Marta es tan inteligente como María.**

dinero   **María tiene tanto dinero como Marta.**

1. enfermarse
2. amigos
3. ropa
4. linda

5. trabajadora
6. estudiar
7. simpática

8. tener resfríos
9. delgada
10. problemas

C. Una charla.   Work with a classmate to complete the following conversation. Use the appropriate forms of **tan** or **tanto**.

TRINI   Lina, ¿qué te pasa? No tienes el pelo (1) _____ largo como antes. Y parece que no estás (2) _____ delgada como el mes pasado.

LINA   Tienes razón. ¡Como (3) _____ en estos días! No sé por qué. Esta mañana comí (4) _____ pasteles que el camarero me miró de una manera muy rara (strange).

TRINI   Me parece que no tienes (5) _____ tiempo libre como nuestras otras amigas. ¿Por qué tienes una vida (6) _____ diferente ahora? ¿Trabajas (7) _____ horas como tu esposo?

LINA   Es que tengo un trabajo nuevo y mi jefe es (8) _____ difícil como don Rafael. ¿Te acuerdas de mi antiguo jefe...? ¡Trabajo (9) _____ horas que...! Pues, tú comprendes, ¿no...?

D. ¿Cómo me comparo con mis parientes o con otra gente? (*How do I compare to my relatives or other people?*)   Form affirmative or negative sentences comparing yourself to your relatives and other people in terms of what you are like, what you have, and what you do. Follow the models.

MODELOS   alto(-a)
No soy tan alto(-a) como mis hermanos.

amigas
Tengo tantas amigas como mi hermana.

estudiar
No estudio tanto como José.

1. libros
2. dinero
3. bajo(-a)
4. correr
5. amable

6. trabajador(a)
7. hacer ejercicios físicos
8. divertirse
9. joven
10. dormir

Preguntas

1. ¿Viaja usted tanto como sus padres?   2. ¿Hace tan buen tiempo hoy como ayer?   3. ¿Comió usted tanto esta mañana como ayer?   4. ¿Es usted tan alto(-a) como su papá?   5. ¿Le gusta a usted el básquetbol tanto como el fútbol? 6. ¿Corre tan rápido como sus amigos?   7. ¿Tiene usted tantos hermanos como hermanas?   8. ¿Sabe usted tanto español como su profesor o profesora?

II. Comparaciones de desigualdad y el superlativo

El Paseo de
Espolón, Burgos

Caminando por una calle de Burgos

EDUARDO   ¿Sabes que tengo un pie *más* grande° *que* el otro?

ADELA   ¡Pero lo dices en broma!° ¡Los dos son *grandísimos!*

EDUARDO   No te burles de mí.° *No* tengo *más que*° un par° de zapatos.
Necesito comprar otro par.

ADELA   No lo puedo creer ...pero, si realmente lo necesitas, ve a esa
zapatería° de la Plaza Mayor. Es *la mejor*° zapatería *de* la ciudad.
Ahí consigues° *los mejores* zapatos y pagas *menos de*° 3.000 pesetas
por cada° par. Mi primo Pedro es el dueño°.

EDUARDO   ¡Imposible! No puede ser ...Imagínate, los últimos zapatos que
compré fueron *carísimos* y los compré allí. Pagué *más de*° 4.750
pesetas. Pero el insulto fue *peor que* el precio. El vendedor°—tu
primo Pedro—me dijo: «¿Señor, sabe que usted tiene los pies *más
grandes de* Burgos?»

ADELA   ¡Realmente! Mi *queridísimo*° primo Pedro insultando a sus clientes!
¡Esto es increíble!

---

más grande *larger*   **¡Pero lo dices en broma!** *You're joking!*   **¡No te burles de
mí!** *Don't kid me, make fun of me!*   **no...más que** *only*   **un par** *one pair*
zapatería *shoe store*   **la mejor** *the best*   **consigues** *you get*   **menos de** *less than*
cada *each*   **dueño** *owner*   **más de** *more than*   **el vendedor** *the salesman*
queridísimo *dearest*

---

1. ¿Tiene Eduardo los pies pequeños? ¿Cómo son?   2. ¿Necesita zapatos Eduardo?
3. Según Adela, ¿adónde debe ir Eduardo a comprar zapatos? ¿Por qué?
4. ¿Cuánto pagó Eduardo la última vez que compró zapatos? ¿Cuánto va a pagar en
la zapatería del primo de Adela?   5. ¿Qué le dijo el vendedor?

A. Comparisons of inequality are expressed with **más...que** or **menos...que.** *More than* is expressed as **más que** and *less than* is **menos que.**

Este medicamento es más caro que el otro.	*This medicine is more expensive than the other.*
Siempre tengo menos enfermedades que él.	*I always have fewer sicknesses than he does.*
María estuvo en cama más que yo.	*María was in bed more than I.*
Nosotros nos enfermamos menos que tú.	*We get sick less than you do.*

Before a number, **de** is used instead of **que** to mean *than.**

¡Que ridículo! Esperamos más de dos horas.	*How ridiculous! We waited more than two hours.*
Tengo menos de tres píldoras.	*I have fewer than three pills.*

B. The superlative forms of adjectives and adverbs (which express the most or the least of a certain quality) use the same forms as the comparative; a definite article is used before a superlative adjective when the noun is not given.

Ana es la doctora más famosa del hospital.	*Ana is the most famous doctor of the hospital.*
Esteban es el más (menos) fuerte del grupo.	*Esteban is the strongest (least strong) in the group.*

Notice that **de** is used after a superlative to express the equivalent of English *in* or *of,* as in the two examples above.

C. Some adjectives and adverbs have irregular comparative and superlative forms:

Adjective	Comparative	Superlative
bueno(-a) *good*	mejor *better*	el, la mejor *best*
malo(-a) *bad*	peor *worse*	el, la peor *worst*
pequeño(-a) *small*	menor *younger*	el, la menor *youngest*
	más pequeño(-a) *smaller*	el, la más pequeño(-a) *smallest*
grande *big*	mayor *older*	el, la mayor *oldest*
	más grande *bigger*	el, la más grande *biggest*

Adverb	Comparative	Superlative
bien *well*	mejor *better*	mejor *best*
mal *badly*	peor *worse*	peor *worst*

*In negative sentences, **que** sometimes appears before a number. Compare the following:
No tengo más de diez dólares. (I have ten or fewer dollars.)
No tengo más que diez dólares. (I only have ten dollars. I've got nothing but ten dollars—no train ticket, no watch, etc.)

The comparative adjectives **mejor, peor, menor,** and **mayor** have the same forms in the feminine as in the masculine; the plurals are formed by adding **-es.**

La doctora Jiménez es mejor que el doctor Ruiz.	Dr. Jiménez is better than Dr. Ruiz.
María está peor hoy que ayer.	María is worse today than yesterday.
Mis dos hermanos menores están enfermos.	My two younger brothers are sick.
¿Cómo se llama el chico que respondió mejor?	What is the name of the boy who answered the best?
¿Dónde están las mejores playas?	Where are the best beaches?

Note that **menor** and **mayor,** which usually follow the nouns they modify, are used with people to refer to age *(younger, older).* When referring to physical size, *bigger* is usually expressed by **más grande** and *smaller* is expressed by **más pequeño.**

Paco y Pancho son menores que Felipe, pero Felipe es más pequeño.	Paco and Pancho are younger than Felipe, but Felipe is smaller.
Adriana es mi hermana mayor; Silvia y Marta son mis hermanas menores.	Adriana is my older sister; Silvia and Marta are my younger sisters.

D. One way to express the exceptional quality of an adjective is to use **muy** with an adjective.

La casa es muy grande.	The house is very large.

A second way is to add **-ísimo (-ísima, -ísimos, -ísimas)** to the adjective. The **-ísimo** ending is the absolute superlative, much stronger than **muy** plus the adjective. If the adjective ends in a vowel, drop the final vowel before adding the **-ísimo** ending.

Sus ojos son lindísimos.	Her eyes are extremely pretty.
El laboratorio es modernísimo.	The lab is extremely modern.
Las noticias son malísimas.	The news is extremely bad.

The **-ísimo** ending can also be added to adverbs.

Luis llegó tardísimo.	Luis arrived extremely late.
Hoy comiste poquísimo.*	Today you ate extremely little.
¡Me duele muchísimo!	It hurts me a lot!

---

*The **c** of **poco** is changed to **qu** to show that the *k* sound of the stem does not change when **-ísimo** is added. Likewise, to maintain the hard sound of *g* a **u** is added: **largo → larguísimo.**

EJERCICIOS

A. Más comparaciones. Choose the appropriate word to complete the sentence.

MODELO Barcelona es (más, menos) famosa que Vigo.
Barcelona es más famosa que Vigo.

1. En Valladolid, hay (más de, más que) cinco museos.
2. Luis perdió quinientas pesetas. Mi amiga perdió mil. Luis perdió (menos de, menos que) mi amiga.
3. El fútbol es el deporte más popular (en, de) España.
4. El océano Pacífico es el océano (mayor, más grande) del mundo.
5. Hablo español bien, pero mi amiga que nació en Burgos habla (mayor, mejor).
6. Aquí hay dos regalos. El (mayor, más grande) costó poco pero el (menor, más pequeño) costó muchísimo.
7. Marisol tiene tres años; es mi hermana (menor, más pequeña).
8. La ciudad de León es más grande (de, que) Burgos.

B. Fidel habla sin rodeos. Fidel likes to tell it like it is. Take the role of Fidel and comment on the statements of his friend, Laura. Follow the model.

MODELO Estos zapatos son caros. **Son carísimos, hombre.**

1. Ese hospital es famoso.
2. *Don Quijote* es una novela importante.
3. Valladolid y León son ciudades lindas.
4. En España, la comida es deliciosa.
5. Este ejercicio es fácil.
6. Hay pocas enfermedades en Ávila.

C. Sí, pero... Complete the comparisons.

MODELOS **Santiago es grande, pero Barcelona es más grande.**

En España hay crimen, pero en los Estados Unidos hay más crimen.

1. Mi amigo canta bien, pero mi tío...
2. La clase de inglés es mala, pero la clase de química...
3. Los portugueses juegan al fútbol, pero los españoles...
4. Mi amigo de veinte años es joven, pero su hermano, de quince años...
5. Carla recibió muchas inyecciones después de enfermarse pero yo recibí...

D. Comparaciones.   Describe the following drawings. Use **tan, tanto(-a, -os, -as), más, menos, mayor, menor,** etc. in your descriptions.

MODELO

Joaquín es mayor que Jimena.
Jimena es menor que Joaquín.

1.

Fidel   Manuel

2.

Ana   Concha

3.

El padre   Roberto
de Roberto

4.

María   Gloria

5.

La casa de los Hernández

La casa de los Rodríguez

6.

Los Sánchez   Los García

E. Traducción.   Give the Spanish equivalent of the following sentences.

1. This is the most important city in Spain.
2. Tomás is a good student, but he is not the best.
3. She is the best nurse in the hospital.
4. Paco gets sick less than Pedro.
5. Adela is our youngest sister, but she is the tallest.
6. Madrid is bigger than Burgos.
7. The headache I have is extremely bad.
8. Her arm hurts very, very much!

Preguntas

1. ¿Tiene usted un(a) hermano(-a) mayor? ¿menor? ¿Hay un bebé en la familia?
2. ¿Es usted el (la) menor de su familia? ¿el (la) mayor? ¿el (la) más fuerte?
3. ¿Quién es el (la) menor de la clase? ¿el (la) mayor? ¿y el (la) más alto(-a)? ¿el (la) más bajo(-a)?   4. ¿Cuál es su mejor clase? ¿y su peor?   5. ¿Cuál es la novela

más interesante que usted conoce?   6. ¿Cuál es la ciudad más grande de España? ¿y de México? ¿y de los Estados Unidos?   7. ¿Es usted más o menos alto(-a) que su madre? ¿que su padre?   8. ¿Tiene usted menos dinero hoy que ayer? 9. ¿Quién es el mejor jugador de tenis del mundo? ¿y la mejor jugadora? ¿el mejor esquiador? ¿y la mejor esquiadora?   10. Para usted, ¿cuál es el peor día de la semana? ¿y el mejor?   11. ¿Tiene usted más de $10 hoy? ¿más de $20?

III. Expresiones de obligación

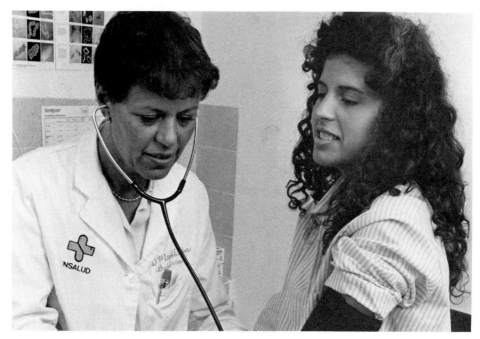

Una doctora española con una paciente

Dos hombres jóvenes hablan en Santander.

EDUARDO	¡Uf! Jugué al fútbol por tanto tiempo que ahora me duele mucho el hombro izquierdo.
RAÚL	¿De veras...? Entonces, *tienes que* ir al doctor ahora mismo.
EDUARDO	¡Pero no hablas en serio!°..No me gusta ir al médico y, además, no *hay que*° ver al doctor por un problema tan pequeño...
RAÚL	¿Cómo sabes que es un problema pequeño? Eso lo *debes* confirmar con un profesional como tu doctor...
EDUARDO	¡Qué va!° Creo que *debes* resolver tus propios° problemas y no los míos°, Raúl...
RAÚL	Bueno, si tú así piensas... Pero yo creo que como tu amigo *tengo que* darte consejos. Realmente pienso que *es necesario* ver al doctor cuando uno tiene problemas... aún° problemas pequeños...¡Para eso están los doctores!,° ¿no?

¡Pero no hablas en serio! *But you're not serious!*   no hay que *it's not necessary to*   ¡Qué va! *Come on!*   propios *own*   los míos *mine*   aún *even*   Para eso...doctores. *That's what doctors are for.*

---

1. ¿Qué le duele a Eduardo? ¿Por qué?   2. ¿Por qué no quiere ir al médico Eduardo?   3. Según Raúl, ¿qué es necesario hacer aún con problemas pequeños? 4. ¿Se enfada Eduardo con Raúl? ¿Qué le dice?   5. Según Raúl, ¿para qué están los amigos? ¿Y para qué están los doctores?

A. Spanish has both personal and impersonal expressions of obligation. **Tener que** + *infinitive* and **deber** + *infinitive* are personal; that is, they have an expressed subject, noun or pronoun, and show agreement. **Hay que** + *infinitive* and **es necesario (es preciso)** + *infinitive* are impersonal; that is, they have no expressed personal subject and do not show agreement.

¡No debiste comer tanto!	*You ought not to have eaten so much!*
Mañana yo tengo que descansar mucho.	*Tomorrow I have to rest a lot.*
Hay que ver al doctor para comprender los síntomas.	*It is necessary to see the doctor in order to understand the symptoms.*
Es necesario practicar el tenis mucho para ser campeón de tenis.	*It's necessary to practice tennis a lot in order to be a tennis champion.*

B. Tener que + *infinitive,* introduced in Chapter 3, is a common expression of necessity meaning *to have to* or *must.* It is a personal expression because it refers specifically to the person(s) who must carry out the action stated.

Tengo que cocinar mucho para la fiesta.	*I have to cook a lot for the party.*
Tuvimos que leer todo el periódico.	*We had to read the entire newspaper.*
Tuvieron que escuchar mis consejos.	*They had to listen to my advice.*

C. Deber + *infinitive* is another common personal expression of duty or obligation, but it does not convey as strong a sense of obligation as **tener que.**

Debo ir al (a la) dentista.	*I must (ought to) go to the dentist.*
Debes buscar empleo.	*You must (ought to) look for employment.*
No debieron hablar así.	*They shouldn't (ought not to) have talked like that.*

Deber de also indicates probability or likelihood.

Debe de ser lunes.	*It must be (probably is) Monday.*
Ellas deben de estar en León.	*They must be in León.*

D. **Hay que** plus infinitive and **es necesario** or **es preciso** + *infinitive* are impersonal expressions of obligation or necessity meaning *one has to, one must, it is necessary to.*

No hay que ir al laboratorio hoy. *It's not necessary to go to the laboratory today.*

Es preciso (necesario) saber nadar *It's necessary to know how to swim*
  si uno quiere dar un paseo en canoa. *if you want to take a canoe ride.*

EJERCICIOS

A. **Los exámenes finales.** Marisol is trying to prepare for her finals, but her little brother is driving her crazy with his questions. Answer for Marisol, using the expression **tener que.** Use object pronouns whenever possible.

> **MODELO** ¿Empezaste las tareas ayer?
> **No, tengo que empezarlas hoy.**

1. ¿Fuiste a la biblioteca ayer?
2. ¿Hiciste los ejercicios de español ayer?
3. ¿Estudiaste química ayer?
4. ¿Escribiste la composición ayer?
5. ¿Encontraste el libro de medicina ayer?
6. ¿Buscaste la receta ayer?

B. **¿Qué hay que hacer?** Play the role of Eduardo's doctor and answer Eduardo's questions using **hay que** + *infinitive.*

> **MODELO** EDUARDO ¿Es necesario comer muchas verduras?
> DOCTOR(A) **Sí, hay que comer muchas verduras.**

1. ¿Es necesario dormir ocho horas por día?
2. ¿Debo tomar jugo de naranja?
3. ¿No es preciso tomar vitamina C todos los días?
4. ¿Tengo que comer menos jamón?
5. ¿Es necesario caminar o nadar dos o tres veces por semana?
6. ¿Debo usar menos sal?

C. **Esta semana...** In pairs, take turns asking and answering questions in Spanish until you find out at least two things your partner thinks he or she should or must do this week. The obligations may be related to school, home, work, health, or family. Here are some ideas.

no tomar café	escribir una carta o una composición
hacer ejercicios	ir a la biblioteca
visitar a un(a) amigo(-a)	trabajar
o pariente en el hospital	tomar un examen
estudiar	ser cortés
leer la lección de español	

D. Traducción.   Give the Spanish equivalent of the following sentences.

1. I have a headache and I must take two aspirins.
2. Yesterday I had to finish three compositions.
3. You ought to eat less, but your mother cooks so well!
4. We have to get up at 6 A.M. tomorrow.
5. Does he have to complain about the medicines?
6. It's necessary to bring the prescription to the pharmacy.

Preguntas

1. ¿Cuándo deben asistir ustedes a clase? ¿mañana? ¿el sábado?   2. ¿Tiene que estudiar usted mucho esta noche?   3. ¿Qué tiene que hacer usted esta noche? ¿mañana? ¿este fin de semana?   4. ¿Qué lengua debemos hablar siempre en esta clase? ¿Practicamos también fuera de (*outside*) la clase?   5. ¿Es necesario tomar muchos líquidos con comida picante?   6. ¿Qué hay que hacer para tocar bien un instrumento musical?   7. ¿Es preciso estudiar mucho para tocar el violín o el piano?   8. ¿Tiene usted que traducir las frases al inglés para comprenderlas? 9. ¿Qué hay que hacer cuando uno tiene la gripe? ¿y cuando tiene tos?

IV. *Por y para*

Vista de Santiago
de Compostela

Manuel y Rosita hablan por teléfono.

MANUEL *¿Por qué* no viajamos a Santiago de Compostela* *por* avión°, Rosita?

ROSITA Es que yo prefiero ir en auto o en tren, Manuel.‡ Dicen que el viaje *por* las montañas° es estupendo, y, además, viajar *por* avión me da mareos°.

MANUEL Pero sólo vamos *por* una semana...tenemos que estar allí *para* el jueves°. ¿Recuerdas que Adolfo nos espera *para* la fiesta de Rosario?

ROSITA ¡Tienes razón! pues... , entonces debemos salir mañana. ¿Tenemos que llevarles regalos?

MANUEL Bueno... , eso depende de ti.

ROSITA Entonces, voy al centro *para* buscar unos recuerdos° de Madrid para Adolfo y Rosario. Después podemos encontrarnos° en casa de mamá *para* cenar juntos°, ¿de acuerdo?

MANUEL De acuerdo.° Prometo estar allí *para* la hora de la cena°.

---

por avión *by plane*   por las montañas *through the mountains*   me da mareos *makes me dizzy*   para el jueves *by Thursday*   recuerdos *souvenirs*   encontrarnos *meet*   juntos *together*   de acuerdo *OK*   para la hora... *by dinnertime.*

---

1. ¿Cómo prefiere ir a Santiago de Compostela Rosita? ¿Por qué?   2. ¿Por cuánto tiempo van Manuel y Rosita a Santiago? ¿Para cuándo tienen que estar allí? ¿Por qué? 3. ¿Qué quiere comprar Rosita para Adolfo y Rosario?   4. ¿Dónde se van a encontrar después Manuel y Rosita? ¿Para qué?   5. ¿Qué promete Manuel?   6. ¿Le da a Ud. mareos viajar por avión? ¿y viajar por auto?

Por and **para** have many uses in Spanish. While both prepositions are often translated by *for* in English, there is a great difference in usage between them.

A. Por is generally used to express:

1. Cause or motive *(because of, on account of, for the sake of)*

El precio de la carne subió por la inflación.	*The price of meat went up because of inflation.*
Me interesa la arquitectura antigua.	*Ancient architecture interests me.*
Por eso voy a Segovia.	*That's why I'm going to Segovia.*
Rosa lo hizo por amor.	*Rosa did it for (the sake of) love.*

2. Time

a. Length or duration of time

La pareja fue a La Coruña por dos semanas.	*The couple went to La Coruña for two weeks.*

---

*See Cultural Note 1 for information about Santiago de Compostela.
‡Both **por avión (auto, tren)** and **en avión (auto, tren)** are acceptable.

b. Part of the day when no hour is mentioned

Dicen que por la tarde hay varios vuelos a Santiago.	*They say that there are several flights to Santiago in the afternoon.*

3. Exchange *(in exchange for)*

Inés pagó cuatrocientas pesetas por las píldoras.	*Inés paid four hundred pesetas for the pills.*
Cambiamos nuestro auto viejo por uno nuevo.	*We exchanged our old car for a new one.*

4. In place of *(as a substitute for, on behalf of)*

Él preparó la cena por su madre.	*He prepared dinner for (in the place of) his mother.*
Luisa bailó por Ana anoche.	*Luisa danced for (instead of, as a substitute for) Ana last night.*

5. The equivalent of *through, along, around, by, by means of*

José caminó por la Avenida de Compostela.	*José walked along Compostela Avenue.*
Pasaron por la casa a las ocho.	*They came by the house at eight o'clock.*
Tomás no puede ver mucho por la ventana.	*Tomás can't see much through the window.*
Se hablaron por teléfono.	*They talked by (on the) telephone.*
Oyeron las noticias por radio.	*They heard the news by (on the) radio.*

6. The object of an errand

Pepe fue al mercado por leche.	*Pepe went to the market for milk.*
Voy a venir por ti a las siete.	*I'm going to come for you at seven o'clock.*
La enfermera vino por una copia de los resultados del laboratorio.	*The nurse came for a copy of the lab results.*

7. Number, measure, or frequency *(per)*

Venden las manzanas por libra.	*They sell apples by the pound.*
¡No lo puedo creer! Fueron a ochenta millas por hora.	*I can't believe it! They went eighty miles per hour.*
Hay que tomar las cápsulas cuatro veces por día.	*It's necessary to take the capsules four times a day.*

8. Por is also used in many set expressions.

¡Por Dios!	*¡Good Lord!*	Por fin	*finally*

por ejemplo	*for example*	por otra parte	*on the other hand*
Por eso	*for that reason, that's why*	¿Por qué?	*why?*
por favor	*please*	por supuesto	*of course*

9. The precise translation of **por** is clarified by the context.

Pasa por Pontevedra.	*She's passing through Pontevedra.*
Pasa por la panadería.	*She's stopping by the bakery.*
Pasa por el periódico.	*She's stopping by for the newspaper.*
Pasa por inteligente.	*She passes for (is considered) intelligent.*

B. **Para** conveys a general sense of destination. It is used to express:

1. Intended recipient (*for* someone or something)

El cocinero preparó una empanada especial para los turistas.	*The cook prepared a special meat pie for the tourists.*

2. The use for which something is intended

Es una taza para té.	*It's a teacup.*
Ese cuarto es para dormir.	*That room is for sleeping.*

3. Direction *(toward)*

Salieron para León ayer.	*They left for León yesterday.*

4. Purpose *(in order to)*

Fueron a Burgos para la boda de María y Tomás.	*They went to Burgos for María and Tomás' wedding.*
Viajamos a Galicia para ver la catedral de Santiago.	*We traveled to Galicia in order to see the cathedral in Santiago.*

5. The person or entity for whom or which one works or acts

Juegan para los Cosmos.	*They play for the Cosmos.*
Trabajó para una doctora española.	*She worked for a Spanish doctor.*

6. A specific event or point in time

Los novios tienen que llegar a la iglesia para las dos.	*The bride and groom have to get to the church by two o'clock.*
Voy a visitarte para tu cumpleaños.	*I'll visit you for your birthday.*

7. Comparisons when there is a lack of correspondence

Pedrito es muy alto para su edad.	*For his age Pedrito is very tall.*
¡Él es muy viejo para ti!	*He is very old for you!*

EJERCICIOS

A. *Por*...**para todos** (**Por**...*for everyone*).   Complete each phrase on the left with an appropriate ending or beginning on the right. Use each verb twice.

MODELOS   No queremos irnos por el frío.

Por eso no queremos irnos.

siempre hablamos	por el frío
ayer no vinieron	por tres meses
no queremos irnos	por el parque
quieren viajar	por empanadas
viste cosas interesantes	por tren
fui a San Francisco	por razones económicas
viajamos a León	por la calle Colón
se mudan a un apartamento	por teléfono
me quedo en Madrid	por avión
dimos un paseo	Por eso
vamos a la panadería	Por fin
	por la noche

B. *Para*...**para practicar**.   Complete each phrase on the left with an appropriate ending on the right. Use each phrase on the left twice.

MODELOS   Carlos viene para cenar con ustedes.

Carlos viene para las once y media.

Mi hermana trabajó mucho	para las once y media
Carlos viene	para Toledo
Esos estudiantes fueron	para comprar ropa de invierno
La pareja se muda	para ir al baile con Susana
Prometí estar allí	para la clase de español
Tienes un recuerdo	para cenar con ustedes
Ese dinero es	para la doctora Díaz
No necesita corbata	para el sur
Tenemos que hacer los ejercicios	para la señora Solé

C. **La casa nueva.**   Complete the following paragraph with **por** or **para**, as needed.

Esta mañana Luisa me llamó _____ teléfono _____ invitarme a cenar en su casa nueva. Ella y Pepe están muy contentos porque _____ fin pudieron comprarse una casa. _____ eso, ellos quieren reunirnos a todos sus amigos esta noche _____ enseñarnos la casa y _____ celebrar juntos esa ocasión. No sé cuánto pagaron _____ la casa, pero sé que _____ poder comprarla tuvieron que pedir prestado (*to borrow*) mucho dinero del banco y de sus padres. Vivieron en un apartamento _____ más de seis años, y pagaron unos $500,00 _____ mes. Decidieron buscar una casa sólo porque supieron que Luisa espera un bebé _____ agosto, y el apartamento va a ser muy pequeño

_____ los tres. Roberto, Luis, Tina, Paulina y yo decidimos contribuir $15,00 cada uno _____ comprarles un lindo regalo _____ la sala. También vamos a llevarles las bebidas y el postre _____ la fiesta. Los muchachos van _____ el vino y la cerveza; Sonia y Paulina pasan _____ la panadería _____ comprar un postre; y yo debo ir _____ el regalo. Creo que les voy a comprar el cuadro (*painting*) que a Luisa le gustó tanto—lo venden _____ $75,00.

D. En acción. Describe the drawings below. Use **por** or **para**, as appropriate.

MODELO

¿Es para mí?

Preguntas

1. ¿Viene usted a esta clase por la mañana? ¿por la tarde? ¿por la noche? ¿A qué hora sale de su casa? ¿vuelve para su casa? 2. ¿Cuántas veces por semana va usted al laboratorio de lenguas? ¿a la biblioteca? ¿al mercado? 3. ¿Compró usted recientemente un regalo para su madre? ¿su padre? ¿su hermana o hermano? ¿qué regalo? 4. ¿Cómo aprende las noticias usted? ¿por radio? ¿por televisión? ¿por los periódicos? 5. ¿Qué hace usted para curar un dolor de cabeza? ¿Toma aspirinas? ¿píldoras? ¿otros medicamentos? Y para curar un dolor de estómago, ¿qué hace? 6. ¿Para cuándo piensa usted terminar sus estudios?

Study Hint: Reading for Comprehension

Like listening comprehension, reading comprehension involves recognizing key vocabulary. Here are some suggestions for improving your reading comprehension in Spanish:

1. Plan on reading an unfamiliar passage at least twice.

2. Before reading the passage itself, notice the title, headings, captions of pictures and other clues to the passage's content.

3. Read the passage quickly without looking up the meanings of unfamiliar words and without stopping to translate into English.

4. Now read slowly, looking up words, and filling in the sections you did not understand the first time.

5. Try to summarize the content to yourself, and be sure that you can answer any comprehension questions that follow. Make up some of your own, too.

6. If there are still sentences or phrases that you do not understand, mark them and ask your instructor to explain them.

SANTIAGO DE COMPOSTELA: CIUDAD DE PEREGRINAJE°

El Hostal de los Reyes Católicos,
Santiago de Compostela

*En una agencia de viajes de Madrid. Una señora norteamericana está
con su familia y hace planes para un viaje a Santiago de Compostela.*[1]

SRA. KINGSLEY	Buenas tardes, señor. Tenemos muchas ganas de visitar Santiago de Compostela y sabemos que está bastante lejos de Madrid... ¿Debemos viajar por avión o es posible hacer el viaje por auto?
AGENTE	Bueno...eso depende...Dígame, señora, ¿cuánto tiempo van a quedarse ustedes en España?
SRA. KINGSLEY	Pues...a ver. Vinimos por diez días y llegamos el martes pasado. Tenemos una semana más, y nos queda un montón de° cosas por ver en Madrid.
AGENTE	Entonces, para visitar Santiago y también tener unos días libres° en Madrid, ustedes tienen que viajar allí por avión. El viaje de ida y vuelta° no cuesta más que cien dólares por persona. El pasaje° para su hija cuesta menos. Y hay cuatro o cinco vuelos por día.
SRA. KINGSLEY	De acuerdo. Prefiero no hacer viajes largos por auto, porque me da mareos. A propósito°, ¿es necesario alquilar° un auto en Santiago?
AGENTE	No, no es necesario. El aeropuerto está a unos veinte minutos de la ciudad y ustedes pueden tomar un taxi hasta el centro.
SRA. KINGSLEY	¿De veras?° ¡Qué bien!
AGENTE	Sí, señora. Una vez en el centro, ustedes pueden caminar por todas partes. Lleven zapatos cómodos o les van a doler los pies. Si caminan, ustedes van a ver mejor los monumentos importantes, como por ejemplo...
SRA. KINGSLEY	...la famosa catedral, por supuesto, y la Plaza de las Platerías, y el Hostal de los Reyes Católicos y...[2]
AGENTE	¡Increíble! Para extranjera,° usted sabe muchísimo.
SRA. KINGSLEY	Es que soy profesora de historia medieval y Santiago fue una de las ciudades más importantes de la Edad Media°, famosa

como sitio de peregrinación°.³ Yo soy una peregrina° moderna. Además, la ciudad de Santiago es conocida por sus monumentos estupendos, y dicen que es lindísima, que tiene restaurantes excelentes donde se preparan mariscos° y empanadas gallegas°.⁴

AGENTE   Sí, señora. ¡Y hay una tuna que pasa por la plaza principal todos los días! Pero, señora, tengan ciudado con los mariscos.

SRA. KINGSLEY   ¿Habla en broma? ¡Los mariscos gallegos son tan famosos!

AGENT   Sí, señora...pero es verano y ustedes tienen que buscar un restaurante con el refrigerador bien visible. Es posible enfermarse comiendo mariscos cuando hace calor.

SRA. KINGSLEY   Pues...mi familia y yo siempre tenemos cuidado... ¡en los EE.UU. también! ¡Y ahora queremos salir para Santiago lo más pronto posible°!

peregrinaje *pilgrimage*   un montón de *a "pile" of, lots of*   libres *free*   ida y vuelta *round-trip*   el pasaje *the passage, ticket*   a propósito *by the way*   °alquilar *to rent*   ¿De veras? *Really?*   extranjera *foreigner*   °la Edad Media *the Middle Ages*   peregrinación *pilgrimage*   peregrina *pilgrim*   mariscos *shellfish*   gallegas *Galician*   lo...posible *as soon as possible*

PREGUNTAS

1. ¿Qué ciudad quiere visitar la señora Kingsley? ¿Está cerca de Madrid?
2. ¿Tienen que viajar por avión o por auto?   3. ¿Cuánto cuesta el viaje de ida y vuelta?   4. ¿Es necesario alquilar un auto para ver la ciudad? ¿Por qué?   5. ¿Es profesora de historia moderna la señora Kingsley?   6. Explique lo que es un(a) peregrino(-a).   7. ¿Cómo es la comida típica de Galicia? Dé unos ejemplos.

NOTAS CULTURALES

1. **Santiago de Compostela** is located in northwestern Spain in the province of **Galicia**. In addition to Spanish, the people there speak **gallego**, a language similar to Portuguese.

2. The cathedral, located in the center of the city, is surrounded by four plazas, a large plaza in front and three smaller ones on the sides. One of the smaller plazas is the lovely **Plaza de las Platerías** or the Silvershops' Square, around which are located the city's silver shops. Facing the large plaza is the **Hostal de los Reyes Católicos**, a magnificent fifteenth-century building which has been made into a hotel.

3. In the Middle Ages, pilgrims from all over Europe visited the cathedral, built on a spot where legend reports that the bones of Spain's patron saint, **Santiago** or Saint James the Apostle, were found. Many modern pilgrims still visit the city, especially on the feast of Saint James, the 25th of July.

4. Galicia is famous for its seafood and for its **empanada gallega**, a very large round meat pie which is cut into slices as one course or a meal in itself. Smaller versions of the **empanada** are popular in Argentina and other Latin American countries.

Funciones y *actividades*

In this chapter, you have seen examples of some important language functions or uses. Here is a summary and some additional information about these functions of language.

EXPRESSING DISBELIEF

Here are some ways to express that you can't quite believe what you've heard.

¿De veras?	*Really?*	No lo puedo creer.	*I can't believe it.*
¿Habla(s) en broma?	*Are you joking?*	¡Qué ridículo!	*How ridiculous!*
¡Pero lo dice(s) en broma!	*But you're kidding!*	¡Qué va!	*Oh, come on!*
		Increíble.	*Incredible.*
¡Pero no hablas en serio!	*But you're not serious!*	Esto (Eso) es increíble.	*This (That) is incredible.*
No puede ser.	*It can't be.*	Imposible.	*Impossible.*
No lo creo.	*I don't believe it.*		

MAKING COMPARISONS

You've learned several ways to make comparisons. Remember that **para** is also used in comparisons to mean *for*.

Es muy alto para su edad.	*He's very tall for his age.*
Para norteamericana, ella habla muy bien el español.	*For an American, she speaks Spanish very well.*

Now do the following activities, using the expressions you have just learned.

A. **¿Lo crees?**   Working with a partner, make at least three statements about yourself, some of them true and some of them false. Your partner should respond with either **Sí, te creo** or an expression of disbelief.

> **MODELOS**   Yo tengo diecinueve años.
> **Sí, te creo.**
>
> Gané un partido de tenis con Martina Navratilova ayer.
> **¡Qué va! Eso es imposible.**

B. **Para...**   React to the following statements using comparisons with **para**.

> **MODELO**   Felipe es atleta. Come muy poco. (Los otros atletas comen mucho más.)
> **Para atleta, Felipe come muy poco.**

1. Jane es de Florida. Habla muy bien el francés. (Los otros norteamericanos no hablan tan bien el francés.)

2. David es policía. No conoce bien la ciudad. (Los otros policías conocen muy bien la ciudad.)

3. Raúl es agente de viajes. No viaja mucho. (Los otros agentes de viajes viajan mucho más.)

4. Carmen es músico. Canta muy mal. (Los otros músicos cantan mejor.)

5. Manuelito tiene dos años. Habla muy bien. (Los otros niños de dos años no hablan tan bien.)

C. Mini-drama.   Your friend, Jenny, is planning to visit Europe and wants to go to Spain, but she has never studied the geography of Spain. You are helping her decide what clothing to bring for a trip from Santander to Santiago de Compostela. She tells you that it's always sunny and hot in Spain. You reply that it rains a lot in Galicia. She doesn't believe you. You tell her she ought to bring an umbrella and a raincoat. She still doesn't believe you. You tell her that it can be cool in the mountains at night. She says you have to be joking. You tell her that it's necessary to wear a sweater from time to time. She says that for a student of Spanish, you don't know much. You tell her that she's not serious and that if she doesn't believe you, she can ask your Spanish professor.

VOCABULARIO ACTIVO

Cognados

el, la atleta	famoso	la parte	usar
el bebé	el líquido	el síntoma	la vitamina
la cápsula	el monumento	el termómetro	

Verbos

acordarse (ue)(de)	*to remember*
cambiar	*to change, exchange*
conservar	*to preserve*
curarse	*to be cured, get well*
descansar	*to rest*
destruir	*to destroy*
doler	*to hurt + indirect object pronoun*
Me duele el pie.	*My foot hurts.*
enfermarse	*to get sick*
prometer	*to promise*
sobrevivir	*to survive, remain*
subir	*to climb, go up, rise*

El cuerpo humano   The human body

la boca	*mouth*
el brazo	*arm*
la cabeza	*head*
la cadera	*hip*
la cara	*face*
el corazón	*heart*
el cuello	*neck*
el dedo	*finger*
el dedo de pie	*toe*
los dientes	*teeth*
la espalda	*back*
el estómago	*stomach*
la garganta	*throat*
el hombro	*shoulder*
la mano	*hand*
la nariz	*nose*
el ojo	*eye*
la oreja	*(outer) ear*
el pecho	*chest*
el pelo	*hair*
el pie	*foot*
la pierna	*leg*
el pulgar	*thumb*
la rodilla	*knee*

La salud   Health

el catarro	*cold*
tener catarro	*to have a cold*
el dolor	*pain*
la enfermedad	*sickness, illness*
el enfermero, la enfermera	*nurse*
fuerte	*strong*
la gripe	*flu*
la inyección	*injection, shot*
el jarabe (de tos)	*(cough) syrup*
los mareos	*dizziness, nausea, motion sickness*
darle (a uno) mareos	*to give (someone) motion sickness*
tener mareos	*to be dizzy, nauseous*
el medicamento	*medication, medicine*
la pastilla	*tablet*
la píldora	*pill*
la receta	*prescription; receipt*
resfriado	
estar resfriado	*to have a cold*
el resfrío	*cold*
tener resfrío	*to have a cold*
la tos	*cough*
tener tos	*to have a cough*

Otras palabras y expresiones

antiguo	*old; ancient*
aún	*even*
derecho	*right (adj)*
la empanada	*meat pie*
hay que	*it is necessary, one must + infinitive*
la iglesia	*church*
izquierdo	*left (adj)*
juntos	*together*
mayor	*greater; larger; older; greatest; largest; oldest*
mejor	*better; best*

menor	*smaller; lesser; younger; smallest; least; youngest*
el mercado	*market*
necesario	*necessary*
es necesario	*it is necessary + infinitive*
las noticias	*news*
la panadería	*bakery*
la pareja	*couple*
peor	*worse; worst*
el periódico	*newspaper*
preciso	*necessary*
es preciso	*it is necessary + infinitive*
el recuerdo	*souvenir; remembrance*
tan	*so, as*
tan...como	*as . . . as*
el vendedor	*salesman*
la zapatería	*shoe store*

Expresiones útiles

¿De veras?	*Really?*
¡Esto es increíble!	*That's incredible!*
¡Imposible!	*Impossible!*
¡No lo puedo creer!	*I can't believe it!*
¡No puede ser!	*It can't be!*
¡Pero lo dices en broma!	*But you're joking!*
¡Pero no hablas en serio!	*But you're not serious!*
¡Qué ridículo!	*How ridiculous!*
¡Qué va!	*Oh, come on!*

Don't forget: Comparisons of equality and inequality and superlatives, pages 252, 255–256

LECTURA V

La España del pasado

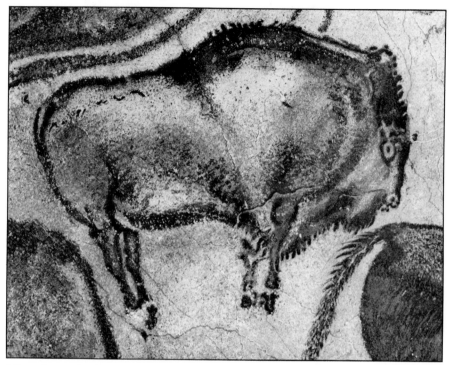

Dibujo de un animal en las Cuevas de Altamira

En las Cuevas° de Altamira, al norte de España, podemos ver algunas° de las   caves/some
pinturas° más antiguas del mundo. Son figuras de animales que tienen entre   paintings
20.000 y 30.000 años. Al sur de la península, por otra parte, floreció° una   flourished
cultura africana que dejó testimonios muy diferentes: figuras estilizadas de
hombres y mujeres.

    La historia de España es una historia de muchas razas y culturas. Los
primeros habitantes históricamente conocidos° de España fueron los iberos°,   known/Iberians
gente de origen europeo. Estos se mezclaron° después con los celtas, inva-   mixed
sores del norte. Luego vinieron los fenicios°, los griegos° y los cartagineses°,   Phoenicians/
éstos del norte de África. Una guerra° terrible y larga entre los cartagineses   Greeks/Car-
y los romanos terminó en el año 218 con el triunfo de los romanos. Es fácil   thaginians
ver la influencia cultural de Roma en la lengua española (el latín hablado°   war
de aquella época formó la base del español moderno), en el sistema de leyes°   spoken
y en la religión cristiana, proclamada como religión oficial por Teodosio,   law
emperador romano nacido° en España. Los romanos construyeron puentes°,   born/bridges
caminos° y acueductos por todo el país. En la foto de la página 276 vemos   roads
el famoso acueducto de Segovia.

El acueducto romano de Segovia

En el año 711 los moros (musulmanes° del norte de África) invadieron la   Moslems
Península Ibérica. Les tomó tres años conquistarla°, pero establecieron allí   to conquer it
una cultura que por mucho tiempo fue la más espléndida del mundo occi-
dental. Durante esos años, sabios° de toda Europa viajaron con frecuencia a   learned persons
las ciudades de Córdoba, Granada, Sevilla y a otras ciudades para aprender
de los moros nuevos conocimientos° en las ciencias en general, y en arqui-   knowledge
tectura, agricultura y arte, en particular. En esta foto vemos la mezquita° de   mosque
Córdoba, donde los arcos y columnas simbolizan el poder° infinito de Alá.   power

La mezquita de Córdoba es un
buen ejemplo de la arquitectura
árabe.

Desde el norte de España los reinos° cristianos empezaron la Reconquista°, guerra que duró casi° ocho siglos. En 1492 las fuerzas militares de Isabel de Castilla y Fernando de Aragón conquistaron Granada, último reino de los moros. Ese mismo año Cristóbal Colón descubrió un nuevo mundo en nombre de España. Los españoles pudieron utilizar después la disciplina militar de la Reconquista para colonizar el Nuevo Mundo y para convertir a la España de los siglos XVI y XVII en la nación más poderosa° del mundo. En la foto vemos la tumba de Isabel y Fernando en Granada.

kingdoms/Reconquest
duró... *lasted almost*

powerful

La tumba de los Reyes Católicos

PREGUNTAS

1. ¿Dónde podemos· ver algunas de las pinturas más antiguas del mundo? ¿Cómo son esas figuras? Descríbalas.   2. ¿Qué grupos llegaron a España después de los iberos?   3. ¿Fue larga o corta *(short)* la guerra entre los cartagineses y los romanos? ¿En qué año terminó esa guerra? ¿Quiénes triunfaron?   4. ¿Qué ejemplos puede dar usted de la influencia romana sobre la cultura española?   5. ¿Quiénes invadieron la Península Ibérica en el año 711? ¿En cuántos años la conquistaron?   6. En aquella época, ¿quiénes viajaron con frecuencia a ciudades como Córdoba, Granada y Sevilla? ¿Para qué?   7. ¿Desde qué parte de España empezaron los cristianos la guerra de la Reconquista? ¿Cuánto tiempo duró?   8. ¿Por qué podemos decir que el año 1492 tiene doble importancia en España?

Razas y culturas.   Fill in the blanks with words chosen from the list below, as appropriate. Follow the model.

> **MODELO**   Los reinos <u>cristianos</u> empezaron la Reconquista desde el norte de España.

romanos	fenicios	cartagineses
moros	europeo	moro
romana	moros	africana
cristianos	celtas	griega
griegos	iberos	europeos

1. En época prehistórica, al sur de España floreció una cultura _____ .
2. Es fácil ver la influencia _____ en la lengua española.
3. Los _____ , gente de origen _____ , fueron los primeros habitantes de España.
4. Los _____ vinieron del norte de África.
5. Los _____ construyeron el acueducto de Segovia.
6. Y los _____ establecieron una cultura espléndida en España.

Elecciones recientes
en El Salvador

LAS NOTICIAS

Funciones

- Telling a story

- Giving the speaker
  encouragement

- Using polite expressions

Vocabulario.   In this chapter you will talk about
the news.
Gramática.   You will discuss and use:
1. The imperfect of regular and irregular verbs
2. The distinctions between the preterit and the
   imperfect
3. The relative pronouns **que** and **quien**
Cultura.   The dialogues take place in Central
America.

¿QUÉ HAY DE NUEVO?

Más inflación: subió el costo de la vida.

Guerrilleros atacaron al ejército; la nación está en guerra (*at war*).

El Papa visitó México.

Hubo una manifestación en la capital de Panamá. Los estudiantes protestaron contra el gobierno.

Ayer hubo un terremoto (*earthquake*) en Guatemala. Murieron miles de personas.

Costa Rica ganó otra vez en fútbol.

Hubo una huelga general de obreros; pidieron aumento de sueldo.

Hubo un incendio en Tegucigalpa. Cinco familias se quedaron sin casa.

El presidente habló de los derechos humanos y de la superpoblación en la última reunión de las Naciones Unidas.

Hubo elecciones generales.

PARA ENTERARSE DE LAS NOTICIAS...

prender (*to turn on*) el televisor el periódico, la revista el canal (*channel*), el noticiero
apagar (*to turn off*) la televisión (*magazine*), los anuncios (*news program*), un reportaje
la radio (*advertisements*) especial, un programa
documental

Preguntas

1. ¿Cuándo prende usted la radio?   2. ¿Qué escucha por radio: música, noticias, deportes?   3. ¿Qué mira por televisión?   4. ¿Cuántas horas mira televisión en un día típico?   5. ¿Hay canales públicos en esta región? ¿Cuántos y cuáles? ¿Qué programas de canales públicos le gustan a usted?   6. Según su opinión, ¿es buena o mala la influencia de la televisión? ¿Por qué?   7. ¿Cómo se entera usted de las noticias? ¿Le interesan mucho las noticias del día?   8. ¿Ve usted el noticiero todas las noches? ¿A qué hora lo ve?   9. ¿Lee el periódico?   10. ¿Lee los anuncios de comida? ¿de ropa?   11. ¿Qué revistas lee usted? ¿Por qué las lee? ¿Qué lee su papá? ¿su mamá?

Asociaciones.   ¿Qué noticias asocia usted con las personas y cosas que siguen?

> **MODELO**   el Papa
> **El Papa viajó a muchos países el año pasado y habló de religión y de política con la gente.**

1. el béisbol o el fútbol
2. Centroamérica
3. el presidente de los Estados Unidos
4. el costo de la vida
5. el tiempo

I. El imperfecto

San José de Costa
Rica es una ciudad
moderna.

Roberto encuentra a Blanca en la biblioteca
de la Universidad de Costa Rica en San José.

ROBERTO Hola, Blanca. ¿Qué lees?

BLANCA Un periódico del dos de mayo de 1968.

ROBERTO ¿En serio?° ¡Es el día que nació mi hermana! Yo *era* muy pequeño...
Sólo *tenía* cinco años, pero recuerdo que mamá *estaba* en el hospital
y papá *estaba* muy nervioso°. Pero volviendo a tu periódico, ¿qué
pasaba en esa época?

BLANCA Pues, *había* guerra en el Medio Oriente°. Recuerdo que las dos
grandes preocupaciones° del momento *eran* las armas nucleares y la
contaminación. *Había* manifestaciones en El Salvador, incendios
forestales° en el Brasil, una huelga de mineros° en Bolivia...

ROBERTO ¡Qué poco cambian las cosas en veinte años!

¿En serio? *Really?* nervioso *nervous* Medio Oriente *Middle East*
preocupaciones *concerns* incendios forestales *forest fires* mineros *miners*

---

1. ¿Qué lee Blanca? 2. ¿Qué edad tenía Roberto el dos de mayo de 1968?
3. ¿Qué recuerda él de su mamá y de su papá? 4. ¿Qué pasaba en el mundo en
esa época? 5. ¿Suceden esas cosas hoy?

A. To form the imperfect of all **-ar** verbs, add the endings **-aba, -abas, -aba,
-ábamos, -abais, -aban** to the stem of the infinitive. The **nosotros** form has a
written accent.

hablar

hablaba	hablábamos
hablabas	hablabais
hablaba	hablaban

B. To form the imperfect of regular **-er** or **-ir** verbs, add the endings **-ía, -ías, -ía, -íamos, -íais, -ían** to the stem of the infinitive. All forms have written accents.

	comer		vivir
comía	comíamos	vivía	vivíamos
comías	comíais	vivías	vivíais
comía	comían	vivía	vivían

C. Stress falls on the ending, not on the stem, in all regular imperfect forms. Stem-changing verbs, therefore, never change their stem in the imperfect.

Infinitive	Present (Stem changes)	Imperfect (No change)
costar (ue)	cuesta	**costaba**
tener (ie)	tiene	**tenía**

Los autos cuestan mucho ahora, pero antes costaban mucho también.

Cars cost a lot now, but they also cost a lot before.

Tiene que ir a muchas reuniones ahora, pero antes tenía que ir a más.

He has to go to a lot of meetings now, but before he had to go to more.

D. Only three verbs are irregular in the imperfect: **ir, ser,** and **ver.**

	ir		ser		ver
iba	íbamos	era	éramos	veía	veíamos
ibas	ibais	eras	erais	veías	veíais
iba	iban	era	eran	veía	veían

E. Haber, which has the form **hay** in the present, in the imperfect has the form **había** *(there was, there were).*

Había mucha gente en la plaza durante la manifestación.

There were a lot of people in the plaza during the demonstration.

F. The imperfect is used:

1. To express customary or repeated past actions.

Les hablaba a los obreros cada vez que los veía.

He would (used to) speak to the workers each time he would see (saw) them.

De vez en cuando veíamos un reportaje sobre el SIDA.

From time to time we would see a report about AIDS.

2. To express past actions as being then in progress.

Subía el precio de la gasolina.	The price of gasoline was going up.
No bajaban los precios de la comida.	Food prices weren't going down.
Anunciaban un concierto en la radio.	They were announcing a concert on the radio.
En agosto los obreros del metro estaban en huelga.	In August the subway workers were on strike.

3. To describe situations or conditions that existed for an indefinite period of time.

Cuando yo era más joven, trabajaba de reportero. ¿De veras?	When I was younger, I worked as a reporter. Really?
Llovía en todo el país.	It was raining all over the country.

4. To describe past mental or emotional states.

Los obreros estaban contentos con el aumento de sueldo.	The workers were happy with the increase in salary.
Sabían que había muchos problemas económicos.	They knew there were many economic problems.
La madre se preocupaba por su familia.	The mother was worrying about her family.

5. To express the time of day or the age of people or things in the past.

Era la una y media.	It was one-thirty.
El presidente sólo tenía cuarenta años en esa época.	The president was only forty years old at that time.

G. The imperfect has several possible equivalents in English.

Ellos estudiaban juntos.
- They used to study together.
- They were studying together.
- They studied together (often, from time to time).
- They would study together (whenever they could).

H. Because the first- and third-person singular forms of a verb in the imperfect are identical, subject pronouns are often used with them for clarity.

Yo sabía que ella miraba el canal público.	I knew she watched the public channel.
Horacio pensaba que yo salía con Juanita.	Horacio thought I was going out with Juanita.

EJERCICIOS

A. Hola, estamos en el aire (*Hi, we're on the air*).   Take the part of José Gómez, a disc jockey with a popular call-in radio program, and respond to the callers' comments. Point out that things are pretty much the same as they used to be.

MODELO   Ahora hay mucha inflación.
Y antes había mucha inflación también.

1. Hay muchas huelgas.
2. La gente se queja mucho.
3. La comida cuesta mucho.
4. Pocos turistas vienen al país.
5. Muchas de nuestras familias se van del país.
6. Los obreros producen mucho.
7. Ahora el costo de la vida sube mucho cada año.

B. ¿Qué hacían?   Tell what the following people were doing when the blackout (*apagón*) occurred in San José yesterday.

MODELO   Felipe / leer el periódico
Felipe leía el periódico.

1. Clara / bañarse
2. Federico / empezar a estudiar
3. Susana y Guillermo / ir de compras
4. tú / prender la radio para escuchar las noticias
5. Anita / escribir una carta
6. nosotros / jugar a los naipes
7. yo / hablar por teléfono
8. los Herrera / comer en un restaurante en el décimo piso de un edificio

C. Cuando tú eras pequeña...   Blanca tells her mother about her daughter Susana. Blanca's mother says Blanca was the same when she was young.

MODELO   Es muy generosa.
Tú también eras muy generosa cuando eras joven.

1. Casi siempre está contenta.
2. Le gusta mucho el chocolate.
3. Tiene muchas amigas.
4. Duerme hasta tarde todos los días.
5. Dice que no tiene problemas.

D. Buenos amigos.   Complete the story about a friendship, using appropriate imperfect forms of the verbs.

Cuando yo (1) _____ (**ser**) menor, (yo) (2) _____ (**jugar**) con mis hermanos. (Yo) (3) _____ (**tener**) una amiga que (4) _____ (**llamarse**) Amalia y que (5) _____ (**vivir**) cerca de nosotros. Ella (6) _____ (**asistir**) a otra escuela y (ella y yo) no (7) _____ (**verse**) durante la semana. (Ella y yo) (8) _____ (**ir**) a jugar al parque todos los fines de semana.

E. Antes del terremoto. Tell what used to go on in this town when it was a great city before the earthquake. Using the verbs **ser**, **ir**, and **ver**, describe the people mentioned and tell where they used to go and whom or what they used to see, as suggested by the cues.

> MODELO   los Díaz / profesores / teatro / muchas obras de teatro
> **Los Díaz eran profesores. Iban al teatro y veían muchas obras de teatro.**

1. nosotros / doctores / hospital / nuestros pacientes
2. tú / reportera / congreso / senadores
3. el tío de Teresa / vendedor / centro / sus clientes
4. yo / reportero / cancha de tenis / jugadores de tenis
5. Jorge / estudiante / café / sus compañeros y amigos

Entrevista

Either in pairs or in groups, interview each other about your childhood. Use the following questions or any others you feel are appropriate.

1. ¿Dónde vivías cuando eras niño(-a)?   2. ¿Cómo era tu casa?   3. ¿A qué escuela asistías cuando tenías ocho años?   4. ¿Trabajaba tu mamá? ¿Dónde te quedabas cuando ella trabajaba?   5. ¿Qué querías ser cuando eras niño(-a)?   6. ¿Qué te gustaba hacer de niño(-a)?   7. ¿Dónde y con quién jugabas?   8. ¿Jugabas al béisbol? ¿al fútbol? ¿al tenis? ¿a otros deportes?   9. ¿Adónde iba tu familia de vacaciones?   10. ¿Qué te gustaba de la escuela? ¿Qué no te gustaba? ¿Eran amables tus profesores?   11. ¿Salías con otros chicos (chicas) cuando tenías catorce años?   12. ¿Veías mucha televisión? ¿Cuáles eran tus programas favoritos?   13. ¿Qué hacías durante tus vacaciones?   14. ¿Eras más feliz antes que ahora? ¿Por qué sí o por qué no?

II.   El imperfecto en contraste con el pretérito

Un mercado en
Chichicastenango,
Guatemala

En un pequeño pueblo° de Guatemala

FEDERICO   *¿Oíste* el noticiero esta tarde?
LETICIA   Sí, lo *escuchaba* mientras° *cocinaba.*
FEDERICO   *¿Hablaron* del terremoto que *hubo* anoche en Nicaragua? Me *decía* Jaime en el autobús que *ocurrió* cerca de las once de la noche... *Había* cientos de personas en las calles porque *celebraban* una fiesta religiosa.
LETICIA   Sí... la Cruz Roja° *mandó* quinientos voluntarios a la región. *Murió* prácticamente° toda la gente que *estaba* en la calle celebrando la fiesta cuando *sucedió* el terremoto.
FEDERICO   ¡Dios mío! ¡Qué terrible!

---

pueblo *town*   mientras *while*   Cruz Roja *Red Cross*   prácticamente *almost, practically*

1. ¿Qué hacía Leticia mientras escuchaba las noticias?   2. En el noticiero, ¿hablaron del terremoto en Nicaragua?   3. ¿Cuándo ocurrió el terremoto? ¿Qué hacía mucha gente a esa hora?   4. ¿Qué hizo la Cruz Roja?   5. ¿Murió mucha gente? ¿Quiénes?

A. Spanish has several verb forms used to report past actions and conditions. A speaker chooses one form or another depending on the way the event is viewed.

B. If a past action or condition is viewed as being completed, the preterit is used. If any time limit, however long or short, is specified for the past action or condition, the preterit, not the imperfect, must be used. The preterit is also used to mention the beginning or end of something in the past, since the beginning or end itself was over the instant it happened. The preterit gives a simple report; it invites the listener to wonder what comes next. Time expressions used with the preterit reinforce the notion that the event or series of events is completed.

Time expressions often associated with the preterit		
ayer	una vez *(once)*	el domingo (pasado)
anoche	dos veces	el mes (el año, etcétera)
a las once	otra vez	pasado

El programa de noticias terminó a las once y media.	*The news program ended at 11:30.*
Empecé el libro que describe la vida del presidente.	*I started the book that describes the president's life.*
El ejército atacó a la gente del pueblo.	*The army attacked the people in the town.*
Subí al autobús en la calle Segunda y bajé en la Avenida Bolívar.	*I got on the bus on Second Street and got off on Bolívar Avenue.*

C. The imperfect is used when the speaker focuses on an action or condition as something going on in the past. The imperfect often invites the listener to wonder what else happened in the same context. Patterns of habitual action, mental states, descriptions of the way things looked or sounded, the time of day, and other background conditions in the past are typically reported with verbs in the imperfect; the speaker's interest is not in their beginning or end, but just that they existed or were occurring. Time expressions used with the imperfect reinforce the focus on the ongoing or habitual aspect of the event.

Time expressions often associated with the imperfect		
todos los días	siempre	mientras
todos los meses	frecuentemente	los domingos

Siempre había robos y otros crímenes allí.	*There were always robberies and other crimes there.*
Los domingos íbamos al campo juntos.	*On Sundays we would go to the country together.*
Protestaban contra la guerra casi todos los días.	*They were protesting against war almost every day.*
No escribían mucho sobre las elecciones mientras Jorge Ubico era presidente.	*They didn't write much about elections while Jorge Ubico was president.*
No hablaban del mismo acontecimiento.	*They weren't talking about the same event.*

D. Often the preterit and imperfect are used in the same sentence to report that an action that was in progress in the past (expressed with the imperfect) was interrupted by another action or event (expressed with the preterit).

Ramón miraba las noticias cuando Teresa lo llamó.	*Ramón was watching the news when Teresa called him.*
Por fin encontraron a los guerrilleros que buscaban.	*Finally they found the guerrillas they were looking for.*
El presidente estaba en la capital cuando tuvieron las elecciones.	*The president was in the capital when they had the elections.*

Study the following paragraph. The tense of each numbered verb is explained on the next page.

Anoche (1) miraba la televisión cuando (2) oí un reportaje especial. A las ocho de la noche, los guerrilleros (3) tomaron el pueblo de San Jacinto. El líder de los guerrilleros (4) era joven. Sólo (5) tenía 29 años y (6) era muy idealista. (7) Hubo una gran celebración. Mientras los guerrilleros (8) tomaban el pueblo, el Presidente de la República (9) estaba de vacaciones en Río de Janeiro. Desde allí, (10) prometió mandar el ejército a San Jacinto. Cuando (11) oí eso, (12) me preocupé mucho porque mis abuelos viven en ese pueblo.

1. **miraba**—an action that was going on, no reference to when it started or ended
2. **oí**—completed action that interrupted something else
3. **tomaron**—completed action
4. **era**—description
5. **tenía**—description of how old he was
6. **era**—description
7. **Hubo**—completed action (the celebration began and ended)
8. **tomaban**—action in progress
9. **estaba**—background condition
10. **prometió**—a promise he gave, finished action
11. **oí**—completed event
12. **me preocupé**—I began to worry (a specific time rather than duration of time is emphasized with the preterit—the beginning)

E. The imperfect of **conocer** means *to know, to be acquainted with,* while the preterit means *to meet, to make the acquaintance of.* The imperfect expresses ongoing acquaintance while the preterit emphasizes meeting for the first time. The imperfect of **saber** means *to know,* while the preterit means *to find out.* Again, the imperfect emphasizes indefinite duration of time in the past, while the preterit indicates a completed action.

Mamá sabía que Eduardo conocía al político.	*Mom knew that Eduardo knew (was acquainted with) the politician.*
Esta mañana supe que tú conocías a mi compañera de cuarto. ¿Dónde la conociste?	*This morning I found out that you knew my roommate. Where did you meet her?*

EJERCICIOS

A. ¡Ya no voy a escuchar las noticias! Elena used to be well informed but has decided that no news is good news. Take Elena's part and tell her friend about some of the upsetting news she heard, using the preterit or imperfect as appropriate.

MODELO Todos los días prendemos la radio temprano
Todos los días prendíamos la radio temprano.

1. Siempre escucho el noticiero de las siete.
2. Esta mañana oigo muchas noticias tristes.
3. Hay un terremoto en la Ciudad de México.
4. Cierran la Universidad Nacional.
5. Doscientas personas mueren en un accidente de avión.
6. Otra vez sube el precio de la gasolina.
7. Apago la radio.

B. **¿Imperfecto o pretérito?** Choose the correct form of the verbs.

> **MODELO** Cuando (ocurrió, ocurría) el terremoto, nosotros (celebrábamos, celebramos) el cumpleaños de papá.
>
> **Cuando ocurrió el terremoto, nosotros celebrábamos el cumpleaños de papá.**

1. Nosotros (llegamos, llegábamos) tarde a la manifestación porque no (supimos, sabíamos) cómo llegar al lugar y (tuvimos, teníamos) que preguntar.
2. Cuando Jorge (salió, salía) hoy (llovió, llovía) y por eso (volvió, volvía) a su apartamento y (se puso, se ponía) el impermeable.
3. Lucía (estuvo, estaba) en El Salvador cuando (empezó, empezaba) la huelga de trabajadores. Ella (vio, veía) las manifestaciones y a toda la gente que (caminó, caminaba) por las calles.
4. (Conocí, Conocía) a Juan en una fiesta, pero no (supe, sabía) que vivía cerca de aquí.

C. **Un robo.** Change the numbered verbs in the following story to the appropriate past-tense forms.

(1) Es una noche de verano. Susana y su esposo Jaime (2) duermen después de su boda (*wedding*). En la sala (*living room*) (3) están todos los regalos. (4) Hay cosas muy lindas. A las doce en punto un hombre (5) entra en la casa. (6) Es el hombre a quien la policía (7) busca desde el sábado. (8) Va a la sala, (9) abre la puerta y (10) ve los regalos allí. Jaime y Susana no lo (11) oyen cuando (12) entra y no lo (13) ven cuando se (14) va. Cuando ellos se (15) despiertan, los regalos ya no (16) están allí. Susana (17) llama a la policía. Los dos (18) están tristes, pero no muy tristes, porque los regalos más importantes, los anillos (*rings*), todavía los (19) tienen.

Now answer the following questions.

1. ¿Qué estación del año era cuando pasó esto? 2. ¿Qué hacían Susana y su esposo? 3. ¿Qué había en la sala? ¿Eran regalos de poco o mucho valor? 4. ¿Qué pasó a las doce? 5. ¿Qué descubrieron Jaime y Susana cuando se despertaron? 6. ¿Qué hizo Susana? 7. ¿Estaban muy tristes los esposos? ¿Por qué sí o por qué no?

D. **Un incendio.** Complete the following news item with the correct preterit or imperfect form of the verbs in parentheses.

Tres personas mueren en un incendio

(1) _____ (haber) un incendio anoche en un edificio de apartamentos en la calle Balboa. (2) _____ (empezar) en el segundo piso mientras la gente (3) _____ (dormir). Una alarma (4) _____ (despertar) a quince personas y ellos (5) _____ (poder) escapar a la calle. Pero (6) _____ (morir) tres personas que (7) _____ (estar) en el tercer piso; parece que (ellos) no (8) _____ (escuchar) la alarma.

Los bomberos (*fire fighters*) (9) _____ (**llegar**) a las 9:47 pero no (10) _____ (**poder**) controlar el incendio hasta las 10:30. Las quince personas que (11) _____ (**quedarse**) sin casa (12) _____ (**pasar**) la noche en el Hotel La Fortuna. La Cruz Roja les (13) _____ (**llevar**) comida y (14) _____ (**empezar**) a buscarles nuevos apartamentos.

In pairs, ask and answer questions about the news item. Use these words in the questions: **¿Dónde...? ¿Qué hacía...? ¿A qué hora...? ¿Por qué...? ¿Cuándo?**

E. El noticiero. Complete the following sentences with appropriate information, using verbs in past tenses.

MODELO La semana pasada el presidente de El Salvador...
> **La semana pasada el presidente de El Salvador pidió ayuda a los Estados Unidos.**

1. Ayer, por televisión, el presidente de los Estados Unidos...
2. La semana pasada Julio Iglesias...
3. Conocí a... cuando...
4. Hoy supe que...
5. En fútbol Costa Rica...
6. Dos personas murieron en el accidente porque...
7. Según el periódico de hoy, el costo de la vida...

Preguntas

1. ¿Trabajaba o estudiaba usted el año pasado?   2. Y anoche, ¿trabajó o estudió? 3. Cuando era niño(-a), ¿qué hacía los fines de semana?   4. ¿Qué hizo el fin de semana pasado?   5. ¿Veía usted muchas películas cuando era un poco menor? 6. ¿Qué película vio el mes pasado?   7. ¿Qué tiempo hacía cuando se levantó esta mañana?   8. ¿Qué hora era cuando se acostó anoche?   9. ¿Tuvo que ir a muchas reuniones el mes pasado?   10. Anoche, ¿qué hizo usted cuando terminó de comer?   11. ¿Qué vio hoy cuando venía a clase?   12. ¿Qué hacía usted cuando entró el profesor hoy?   13. En general, ¿a qué hora se levantaba el semestre pasado? ¿A qué hora se levantó hoy?   14. ¿Ocurrió un acontecimiento muy importante la semana pasada? ¿Cómo lo supo usted? ¿Qué hacía cuando oyó la noticia?

III.   Los pronombres relativos *que* y *quien*

Rubén Darío (1867-1916),
nicaragüense, poeta máximo
del modernismo literario
hispanoamericano

Un grupo de amigos juegan «trivia» en un café en Tegucigalpa, Honduras.

FELIPE   ¿Cómo se llama el poeta° de Nicaragua *que* escribió el libro de
poesías° *Azul?*

MANUEL   ¡Qué fácil!

ANA   Rubén Darío. Ahora tiene que contestar Pilar. ¿Qué país
centroamericano no tiene ejército?

MANUEL   Otra pregunta fácil.

PILAR   Costa Rica. Y ahora una pregunta para Manuel. ¿Cómo se llama el
explorador a *quien*° Fernando de Aragón e Isabel de Castilla le dieron
el dinero para el viaje de la Niña, la Pinta y la Santa María a América?

MANUEL   Pues... a ver. ¿Por qué me dan a mí todas las preguntas difíciles...?

---

el poeta   *poet*   poesías   *poetry*   el explorador a quien   *the explorer to whom*

---

1. ¿Qué hace el grupo de amigos?   2. ¿Quién es Rubén Darío?   3. ¿Tiene
ejército Costa Rica?   4. ¿Quién cree que las dos primeras preguntas son fáciles?
¿Qué le preguntan a él?   5. ¿Sabe Manuel quién es ese explorador? ¿Lo sabe usted?
(Cristóbal Colón, ¿verdad?)

A. Relative pronouns replace nouns or pronouns and are used to join simple
sentences. For example:

Conozco a un político. Ese político
vive en Panamá. → Conozco a un
político que vive en Panamá.

*I know a politician. That politician
lives in Panama. → I know a
politician who lives in Panama.*

Ana y Luis son amigos. Recibí noticias de ellos ayer. → Ana y Luis son los amigos de quienes recibí noticias ayer.	*Ana and Luis are friends. I heard (received news) from them yesterday. → Ana and Luis are the friends from whom I heard (received news) yesterday.*

B. **Que** is the most commonly used equivalent for *that, which, who,* or *whom;* it is used to refer to either persons or things.

El reportaje sobre los derechos humanos en Centroamérica que vimos anoche fue muy interesante.	*The report about human rights in Central America that (which) we saw last night was very interesting.*
La mujer que vi en el Congreso ayer es de Honduras.	*The woman whom I saw at the Congress (building) yesterday is from Honduras.*
¿Quién es el senador que habló del problema de la superpoblación?	*Who is the senator who talked about the overpopulation problem?*

C. After the prepositions **a, con, de,** and **en, que** is used when referring to things.

Éstos son los problemas de que hablo.	*These are the problems (that) I'm talking about.*

D. Relative pronouns are often omitted in English, but they are always used in Spanish.

Éste es el libro que terminé de leer anoche.	*This is the book (that) I finished reading last night.*

E. **Quien** (**quienes** in the plural) refers only to people. It is usually used as the object of a preposition. When used as an indirect object, **quien(es)** must be preceded by the preposition **a.**

Es el político de quien tú me hablabas, ¿verdad?	*He's the politician you were telling me about, right?*
Ésos son los amigos con quienes cenamos esta noche.	*Those are the friends we are having dinner with tonight.*
Ernesto Cardenal es el poeta de Nicaragua a quien le dieron el puesto de Ministro de Cultura.	*Ernesto Cardenal is the poet from Nicaragua to whom they gave the position of Minister of Culture.*

Notice that although in informal English a sentence may end with a preposition, this is not possible in Spanish.

Es el líder contra quien protestaba la gente.	*He's the leader the people were demonstrating against (against whom the people were demonstrating).*

Note that **quien** cannot be used in the first example under A or the first two examples under B; **que** is essential in those cases. **Quien(es)** is normally used only after a preposition.

EJERCICIOS

A. Agenda del presidente. The president's aide is telling him who the people he has to see today are. Complete the sentences with **que** or **quien(es)**.

1. El señor Calero es el representante _____ va a viajar a Chile.
2. El señor Ramos y la señora López son los senadores con _____ usted cenó la semana pasada.
3. Ramón Ramírez es el atleta _____ ganó en los Juegos Panamericanos.
4. El señor García es el experto _____ estudia la situación de derechos humanos en Centroamérica.
5. El señor Soler es el doctor con _____ usted tiene cita *(appointment)* esta tarde.
6. La doctora Vega es la persona _____ representa a Panamá en las Naciones Unidas.
7. La señorita Castillo es la persona de _____ usted recibió una carta sobre la huelga de profesores.
8. El señor Schmidt es el experto alemán a _____ le vamos a pedir consejos sobre el transporte público.

B. Opiniones. Complete the first blank in each sentence with an appropriate noun that expresses your opinion and the second blank with **que** or **quien(es)**.

1. _____ es un líder _____ es muy inteligente.
2. _____ son personas de _____ prefiero no hablar.
3. _____ son dos películas _____ pienso ver.
4. _____ es una persona a _____ le interesan mucho las noticias.
5. _____ son dos estudiantes _____ siempre están en clase.
6. _____ es un profesor (una profesora) con _____ sigo un curso muy interesante.
7. _____ son ciudades _____ quiero visitar.
8. _____ es un canal _____ tiene muchos anuncios aburridos.
9. _____ es un país _____ quiero conocer.

Preguntas

1. ¿Qué países están en guerra en este momento? Según su opinión, ¿cuáles son los países que tienen más problemas económicos en estos días? 2. ¿Cuál es el líder mundial *(world)* de quien hablan mucho ahora en las noticias? 3. ¿Cómo se llama un(a) político(-a) que usted admira mucho? 4. ¿Quién es un(a) reportero(-a) en quien usted tiene mucha confianza *(confidence)*? 5. ¿Cómo se llama un(a) profesor(a) que lo (la) ayudó mucho a usted? ¿a quien le pidió consejos? 6. ¿De dónde es la persona con quien usted vive?

PRIMERO, LAS MALAS NOTICIAS

El Mercado Coca-Cola,
San José, Costa Rica

Juan visita a su abuelo en un hospital de San José, Costa Rica.[1]

JUAN — Escuchaba el noticiero en el auto mientras venía para acá°. Todas las noticias eran malas. Después te compré una revista en el Mercado Coca-Cola...[2] *(La busca entre sus cosas.)*

DON AURELIO — Creo que ahora dan las noticias por televisión. *(Prende el televisor.)*[3]

EL REPORTERO — Mataron° al senador Sánchez mientras iba al Congreso. Guerrilleros salvadoreños atacaron al ejército esta mañana. Murieron dos personas... . Hubo un terremoto en Tegucigalpa a las cuatro de la mañana. No saben el número de muertos°. Ahora vamos a hablar con una mujer que estaba allí cuando ocurrió el terremoto...

DON AURELIO — *(Apaga el televisor.)* ¡Qué horror! Guerrilleros, asesinatos° de líderes políticos, terremotos, inflación, huelgas...[4] Cuando yo era joven, no teníamos tantos problemas. Pero, hijo, cuéntame qué pasa en Cartago.[5]

JUAN — Pues, tía Leonora tuvo hijo—¡un niño de cuatro kilos° y medio!—en el auto mientras su esposo la llevaba al hospital.

DON AURELIO — ¡Dios mío! ¿Y cómo están?

JUAN — Por suerte, están bien.

DON AURELIO — ¡Gracias a Dios! Pues ésa en realidad no es una mala noticia. ¿Qué más está pasando?

JUAN — ¿Recuerdas los arqueólogos que trabajaban cerca de Cartago?

DON AURELIO	Sí... ¿qué pasó? La enfermera hablaba de eso esta mañana. Pero no la oí bien.
JUAN	Pues encontraron unas ruinas muy interesantes. Creen que son de los indios° que vivían en esa región.
DON AURELIO	¡Otra buena noticia! *(Entra una enfermera.)*
LA ENFERMERA	Don Aurelio, el doctor decidió que usted puede volver a su casa hoy mismo°.
DON AURELIO	¡Y ésta es para mí la mejor noticia del año!

para acá = para aquí *over here*   Mataron *They killed*   muertos *dead*   asesinatos *assassinations*   kilos *kilograms*   indios *Indians*   hoy mismo *this very day*

PREGUNTAS

1. ¿Dónde escuchaba el noticiero Juan?   2. ¿Cómo eran las noticias? 3. ¿Cuáles son las noticias en la televisión?   4. ¿Por qué apaga don Aurelio el televisor?   5. Según don Aurelio, ¿eran mejores las noticias cuando él era niño? 6. ¿Qué pasó con la tía Leonora?   7. ¿Dónde encontraron los arqueólogos unas ruinas? ¿Qué creen ellos?   8. ¿Qué noticia trajo la enfermera? ¿Qué piensa don Aurelio de esta noticia?   9. Para usted, ¿cuál fue la mejor noticia del año pasado?

NOTAS CULTURALES

1. Costa Rica, with a population of about three million, has a long history of democracy and political stability.

2. An important avenue and the second-largest market of San José are named Coca-Cola, perhaps as the result of large signs formerly displayed there. United States influence throughout Central America is very noticeable.

3. The terms **don** and **doña** are used to show respect, because of age or position. They are used with first names.

4. For Latin America in general, and Central America in particular, the 1980s have been the worst decade in history economically. Nearly every Spanish-American country is worse off now than it was ten or twenty years ago. Costa Rica is one of the least poor Central American countries, but poverty is crushing in most of the area. In El Salvador, half the children born die before they are five years old. In Central America, Costa Rica stands out as a true democracy with a relatively high standard of living.

5. Cartago was the administrative center of Costa Rica from 1563 to 1821, when Costa Rica won its independence from Spain and San José became its capital. Located in a rich coffee-growing area on the central plateau, it was totally destroyed in 1723 by an eruption of the Irazù volcano. Partially rebuilt, it was destroyed again by earthquakes in 1822, 1841, and 1910. Its buildings today are squat structures designed to resist earthquakes.

Funciones y *actividades*

In this chapter, you have seen examples of some important language functions, or uses. Here is a summary and some additional information about these functions of language.

TELLING A STORY

Here are some expressions that are often used in telling a story.

¿Sabe(s) qué le pasó a Julio (me pasó a mí) ayer?	*Do you know what happened to Julio (to me) yesterday?*
¿Sabía(s) que...?	*Did you know that . . .?*
Eso me recuerda...	*That reminds me of . . .*
Siempre recuerdo...	*I('ll) always remember . . .*
Después (Entonces)...	*Then . . .*
¿Y sabe(s) qué?	*And do you know what?*

GIVING THE SPEAKER ENCOURAGEMENT

When someone is telling a story, it's important to give the speaker some sort of response to show you are listening and want him or her to continue. Here are some ways to do this in Spanish.

¿Y después?	*And then what?*
¿Y qué pasó después?	*And then what happened?*
¿Y qué hacía(s) mientras pasaba eso?	*And what were you doing while that was happening?*
¿Y qué hizo (hiciste) después?	*And then what did you do?*
Sí, entiendo.	*Yes, I understand.*
Sí, claro.	*Yes, sure.*
Sí, cómo no.	*Yes, of course.*
¿En serio? ¿De veras?	*Really?*

USING POLITE EXPRESSIONS

Con permiso means *Excuse me* when you are about to pass in front of someone, eat something in front of someone, etc. It literally means "With your permission." **Perdón** means *Excuse me* when you have done something for which you are apologizing (like stepping on someone's toe or spilling something on someone).

¡**Salud!** (literally, "*Health!*") is used when making toasts to mean *Cheers!* and also when someone sneezes to mean *Gesundheit!*

¡**Felicitaciones!** means *Congratulations!*

There are two ways to say *You're welcome*: **De nada** and **No hay de qué**, both of which express *It's nothing.*

Now do the following activities, using the expressions you have just learned.

A. ¿Es usted una persona cortés? Referring to the drawings, use the polite expression that best fits each of the following situations. To evaluate your results, see page 300.

¡Bienvenido!

Gracias.

Me llamo Juan Vargas.

AH-CHÍS!

¿Qué dice usted...?

1. si le dan un regalo
2. si le dan las gracias por un favor
3. si quiere pasar delante de una persona o de un grupo de gente

4. si usted no conoce a una persona, pero quiere decirle su nombre
5. antes de tomar vino
6. a unas personas que empiezan a comer
7. si usted tropieza con *(bump into)* una persona en la calle
8. si alguien estornuda *(if someone sneezes)*
9. si un(a) amigo(-a) viene a visitarlo(-la); ustedes están en el aeropuerto
10. si un(a) buen(a) amigo(-a) anuncia que se va a casar
11. si alguien a quien usted no conoce le dice: «Hola, me llamo Julio Rendón.»
12. si usted está en un ascensor *(elevator)* lleno *(full)* de gente y quiere salir

B. ¿Y sabes qué...? With a partner, tell a story about something that happened to you or someone you know. Your partner will ask questions and give encouragement; use words and expressions from this chapter. Then change roles and your partner will tell a story.

C. Compañero(-a) de cuarto. Tell a story about a roommate you've had, or invent one. Include the answers to the following questions.

1. ¿Cómo era su compañero(-a)? ¿Qué estudiaba? ¿Estudiaban juntos(-as)?
2. ¿Les gustaban las mismas cosas? Por ejemplo, ¿les gustaba el mismo tipo de música? ¿de comida? ¿de ropa?
3. ¿Qué diferencias había entre su compañero(-a) y usted? Por ejemplo, ¿se levantaban más o menos a la misma hora? ¿Eran corteses los (las) dos?

D. Los sospechosos *(The suspects).* Imagine that a break-in occurred last night. Two students, **los sospechosos,** leave the room to devise their alibi. After a few minutes, call one of the suspects back into the room to answer your questions. Take notes on the answers, and be sure the second suspect is out of earshot. Then send the first suspect back out of the room and call in the second. If the second suspect's answers corroborate those of the first, they are **inocentes,** but if they contradict each other, both are **culpables** *(guilty).* Use the following questions or others of your own.

1. ¿Qué hiciste anoche? ¿Con quién estabas?   2. ¿Adónde fueron?   3. Si fueron al cine, ¿qué película vieron?   4. ¿Dónde se sentaron?   5. ¿Había mucha o poca gente allí?   6. ¿Comieron? ¿Qué comieron? ¿Cuánto costó? 7. ¿Quién les sirvió la comida? ¿Cómo era él o ella?   8. ¿Cómo llegaron al lugar donde fueron? ¿Fueron en auto? ¿en autobús?   9. ¿Cómo era el auto? ¿De qué color era?   10. ¿Qué ropa llevabas? ¿y tu amigo(-a)?   11. ¿A qué hora volvieron a casa?   12. ¿Dónde vive tu amigo(-a)?   13. ¿Cuántas horas pasaron juntos anoche?   14. ¿De qué cosas hablaron?

E. Mini-drama. Imagine that a Spanish-speaking visitor comes to see you. Tell him or her about what things were like at your school last year. Mention your daily routine, the courses you took, your professors and friends, and anything significant that was going on in the world.

VOCABULARIO ACTIVO

Cognados

el congreso	la gasolina	el programa documental
económico	el líder	público
la elección	las Naciones Unidas	la región
el experto, la experta	el, la poeta	el reportaje
el explorador, la exploradora	el político, la política	el senador, la senadora

Verbos

admirar	to admire
anunciar	to announce
apagar (gu)	to turn off, extinguish
atacar (qu)	to attack
bajar	to go down, decrease
celebrar	to celebrate
haber	there is, are
ocurrir	to happen, occur
pasar	to happen, occur
poner (g)	to turn on; to light
prender	to turn on; to light; to grasp
protestar	to protest
terminar	to finish, end

Las noticias

el acontecimiento	event, happening
el anuncio	announcement
las armas	arms, weapons
el aumento	increase, raise
el aumento de sueldo	raise in salary
el costo de la vida	cost of living
la cruz	cross
la Cruz Roja	Red Cross
el derecho	right
los derechos humanos	human rights
el ejército	army
la guerra	war
en guerra	at war
el guerrillero, la guerrillera	guerrilla (warrior)
el incendio	fire
el noticiero	news program
el obrero, la obrera	worker
el Papa	Pope
la revista	magazine
el SIDA	AIDS
la superpoblación	overpopulation
el terremoto	earthquake

Otras palabras y frases

cada	each, every
el compañero, la compañera	companion
el compañero, la compañera de cuarto	roommate
don, doña	terms of respect used with first names
la época	time, era, epoch
mientras	while
mismo	same
el pueblo	town; people
sin casa	homeless

Expresiones útiles

¿De veras?	Really?
¿En serio?	Really?

Cognados falsos

el canal	channel
la manifestación	demonstration
la reunión	meeting
suceder	to happen, occur

¡Comienzan
nuestras vacaciones
en México!

VIAJES Y PASEOS

Funciones

- Asking for directions
- Understanding directions
- Getting someone's attention

Vocabulario.   In this chapter you will talk about traveling.

Gramática.   You will discuss and use:

1. Past participles (corresponding to English verb forms in -ed, like *painted*) used as adjectives (*a painted wall*)

2. The present and past perfect tenses, corresponding to English constructions like *I have painted, I had painted*

3. The contrasts among the past indicative tenses

4. **Hace** with time expressions, to express how long something has been going on or how long ago it happened

Cultura.   The dialogues take place in various cities in Mexico.

¿CÓMO VIAJA USTED?

¿Anda en bicicleta?

¿Va a pie?

¿Hace autostop?

¿Viaja usted por tren?

la estación de trenes (de ferrocarril)
el horario
la salida, la llegada

¿Viaja usted por barco?

el puerto

¿Viaja usted por avión?

el aeropuerto
Los pasajeros suben al avión.

Si usted sale del país, tiene que pasar por la aduana.

El agente de aduana revisa las maletas (el equipaje).

En un banco usted cambia dinero o cheques de viajero.

la caja
el (la) cajero(-a)

Usted se queda en un hotel o en una pensión.

el hotelero
la recepción
la habitación (room)

Las definiciones. Dé la palabra que corresponde a la definición.

MODELO una cosa en que viajamos por mar: un... **barco**

1. un lugar donde las habitaciones cuestan poco: una...
2. un lugar donde cambiamos los dólares por pesos: un... o la...
3. un lugar donde revisan las maletas: la...
4. el lugar donde hay muchos barcos: el...
5. las maletas que llevamos cuando viajamos: el...
6. el lugar donde nos ayudan con los boletos y las reservaciones: la...
7. una persona que hace un viaje por avión: un(a)...

¿QUÉ HACE EL VIAJERO (*TRAVELER*) EXPERTO?

1. No deja las cosas para el último momento. Va a una agencia de viajes. Decide cómo va a viajar: por barco, por tren, por avión o a pie. Compra boletos de ida y vuelta (*round-trip*).

2. Decide si quiere quedarse en una pensión o en un hotel. Estudia los precios antes de decidir. Hace sus reservaciones antes de salir.

3. Lee varios libros sobre el sitio (*place*) que va a visitar. También consulta mapas.

4. Hace la maleta varios días antes de salir. No lleva mucho equipaje.

5. Siempre recuerda las tres cosas más importantes: los boletos, el dinero (o los cheques de viajero) y el pasaporte.

6. Llega temprano al aeropuerto, al puerto o a la estación de autobuses o del ferrocarril.

7. Siempre conoce las regulaciones de la aduana.

¿Verdadero o falso? Indique si las siguientes frases (*following sentences*) son verdaderas (*true*) o falsas.

1. El viajero experto compra los boletos en el aeropuerto antes de subir al avión.
2. Lleva mucho equipaje.
3. Hace la maleta la noche antes de salir.
4. Si el avión sale a las tres, el viajero experto llega a las 2:45.
5. Lee libros y consulta mapas del sitio que va a visitar.
6. Recuerda tres cosas importantes: el dinero, el pasaporte y las aspirinas.
7. No lleva cheques de viajero porque es difícil cambiarlos.
8. Pregunta el precio de las habitaciones antes de hacer la reservación.

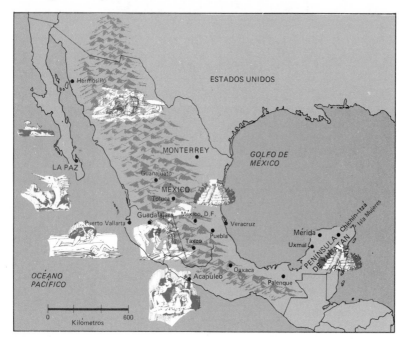

Preguntas

Para las preguntas 7–10, consulte el mapa de arriba.

1. ¿Le gusta viajar? ¿Qué ciudad o sitio visitó durante su último viaje? 2. ¿Piensa hacer un viaje largo este año? ¿un viaje corto (*short*)? ¿Adónde? ¿Cuándo? ¿Con quiénes? 3. Uno de los paseos favoritos de muchos niños es ir al parque zoológico. ¿Cuál es su paseo favorito? 4. ¿Cómo viaja usted? ¿Pasea mucho en auto usted? ¿Hace autostop a veces? 5. ¿Piensa hacer un paseo este fin de semana? ¿Adónde? 6. ¿Qué es un(a) cajero(-a)? Explique (*Explain*). ¿y un(a) hotelero(-a)? 7. Si usted quiere visitar ruinas de México, ¿adónde va? 8. Si usted quiere comprar recuerdos de su viaje a México, ¿qué ciudades debe visitar? 9. Si usted quiere ver los grandes museos y viajar por metro, ¿qué ciudad debe visitar? 10. Si usted quiere pescar en México, ¿adónde va?

I. El participio pasado usado como adjetivo

La recepción de un hotel nunca está cerrada.

Un estudiante norteamericano llega a la recepción de un hotel en la Ciudad de México.

EDWARD	Perdón, señor. Necesito cambiar un cheque de viajero y el banco de al lado está *cerrado*.
RECEPCIONISTA	Sí, señor, a esta hora ya todos los bancos están *cerrados*... Pero...usted puede cambiar dinero aquí en el hotel.
EDWARD	¡Fantástico! Entonces mi problema está *resuelto°*... ¿Me puede decir cómo llegar a...?
RECEPCIONISTA	¿...a la caja? ¡Cómo no!° Es muy fácil. ¿Ve aquel piano *cubierto°*? Pues...vaya *derecho°* y después de pasar el piano, la caja va a estar a su izquierda. ¡Y no se preocupe! La caja siempre está *abierta*.
EDWARD	Muchas gracias. ¿Sabe usted si los museos están *abiertos* hoy? Y las librerías... ¿hasta qué hora están *abiertas*?
RECEPCIONISTA	Bueno... las librerías están *abiertas* hasta tarde, pero los museos en general no abren los lunes... Pero la tienda de este hotel ¡es un pequeño museo! Allí usted va a encontrar de todo: *cuadros° pintados* por pintores *conocidos,* mapas muy *detallados°*, cosas *hechas°* a mano, ¡guías *escritas* en inglés... ! ¡Y la tienda está al lado de la caja... !
EDWARD	¡ ...muy bien *situada°*!
RECEPCIONISTA	¡También aceptan tarjetas de crédito°!
EDWARD	¡Muchas gracias, señor! Hasta luego.

---

resuelto *solved*   ¡Cómo no! *Sure!*   cubierto *covered*   derecho *straight ahead*
cuadros *paintings*   detallados *detailed*   hechas *made*   situada *located*   tarjetas
de crédito   *credit cards*

1. ¿Qué necesita hacer Edward?   2. ¿Están abiertos los bancos?   3. ¿Dónde está la caja en el hotel?   4. ¿Están abiertos los museos los lunes?   5. ¿Aceptan tarjetas de crédito en la tienda del hotel? ¿Qué venden allí?   6. ¿Está bien situada la tienda del hotel? ¿Por qué?

A. The past participles of regular English verbs end in -ed: *closed.* To form the past participle of regular Spanish **-ar** verbs, add **-ado** to the stem of the infinitive.

cerr-ar	**cerrado**	*closed*
situ-ar	**situado**	*situated*

B. To form the past participle of regular **-er** and **-ir** verbs, add **-ido** to the stem of the infinitive.

aprend-er	**aprendido**	*learned*
viv-ir	**vivido**	*lived*
conoc-er	**conocido**	*known*

When **-ido** is added, if the verb stem ends in **a, e,** or **o,** an accent mark must be written on the **i** to show that the two adjacent vowels do not merge to form a diphthong.

tra-er	**traído**	*brought*
cre-er	**creído**	*believed*
o-ír	**oído**	*heard*

The past participle of **ser** is **sido,** and of **ir, ido.**

C. Here are some irregular past participles. All end in **-to** except **dicho** and **hecho.**

abrir	**abierto**	*open, opened*
cubrir	**cubierto**	*covered*
describir	**descrito**	*described*
descubrir	**descubierto**	*discovered*
decir	**dicho**	*said*
devolver	**devuelto**	*returned, taken back*
escribir	**escrito**	*written*
hacer	**hecho**	*made, done*
morir	**muerto**	*died, dead*
poner	**puesto**	*put*
resolver	**resuelto**	*solved*
romper	**roto**	*broken*
ver	**visto**	*seen*
volver	**vuelto**	*returned*

D. The past participle is often used as an adjective and agrees in gender and number with the noun it modifies. It is frequently used with **estar** to describe a condition or state that results from an action.

¿Está escrito en español el poema? Sí... , creo que sí.
Is the poem written in Spanish? Yes, I think so.

La maleta está cerrada y no la puedo abrir.
The suitcase is closed and I can't open it.

Las reservaciones ya están hechas.
The reservations are already made.

EJERCICIOS

A. La búsqueda (*The search*). Juanita busca cosas hechas en países hispánicos. Haga el papel (*play the role*) de ella y forme preguntas según el modelo.

MODELO ¿Venden aquí cuadros pintados en México? (cerámica)
¿Venden aquí cerámica pintada en México?

1. ¿Tienen cosas hechas en México? (una guitarra, un poncho, dos maletas, un bolso, sandalias, un sombrero)
2. ¿Lees una novela escrita en español? (libros, una obra, un periódico, cartas, un calendario, una guía)

B. Imaginación y lógica. Forme frases lógicas usando una expresión de cada columna. Ponga atención a la forma del participio pasado.

MODELO una maleta cerrada

un libro	usar
una maleta	vestir
un viaje	conocer
unos problemas	hacer
un museo	romper
unas cosas	pintar
una casa	devolver
unos boletos	resolver
unas personas	abrir
unas reservaciones	cerrar

C. Sí, ya está hecho. Haga el papel de Graciela y dígale a su esposo que todas las preparaciones necesarias para su viaje a Puebla están hechas.

MODELO ¿Cerraste las ventanas?
Sí, las ventanas ya están cerradas.

1. ¿Informaste a los vecinos?
2. ¿Resolviste todos los problemas?
3. ¿Escribiste las cartas?
4. ¿Hiciste las reservaciones?
5. ¿Compraste los boletos?
6. ¿Pusiste las maletas en el auto?

D. ¡Un asesinato en la casa Solís! Descubrieron un asesinato (*murder*) en la casa de los señores Solís. Después de examinar la casa, el detective Rocha resuelve el crimen. Descubra quién es el asesino llenando los espacios (*filling in the blanks*) con el participio pasado de los verbos indicados.

MODELO romper Rocha vio muchas cosas **rotas** en el cuarto.

A la derecha de la silla el detective Rocha vio a un hombre (1) _____ (**morir**). La mesa ya estaba (2) _____ (**poner**) y allí había cosas muy caras, (3) _____ (**comprar**) en Francia. Rocha vio que los Solís eran gente rica. Tenían obras de arte (4) _____ (**pintar**) por Picasso, varias cosas bonitas (5) _____ (**traer**) de sus viajes a Europa, y unos libros (6) _____ (**escribir**) en el siglo XVI. Pero, allí también había una persona (7) _____ (**morir**). Era el señor Solís y tenía las manos muy (8) _____ (**cerrar**). En la mano derecha tenía un papel. Era una carta (9) _____ (**escribir**) por una mujer (10) _____ (**llamar**) Carolina. La carta decía: «(11) _____ (**querer**) amor (*love*), Tu esposa lo sabe todo (*knows all about it*). Hay que tener cuidado de ella. Carolina.» Rocha descubrió después que en la mano izquierda que estaba (12) _____ (**cerrar**) el señor Solís tenía un botón verde. Observó también que Solís tenía la camisa (13) _____ (**cubrir**) de sangre (*blood*). Después Rocha fue a la sala y allí encontró a la señora Solís, (14) _____ (**vestir**) de verde y (15) _____ (**sentar**) en el sofá. Parecía (16) _____ (**dormir**) pero estaba (17) _____ (**morir**). Rocha dijo: «El misterio está (18) _____ (**resolver**).» ¿Qué vio el detective en la sala? Había un bolso (19) _____ (**abrir**) al lado de la señora Solís. También en el sofá había una botella vacía (*empty bottle*) de píldoras para dormir. En la mano derecha de la señora había un cuchillo (20) _____ (**cubrir**) de sangre.

E. ¿Puede usted contestar estas preguntas?

1. ¿Cómo estaba la mesa? 2. ¿Qué clase de obras de arte tenían los Solís? 3. ¿Qué tenía en la mano derecha el señor Solís? ¿y en la izquierda? ¿Cómo estaban sus manos? 4. ¿Cómo estaba la camisa del señor Solís? 5. ¿De qué color estaba vestida la señora Solís? 6. ¿Dormía o descansaba la señora Solís? ¿Cómo estaba ella? 7. ¿En qué condición estaba el cuchillo? 8. ¿Quién fue el asesino?

Preguntas

1. ¿Cómo está usted en este momento? ¿cansado(-a)? ¿preocupado(-a)? 2. ¿Está usted sentado(-a) cerca de la ventana? ¿de la puerta? 3. ¿Tiene usted el libro abierto o cerrado ahora? ¿y el cuaderno? 4. ¿Está usted preocupado(-a) por sus clases? ¿Por qué otras cosas está preocupado(-a)? 5. En sus clases de inglés, ¿leyó usted obras escritas por Hemingway? ¿por Cervantes? ¿por García Márquez? 6. ¿Está muy contaminado el aire de esta ciudad? ¿de la ciudad donde usted vive? ¿de Nueva York? 7. ¿Tiene usted una cosa—un libro, ropa, un auto—hecha en otro país? 8. ¿Puede usted explicar el refrán (*saying*) que dice: «En boca cerrada no entran moscas (*flies*)»?

II. **El presente perfecto y el pluscuamperfecto**

Vista de
Guanajuato, México

Un suceso° misterioso en el pueblo de Guanajuato

HOMBRE Nº 1	Perdón, señor. ¿*Ha visto* usted policías por esta calle? *He oído* que no hay policías en esta parte de la ciudad.
HOMBRE Nº 2	Por aquí, no, no *he visto* policías, pero *me he encontrado* con° dos o tres en la Plaza Hidalgo.
HOMBRE Nº 1	¿Está cerca de aquí la Plaza Hidalgo?
HOMBRE Nº 2	No, está bastante lejos... Está en el centro, a unas veinte cuadras° de aquí...
HOMBRE Nº 1	Bien lejos...Bueno, gracias... ¿Pero está seguro de que no *ha visto* policías por aquí?
HOMBRE Nº 2	Segurísimo. Antes de encontrarme con usted, ¡no *había visto* un alma° por estas calles...!
HOMBRE Nº 1	Entonces, ¡arriba las manos!°

---

suceso *event*   me he encontrado con *I have run into, met up with*   cuadras *blocks*
un alma *a soul*   ¡arriba las manos! *hands up!*

---

1. ¿Hay policías por la calle?   2. ¿Dónde se ha encontrado con policías el segundo hombre? ¿Cuántos?   3. ¿Dónde está la Plaza Hidalgo?   4. ¿Qué quiere el primer hombre?

In English the present perfect and past perfect tenses are formed with the auxiliary verb *have* plus a past participle: *I have practiced, I had practiced.*

A. The present perfect tense

1. To form the Spanish present perfect tense, use a present-tense form of **haber** plus a past participle.

haber	+ *past participle*
he hemos ⎫ has habéis ⎬ practicado ha han ⎭	

2. The past participle always ends in **-o** when used to form a perfect tense; it does not agree with the subject in gender or number.

Ya hemos viajado a Guanajuato.	*We have already traveled to Guanajuato.*
No, ella no ha vuelto aún.	*No, she hasn't returned yet.*

3. The present perfect is used to report an action or event that has recently taken place or been completed and still has a bearing upon the present. It is generally used without reference to any specific time in the past (that is, without words such as **ayer, la semana pasada,** etc. which would require the preterit), since it implies a reference to the present day, week, month, etc.

Todavía no han llegado los García. ¿Los esperamos o salimos sin ellos?	*The Garcías still haven't arrived.* *Do we wait for them or do we leave without them?*
¿Estás listo? Sí, ya he comprado recuerdos para todos.	*Are you ready? Yes, I've already bought souvenirs for everybody.*

Contrast the following sentences:

Hemos revisado el horario y no hay otro tren.	*We've checked the schedule and there isn't another train.*
Ayer revisamos el horario y no había otro tren.	*Yesterday we checked the schedule and there wasn't another train.*

B. The past perfect tense

1. The past perfect tense **(pluscuamperfecto)** is formed with an imperfect form of **haber** plus a past participle.

haber	+ *past participle*
había habíamos ⎫ habías habíais ⎬ vuelto había habían ⎭	

2. It is used to indicate that an action or event had taken place at some time in the past prior to another past event, stated or implied. If the other past event is stated, it is usually expressed with the preterit or imperfect.

¿Habías paseado por aquí antes?	*Had you walked around here before?*
Ya habían comprado el pasaje de ida y vuelta cuando llamaste.	*They had already bought the round-trip ticket when you called.*
Cuando tú hacías las compras, yo todavía no había cambiado el dinero que tenía.	*When you were doing the shopping, I still hadn't exchanged the money I had.*

3. The auxiliary form of **haber** and the past participle are seldom separated by another word. Pronouns and negative words normally precede the form of **haber.**

¿Ya me han enviado la cuenta?	*Have they already sent me the bill?*
No, no te la han enviado todavía.	*No, they haven't sent it to you yet.*

When **haber** is used as an infinitive, the pronouns are attached to the infinitive and thus come between **haber** and the past participle.

Después de haberte visto, me encontré con tu hermana.	*After having seen you, I met (ran into) your sister.*

EJERCICIOS

A. Viajeros. ¡Todos han viajado recientemente! Incluyan a todos los viajeros, según el modelo.

MODELO Susana ha ido a Francia. (Jorge)
Jorge también ha ido a Francia.

1. Javier ha visitado ese museo en Londres varias veces. (nosotros, yo, Luis y Estela, tú, los turistas)
2. Ellos ya han viajado por México. (mi tía y yo, mis padres, tú, el profesor, la profesora, yo)
3. Cuando llegué, ellos ya habían salido. (mi novia, la doctora, ustedes, los turistas)

B. ¿Qué han hecho? Trabaje con un(a) amigo(-a) de la clase. Uno de ustedes hace el papel del Señor Castro y forma preguntas. El otro hace el papel de Matilde o Franco Díaz, y contesta las preguntas sobre las cosas que ya han hecho en México.

MODELO viajar en metro
CASTRO **¿Han viajado ustedes en metro?**
DÍAZ **Sí, hemos viajado en metro.**

1. ver el Museo de Antropología
2. asistir al Ballet Folklórico
3. subir a la Pirámide del Sol
4. visitar la Universidad Nacional
5. hacer un viaje a Puebla
6. ir al Palacio Nacional para ver los famosos murales

C. Pensar y hablar.   Complete las oraciones. Para cada espacio, escoja (*choose*) el verbo más apropiado y úselo en el presente perfecto.

1. (abrir, pasear) Nosotros _____ mucho hoy pero todavía no _____ la guía.
2. (ver, estar) Dices que tú _____ en México. ¿_____ las ruinas en Yucatán?
3. (bañarse, acostarse) Los niños ya _____ pero todavía no _____ .
4. (leer, ver) Yo _____ varias películas de terror pero todavía no _____ la novela «Frankenstein».
5. (morirse, volver) Los vecinos fueron al hospital a las cinco y todavía no _____ . ¿Crees que _____ don Carlos?

Ahora en el pluscuamperfecto.

6. (descubrir, morirse) Vi en el periódico esta mañana que _____ dos mexicanos famosos y también que unos ingenieros _____ petróleo cerca de Puebla.
7. (viajar, terminar) Cuando nació tu primer hijo yo ya _____ mis estudios. También ya _____ por todo México.
8. (levantarse, irse) Llamé a los Suárez esta mañana y todavía no _____. Los llamé otra vez por la tarde y (ellos) ya _____ de vacaciones.
9. (hablar, volver) No les dijimos a los tíos que nosotros _____ el sábado pasado porque no _____ con ellos hasta ayer.
10. (prometer, decir) Ustedes nos _____ que iban a llegar temprano. Nos lo _____ .

D. En acción.   ¿Qué han hecho estas personas recientemente? Describa cada uno de los siguientes dibujos (*following drawings*).

MODELO

**El hombre se
ha acostado.**

1.

2.

3.

4.

5.

6.

7.

8.

Preguntas

1. ¿Cuántos exámenes ha tenido esta semana? ¿este semestre? 2. ¿Qué ha hecho usted esta mañana? ¿y esta semana? 3. ¿Qué lugares interesantes ha visitado usted? 4. ¿Ha viajado usted a otros estados (*states*)? ¿a otros países? 5. ¿Qué películas buenas ha visto este año? ¿este mes? 6. ¿Quién le ha escrito a usted este mes? ¿Cuántas cartas ha enviado usted este mes? ¿A quién(es)? 7. En su vida, ¿ha perdido cosas de mucho valor? ¿Qué ha perdido? 8. ¿Ha tenido problemas usted en sus clases? 9. ¿Ha viajado usted por avión? ¿por barco? ¿por tren? ¿Adónde ha ido? 10. ¿Se ha quedado usted en un hotel caro? ¿en una pensión? ¿Dónde?

III. Contraste entre los tiempos pasados

Las playas de Isla Mujeres son estupendas.

En una casa de Taxco

PEDRO Te *llamé* el viernes pasado pero tu mamá me *dijo* que ya *habías salido* para Isla Mujeres. Me *han dicho* que es un lugar muy lindo. ¿Te *gustó*?

ELBA ¡Me *encantó*! ¡*Pasé* una semana fantástica! Nunca *me había imaginado*° un sitio tan lindo. ¡Las playas son estupendas!

PEDRO ¿Dónde está esa isla?

ELBA Está cerca de la península de Yucatán. El viaje por barco *llevó*° menos de una hora.

PEDRO ¿Tan poco...? ¿Y qué *hiciste* allí?

ELBA Pues... todas las mañanas *nadaba* y *tomaba* sol°. Después, a mediodía°, *almorzaba* y luego *descansaba* un rato°.

PEDRO Y por las noches, ¿qué *hacías*?

ELBA Pues...realmente *salí* sólo una noche en toda esa semana... La verdad es que no *era* necesario salir para divertirse. El hotel *tenía* de todo: restaurantes abiertos hasta medianoche°, una discoteca también abierta hasta muy tarde, y...¡mucha gente interesante!

nunca me había imaginado	*I had never imagined*	llevó *took*	tomaba sol *I sunbathed*
mediodía *noon*	un rato *awhile*	medianoche midnight	

1. ¿Por qué no estaba en casa Elba cuando Pedro la llamó?   2. ¿Le gustó a Elba Isla Mujeres?   3. ¿Cuánto tiempo llevó el viaje por barco a Isla Mujeres? 4. ¿Qué hacía Elba por la mañana? ¿y por la tarde?   5. ¿Qué tenía el hotel?

Spanish has four widely used tenses in the indicative mood that deal with past actions or events. Two of them—the preterit and the imperfect—are simple tenses, and two—the present perfect and the past perfect—are compound tenses. Although all four tenses describe past events, we have seen in this and previous chapters how they differ in interpretation and emphasis.

A. The preterit is used to give a simple report of past actions and conditions that are over. It is often used with adverbs of time that suggest a precise limit for the action (**ayer, por la mañana, la semana pasada, anoche,** etc.). No particular implications for the present are suggested.

B. The imperfect focuses on a past action or condition as something going on or repeated in the past, often as a context for understanding some other event. It is not used with adverbs of time that suggest that the action or condition is over, but with adverbs or expressions that indicate customary or repeated actions (**siempre, todos los días,** etc.).

C. The present perfect emphasizes that a past action has implications for the present. It is not used with references to a specific time in the past, but is often used with adverbs like **recientemente, últimamente, todavía, aún, ya,** etc. that include the idea of present time.

El barco todavía no ha llegado al puerto.	*The ship hasn't arrived in port yet.*
Últimamente, han viajado mucho, ¿no?	*You've traveled a lot recently, haven't you?*
Sí, hemos visitado tres países en los últimos dos meses.	*Yes, we've visited three countries in the last two months.*

D. The past perfect makes clear that a past action happened before another past action, stated or implied.

¿Ya habías estado en Cuernavaca?	*Had you already been in Cuernavaca?*
Yo ya había pagado las entradas cuando él llegó al teatro.	*I had already paid for the tickets when he arrived at the theater.*

E. Sentences may report speech directly or indirectly. Compare:

Ella dice «me voy».	*She says, "I'm going."*
Ella dice que se va.	*She says that she's going.*

Notice the sequence of tenses used when sentences indirectly report past speech.

Present speech:	**Dice que se va.** *She says that she is going.*
Past speech:	**Dijo que se iba.** *She said that she was going.*
Present speech:	**Dice que ya se ha ido al museo.** *She says that she has already gone to the museum.*
Past speech:	**Dijo que se había ido al museo.** *She said that she had gone to the museum.*

EJERCICIOS

A. ¿Cómo se dice en español?   Escoja *(Choose)* la frase en español que corresponde mejor a la oración *(sentence)* o frase en bastardilla *(italics)*.

1. *He used to come at eight o'clock.*
   a. Vino a las ocho.
   b. Venía a las ocho.
   c. Había venido a las ocho.
2. *They have already seen that museum.*
   a. Ya han visto ese museo.
   b. Ya vieron ese museo.
   c. Ya habían visto ese museo.
3. We were eating *when he came in.*
   a. cuando entraba
   b. cuando ha entrado
   c. cuando entró
4. *What have you done?*
   a. ¿Qué habías hecho?
   b. ¿Qué hiciste?
   c. ¿Qué has hecho?
5. I knew how to do it because *I had done it* before.
   a. lo hice
   b. lo había hecho
   c. lo he hecho
6. We did our homework while *we waited for you.*
   a. te hemos esperado
   b. te esperábamos
   c. te habíamos esperado

B. ¿Qué dijo Juana?   Haga el papel de la amiga de Juana y cuente qué dijo Juana. Empiece cada frase con: **Juana dijo...**

MODELO   Quiero viajar a Oaxaca.
          Juana dijo que quería viajar a Oaxaca.

1. Camino diez cuadras para llegar a mi oficina.
2. Ya he hecho las reservaciones.
3. Pienso invitar a mi prima.
4. Todavía no he decidido dónde quedarme.
5. He leído dos libros sobre la civilización azteca.
6. Voy a comprar muchos recuerdos para mi familia.

Preguntas

1. ¿Ha viajado usted a México? ¿a España? ¿a otro país hispano? ¿Cuándo? ¿Compró recuerdos? ¿cerámica? ¿una guitarra? ¿Vio ruinas? ¿de qué civilización?
2. ¿Adónde fue usted de vacaciones el verano pasado? ¿Había estado allí antes?
3. De niño(-a), ¿adónde iba de vacaciones con su familia? ¿Le gustaba ir allí? ¿Por qué?   4. ¿En qué ciudades ha vivido usted? ¿Cuál le ha gustado más? ¿Por qué?
5. Antes de estudiar aquí, ¿asistió a otra universidad? ¿Por qué cambió de universidad?   6. En uno de sus viajes, ¿ha tenido usted que pasar por la aduana? ¿en qué país(es)? ¿Cuándo? ¿Revisaron sus maletas? ¿Conocía usted las regulaciones?   7. La última vez que usted viajó, ¿se quedó usted en un hotel o en una pensión? ¿Hizo sus reservaciones de hotel por teléfono o por carta?   8. ¿Ha cambiado cheques de viajero últimamente? ¿en un banco? ¿en la caja de un hotel? ¿en otro lugar? ¿O prefiere usar sólo tarjetas de crédito cuando viaja?

IV. *Hacer* en expresiones de transcurso de tiempo

Una estación de trenes en Ciudad de México

En una estación de trenes en la Ciudad de México

JANE	¡Por fin llegas!
FERNANDO	¿«Por fin»? *¿Cuánto tiempo hace que* me esperas?°
JANE	*Hace una hora que* estoy aquí. ¿Dónde estabas?
FERNANDO	En casa, hasta que salí *hace media hora*°. ¿Por qué?
JANE	¿No teníamos que encontrarnos a las cinco para tomar el tren de las cinco y cuarto? Son las seis... Cuando tú saliste de tu casa, ya *hacía media hora que* yo estaba aquí...° ¡y el tren salió *hace cuarenta y cinco minutos!*
FERNANDO	Tú y tu puntualidad yanqui. Hay otros trenes... Estás en América Latina, Jane, ¿recuerdas?

JANE   Pero...dime, Fernando, en general, si tú tienes una cita° a las cinco, ¿a qué hora llegas...?

FERNANDO   Un poco más tarde, por supuesto. A las cinco y media, o a las seis, o...

¿Cuánto tiempo...   *How long have you been waiting for me?*   hace media hora   *half an hour ago*   ya hacía media hora...   *I had already been here for half an hour*   cita   *appointment*

---

1. ¿Cuánto tiempo hace que Jane espera a Fernando?   2. ¿Dónde estaba Fernando?   3. ¿A qué hora tenían que encontrarse ellos? ¿Por qué?   4. ¿Cuánto tiempo hacía que Jane esperaba cuando Fernando salió de su casa?   5. Si Fernando tiene una cita a las cinco, en general ¿a qué hora llega?   6. Para usted, ¿es importante la puntualidad? ¿Cree usted que la puntualidad es una característica yanqui? ¿Tiene amigos hispanos que son puntuales? ¿Y amigos norteamericanos que no son puntuales?

A. To express an action or event that began in the past and continues into the present use the construction:

> **Hace** + *time period* + **que** + *verb in the present tense*

Hace dos años que vivo en México.   *I have been living in Mexico for two years.*

Hace tres horas que están en la oficina de la aduana.   *They have been in the customs office three hours.*

The verb in the main clause is in the present tense, since the action is still in progress.

B. To express an action or event that began at some point in the past and continued up to some other point in the past, use:

> **Hacía** + *time period* + **que** + *verb in the imperfect tense*

Hacía dos años que vivía en Nueva York cuando volvió a Guadalajara.   *She had been living in New York for two years when she returned to Guadalajara.*

Hacía ocho días que estaban en esa pensión.   *They had been in that boardinghouse for eight days.*

C. The clause in the present or imperfect can occur at the beginning of the construction. In that case, **que** is omitted.

Viajo por la península hace quince días. (Hace quince días que viajo por la península.)   *I have been traveling around the peninsula for fifteen days.*

Viajaba por la península hacía quince días. (Hacía quince días que viajaba por la península.)	*I had been traveling around the peninsula for fifteen days.*

D. Hace can also mean *ago*. In this case the verb is in the preterit or imperfect.

Subieron al avión hace media hora.	*They got on the plane half an hour ago.*
¿Dormías hace dos horas?	*You were sleeping two hours ago?*

E. To ask a question with these expressions, use the construction:

> ¿**Cuánto tiempo hace (hacía) que** + *verb*?

¿Cuánto tiempo hace que están en la oficina de la aduana?	*How long have they been in the customs office?*
¿Cuánto tiempo hacía que estaban en esa pensión?	*How long had they been in that boardinghouse?*
¿Cuánto tiempo hace que subieron al avión?	*How long ago did they get on the plane?*

EJERCICIOS

A. En otras palabras. Exprese las oraciones en otras palabras, cambiándolas según el modelo.

MODELOS Hace un año que vivo en Oaxaca.
Vivo en Oaxaca hace un año.

Hace un año que viví en Oaxaca.
Viví en Oaxaca hace un año.

1. Hace dos horas que esperan a su amigo en el Hotel Colón.
2. Hace una hora que los niños se acostaron.
3. Hace tres años que mi esposa estudia en Cuernavaca.
4. Hace años que fui a Yucatán por barco.
5. Hace una semana que Rita no anda en bicicleta.
6. Hace seis meses que compré esos pasajes con mi tarjeta de crédito.
7. Hace una hora que subieron al avión y todavía no ha salido.
8. Hace media hora que Silvia toma sol en la playa.

B. Lo hice hace tiempo. Silvia se ha preparado para su viaje a la Ciudad de México. Haga el papel de Silvia y conteste las preguntas de su mamá, usando **hace** + una expresión de tiempo.

MODELO ¿Ya hablaste con la agente de viajes? (tres semanas)
Sí, hablé con la agente de viajes hace tres semanas.

1. ¿Ya compraste los pasajes de ida y vuelta? (diez días)
2. ¿Fuiste al banco? (una semana)
3. ¿Pusiste los cheques de viajero en tu bolso? (unas horas)
4. ¿Hiciste las maletas? (dos semanas)
5. ¿Leíste tu guía turística? (mucho tiempo)
6. ¿Ya pediste una habitación en el hotel? (dos meses)
7. ¿Revisaste el horario del avión? (dos días)
8. ¿Llamaste un taxi? (media hora)

C. Entrevista. Gloria Torres tiene entrevista para un empleo como secretaria bilingüe en una compañía grande de México. Haga el papel de Gloria y conteste las preguntas afirmativamente, usando **hace** + una expresión de tiempo.

MODELO   Usted busca trabajo como secretaria bilingüe, ¿no? (diez días)
Sí, hace diez días que busco trabajo como secretaria bilingüe.

1. Su familia vive en la capital, ¿no? (veinte años)
2. Usted estudia inglés con una profesora norteamericana, ¿no? (diez años)
3. Usted da clases de inglés por la noche, ¿no? (un año)
4. Uno de sus amigos trabaja aquí, ¿no? (tres años)
5. Usted sabe escribir cartas comerciales, ¿no? (mucho tiempo)
6. Usted conoce las regulaciones de la aduana, ¿no? (varios años)
¡Pues hace varios años que necesito una persona como usted!

D. Traducción.   Exprese en español.

1. The ship arrived at the port two days ago.
2. I had been sleeping for an hour when the train passed and woke me up.
3. We've been traveling on foot for three hours. Wouldn't you prefer to ride a bicycle?
4. She's been waiting in the hotel for twenty minutes.
5. You (**tú**) have been complaining about the train schedule for two hours!
6. I cashed my last traveler's check three days ago! I've had to use my credit card five times!
7. They had been looking for the luggage for an hour when she found one suitcase near the door.

Preguntas

1. ¿Cuántas semanas hace que comenzó el semestre? ¿Y cuánto tiempo hace que comenzó la clase de hoy?   2. ¿Cuánto hace que usted viajó a otra ciudad o país? ¿a qué ciudad? ¿a qué país?   3. ¿Cuánto tiempo hace que usted conoció a su profesor(a) de español? ¿Dónde se conocieron?   4. ¿Cuánto hace que usted comió su última comida? ¿y que usted se levantó?   5. ¿Cuánto hace que usted está en la universidad?   6. ¿Cuánto hace que usted estudia español?   7. ¿Va usted mucho al cine con sus amigos(-as)? ¿Cuánto tiempo hace que usted vio una película interesante? ¿qué película? Descríbala en tres o cuatro oraciones.

EN LA ANTIGUA CAPITAL AZTECA

La Torre Latinoamericana y el Palacio de Bellas Artes están cerca del Parque Alameda.

En una oficina del Zócalo, México, D.F.[1] Dos agentes de la Compañía Turismo Mundial le dan la bienvenida° a Amalia Mercado, una agente uruguaya en viaje de negocios°.

HÉCTOR   ¡Bienvenida, señorita Mercado! ¿Qué tal el viaje?

AMALIA   Bastante bueno, gracias. Pero... ¡No me llame «señorita»! Llámeme Amalia, por favor. ¿Y usted es...?

HÉCTOR   ¡Oh, perdóneme! Yo soy Héctor Peralta, y éste es Alonso Rodríguez. Él está a cargo de° las excursiones al Caribe°...

AMALIA   ¡Pero si ya nos hemos conocido! Fue en Montevideo. ¿Recuerdas?

ALONSO   ¡Claro! Me llevaste a pasear por la playa después de haber asistido a una reunión de trabajo muy aburrida.

AMALIA   No sabía que ahora vivías en México.

ALONSO   Vine aquí hace dos años.

HÉCTOR   Cuéntenos algo de usted, Amalia. ¿Es éste su primer viaje a México?

AMALIA   Sí. Vine por invitación de la Compañía Mexicana de Aviación. ¡Y vean mi suerte! La invitación incluye° pasaje de ida y vuelta y seis días en el mejor hotel de esta ciudad, que me parece misteriosa y fascinante.

HÉCTOR   Es verdad. La ciudad está construida sobre las ruinas de la antigua capital azteca...

ALONSO   ...que estaba en medio de un lago°,[2] algo así como una antigua Venecia mexicana, ¿no?

HÉCTOR   Exacto. Dicen que los aztecas tenían su gran templo aquí cerca, en el sitio donde está ahora la catedral.

AMALIA   ¿Realmente? ¡Qué interesante!...¿Y qué les parece si me llevan a conocer el centro? ¡Recuerden que sólo tengo seis días!

ALONSO   Tus deseos° son órdenes, Amalia. Síganme. Los invito a tomar una copa° en el bar de la Torre Latinoamericana.[3]

HÉCTOR   Desde allí usted va a poder admirar la belleza° de esta ciudad. ¡La vista° es tan hermosa°!

AMALIA   ¡Qué suerte!...Pero, por favor, espérenme allá. No he comprado película para mi cámara y ¡quiero sacar muchas fotos! ¿Cuál es la dirección° de la Torre Latinoamericana?

ALONSO   Está en la esquina de la Avenida San Juan de Letrán y la Avenida Madero. Mira, te explico: ve a la salida° del hotel y cruza la calle. Allí enfrente hay una parada de taxis°. Toma un taxi y dile al taxista que te lleve a la Torre Latinoamericana. ¡Más fácil, imposible!, ¿no...? El bar está muy bien situado: en el último piso, donde también hay un observatorio ¡y una vista magnífica de la ciudad!

AMALIA   ¡Qué bien! Entonces, hasta muy pronto...

---

dan la bienvenida *welcome*   negocios *business*   a cargo de *in charge of* Caribe *Caribbean*   incluye *includes*   en medio de un lago *in the center of a lake*   deseos *wishes*   una copa *a drink*   belleza *beauty*   vista *view*   hermosa *beautiful* dirección *address*   salida *exit*   parada de taxis *taxi stand*

PREGUNTAS

1. ¿Se han conocido Amalia y Alonso? ¿Dónde?   2. ¿Cuánto tiempo hace que Alonso vino a México?   3. ¿Qué incluye la invitación que recibió Amalia? 4. Describa la antigua capital azteca.   5. ¿Adónde van a tomar una copa los tres amigos?   6. ¿Qué no ha comprado Amalia?   7. ¿Dónde está situada la Torre Latinoamericana? Y el bar, ¿dónde está situado? ¿Hay una vista de la ciudad?

NOTAS CULTURALES

1. **El Zócalo** (officially called **Plaza de la Constitución**), one of the biggest squares in the world, is located in the center of Mexico City (**México, Distrito Federal**). One side is occupied by the cathedral, one of the largest in America, built on the site of a former Aztec temple. Another side is occupied by the **Palacio Nacional**, which contains the offices of the president and other government officials. It was built over the site of Moctezuma's palace. Moctezuma was the emperor of the Aztecs, who had conquered most of the other Indians of Mexico by the time the Spanish arrived.

2. The subsoil of Mexico City is like a sponge; about 85 percent of it is water, much of which is extracted from time to time for use in the growing city. For that reason, many of the older public buildings have been thrust upward and must be entered by stairways added later to the original structure, while others have sunk and must now be reached by descending a stairway.

3. The **Torre Latinoamericana** is a forty-four-story skyscraper, one of the tallest in Latin America. It literally floats on its foundation, which consists of piers sunk deep into the clay beneath Mexico City. The observatory on top is popular with tourists.

Funciones y *actividades*

In this chapter, you have seen examples of some important language functions, or uses. Here is a summary and some additional information about these functions of language.

ASKING FOR DIRECTIONS

The ability to ask for and understand directions is one of the most important language functions you will need when traveling in a Spanish-speaking country. Here are some ways to ask for directions.

¿Dónde está...?	*Where is . . .?*
Busco la calle...	*I'm looking for . . . Street.*
¿Hay un correo (una estación de autobuses) cerca de aquí?	*Is there a post office (a bus station) near here?*
Por favor, señor(a), ¿está lejos (cerca) el mercado?	*Please, sir (ma'am), is the marketplace far away (nearby)?*
¿Cuál es la dirección de... ?	*What's the address of . . . ?*
¿Me puede decir cómo llegar a...?	*Can you tell me how to get to . . . ?*
¿Por dónde va uno a... ?	*How do you get to . . . ?*

UNDERSTANDING DIRECTIONS

Here are some responses you may hear when you ask for directions.

Siga por la calle...	*Follow . . . Street . . .*
Doble a la izquierda (derecha).	*Turn left (right).*
Siga adelante (derecho).	*Keep going straight.*
Vaya derecho hasta llegar a...	*Go straight until you get to . . .*
Sígame hasta llegar a...	*Follow me until you get to . . .*
Camine dos cuadras hasta llegar a...	*Walk two blocks until you arrive at . . .*
Cruce la calle y...	*Cross the street and . . .*
Está al lado de...	*It's next to . . .*
Está al norte (sur, este, oeste) de...	*It's north (south, east, west) of . . .*
Está en la esquina de...	*It's on the corner of . . .*
Está en el centro.	*It's downtown.*
Después de pasar por... , está...	*After you pass . . . , it's . . .*

GETTING SOMEONE'S ATTENTION

One way to get attention is to simply say, **¡Oiga, señor (señora, señorita)! Oiga** is a word that never fails to get people to lend an ear. **Perdón, perdóneme,** or **discúlpeme** are also often used and are more polite.

Ahora haga las siguientes actividades, usando las expresiones que acaba de aprender (*you have just learned*).

A. **En la Ciudad de México.** Usted está en la Ciudad de México, en la cruce (*intersection*) de la Avenida Insurgentes y el Paseo de la Reforma. Siga las instrucciones. ¿Dónde está usted ahora y qué sitios turísticos ve usted? (Empiece siempre desde Insurgentes y Paseo de la Reforma; vea el mapa que sigue.) Las respuestas están en la página 324.

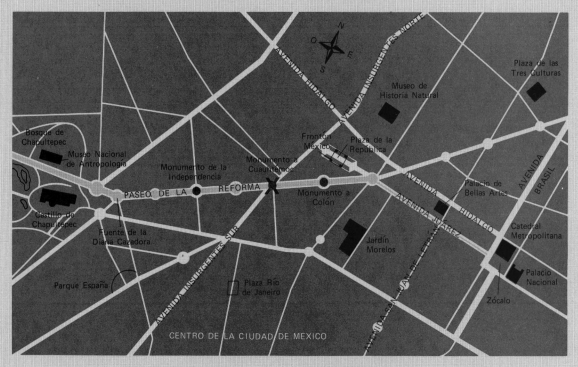

MODELO   Tome la Avenida Insurgentes Norte hasta llegar a la Avenida Hidalgo. Doble a la derecha. Siga derecho hasta la Avenida San Juan de Letrán y doble a la derecha. Camine media cuadra y lo va a ver a su derecha.
         el Palacio de Bellas Artes

1. Vaya derecho por Paseo de la Reforma hasta llegar a la Fuente de la Diana Cazadora. Allí no vaya derecho. Usted va a entrar al Parque de Chapultepec, pero siga por Paseo de la Reforma hasta llegar a un gran edificio a su derecha.
2. Tome Paseo de la Reforma hacia el Monumento a Colón y vaya hasta la Avenida Juárez. Doble a la derecha. Cruce las Avenidas San Juan de Letrán y Brasil. Siga adelante. Es una gran plaza que va a ver enfrente de usted.
3. Tome Paseo de la Reforma hasta llegar a la Avenida Juárez. Doble a la izquierda. Está en la Plaza de la República.
4. Tome Insurgentes Norte hasta la Avenida Hidalgo. Doble a la derecha. Cruce las Avenidas San Juan de Letrán y Brasil. Está en la esquina de Hidalgo y Brasil.

B. Perdidos. Usando el mapa de la Ciudad de México en la página 323 y los sitios del ejercicio A que usted encontró, trabaje con un(a) amigo(-a) de la clase y describa cómo ustedes no encontraron los sitios y se perdieron *(got lost)* en la Ciudad de México.

C. ¿Por dónde va uno para llegar a... ? Trabajando con un(a) amigo(-a) de la clase, pregunte y conteste cómo van desde la clase hasta los siguientes lugares:

1. el aeropuerto
2. la estación de autobuses o de trenes
3. un parque o un lugar bonito para dar un paseo
4. un buen restaurante
5. un sitio de interés que usted quiere visitar

D. Un viaje imaginario. Trabaje con un(a) amigo(-a) de la clase y describa un viaje imaginario que hicieron ustedes. Use verbos en el pasado (pretérito, imperfecto, presente perfecto, etc.) y también expresiones con **hacer.** Cuente cuándo salieron, adónde fueron, qué vieron, qué sitios similares habían visto antes, cuánto tiempo hacía que tenían planes, etcétera.

Respuestas, Ejercicio A, página 323.
1. el Museo Nacional de Antropología 2. el Zócalo 3. el Frontón México
4. la Catedral Metropolitana

VOCABULARIO ACTIVO

Cognados

la cerámica	la puntualidad	las ruinas
fantástico	las regulaciones	el secretario, la secretaria bilingüe
misterioso	las reservaciones	yanqui
la península		

Verbos

consultar	*to consult*
cubrir	*to cover*
devolver	*to return, take back*
encontrarse con	*to meet (up with), run into*
enviar	*to send*
llevar	*to take (a period of time)*
pasear	*to take a walk, ride*
romper	*to break*
situar	*to situate, locate*
tomar sol	*to sunbathe*

Los viajes

a pie	*on foot*
la aduana	*customs, customs house*
andar en bicicleta	*to ride a bicycle*
el autostop	*hitchhiking*
hacer autostop	*to hitchhike*
el barco	*boat, ship*
la caja	*cashier's office; cash register*
el cajero, la cajera	*cashier*
el cheque de viajero	*traveler's check*
de ida y vuelta	*round-trip*
el equipaje	*baggage, luggage*
el ferrocarril	*railway*
la habitación	*room*
el horario	*schedule, timetable*
el hotelero	*hotel-keeper*
la pensión	*boardinghouse*
el puerto	*port; harbor*
el sitio	*place, spot, site*
la tarjeta de crédito	*credit card*
el viajero	*traveler*

Otras palabras y frases

el alma *f*	*soul*
la cita	*appointment*

la cuadra	*block*
el cuadro	*painting*
Hace (dos años) que... + verb in present	*For (two years) . . .*
Verb in past + hace (dos años)	*two years ago . . .*
la isla	*island*
la medianoche	*midnight*
el mediodía	*noon*
todavía	*still, yet*
últimamente	*recently*

Expresiones útiles

Después de pasar...	*After passing . . .*
Está al lado de...	*It's next to . . .*
Está en el centro.	*It's downtown.*
Está en la esquina de...	*It's on the corner of . . .*
Vaya derecho.	*Go straight ahead.*

Cognados falsos

el pasaje	*ticket*
la recepción	*reception desk*
resolver	*to solve*
revisar	*to check, examine*

> Don't forget: Irregular past participles, page 306

LECTURA VI

Hispanoamérica: Antes y después de la conquista

Mucho antes del siglo XVI, cuando llegaron los españoles al Nuevo Mundo— ya existían en estas tierras° varias civilizaciones indígenas, como por ejemplo: los mayas en Centroamérica, los toltecas y los aztecas en México, y los incas en lo que es hoy° Perú, Ecuador y Bolivia.

    Una civilización muy avanzada fue la de° los mayas, quienes sabían mucho sobre matemáticas, astronomía y arte. Construyeron observatorios y pirámides con decoraciones muy impresionantes°. También tenían su propio° sistema de escritura° y un calendario muy exacto.

    Otra civilización bastante avanzada fue la de los toltecas. Construyeron ciudades imponentes° y sabían mucho de agricultura. También tenían com-

°lands

lo... what is today

°that of

impressive/own

writing

impressive

La Pirámide del Sol, Teotihuacán

plicadas leyes° sociales, políticas y religiosas. Cuando llegaron a Teotihuacán, un lugar en el centro de México, cerca del año 900 d.C., encontraron allí pirámides enormes, entre ellas la Pirámide del Sol—construida aproximadamente en el año 500 a.C.—que vemos en la foto. Cuando el conquistador español Hernán Cortés llegó a México en 1519, Teotihuacán estaba en manos de° los aztecas.

    En los siglos XV y XVI, los aztecas dominaban a los otros pueblos de México. La capital azteca era la ciudad de Tenochtitlán, sitio de la actual° capital del país. Era una ciudad magnífica, construida en medio de un lago° y en islas conectadas por puentes°. Tenía templos, palacios y mercados. Los aztecas tenían un gran imperio°, pero también tenían muchos enemigos°. Con la ayuda de las otras tribus indígenas de la región, Cortés capturó a

laws

in the possession of

present
lake
bridges
empire/enemies

El conquistador Hernán Cortés (1485-1547)

Moctezuma, el emperador azteca, y en tres años conquistó todo el imperio azteca.

Otra gran civilización indígena de hispanoamérica fue la de los incas. Vivían en la región de los Andes (hoy Ecuador, Perú y Bolivia). La sociedad incaica tenía una estructura social piramidal, con un jefe° supremo (el Inca) y varias clases sociales. Los nobles eran muy ricos, pero la gente común trabajaba en tierras colectivas y solamente recibía la comida necesaria para vivir. Los viejos y los enfermos recibían ayuda del estado°, un sistema bastante socialista. Los incas sabían mucho de medicina e ingeniería. Usaban anestesia y hacían operaciones delicadas. Construyeron excelentes caminos°, puentes, acueductos y fortalezas°, como la que vemos en la foto.

chief

state

roads

fortresses

Una fortaleza incaica

El Padre Miguel Hidalgo, líder de la rebelión

Durante los tres siglos de la Colonia—desde el siglo XVI hasta el XIX—, la sociedad hispanoamericana fue básicamente feudal. Estaba formada por cuatro grupos: los indios, los mestizos (hijos de madres indias y padres españoles), los criollos (blancos nacidos en América) y los españoles (nacidos en España). Los indios trabajaban para los españoles y para los criollos. Trabajaban muy duro en las minas o en las haciendas° de los ricos. Poco a poco° el número de mestizos crecía°. Los españoles tenían casi todo el poder°, porque el gobierno español les daba a ellos todos los puestos políticos. Esta discriminación causaba resentimientos entre los criollos y, por eso, eran inevitables los movimientos de independencia.

Los movimientos revolucionarios de independencia empezaron en el siglo XIX. En México, el Padre Miguel Hidalgo empezó una rebelión que llevó a° la independencia. En la Argentina, el General José de San Martín, un criollo, fue el jefe de las fuerzas revolucionarias que lucharon° por la independencia de Argentina y Chile. Otro jefe criollo, Simón Bolívar, ganó la liberación del norte de Sudamérica. Para 1825 ya toda Hispanoamérica era independiente.

Aunque Bolívar quería unir todos los países de Hispanoamérica para formar un solo país poderoso°, la unidad fue imposible, y los países permanecieron° separados e independientes entre sí. El sueño° de Bolívar no se realizó° y muchas naciones pasaron a manos de dictadores. Para la mayoría de los países de Hispanoamérica, la independencia política de España no fue una verdadera° liberación. Sin embargo,° siguen buscando la democracia.

estates, large farms
little by little / grew/power

led to

struggled

powerful
remained/dream
didn't come about
true/However

PREGUNTAS

1. Antes del siglo XVI, ¿existían civilizaciones indígenas en el Nuevo Mundo? Dé ejemplos.   2. ¿Qué construyeron los mayas?   3. ¿Dónde está la Pirámide del Sol?   4. ¿Cómo era la capital de los aztecas?   5. ¿En qué región vivían los incas? 6. Describa la estructura social de los incas.   7. ¿Qué construyeron ellos? 8. ¿Por qué fue feudal la estructura social de Hispanoamérica durante los tres siglos de la Colonia?   9. ¿Cuándo empezaron los movimientos de independencia? 10. ¿Quién fue Miguel Hidalgo? ¿y José de San Martín? ¿y Simón Bolívar?

¿Verdadero o falso?
1. Los mayas tenían su propio sistema de escritura.   2. La capital azteca era Tenochtitlán.   3. Moctezuma era un conquistador español.   4. El sistema de gobierno de los incas era bastante socialista.   5. Los incas hacían operaciones delicadas.   6. Durante los tres siglos de la Colonia, los mestizos tenían mucho poder político.   7. El General José de San Martín era criollo.   8. Para 1825 toda Hispanoamérica era independiente.

CAPÍTULO TRECE

En el Museo del Prado, hay obras de arte maravillosas.

ARTES Y LETRAS

Vocabulario. In this chapter you will talk about art and literature.

Gramática. You will discuss and use:

1. The subjunctive mood, an alternative system of verb forms; the expressions **ojalá**, **tal vez**, and **quizá(s)**
2. The present subjunctive of regular verbs
3. The present subjunctive of irregular, stem-changing, and spelling-changing verbs
4. Other command forms in the subjunctive; the **nosotros** (*let, let's*) and **vosotros** commands

Cultura. The dialogues take place in Madrid.

Funciones

- Extending invitations
- Accepting invitations
- Declining invitations
- Making a toast
- Making introductions

el arte realista, el realismo

Retrato de Felipe IV (1623),
Diego Rodríguez de Silva y Velázquez
(1599–1660)

el arte abstracto

Los tres músicos (1921), cuadro de Pablo Ruiz y Picasso (1881–1973)

ARTES...

el cuadro   el retrato

el pintor (la pintora)
la pintura

el (la) modelo

la escultura
la escultora (el escultor)

el museo, la galería
la exposición *(exhibit)*

El Teatro Nacional

el baile
el bailarín, la bailarina
la función

el ballet; la ópera
la música
el compositor, la compositora
el, la cantante *(singer)*
la orquesta
el director, la directora

...Y LETRAS

El Teatro Popular

una obra de teatro
los personajes *(characters)*
Escena 3
el actor (el artista)
la actriz (la artista)

la novela; el, la novelista
el cuento *(short story);* el, la cuentista
la poesía, el poema; el, la poeta
el ensayo *(essay);* el, la ensayista
el escritor (el autor)
la escritora (la autora)
la antología

La palabra inapropiada.   ¿Qué palabra no se relaciona con las otras de la serie? Explique por qué.

> **MODELO**   artista, romántico, realista, abstracto
> **artista (es persona; no es estilo)**

1. escritor, compositor, pintora, poema
2. cuadro, pintura, retrato, ballet
3. teatro, periódico, novela, cuento
4. pintar, escribir, leer, bailar
5. ensayista, cuentista, novelista, artista
6. galería, exposición, antología, museo
7. escena, drama, actriz, noticiero
8. revista, libro, autor, antología

El examen final.   ¿Qué sabe usted de arte y literatura españolas? Escoja (*choose*) la descripción apropiada de la columna derecha para cada nombre de la columna izquierda.

1. *Don Quijote*
2. Pablo Picasso
3. Plácido Domingo
4. *Las Meninas*
5. Andrés Segovia
6. Julio Iglesias

a. cantante español contemporáneo
b. famoso guitarrista clásico español del siglo XX
c. novela famosísima de Miguel de Cervantes
d. famoso pintor español del siglo XX
e. obra de arte pintada por Diego de Velázquez
f. cantante de ópera

Los gustos artísticos (*Artistic tastes*).   Entreviste a otra persona de la clase. ¿Cuáles son los intereses culturales de esa persona?

1. ¿Prefieres leer cuentos, novelas, revistas o sólo el periódico?
2. ¿Cuál es tu autor o autora favorita? ¿tu novela o cuento favorito?
3. ¿Lees más de diez libros por año? ¿veinte? ¿Qué clase de libros lees?
4. ¿Te gusta escribir? ¿Sabes pintar? ¿cantar? ¿tocar el violín?
5. ¿Te gustan los cuadros realistas o prefieres el arte abstracto?
6. ¿Sabes los nombres de tres pintores famosos? ¿de tres pintores españoles?
7. ¿Te interesa el teatro? ¿O prefieres el cine? ¿Por qué?
8. ¿Lees el periódico todos los días? ¿Lees revistas? ¿Cuáles?
9. ¿Lees poesía? ¿Quién es tu poeta preferido(-a)? ¿tu poema favorito? ¿Puedes describírnoslos?

I. El modo subjuntivo; *ojalá, tal vez, quizá(s)*

Plácido Domingo, cantante español muy conocido, canta *Lohengrin*.

En un teatro de Madrid

AGENTE Con o sin catarro, Matilde siempre canta bien. Come naranjas y ya está°.

DIRECTOR *Ojalá que cante* bien esta noche.°

AGENTE ¿Por qué? ¿Asiste el presidente de los Estados Unidos... ?

DIRECTOR No, pero ¡*tal vez asistan* los reyes de España!°

AGENTE Entonces, ¡*ojalá que Matilde coma* muchas naranjas!°

---

ya está *that's it, everything is OK*   Ojalá...noche *I hope she sings well tonight.*
¡tal...España! *perhaps the King and Queen of Spain will attend!*   ¡ojalá...naranjas! *let's hope Matilde eats many oranges!*

---

1. Según el director, ¿canta mal Matilde cuando está enferma?   2. ¿Qué hace Matilde para cantar bien con catarro?   3. ¿Cree usted que Matilde va a comer tantas naranjas como dice el agente? ¿Por qué?

A. Verb forms differ in mood as well as in person, number, and tense. So far in this text, except for command forms, all verb forms have been in the indicative mood. Verbs in the indicative are used to report facts. They affirm the existence of an action or condition.

Matilde siempre canta bien.	*Matilde always sings well.*
Matilde come naranjas.	*Matilde eats oranges.*

That Matilde always sings well, and that she eats oranges, are reported as simple facts, so the verbs are indicative. The indicative is also used in direct questions.

¿Asisten los reyes? *Are the king and queen attending?*

B. Subjunctive verb forms do not affirm or ask whether or not an action happens or a condition exists. Instead, they mention an action or condition as a possibility whose existence is commented on in the same sentence.

Ojalá que Matilde cante bien. *I hope Matilde sings well.*
Tal vez asista el rey. *Perhaps the king will attend.*

1. In the sentences above, **cante** and **asista** are subjunctive forms. The next section presents all the subjunctive forms; for now, notice how the theme vowels of the endings switch.

	Indicative	*Subjunctive*
-ar *verbs*	a →	e
cantar	(ella) cant**a**	(ella) cant**e**
-er, -ir *verbs*	e →	a
comer	com**e**	com**a**
asistir	asist**e**	asist**a**

2. The subjunctive forms **cante** and **asista** are used because in these sentences, the speakers are not reporting actions as facts. *Singing* and *attending* are just concepts that the speakers hope to see **(ojalá)** or speculate that they may see **(tal vez)** become realities.

C. The subjunctive occurs more frequently in Spanish than in English; the discussion of its uses continues into Chapter 17. You have already seen two short phrases, however—**ojalá (que)** and **tal vez**—, that often serve as comments introducing subjunctive forms.

1. Ojalá is derived from Arabic *na xa Alah* meaning *Allah grant that* . . . It is variously translated into English as *I hope that, we hope that, let's hope that,* and *hopefully.* When a verb is mentioned subject to the comment **ojalá,** the verb mood is subjunctive. The use of **que** after **ojalá** is optional before a verb.

Ojalá que sí. *Hopefully, yes. (We hope so.)*
Ojalá (que) ellos no peleen. *I hope they don't fight.*

2. Both **tal vez** and **quizá(s)** mean *perhaps.* When a verb is tagged with either of them as a comment, the verb is subjunctive if the speaker is expressing real doubt. Otherwise the verb is indicative.

Tal vez (quizás) asistan los reyes. *Perhaps the king and queen will attend. (Speaker is honestly doubtful; verb is subjunctive.)*

Quizás (tal vez) ganan mucho las cantantes. *Maybe singers earn a lot. (Speaker is really pretty sure they do; verb is indicative.)*

EJERCICIOS

A. ¡Ojalá! Juliana y Fabio hablan de la clase de literatura española. Ella ya ha seguido la clase y se la describe a su amigo porque él la va a seguir este año. Dé las reacciones de Fabio. Use **ojalá que** y el verbo en el subjuntivo. (Para formar el subjuntivo de los verbos de este ejercicio, sólo hay que cambiar la **a** por **e** o la **e** por **a**.)

MODELO La profesora expresa mucho entusiasmo.
Ojalá que la profesora exprese mucho entusiasmo.

1. La profesora habla de dos novelas modernas.
2. Comprende el teatro de Alejandro Casona.
3. Y lee unos cuentos de ciencia ficción.
4. La profesora describe la poesía romántica.
5. Enseña fotos de los grandes autores contemporáneos.
6. Invita a la clase a sus amigos escritores.

B. ¡Tal vez tengamos otro Picasso! *(Perhaps we have another Picasso!)* Juan Antonio quiere ser pintor. Haga el papel de su primo Diego y conteste las preguntas. Use **tal vez** y el subjuntivo.

MODELO ¿Pinta Juan Antonio como Pablo Picasso?
Tal vez pinte como Pablo Picasso.

1. ¿Enseña Juan Antonio su nuevo cuadro?
2. ¿Aprende mucho Juan Antonio en sus clases de arte?
3. ¿Compra ese señor rico el nuevo cuadro de Juan Antonio?
4. ¿Viaja Juan Antonio al Museo de El Greco en Toledo?
5. ¿Le gusta a Juan Antonio el estilo de El Greco?
6. ¿Cree el director del Museo del Prado en el talento de Juan Antonio?

C. ¿Con confianza o con duda? *(With confidence or doubt?)* Diga si Armando habla con confianza o con duda. Explique por qué.

MODELOS Tal vez viajamos a Madrid este verano.
Habla con confianza porque usa el indicativo de *viajar*.

Quizás compre pronto un auto nuevo.
Habla con duda porque usa el subjuntivo de *comprar*.

1. Ernesto se enferma mucho. Quizás trabaja demasiado.
2. Tal vez se cure si se va de vacaciones.
3. ¿No encuentras el periódico? Tal vez lo lea Enrique.
4. El secretario parece muy ocupado. Quizás escribe a todos los senadores.

II. El presente de subjuntivo de los verbos regulares

El instructor de ballet quiere que sus estudiantes practiquen mucho.

En una escuela de teatro, en Madrid

RAMONA   ¡Ay, Carmen, el instructor de baile quiere que yo *baile* con Carlos! Pero yo no quiero bailar con él. ¡Él y yo no bailamos bien juntos!

CARMEN   ¡Qué suerte tienes! Yo siempre le pido que me *permita* bailar con Carlos, pero él manda que yo *practique* y *trabaje* con Luis. Prohíbe que nosotros *bailemos* con otra persona.

RAMONA   ¡Qué injusticia! ¿Sabes que Luis y yo... ?

CARMEN   ¡Claro que lo sé!° ¡Todo el mundo° lo sabe... y creo que el instructor también! Probablemente por eso él prohíbe que tú y Luis *bailéis* juntos. ¿Por qué no te quejas?

RAMONA   Me gustaría°...pero ¿para qué? Ya sabemos que él no va a cambiar de idea... ¿Sabías que ahora quiere que también *practiquemos* los fines de semana?

CARMEN   Sí, lo supe ayer. Es como una vez° tú dijiste: si el instructor quiere que *bailemos* con una mesa, lo hacemos, y si nos pide que *asistamos* a clase los sábados y domingos, pues...¡también lo vamos a hacer!

¡Claro...sé!   *Of course I know it!*   **Todo el mundo**   *Everyone*   **Me gustaría**   *I would like to* una vez   *once*

---

1. ¿Dónde están Ramona y Carmen? ¿De qué están hablando? ¿Se están quejando? ¿Por qué?   2. ¿Qué quiere el instructor? ¿Está de acuerdo Ramona? ¿Por qué? 3. ¿Qué le pide siempre al instructor Carmen? ¿Qué manda él?   4. Según su opinión, ¿qué relación hay entre Luis y Ramona? ¿Son hermanos? ¿amigos? ¿novios? 5. ¿Por qué no quiere quejarse Ramona?   6. ¿Qué dice Carmen de la situación?

7. Según las dos amigas, ¿es el instructor una persona buena y simpática? ¿Cómo es él? Descríbalo con dos o tres adjetivos.   8. ¿Conoce usted a alguien como este instructor? ¿Quién?

A. As stated before, the indicative and the subjunctive moods are two different ways of expressing facts or ideas. While the indicative mood is used to state facts or ask direct questions, the subjunctive is used for:

1. Indirect commands or requests.

My boss requests that I be at work at eight o'clock sharp.
Mary's mother asks that she celebrate Christmas with the family.

2. Situations expressing doubt, probability, or something hypothetical or contrary to fact.

If I were rich, I would go to Spain for the whole summer.
Be that as it may . . .

3. Statements of emotion, hope, wishing, or wanting.

May you succeed at everything you do.
Sally wishes that Tom were going to the party.

4. Statements of necessity.

It is necessary that he finish the painting for the exhibition.

5. Statements of approval or disapproval, permission, or prohibition.

Father forbids that she even think about going to Madrid next month.
It's better that we stay home.

Although the subjunctive is used in Spanish far more than it is in English, its use in this chapter will be limited to phrases with **ojalá** and **tal vez** (or **quizás**), and to indirect requests and commands with six verbs: **mandar** *(to order)*, **pedir** *(to ask, request)*, **permitir** *(to allow, let)*, **preferir** *(to prefer)*, **querer** *(to wish, want)*, and **prohibir** *(to prohibit, forbid)*. First, you'll see how the subjunctive of regular verbs is formed.

B. To form the present subjunctive of regular verbs, drop the ending **-o** from the **yo** form of the present indicative and add a subjunctive ending, as follows:

| **-ar *verbs:*** | -e, -es, -e, -emos, -éis, -en |
| **-er *and* -ir *verbs:*** | -a, -as, -a, -amos, -áis, -an |

hablar		**comer**		**vivir**	
hable	hablemos	coma	comamos	viva	vivamos
hables	habléis	comas	comáis	vivas	viváis
hable	hablen	coma	coman	viva	vivan

El pintor está enfermo pero tal vez (quizás) se cure pronto.

The painter is sick, but maybe he'll get well soon.

Quizás leamos *Don Quijote* en esta clase. ¿Es don Quijote el personaje principal de la novela?	*Perhaps we'll read* Don Quijote *in this class. Is Don Quijote the main character of the novel?*
Mis padres no quieren que yo estudie para escultora.	*My parents don't want me to study to be(come) a sculptor.*
Esa escritora prefiere que sus hijos no lean sus obras.	*That writer prefers that her children not read her works.*
El profesor Robles pide que no hablemos en la galería.	*Professor Robles asks that we not talk in the gallery.*

C. You may have noticed that these subjunctive forms are mostly the same as the command forms presented in Chapter 7. Compare the following sentences.

Lean la novela.	*Read the novel.*
Ojalá que ustedes lean la novela.	*I hope you read the novel.*
Llame a mi tía, por favor.	*Call my aunt, please.*
Quiero que usted llame a mi tía.	*I want you to call my aunt.*
No abras la puerta.	*Don't open the door.*
Piden que no abras la puerta.	*They ask you not to open the door.*

D. There are a number of things to notice about the structure of the sentences with the subjunctive that you have just seen. One is that the verbs **mandar, pedir, permitir, preferir, prohibir,** or **querer** are in the indicative in clauses that could (grammatically) stand alone as sentences; for instance: **Piden.** *(They request.)* This clause is called an independent clause. The *independent* clause is followed by **que** *(that)* plus another clause that contains a verb in the subjunctive. This clause beginning with **que** is called a *dependent* clause—it cannot stand alone as a sentence. For example, in the sentence **Piden que asistamos a clase,** the phrase **que asistamos a clase** *(that we attend class)* is not a complete sentence. The **que** is essential in the Spanish sentence, although *that* is not always used in English. In English, an infinitive construction is frequently used where Spanish uses the subjunctive.

Papá prohíbe que ella lea ese ensayo.	*Dad forbids her to read that essay. (Dad forbids that she read that essay.)*

If the subject of the independent clause is different from the subject of the dependent clause, the subjunctive must be used in Spanish rather than an infinitive construction. However, an infinitive must be used in Spanish when there is no change of subject. Compare:

Quiero asistir al concierto.	*I want to attend the concert.* (no change in subject)
Quiero que tú asistas al concierto.	*I want you to attend (that you attend) the concert.* (change in subject)
No quieren leer hasta medianoche.	*They don't want to read till midnight.* (no change in subject)
No quieren que sus hijos lean hasta medianoche.	*They don't want their children to read till midnight. (They don't want that their children read till midnight.)* (change in subject)

EJERCICIOS

A. Piense y hable. Termine las frases. Escoja el más apropiado de los dos verbos entre paréntesis y úselo en el subjuntivo.

1. (decidir, levantarse) Ojalá que tú _____ temprano mañana y tal vez _____ visitarme.
2. (comprender, ganar) El director quiere que los músicos _____ bien la música. También quiere que _____ mucho dinero.
3. (tomar, correr) El director permite que yo _____ dos kilómetros por día. Pero no permite que yo _____ mucho vino.
4. (llevar, permitir) Tal vez ustedes nos _____ ayudarlos. Quizás nos _____ a la galería después.
5. (estudiar, casarse) Sus padres no permiten que Estela _____ para escultora. Tampoco permiten que ella _____ con un escultor.
6. (enseñar, responder) El pintor quiere que tú _____ a sus preguntas. Tú tal vez le _____ a tener paciencia.
7. (vivir, viajar) Mamá quiere que nosotros _____ por toda España. Quiere que _____ unos meses en Barcelona.
8. (leer, comprender) Nosotros tal vez _____ esa antología. Ojalá la _____.

B. Por favor, ¡usen el subjuntivo! Repita las frases, cambiándolas a pedidos (*requests*) que hace(n) otra(s) persona(s). Siga el modelo.

MODELO Hablo con el pintor. Me pide que...
Me pide que hable con el pintor.

1. Pedro nos invita al teatro. Quiero que...
2. Tus hijos miran la exposición. ¿No quieres que... ?
3. Vivimos cerca de la universidad. Nos piden que...
4. Leo esta revista. ¿Prohíbes que... ?
5. Toman vino después de la función. No quiero que...
6. Estudian un poema difícil. Manda que...
7. Recibimos a los cantantes. Prefieren que...
8. Teresa y Jorge hablan con la directora. Prohíben que...

C. Entrevista. Es el año 1592. Miguel de Cervantes está en la cárcel (*jail*). Haga el papel de don Miguel y conteste las preguntas que le hacen. Use **tal vez** y el subjuntivo.

MODELO Don Miguel, ¿va a escribir usted una novela larguísima?
Tal vez escriba una novela larguísima.

1. ¿Va a llamarse «don Quijote» el personaje principal?
2. ¿Va a leer muchas novelas románticas don Quijote?
3. ¿Va a viajar otra persona con don Quijote?
4. Y esa otra persona, ¿va a dejar a su familia?
5. Y los dos, ¿van a vivir en el campo?
6. ¿Se va a casar don Quijote?
7. ¿Van a comprar el libro muchas personas?
8. ¿Y vamos a creer que es la mejor novela del mundo?

D. Los sueños de Alberto. Alberto sueña con ser director de orquesta. Haga el papel de Alberto y conteste con **ojalá** y el subjuntivo.

MODELO ¿Vas a casarte con una compositora?
Ojalá que me case con una compositora.

1. ¿Vas a estudiar en Madrid?
2. ¿Vas a trabajar mucho?
3. ¿Vas a aprender a ser buen músico?
4. ¿Vas a viajar a muchas partes del mundo?
5. ¿Vais a vivir tú y tu esposa en una casa cómoda?
6. ¿Van a decidir tener muchos niños?
7. ¿Vas a escribir música original?
8. ¿Vamos a leer tu nombre en los periódicos?

III. Formas subjuntivas irregulares

El Museo de Arte Contemporáneo, Madrid

En casa de Alicia

ALICIA   Mama, quiero que *conozcas* a Guillermo°, el pintor de quien te hablé° ayer. Me pide que *vaya* con él a la exposición de sus pinturas en el Museo de Arte Contemporáneo.

ENCARNACIÓN   Mucho gusto, Guillermo.

GUILLERMO   Igualmente, señora.

ENCARNACIÓN   Alicia, tal vez *sea* buena idea pedirle permiso° a tu padre, ¿no lo crees?

ALICIA   Sí, mamá, tienes razón. Ojalá que papá *esté* de buen humor°...

---

quiero...Guillermo   *I want you to meet Guillermo*   de...hablé   *I told you about*   pedirle permiso   *to ask permission*   Ojalá...humor   *I hope Dad is in a good mood*

---

1. ¿A quién quiere Alicia que su mamá conozca? ¿Quién es Guillermo?
2. ¿Adónde quiere él que vaya Alicia?   3. ¿Para qué quiere Encarnación que Alicia hable con su padre?   4. ¿Cree usted que Alicia y su padre son buenos amigos? ¿Por qué sí o por qué no?

A. As in **usted** commands, verbs that have an irregularity in the **yo** form of the present indicative carry this irregularity over into the present subjunctive. The subjunctive endings are the same for irregular verbs as for regular verbs.

> **-ar:** -e, -es, -e, -emos, éis, -en
> **-er, -ir:** -a, -as, -a, -amos, -áis, -an.

decir		conocer		tener	
diga	digamos	conozca	conozcamos	tenga	tengamos
digas	digáis	conozcas	conoczáis	tengas	tengáis
diga	digan	conozca	conozcan	tenga	tengan

Here are some other verbs that follow this pattern.

construir	construy-	**salir**	salg-
destruir	destruy-	**traer**	traig-
hacer	hag-	**valer**	valg-
oír	oig-	**venir**	veng-
poner	pong-	**ver**	ve-

¿El ministro de cultura quiere que destruyan un teatro para construir una piscina... ?	*The minister of culture wants them to destroy a theater in order to build a swimming pool . . . ?*
Pablo prefiere que los niños oigan un concierto de música española.	*Pablo prefers that the children hear a concert of Spanish music.*
Ojalá ustedes digan la verdad.	*I hope you're telling the truth.*
¿Qué quieres que te traiga?	*What do you want me to bring you?*
Tal vez valga la pena leer eso.	*Perhaps it's worth it to read that.*

B. The following verbs with irregular **usted** commands are irregular in the subjunctive:

dar		estar		haber	
dé	demos	esté	estemos	haya	hayamos
des	deis	estés	estéis	hayas	hayáis
dé	den	esté	estén	haya	hayan

ir		saber		ser	
vaya	vayamos	sepa	sepamos	sea	seamos
vayas	vayáis	sepas	sepáis	seas	seáis
vaya	vayan	sepa	sepan	sea	sean

Ojalá que abuela no esté enferma.
Tal vez haya una obra nueva en el
 teatro María Guerrero.
Ojalá que sea buena. Si lo es, ¿te
 gustaría ir a verla conmigo?

We hope Grandma isn't sick.
Perhaps there's a new play at the
 María Guerrero theater.
I hope it's good. If it is, would you
 like to go to see it with me?

C. Most stem-changing **-ar** and **-er** verbs retain the same pattern of stem change in the present subjunctive that they have in the indicative.

encontrar		**poder**	
encuentre	encontremos	pueda	podamos
encuentres	encontréis	puedas	podáis
encuentre	encuentren	pueda	puedan

entender		**pensar**	
entienda	entendamos	piense	pensemos
entiendas	entendáis	pienses	penséis
entienda	entiendan	piense	piensen

La pintora quiere que entendamos
 su pintura...¡y tú quieres que la
 destruyamos!
Tal vez él encuentre trabajo aquí.

The painter wants us to understand
 her painting . . . and you want us
 to destroy it!
Perhaps he will find work here.

D. Stem-changing **-ir** verbs that have a change in stem of **e** to **ie**, **e** to **i**, or **o** to **ue** in the present indicative follow the same pattern in the subjunctive with an additional change: in the **nosotros** and **vosotros** forms, the **e** of the stem is changed to **i**; the **o** is changed to **u**.

sentirse (ie, i)		**morir (ue, u)**		**dormir (ue, u)**	
me sienta	nos sintamos	muera	muramos	duerma	durmamos
te sientas	os sintáis	mueras	muráis	duermas	durmáis
se sienta	se sientan	muera	mueran	duerma	duerman

pedir (i)		**vestirse (i)**	
pida	pidamos	me vista	nos vistamos
pidas	pidáis	te vistas	os vistáis
pida	pidan	se vista	se vistan

Ojalá que se sientan cómodos.
El director pide que la actriz se vista
 rápido.
Tal vez muera el protagonista.
 ¿Todavía quiere ver la obra?

I hope you feel comfortable.
The director asks that the actress
 get dressed fast.
Perhaps the protagonist dies. Do
 you still want to see the play?

E. When endings are added to the stems of verbs and other words, the pronunciation of the stem rarely changes. To show that no change in sound occurs, certain changes in spelling are made.

1. **c** changes to **qu** before **e.**

	Yo Form	
	Present Indicative	Present Subjunctive
buscar	busco	busque
sacar	saco	saque
tocar	toco	toque

Mamá, ¿quieres que saque mi violín y que te toque una canción?	*Mom, do you want me to take out my violin and play you a song?*
¿Qué nota sacaste en el examen?	*What grade did you get on the exam?*

2. **g** changes to **gu** before **e.**

jugar	juego	juegue
llegar	llego	llegue
pagar	pago	pague

Tal vez lleguemos tarde a la ópera.	*Maybe we'll arrive late to the opera.*
No quieren que yo le pague al escultor.	*They don't want me to pay the sculptor.*

3. **z** changes to **c** before **e.**

almorzar	almuerzo	almuerce
comenzar	comienzo	comience
empezar	empiezo	empiece

La cantante quiere que la función comience antes de las ocho.	*The singer wants the show to start before eight.*

Remember that these changes are in spelling only; the pronunciation of the stem does not change.

EJERCICIOS

A. **Piense y hable.**   Termine las frases. Escoja el más apropiado de los dos verbos entre paréntesis y úselo en el subjuntivo.

   1. (ir, tener) Ojalá que nosotros _____ tiempo de almorzar. Quizás _____ al restaurante nuevo.

2. (conocer, poder) Quizás usted _____ a esa cantante española. Tal vez _____ decirme su nombre.

3. (conducir, saber) Yo prefiero que tú _____ . ¡No quiero que Marta _____ que no conduzco bien!

4. (conocer, vestirse) Ojalá que los niños _____ bien para ir al teatro. Quiero que (ellos) _____ al director.

5. (dormir, llegar) El director quiere que nosotros _____ ocho horas esta noche. Quiere que _____ temprano al teatro mañana.

6. (empezar, ser) El director prefiere que la función _____ a las seis pero quizás eso _____ imposible.

7. (poder, tener) Ojalá que yo _____ dinero para las entradas. Si no lo tengo, tal vez _____ pedírselo a mi padre.

8. (encontrar, entender) Nosotros tal vez _____ la antología en la biblioteca. Dicen que los cuentos son difíciles de entender. Ojalá que los _____ .

9. (irse, sentirse) La escultora quiere que el modelo _____ cómodo. No quiere que él _____ antes de terminar.

10. (cerrar, ponerse) El director prohíbe que los actores _____ la puerta del teatro. Ojalá que ellos no _____ nerviosos.

B. Daniel y su papá. Haga el papel del señor Ramón Vives de Luna, papá de Daniel. Hable con Daniel y dígale que usted quiere que él se porte mejor (*behave better*). Use **quiero que** o **no quiero que** y el subjuntivo.

MODELO Daniel duerme todo el día.
Daniel, no quiero que duermas todo el día.

1. Daniel no sabe sus lecciones.
2. Daniel no se viste bien.
3. Daniel no hace sus tareas.
4. Daniel saca malas notas.
5. Daniel no va a la escuela todos los días.
6. Daniel llega tarde a sus clases.
7. Daniel se acuesta después de medianoche.
8. Daniel juega en la calle.
9. Daniel no dice siempre la verdad.
10. Y Daniel tiene problemas con su mamá.

C. La venganza (*The revenge*). Ofrezca a su profesor(a) las siguientes sugerencias (*suggestions*) y mandatos. Use el subjuntivo, según el modelo.

MODELO ir a la puerta
Quiero que usted vaya a la puerta.

1. abrir la puerta
2. cerrar la puerta
3. ir a su escritorio
4. sacar un libro
5. abrir el libro
6. leer una frase
7. poner el libro en el escritorio
8. ir a la pizarra
9. escribir su nombre
10. decirnos «Muchas gracias por su atención»

D. Proyectos (*Plans*). Julia vive en los Estados Unidos pero tiene una galería de arte en Madrid. Haga el papel de Julia y conteste las preguntas que le hace una amiga. Diga que no sabe (**«No sé»**) y use **tal vez** y el subjuntivo, según el modelo.

> MODELO   ¿Cuándo vas a salir para Madrid? (la semana próxima)
> **No sé. Tal vez salga la semana próxima.**

1. ¿Con quién vas a ir a España? (con Howard y Ana)
2. ¿Cuándo vas a tener la recepción en la galería? (el último día de la exposición)
3. ¿Vas a tener mucho tiempo? (cuatro o cinco días)
4. ¿Cómo van a divertirse ustedes? (visitando galerías y museos)
5. ¿Qué clase de cuadros vas a buscar? (realistas y abstractos)
6. ¿Qué exposiciones de arte vas a ver? (sólo la exposición de arte moderno)
7. ¿Cuándo van a volver a casa? (el mes próximo)
8. ¿Vas a traer cuadros de Madrid? (unos cuadros de Velázquez y de Picasso)

Preguntas

Use **ojalá**, **tal vez** o **quizá(s)** en las respuestas.

1. ¿Va a casarse usted en menos de dos años?   2. ¿Va a ir a España el año próximo?   3. ¿Vale la pena asistir a la universidad? ¿Para qué?   4. ¿Va a haber muchas guerras en el futuro? ¿Por qué?   5. Según su opinión, ¿qué cosas positivas tal vez pasen en el futuro? Hable de cuatro cosas que usted quiere ver en el futuro.

IV. Mandatos de *nosotros*, de *vosotros* y de tercera persona

Horacio Gutiérrez, pianista distinguido de origen cubano

En casa de los Pereda, en un barrio céntrico° de Madrid

AMPARO   *Salgamos* esta noche,° Javier...¿Qué te parece si vamos al cine?°

JAVIER   Sí... , ¡qué buena idea! *Veamos°* esa película nueva que muestran en el Cine Delicias.

AMPARO   ¡Ay, no Javier! Me dijo Gloria que era muy juvenil. *¡Que la vean Carlitos y Rosita!°*

JAVIER   Pues, *pongámonos* de acuerdo°... Escoge tú.
AMPARO   Entonces, *olvidémonos* del cine y *asistamos* al concierto en el Teatro
 Español. El pianista Horacio Gutiérrez* va a tocar sonatas de Scarlatti...
MAMÁ   *(Entra en la sala.)* ¿Vais al concierto de Gutiérrez? *Que toque°* tan
 bien como dicen que tocó en Moscú. *Pasad* una noche linda° y *tened*
 cuidado con el coche.
JAVIER   Gracias, mamá. *Vámonos,°* Amparo.

---

barrio céntrico   *downtown neighborhood*   Salgamos...noche   *Let's go out tonight*   ¿Qué...cine?
How do you feel about going to the movies?   Veamos   *Let's see*   ¡Que...Rosita!   *Let Carlitos and*
Rosita see it!   pongámonos...acuerdo   *let's agree*   Que toque   *May he play (I hope he plays)*
Pasad...linda   *Have a lovely evening*   Vámonos   *Let's go*

---

1. ¿Qué quiere hacer Amparo? ¿Cuál es su primera sugerencia?   2. ¿Cuál es la
película que muestran en el Cine Delicias? ¿Le interesa esa película a Amparo? ¿Por
qué sí o por qué no?   3. ¿Quién es el pianista que va a tocar? ¿De quién es la
música que va a tocar?   4. ¿Ha estado la mamá en Rusia? ¿Por qué habla de
Moscú?

A. The affirmative and negative **usted** commands and the negative **tú** commands
presented in Chapters 7 and 8 are subjunctive forms. Subjunctive forms are also
used for third person or indirect commands, **nosotros** commands, and the negative **vosotros** commands.

B. Third person or indirect commands are used after **que** with the meaning of
have or *let (somebody do something)*. **Nosotros** commands have the meaning
let's (do something). **Vosotros** commands are used in Spain instead of the
ustedes form for informal plural commands (i.e., plural of **tú**).

	Affirmative	*Negative*	
-ar verbs **tomar**	que tome	que no tome	**(él, ella)**
	que tomen	que no tomen	**(ellos, ellas)**
	tomemos	no tomemos	**(nosotros, nosotras)**
	tomad	no toméis	**(vosotros, vosotras)**
-er verbs **comer**	que coma	que no coma	**(él, ella)**
	que coman	que no coman	**(ellos, ellas)**
	comamos	no comamos	**(nosotros, nosotras)**
	comed	no comáis	**(vosotros, vosotras)**
-ir verbs **escribir**	que escriba	que no escriba	**(él, ella)**
	que escriban	que no escriban	**(ellos, ellas)**
	escribamos	no escribamos	**(nosotros, nosotras)**
	escribid	no escribáis	**(vosotros, vosotras)**

*Cuban-born and a leading international piano virtuoso, Horacio Gutiérrez won the silver medal in the 1970
Tchaikovski piano competition in Moscow.

C. **Vamos** is the only affirmative **nosotros** command that does not use the subjunctive form.

Vamos al concierto. ¡Cómo no!	*Let's go to the concert. Sure!*

In the negative, however, **vayamos** is used.

No vayamos al concierto hoy. Otro día tal vez...	*Let's not go to the concert today. Another day, perhaps . . .*

For the affirmative **nosotros** command of a reflexive verb, **nos** is attached to the end of the command. The **-s** of the command ending is omitted. An accent is written to show that the stress has not shifted.

irse

Vamos + nos = Vámonos.	*Let's go.*
No nos vayamos. Tenemos mucho que hacer hoy.	*Let's not go. We have a lot to do today.*

levantarse

Levantemos + nos temprano = Levantémonos temprano.	*Let's get up early.*
No nos levantemos tarde.	*Let's not get up late.*

D. A widely used alternative to the affirmative **nosotros** or *let's* command is the construction **Vamos a** + *infinitive*.

Vamos a { tomar. comer. escribir. }   Let's { take. eat. write. }

In the negative, this construction is not a command but a simple statement.

No vamos a comer.	*We're not going to eat.*

E. Affirmative **vosotros** commands are formed by replacing the **-r** of the infinitive with **-d.** The negative **vosotros** commands are present subjunctive forms.

¡Pasad una noche maravillosa!	*Have a wonderful evening!*
No lleguéis tarde, por favor.	*Don't arrive late, please.*

F. Examples of every Spanish command form have now been presented. All are subjunctive forms except the affirmative familiar **tú** commands (practiced in Chapter 7) and the affirmative **vosotros** commands (presented in section E above).

EJERCICIOS

A. Cambiemos. Diga cada mandato de otra forma, confirmando o negando las frases que siguen, según las indicaciones. Siga los modelos.

MODELOS Vamos a bailar. **Sí, bailemos.**

Vamos a estudiar. **No, no estudiemos.**

1. Vamos a ver televisión.   Sí, ...
2. Vamos a jugar con los niños.   No, ...
3. Vamos a dormir hasta las diez.   No, ...
4. Vamos a tocar el piano.   No, ...
5. Vamos a mirar los cuadros de Goya.   Sí, ...
6. Vamos a cenar después de la función.   Sí, ...

B. Ahora, ¡hacedlo vosotros...!   Cambie del mandato plural en primera persona (**nosotros**) al mandato en segunda persona (**vosotros**), siguiendo el modelo.

MODELO   Trabajemos.   **¡No, yo no! ¡Trabajad vosotros!**

1. Almorcemos en el centro.   4. Volvamos al hotel.
2. Pidamos más comida.   5. Leamos las noticias del país.
3. Visitemos un museo.   6. Pongámonos de acuerdo.

C. Conozcamos Madrid.   Sonia, Francisca y Yolanda son estudiantes de bellas artes (*fine arts*) en la Universidad de Salamanca. Deciden viajar a Madrid para ver las maravillas del arte español en la capital. Conteste por Yolanda, siguiendo los modelos. Use pronombres objetos cuando sea posible.

MODELOS   SONIA   ¿Viajamos a Barcelona o a Madrid?
                YOLANDA **Viajemos a Madrid, pero ¡no viajéis sin mí!**

                SONIA   ¿Compramos los pasajes hoy o mañana?
                YOLANDA **Comprémoslos mañana, pero ¡no los compréis sin mí!**

1. ¿Nos vamos en tren o en auto?
2. ¿Compramos maletas grandes o pequeñas?
3. ¿Salimos mañana o el sábado?
4. ¿Visitamos primero el Museo del Prado o la nueva galería de arte?
5. ¿Asistimos a una ópera o a un ballet?
6. ¿Vamos de compras aquí o en Madrid?
7. ¿Volvemos en una o dos semanas?
8. ¿Reservamos dos o tres habitaciones?

D. Julio el terco.   Julio no coopera con sus amigos—es terco (*stubborn*). Cuando le piden que haga algo, siempre quiere que lo haga otra persona. Conteste las preguntas por Julio.

MODELO   Julio, ¿quieres leer el último cuento de Santiago? (Abel)
                Yo no, que lo lea Abel.

1. ¿Quieres ver la obra de Casona? (Camilo)
2. ¿Quieres aprender este nuevo baile? (Trini)
3. ¿Quieres ir al concierto? (René y Juan)
4. ¿Quieres conducir el auto? (Melinda)
5. ¿Quieres conocer al escritor Jorge Muñoz? (los otros)
6. ¿Quieres escuchar el disco de Horacio Gutiérrez? (mi mamá)

EN EL MUSEO DEL PRADO

Las Meninas (1656),
cuadro de Diego
Rodríguez de Silva y
Velázquez

*Una profesora de arte y unos estudiantes visitan
el Museo del Prado¹, en Madrid.*

PROFESORA   Descansemos aquí. Ya hemos visto las obras de Velázquez, de
El Greco y de Goya. Ahora quiero que me digáis cuál de los
tres pintores os ha gustado o interesado más...

ANA   A mí me ha gustado el Greco por su estilo único y original.

JORGE   ¿Esas figuras largas y deformadas°?² ¡Son horribles!

ANA   Son las visiones de un místico.

JORGE   ¡O quizás de un loco! Pero veamos qué piensan los demás. Pablo, danos tu opinión...

PABLO   Pues...me parece interesante el estilo de El Greco, pero en realidad me han impresionado más los retratos de Velázquez. Son
tan realistas que las personas que pinta parecen estar vivas°, ¿no?

San Martín y el mendigo (1597-99), cuadro de Domenico Theotocopuli, llamado El Greco (1541-1614)

ANA   Sí, son bastante realistas... Y hablando de Velázquez, tengo una pregunta sobre *Las Meninas*. ¿Por qué lo han puesto en una sala aparte°?[3]

PROFESORA   Porque es uno de los cuadros más famosos del museo. En la historia del arte significa un problema resuelto: la representación perfecta del espacio en sus tres dimensiones por medio de la manipulación de distintas° intensidades de luz.

ANA   Mientras lo miraba, me di cuenta° de que el cuadro juega muy bien con los conceptos de ilusión y realidad, ¿verdad que sí?

JORGE   Sí, pero me parece que Goya tiene más valor universal. Sus obras son una sátira de la humanidad.

ANA   Estoy de acuerdo con eso. Pero no olvidemos que el realismo de Velázquez era importante para los hombres del siglo XVII porque entonces todavía no habían inventado la fotografía. Hoy día a la gente le interesa más la expresividad° de Goya.

Aguafuerte (*etching*)
de *Los caprichos*
(1799), por
Francisco de Goya
y Lucientes
(1746-1828)

PABLO   Son obras demasiado deprimentes° para mí. No me gusta ver
escenas brutales, cuerpos fracturados, monstruos grotescos[4]...

ANA   Sin embargo, sus obras han tenido una gran influencia en el
arte del siglo XX. ¿No es así, profesora?

PROFESORA   Así es, muchachos... Pero prefiero que vosotros mismos descu-
bráis esa influencia en los cuadros que vamos a ver después...

JORGE   ...¡después de comer!... ¿Qué os parece si continuamos esta dis-
cusión en la cafetería? ¡No veo la hora de almorzar!° Estoy a
punto de morder° una naturaleza muerta.[5]

---

deformadas *deformed*   estar vivas *to be alive*   sala aparte *separate room, room by itself*
distintas *different*   me di cuenta *I realized*   expresividad *expressiveness*   deprimentes
depressing   ¡No...almorzar! *I can't wait to have lunch!*   Estoy...morder *I'm about to bite*

PREGUNTAS

1. ¿Dónde están la profesora y sus estudiantes?   2. ¿De qué pintores hablan?
3. ¿Cómo son las figuras que pintó El Greco?   4. ¿Quién pintó *Las Meninas*?
5. ¿Por qué han puesto esta obra en una sala aparte?   6. ¿Con qué conceptos juega el cuadro?   7. Según Jorge, ¿por qué tienen más valor universal las obras de Goya?   8. ¿Por qué era importante el estilo de Velázquez para los hombres del siglo XVII?   9. ¿Cuál de los tres pintores le gusta más a usted? ¿Por qué?
10. ¿Hay ejemplos de sus cuadros en este capítulo? ¿Qué cuadros? ¿Y cuál de ellos le gusta más a usted? ¿Por qué?

NOTAS CULTURALES

1. The **Museo del Prado** of Madrid, founded in the early nineteenth century, is one of the great art museums of the world, particularly noted for its fine collections of Spanish and Flemish paintings.

2. Domenico Theotocopoulos (1541–1614), known as **El Greco** *(the Greek),* is usually considered a Spanish painter since his greatest works were done after his arrival in Spain and reflect the fervent mysticism sometimes associated with that country. The figures in his paintings appear elongated, and for many years this was thought to be due to a visual problem of the artist. Modern critics, however, have classified **El Greco** as one of the world's great painters who distorted outward form in order to express the inward spirit.

3. **Las Meninas** (*The Maids of Honor)* is one of the most important paintings of Diego Veláz-quez. The effect of three dimensionality is not achieved by the traditional method of geometric perspective, but by the contrasting of light and shadow, a technique which was to have a great impact on later artists.

The painting seems to be totally unposed. The princess Margarita, two maids of honor, two dwarfs (**enanos**, used for entertainment in the court), and a dog seem to have entered the painter's studio and appear in the foreground. To the left behind them is Velázquez himself busily painting on his canvas. To the right are two ladies of the court. On the far back wall hangs a mirror in which appear the reflections of the king and queen, who would therefore seem to be standing in the place where we, the observers, now are. Finally, farther back still, a court official stands in an open doorway. By looking at the picture, we are seeing—as though we looked through the eyes of the king and queen—an impromptu view of the daily reality of the court. Is the painting the artist is shown doing of the royal couple, of us, or is it the very painting we now see, assuming he is gazing into a mirror directly in front of him? The observer is invited to ponder on a theme suggested by the painting: where is the line between illusion and reality?

4. Francisco de Goya (1746–1828) was a Spanish painter who produced an enormous variety of paintings, drawings, and engravings. His later works portray in grotesque detail the horrors of war (which he viewed close at hand), the cruelty and vices of society, and terrifying images drawn from witchcraft, superstition, dreams, and myths.

5. **Naturaleza muerta** is the Spanish term for *still life,* a painting which portrays small inanimate objects (such as bottles, flowers, and—very often—food) painted in a very realistic manner.

Funciones y *actividades*

In this chapter, you have seen examples of some important language functions, or uses. Here is a summary and some additional information about these functions of language:

EXTENDING INVITATIONS

¿Le (te) gustaría ir a... (conmigo)?	Would you like to go to . . . (with me)?
¿Qué le (te) parece si vamos a... ?	How do you feel about going to . . . ?
Si está(s) libre hoy, vamos a...	If you're free today, let's go to . . .
¿Quiere(s) ir a... ?	Do you want to go to . . . ?
¿Me quiere(s) acompañar a... ?	Do you want to go with (accompany) me to . . . ?

ACCEPTING INVITATIONS

Sí, ¡con mucho gusto!	Yes, gladly (sure)!
¡Cómo no! ¿A qué hora?	Sure. What time?
¡Listo(-a)! Gracias por la invitación.	OK! (literally, I'm ready to go!) Thanks for the invitation.
Sí, ¡qué buena idea!	Yes, what a good idea!
No veo la hora de verte (de hablar contigo, de almorzar, etc.).	I can't wait to see you (to talk to you, to have lunch, etc.).
De acuerdo, ¡tengo todo el día libre!	OK, I have the whole day free!

DECLINING INVITATIONS

(Es que) tengo mucho que hacer esta semana. La semana que viene, tal vez.	I have a lot to do this week. Next week, perhaps.
Me gustaría (mucho), pero (no puedo ir)...	I'd like to (very much), but (I can't go) . . .
Otro día tal vez; hoy estoy muy ocupado(-a).	Another day, perhaps; today I'm very busy.
¡Qué lástima! Esta tarde tengo que estudiar.	What a shame! This afternoon I have to study.

MAKING A TOAST

The most common way to make a toast is **¡Salud!** *(To your health!),* as you saw earlier. Three longer versions that you may hear are

Salud, amor y pesetas.	Health, love, and money.
Salud, amor y pesetas y el tiempo para gozarlos (gastarlos).	Health, love, and money, and the time to enjoy (spend) them.
Salud y plata y un(a) novio(a) de yapa.	Health, money (silver), and a sweetheart besides.

MAKING INTRODUCTIONS

If you are introducing yourself, you can say **Déjeme presentarme. Me llamo...**
To introduce someone else to another person, you can say:

Ésta es... , una amiga de México
  (California, etcétera).
This is . . . , a friend from Mexico
  (California, etc.).

Éste es mi hermano.
This is my brother.

Quiero que conozca(s) a...
I want you to meet . . .

Quiero presentarle(-te) a...
I want to introduce you to . . . (or:
I want to introduce . . . to you)

As you have seen, **Mucho gusto** is generally used for *Glad to meet you.*

Ahora haga las siguientes actividades, usando las expresiones que acaba de aprender.

A. Invitaciones. Trabaje con un(a) compañero(-a) de clase y hágale cada una de las siguientes invitaciones. Su compañero(-a) debe aceptar algunas de sus invitaciones y rechazar (*decline*) las otras.

1. ir a una exposición de arte
2. ir a una fiesta de cumpleaños para su mamá (de usted)
3. ir a una conferencia (*lecture*) sobre Centroamérica
4. ir a un concierto de Madonna
5. ir al parque zoológico
6. ir a un partido de jai alai
7. ir a las montañas para esquiar
8. ir a una corrida de toros
9. ir con él (ella) al teatro
10. ir al barrio italiano para comer pizza

B. Mini-dramas. Dramatice en clase las siguientes situaciones.

1. El día de San Valentín (*Valentine's Day*) usted y un(a) amigo(-a) están cenando en un restaurante muy bueno. Usted pide vino y el camarero (*waiter*) se lo trae. Su amigo(-a) le cuenta que ayer tuvo una entrevista para un trabajo en una galería de arte y ¡le dieron el trabajo! El director quiere que empiece a trabajar inmediatamente. Usted felicita (*congratulate*) a su amigo(-a). Para celebrar su buena suerte, su amigo(-a) lo (la) quiere llevar al teatro después de la cena. Usted acepta la invitación y dice que le encanta el teatro.
2. Una persona que usted conoce y que tiene un carácter muy difícil lo (la) invita regularmente a salir: al teatro, al cine, a conciertos, a cenar, etc. A esa persona no le gusta que le digan que «No» cuando invita... Esta vez (*This time*) la invitación es para asistir a un concierto el viernes. Usted le dice que no va a poder porque ese día va a ver una obra de teatro. Entonces él (ella) repite la invitación para el sábado, después para el domingo, etcétera. Usted debe buscar (¡y encontrar!) una buena excusa para cada invitación y rehusarla (*decline it*) ¡muy cortésmente (*politely*)!

¿Sabe Ud. quién pintó este cuadro?

C. **¡Trivia en español!**   ¿Qué sabe usted de las artes españolas? Conteste las preguntas que siguen y va a saber si usted es experto, aficionado o ignorante.

1. ¿Quién escribió la obra *Don Quijote*?
2. ¿Quién pintó un famoso cuadro titulado *Guernica*?
3. ¿Puede dar el nombre de un compositor español famoso?
4. ¿Fue El Greco escritor, poeta, pintor o arquitecto?
5. ¿En qué siglo vivió Velázquez?
6. ¿Puede dar el nombre de un pintor español famoso de este siglo?
7. ¿Quién nació primero: Goya o El Greco?
8. ¿Puede indicar cuál de las personas que siguen no se relaciona con las otras: Goya, Segovia, El Greco?
9. ¿De quién fue contemporáneo Cervantes: del Rey Arturo, de Shakespeare o de George Washington?
10. ¿Cómo se llama el museo más famoso de España?

Clave (Key):
1. Miguel de Cervantes 2. Pablo Picasso 3. Domenico Scarlatti, Enrique Granados, Isaac Albéniz... 4. pintor 5. XVII (1599–1660) 6. Picasso, Miró, Gris... 7. El Greco 8. Segovia 9. Shakespeare 10. Museo del Prado

Significado:
9–10 correctas: ¡Excelente! Usted sabe mucho sobre la cultura española.
6–8 correctas: Usted sabe un poco, pero debe leer más sobre la cultura española.
0–5 correctas: ¡Pobrecito(-a)! Realmente debería (*should*) dormir menos en clase...

D. **Un mini-drama más...**   Con otros dos compañeros de clase, dramatice la siguiente situación.

LUGAR: un mercado de artesanías (*handicrafts*) en Madrid
PERSONAJES: una persona que vende cuadros y estatuas (*statues*); Julie y Eric, dos turistas norteamericanos (ambos profesores de español)

ERIC: «Mira, Julie, qué lindos cuadros.»

JULIE: responde que sí, que son muy bonitos, que le gustan los colores, las figuras, etcétera...Le interesa especialmente uno de un pintor pintándose a sí mismo *(painting himself)* porque le parece muy artístico. Le pregunta a la persona que los vende quién los ha pintado.

VENDEDOR(A): dice que su hermano los pintó hace dos semanas. Dice que también tiene estatuas muy lindas.

ERIC: declara que le gustan más las estatuas, que nunca ha visto estatuas tan lindas. Le pregunta al (a la) vendedor(a) cuánto cuestan.

VENDEDOR(A): responde que las estatuas cuestan cinco dólares cada una.

JULIE: «¡Qué lástima!», dice, y comenta que ella pensaba comprar cuatro por diez dólares.

VENDEDOR(A): dice que por esa cantidad le puede dar dos estatuas y un cuadro.

JULIE: dice que está de acuerdo y que va a llevar dos estatuas y el cuadro del pintor pintándose a sí mismo. El cuadro es para una amiga a quien le gusta este tipo de arte.

ERIC: «Estoy seguro que es para Teresa...», comenta, y escoge otras estatuas.

JULIE Y ERIC: dan las gracias y se van.

VOCABULARIO ACTIVO

Cognados

abstracto
el actor
la actriz
la antología
el arte, las artes

el autor, la autora
el ballet
contemporáneo
el director, la directora
la escena

la galería
el instructor, la instructora
el, la novelista
la orquesta
el, la pianista

el poema
el público
el realismo
romántico

Verbos

construir — *to build, to construct*
escoger — *to choose*
mandar — *to order, to command*
pelear — *to fight*
permitir — *to allow, to permit*
prohibir — *to forbid, to prohibit*
sacar — *to take out; to get*
valer — *to be worth*
  valer la pena — *to be worth it, to be worth the trouble*

Artes y Letras — Arts and Letters

el, la cantante — *singer*
el compositor, la compositora — *composer*
el, la cuentista — *short-story writer*
el cuento — *short story, tale*
el, la ensayista — *essayist*
el ensayo — *essay*
el escritor, la escritora — *writer*
el escultor, la escultora — *sculptor*
la escultura — *sculpture*
la exposición — *exhibit, exhibition*
la función — *show, performance; function*
el, la músico — *musician*
la obra maestra — *masterpiece*
papel: hacer un papel — *to play a role*
el personaje — *character*
el personaje principal — *main character, protagonist*
la pintura — *painting, paint*
el retrato — *portrait*

Otras palabras y frases

estar de buen humor — *to be in a good mood*
ojalá (que) — *I (we, let's) hope (that); hopefully*
la reina — *the queen*
el rey — *the king*
tal vez — *perhaps, maybe*

Expresiones útiles

¡Cómo no! — *Sure!*
¿Le (te) gustaría ir a...(conmigo)? — *Would you like to go to . . .(with me)?*
Me gustaría... , pero... — *I'd like to . . . , but . . .*
¡No veo la hora de (verte, almorzar...)! — *I can't wait to (see you, have lunch . . .)!*
Otro día tal vez... — *Another day perhaps . . .*
¿Qué le (te) parece si vamos a... ? — *How do you feel about going to . . .?*
¿Quiere(s) ir a... ? — *Do you want to go to . . .?*
Quiero que conozcas a... — *I want you to meet . . .*
¡Sí... , qué buena idea! — *Yes . . . , what a good idea!*

Algunos mexicanos
de Guadalajara
celebran el Día de la
Independencia.

FIESTAS Y ANIVERSARIOS

Funciones

- Expressing agreement

- Expressing
  disagreement

Vocabulario. In this chapter you will describe
parties and special days.

Gramática. You will discuss and use:

1. The subjunctive in noun clauses
2. The subjunctive versus the indicative in noun
   clauses and after impersonal expressions
3. Affirmative and negative words
4. Adverbs ending in **-mente**

Cultura. The dialogues take place in various
Mexican cities.

FIESTAS Y ANIVERSARIOS

el cumpleaños
el pastel, la torta

el pavo
el Día de Acción
de Gracias

el candelabro
la fiesta de Janucá

el árbol de Navidad
la Navidad
el 25 de diciembre

unas flores
el Día de la Madre

unas tarjetas
el Año Nuevo
el 1° de enero

ALGUNAS FIESTAS HISPÁNICAS

los Reyes Magos
el Día de (los) Reyes
el 6 de enero

el Día de los Trabajadores
el 1° de mayo

el Día de los Muertos
el 2 de noviembre

TRES FIESTAS MEXICANAS TÍPICAS

La fiesta del Grito de
Dolores
(de la Independencia)
el 16 de septiembre

el Día de la Virgen
de Guadalupe (santa
patrona de México)
el 12 de diciembre

la piñata, los dulces
Las Posadas
    desde el 16 hasta
    el 24 de diciembre

¡Fiestas!   Complete las oraciones con la(s) palabra(s) apropiada(s).

1. El sábado próximo es el _____ de mamá; vamos a hacerle un _____
   de chocolate para celebrarlo.
2. Los niños hispanos creen que _____ les traen regalos el 6 de enero
   (Día de los Reyes).*
3. ¿Dónde están los adornos para el _____ de Navidad?
4. Nuestros amigos judíos (*Jewish*) tienen un _____ de Janucá.
5. En los Estados Unidos mucha gente come _____ para celebrar el Día
   de Acción de Gracias (*Thanksgiving*).
6. El 4 de julio siempre celebramos _____ de los Estados Unidos.
7. Siempre les envío _____ de Navidad a mis amigos.
8. Hay muchos _____ en la piñata que ella trae para sus sobrinos.
9. Vamos a comprar unas _____ muy bonitas para Mamá.

Preguntas

1. ¿Cuáles son las fiestas que se celebran en los Estados Unidos y también en
México?   2. ¿Cuál es su día de fiesta favorito? ¿Por qué?   3. ¿Cuándo es su
cumpleaños? En general, ¿cómo lo celebra? ¿Cómo lo celebró o lo va a celebrar
este año?   4. ¿Les envía muchas tarjetas a sus amigos? ¿Cuándo? ¿Se las envían
también ellos a usted? ¿Cuándo?   5. ¿En qué fiestas recibe regalos usted?
6. ¿Come pavo su familia el Día de Acción de Gracias? ¿Y en Navidad?

---

*Hispanic children believe that the Three Kings bring them presents on January 6, the Epiphany. The chil-
dren leave straw out at night for the kings' camels.

I. El subjuntivo en las cláusulas sustantivas

Roberto tiene 40 años... ¡es su cumpleaños!

En una clínica

LA DOCTORA	Primero quiero que la enfermera le *tome* la temperatura... Dudo° que *tenga* fiebre pero... Dígame, ¿qué ha hecho esta semana?
LA ENFERMA	Pues... el martes hubo una fiesta en casa de Gloria; el miércoles celebramos el cumpleaños de Roberto... , anoche fui a un baile... Y ahora estoy aquí porque me estoy sintiendo muy mal desde esta mañana.
LA DOCTORA	Después de tantas fiestas, no me sorprende° que *se sienta* mal... Le pido que *vaya* al hospital ahora mismo. Quiero que allí le *hagan* unos exámenes.
LA ENFERMA	Pero... ¡doctora! ¿Qué tengo?
LA DOCTORA	Aún no lo sé. Por ahora sólo puedo decirle que su aspecto físico es horrible. Mírese en ese espejo°. Usted está muy pálida°, tiene los ojos nublados°, los labios...°
LA ENFERMA	¡Basta ya!° ¡Tampoco es usted una Venus!

Dudo... *I doubt*   no me sorprende *It doesn't surprise me*   espejo *mirror*
pálida *pale*   nublados *cloudy*   los labios *lips*   ¡Basta ya! *That's enough for now!*

---

1. Según la doctora, ¿tiene fiebre la enferma?   2. ¿Qué ha hecho recientemente la enferma?   3. ¿Le sorprende a la doctora que la muchacha se sienta mal? 4. ¿Qué le pide la doctora a la enferma?   5. ¿Por qué se enoja la enferma?

A. A dependent clause that takes the place of a noun is called a noun clause.

	Noun	
Quiero /	dinero.	_I want money._
	Noun Clause	
Quiero /	que mi esposa gane dinero.	_I want my wife to earn money._

In Spanish, noun clauses are always introduced by **que.**

B. The verb in the noun clause is subjunctive if:

1. It has a different subject from the verb in the main clause.

2. The action it describes is commented on as a concept, not just reaffirmed as a fact, by the main clause.

C. Specifically, the subjunctive usually follows main clauses that express:

1. Will, desire, preference, an order, or a request. These are expressed with **verbos de voluntad** which include:

decir	_to tell, to command_	pedir (i)	_to request, to ask_
desear	_to want, to wish_	preferir (ie, i)	_to prefer_
insistir (en)	_to insist_	querer (ie)	_to want, to wish_
mandar	_to command, to order_	rogar (ue)	_to beg_

Insisten en que todos en la procesión lleven el traje tradicional.	_They insist that everyone in the procession wear the traditional costume._
¡Te digo que vengas al baile!	_I'm telling you to come to the dance!_
Ella prefiere que vayamos al desfile.	_She prefers that we go to the parade._
Deseo que me enseñes a bailar.	_I want you to teach me to dance._

2. Hope, emotion, and feeling. Typical expressions include:

alegrarse (de)	_to be glad_	sorprender	_to surprise_
esperar	_to hope, to wait_	temer	_to fear, to be afraid_
sentir (ie, i)	_to be sorry_	tener miedo (de)	_to be afraid_

¿Tienes miedo de que Tomás no recuerde tu cumpleaños?	_Are you afraid that Tomás won't remember your birthday?_
Se alegran de que participemos en la celebración.	_They are happy that we are participating in the celebration._

3. Approval, permission, prohibition, or advice. Typical verbs include:

aconsejar	_to advise_	prohibir (i)	_to prohibit_
gustar	_to please, to be pleasing_	recomendar (ie)	_to recommend_
permitir	_to permit, to allow_		

| Me gusta que Ana lleve los adornos para el árbol. | *I'm pleased (it pleases me) that Ana is bringing the decorations for the tree.* |
| Te recomendamos que compres un pavo bien grande. | *We recommend that you buy a very big turkey.* |

4. Necessity. The most common verb is **necesitar**.

| Necesitan que llevemos la piñata. | *They need us to take the piñata.* |

5. Doubt or uncertainty. Typical verbs are:

| dudar | *to doubt* |
| no estar seguro(-a) | *to not be sure* |

| No estoy seguro que los turistas sepan que hoy es un día feriado. | *I'm not sure the tourists know that today is a holiday.* |

Remember that **que** is always used in these expressions, although in English *that* can be omitted or an infinitive used.

| ¿Esperas que yo aprenda a bailar antes de tu fiesta de cumpleaños? | *Do you hope (that) I learn to dance before your birthday party?* |
| Quieren que traigamos flores a tía Eulalia. | *They want us to bring flowers for Aunt Eulalia.* |

Remember also that the subjunctive is used only when there is a change of subject; when the subject of the main and dependent clauses is the same, an infinitive is used.

| Necesito que compres el árbol antes de venir a casa. | *I need you to buy the tree before you come home.* |
| Ellos quieren comprar los adornos hoy. | *They want to buy the ornaments today.* |

A. ¿Quién hace qué? Los amigos de José están organizando una fiesta. Ayúdelos a decidir quién hace las diferentes cosas. Complete las frases según el modelo.

> **MODELO** Espero que ustedes compren los adornos. (traer el pavo)
> **Espero que ustedes traigan el pavo.**

1. No permitimos que tú compres todo el vino. (hacer eso, olvidar el pastel de cumpleaños, cambiar la tradición, irse temprano)
2. Yo les aconsejo que inviten a todos. (comprar más regalos, empezar la fiesta a las seis, llamar a los músicos, ir al mercado temprano)
3. Ella duda que tengamos bastante comida. (tomar demasiado vino, preferir llegar temprano, poder pagar a los músicos, terminar antes de medianoche)

B. El aniversario de los Gómez. Haga el papel de la señora Moreno. Añada (*Add*) las palabras entre paréntesis para describir la fiesta sorpresa que prepara para el aniversario de sus amigos, Marta y Jorge Gómez.

> **MODELO** Marta y Jorge llegan aquí a las seis. (no estar segura)
> **No estoy segura que Marta y Jorge lleguen aquí a las seis.**

1. Todos traen regalos. (dudar)
2. Invitamos a todos los vecinos. (querer)
3. Diez personas traen vino y dos compran pavo. (recomendar)
4. La fiesta es una sorpresa para ellos. (preferir)
5. Tú cantas en la fiesta. (esperar)

C. En acción. Describa lo que (*what*) pasa en cada uno de los siguientes dibujos (*drawings*).

MODELO

prohibir / comer dulces
La madre prohíbe que la niña coma dulces.

1.

alegrarse / darle un regalo

2.

dudar / llover

3.

rogar / ir al baile

4.

preferir / no fumar
(*smoke*) en la casa

5.

tener miedo de / llegar
tarde / fiesta

D. La transformación. Use las palabras siguientes para formar frases. Añada todas las palabras necesarias.

MODELO Adela / preferir / esposo / no comer / tanto
Adela prefiere que su esposo no coma tanto.

1. yo / aconsejar / tú / descansar / antes del baile
2. nosotros / desear / ella / volver / temprano
3. él / insistir / nosotros / traer / la torta
4. Raúl / dudar / ellos / venir / la fiesta de cumpleaños
5. ellos / pedir / todos / quedarse / en la plaza durante el desfile
6. los niños / querer / los Reyes / traer / muchos regalos

II. El uso del subjuntivo y del indicativo en expresiones impersonales y en otras cláusulas sustantivas

Una fiesta de graduación, México

En casa de los Álvarez en México

SR. ÁLVAREZ   Si usted quiere tocar el piano en la fiesta de mi hija, es importante que *hablemos* de la música que le gusta tocar.

PIANISTA   Pues... es cierto que no me *gusta* la música popular. Es aburrida y estoy seguro° que usted no quiere que sus invitados *se aburran*° en la fiesta...

SR. ÁLVAREZ   ¡Al contrario!° Quiero que lo *pasen* bien°. Por eso recomiendo que usted *presente* un programa de música clásica y música popular. Mi hija le pide que usted *tenga* un poco de todo. A sus amigos les gusta la música clásica...pero prefieren bailar rock, salsa, disco, música muy rítmica... Creo que uno de ellos es músico también... Toca el tambor...°

PIANISTA   ¡Qué tontería!° ¡Es ridículo que a ellos les *guste* ese tipo de música! Yo no toco música popular... ¡ni por todo el dinero° del mundo! Para un buen pianista, es imposible hacer eso sin destruir sus ideales profesionales.

SR. ÁLVAREZ Pues... no estoy de acuerdo con usted. Queremos que todos *bailen* y *se diviertan.* Es una fiesta de graduación; no un concierto. Es una lástima° que usted *pierda* la oportunidad de tocar para la familia del presidente. Ellos van a estar en la fiesta.

PIANISTA Bueno... En realidad, la música popular...

---

estoy seguro *I'm sure*   se aburran *get bored*   ¡Al contrario! *On the contrary!*   que
lo pasen bien *that they have a good time*   tambor *drum*   ¡Qué tontería! *How ridiculous!*
ni por todo el dinero *not even for all the money*   Es una lástima *It's a pity*

---

1. ¿Le gusta al pianista la música popular? ¿Por qué?   2. ¿Qué le recomienda al pianista el señor Álvarez?   3. ¿Qué música prefieren bailar los amigos de la señorita Álvarez?   4. ¿Qué instrumento toca uno de los amigos de ella?   5. ¿Qué familia famosa va a asistir a la fiesta de graduación?   6. ¿Es flexible o inflexible el músico?

A. Impersonal expressions have no obvious subject, and equivalent English expressions often begin with the pronoun *it.* The subjunctive is used after many impersonal expressions of doubt, emotion, expectation, permission or prohibition, and personal judgment. The clauses are generally linked by **que.** Some of the more common impersonal expressions that require the subjunctive in a following clause are:

Es bueno.	*It's good.*	Es (una) lástima.	*It's a pity.*
Es malo.	*It's bad.*	Es probable.	*It's probable.*
Es mejor.	*It's better.*	Es necesario.	*It's necessary.*
Es imposible.	*It's impossible.*	Es ridículo.	*It's ridiculous.*
Es posible.	*It's possible.*	Es difícil.	*It's difficult.*
Es importante.	*It's important.*	Está bien.	*It's all right (OK).*
Es sorprendente.	*It's surprising.*		

Es importante que pidas una torta para más de veinte personas.

It's important that you order a cake for more than twenty people.

¿Es bueno que coman tanto pavo?

Is it good that they are eating so much turkey?

No, no es bueno que coman tanto.

No, it's not good that they are eating so much.

All the preceding impersonal expressions are followed by the subjunctive in dependent clauses in affirmative, negative, or interrogative sentences.

Remember that the subjunctive is used only when a subject is mentioned in the dependent clause. If there is no subject mentioned, the impersonal expression is followed by an infinitive.

Es necesario empezar las preparaciones un mes antes de la fiesta.

It's necessary to begin the preparations a month before the party.

B. When the impersonal expression in the main clause reaffirms the reality of the action or thought mentioned in the dependent clause, the verb in the dependent clause is indicative.

Es cierto que Ana canta bien.	*It's certain that Ana sings well.*

Some impersonal expressions are followed by the indicative when they are affirmative but require the subjunctive when used in the negative. They take the subjunctive in interrogative sentences only if doubt is strongly implied. Here are some examples:

(No) es verdad.	*It's (not) true.*	(No) es (está) claro.	*It's (not) clear.*
(No) es cierto.	*It's (not) certain.*	(No) es seguro.	*It's (not) certain.*
(No) es evidente.	*It's (not) evident.*	(No) es obvio.	*It's (not) obvious.*

No hay duda de que... takes the indicative. The affirmative **Hay duda de que...** takes the subjunctive.

Elena, ¿estás lista? Es seguro que la mayoría de los invitados van a llegar temprano.	*Elena, are you ready? It's certain that most of the guests are going to arrive early.*
Pues, querido, también es cierto que yo voy a llegar muy tarde.	*Well, dear, it is also certain that I am going to arrive very late.*
¿Es verdad que todo se vaya a arreglar?	*Is it true that everything is going to turn out all right?* (doubt implied)
¿Es verdad que todo se va a arreglar?	*Is it true that everything is going to turn out all right?* (no doubt implied)
No, no es verdad que todo vaya a arreglarse.	*No, it isn't true that everything is going to turn out all right.* (negative)

C. Verbs normally followed by the subjunctive in dependent noun clauses are sometimes followed by the indicative. Here are some examples:

1. Decir is followed by the subjunctive if a command is implied, and by the indicative if a fact is stated.

Le digo al perro que no cante más.	*I'm telling the dog not to sing any more.*
Ella dice que Ana canta bien.	*She says that Ana sings well.*

2. The verbs **creer** and **pensar** require the subjunctive in interrogative or negative sentences when surprise or doubt is implied. The indicative is used in affirmative sentences or when there is no uncertainty or doubt in the speaker's mind.

¿Crees que Alicia esté en el desfile?	*Do you think that Alicia is in the parade?* (doubt implied)
¿Crees que Alicia está en el desfile?	*Do you think that Alicia is in the parade?* (simple question)
No creo que Alicia esté en el desfile.	*I don't think Alicia is in the parade.*

EJERCICIOS

A. Imaginación y lógica. Forme frases lógicas usando una expresión de cada columna. ¡Ponga atención a la forma del verbo!

MODELO **Es importante que los mexicanos recuerden el pasado.**

Es importante		el gobierno	celebrar muchas fiestas religiosas
Es cierto		los mexicanos	recordar el pasado
Es difícil	que	nosotros	aprender los bailes tradicionales
Es probable		los niños	ayudar en la fiesta de cumpleaños
Es verdad		tú	divertirse con la piñata
No es evidente			necesitar el candelabro para Janucá
No es obvio			recibir tarjetas de Navidad
No es seguro			

B. ¡Dio en el clavo! (*You hit the nail on the head!*) Haga el papel del alcalde (*mayor*) de Querétaro. Conteste las preguntas que le hace un reportero norteamericano. Use las palabras entre paréntesis para mostrar que usted está seguro de las respuestas.

MODELO ¿A los turistas les interesan las fiestas mexicanas? (es verdad)
Sí, es verdad que les interesan las fiestas mexicanas.

1. ¿A los mexicanos les gustan mucho las fiestas? (es obvio)
2. ¿Hay muchas fiestas religiosas en México? (es evidente)
3. ¿Ayuda el gobierno con los gastos (*expenses*) de las fiestas locales? (No hay duda)
4. ¿Son un poco diferentes las celebraciones en los varios pueblos mexicanos? (yo estoy seguro)
5. ¿Celebran en México muchas fiestas con corridas de toros? (es cierto)

C. ¿Qué dijiste, Patricia? Lola no oye bien a Patricia, su hermana mayor. Haga el papel de Patricia y repita lo que (*what*) le dice a Lola, cambiando el verbo al subjuntivo si es necesario.

MODELO Prepara las bebidas para la fiesta. (te digo que)
Te digo que prepares las bebidas para la fiesta.

1. No te pongas el vestido azul. (Insisto en que)
2. Llama a Antonio ahora mismo. (Quiero que)
3. Ve al mercado por refrescos. (Necesito que)
4. María va a llegar tarde. (Creo que)
5. Viene mucha gente. (Es cierto que)
6. Conoces a todos mis amigos. (Dudo que)

Preguntas

1. ¿Siente o se alegra usted de que no haya clases los sábados? ¿Por qué es importante no tener clases todos los días?   2. ¿Qué quiere usted que le den sus amigos para su cumpleaños? ¿Recomienda que busquen regalos baratos o caros? 3. ¿Cuántas horas por semana estudia usted español? ¿Está seguro(-a)? ¿Duda su profesor(a) que usted estudie tantas horas?   4. ¿Ha ido usted a muchas fiestas este semestre? ¿este mes? ¿esta semana? ¿A qué tipo de fiestas?   5. ¿Qué quieren los estudiantes que hagan los profesores? ¿Y qué quieren los profesores que hagan los estudiantes? ¿Qué le recomienda usted a su profesor(a) de español que cambie en la clase?   6. Cuando usted tiene problemas, ¿duda que todo vaya a arreglarse?

III. **Palabras afirmativas y palabras negativas**

Los mexicanos celebran su independencia con un desfile en el Zócalo.

Un 15 de septiembre (la «Noche del Grito») en la Ciudad de México. Dos estudiantes están en el Zócalo y esperan el grito tradicional del Presidente desde el balcón del palacio.*

ESTUDIANTE 1   ¡Hay tanta gente! ¡No veo *nada*!° ¿Ves tú a *alguien*°? ¿Ya ha dicho *algo*° el presidente?

ESTUDIANTE 2   Pues... no veo a *nadie*° en el balcón... En cambio,° hay miles de° personas aquí en la plaza. ¿Ves ese grupo de muchachas? Hay *algunas* muy bonitas... me pregunto° de dónde son...

ESTUDIANTE 1   Yo no veo a *ninguna*° muchacha bonita. Además, no vinimos *ni* para mirar *ni*° para admirar muchachas... ¡Estamos aquí para escuchar al presidente! En unos minutos todo el mundo va a gritar° «¡Viva México!» para recordar el grito que empezó la

*September 16 is the anniversary of the proclamation of Mexican Independence. On the 15th, «la Noche del Grito» commemorates the **grito** or *shout* of Father Hidalgo who in 1810 led the popular revolt that began the struggle for independence. The bell Father Hidalgo rang to summon the people was later installed in the **Palacio Nacional**. Thousands of Mexicans gather in the **Zócalo** or central plaza of Mexico City waiting for the bell to ring and for the President to begin the cry of «**¡Viva México!**»

guerra de la independencia, ¿recuerdas? Es un momento muy importante y es necesario que tú y yo participemos... Mira...veo a *alguien* en el balcón. ¡Debe ser el presidente!

ESTUDIANTE 2   ...Y también hay una rubia muy linda allá con...

ESTUDIANTE 1   ¡*Nunca*° me escuchas!

¡No veo nada! *I don't see anything!*   alguien   *anyone*   algo   *anything*   no veo a nadie   *I don't see anyone*   En cambio   *On the other hand*   miles de   *thousands of*   me pregunto   *I wonder*   ninguna   *any*   ni...ni   *neither . . . nor*   todo el mundo va a gritar   *everyone is going to shout*   ¡Nunca... !   *You never . . .!*

---

1. ¿A quién quiere ver el primer estudiante?   2. ¿Hay alguien en el balcón?
3. ¿Dónde están los dos estudiantes?   4. ¿Para qué está allí el primer estudiante?
5. ¿Qué grita todo el mundo? Explique para qué gritan todos.

Affirmative Words		Negative Words	
sí	*yes*	no	*no*
alguien	*someone, anyone*	nadie	*no one, not anyone*
algo	*something, anything*	nada	*nothing, not anything*
algún, alguno(-a; -os; -as)	*some, any*	ningún, ninguno(-a)	*none, not any, no, neither (of them)*
también	*also, too*	tampoco	*not either, neither*
siempre	*always*	nunca, jamás	*never, not ever*
o...o	*either . . . or*	ni...ni	*neither . . . nor*
		ni siquiera	*not even*

A. The negative words **nadie, nada, ninguno, tampoco,** and **nunca** can be placed either before or after a verb.

No me invitó nadie. Nadie me invitó.	*No one invited me.*
No trajimos nada para la fiesta. Nada trajimos para la fiesta.	*We didn't bring anything for the party.*
No fue al desfile tampoco. Tampoco fue al desfile.	*She (He) didn't go to the parade either.*

Notice that **no** precedes the verb when a negative word follows it. **No** is omitted when another negative word precedes the verb.

B. Alguno and **ninguno** can refer either to people or to things, while **alguien** and **nadie** refer only to people. **Alguno** and **ninguno** usually refer to certain members or elements of a group that the speaker or writer has in mind. Before a masculine singular noun, **alguno** becomes **algún** and **ninguno** becomes **ningún.** Note that **ningún, ninguno,** and **ninguna** are generally used in the singular.

Nadie trajo la piñata.	*No one brought the piñata.*
Ninguna de ellas hizo la torta.	*Neither one of them made the cake.*
¿Hay alguien en la plaza?	*Is there anyone in the square?*

¿Hay algunos músicos en la procesión?	Are there any musicians in the procession?
No hay ningún cantante aquí.	There is no singer here.

With **alguien** and **nadie** and with **alguno** and **ninguno** when they refer to people, the personal **a** is used just as it is with nouns or other pronouns.

¿Busca usted a alguien?	Are you looking for someone?
No se lo voy a decir a nadie.	I'm not going to tell it to anyone.

c. Several negatives can be used in the same sentence.

¡No dio nada a nadie nunca!	He (She) never gave anything to anyone!

D. *Neither . . . nor* is expressed with **ni...ni** and *either . . . or* with **o...o.** When used with the subject of a sentence, both expressions usually take the plural form of the verb.

Doña Emilia no quiere servir ni jamón ni pavo en la fiesta.	Doña Emilia doesn't want to serve either ham or turkey at the party.
Ni el postre ni la ensalada están listos.	Neither the dessert nor the salad is ready.
O la torta o el pastel son para la fiesta.	Either the cake or the pie is for the party.

EJERCICIOS

A. La transformación. Cambie las frases al negativo.

> **MODELO** Los hijos le dan algún regalo a su madre el Día de la Madre.
> **Los hijos no le dan ningún regalo a su madre el Día de la Madre.**

1. Siempre cenamos en un restaurante el Día de la Madre.
2. También vamos a un restaurante para el Año Nuevo.
3. El Día de (los) Reyes, recibimos o regalos o dinero de los abuelos.
4. Venden algunas tarjetas bonitas en esa tienda.
5. Alguien tiene que trabajar el Día de la Independencia.
6. ¿Vamos a hablar de algo interesante?
7. Hay algún candelabro en la casa?

B. ¡Ya te dije que no! Haga el papel de Eliana y conteste las preguntas que le hace Guillermo. Todas las respuestas de Eliana son negativas.

> **MODELO** GUILLERMO Hola, Eliana, ¿me llamó alguien?
> ELIANA **No, no te llamó nadie.**

GUILLERMO	¿Viste a Jorge o a Lucía?
ELIANA	No, _____.
GUILLERMO	¿Hay algún problema?
ELIANA	No, _____.

GUILLERMO   ¿Quieres salir a cenar o a bailar?

ELIANA   No, _____.

GUILLERMO   ¿No quieres ir al cine tampoco?

ELIANA   No, _____.

GUILLERMO   Entonces, no quieres hacer nada, ¿verdad?

ELIANA   Al contrario...

C. Traducción.   Traduzca las frases siguientes al español.

1. She didn't bring anything to the party.
2. I'm going to bring her either a cake or flowers for her birthday.
3. Do you need something before dinner?
4. No one ate cheese or bread at the party.
5. Did any of your friends go to the parade downtown last night?
6. Rogelio never drinks anything at these celebrations.

Preguntas

1. Cuando usted hace una fiesta en su casa, ¿qué platos prepara? ¿Traen sus amigos algún plato especial? ¿Qué traen?   2. ¿Conoce usted algún restaurante mexicano? ¿Sirven allí alguna comida típica? ¿Qué sirven? ¿Tienen decoraciones típicas como piñatas, por ejemplo?   3. ¿Invitó usted a alguien a su casa para una fiesta la semana pasada? ¿Qué hicieron en la fiesta?   4. ¿Ha ido usted a alguna celebración interesante este mes? ¿Qué celebración? Descríbala.   5. ¿Vio usted anoche a algún (alguna) estudiante de la clase de español? ¿A quién? ¿Estuvieron en una fiesta o en la biblioteca?

IV. Adverbios terminados en -*mente*

Esta gente baila bien, ¿no?

En una fiesta

LUPE ¿Ves qué bien baila Bernardo? Algunas personas aprenden *fácilmente*° los bailes tradicionales, pero otras, como yo... , los aprende muy difícil y *lentamente*°.

ANTONIO Sí, es verdad...pero ¡tú bailas *estupendamente*!...

LUPE Estoy de acuerdo... Pensaba en...pues, ... *probablemente* en alguien que no conoces.

ANTONIO ¡Qué va! Sabes que *realmente* no puedo bailar *correctamente* ninguno de los bailes tradicionales. *Verdaderamente* tengo las piernas como palos° cuando bailo...

LUPE Eso es... Yo no quería decirlo *directamente*... ¿Ves cómo Bernardo sigue *perfectamente* el ritmo de la música?

ANTONIO Sí, tienes razón. Pero no olvides que los bailarines practican *diariamente*° durante semanas antes de las celebraciones. No es sorprendente ni impresionante que bailen bien... Yo tengo que hacer cosas más importantes... como...

LUPE ¡Encantada, Bernardo! Claro que quiero bailar... Justo le decía° a Antonio que *realmente* da gusto° verte bailar...

---

fácilmente *easily*   difícil y lentamente *with difficulty and slowly*   las piernas como palos *two left feet*   diariamente *daily*   Justo le decía *I was just saying . . .* da gusto *it's a pleasure*

---

1. ¿Baila bien Lupe?   2. Y Antonio, ¿puede bailar correctamente los bailes tradicionales?   3. ¿Quién baila perfectamente?   4. ¿Practican frecuentemente los bailarines?   5. ¿Quiere Lupe bailar con Bernardo?

A. Adverbs modify verbs, adjectives, or other adverbs. Some adverbs you have learned are associated with place—**cerca, allí, aquí,** etc.—and others are associated with time—**siempre, ayer, ahora,** etc.

B. Many adverbs are formed by adding **-mente** (which corresponds to the English *-ly*) to the feminine singular form of an adjective. Below are some of them.

alegre	**alegremente**	*happily*
clara	**claramente**	*clearly*
correcta	**correctamente**	*correctly*
diaria	**diariamente**	*daily*
difícil	**difícilmente**	*with difficulty*
directa	**directamente**	*directly*
entusiasta	**entusiastamente**	*enthusiastically*
especial	**especialmente**	*especially*
estupenda	**estupendamente**	*stupendously*
extremada	**extremadamente**	*extremely*
fácil	**fácilmente**	*easily*
natural	**naturalmente**	*naturally*

perfecta	**perfectamente**	*perfectly*
probable	**probablemente**	*probably*
real	**realmente**	*really*
verdadera	**verdaderamente**	*truly, really*

C. An adverb generally follows the verb it modifies but precedes the adjective or adverb it modifies.

Bernardo sabe bailar perfectamente.	*Bernardo knows how to dance perfectly.*
Antonio es extremadamente celoso.	*Antonio is extremely jealous.*

D. When two or more adverbs ending in **-mente** occur in a series, **-mente** is added only to the final one.

Celebraron entusiasta y alegremente.	*They celebrated happily and enthusiastically.*

EJERCICIOS

A. De adjetivos a adverbios.   Convierta los adjetivos en adverbios.

MODELO   verdadero   **verdaderamente**

1. total
2. amable
3. claro
4. generoso
5. posible
6. inmediato
7. natural
8. especial
9. agradable
10. cortés
11. alegre
12. extremado
13. diario
14. perfecto
15. natural

B. Estamos prácticamente listos.   Haga el papel de don Antonio. Hable con Juanita de la celebración que tiene lugar la semana que viene.

MODELO   Es necesario que practiques el baile. (diario)
Es necesario que practiques el baile diariamente.

1. Este traje es para ti. (especial)
2. Aprendiste el baile tradicional. (fácil)
3. Ojalá que bailes bien. (real)
4. Es importante que salgamos después del desfile. (inmediato)
5. La gente va al centro. (directo)
6. Ella está nerviosa. (extremado)

Preguntas

1. ¿Habla usted correctamente el español? ¿y el inglés? ¿y el francés?   2. ¿Qué hace generalmente por la noche?   3. ¿Practica algún deporte regularmente? ¿Qué deporte(s)?   4. ¿Qué día feriado le gusta especialmente? ¿Por qué?   5. En la clase, ¿habla el profesor o la profesora totalmente en español? ¿Comprende usted perfectamente lo que *(what)* él/ella dice?   6. Generalmente, ¿qué hace usted inmediatamente después de esta clase? ¿y antes? ¿Qué va a hacer hoy?

LAS POSADAS

Un niño hace el papel de San José en las Posadas.

Don Antonio, un español de 75 años, está en un pequeño pueblo de México, de visita en casa de su hija Paula. Es época de Navidad. Algunas familias se han reunido en la casa de Paula para celebrar las Posadas.[1]

PAULA	Entren, por favor. Están en su casa.[2]
UNA VECINA	¡Qué bonito está todo! ¡Nunca había visto adornos tan lindos! ¡...y el nacimiento° es precioso°!
PAULA	Gracias. Diles a tus hijos que se sienten aquí al lado de mi padre. Quiero que vean bien las Posadas.
VECINA	Muchas gracias. Como don Antonio no sabe nada de esto, ¿quieres que le explique el origen de la celebración?
PAULA	Sí, por favor. Es importante que comprenda todo lo que pasa.
VECINA	Pues...¡es una celebración totalmente mexicana! Creo que viene de la época de los aztecas.
VECINO	Probablemente no. Es evidente que es una ceremonia muy cristiana...
VECINA	No, querido, en eso no estoy de acuerdo contigo... No «es evidente» pero sí es verdad que algunas cosas son típicamente indias y...
DON ANTONIO	¡Escuchen! Ya han empezado las canciones.
VECINA	Dos hombres empiezan a cantar; uno hace el papel de San José y el otro hace el papel del dueño de la casa.
SAN JOSÉ	En nombre del cielo, danos posada. Ábrele la puerta a mi esposa amada.
EL DUEÑO	Aquí no hay mesón. Sigan adelante, y no me hables más, ¡ladrón o tunante![3]

Una hora después. Las canciones han terminado.

PAULA	Pues, que pasen todos al comedor°. La comida está lista. Sí, ahora es mejor que todos entren, coman, beban ¡y se diviertan! A ver... , ¡que traigan la piñata!⁴
NIÑO	¡Mira qué grande es la piñata, abuelo! ¿Tienen piñatas en España?
DON ANTONIO	No, mi tesoro°. No es nuestra costumbre°.
NIÑO	¡Pobres niños españoles!

---

nacimiento *nativity scene*   precioso *lovely*   comedor *dining room*   mi tesoro *my dear (literally, "my treasure")*   costumbre *custom*

PREGUNTAS

1. ¿Para qué se han reunido varias familias del pueblo? 2. ¿Qué quiere la vecina explicarle a don Antonio? ¿Por qué no sabe mucho de eso? 3. ¿Es de origen azteca o cristiano la celebración de las Posadas? 4. ¿Cuáles son los papeles que hacen los dos hombres que cantan? 5. Después de las canciones, ¿adónde quiere Paula que pasen todos? 6. ¿Tienen piñatas los niños españoles? 7. ¿Ha visto usted una piñata alguna vez?

NOTAS CULTURALES

1. The **Posadas** (literally, "the inns") are Christmas celebrations in Mexico commemorating the search of Joseph and Mary for lodging in Bethlehem. The festivities are held on nine consecutive nights, beginning on December 16 and ending on Christmas Eve. Nine families usually participate, with each family sponsoring one evening. The celebration begins around eight o'clock with prayers and songs; then the company divides into two groups, one acting as Joseph and Mary seeking lodging, the other acting as the innkeepers. The groups converse in song. At the end of the evening, the identity of those seeking shelter is revealed, they are admitted to the "inn," and there is much celebrating. For the first eight nights, there are fruits, nuts, candies, and punch; on Christmas Eve the host family for that year (the **padrinos**) provides a large dinner after Midnight Mass **(Misa de gallo)**. The origin of the custom is said to be an Aztec ceremony that a Spanish priest, Diego de Soria, adapted to Christian purposes.

2. This is the traditional greeting a host or hostess in the Hispanic world uses to welcome a guest. It means *You are in your own house.*

3. SAINT JOSEPH: In the name of heaven, / give us shelter. / Open the door / to my beloved wife. / OWNER: There is no inn here. / Continue (on your search), / speak to me no further, / thief or rogue!

4. The **piñata** is a brightly colored figure, usually in the shape of an animal or toy, made of tissue paper, which covers a clay or cardboard container full of fruits, candies, and coins. The children take turns at being blindfolded and trying to break the **piñata** with a bat. When it is finally broken, the contents spill out and all the children leap upon them happily. **Piñatas** are also used for children's parties.

Funciones y *actividades*

In this chapter, you have seen examples of some important language functions, or uses. Here is a summary and some additional information about these functions of language.

EXPRESSING AGREEMENT

Here are some ways to indicate agreement.

Exacto.	*Exactly.*	Estoy de acuerdo.	*I agree.*
Claro. (Seguro. Por supuesto. Naturalmente.)	*Certainly. (Sure. Of course. Naturally.)*	Sí, es verdad.	*Yes, it's (that's) true.*
		Así pienso.	*That's how I think.*
Eso es.	*That's it.*		
Sí, ¡cómo no!	*Yes, of course!*	¡Ya lo creo!	*I believe it!*
Sí, tiene(s) razón.	*Yes, you're right.*	Probablemente sí. (Es probable que sí.)	*Probably. (Probably so.)*
Sí, así es.	*Yes, that's so.*	Correcto.	*Right. (Correct.)*

EXPRESSING DISAGREEMENT

Here are some ways to indicate disagreement.

No, no es verdad.	*No, it's (that's) not true.*	Pero en cambio...	*But on the other hand . . .*
No, no estoy de acuerdo.	*No, I don't agree.*	¡Qué tontería!	*How ridiculous!*
No, no es así.	*No, it's not so.*	¡Qué absurdo (ridículo)!	*How absurd (ridiculous)!*
Probablemente no. (Es probable que no.)	*Probably not.*	Al contrario.	*On the contrary.*
		No, no tienes razón.	*No, you're not right.*
		¡Qué va!	*Oh, come on!*

You can use the following expressions to disagree with a suggestion that you or someone else do something.

¡Ni por todo el dinero del mundo!	*Not for all the money in the world!*
¡Ni hablar!	*Don't even mention it!*
¡De ninguna manera!	*No way!*

Ahora haga las siguientes actividades, usando las expresiones que acaba de aprender.

A. Al contrario... Trabaje con un(a) amigo(-a) de la clase. Uno(-a) de ustedes va a expresar cinco opiniones. El (la) otro(-a) hace el papel del «abogado del diablo» ("devil's advocate"): no está de acuerdo y dice lo contrario. Use tantas expresiones de desacuerdo (*disagreement*) como e sea posible.

MODELO   La comida de la cafetería de la universidad es excelente.
            Al contrario, ¡es horrible!

Use sus propias ideas o escoja algunas de la lista siguiente:

1. el número de días feriados en los Estados Unidos
2. los exámenes de la clase de español
3. las restricciones sobre fiestas en su universidad
4. la edad legal de tomar bebidas alcohólicas en este estado
5. el arte de su pintor(a) favorito(-a)
6. las novelas de su escritor(a) favorito(-a)
7. los lunes por la mañana / los sábados por la noche

B. Mini-drama.   Usted y un(a) amigo(-a) organizan una fiesta para otro(-a) amigo(-a). Tienen que decidir a quiénes invitar, y qué pedirles que traigan. Usted y su amigo(-a) no están de acuerdo en nada. Finalmente deciden qué cosas la gente debe traer, y cuándo y dónde la fiesta va a tener lugar. Usen expresiones de desacuerdo y después expresiones de acuerdo.

VOCABULARIO ACTIVO

Cognados

el aniversario	la celebración	la graduación	la procesión
el balcón	clásico	la piñata	religioso
el candelabro	diferente	popular	tradicional

Verbos

arreglarse	*to work out, turn out all right*
celebrar	*to celebrate*
dudar	*to doubt*
gritar	*to shout*
insistir (en)	*to insist (on)*
rogar (ue)	*to ask*
sorprender	*to surprise*
temer	*to fear*

Adverbios

alegremente	*happily*
claramente	*clearly*
correctamente	*correctly*
diariamente	*daily*
directamente	*directly*
especialmente	*especially*
extremadamente	*extremely*
generalmente	*generally*
inmediatamente	*immediately*
naturalmente	*naturally*
perfectamente	*perfectly*
probablemente	*probably*
totalmente	*totally*
verdaderamente	*truly, really*

Fiestas y aniversarios

el adorno	*decoration, ornament*
el Año Nuevo	*New Year's Day*
el árbol	*tree*
el desfile	*parade*
el Día de Acción de Gracias (U.S.)	*Thanksgiving*
el Día de la Madre	*Mother's Day*
el Día de los Reyes	*Three King's Day, Epiphany*
el día feriado	*holiday*
la fiesta de Janucá	*Chanukah*
las flores	*flowers*

la Navidad	*Christmas*
el pavo	*turkey*
la tarjeta	*card, greeting card*

Expresiones útiles

Al contrario	*On the contrary*
En cambio	*On the other hand*
Eso es.	*That's it.*
Estoy de acuerdo.	*I agree.*
No, no estoy de acuerdo.	*No, I don't agree.*
¡Qué va!	*Oh, come on!*
Sí, es verdad.	*Yes, it's true.*
Sí, tiene(s) razón.	*Yes, you're right.*

Don't forget: Negative and affirmative words, page 371
Impersonal expressions, page 367

LECTURA VII

Las fiestas

A los hispanos les gustan las fiestas—fiestas con familiares° y amigos, fiestas nacionales, regionales, folklóricas, religiosas... En general, cada comunidad o pueblo celebra anualmente varias fiestas. A la gente hispana le gusta reunirse°. Cualquier° pretexto es bueno.

family members

to get together/ Any

Representan acontecimientos históricos, como por ejemplo: la conquista de América por los españoles, o la independencia de las naciones americanas de España. En el pueblo de Guatemala que vemos en la foto, los indios,

Representación de la Conquista, en Guatemala

vestidos de conquistadores españoles o de jefes indígenas, participan en una representación de la conquista. En México, mucha gente se reúne en la plaza de su pueblo o ciudad todos los 15 de septiembre a las 11 de la noche, para gritar y recordar la Noche del Grito°, cuando el padre Hidalgo había empezado la rebelión que después terminó en la independencia mexicana.

Night of the Cry

Como la mayoría de la gente hispana es católica, las fiestas católicas son muy importantes, tanto en España como en Hispanoamérica. Por esa razón, muchos pueblos y ciudades celebran el día de su santo(-a) patrón(a) y muchas personas también celebran el día de su santo(-a). Por ejemplo, si alguien se llama José, es muy probable que celebre—además de° su cumpleaños—el 19 de marzo, día de San José.

besides, in addition to

Una de las festividades religiosas más importantes del mundo hispano es la celebración de la Semana Santa. En Sevilla, por ejemplo, toda la ciudad se transforma durante esa semana. Adornan las casas con mantos violetas°, estatuas y flores. Los niños se visten de° ángeles o de Jesús, y muchos adultos se visten de penitentes. Hay procesiones lentas y silenciosas de enormes pasos, que son plataformas decoradas con estatuas que representan escenas

purple mantles

dress as

Una procesión religiosa
durante la Semana Santa
en Sevilla

religiosas. Los hombres de Sevilla, vestidos de penitentes, llevan esos pasos. Después de las Pascuas°, hay una gran celebración con bailes, música y fuegos artificiales°.

Easter
fireworks

En las fiestas religiosas de los pueblos pequeños de Hispanoamérica encontramos, muchas veces, una mezcla° curiosa de cristianismo y religión

mixture

Fiesta de la Diablada, Oruro, Bolivia

indígena. Así,° por ejemplo, en algunas partes del Perú y de Bolivia, la gente honra° simultáneamente a la Virgen María y a la Pachamama o Madre Tierra°. En la Fiesta de la Diablada°, los indios bolivianos llevan máscaras° que representan el bien y el mal° en forma de ángeles y diablos, o de los antiguos demonios de los Andes. Hay bailes dramáticos y la celebración termina con una ceremonia religiosa.

Thus
honor/Mother Earth
devilry/masks
el bien... good and evil

PREGUNTAS

1. ¿Por qué les gustan las fiestas a los hispanos?   2. ¿Qué tipo de fiestas les gustan?   3. ¿Qué acontecimiento histórico representan los indios de Guatemala en la foto?   4. ¿Qué ciudad tiene una celebración muy famosa relacionada con la Semana Santa? Descríbala y explique qué es un «paso».   5. ¿Qué mezcla curiosa encontramos en muchas fiestas hispanas? Dé un ejemplo.   6. ¿Existe una mezcla de elementos cristianos y no cristianos en algunas de las fiestas que celebramos en los Estados Unidos? Dé ejemplos.

¿Qué recuerda?   Llene los espacios con las palabras apropiadas.

1. En México mucha gente _____ en la plaza todos los 15 de septiembre para celebrar la Noche del Grito.
2. La mayoría de la gente hispana es _____.
3. Muchos hispanos celebran el día de su _____.
4. La _____ es una de las festividades religiosas más importantes del mundo hispano.
5. Para las festividades, los niños de Sevilla se visten de _____.
6. En algunas partes del Perú y de Bolivia, la gente _____ a la Virgen María y a la Pachamama.
7. En la Fiesta de la Diablada, los indios llevan _____ que representan el bien y el mal.

Novios en la
Alhambra, Granada,
España

CAPÍTULO
QUINCE

NOVIOS Y AMIGOS

Vocabulario. In this chapter you will talk about friendship and romance.

Gramática. You will discuss and use:

1. The future tense
2. The conditional (*she would write if . . .*)
3. Long-form possessives, both adjectives (*of mine, of hers*) and pronouns (*mine, hers*)
4. Reciprocal constructions like *they see each other*

Cultura. The dialogues take place in the Spanish cities of Granada, Málaga, and Sevilla.

Funciones

- Making deductions
- Stating intentions
- Expressing probability and possibility

LOS AMIGOS

llevarse bien (con)
quererse

tener una cita
salir con
salir juntos
acompañar

abrazar(se)
el abrazo

LOS NOVIOS

enamorarse de
estar enamorado(-a) (de)
el amor

besar(se)
el beso

tener celos (de)
ser (ponerse) celoso(-a)

los novios
el novio
la novia
la pareja
el noviazgo

Los novios are a couple in love intending to marry or recently married. Their relationship, **el noviazgo**, may last for years, and is not entered into lightly. **Los prometidos** are engaged persons; they have formally agreed to marry. ♡

el anillo (de oro, de platino...)
darle un anillo a alguien
el prometido, la prometida

EL MATRIMONIO

EL DIVORCIO

casarse (con)
el casamiento,
   la boda
la iglesia, la sinagoga
el matrimonio civil

la separación provisional
la anulación matrimonial
divorciarse

Para completar.   Escoja las palabras o expresiones apropiadas para completar estas oraciones sobre el noviazgo de Ana y Luis.

1. Anoche Luis tuvo una (cita / sinagoga) con Ana, su (abrazo / novia). La (salió / llevó) al teatro.
2. Después Luis le dio un (anillo / beso) de oro.
3. Lo hizo porque él está (aburrido / enamorado) de ella.
4. Luis y Ana van a (casarse / divorciarse) el 21 de mayo próximo en la iglesia San Miguel.
5. Después de la (boda / anulación matrimonial), ellos piensan ir a Toledo por tres semanas.
6. Ana y Luis se (quieren / gritan) muchísimo, pero éste se pone un poco (romántico / celoso) cuando Ana habla con otros hombres.
7. La verdad es que ellos siempre salen (enamorados / juntos). Ana sólo sale (con / sin) Luis ¡y viceversa!
8. No hay duda de que ellos se (besan / llevan) muy bien y por eso creo que no van a hablar de (divorcio / matrimonio civil) ¡jamás!

Opiniones.   ¿Está usted de acuerdo o no? Explique por qué.

1. Una pareja debe tener una boda religiosa.
2. No es malo ser un poco celoso o celosa.
3. Es importante llevarse bien con los suegros.
4. Si el esposo y la esposa no se llevan bien, (ellos) deben divorciarse.
5. El amor es eterno y por eso no debe existir el divorcio.
6. La falta (lack) de dinero causa muchos divorcios.
7. Por eso, si los esposos tienen poco dinero, deben vivir con los suegros.
8. Todas las religiones deben tolerar el divorcio.
9. Los novios deben conocerse por más de un año antes de casarse.
10. Los novios no deben vivir juntos antes de casarse.

Preguntas

1. ¿Tiene usted muchos amigos? ¿un(a) amigo(-a) favorito(-a)? ¿Dónde y cuándo se conocieron?   2. En general, ¿cómo se lleva usted con sus amigos? ¿Los ve mucho? ¿Cuándo?   3. ¿Se ha enamorado usted alguna vez? ¿De quién? ¿Cuándo? ¿Pensó casarse con esa persona? ¿Por qué sí o por qué no?   4. ¿Tiene usted novio(-a) ahora? ¿Se llevan bien? ¡mal? ¿más o menos bien? ¿Tiene celos de los amigos de su novia (las amigas de su novio)? ¿Piensa casarse con él (ella)? ¿Por qué sí o por qué no?   5. ¿Cree usted que puede existir una amistad (*friendship*) profunda y sincera (sin implicaciones románticas) entre un hombre y una mujer?

I. El futuro

Unas estudiantes de la Universidad de Granada

Dos compañeros de la Universidad de Granada hablan de su amiga Rita.

ERNESTO   ¿Sabías que Rita ya tiene planeados los próximos dos años°?
GUSTAVO   No me digas.° ¿Qué piensa hacer?°
ERNESTO   *Estudiará, leerá, asistirá* a todas las conferencias...
GUSTAVO   ¡Qué aburrido! ¿Qué *sacará* ella llevando una vida tan monótona?° Invítala al cine y *verás* lo rápido que cambia de idea°.
ERNESTO   Realmente lo dudo... ¡Una chica así no *tendrá* tiempo ni para enamorarse!

---

ya...años   *already has the next two years planned*   No me digas.   *Don't tell me. (You don't say.)*
¿Qué piensa hacer?   *What does she plan to do?*   ¿Qué...monótona?   *What will she get out of living such a monotonous life?*   lo...idea   *how fast she changes her mind*

---

1. Según Ernesto, ¿qué hará Rita este año y el próximo?   2. ¿Qué le recomienda Gustavo a Ernesto?   3. ¿Cree usted que Ernesto va a invitar al cine a Rita? ¿Por qué?   4. ¿Piensa usted que Rita es una persona interesante? ¿Por qué?

A. To form the future tense of regular verbs, add to the complete infinitive the endings **-é, -ás, -á, -emos, -éis, -án.** The endings are the same for **-ar, -er,** and **-ir** verbs. Except for the **nosotros** form, all forms have written accents. One use of this tense is to ask about or affirm what will happen in the future.

hablar		**comer**		**vivir**	
hablaré	hablaremos	comeré	comeremos	viviré	viviremos
hablarás	hablaréis	comerás	comeréis	vivirás	viviréis
hablará	hablarán	comerá	comerán	vivirá	vivirán

Hoy supe que tu hermano se casará con mi prima.

La nueva pareja vivirá aquí por un tiempo.

Seguramente te prometerá un anillo de platino, ¿no...?

Today I learned that your brother will marry my cousin.

The new couple will live here for awhile.

Surely he will promise you a platinum ring, right . . . ?

B. Some verbs have irregular stems in the future; their endings, however, are the same as for regular verbs.

1. Verbs that drop the vowel of the infinitive ending.

Infinitive	Infinitive Stem	Future Tense (yo form)
habér	habr-	**habré**
podér	podr-	**podré**
querér	querr-	**querré**
sabér	sabr-	**sabré**

The future form of **hay** is **habrá.**

2. Verbs that replace the vowel of the infinitive ending with **d.** (Note that these are the same verbs that insert **g** in the present tense **yo** form.)

ponér + d	pondr-	**pondré**
salír + d	saldr-	**saldré**
tenér + d	tendr-	**tendré**
valér + d	valdr-	**valdré**
venír + d	vendr-	**vendré**

3. Verbs that drop the stem consonant, plus a vowel.

decir	dir-	**diré**
hacer	har-	**haré**

Jaime no podrá visitar a sus suegros. No tendrá tiempo.

Los novios querrán pasar su luna de miel en Toledo.

Habrá que comprarles un regalo a los recién casados.

Jaime won't be able to visit his in-laws. He won't have time.

The bride and groom will want to spend their honeymoon in Toledo.

We (One) will have to buy a gift for the newlyweds.

C. The future tense can also be used to express probability in the present.

¿Qué hora será?	*What time can it be? (I wonder what time it is.)*
Serán las ocho.	*It must be (It's probably) eight o'clock.*
¿Valdrá la pena decirle a papá que tengo una cita con mi novio?	*Can it be worth the trouble to tell Dad I have a date with my boyfriend?*
¿Estará en clase Tomás? Lo dudo. Él estará con Beatriz.	*I wonder if Tomás is in class. (Can Tomás be in class?) I doubt it. I'll bet he is with Beatriz. (He's probably with Beatriz.)*

D. The present indicative or a form of **ir a** + *infinitive* is often used instead of the future to express actions that will occur in the near future or that are regarded as sure to happen.

Se casarán en 1995.	*They'll get married in 1995.*
Se casan mañana.	*They're getting married tomorrow.*
No hay duda de que vas a llegar tarde a tu cita.	*There's no doubt that you're going to be late for your appointment.*

When the subjunctive is required in a dependent clause, the future may not take its place.

Lola espera que te guste Granada.	*Lola hopes that you will like Granada.*

While the present subjunctive merely poses a concept ("your liking Granada") about which a comment is made (Lola hopes), the future indicative is often used to affirm that an action will happen. Compare the following sentences:

Espero que ese matrimonio dure.	*I hope that marriage will last.*
Sé que ese matrimonio durará.	*I know that marriage will last.*

EJERCICIOS

A. Para llenar. Complete las frases con la forma apropiada del futuro de los verbos entre paréntesis.

yo
1. (decir) Te _____ la verdad.
2. (hacer) Les _____ un favor a mis futuros suegros.
3. (venir) _____ a visitarte el domingo.
4. (dar) Le _____ un anillo a mi novia.

tú
5. (salir) Constancia, ¿ _____ conmigo el sábado?
6. (ponerse) ¿ _____ algo elegante?
7. (bailar) ¿ _____ conmigo toda la noche?
8. (decir) ¿Le _____ a tu padre que me quieres?

nosotros

9. (vivir) Tú y yo _____ juntos toda la vida.
10. (tener) _____ muchos niños.
11. (trabajar) _____ para un futuro mejor.
12. (ser) Nunca _____ celosos.

ellos

13. (enamorarse) Muchos jóvenes _____ este año.
14. (pensar) _____ que el amor es eterno.
15. (dar) Los chicos les _____ anillos a las chicas.
16. (casarse) Pero, ¿cuántos _____ ?

él, ella

17. (hacer) Antonio _____ una cita con Sarita.
18. (llevar) Él la _____ al restaurante.
19. (querer) Sarita _____ pedir algo caro. También _____ tomar vino con la cena.
20. (tener) El pobre Antonio _____ que pedir algo muy barato.

B. Visitaremos Granada.   Cambie las oraciones de la forma *ir a* al tiempo futuro para decir lo que harán estos turistas.

MODELO   Vamos a visitar Granada.   **Visitaremos Granada.**

1. El autobús va a llegar al hotel a las ocho.
2. Vamos a salir para La Alhambra a las ocho y cuarto.
3. Nadie va a querer perder el autobús.
4. También vamos a ver la universidad.
5. Otros van a preferir otro restaurante.
6. Una gitana (*gypsy*) te va a vender recuerdos.
7. La señora González va a comprar un anillo.
8. Vamos a volver al hotel después de las cuatro.

C. En el año 2001.   En cinco frases, diga cómo será la vida en el año 2001.

MODELO   **En el año 2001 no tendremos que trabajar.**

D. Cuentos progresivos.   En grupos de cuatro o más estudiantes, preparen ustedes un cuento progresivo. La primera persona empieza el cuento con una oración como «Mañana saldré de casa temprano...» Luego, otra persona repetirá lo que dijo la primera y añadirá (*will add*) otra acción al cuento. Y así siguen las otras personas del grupo. Cada estudiante debe seguir participando hasta añadir por lo menos una cosa nueva al cuento. Algunos cuentos pueden empezar así:

1. Mañana me despertaré a las seis y...
2. El año que viene mis amigos y yo iremos a España y...
3. En el futuro una mujer será presidenta y...

Preguntas

Escoja a un(a) estudiante y dígale que se siente enfrente de la clase. Luego hágale preguntas sobre el futuro. Las preguntas que siguen quizás sean útiles pero usted debe hacerle otras preguntas también.

1. ¿Serás rico(-a) algún día?   2. ¿Dónde vivirás después de terminar tus estudios?
3. ¿Cuándo te casarás?   4. ¿Harás muchos viajes en el futuro? ¿Adónde viajarás?
5. ¿Adónde irás el verano que viene?   6. ¿Quién será presidente(-a) en el futuro?
7. ¿Qué harás para divertirte este fin de semana?   8. ¿Te quedarás en casa o saldrás el domingo?   9. ¿A qué hora te acostarás esta noche? ¿A qué hora te levantarás?

II. El condicional

Las famosas palomas blancas viven en el Parque María Luisa, en Sevilla.

En un hotel de Sevilla

MARUJA   ¡Ay, me habían dicho que no *sería* fácil la vida de casada°!
ISMAEL   ¿Por qué dices eso, mi amor°?
MARUJA   ¿No recuerdas la promesa que me hiciste la semana pasada?
ISMAEL   ¿Qué te *prometería* yo? ¿Te dije que *iríamos* al cine...o que *saldríamos* todas las noches?
MARUJA   ¡Dios mío! ¡Qué clase de esposo tengo yo! Me prometiste que no *fumarías* más°.
ISMAEL   Y cumplí mi promesa, cariño°. No fumo más. Fumo exactamente lo mismo que siempre°.

---

vida de casada   *married life*   mi amor   *my love*   no fumarías más   *you wouldn't smoke any more*   cumplí...cariño   *I kept my promise, dear*   lo...siempre   *the same as ever*

---

1. ¿Qué le habían dicho a Maruja del matrimonio?   2. ¿Recuerda Ismael la promesa que le hizo a su esposa? ¿Cuál fue la promesa?   3. Según Ismael, ¿cumplió él su promesa? ¿Por qué?

A. To form the conditional of regular verbs, add to the complete infinitive the endings **-ía, -ías, -ía, -íamos, -íais, -ían.** The conditional usually conveys the meaning *would.*

hablar		comer		vivir	
hablaría	hablaríamos	comería	comeríamos	viviría	viviríamos
hablarías	hablaríais	comerías	comeríais	vivirías	viviríais
hablaría	hablarían	comería	comerían	viviría	vivirían

No, Graciela y Diego no se llevarían bien.	*No, Graciela and Diego wouldn't get along well.*
No viviríamos juntos antes de casarnos.	*We wouldn't live together before getting married.*
Nuestros padres no lo permitirían.	*Our parents wouldn't permit (allow) it.*

Remember that verbs in the imperfect expressing repeated events in the past are often also translated *would* meaning *used to.* In Spanish, the imperfect and the conditional are not interchangeable.

Durante el verano, comíamos en el patio todos los días.	*During the summer, we would eat on the patio every day.*
Cuando eran novios, su prometido la llamaba todas las noches.	*When they were engaged, her fiancé would call her every night.*

B. The conditional is used to express an action that was projected as future or probable from the point of view of a time in the past.

Roberto y Emilia dijeron que se quedarían solteros.	*Roberto and Emilia said that they would stay single.*
Yo creía que una boda tradicional sería más elegante.	*I thought a traditional wedding would be more elegant.*

C. The verbs that have irregular stems in the future have the same irregular stems in the conditional. They use the same conditional endings as verbs with regular stems.

haber, **habr-**	poner, **pondr-**	valer, **valdr-**	decir, **dir-**
poder, **podr-**	salir, **saldr-**	venir, **vendr-**	hacer, **har-**
querer, **querr-**	tener, **tendr-**		
saber, **sabr-**			

The conditional form corresponding to **hay** is **habría.**

No, Lucía nunca diría eso.	*No, Lucía would never say that.*
Te dije que vendrían a la boda los padres de Juan.	*I told you Juan's parents would come to the wedding.*
Creo que usted podría encontrarles un apartamento a los recién casados.	*I think you could (would be able to) find an apartment for the newlyweds.*

D. The conditional may be used to express probability in the past.

¿Qué hora sería cuando ellos llegaron?	What time was it (probably) when they arrived?
Sería la una de la tarde.	It was probably one in the afternoon.
¿Qué edad tendría Pepito cuando sus padres se mudaron a Sevilla?	Approximately how old was Pepito when his parents moved to Sevilla?
Tendría once o doce años.	He was around eleven or twelve years old (He must have been eleven or twelve).

E. Speakers often use the conditional to soften requests or suggestions.

Nosotros deberíamos tomar un taxi.	We should take a taxi.
¿Me podría decir cómo llegar al Hotel Cuatro Naciones?	Could you tell me how to get to the Cuatro Naciones Hotel?

EJERCICIOS

A. Yo te lo dije, Rosa. A pesar de (*in spite of*) todo lo negativo que le dijo su amigo Pedro, Rosa aceptó un puesto en la compañía Suárez. Haga el papel de Rosa y complete las oraciones para indicar lo que le había dicho Pedro.

Pedro me dijo que...

MODELO (gustar)...no me **gustaría** la compañía.

1. (ser) ...el trabajo _____ muy difícil.
2. (tener) ...los trabajadores no _____ tiempo de almorzar.
3. (decir) ...mi jefe (*boss*) nunca _____ la verdad.
4. (llevarse) ...aquellos dos secretarios no _____ bien.
5. (andar) ...el nuevo sistema no _____ bien.
6. (pedir) ...la compañía les _____ mucho a los trabajadores.
7. (valer) ...no _____ la pena hablar con el director.
8. (estar) ...los trabajadores _____ en huelga.

B. Marisol la atrevida. Marisol la atrevida (*daring*) haría cosas que no harían sus amigos. Haga el papel de Marisol y responda a los comentarios de sus amigos.

MODELO FÉLIX Yo no trabajo en aquella compañía.
       MARISOL **Pues yo sí trabajaría en aquella compañía.**

1. MIGUEL Yo no como sopa fría.
2. JUANA No me caso con un hombre celoso.
3. TERESA Yo no salgo sola de noche.
4. VÍCTOR No les digo la verdad a mis suegros.
5. SUSANA No voy a la boda de mi ex-novio.
6. JOAQUÍN Yo no trabajo de secretario.
7. SANCHO No hago un viaje a Granada.
8. CARLOS No paso mi luna de miel en Málaga.

C. Castillos en el aire.   Esteban sueña con ser millonario. Con las palabras que siguen, haga oraciones para decirle a la esposa de Esteban cómo él gastaría (*would spend*) su dinero.

> **MODELO**   yo / dar / dinero a los pobres
> **Yo daría dinero a los pobres.**

1. tú y yo / viajar / por todo el mundo
2. nuestros hijos / asistir / a una buena universidad
3. yo / ponerme / ropa elegante
4. nosotros / vivir / en una casa muy grande
5. tú / no trabajar / en la casa
6. Anita / poder / tener / muchas cosas lindas
7. yo / hacer / muchas cosas que ahora no puedo hacer
8. todos / ser / muy felices

D. ¿Por qué no irían?   Anoche Mirta y Mario tuvieron una fiesta fantástica pero muchos amigos no fueron. Diga las razones probables por las cuales (*for which*) no fueron, completando las frases, según los modelos.

> **MODELOS**   Marta / tener invitados   **Marta tendría invitados de otra ciudad.**
>
> Rosa / no estar en casa   **Rosa no estaría en casa.**

1. Toño / estar enfermo
2. Alfonso / tener una cita
3. Rafael / estar cansado
4. Miguel / no llevarse bien con Mario
5. Juan / tener que trabajar
6. María / estudiar para un examen
7. Jacinta / jugar al tenis
8. Camilo / no querer ver a Mirta

E. Otro don Quijote.   Después de leer unos capítulos de *Don Quijote,* usted ya empieza a pensar y ver el mundo como el estimado «don». Usted cree que debe cambiar el mundo. En cinco frases, diga qué cambios haría.

> **MODELO**   **Yo terminaría con la pobreza.**

Entrevista

Divídanse en grupos de cuatro o cinco personas. Escojan a alguien del grupo para hacerle las siguientes preguntas. Luego escojan a otra persona y procedan de la misma forma hasta entrevistar a todos los miembros del grupo.

1. ¿Dónde te gustaría vivir?   2. ¿Vivirías en Rusia?   3. ¿Darías tu vida por un amigo o una amiga?   4. ¿Mentirías para ayudar a un amigo o a una amiga? 5. ¿Votarías por una mujer para presidenta?   6. ¿Qué harías con un millón de dólares?   7. ¿Te gustaría vivir en Andalucía? ¿Qué harías allí?   8. ¿Dónde te gustaría pasar tu luna de miel?

III. **La forma enfática de los adjetivos posesivos**

El aeropuerto de
Málaga

En el aeropuerto de Málaga

ÓSCAR	Esta llave es *mía,*° ¿no?
RAÚL	Sí, es *tuya*°. Y dime, ¿es éste el pasaporte de Enrique?
ÓSCAR	Pues...sí, creo que es *el suyo*°. Pero...no veo mi maleta.
EMPLEADA	¿La maleta azul era de usted? ¡Yo creía que era de esos turistas venezolanos!
ÓSCAR	No, señorita, *la mía* era la única azul°. Las de ellos eran todas negras.
EMPLEADA	¡Dios *mío!*° Vino un hombre con barba°, dijo que era amigo de ellos...¡y se la llevó!

Esta...mía *This key is mine*   tuya *yours*   el suyo *his*   la...azul *mine was the only blue one*   ¡Dios mío! *Good heavens! (literally, "My God!")*   barba *beard*

---

1. ¿Es de Óscar la llave?   2. ¿De quién es el pasaporte? ¿Es también suya la maleta perdida?   3. ¿De qué color era la maleta de Óscar?   4. ¿De quiénes eran las maletas negras?   5. ¿Quién se llevó la maleta azul?   6. ¿Cree usted que Óscar va a recuperar (*recover*) su maleta? ¿Por qué sí o por qué no?

A. There are other forms of possessive adjectives than those presented in Chapter 5. These longer forms follow rather than precede the nouns they modify and agree with them in gender and number.

Singular	*Long Forms of Possessive Adjectives* Plural	
mío, mía	míos, mías	*my, of mine*
tuyo, tuya	tuyos, tuyas	*your, of yours*
suyo, suya	suyos, suyas	*his, of his; her, of hers; your, of yours*
nuestro(-a)	nuestros(-as)	*our, of ours*
vuestro(-a)	vuestros(-as)	*your, of yours*
suyo, suya	suyos, suyas	*their, of theirs; your, of yours*

Esos amigos tuyos se llevan bien. — *Those friends of yours get along well.*

Mario se casa con una antigua compañera suya. — *Mario is marrying a former classmate of his.*

B. Possessive pronouns have the same forms as the long forms of the possessive adjectives. They are usually preceded by the definite article. The article and the pronoun agree in gender and number with the noun referred to, which is omitted.

Voy a vender el *(anillo)* mío porque Juan y yo nos hemos divorciado. — *I'm going to sell mine* (my ring) *because Juan and I have divorced.*

¿Pagaste tanto por la *(casa)* tuya? Nosotros pagamos menos por la · *(casa)* nuestra. — *Did you pay that much for yours* (your house)? *We paid less for ours* (our house).

C. After the verb **ser** the definite article is usually omitted.

Las rojas son nuestras. — *The red ones are ours.*
Esas fotos no son tuyas. — *Those photos aren't yours.*
¿Son míos estos pasajes? — *Are these tickets mine?*

D. As seen in section A, **suyo(-a)** and **suyos(-as)** can have different meanings, depending on the possessor: for instance, **la casa suya** could mean *his house, her house, your house* (**Ud.** or **Uds.**), or *their house*. For clarity, a prepositional phrase with **de** is sometimes used instead.

de + él (ella, usted, ellos, ellas, ustedes)	
El amigo mío es soltero. Y el suyo (Y el de usted), ¿es casado?	My friend is single. And yours, is he married?
Las *(llaves)* mías están aquí, pero no veo las suyas (las de ella)...	Mine *(My keys)* are here, but I don't see hers...

EJERCICIOS

A. **¿Con quiénes vamos?**   Su profesor(a) les ha pedido que visiten un mercado al aire libre (*open-air market*). Diga quién(es) fue(ron) con quién(es).

> **MODELO**   yo / amigos
> **Yo fui con unos amigos míos.**

1. Miguel y Jorge / compañeros
2. Susana / hermana
3. tú / primos
4. ustedes / tías
5. nosotros / vecino
6. la profesora / estudiantes

B. **¡Qué coincidencias tiene la vida!**   El señor Ruiz le habla a su hijo Alberto de sus buenos tiempos pasados. Haga el papel de Alberto y respóndale a su padre que las cosas siguen igual que antes.

> **MODELO**   SR. RUIZ   Mi apartamento era grandísimo.
> ALBERTO   **El mío es grandísimo también.**

1. Mis clases eran muy interesantes.
2. Mi compañero de cuarto era peruano.
3. Mis diversiones favoritas eran nadar y bailar.
4. Pagaba muy poco por mi apartamento.
5. Mis profesores eran muy buenos.

C. **¿Es tuyo esto?**   La Sra. Ruiz está ayudando a una amiga a desempacar (*unpack*) sus maletas. Haga el papel de la amiga y conteste que sí a las preguntas de la Sra. Ruiz.

> **MODELO**   ¿Es tuyo este anillo?   **Sí, es mío.**

1. ¿Es tuya esta falda?
2. ¿Son de Irene estas sandalias?
3. ¿Es de Luisito esta camisa?
4. ¿Es de Luis este poncho?
5. ¿Son de ustedes estos cuadros?

IV. El recíproco

La Catedral de Sevilla, con la (torre) Giralda

Natalia y Fernando se encuentran en un parque de Sevilla.

FERNANDO	¡Natalia, tanto tiempo que no *nos vemos*!
NATALIA	¿Qué tal, Fernando?
FERNANDO	Pues, muy bien. ¿Sabes que tengo una nueva obra, una comedia... ?
NATALIA	¿Ah...sí? ¿Y cómo se llama?
FERNANDO	Se llama «Tragedia de amor». Oye, te la cuento en pocas palabras. Al comienzo° el hombre y la mujer *se conocen*°, empiezan a *quererse*°, *se besan*°, *se confiesan su amor*°. Segundo acto: no *se saludan*°, no *se hablan*, no *se miran*, ya no *se llevan bien*°, ya no *se quieren*°. Tercer acto...
NATALIA	Ya me lo imagino...*Se insultan, se odian*°, lloran, rompen°. ¡Fin!
FERNANDO	Así mismo.° ¿Te consigo entrada?°
NATALIA	No sé...Estoy muy ocupada. *Nos hablamos*° la semana próxima... ¡y espero que pronto *nos veamos otra vez*°!

Al comienzo *At the beginning* **se conocen** *meet (each other)* **a quererse** *to love each other* **se besan** *they kiss (each other)* **se...amor** *they confess their love for each other* **no...saludan** *they don't greet each other* **ya...bien** *they don't get along any more* **ya...quieren** *they no longer love each other* **se odian** *they hate each other* **rompen** *they break up* **Así mismo.** *Exactly so.* **¿Te...entrada?** *Should I get you a ticket?* **Nos hablamos** *We'll talk (to each other)* **nos...otra vez** *we'll see each other again*

---

1. ¿Dónde se encuentran los dos amigos?   2. ¿Cómo se llama la nueva obra de Fernando?   3. ¿Qué pasa al comienzo de la obra? ¿y en el segundo acto?   4. ¿Se imagina Natalia qué pasa en el tercer acto? ¿Qué pasa?   5. ¿Cree usted que Natalia y Fernando van a hablarse la semana próxima? ¿Por qué cree eso?

The reflexive pronoun **nos** may be used with a **nosotros** form of a verb, **se** with an **ellos** form, and **os** with a **vosotros** form to express a reciprocal action. This construction corresponds to English *each other, one another.*

Se hablan por teléfono.	*They talk to each other on the phone.*
Todos se miran.	*They all look at one another.*
Vosotros os entendéis mucho.	*You understand each other very well.*
Roberto y yo nos llevamos bien.	*Roberto and I get along (with each other) well.*
No nos vemos mucho y, gracias a eso, no nos gritamos nunca.	*We don't see each other much and, thanks to that, we never scream at each other.*

At times, a phrase in the general form **el uno al otro, la una a la otra, los unos a los otros, las unas a las otras,** etc. is added for emphasis or clarification. The definite article is often dropped. Other prepositions besides **a** are used: **se divierten unos con otros.**

Se cuentan historias el uno al otro.	*They tell each other stories.*
Lola y Ana se ayudan la una a la otra.	*Lola and Ana help each other.*
En clase todos se saludan unos a otros.	*In class everyone greets each other.*

EJERCICIOS

A. Nos conocemos bien. Haga el papel de Mario y diga cómo es vivir con Martín, su hermano gemelo (*twin brother*). Añada los detalles que sean necesarios.

MODELOS ver **Martín y yo nos vemos todos los días.**

escribir **No nos escribimos porque vivimos juntos.**

1. hablar
2. no insultar
3. dar regalos
4. llamar por teléfono
5. no prestar la ropa
6. ayudar en todo
7. no gritar nunca
8. querer mucho

B. Historia de un amor recíproco. Complete el párrafo con la forma apropiada del verbo indicado. Use el presente, el pretérito o el imperfecto, según corresponda.

Un día Ramón y Ramona (1) _____ (conocer) en un baile. Otro día (2) _____ (ver) en la Plaza de Cataluña. Esa noche (3) _____ (confesar) su amor. Después (4) _____ (querer) cada día más. Todos los días (5) _____ (hablar) por teléfono y (6) _____ (ayudar) siempre. Los dos (7) _____ (entender) y (8) _____ (llevar) muy bien.

C. Historia de otro amor recíproco. Ahora vuelva a contar la historia anterior cambiando **Ramón y Ramona** por **Luis(a) y yo.** Si quiere agregar (*add*) una o dos frases más para completar la historia, por favor ¡hágalo!

Entrevista

Trabaje con un(a) compañero(-a) para hacerse y contestar las siguientes preguntas.

1. ¿Cuándo nos vemos tú y yo? ¿Y cuándo se ven tú y tu profesor(a) de matemáticas (literatura, historia, química, física...)? 2. ¿Se hablan en español tú y tus amigos cuando no están en clase? 3. ¿Quiénes se saludan al comienzo de la clase? 4. ¿Tienes hermano (hermana, novio, novia)? ¿Cómo se llama? 5. ¿Se ven todos los días tú y tu hermano (hermana, novio, novia)? ¿Se llevan bien ustedes? ¿Se ayudan mutuamente? ¿Se cuentan sus problemas? 6. ¿Se comunican bien tú y tus padres? ¿tú y tus amigos? ¿tú y tu compañero(-a) de cuarto? ¿tú y tus profesores?

AMOR A PRIMERA VISTA°

Sevilla es una ciudad muy romántica.

Un autobús turístico entra a la ciudad de Sevilla[1].

GUÍA°   Dentro de unos minutos llegaremos al Barrio de Santa Cruz[2].

SRA. VEGA   Para ser tan joven, el guía sabe mucho, ¿no lo crees?

SOFÍA   Será muy inteligente...o tendrá mucha memoria...Yo no podría recordar tantos hechos° históricos.

DAVID   Perdón, señorita, por casualidad°, ¿ha estado alguna vez en la Argentina?

SOFÍA   ¿Yo...? No, nunca. ¿Por qué me pregunta eso?

DAVID   Pues, por nada°. Yo soy argentino. Me llamo David Blum.

SOFÍA   ¿Blum? Ése es mi apellido° también. ¡Qué casualidad!° Y me gustaría conocer la Argentina. Mis padres pasaron la luna de miel en Buenos Aires. Pienso ir allí algún día.

DAVID   Me encantaría enseñarle la ciudad. A propósito°, ¿adónde irá después de visitar Sevilla?

SOFÍA   Seguiré° con la misma compañía hasta Granada[3]. El sábado próximo se casa mi prima. Estaré allá para la boda. Ella y su novio se conocieron en la Universidad de Granada el año pasado. ¿Y usted...? ¿Volverá a la Argentina pronto?

DAVID   No... Me encontraré con mi hermano en Málaga[4]. Pero tengo tres días libres. Tal vez los pasaré en Granada. Podríamos visitar la Alhambra juntos...y así tendríamos tiempo de conocernos mejor...

Dos horas después, el autobús está por partir.

SRA. VEGA   No me gusta hacer este tipo de preguntas...pero, ¿querrías decirme cuánto pagaste por esa pulsera° de filigrana[5]...?

SOFÍA   ¡Por supuesto! Pagué tres mil doscientas pesetas por ella y se la compré a una gitana[6].

DAVID   ¡Tres mil doscientas pesetas! Me parece un precio exagerado... ¿No trataste de regatear°? A veces la gente que anda por la calle pide mucho más de lo que se pagaría en las tiendas.

Cuatro días después, en Granada

SOFÍA   Pero...David, ¿qué hará tu hermano? ¿Te esperará en Málaga o se irá sin ti?

DAVID   No importa que se vaya sin mí. Lo único° que tiene importancia para mí ahora es estar contigo. Y aquí me quedaré hasta que tú me digas cuándo nos volveremos a ver.

SOFÍA   La verdad es que ahora no podría vivir sin ti. ¿Será que me he enamorado de ti...? Te daré mi dirección en Nueva York. Pero dime, ¿vendrás a verme...?

DAVID   ¡Por supuesto, Sofía! Creo que en este momento ¡yo iría al fin del mundo por ti!

Amor...vista *Love at first sight*   guía *guide*   hechos *facts*   por casualidad *by chance*   por nada *for no reason*   apellido *last name*   ¡Qué casualidad! *What a coincidence!*   A propósito *By the way*   Seguiré *I will continue (go on)*   pulsera *bracelet*   trataste de   regatear *try to bargain*   Lo único *The only thing*

PREGUNTAS

1. ¿Adónde llegarán los turistas dentro de unos minutos?   2. ¿Qué dice Sofía del guía? ¿Por qué?   3. ¿Qué le parece a usted la interrupción de David? ¿Por qué será que le hizo una pregunta tan rara a Sofía?   4. ¿Qué país le gustaría conocer a Sofía? ¿Por qué?   5. ¿Adónde irá Sofía después de visitar Sevilla? ¿Para qué quiere ir allí? ¿Dónde y cuándo se conocieron la prima de Sofía y su novio? 6. ¿Cuánto pagó Sofía por la pulsera de filigrana? ¿A quién se la compró? 7. Según David, ¿por qué hay que tener cuidado?   8. ¿Por qué se quedó David en Granada? ¿Qué hará su hermano?   9. Para David, ¿vive muy lejos Sofía? ¿Qué dice él?   10. ¿Cree usted que es posible enamorarse en cuatro días? ¿Cree que Sofía y David volverán a verse? ¿Por qué?

NOTAS CULTURALES

1. **Sevilla**, an exceptionally beautiful port city in southwest Spain, is the chief city of Andalucía, one of Spain's autonomous regions, famous for its olive trees, wines, fine horses and cattle, flamenco dancing, and rich cultural history. For eight centuries it was part of various Moorish kingdoms.

2. **El Barrio de Santa Cruz** was Seville's Jewish quarter during its centuries as a Moorish city. It is famous for its narrow streets, plazas, and white houses with **rejas**, barred windows lush with flowers through which lovers traditionally converse.

3. Granada, located in southern Spain at the foot of the snow-capped **Sierra Nevada**, was capital of the last great Moorish kingdom in Spain. From the 13th to the 15th centuries, it was one of the richest, most populous cities in the world. In 1492, it fell to the Christians. Granada's **Alhambra** palace, completed in the 14th century, is considered the finest example of civil architecture surviving from the first thousand years of Islam.

4. Málaga is a resort city on Spain's southern **Costa de Sol**.

5. Filigreed jewelry is a characteristic product of Seville, reflecting its Islam heritage.

6. Gypsies, a nomadic people perhaps originally from India though named for Egypt, live in several parts of **Andalucía**. Many achieved fame as flamenco guitarists and dancers.

Funciones y actividades

In this chapter, you have seen examples of some important language functions, or uses. Here is a summary and some additional information about these functions of language.

MAKING DEDUCTIONS

Por eso	*For that reason*
Por estas (esas) razones	*For these (those) reasons*
Por lo tanto	*Therefore*
Como consecuencia (resultado)	*As a consequence (result)*
Será que	*It must be that*
Sería que	*It must have been that*

STATING INTENTIONS

In addition to using the future tense, you can state intentions with these expressions:

Pienso	*I intend (plan)*
No pienso	*I don't intend (plan)*
Voy a	*I'm going to*
No voy a	*I'm not going to*

EXPRESSING PROBABILITY AND POSSIBILITY

Besides the use of future and conditional forms to express probability and possibility, as you saw in this chapter, there are some other ways to express the same idea. The following are given in order, from most highly probable to least likely:

No hay duda de que (+ *indicative*)	*There's no doubt that*
Seguramente (+ *indicative*)	*Surely* (also: *Probably*)
Por cierto (+ *indicative*)	*Certainly*
Estoy seguro(-a) que (+ *indicative*)	*I'm sure that*
Es verdad (indudable, etc.) que (+ *indicative*)	*It's true (certain, etc.) that*
Creo (Pienso) que (+ *indicative*)	*I believe (think) that*
Es probable que (+ *subjunctive*)	*It's probable that*
Es posible que (+ *subjunctive*)	*It's possible that*
Tal vez (Quizás) (+ *subjunctive or indicative*)	*Perhaps*
Es poco probable que (+ *subjunctive*)	*It's unlikely that*
No hay ninguna posibilidad de que (+ *subjunctive*)	*There's no possibility that*

For more information on when to use the subjunctive and when to use the indicative with these forms, review Chapters 13 and 14.

Ahora haga las siguientes actividades usando las expresiones que acaba de aprender.

A. En treinta años... Las siguientes oraciones son predicciones que algunas personas han hecho sobre el mundo del futuro. Primero, complete las oraciones con el futuro de los verbos entre paréntesis. Luego exprese su opinión sobre cuán probables (*how probable*) o posibles usted cree que son esas predicciones.

MODELO En los países industrializados, casi todo el mundo <u>tendrá</u> (**tener**) un robot para limpiar la casa, cocinar, etc. y <u>será</u> (**ser**) muy común el uso de los robots en la industria.
Es posible que el uso de los robots en la industria sea muy común; tal vez mucha gente tenga robots en la casa también.

1. Mucha gente _____ (**vivir**) y _____ (**trabajar**) en colonias en el espacio; esas colonias _____ (**tener**) su propio (*own*) sistema de producción de comida.
2. _____ (**existir**) órganos humanos artificiales de toda clase y el transplante de órganos _____ (**ser**) algo muy común; también _____ (**haber**) sangre (*blood*) artificial que se _____ (**poder**) usar para cualquier persona—sin importar la clase de sangre que tenga (de tipo A, B, O, etc.).
3. La gente _____ (**hacer**) sus compras por computadora; _____ (**ser**) posible seleccionar (*select*) algo entre una gran variedad de artículos y comprarlo sin salir de la casa. También, gracias al uso de las computadoras, mucha gente _____ (**trabajar**) en casa en vez de ir a la oficina.
4. La gente _____ (**vivir**) hasta la edad (*age*) de cien años o más porque _____ (**haber**) curas para muchas enfermedades (como el cáncer, por ejemplo). Como consecuencia, mucha gente _____ (**casarse**) más de una vez, y la jubilación (*retirement*) _____ (**ser**) a una edad más avanzada.
5. _____ (**aumentar**) dramáticamente el número de personas que vivan en nuestro planeta: la tierra _____ (**tener**) unos diez mil millones (10.000.000.000) de habitantes en el año 2030.
6. _____ (**haber**) menos gente «super-rica» y la situación económica del tercer mundo _____ (**estar**) peor que ahora.
7. Los futuros papás _____ (**poder**) escoger el sexo de sus hijos. Más padres _____ (**quedarse**) en casa con los niños mientras las madres trabajen fuera de casa.
8. Los trenes _____ (**ir**) a 300 millas por hora; los coches _____ (**ser**) más pequeños y más rápidos; los aviones _____ (**ser**) de plástico.

9. En los Estados Unidos, el 60 por ciento de los jóvenes del futuro
_____ (asistir) a una universidad o «college», en comparación con el
30 por ciento de ahora.

10. Los apartamentos y casas de los Estados Unidos y de otras partes del
mundo _____ (ser) más pequeños, pero muchos muebles (furniture)
_____ (tener) más de un uso y las paredes _____ (ser) movibles.

B. Como consecuencia...   Escoja dos de las predicciones del ejercicio A que
a usted le parezcan posibles o probables en el futuro. (O exprese otras
predicciones que usted quiera hacer.) Si esas predicciones llegan a cumplirse
(turn out to be true), ¿qué consecuencias tendrán? Haga por lo menos dos
afirmaciones usando algunas de las expresiones para hacer deducciones que
están en este capítulo.

MODELO   Mucha gente trabajará en su casa; por lo tanto, aumentará el
número de madres que trabajen (who might work) por dinero
sin salir de la casa.

C. Intenciones.   En grupos de dos, pregunte a un(a) compañero(-a) si él/ella
piensa o no hacer las siguientes cosas este fin de semana; él/ella responde sus
preguntas y después le hace las mismas preguntas (o preguntas similares) a
usted. Averigüe (find out) por lo menos tres cosas que cada uno de ustedes va
a hacer este fin de semana.

MODELO   limpiar tu cuarto
¿Limpiarás tu cuarto? (¿Piensas limpiar tu cuarto? ¿Es posible
que limpies tu cuarto?)

1. ir a un concierto de música «rock»
2. estudiar
3. trabajar en el jardín
4. jugar al vólibol
5. cumplir una promesa o romper una promesa
6. celebrar un cumpleaños
7. hacer ejercicios
8. ir a alguna parte (a un sitio de interés, a un parque, etc.)

Entrevista

Hágale las preguntas que siguen a un(a) compañero(-a). Luego comparta (share) la
información con los otros del grupo.

1. ¿Cuánto tiempo deben conocerse un hombre y una mujer antes de casarse?
2. ¿Es mejor que una mujer con hijos se quede en casa en vez de trabajar? ¿Por
qué?   3. ¿Son más felices las mujeres casadas o las solteras? ¿y los hombres
casados o solteros? ¿Por qué?   4. ¿Quiénes son más celosos: los hombres o las
mujeres?   5. ¿Puede usted explicar los refranes (proverbs) que siguen? a. «Donde
hay amor, hay dolor.» y b. «Ojos que no ven, corazón que no siente.»

Melodrama de amor.   Según los dibujos, cuente la historia de Ana y Rodrigo.

1.   2.   3.   4.

5.   6.   7.   8.

9.   10.

VOCABULARIO ACTIVO

Cognados

el divorcio	el matrimonio	platino	la sinagoga
eterno	monótono	la promesa	

Verbos

abrazar	to hug, to embrace
besar	to kiss
cumplir	to carry out, to fulfill
divorciarse	to (get a) divorce
durar	to last
enamorarse (de)	to fall in love (with)
estar enamorado (de)	to be in love (with)
fumar	to smoke
llevarse (bien)	to get along (well)
planear	to plan
salir (con)	to go out (with)
saludar(se)	to greet (each other)
tener celos (de)	to be jealous (of)
tener una cita	to have a date; to have an appointment
tolerar	to tolerate

Novios y amigos

el abrazo	hug
el amor	love
el anillo	ring
la anulación matrimonial	marriage annulment
el beso	kiss
la boda	wedding
casado	married
el casamiento	marriage; wedding
la luna de miel	honeymoon
el matrimonio civil	civil marriage
la novia	girlfriend
el novio	boyfriend
el noviazgo	engagement, courtship
la prometida	fiancée
el prometido	fiancé
el recién casado, la recién casada	newlywed
la separación provisional	trial separation
soltero	single

Otras palabras y frases

la falta	lack
la llave	key

Expresiones útiles

Creo que (+ indicativo)	I believe that
No hay duda de que (+ indicativo)	There's no doubt that
Pienso	I intend (plan)
Seguramente	Surely, Probably
Será que	It must be that
Tal vez	Perhaps
Voy a	I'm going to

Don't forget: Long-form possessives, page 396

Este joven
paraguayo parece
contento, ¿no?

**CAPÍTULO
DIECISÉIS**

SENTIMIENTOS Y EMOCIONES

Funciones

- Apologizing

- Expressing forgiveness

- Giving advice

Vocabulario.   In this chapter you will talk about feelings and emotions.

Gramática.   You will discuss and use:

1. The subjunctive in dependent clauses that function as adjectives

2. The subjunctive after adverbial conjunctions (**antes que** *before* **a menos que** *unless,* etc.), and the subjunctive or indicative after conjunctions of time (**cuando** *when,* **tan pronto como** *as soon as,* etc.)

3. Uses of the infinitive

Cultura.   The dialogues take place in Asunción, Paraguay, and the surrounding area.

¿CÓMO SE SIENTE ALBERTO? ¿CÓMO ESTÁ ÉL?

está $\begin{cases} \text{feliz} \\ \text{contento} \\ \text{alegre} \end{cases}$
alegrarse

se siente $\begin{cases} \text{triste} \\ \text{deprimido} \\ \text{llorar} \end{cases}$
deprimirse

está enamorado
enamorarse (de)

está $\begin{cases} \text{asustado} \\ \text{sorprendido} \end{cases}$
asustarse
sorprenderse

está $\begin{cases} \text{aburrido} \\ \text{cansado} \end{cases}$
aburrirse
cansarse

está orgulloso
se siente orgulloso

está $\begin{cases} \text{frustrado} \\ \text{enojado} \end{cases}$
frustrarse
enojarse

se siente mal
está enfermo
enfermarse

se siente bien
reírse (i)
darle risa

está avergonzado
avergonzarse
darle vergüenza

¿QUÉ HACE ANA? ¿CÓMO ESTÁ ELLA?

se alegra
está feliz
está contenta

se enoja
está enojada
está furiosa

llora
está triste
está deprimida

¿QUÉ LE DA A ANA? ¿CÓMO SE SIENTE ELLA?

le da vergüenza
se siente
avergonzada

le da rabia
se siente frustrada

le da risa
se siente feliz

Palabras relacionadas. Dé el adjetivo o participio pasado (usado como adjetivo) relacionado con cada uno de los siguientes verbos.

   MODELO   sorprenderse   **sorprendido(-a)**

1. enfermarse	5. enojarse	8. aburrirse
2. alegrarse	6. asustarse	9. cansarse
3. avergonzarse	7. deprimirse	10. frustrarse
4. enamorarse		

Preguntas

1. ¿Cómo está la persona que tiene un mes de vacaciones? ¿que dice o hace algo malo en público? ¿que descubre que su mejor amigo(-a) va a mudarse a otra ciudad? ¿que pierde su pasaporte y su dinero?   2. ¿Qué hace la persona que ve una película trágica? ¿que escucha un chiste (*joke*)?   3. ¿Cómo se siente la persona que está sola en la casa a medianoche y oye ruidos (*noises*) extraños?   4. ¿Cómo se siente usted cuando gana un partido de béisbol (básquetbol, tenis, etc.) o un juego de cartas (trivia, dominó, etc.)?   5. Cuando esperamos a una persona por mucho tiempo, ¿cómo nos sentimos?   6. ¿Cuándo llora usted?   7. ¿Cuándo tiene vergüenza usted? ¿Qué cosas le dan vergüenza? ¿le dan rabia? ¿le dan risa?   8. ¿Hay cosas que lo (la) asustan a usted? ¿Puede dar un ejemplo?

I. El subjuntivo en cláusulas adjetivales

Unos estudiantes paraguayos se alegran de la construcción de un nuevo edificio para su liceo.

En un liceo° de Asunción

SR. MÉNDEZ	¿Es usted la persona que quiere trabajar aquí?
SR. GÓMEZ	Sí, señor, yo soy profesor y busco un empleo° *que me guste.* Puedo enseñar historia, literatura o cualquier otro curso *que usted mande°.*
SR. MÉNDEZ	¡Qué bien! Por fin conozco a alguien que sabe más que yo... Dígame, ¿sabe usted quién mató° a Julio César?
SR. GÓMEZ	Pero señor, pregúntele eso a alguien *que sea detective.*
SR. MÉNDEZ	¡Bruto!°
SR. GÓMEZ	Esto es demasiado, señor. Por favor, sin ofender...

---

liceo *high school*   empleo *job*   cualquier...mande *any other course you like (literally "order")*   mató *killed*   ¡Bruto! *Brutus! (also "Brute! Ignoramus!")*

---

1. ¿Quién busca un empleo que le guste?   2. ¿Qué es el señor Gómez?
3. ¿Qué puede enseñar él?   4. Aparentemente, ¿sabe él quién mató a Julio César?
5. Según el señor Gómez, ¿a quién hay que preguntarle quién lo mató?   6. ¿Sabe usted quién fue Julio César? ¿y Bruto?

A dependent clause that modifies a noun or pronoun is called an adjective clause.

Asunción es una ciudad *que tiene más de 400 años.*	*Asunción is a city that is over 400 years old.*
Me da rabia pensar en eso *que me dio tanta vergüenza.*	*It makes me angry to think of that (thing, circumstance) that made me so ashamed.*

The noun or pronoun being described is called the antecedent. In the sentences above, the antecedents are **ciudad** and **eso**. Pronouns that often appear as the antecedents of adjective clauses include **alguien** (someone), **algo** (something), and **alguno** (some, someone).

Sandra habló con alguien que conoce a un buen detective.	Sandra spoke to someone who knows a good detective.
¿Dije algo que te ofendió?	Did I say something that offended you?

B. The verb in an adjective clause may be indicative or subjunctive, depending on whether the antecedent is definitely known to exist.

1. Antecedent definitely exists and is known: indicative.

El alcalde es un médico que sabe guaraní.*	The mayor is a doctor who knows Guaraní.
La pobreza es algo que lo asusta.	Poverty is something that scares him.

2. Antecedent unknown, indefinite, uncertain, or nonexistent: subjunctive.

Necesitan un camarero que sepa guaraní.	They need a waiter who knows Guaraní.
No hay nada que lo asuste.	There isn't anything that scares him.

Study the contrasts in the following examples.

¿Hay alguien aquí que comprenda la lengua de los guaraníes?	Is there anybody here who understands the language of the Guaraní Indians?
Sí, aquí hay alguien que la comprende.	Yes, there's someone here who understands it.
No, aquí no hay nadie que la comprenda.	No, there's nobody here who understands it.

C. The personal **a** is used before a direct object standing for a person when the speaker has someone definite in mind, but not when the person is indefinite or unspecified. (However, when the pronouns **alguien, nadie, alguno,** and **ninguno** are used as direct objects referring to a person, the personal **a** is nearly always used, whether the person is known or not.)

Buscan un profesor que sea experto en lenguas indígenas.	They're looking for a professor who is an expert on Indian languages.
Le pagan a un profesor que es experto en lenguas indígenas.	They're paying a professor who is an expert on Indian languages.
Necesitamos a alguien que sepa hablar español y guaraní.	We need someone who knows how to speak Spanish and Guaraní.
Encontramos a alguien que sabe hablar español y guaraní.	We found somebody who knows how to speak Spanish and Guaraní.

*See cultural note 2, p. 423

EJERCICIOS

A. El candidato ideal. La universidad paraguaya busca a alguien que se encargue de (*that would be in charge of*) la clase de lengua guaraní. ¿Cuál es la descripción del candidato ideal?

> **MODELO** tiene buen carácter
> **Buscamos a alguien que tenga buen carácter.**

1. sabe hablar español y guaraní
2. es experto en lenguas indígenas
3. tiene mucha experiencia
4. nunca se enoja con nadie
5. puede trabajar largas horas
6. se lleva bien con los estudiantes

B. ¿Por qué se mudan? Los señores Ruiz piensan mudarse a otro barrio. Complete las oraciones para saber por qué.

> **MODELO** (gustar) Vivimos en un barrio que no nos **gusta** mucho.
> Buscamos un barrio que nos **guste** más.

1. (ser) Tenemos una casa que _____ muy pequeña.
   Necesitamos una casa que _____ más grande.
2. (estar) Los niños quieren jugar en un parque que _____ cerca de casa.
   Ahora juegan en un parque que _____ muy lejos.
3. (haber) Vivimos en un pueblo donde no _____ universidad.
   Buscamos una ciudad donde _____ universidad.
4. (interesar) En este pueblo hay poca gente que nos _____ .
   En realidad, aquí no hay nadie que nos _____ .
5. (enseñar) Mi hija asiste a una escuela donde no _____ música.
   Quiere asistir a una escuela donde _____ música.

C. ¿No hay nadie que piense igual? Use las palabras que están entre paréntesis para dar los comentarios de Andrés, siempre opuestos (*opposite*) a los deseos de los demás (*others*).

> **MODELO** Quiero asistir a la conferencia que empieza a las diez.
> (una conferencia / más tarde)
> **Pues yo quiero asistir a una conferencia que empiece más tarde.**

1. Queremos visitar las ruinas que son de la época colonial. (unas ruinas / época de los jesuitas)
2. Necesito encontrar al señor que habla guaraní. (una persona / español)
3. La compañía busca a los jóvenes que quieren trabajar aquí. (unos jóvenes / en el Chaco)
4. Vamos a la cafetería donde tienen buenos postres. (un restaurante)
5. Aquí hay alguien que sabe cuál es la capital de Paraguay. (no hay nadie / Bolivia)
6. Alfredo va a quedarse en el hotel que está cerca de la calle Palma. (buscar / un hotel / lejos del centro)
7. Quiero comprarle a Sonia los zapatos que le gustan. (un suéter)
8. Constancia y Alfredo van a leer el libro que describe la cultura maya. (querer leer / un libro / cultura guaraní)

D. Para completar. Complete las oraciones.

> **MODELO** Quiero comprar un disco que...
> **Quiero comprar un disco que tenga canciones paraguayas.**

1. Necesito una amiga que...
2. Tengo un libro que...
3. En Paraguay hay gente que...
4. En esta clase no hay nadie que...
5. Conozco a un señor que...
6. No hay político que...
7. ¿Dónde está ese secretario que... ?
8. En esta ciudad yo he visto casas que...

E. Su opinión personal. Complete las oraciones con su opinión personal.

1. Quiero casarme con un hombre (con una mujer) que...
2. Quiero comprar una casa que...
3. Quiero comprar un auto que...
4. Quiero trabajar en un lugar que...
5. Quiero votar por un(a) presidente(-a) que...
6. Quiero comer en un restaurante que...
7. Quiero ir al teatro con alguien que...
8. Quiero escuchar unos discos que...

Preguntas

1. ¿Tiene usted amigos que viven cerca de su casa? ¿Prefiere que sus amigos vivan cerca o lejos de su casa? ¿Por qué?   2. ¿Es usted amigo(-a) de alguien que sea muy interesante? ¿que tenga muchos problemas? ¿que siempre esté contento(-a)? 3. ¿Conoce usted a alguien que tenga más de cien años? ¿que escriba poemas o cuentos? ¿que viaje mucho?   4. ¿Prefiere usted ver películas que le den risa? ¿que le hagan llorar? ¿que le hagan pensar?   5. ¿Hay alguien en esta clase que sepa hablar árabe? ¿japonés? ¿Hay alguien que pueda tocar la guitarra? ¿cantar?

II. El subjuntivo y las conjunciones adverbiales

Estos campesinos (*farmers*), descendientes de los guaraníes, toman mate, una bebida similar al té.

En una casa paraguaya

JANE	Discúlpeme°, doña Ramona. Me siento muy avergonzada. Creo que rompí este reloj.
DOÑA RAMONA	No importa°, Jane. Ya estaba roto, pero vamos a dejarlo aquí *para que Luis lo arregle°* cuando llegue. Él es muy bueno en estas cosas.
JANE	Oh, ¡qué alivio!°
DOÑA RAMONA	Pero pareces un poco deprimida. Debe ser por° el viaje... Entonces, *para que no pienses* en eso, ¿qué te parece si te enseño algunas palabras en guaraní *antes de que vuelvas* a tu país?
JANE	¡Sí, doña Ramona! Las despedidas° siempre me causan tristeza°. Pero puede empezar a enseñarme guaraní *cuando desee*. Por ejemplo, ¿cómo se dice «yo to quiero»? Quiero decírselo a Teddy *en cuanto°* lo vea.
DOÑA RAMONA	Pues eso se dice «che ro jaijú». Sé que él se va a sentir muy feliz *tan pronto como°* le digas qué significa.

Discúlpeme *Forgive me*   **No importa** *It doesn't matter*   **para...arregle** *so that Luis will fix it*   **¡qué alivio!** *what a relief!*   **Debe ser por** *It must be because of*   **despedidas** *farewells*   **tristeza** *sadness*   **en cuanto** *as soon as*   **tan pronto como** *as soon as*

---

1. ¿Por qué está Jane un poco deprimida?   2. ¿Qué quiere aprender ella antes de volver a su país?   3. ¿Qué le causa tristeza a Jane?   4. ¿Qué le quiere decir Jane a Teddy cuando lo vea?   5. ¿Cómo se dice «yo te quiero» en guaraní?

A. Adverbs describe the conditions under which actions take place. They often answer the questions why?, when?, where?, how?, or how much? Dependent clauses that function as simple adverbs are called adverbial clauses.

(When?)	He's leaving *now* (= adverb).
(Why?)	He's going to Lambaré *so that Ana will be happy* (= adverbial clause).
(How?)	He's going *provided that we buy the ticket* (= adverbial clause).

B. The following adverbial conjunctions always require the subjunctive in a clause following them; they indicate that an action or event is indefinite or uncertain (it may not necessarily take place):

a menos que	*unless*	en caso (de) que*	*in case*
antes (de) que*	*before*	para que	*so that*
con tal (de) que*	*provided that*	sin que	*without*

No voy a ir a menos que me sienta mejor.	*I'm not going to go unless I feel better.*

---

*The **de** may be omitted.

Sea cortés, para que no se ofendan.	*Be polite, so that they are not offended.*
¿Por qué no salen ahora, antes de que papá se ponga nervioso?	*Why don't you go out now, before Dad gets nervous?*
Ana ve a Carlos todos los días sin que su familia lo sepa.	*Ana sees Carlos every day without her family's knowing it.*

C. Aunque is followed by the subjunctive to indicate conjecture or uncertainty, but by the indicative to indicate fact or certainty.

Voy a salir, aunque llueva.	*I'm going to go out even though it may rain.*
Voy a salir, aunque llueve.	*I'm going to go out even though it is raining.*

D. Either the subjunctive or the indicative may follow these conjunctions of time:

cuando	*when*	hasta que	*until*
después (de) que	*after*	mientras (que)	*while*
en cuanto	*as soon as*	tan pronto como	*as soon as*

The indicative is used if the adverbial clause expresses a fact or a definite event; for instance, a customary or completed action. However, if the adverbial clause expresses an action that may not necessarily take place or that will probably take place, but at an indefinite time in the future, the subjunctive is used.

Elena va a alegrarse mucho tan pronto como lo sepa.	*Elena is going to get very happy as soon as she finds out.*
Elena se alegró mucho tan pronto como lo supo.	*Elena got very happy as soon as she found out.*
Cuando les cuente el chiste, ellos van a morirse de risa.	*When I tell them the joke, they're going to die of laughter.*
Cuando les conté el chiste, ellos se murieron de risa.	*When I told them the joke, they (nearly) died of laughter.*
No le digamos eso al jefe hasta que se calme.	*Let's not tell the boss that until he calms down.*
No le dijimos eso al jefe hasta que se calmó.	*We didn't tell the boss that until he calmed down.*
Vamos a poner la mesa después que llegue Jorge.	*We are going to set the table after Jorge arrives.*
Pusimos la mesa después que llegó Jorge.	*We set the table after Jorge arrived.*

E. Some of the conjunctions just discussed are prepositions or adverbs combined with **que** or **de que (para que, sin que, antes de que, hasta que, después de que).** These conjunctions (without **que**) are often followed by infinitives if there is no change of subject.

Después de enojarse, Juan se puso muy triste.	*After getting angry, Juan became very sad. (no change of subject)*
Después de que ella se enojó, Juan se puso muy triste.	*After she got angry, Juan became very sad. (change of subject)*

EJERCICIOS

A. Para completar...   Complete cada una de las siguientes oraciones con la forma correcta de uno de los dos verbos sugeridos (entre paréntesis) y agregue (*add*) información apropiada o necesaria.

> **MODELO**   Voy a pasar la noche aquí para que... (estar/ser)
> **Voy a pasar la noche aquí para que tú no estés solo.**

1. Quieren irse antes de que... (volver/pedir)
2. Susana hace eso para que usted... (ofenderse/saber)
3. Pensamos llegar a las siete a menos que... (estar/llamar)
4. ¿Por qué no vamos al cine antes de que...? (llover/viajar)
5. Ellos van a clase a menos que... (hacer/ser)
6. ¿Piensan hacerlo sin que ella...? (saber/ponerse)
7. El profesor habla claramente para que nosotros lo... (poder/entender)
8. ¿Realmente no puedes hacer nada sin que ellos...? (venir/dar)

B. La historia de Inés.   Combine las frases usando la conjunción dada entre paréntesis y así sabrá algo de la vida personal de Inés. Siga el modelo.

> **MODELOS**   Inés vivió con sus padres. Compró un apartamento. (hasta que)
> **Inés vivió con sus padres hasta que compró un apartamento.**
>
> Inés y Bob van a trabajar. Ellos pueden casarse y mudarse a una casa grande. (hasta que)
> **Inés y Bob van a trabajar hasta que ellos puedan casarse y mudarse a una casa grande.**

1. Su papá se puso furioso. Inés se fue de la casa. (cuando)
2. Ella no le habló más a su papá. Él se calmó. (hasta que)
3. Inés se va a alegrar. Su padre la disculpa. (cuando)
4. Inés le escribió una carta. Su padre la llamó. (tan pronto como)
5. Su mamá se puso muy contenta. Ella supo la noticia. (después que)
6. Inés quiere mucho a su novio. Él es mucho mayor que ella. (aunque)

C. Imaginación y lógica.   Combine elementos de las tres columnas y forme oraciones lógicas en el indicativo o subjuntivo, según sea apropiado. Use cada una de las conjunciones de la segunda columna por lo menos una vez.

> **MODELOS**   **Lo hacen mientras los niños duermen.**
>
> **Debes comer para que ellos no se enojen.**

debes comer	mientras	Sergio / volver
vamos a estar tristes	aunque	ellos / no enojarse
lo hacen	tan pronto como	ustedes / irse
pienso esperar aquí	cuando	tú / no tener hambre
siempre vamos al cine	hasta que	los niños / dormir
se pone furioso(-a)	para que	su amante / mentirle
van a sentirse felices	a menos que	sus amigos / mudarse
en general, estudio	antes (de) que	los Pérez / estar lejos

D. Traducción.   Dé la traducción al español de las siguientes oraciones.

1. They will call me before she leaves.
2. She is going to his birthday party, although she doesn't feel well.
3. I usually play the piano whenever I am a little depressed.
4. They are going to wait for us until we arrive.
5. He is going to use the car without his father's knowing about it.
6. You (**tú**) can't sleep unless you are very tired, right?

Preguntas

1. ¿Adónde piensa ir usted cuando termine esta clase? ¿cuando lleguen las vacaciones? ¿cuando complete sus estudios universitarios?   2. ¿Qué quiere hacer usted cuando sepa hablar bien el español? ¿antes de que termine esta década *(decade)*?   3. ¿Asiste usted a clase aunque llueva? ¿aunque esté muy cansado(-a)?   4. ¿No puede estudiar usted a menos que tome café? ¿a menos que esté solo(-a)?   5. ¿Qué cree usted que debe hacer un(a) estudiante para que le sea más fácil aprender español?

III.   Usos del infinitivo

Asunción, capital del Paraguay, está a unos trescientos kilómetros de Encarnación.

De Asunción a Encarnación, un pueblo al sur de Paraguay

LA VIAJERA   Señor, *¿es posible ir* a Encarnación en tren?
EL AGENTE   Sí, señorita. *Puede tomar* el tren de las 6:00 A.M. (de la mañana) si *desea viajar* de día° o el expreso si no *teme viajar* de noche°. ¿Cuándo *quiere salir?*
LA VIAJERA   Esta misma noche. *Espero estar* allí mañana antes de las 4:00 P.M. (de la tarde). ¡Estoy ansiosa *por ver* a mi familia!
EL AGENTE   Pues, *vamos a ver*... Ahora son las doce menos cinco. *Acaba de salir* el expreso... ¡Pero hoy es su día de suerte°, señorita! Dentro de diez minutos *va a salir* otro expreso para Encarnación...
LA VIAJERA   ¡Qué suerte! ¿Y a qué hora llega allí?

EL AGENTE   Mañana a las 2:15 P.M. Éste lleva un coche-cama°. *Puede dormir unas horas, si quiere.*

LA VIAJERA   ¡Buena idea! Déme un pasaje de ida y vuelta. ¡Pero, dése prisa, por favor! ¡No *quiero perderlo*°!

---

de día *by day*   de noche *at night*   su...suerte *your lucky day*   coche-cama *sleeping car*   perderlo *to miss it*

---

1. ¿Es posible viajar de Asunción a Encarnación en tren?   2. ¿Qué tren debe tomar la viajera si quiere viajar de noche? ¿de día?   3. ¿A qué hora quiere estar la señorita en Encarnación? ¿Por qué?   4. ¿Perdió ella el expreso de las doce menos cinco? ¿y el de las doce y cinco?   5. ¿A qué hora llega ese expreso a Encarnación? ¿Lleva o no un coche-cama?   6. ¿Qué clase de pasaje quiere ella? ¿sólo de ida o de ida y vuelta?

In Spanish the infinitive can be used in the following ways:

1. As a noun. The infinitive is often used as the subject or object of a verb in much the same way that the *-ing* form of the English verb is used. It can be used with or without the definite article **el.**

Creo que (el) viajar es estupendo.   *I believe that traveling is great.*

2. As a verb complement. Most verbs may be followed directly by an infinitive. Certain verbs require a preposition (most often **a** or **de,** but in some cases **en** or **con**) before the infinitive. **Tener** and **haber** are followed by **que** plus an infinitive to express obligation.

Francisca puede reír y llorar de alegría a la vez.	*Francisca can laugh and cry from happiness at the same time.*
Fuimos a ver *La venganza del Zorro.*	*We went to see The Revenge of Zorro.*
Tratan de llegar temprano.	*They try to arrive early.*
Tenemos que comprar el pasaje.	*We have to buy the ticket.*
Hay que comprarlo hoy.	*One has (you have) to buy it today.*

The expression **acabar de** is followed by the infinitive to mean *to have just (done something).*

Acabo de hablar con Enrique. ¡Por fin!	*I have just spoken to Enrique. Finally!*
Acaban de oír las malas noticias. ¡Esto es el colmo!	*They have just heard the bad news. This is the last straw!*

3. As the object of a preposition.

Antes de recibir tu carta, Marta estaba muy enojada.   *Before receiving (she received) your letter, Marta was very angry.*

Después de llorar casi una hora, Ana se calmó.	*After crying almost an hour, Ana calmed down.*
En vez de trabajar, él va a la playa todos los días.	*Instead of working, he goes to the beach every day.*
Sin exagerar nada, le conté todo.	*Without exaggerating anything, I told him everything.*
Para ir a Asunción, hay que manejar dos horas.	*To go to Asunción, you have to drive two hours.*

4. With **al. Al** plus infinitive expresses the idea of *on* or *upon* plus the *-ing* form of the English verb.

Al verla, supe que estaba desilusionada. Lo siento, le dije.	*Upon seeing her (When I saw her) I knew she was disappointed. I'm sorry, I said to her.*
Al recibir la noticia, Pedro se sintió avergonzado.	*Upon receiving the news (When he received the news), Pedro felt embarrassed.*
Al saber que su marido tenía una amante, Olga se puso furiosa.	*Upon learning that her husband had a lover, Olga became furious.*

5. On signs, as an alternative to an **usted** command form.

Empujar.
Empuje. } *Push.*
No fumar. *No smoking.*

EJERCICIOS

A. Entonces, ¿qué vamos a hacer? Pedro y Miguel discuten (*are discussing*) cómo llegar al picnic de la clase. Haga el papel de Miguel y conteste negativamente las preguntas de Pedro. Siga el modelo.

MODELO ¿Viene Susana a buscarnos? (poder)
No, ella no puede venir a buscarnos.

1. ¿Va al picnic en taxi Ramón? (pensar)
2. ¿Lo llevan sus padres? (ir a)
3. ¿Pasan tus primas por Teresa y Ramón? (querer)
4. ¿Lo saben ellos? (deber)
5. ¿Maneja Inés el auto de sus padres? (querer)
6. ¿Lo hace Pepito? (tener ganas de)
7. ¿Tomamos el tren? (poder)
8. Entonces, ¿nos olvidamos del picnic? (deber)

B. **¡Vamos a darnos prisa!** (*Let's hurry!*)   Lelia y Rolando están organizando
una fiesta de despedida (*farewell*) para Alicia, una amiga que pronto viaja al
Brasil. Haga el papel de Rolando y conteste las preguntas de Lelia siguiendo los
modelos. Use pronombres objetos cuando sea posible.

> **MODELOS**   ¿Quién llama a Paco? (yo / ir a)
> **Yo lo voy a llamar.**
>
> ¿Quién trae la torta? (Marisa / prometer)
> **Marisa prometió traerla.**

1. ¿Quién compra el regalo? (Daniel / ir a)
2. ¿Quién habla con Sofía? (mi hermana / pensar)
3. ¿Quién le da el regalo a Alicia? (yo / querer)
4. ¿Quién trae los discos? (Ernesto y Mario / prometer)
5. ¿Quién cuenta los chistes? (los Gómez / deber)
6. ¿Quién hace el postre? (Rogelio / tener ganas de)
7. ¿Quién busca a Alicia? (su novio / querer)
8. ¿Quién prepara la sangría? (los muchachos / prometer)
9. ¿Quién toca la guitarra y canta? (tú y yo / poder)

C. **Sí, abuela, acabo de hacerlo.**   Conteste afirmativamente las preguntas de la
Sra. Bello, como lo haría su nieto. Siga el modelo y use pronombres objetos
cuando sea posible.

> **MODELO**   ¿Viste a tu prima?
> **Sí, acabo de verla.**

1. ¿Terminaron el trabajo tus padres?
2. ¿Lavaste el auto?
3. ¿Les habló Lucía a ustedes?
4. ¿Recibiste mi carta?
5. ¿Leyeron mis chistes tus hermanos?

D. **Los letreros de José.**   José está preparando unos letreros (*signs*) que le
pidieron. Siguiendo el modelo, diga qué va a escribir él en cada uno de los
letreros que siguen.

MODELO

 NO FUMAR

1

2

3

4

5

E. Traducción. Traduzca al español las siguientes oraciones.

1. I have just watched that program.
2. We left before eating.
3. Was he angry? He went away without saying anything.
4. Seeing is believing.
5. When he saw (Upon seeing) his grade, Pablo felt very happy.
6. Why doesn't she laugh instead of crying?
7. I'm trying to study.
8. Luis is anxious to see his girlfriend.

Preguntas

1. ¿Qué hizo usted anoche al llegar a su casa? ¿esta mañana al levantarse? 2. ¿Se sintió triste o feliz al terminar sus estudios secundarios? ¿al recibir la nota de su primer examen de español? 3. ¿Prefiere usted viajar de día o de noche? ¿Teme viajar en avión? ¿Por qué sí o por qué no? 4. ¿Qué debe decir uno al encontrarse con un amigo? ¿al recibir un regalo? ¿al entrar a clase? ¿al salir?

ASUNCIÓN:[1]
EL
HOMBRE
Y LA
MUJER

Vista de Asunción, Paraguay

Dos mujeres se encuentran en la
«Peluquería° Guaraní»[2] *de Asunción, Paraguay.*

GLORIA   ¡Hola, Elena! ¡Cuánto me alegro de verte! ¿Cómo estás?

ELENA   Muy bien, Gloria. ¡Qué sorpresa! Hacía tanto que no te veía. ¿Qué haces aquí?

GLORIA   Vengo todos los meses para que me cambien el color del pelo. Hay una muchacha aquí que me lo hace muy bien, sin que nadie pueda notarlo°. No quiero que mi novio descubra que no soy rubia° natural. Me de vergüenza decírselo.

ELENA   Pero cuando él sepa la verdad, se va a sentir desilusionado, ¿no lo crees?

GLORIA   Tal vez sí, pero no importa. Por ahora no lo sabe y está contento.

MARÍA   Buenas tardes, señorita Martínez. Tan pronto como termine con la señora Ospina, la atiendo°.

GLORIA   Gracias, María. No tengo prisa.

MARÍA   *(a Elena)* ¿Y usted, señorita? ¿En qué puedo servirla?

ELENA   Tengo que dar una charla° y necesito un peinado° que sea elegante y sencillo° a la vez.

MARÍA   No hay ningún problema... si usted puede esperar unos veinte minutos hasta que termine con otra cliente.

ELENA   Cómo no... Francamente, Gloria, me parece triste que una mujer le tenga que mentir a su novio o a su esposo.

GLORIA   ¿Por qué? Ellos nos mienten a nosotras. Hace algunos días—para darte un ejemplo—Olga me llamó por teléfono para contarme que su esposo tiene una amante. Y tú sabes que han tenido otros problemas también. ¡Lloraba tanto la pobre!

ELENA   ¡Qué barbaridad! ¿Y qué va a hacer?

GLORIA   Nada. ¿Qué puede hacer?

ELENA   Puede buscarse un amante ella también.

GLORIA   ¿Para qué? La venganza es estúpida.

ELENA   Entonces puede divorciarse.

GLORIA   Tampoco. Aunque su esposo no le es fiel°, Olga todavía lo quiere. Creo que cuando te cases, Elena, vas a pensar de otra manera°.

ELENA   Lo dudo. Es obvio que mis ideas sobre el matrimonio son muy diferentes a las que tienen ustedes dos... Además es difícil que me case aquí.[3]

GLORIA ¿No conoces a ningún hombre que te interese?

ELENA   Sí, pero no hay ninguno que me guste para esposo.

GLORIA ¡Qué increíble! Espero que no te mueras soltera.

ELENA   ¿Por qué no? Mi abuela siempre decía que «más vale° estar solo que mal acompañado». Y en mi caso, realmente prefiero estar soltera que mal casada...

---

peluquería *beauty parlor*   notarlo *notice it*   rubia *blond*   la atiendo *I'll wait on you*
charla *talk*   peinado *hairdo*   sencillo *simple*   fiel *faithful*   de otra manera *otherwise*   más vale *it's better*

PREGUNTAS

1. ¿Dónde se encuentran Gloria y Elena?   2. ¿Por qué viene Gloria a este lugar todos los meses?   3. Según Elena, ¿cómo se va a sentir el novio de Gloria cuando sepa la verdad?   4. ¿Qué le parece triste a Elena? ¿Le parece triste eso a usted también? ¿Por qué sí o por qué no?   5. ¿Qué le contó a Gloria su amiga Olga cuando la llamó por teléfono?   6. ¿Qué va a hacer Olga? ¿Por qué no va a divorciarse? ¿Qué cree usted que ella debe hacer?   7. ¿Piensa casarse Elena? ¿Por qué?   8. ¿Está usted de acuerdo en que es mejor estar soltero(-a) que mal casado(-a)? ¿Por qué?

NOTAS CULTURALES

1. **Asunción,** one of the oldest cities of South America (founded in 1537), is the capital city and port of Paraguay, on the eastern bank of the Paraguay River. The center of trade and government of the nation, it has a picturesque charm with its pastel-colored buildings and numerous orange trees.

2. **Guaraní** is the language of the Indians who inhabited Paraguay before the Spanish conquest. Paraguay is the only Latin American country that has adopted an Indian language as one of its two official languages. Almost all Paraguayans are **mestizo** and bilingual, and street signs, newspapers, and books often appear in both Spanish and **guaraní**. Spanish is the language used for instruction and business in general, but **guaraní** is favored for social discourse at all levels of society.

3. In Paraguay the ratio of men to women is rather low because many men emigrate to nearby Brazil and Argentina, where there are more opportunities for work. The scarcity of males dates from the War of the Triple Alliance (1865–70), when President Solano López waged a war against Argentina, Brazil, and Uruguay that killed about half of Paraguay's population. Only 13 percent of the survivors were male, mostly old men and very young boys. It took many years for the sex ratio of young people of a marriageable age to return to an approximately even balance. It is said that some of the priests in those times went so far as to advocate polygamy.

Funciones y *actividades*

In this chapter, you have seen examples of some important language functions, or uses. Here is a summary and some additional information about these functions of language.

APOLOGIZING

Lo siento (mucho).	*I'm (very) sorry.*
Siento mucho que (+ *subj*)...	*I'm very sorry that . . .*
Perdón. Perdóneme. (Perdóname.)	*Excuse me. (also: Forgive me. I'm sorry.)*
Discúlpeme. (Discúlpame.)	*Excuse me. (also: I'm sorry.)*

EXPRESSING FORGIVENESS

Está bien.	*It's OK.*
No hay (ningún) problema.	*There's no problem.*
No importa.	*It doesn't matter.*
No hay pena.	*No need to be embarrassed.*
No hay de qué.	*It's nothing. (also: You're welcome.)*

GIVING ADVICE

Usted debe (Tú debes)...	*You should...*
Le (Te) aconsejo que (+ *subj*)...	*I advise you to...*
Es mejor que usted (tú) (+ *subj*)...	*It's better for you to...*
Recomiendo que usted (tú) (+ *subj*)...	*I recommend that you...*

Ahora haga las siguientes actividades, usando las expresiones que acaba de aprender.

A. Mini-drama.   Dramatice la siguiente situación. Su novio(-a) la (lo) llama dos horas después de cuando ustedes tenían planeado salir. Él (Ella) había olvidado totalmente la cita. Usted está furiosa(-o) y le recuerda: «Ésta es la segunda vez que pasa lo mismo esta semana...» Él (Ella) le dice: «Discúlpame. Te prometo que no volverá a pasar.» Al principio (*At first*) usted no quiere perdonarlo(-a) pero después decide darle una «tercera» oportunidad...

B. Refranes (*Proverbs*).   Aquí hay algunos proverbios sobre el tema del amor y la amistad. ¿Qué significado tienen? ¿Está usted de acuerdo con estos refranes? Comente.

1. Donde hay amor, hay dolor.
2. Ni el que ama ni el que manda quieren compañía.
3. Amores nuevos olvidan viejos.
4. Ni ir a la guerra ni casar se debe aconsejar.
5. Donde hay celos, hay amor.
6. Más vale estar solo que mal acompañado.

C. Entrevista. Haga las siguientes preguntas a un(a) compañero(-a) y luego presente la información a la clase.

1. ¿Qué cosas te dan rabia? ¿Te has enojado recientemente por alguna razón? ¿Por qué? ¿Cuándo fue la última vez que te enojaste?
2. ¿Cuál fue una de las sorpresas más lindas que has recibido últimamente?
3. A muchos hispanos la mujer norteamericana les parece «liberada», libre de hacer lo que quiera (*free to do whatever she likes*). Según tu opinión, ¿está «liberada» la mujer norteamericana? ¿Crees que las mujeres de este país tienen los mismos derechos que los hombres, tanto en el trabajo como en la casa?
4. ¿Existe la «norteamericana típica» o no? Si crees que existe, descríbela.
5. ¿Crees que es mejor que una mujer con hijos se quede en su casa en vez de trabajar fuera de casa (*outside the home*)? ¿Por qué sí o por qué no?
6. ¿Piensas que son más felices las mujeres casadas que las solteras? ¿los hombres casados que los solteros? ¿Por qué?

D. El (La) espiritista (*The spiritualist*). Tina (Toño) tiene muchos problemas y va a ver a Monsieur Leo (Madame Leona), un(a) espiritista muy conocido(-a). Con un(a) compañero(-a) dramatice una conversación entre ellos(-as), siguiendo las ideas sugeridas abajo.

TINA (TOÑO)	Dice que últimamente se siente mal, que siempre tiene dolores de cabeza y que está muy nerviosa(-o). Le pregunta qué puede ser.
ESPIRITISTA	Le hace varias preguntas sobre su rutina diaria: a qué hora se levanta, a qué hora se acuesta, qué come, etcétera.
TINA (TOÑO)	Dice que no duerme mucho y que tampoco come mucho porque no tiene tiempo. Trabaja unas dieciocho horas por día.
ESPIRITISTA	Le hace algunas preguntas sobre su vida social: si tiene novio(-a), etcétera.
TINA (TOÑO)	Describe a su novio(-a).
ESPIRITISTA	Le da los siguientes consejos.

No es bueno:
  tomar café
  seguir viendo (*keep seeing*)
    a su novio(-a)
  salir los martes
  trabajar tantas horas al día
  ? (*add two items of your own*)

También le dice que es bueno:
  hacer más ejercicios
  dormir más
  comer tres comidas al día
  leer su horóscopo todos los días
  salir más para conocer a más muchachos(-as)
  ? (*add two items of your own*)

E. Consejos. Con un compañero(-a), dense consejos mutuamente. Una persona menciona un problema, real o imaginario; la otra persona le dice qué hacer o qué no hacer.

MODELO Siempre estoy cansado(-a).
Te aconsejo que descanses más (que tomes vitaminas, etcétera).

VOCABULARIO ACTIVO

Cognados

ansioso   el, la detective   frustrado   furioso

Verbos

aburrirse	to be (get) bored
acabar de + *inf*	to have just (done something)
alegrarse	to be (get) happy
asustar	to scare, to frighten
asustarse	to be (get) scared, frightened
avergonzarse (ue)	to be (get) embarrassed, ashamed
calmarse	to calm down
cansarse	to be (get) tired
deprimirse	to be (get) depressed
disculpar	to forgive
empujar	to push
frustrarse	to be (get) frustrated
llorar	to cry
manejar	to drive
ofender	to offend
ofenderse	to be (get) offended; to take offense
perdonar	to forgive
ponerse + *adj*	to become + *adj.*
reírse	to laugh
sentirse + *adj* or *adv*	to feel + *adj. or adv.*
tratar (de)	to try (to)

Sentimientos y emociones / Feelings and emotions

alegre	*happy*
la alegría	*happiness*
asustado	*scared, frightened, startled*
avergonzado	*embarrassed, ashamed*
cansado	*tired*
deprimido	*depressed*
desilusionado	*disappointed*
enojado	*angry*
orgulloso	*proud*
la rabia	*anger, rage*
darle rabia (a alguien)	*to make (someone) angry*

la risa	*laughter*
darle risa (a alguien)	*to make (someone) laugh*
la venganza	*revenge*
la vergüenza	*shame*
darle vergüenza (a alguien)	*to make (someone) ashamed*

Conjunciones

a menos que	*unless*
antes (de) que	*before*
aunque	*although*
con tal (de) que	*provided that*
después (de) que	*after*
en caso (de) que	*in case*
en cuanto	*as soon as*
hasta que	*until*
mientras (que)	*while*
para que	*so that*
sin que	*without*
tan pronto como	*as soon as*

Otras palabras y frases

el, la amante	*lover*
el chiste	*joke*
la despedida	*farewell, leave-taking*
los recursos naturales	*natural resources*
la represa	*dam*

Expresiones útiles

Discúlpeme.	*Excuse me. (also: I am sorry.)*
No importa.	*It doesn't matter.*
Perdóneme. (Perdóname.)	*Forgive me. (also: Excuse me. I am sorry.)*
No hay (ningún) problema.	*There's no problem.*

El Zócalo es la plaza principal de la Ciudad de México que está construida sobre la antigua capital azteca. En el Zócalo se encuentran la Catedral, el Palacio Nacional y otros edificios del gobierno. ¿Qué lugar en los EEUU se puede comparar con el Zócalo?

Se sabe mucho de la gran civilización incaica gracias a las ruinas de Machu Picchu. «La ciudad perdida de los incas» está en los Andes cerca del Cuzco. ¿Dónde hay ciudades indias en los EEUU?

El producto más importante de Venezuela es el petróleo. Caracas, su capital, es un buen ejemplo de una ciudad en crecimiento *(growing)*. ¿Cómo se compara con otros lugares en Sudamérica?

Muchos mexicanos y turistas pasan los domingos en los jardines flotantes de Xochimilco en las afueras de la capital. Se divierten escuchando música de los mariachis, mirando las flores y charlando con los amigos. En su opinión, ¿por qué es tan popular Xochimilco?

Chichén Itzá, una antigua ciudad maya en Yucatán, es famosa por su gran pirámide El Castillo y otras ruinas. También hay una estatua de Chac Mool, el dios de la lluvia. ¿Por qué cree Ud. que los mayas construyeron ésta y otras pirámides?

Cada año miles y miles de personas vienen a esta basílica para dar gracias y mirar la famosa imagen de la Santa Patrona de México—la Virgen de Guadalupe. ¿Cómo es la basílica?

Se puede pasar unas vacaciones magníficas en las islas del Caribe. Allá se practican todos los deportes acuáticos. También se puede visitar monumentos como El Morro de San Juan. Esta fortaleza fue construida para defender a Puerto Rico de los piratas ingleses en el siglo XVI. ¿Qué le gustaría a Ud. visitar?

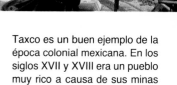

Taxco es un buen ejemplo de la época colonial mexicana. En los siglos XVII y XVIII era un pueblo muy rico a causa de sus minas de plata. ¿A qué se refiere la época colonial en México? ¿Y en los EEUU?

A Buenos Aires se le conoce como «el París de Sudamérica».
Aquí se ve el famoso obelisco en la Avenida 9 de Julio, la calle
más ancha del mundo. ¿Por qué se le llama a Buenos Aires
«el París de Sudamérica»?

Las Cataratas del Iguazú son cuatro veces más anchas que las Cataratas del
Niágara. Se encuentran en la frontera *(border)* entre la Argentina y el Brasil.
¿Ha visitado Ud. unas cataratas? ¿Cuáles?

La economía de Panamá depende de su canal que se inauguró en 1914. Unos
catorce mil barcos pasan por el canal de un océano al otro. ¿Por qué construyeron el canal en Centroamérica?

LECTURA VIII

ESPAÑA EN EL SIGLO VEINTE

Actualmente° España celebra más de una década de democracia después de At present los treinta años de dictadura que siguió a la Guerra Civil. Parece que el siglo XX va a terminar con un gobierno democrático y liberal, aunque empezó en un clima de inestabilidad, rebeliones y guerras.

Durante los primeros veinticinco años de este siglo España sufrió un verdadero caos político. El rey Alfonso XIII cambió arbitrariamente los ministros de gobierno y hubo treinta y tres gobiernos diferentes en veintiún años (1902–1923). Además, España estaba en guerra con Marruecos° (en esa Morocco época, territorio dividido entre Francia y España), que luchaba por° su independencia. Muchos españoles protestaron contra esa guerra y también contra las injusticias sociales dentro de España. Los conflictos regionales empeoraron° el estado de cosas. Para mejorar° esa difícil situación, el rey worsened/
improve permitió que el general Miguel Primo de Rivera estableciera° una dictadura° to establish/
dictatorship militar. Esa dictadura duró desde 1923 hasta 1930 cuando Primo de Rivera finalmente dejó el poder°. power

La Segunda República, después de un proceso de elecciones democráticas, se proclamó en 1931. Desgraciadamente,° esta Segunda República no duró Unfortunately más que cinco años. La constitución republicana de 1931 era tan liberal que provocó una reacción de la derecha. Esto causó una serie de conflictos entre la izquierda y la derecha que llevó finalmente a° la Guerra Civil, iniciada° led to/begun con el pronunciamiento del 17 de julio de 1936. Desapareció° la unidad de disappeared España: en todo el territorio español los franquistas° o «nacionales» luchaban followers of
Franco

Soldados rebeldes (en contra de la república) de la Guerra Civil Española

contra los izquierdistas o «republicanos». Varios otros países intervinieron con armas y soldados para ayudar a ambos° lados a tal punto que° la guerra en España se convirtió° entonces en una preparación para la Segunda Guerra Mundial.

both/to such an extent that
turned into

Después de casi tres años de muerte° y destrucción, la guerra terminó con el establecimiento de la dictadura de Francisco Franco. España quedó° aislada del resto de Europa y sólo empezó a recuperarse económicamente a fines de la década del cuarenta. La situación económica mejoró° muchísimo en los años cincuenta cuando el turismo llevó mucho capital extranjero° al país. El régimen de Franco también impuso una censura rígida en la prensa° y en las

death
remained
improved
foreign
press

El Generalísimo Francisco Franco conmemora otro aniversario del fin de la Guerra Civil, 1950.

artes. Las tensiones regionales no dejaron de° producir conflictos, especialmente en el País Vasco. En 1973 un grupo guerrillero vasco asesinó al almirante° Luis Carrero Blanco, candidato preferido de Franco para sucederlo eventualmente en el poder.

did not cease to
admiral

Con la muerte de Franco el 20 de noviembre del 1975, el gobierno pasó a manos de Juan Carlos de Borbón, nieto del rey Alfonso XIII y continuador de la monarquía borbónica. El rey nombró° ministros progresistas y en 1977 tuvieron lugar° las primeras elecciones nacionales desde 1936. En 1978 fue aprobada una nueva constitución que, entre varios cambios progresistas, permitió cierta° autonomía a los parlamentos regionales. El nuevo gobierno demostró gran estabilidad en 1981 cuando un grupo de militares intentó° un golpe de estado° al entrar armados en el Congreso de Diputados en Madrid. El rey Juan Carlos apoyó° la constitución y denunció los hechos° de los militares. Estos se entregaron° y fueron detenidos°.

named
took place
a certain
attempted
coup d'etat
supported/deeds
surrendered/
were arrested

El rey Juan Carlos
de España y su
esposa, la reina
Sofía

En 1982 el Partido Socialista Obrero Español (PSOE), encabezado° por
Felipe González Márquez, ganó las elecciones y tuvo el 47 por ciento del
voto popular. Felipe González prometió crear 800.000 nuevos empleos pero,
desgraciadamente, hoy día el problema del desempleo es cada vez más° serio.
En 1987 hubo una serie de huelgas de obreros y profesionales: mineros en
Asturias, estudiantes, médicos, y empleados del transporte público (aerolí-
neas y ferrocarriles°). En un solo día de huelga—el 15 de abril—la economía

headed

more and more

railroads

Hubo una huelga de
obreros del metro
en Madrid, el 2 de
abril de 1987.

española perdió 35 billones de pesetas durante la Semana Santa, época de muchos viajes para turistas y españoles. Los estudiantes también protestaron el desempleo que había llegado al 45 por ciento para los jóvenes de 16 a 24 años. Sin embargo°, es importante indicar que en esa época difícil el presidente González tuvo el apoyo° de las Cortes°. El partido socialista se mantuvo° en el poder después de las elecciones de junio de 1987.

En conclusión, podemos afirmar que España ha progresado en los últimos años, pero también hay problemas graves. El gobierno del rey se mantiene fuerte. El país se ha europeizado bastante y continúa integrándose en la comunidad europea. En cuanto a° la vida intelectual, muchos exiliados, escritores y artistas, han vuelto a su patria y los artistas se expresan en un clima de libertad. Sin embargo, varias situaciones peligrosas° amenazan° la estabilidad del país. El número de crímenes ha aumentado y el desempleo es un problema verdaderamente grave. Algunos desilusionados dicen que con Franco vivían mejor. Es difícil predecir el futuro de España, pero esperamos que el amor a la libertad continúe manteniéndose firme.

Nevertheless
support/Spanish Parliament
remained

With regard to

dangerous/ threaten

A. ¿Verdadero o falso?

1. Actualmente España celebra más de una década de democracia.
2. Durante la primera parte del siglo XX, España estaba en guerra con Marruecos.
3. El general Miguel Primo de Rivera estableció un gobierno liberal.
4. La Guerra Civil empezó en 1931.
5. Varios otros países intervinieron en la Guerra Civil.
6. En la década del cuarenta, el turismo llevó mucho capital extranjero a España.
7. Juan Carlos de Borbón es el nieto del rey Alfonso XIII.
8. Los franquistas ganaron las elecciones de 1982.
9. Hoy día, el desempleo es un problema serio en España.
10. A causa de las huelgas de 1987, Felipe González perdió el apoyo de las Cortes.

B. ¿Querría usted saber más?

¿Qué le preguntaría usted a un(a) amigo(-a) español(a)? Después de terminar esta lectura sobre España en el siglo XX, ¿qué más querría saber usted? Haga una lista de cinco o seis preguntas que usted le haría a un(a) amigo(-a) español(a).

Uno puede comprar
de todo en las tiendas
de «Bellas Artes».

DE COMPRAS

Funciones

- Expressing satisfaction and dissatisfaction

- Summarizing

Vocabulario. In this chapter you will talk about shopping and stores.

Gramática. You will discuss and use:

1. The imperfect subjunctive
2. *If* clauses
3. Change of the conjunctions **y** to **e** and **o** to **u**
4. Diminutives

Cultura. The dialogues take place in Caracas, Venezuela and the surrounding area.

to lend

spend/cheap

save

En la tienda hay blusas, faldas, pantalones, calcetines...

En el almacén (*grocery store*) hay verduras, carne, queso, frutas...

En la panadería hay pan, galletas (*crackers*), bizcochos (*cookies*)...

En la farmacia compramos aspirinas, medicinas, cosméticos...

En el banco compramos cheques de viajero y cambiamos dinero...

En la mueblería compramos mesas sillas, sofás...

En el mercado los artesanos muestran sus obras: alfarería (*pottery*), tapices (*tapestries*), cerámica (*pottery*)...

Asociaciones.   Indique la palabra que no pertenece al grupo.

MODELO   tienda: ropa, calcetines, galletas, faldas   **galletas**

1. liquidación: barato, rebajado, oferta, viajero
2. banco: cambiar, cheques, dinero, cosméticos
3. mercado: autos, ponchos, tapices, frazadas
4. almacén: queso, azúcar, faldas, frutas
5. panadería: pan, bizcochos, galletas, alfarería
6. mueblería: calcetines, escritorios, sillas, mesas

¿Verdadero o falso?   Si es falso, diga por qué.

1. En el banco cambiamos y ahorramos dinero.
2. En Venezuela, para cambiar los dólares a bolívares vamos a la panadería.
3. Si necesitamos carne, vamos a la mueblería.
4. Si me duele la cabeza y necesito aspirinas, voy a la farmacia.
5. En el mercado hay de todo: papas, ponchos, frutas, tapices.

Preguntas

1. Cuando usted necesita ropa, ¿le gusta ir a tiendas grandes, a boutiques exclusivas, o prefiere hacer sus compras en tiendas más baratas? ¿Dónde compra su ropa?   2. Cuando va de compras, ¿busca ofertas o compra lo primero (*the first thing*) que ve?   3. ¿Ahorra usted dinero todos los meses?   4. ¿En qué gasta más dinero: en comida, en el costo de su apartamento, en su auto, en sus estudios— el costo de la universidad, de los libros, etc.—o en diversiones?   5. ¿Adónde va usted para comprar pan?   6. Si usted necesita medicina, ¿adónde va?   7. En estos días, ¿hay ofertas en las tiendas locales? ¿Qué ofertas hay?   8. ¿Cuesta demasiado la ropa? ¿Qué cuesta demasiado?   9. ¿Cuánto vale este libro? ¿un buen vestido? ¿un kilo de bananas?   10. Cuando usted tiene más dinero del que necesita (*than you need*), ¿qué hace con el resto... ?

I. El imperfecto del subjuntivo

Ana necesita zapatos nuevos para su entrevista.

En casa de los Bello

RAÚL   ¿Dónde estabas, Marta?

MARTA   Ana me pidió que *fuera* de compras con ella. Quería que la *ayudara* a escoger unos zapatos para su entrevista en Caracas.

RAÚL   ¿Encontraron algo que les *gustara*?

MARTA   No, no compramos nada. A Ana no le gustaron los zapatos que estaban en oferta°. Buscaba algo que *hiciera* juego° con su traje nuevo.

RAÚL   Total que° todavía no tiene zapatos para su entrevista... Sé que quiere conseguir ese puesto° en la capital.

MARTA   Yo le dije que tú no te opondrías° con tal que ella *ahorrara* dinero para venir a vernos de vez en cuando. Después de todo°, ¡es nuestra hija y hay que ayudarla!

RAÚL   La verdad es que vamos a estar muy tristes y muy solos sin nuestra hija. Me gustaría que *trabajara* en nuestro almacén, pero reconozco° que ella necesita hacer su propia vida°... , ¿no?

---

en oferta *on sale*   hiciera juego *would match*   Total que *So*   conseguir ese puesto *to get that job*   no te opondrías *you would not be opposed*   Después de todo *After all*   reconozco *I recognize*   su propia vida *her own life*

---

1. ¿Qué le pidió Ana a su madre?   2. ¿Por qué quería Ana zapatos nuevos?
3. ¿Qué le dijo Marta a Ana?   4. ¿Cómo van a estar Raúl y Marta sin Ana?
5. ¿Qué le gustaría a Raúl?   6. ¿Qué reconoce él?

A. To form the imperfect subjunctive of all verbs, remove the **-ron** ending from the **ustedes** form of the preterit and add the imperfect subjunctive endings: **-ra, -ras, -ra, -́ramos, -rais, -ran.** Notice that the **nosotros** form requires a written accent on the vowel preceding the ending.

hablar		**comer**		**vivir**	
hablara	habláramos	comiera	comiéramos	viviera	viviéramos
hablaras	hablarais	comieras	comierais	vivieras	vivierais
hablara	hablaran	comiera	comieran	viviera	vivieran

Only those stem-changing verbs that change their stems in the preterit change their stems in the imperfect subjunctive.

pensar		**volver**		**pedir**	
pensara	pensáramos	volviera	volviéramos	pidiera	pidiéramos
pensaras	pensarais	volvieras	volvierais	pidieras	pidierais
pensara	pensaran	volviera	volvieran	pidiera	pidieran

Verbs with spelling changes or irregularities in the **ustedes** form of the preterit have the same changes in the imperfect subjunctive.

Infinitive	Ustedes Form: Preterit	Yo Form: Imperfect Subjunctive
andar	anduvieron	anduviera
construir	construyeron	construyera
creer	creyeron	creyera
dar	dieron	diera
decir	dijeron	dijera

Infinitive	Ustedes Form: Preterit	Yo Form: Imperfect Subjunctive
estar	estuvieron	estuviera
haber	hubieron	hubiera
hacer	hicieron	hiciera
ir, ser	fueron	fuera
leer	leyeron	leyera
morir	murieron	muriera
poder	pudieron	pudiera
poner	pusieron	pusiera
querer	quisieron	quisiera
saber	supieron	supiera
tener	tuvieron	tuviera
traer	trajeron	trajera
venir	vinieron	viniera
ver	vieron	viera

B. The imperfect subjunctive is used in the same situations as the present subjunctive, but usually when the verb in the main clause is in some past tense rather than in the present. Compare the following examples.

No quiero que usted gaste tanto dinero.	*I don't want you to spend so much money.*
No quería que gastara tanto dinero.	*I didn't want you to spend so much money.*
Es mejor que ahorres parte de tu sueldo... ¡o nunca serás rico!	*It's better that you save part of your salary . . . or you'll never get rich!*
Era mejor que ahorraras parte de tu sueldo.	*It was better that you saved part of your salary.*
El dependiente dice el precio claramente para que los turistas lo puedan entender.	*The salesclerk is saying the price clearly, so the turists can understand it.*
El dependiente dijo el precio claramente para que los turistas lo pudieran entender.	*The salesclerk said the price clearly so that the tourists could understand it.*

Sometimes the verb in the main clause is in the present, but the imperfect subjunctive is used in the dependent clause to refer to something in the past.

¿Es posible que el tapiz valiera tanto?	*Is it possible that the wall hanging was worth that much?*
No, no es posible que costara 500.000 bolívares.	*No, it's not possible that it cost 500,000 bolívares.*

C. As you have learned, **ojalá** plus present subjunctive is used to express a genuine hope or wish.

Ojalá que sea barato el alquiler.	*I hope the rent will be cheap.*

The speaker shifts to the imperfect subjunctive to express a wish that is only hypothetical or unlikely to be fulfilled.

Ojalá que fuera barato el alquiler.	*I wish the rent were cheap (but I know it is not).*

D. The imperfect subjunctive of **querer, poder,** and **deber** is sometimes used to soften a statement or question, for politeness.

Yo quisiera mostrarle otro coche al cliente.	*I would like to show another car to the client.* (wish)
Quiero mostrarle otro coche al cliente.	*I want to show another car to the client.* (will)
Debiéramos pagar.	*We should pay.* (weak obligation)
Debemos pagar.	*We should (must) pay.* (stronger obligation)

E. An alternate set of endings for the past subjunctive is often used in Spain and is found in many literary works: **-se, -ses, -se, -´semos, -seis, -sen.** The **-se** endings are added to the same stem as the **-ra** endings and have the same uses, except that the **-se** forms are not used to indicate politeness. You should learn to recognize the **-se** forms. The **-ra** forms, however, are preferred for conversation in Spanish America.

Me alegraba de que tú regatearas.	*I was happy that you bargained.*
Esperaban que aumentasen las ventas.	*They hoped that sales would go up.*
Ella tenía miedo de que el empleado pidiese un aumento de sueldo.	*She was afraid the employee would ask for a salary increase.*

EJERCICIOS

A. Imaginación y lógica. Forme oraciones nuevas con una expresión de cada columna.

MODELO Ojalá que ellos hablaran español.

				el coche
				en Chile
		compraron		la lección
		escucharon		una carta
	usted	hablaron	-ra	en México
	Emilia	prepararon	-ras	la casa
	Diego y yo	terminaron	-ra	los ejercicios
Ojalá que	tú	trabajaron	-´ramos	la radio
	ellos	comieron	-rais	español
	yo	escribieron	-ran	a la profesora
		vendieron		las tortillas
		vivieron		inglés
				la comida
				el desayuno

B. Hoy igual que ayer. Hace dos años don Andrés se jubiló (*retired*) y le dejó su almacén a su nieto Ramón. Haga el papel de don Andrés y responda a los comentarios de Ramón. Dígale que lo que ocurre hoy también ocurría en el pasado. Empiece sus comentarios con una expresión apropiada (**¡Qué interesante!**, **¡Qué coincidencia!**, **¡Qué lástima!**, etc.), siguiendo el modelo.

> MODELO   Busco un dependiente que sea bilingüe.
> **¡Qué coincidencia! Hace unos años yo también buscaba un dependiente que fuera bilingüe.**

1. No puedo pagar buenos sueldos hasta que aumenten nuestras ventas.
2. Siempre tengo cosas en oferta para que los clientes estén contentos.
3. A veces tengo miedo de que los precios sean muy altos.
4. Quiero mudar el negocio al centro tan pronto como tengamos más dinero.
5. No hay empleado que ahorre más de cincuenta dólares por mes.
6. Tampoco hay nadie que sepa regatear.
7. No es legal que vendamos tapices importados.
8. No creo que los clientes quieran pagar tanto por una camisa.

C. ¡Más imaginación... ! Forme oraciones nuevas con una expresión de cada columna.

> MODELO   **Mi padre quería que yo dijera la verdad.**

Mi padre (no) quería que	mi hermano	ser médico(-a)
Los profesores esperaban que	usted	decir la verdad
Los políticos temían que	yo	llegar tarde a la clase
Mis abuelos dudaban que	las mujeres	tener más libertad
Me alegraba que	los periódicos	fumar
	los empleados	pedir mejores sueldos
		ir de compras con Sonia
		continuar la huelga

D. Oraciones incompletas. Complete las oraciones con la información apropiada.

1. Mi abuela buscaba una medicina que...
2. Mis padres querían que yo...
3. El dueño mandó que los empleados...
4. Yo saldría de compras contigo con tal que tú...
5. Anoche en la fiesta no había nadie que...
6. En 1776 Inglaterra no quería que las colonias americanas...
7. Durante los años de Vietnam muchos americanos temían que...

Preguntas

1. Cuando usted era niño(-a), ¿querían sus padres que usted se acostara temprano? ¿que terminara toda la comida de su plato? ¿Qué otras cosas querían que hiciera?   2. ¿Le prohibían ellos que fuera al cine a ver películas violentas? ¿que

saliera con alguien del otro sexo?   3. ¿Le permitían que organizara fiestas en su casa? ¿que condujera el auto de la familia?   4. ¿Querían ellos que usted trabajara durante las vacaciones? ¿que ahorrara un poco? ¿que no les prestara dinero a sus amigos?   5. ¿Hacía usted muchas cosas sin que sus padres lo supieran? ¿Qué cosas?

II. El imperfecto de subjuntivo en cláusulas con *si*

Venden ponchos y muchas cosas más en los mercados venezolanos.

En un mercado de artesanos, en Caracas

DOÑA CARLA	¿Cuánto cuesta este poncho, señorita?
VENDEDORA	Quinientos bolívares, señora. Es de lana pura, sabe...
DOÑA CARLA	¿Quinientos bolívares? No los tengo...y si los *tuviera* no lo podría comprar... ¡Es demasiado caro!°
VENDEDORA	¿Y *si* se lo *vendiera* por cuatrocientos ochenta?
DOÑA CARLA	Pues, lo *preferiría* en otro color. Éste no me gusta porque...
VENDEDORA	Es el último que me queda°. Hace unos diez minutos vendí uno rojo muy bonito. ¿Sabe que en las tiendas del centro estos ponchos cuestan el doble°? ¡Y en esos lugares tienen precios fijos°... ! Pero lléveselo por cuatrocientos cincuenta, señora...
DOÑA CARLA	*Si* me lo *diera* por cuatrocientos veinte, me lo llevaría.
VENDEDORA	Está bien. Se lo doy por cuatrocientos veinte.
DOÑA CARLA	¡De acuerdo!° Muchas gracias.

¡Es...caro!   *It's too expensive!*   me queda   *I have left*   el doble   *double, twice as much*
precios fijos   *fixed prices*   ¡De acuerdo!   *Agreed!, OK!*

---

1. ¿Cuánto cuesta el poncho?   2. ¿Cree doña Carla que el poncho es muy caro o muy barato?   3. Si ella tuviera quinientos bolívares, ¿compraría el poncho?

4. Si la vendedora le vendiera el poncho por cuatrocientos ochenta bolívares, ¿lo compraría?   5. ¿De qué color era el poncho que la vendedora había vendido unos minutos antes?   6. Según la vendedora, ¿cuánto cuestan esos ponchos en el centro? En general, ¿es posible regatear en las tiendas del centro? ¿Por qué sí o por qué no? 7. ¿Compraría ella el poncho si la vendedora se lo diera por cuatrocientos veinte bolívares?

A. When an *if* clause expresses a situation that the speaker or writer thinks of as true or definite, or makes a simple assumption, the indicative is used.

Si llueve, Carlos no va de compras.	*If it rains, Carlos isn't going shopping.*
Si llovió ayer, Carlos no fue de compras.	*If it rained yesterday, Carlos didn't go shopping.*
Si Manuel va al mercado, yo voy también.	*If Manuel goes to the market, I will go too.*

When the verb in an *if* clause is in the present tense, it is always in the indicative, whether the speaker is certain or not.

Si vienes, me alegraré.	*If you come, I'll be happy.*
Si recibimos dinero hoy, iremos al supermercado.	*If we receive money today, we'll go to the supermarket.*

B. However, when the *if* clause expresses something that is hypothetical or contrary to fact and the main clause is in the conditional, the *if* clause is in the imperfect subjunctive.

Esa cámara es estupenda; si tuviera dinero, la compraría.	*That camera is wonderful; if I had money, I would buy it.*
Luis y Mirta irían con nosotros si estuvieran aquí.	*Luis and Mirta would go with us if they were here.*
Si las frazadas fueran de mejor calidad, las compraríamos.	*If the blankets were of better quality, we'd buy them.*
Si fueras más cuidadoso, no romperías las cosas.	*If you were more careful, you wouldn't break things.*

C. *If* clauses in the imperfect subjunctive refer to the present.

Si tuviera dinero, te lo daría.	*If I had money (now), I'd give it to you.*

To express an *if* clause about the past, a compound tense (imperfect subjunctive of **haber** + *past participle*) must be used.

Si hubiera tenido dinero, te lo habría dado.	*If I'd had any money (at that time), I'd have given it to you.*

D. The expression **como si** *(as if)* implies a hypothetical, or untrue, situation. It is followed by the imperfect subjunctive.

¡Regateas como si supieras lo que haces!	*You bargain as if you knew what you were doing!*
Andrés gasta dinero como si fuera millonario.	*Andrés spends money as if he were a millionaire.*
Elena se viste como si tuviera una fortuna.	*Elena dresses as if she had a fortune.*

EJERCICIOS

A. Esperanzas frustradas. Raquel pensaba pasar el día con sus amigos pero, cuando estaba por salir, su mamá le dijo que tenía que ayudarla a limpiar la casa. Haga el papel de Raquel y cambie las oraciones para decir cómo sería su día si no tuviera que quedarse en casa.

MODELO Si hace buen tiempo, iremos al Parque Central.
Si hiciera buen tiempo, iríamos al Parque Central.

1. Si tía Julia me manda dinero, compraré un vestido nuevo.
2. Si Carmen y su hermano tienen tiempo, me acompañarán.
3. Si tenemos hambre, comeremos en un restaurante.
4. Si veo a mis amigos, los invitaré a almorzar con nosotros.
5. Si los precios están bajos, le diré a Ramón que se compre unas corbatas nuevas.
6. Si encontramos algunas ofertas, valdrá la pena gastar dinero.

B. Puros sueños. Complete las oraciones que siguen.

MODELO Si fuera actor (actriz),...
Si fuera actor (actriz), saldría en muchas películas románticas.

1. Si tuviera un millón de dólares,...
2. Si yo fuera dueño(-a) de una tienda,...
3. Si me quedaran sólo tres meses de vida,...
4. Si tuviera que vivir solo(-a),...
5. Si yo volviera a nacer en otra forma,...
6. Si yo fuera hombre (mujer),...
7. Si yo tuviera tres días libres,...
8. Si yo fuera invisible,...
9. Si mañana fuera mi cumpleaños,...
10. Si yo estuviera hoy en América del Sur,...

C. Cuando ganemos la lotería...   Todas las semanas el señor Benítez compra un billete de lotería. Está absolutamente seguro que un día se sacará «la grande» *(he will win the grand prize)*. Haga el papel del señor Benítez y forme oraciones para decir qué hará cuando gane la lotería.

MODELO   yo / recibir un millón de pesos / comprar un barco grande
Cuando yo reciba un millón de pesos, compraré un barco grande.

1. nosotros / comprar ese barco / viajar mucho
2. nosotros / viajar / conocer muchos países
3. ellos / darme el dinero / también / comprar una casa elegante
4. nosotros / vivir en una casa elegante / estar muy contentos
5. mi familia / estar contenta / yo / sentirme muy feliz

D. Si ganáramos la lotería...   Hablemos ahora de la señora Benítez. Ella no es tan optimista como su esposo, pero también sueña con ser rica. Haga el papel de la señora Benítez y cambie las oraciones del ejercicio anterior para decir qué haría usted si ganara la lotería.

MODELO   yo / recibir un millón de pesos / comprar un barco grande
Si yo recibiera un millón de pesos, compraría un barco grande.

E. Si así fuera...   Para cada pregunta, escoja una de las dos respuestas dadas *(a o b)* y agregue otra de su propia invención. Siga el modelo.

MODELO   ¿Qué haría usted si ganara el Premio Nobel?
          a. no lo aceptaría
          b. seguiría trabajando igual que antes
          c. ?
          Si ganara el Premio Nobel, yo seguiría trabajando igual que
          antes y ahorraría el dinero para gastarlo en el futuro.

1. ¿Qué haría usted si fuera rico(-a)?
   a. viajaría por todo el mundo
   b. ayudaría a los pobres
   c. ?
2. ¿Qué haría usted si estuviera de vacaciones?
   a. esquiaría en las montañas
   b. me levantaría tarde todos los días
   c. ?
3. ¿Qué haría usted si recibiera malas notas?
   a. estudiaría más
   b. les pediría ayuda a mis profesores
   c. ?
4. ¿Qué haría usted si su novio(-a) se enamorara de su mejor amiga(-o)?
   a. lloraría mucho
   b. buscaría otro(-a) novio(-a) («Un amor se cambia por otro», ¿no?)
   c. ?

5. ¿Qué haría usted si pudiera viajar al pasado o al futuro?
   a. viajaría a 1492 para estar con Colón durante su primer viaje a América
   b. volvería a visitar esta universidad en el año 2010
   c. ?

Entrevista

Hágale las siguientes preguntas a un(a) compañero(-a) de clase. Luego compare la información con lo que dijeron otros.

1. Si tuvieras mucho dinero, ¿qué comprarías? 2. Si pudieras dar un millón de dólares a una organización, ¿a qué organización se lo darías? ¿Por qué? 3. Si te quedara sólo un año de vida, ¿qué harías? 4. Si sólo pudieras leer tres libros, ¿qué libros leerías? ¿Por qué esos tres? 5. ¿Qué problemas nacionales resolverías si fueras presidente(-a)? 6. ¿Qué harás mañana si hace buen tiempo? 7. Si recibes una nota mala en el próximo examen, ¿qué harás? 8. Si no tienes obligaciones este sábado, ¿qué harás?

III. Cambio de las conjunciones y en e y o en u

Un edificio moderno
de apartamentos,
Caracas

En un edificio de apartamentos cerca de Caracas

DON CARLOS   ¿Está en casa el señor o la señora González?

ROSITA   ¿A qué señores González busca usted? ¿Busca a mis padres, Fernando *e* Isabel, o a mis tíos, Juana *e* Ignacio?

DON CARLOS   La verdad es que no me importa: unos u otros,° me da igual°...

ROSITA   Bueno, mamá y papá salieron de compras y mis tíos Juana *e* Ignacio están aquí pero hoy no reciben°.

DON CARLOS   Pues, en este caso no deben recibir sino° dar. Vengo por el alquiler.

---

unos u otros   *either*   me da igual   *it's all the same to me*   no reciben   *they're not receiving visitors*   sino   *but rather*

---

1. ¿A quién busca don Carlos?   2. ¿Quiénes están en casa, los padres o los tíos de Rosita?   3. ¿Cómo se llaman los padres de Rosita? ¿y sus tíos?   4. ¿Qué quiere don Carlos?

A. When the word following the conjunction **y** *(and)* begins with the sound /i/, spelled **i** or **hi,** the **y** is changed to **e.**

noticias e información	*news and information*
trabajador e inteligente	*hard-working and intelligent*
verano e invierno	*summer and winter*
madre e hija	*mother and daughter*

Y does not change to **e** when followed by a word beginning with the letters **hie,** since the initial sound is the glide /y/.

nieve y hielo   *snow and ice*

B. When the word following the conjunction **o** *(or)* begins with an **o** or **ho,** the **o** is changed to **u.**

diez u once	*ten or eleven*
primavera u otoño	*spring or fall*
plata u oro	*silver or gold*
ayer u hoy	*yesterday or today*

EJERCICIOS

A.   ¿Están seguros... ?   En las dos oraciones que siguen, sustituya los nombres en bastardilla *(italics)* por los que están entre paréntesis.

1. Carlos *e Inés* han visto el programa. (Roberto, Isabel, Hilda, Teresa, Ignacio)
2. Sé que o Anita u *Olga* conocen bien Caracas. (Ofelia, Silvia, Oscar, Héctor, Homero)

B. Traducción. Traduzca al español las siguientes frases.

1. French and Italian
2. mathematics and history
3. sons and daughters
4. father and son
5. meat and fruits
6. to bargain and to buy
7. to live or to die
8. seven or eight
9. woman or man
10. one or another
11. train or bus
12. minutes or hours

Preguntas

1. ¿Habla usted español e inglés? ¿francés e italiano? 2. ¿Ha visitado usted Guatemala u Honduras? 3. ¿Son simpáticos e inteligentes sus profesores? 4. ¿Sabe mucho de economía e historia el presidente de este país? 5. ¿Es buena e interesante esta clase? 6. ¿Prefiere usted comer comida italiana u otro tipo de comida? ¿Qué comida? ¿Por qué?

IV. Formas diminutivas

El pequeño pueblo de Llanos, Venezuela

En un pueblecito° venezolano

CARMEN   ¿Vas a la fiesta mañana? *Carlitos°* me dijo que te había invitado.

ISABEL   No, no puedo... Me gustaría ir pero tengo que cuidar° a mi *hermanita°*. Mis padres van a hacer un *viajecito°* a la capital...y los vecinos° que siempre la cuidan ¡también van a salir mañana... !

CARMEN   Pero... ¡eso es terrible... ! ¿Qué dirá *Carlitos*? ¿Por qué no llevas a tu *hermanita* contigo?

ISABEL   ¡Imposible! Ella es demasiado *chiquita°* para salir de noche.

---

pueblecito	*small town*	Carlitos	*Charlie*	cuidar	*to take care of, babysit*
hermanita	*little sister*	viajecito	*short trip*	vecinos	*neighbors* demasiado
chiquita	*too small, extremely young*				

---

1. ¿Qué le dijo Carlitos a Carmen?   2. ¿Por qué no puede ir Isabel a la fiesta? ¿Qué van a hacer sus padres? ¿Por qué no puede dejar a la niñita con los vecinos? 3. ¿Sabe Carlitos que Isabel no puede ir a la fiesta con él? ¿Cómo lo sabe usted? 4. ¿Cuál es la idea de Carmen? ¿Piensa Isabel que es una buena idea? ¿Por qué?

A. Certain endings in Spanish may be added to words to form diminutives. A diminutive is often used to express smallness, cuteness, or affection. The number of diminutive endings is large; particular combinations have special shades of meaning. Here are two rules of thumb, just as examples; each would have to be greatly elaborated to cover all possible formations.

1. **-(e)cito(-a)** is added to words of more than one syllable that end in **-n**, **-r**, **-e**, or certain diphthongs; to some two-syllable words ending in **-o** or **-a** if the word contains certain diphthongs; and to one-syllable words ending in a consonant.

jovencitos	*youngsters*	rubiecito	*little blond boy*
mujercita	*little woman*	trencitos	*small trains*
hombrecito	*little man*	solcito	*little sun*

2. **-ito(-a)** is added to most other words that end in **-o** or **-a**, and to more-than-one-syllable words that end in any consonant other than **n** or **r.**

casita	*cute little house*	Miguelito	*little Miguel*
autitos	*little cars*	relojito	*small watch*
ahorita	*right away*	perrito	*little dog*

B. Some words require a spelling change before the diminutive ending to show that the pronunciation of the base word does not change.

amigo	**amiguito**	*little friend*
poco	**poquito**	*little bit*
luz	**lucecita**	*little light*
voz	**vocecita**	*soft little voice*

EJERCICIOS

A. ¡Pobrecita! Cambie las palabras en bastardilla (*in italics*) a la forma diminutiva.

> **MODELO** La *hermana* de *Pedro* continúa *enferma*.
> **La hermanita de Pedrito continúa enfermita.**

1. ¿Quién es ese *chico*?
2. Es el *hermano* de *Teresa*.
3. ¿No se siente bien tu *amiga*?
4. Ella tiene un *dolor* en el *brazo, Inés*.
5. Creo que las aspirinas están encima de la *mesa, hijo*.
6. Dale a *Carlos* un *poco* de agua.
7. Hay un *vaso cerca* de las aspirinas.
8. Espera un *momento*, voy a hacer una *llamada*.

B. Muchas cositas lindas. Gloria le cuenta a su compañera de cuarto qué regalos le dieron sus parientes y amigos por su compleaños.

> **MODELO** abuelo / perro **Mi abuelo me regaló un perrito.**

1. amigas / unas flores
2. José / un libro
3. tía / una blusa
4. Carlos / un anillo
5. abuela / mil bolívares
6. papá / un viaje a París

Preguntas

Conteste las preguntas con la forma diminutiva cuando sea posible.

1. ¿Vive usted cerca de la universidad? 2. ¿Se levanta temprano todos los días? ¿y hoy? 3. ¿Tiene usted hermanas? ¿y hermanos? 4. ¿Quiere que alguien le dé un regalo? ¿Quién? ¿Cuándo? 5. ¿Quiere mucho a sus abuelos? ¿Tiene un(a) abuelo(-a) favorito(-a)? 6. ¿Tiene usted un poco de dinero? ¿Cómo piensa gastarlo? Si usted necesita dinero, ¿a quién se lo pedirá... ?

CARACAS: DIFERENCIAS ENTRE PADRES E HIJOS

Vista de Caracas, Venezuela

Una pareja de un pequeño pueblo venezolano toma café con sus vecinos.

EL VECINO — No nos han dicho nada de su viaje a Caracas. ¿Qué les pareció la capital?

LA SEÑORA — ¡Horrible!

EL SEÑOR — Una gran desilusión°. Todo era muy caro y de mala calidad. Además, las cosas tenían precios fijos y no se podía regatear°. Nosotros hicimos el viaje principalmente para que los muchachos vieran los sitios importantes: los museos, la casa de Bolívar...[1]

LA SEÑORA — Pero también vieron otras cosas sin que lo pudiéramos evitar°.

LOS VECINOS — Total que° no les gustó Caracas... ¿Pero qué cosas tan horribles vieron... ?

EL SEÑOR — Fuimos al Parque del Este[2] y vimos novios que se besaban en público, como si estuvieran solos en el mundo. En resumen,° Caracas es un centro de perdición°...

EL VECINO — ¡Qué escándalo!

EL SEÑOR — Pero eso no es todo... Había muchachos de once o doce años que fumaban en la calle.

LA VECINA — ¡Como si no tuvieran otra cosa que hacer!

EL SEÑOR — Por eso regresamos pronto. Queríamos volver antes de que los muchachos empezaran a imitar las malas costumbres°.

En otra parte de la casa, el hijo de catorce años y la hija de dieciséis toman refrescos con sus amigos.

EL AMIGO — ¿Y el viaje a Caracas? ¿Qué les pareció la ciudad?

EL HIJO — ¡Fabulosa! Allí todo es muy barato y de buena calidad. En las tiendas se venden miles de cosas.

LA HIJA — Sí, es un sueño. Los jóvenes se visten a la moda y tienen mucha libertad.

EL HIJO	Los edificios son muy lindos y modernos.³
LA AMIGA	¿Vieron la Rinconada?⁴
EL HIJO	Sí, por fuera°. Yo quería que entráramos, pero mi padre dijo que no.
LA HIJA	Es una lástima que no pudiéramos pasar más tiempo en las playas. Conocimos allá a un grupo de chicos que nos invitaron a una fiesta.
EL HIJO	Sí, pero mamá nos prohibió que aceptáramos la invitación.
LA AMIGA	¡Qué lástima! A mí me gustaría vivir algún día en Caracas.
EL HIJO	A mí también. Si yo pudiera vivir en esa ciudad, sería la persona más feliz del mundo.

desilusión *disappointment*   no...regatear *one couldn't bargain*   evitar *to avoid*   Total
que *So*   En resumen *In conclusion*   perdición *immorality, sin*   costumbres *habits*
por fuera *from outside*

PREGUNTAS

1. ¿A qué ciudad viajó la pareja venezolana? ¿Para qué hicieron el viaje?   2. ¿Qué vieron en el Parque del Este?   3. ¿Por qué querían volver los padres?   4. ¿Qué les pareció la ciudad a los jóvenes? ¿Por qué les gustó hacer compras allí?   5. ¿A quiénes conocieron en la playa?   6. ¿Por qué no aceptaron la invitación que les hicieron?   7. ¿Cómo se sentiría el hijo si pudiera vivir en Caracas?   8. ¿Hay muchas diferencias de opinión entre usted y sus padres? ¿Le gustaría a usted viajar con ellos? ¿Por qué sí o por qué no?

NOTAS CULTURALES

1. Caracas is the birthplace of **Simón Bolívar**, one of South America's greatest heroes, and the site of the **Museo Bolívar**, which houses his personal effects and documents. **Bolívar** was born in 1783 and was a major figure in the movement for independence from Spain. He was a brilliant general and a greatly admired politician who dreamed of uniting the countries of South America as one nation. He died brokenhearted in 1830 without realizing his dream.

2. **El Parque del Este** in Caracas is a large park with artificial lakes, a zoo, playgrounds, and a train with fringe-topped cars. A great variety of orchids can be seen in its gardens, and in its excellent aviary there are specimens of the many tropical birds for which Venezuela is famous.

3. Caracas is a city of modern and ultramodern architecture. In the last several decades the government has sponsored many low-rent apartment complexes. The money for such projects comes from Venezuela's oil industry.

4. **La Rinconada** is one of the world's most luxurious racetracks, complete with escalators, an air-conditioned box for the president, and a swimming pool for the horses.

Funciones y *actividades*

In this chapter, you have seen examples of some important language functions, or uses. Here is a summary and some additional information about these functions of language.

EXPRESSING SATISFACTION AND DISSATISFACTION

Here are some ways to express that you are pleased or displeased with something you have bought, seen, etc.

Esto (Eso) es buenísimo (fabuloso, justo lo que nos faltaba, etcétera).	*This (That) is very good (great, just what we needed, etc.).*
¡Esto (Eso) es terrible (feo, malo, aburrido, insoportable)!	*This (That) is terrible (ugly, bad, boring, unbearable)!*
Esto (Eso) (no) es aceptable.	*This (That) is (un)acceptable.*
Es demasiado...	*It's too . . .*
Esto (Eso) no funciona (no sirve).	*This (That) doesn't work.*
(No) me gusta... porque...	*I (don't) like . . . because . . .*
Me gustaría + *infinitive*... porque (pero, etc.)...	*I would like + infinitive . . . because (but, etc.) . . .*

SUMMARIZING

Here are some ways to conclude, to express that you are coming to the point.

Total que...	*So . . .*
A fin de cuentas...	*After all . . . (All things considered . . .)*
Después de todo...	*After all . . .*
Al fin y al cabo...	*In the end . . . (To make a long story short . . .)*
En resumen... (En conclusión...)	*In summary . . . (In conclusion . . .)*

Ahora haga las siguientes actividades, usando las expresiones que acaba de aprender.

A. ¿Qué dicen? Observe los dibujos e imagine qué estarán diciendo estas personas. Exprese satisfacción o insatisfacción, según sea apropiado. Siga el modelo.

> **MODELO** **Esta maleta no sirve. Me gustaría devolverla.**

B. En conclusión. Dé un comentario o una frase que sirva de conclusión a cada una de las siguientes situaciones.

1. Alguien que usted conoce acaba de hablar durante una hora sobre economía y especialmente sobre temas relacionados con la inflación. La tesis de esa persona es que no es bueno ahorrar dinero en tiempos de mucha inflación.
2. Uno(-a) de sus amigos(-as) se está quejando de su compañero(-a) de cuarto—desde hace diez minutos—y llega a la conclusión de que va a buscar otro lugar para vivir.
3. Usted está escribiendo una composición sobre la costumbre *(custom)* de regatear en América Latina. Termina su trabajo diciendo que está bien regatear en los mercados, pero que no está bien regatear en las tiendas donde los precios son generalmente fijos.
4. Ahora haga un comentario final—de resumen *(summary)*—sobre su clase de español.

VOCABULARIO ACTIVO

Cognados

el artesano, la artesana	los cosméticos	el inventario	millonario
la boutique	el costo	el kilo	la organización
la calidad	fabuloso	la liquidación	el poncho
el cliente	la fortuna	local	puro
continuar (ú)			

Verbos

ahorrar	*to save (time, money)*
aumentar	*to increase, to go up*
cuidar (a)	*to take care of*
deber	*to owe*
gastar	*to spend; to waste*
prestar	*to lend*
rebajar	*to reduce; to mark down*
reconocer	*to recognize, to admit*
regatear	*to bargain (over prices)*

De compras — Shopping

la alfarería	*pottery; potter shop*
el almacén	*grocery store*
barato	*cheap, inexpensive*
el bizcocho	*cookie, biscuit*
el bolívar	*monetary unit of Venezuela*
caro	*expensive*
el, la dependiente	*salesclerk; shop assistant; clerk*
el empleado, la empleada	*employee*
la frazada	*blanket*
la galleta	*cracker*
la mueblería	*furniture store*
la oferta	*sale, (special) offer*
el precio fijo	*fixed price*
rebajado	*reduced; marked down; on sale*
el tapiz	*tapestry*
la venta	*sale, selling*
en venta	*on sale*

Otras palabras y frases

el alquiler	*rent*
el coche	*car*
hacer juego con	*to match, to go with*
rico	*rich*
el sueldo	*salary*
el vecino, la vecina	*neighbor*

Expresiones útiles

Después de todo...	*After all . . .*
En resumen...	*In summary (or: In conclusion) . . .*
Es demasiado...	*It's too . . .*
¡Eso es terrible (aburrido, etc.)!	*That's terrible (boring, etc.)!*
Me gustaría + infinitive...porque (pero, etc.)...	*I would like + infinitive . . . because (but, etc.) . . .*
(No) me gusta... porque...	*I (don't) like . . . because . . .*
Total que...	*So . . .*

Una mujer de
negocios en su oficina
de Lima, Perú

PROFESIONES Y OFICIOS

Funciones

- Expressing doubt
- Asking for permission
- Granting or denying
  permission

Vocabulario. In this chapter you will talk about jobs, professions, and occupations.

Gramática. You will discuss and use:

1. Other uses of the progressive
2. Other uses of **se**: as an impersonal pronoun equivalent to English *one, people, they;* as an alternative to the passive in such sentences as *Newspapers are sold here;* and as a way to express unplanned occurrences (e.g., **olvidarse** *to forget*)
3. Adjectives used as nouns (*I'll take the red one.*)
4. Future perfect and conditional perfect tenses (*for recognition only*)

Cultura. The dialogues take place in the Peruvian cities of Lima and Cuzco.

el abogado, la abogada

el policía, la mujer policía

el vendedor,
la vendedora

el secretario,
la secretaria

el ingeniero,
la ingeniera

el, la comerciante
el hombre (la mujer)
de negocios

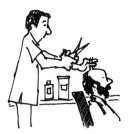

el peluquero,
la peluquera

el, la músico

el doctor, la doctora
el médico, la médica

el programador
la programadora
(de computadoras)

el cura, el sacerdote

el camarero, la camarera
el mesero, la mesera

el jardinero,
la jardinera

el bombero, la bombera

el ama de casa

el, la cantante

el, la agente de viajes

el consejero
(la consejera)
de trabajo

Asociaciones. ¿Qué profesiones u oficios (*jobs*) asocia usted con las personas y cosas que siguen?

1. el dinero
2. las vacaciones
3. un restaurante
4. el divorcio
5. una oficina
6. una computadora
7. una boda
8. la construcción
9. una persona que busca trabajo
10. la música
11. las plantas
12. la gente enferma
13. los incendios
14. el trabajo de la casa
15. el pelo

Preguntas

1. ¿Cuál era la profesión de J.C. Penney? ¿de Jonas Salk? ¿Y cuál es la profesión de Michael Jackson?   2. ¿Quiénes trabajan en un hospital? ¿en el campo? ¿en una oficina? ¿en una tienda? ¿en casa? ¿muy lejos de la casa?   3. ¿Qué profesión le gustaría tener si tuviera el dinero y el talento necesarios?   4. ¿Qué le gusta a usted de esa profesión?   5. ¿Qué carrera (*career*) piensa usted seguir?   6. ¿Hay algo que no le guste de la carrera que piensa seguir?   7. ¿Cuáles son algunas de las profesiones consideradas de servicio público?   8. ¿Cuáles son algunas profesiones u oficios que pagan bien? ¿que pagan mal?   9. ¿Trabaja usted? ¿Dónde trabaja? ¿Le gusta su trabajo? ¿Por qué sí o por qué no?   10. ¿Le gustaría ser profesora? ¿Por qué sí o por qué no?

I. Otros usos del progresivo

Una tienda de
computadoras, Lima

En Lima, Perú, Ricardo está hablando *con un consejero de trabajo.*

CONSEJERO	Así que usted *está buscando* trabajo en... ¿qué área?
RICARDO	En programación°... Soy programador de computadoras. Por ahora *estoy trabajando* en una oficina, pero me gustaría *estar haciendo* otra cosa. Hasta hace unos meses *estaba trabajando* en una agencia de viajes.
CONSEJERO	¿Y qué hacía antes de eso?
RICARDO	Entre el 85 y el 87 trabajé de vendedor de ropa en una tienda, pero como *estaba trabajando* tanto y *ganando* tan poco, decidí *seguir estudiando* en la universidad.
CONSEJERO	¡Qué bien! ¿Y qué estudió?
RICARDO	Estudié sociología y psicología. Pero como usted puede ver, *andaba trabajando* mucho sin mucho provecho.° Ahora no sé qué hacer.
CONSEJERO	Tengo una idea. Con toda su experiencia, ¿por qué no trabaja aquí... de consejero de trabajo? En este momento, *¡estamos buscando* a alguien con sus calificaciones°!

programación *programming*   provecho *progress, gain*   calificaciones *qualifications*

1. ¿Dónde está trabajando Ricardo ahora? ¿Qué hace?   2. ¿Dónde estaba trabajando hasta hace unos meses?   3. ¿Qué hacía antes de eso?   4. ¿Por qué decidió seguir estudiando en la universidad? ¿Qué estudió?   5. ¿Qué tipo de empleo quiere Ricardo?   6. ¿Qué le recomienda el consejero?

A. The formation of present participles and the formation and use of the present progressive was discussed in Chapter 3. Remember that present participles of verbs whose stem ends in a vowel take the ending **-yendo** rather than **-iendo.**

creer	**creyendo**	oír	**oyendo**
leer	**leyendo**	traer	**trayendo**

The present participle of **ir** is **yendo.**

B. The **-ir** verbs that change stem vowel **e** to **i** or **o** to **u** in the third person preterit show the same change in the stem of the present participle.

decir	**diciendo**	preferir	**prefiriendo**
dormir	**durmiendo**	seguir	**siguiendo**
morir	**muriendo**	servir	**sirviendo**
pedir	**pidiendo**		

Poder is the only **-er** verb with a change in the present participle.

poder	**pudiendo**

C. Remember that the present progressive is used to emphasize that an action is going on at the moment.

¿Qué tipo de oficio estás buscando?	*What type of job are you looking for?*
No puedo salir ahora; estoy comiendo.	*I can't go out now; I'm eating.*

D. A form of **estar** in the imperfect (or sometimes in the preterit) may be combined with a present participle to form the past progressive tense. This tense indicates that an action was in progress at a given moment in the past.

¿Qué estaban haciendo los comerciantes aquí ayer? Estaban hablando del nuevo negocio.	*What were the business people doing here yesterday? They were talking about the new business.*
La secretaria estaba hablando por teléfono.	*The secretary was talking on the phone.*

E. Verbs of motion, including **seguir, ir, venir,** and **andar,** are sometimes used instead of **estar** in a progressive tense to imply that an action is or was unfolding little by little or in spite of an interruption.

Andaba buscando trabajo.	*He was (going along) looking for work.*
El médico sigue diciendo que Raúl está bien, pero tengo mis dudas.	*The doctor keeps on saying that Raúl is fine, but I have my doubts.*

F. Spanish speakers use progressive tenses much less frequently than English speakers.

1. The simple present tense is used to describe most actions going on in the present; the preterit and imperfect are used for most past actions.

¿Qué haces en estos días? Trabajo en una peluquería. Soy peluquero.	*What are you doing these days? I'm working in a barbershop. I'm a barber.*

¿Qué hacía Ramón por la tarde?
Hablaba con los músicos.

What was Ramón doing this afternoon? He was talking to the musicians.

With the progressive there is sometimes the sense that an action is (was) going on at the same time as something else or in conflict with it.

Vámonos—el cura está esperando.
¿No quiso ayudarte? No, estaba leyendo.

Let's go—the priest is waiting.
Wouldn't he (she) help you? No, he (she) was reading.

2. The Spanish progressive is seldom used to refer to future actions; the present tense, **ir a** + *infinitive,* or the future tense is used instead.

Voy a la peluquería el sábado.

I'm going to the hairdresser's on Saturday.

Dejaré este trabajo para la próxima semana.

I'll leave this work for next week.

3. Ir and **venir** are usually not used in the progressive. A simple tense is used instead.

Que yo sepa, Joaquín va (viene) a Lima.

As far as I know, Joaquín's going (coming) to Lima.

G. Remember that when object pronouns are attached to the end of the present participle, an accent mark is written on the participle to show that the stress has not changed.

Mi jefe se estaba quejando de su carrera.
Mi jefe estaba quejándose de su carrera.

My boss was complaining about his career.

EJERCICIOS

A. Piense y hable.   Termine las frases. Escoja el más apropiado de los dos verbos entre paréntesis y úselo en la forma progresiva.

> **MODELO**   (hablar, tratar) El pobre Jacinto está <u>tratando</u> de dormir pero los chicos están <u>hablando</u> mucho.

1. (pedir, gastar) Los niños están _____ mucho dinero recientemente. ¿En qué lo están _____?
2. (divertirse, quedarse) Julia me contó en su carta que está _____ en un hotel elegante en Quito y que está _____ mucho.
3. (morir, leer) Yo estaba _____ un libro cuando me llamó mi tía para decirme que mi abuela estaba _____.
4. (construir, dejar) Nosotros estamos _____ un garaje (*garage*) en casa. Mientras tanto estamos _____ el coche en la calle.

5. (buscar, aprender, repetir) ¿Cuánto tiempo hace que ese joven anda
   _____ esposa? Sigue _____ la misma cosa: «Estoy _____ mucho
   sobre las mujeres».

6. (subir, costar) Me parece que los precios están _____ mucho. La
   comida me está _____ más y más todas las semanas.

7. (bañarse, hablar por teléfono, esperar) Estuve _____ a mi novia en su
   casa por más de media hora. Su mamá me dijo que estaba _____ pero
   creo que estaba _____.

B. El terremoto. ¿Qué estaban haciendo las siguientes personas cuando ocurrió
el terremoto en Lima, Perú? Siga el modelo.

MODELO **La mesera estaba sirviéndoles café a unos comerciantes. Los
comerciantes estaban hablando de una nueva tienda que
iban a abrir.**

MODELO   1.   2.

3.   4.   5.

6.   7.   8.

C.   **¿Qué están haciendo?**

> **MODELO**   un empleado de Taquito King
> **Está vendiendo tacos.**

1. el presidente de los Estados Unidos
2. sus padres (de usted)
3. el jugador de béisbol Fernando Valenzuela
4. el escritor peruano Mario Vargas Llosa
5. el cantante Julio Iglesias
6. el bailarín Fernando Bujones
7. los reyes de España

D.   **Mini-drama.**   Vamos a imaginar que no estábamos aquí en la clase la semana pasada. Estábamos en otro lugar, haciendo otra cosa. Escriba tres o cuatro oraciones describiendo la escena que usted imagina.

> **MODELOS**   Estaba descansando en una playa de España. Estaba diciéndoles a las chicas que lo sentía pero que estaba leyendo y por eso no podía jugar al vólibol con ellas. Les estaba diciendo que jugaría con ellas otro día.
>
> Estaba esquiando en las montañas de Chile. Estaba pasando rápido cerca de unos jóvenes muy guapos (*handsome*), diciéndoles que tal vez nos veríamos por la noche.

Preguntas

1. ¿Está usted descansando ahora?   2. ¿Qué está haciendo usted en este momento?   3. ¿Cuáles son diez cosas que están pasando en el mundo en este momento?   4. ¿En qué estaba pensando usted hoy cuando entró a la clase?   5. ¿Qué estaba haciendo usted ayer a las ocho de la noche?   6. ¿Puede dar una lista de cinco cosas que usted no estaba haciendo anoche a las diez?

II.   Usos adicionales del pronombre se

Una agencia de empleos, Lima

Una mujer de negocios habla con una turista norteamericana en el Perú.

JANICE ¿Es verdad que en este país *se cierran* las tiendas entre el mediodía y las tres?

PATRICIA Pues, depende. En general, en los pueblos todavía *se cierran* las tiendas durante esas horas, pero en las ciudades más grandes ya prácticamente° *se ha perdido* esa costumbre°.

JANICE Pero *se trabaja* mejor después de una buena siesta, ¿no?

PATRICIA Cómo no, pero con el horario de nueve a cinco *se puede* conservar energía, especialmente en el invierno. *Se dice* que *se nos va a acabar*° el petróleo en treinta años si no lo conservamos. Así que ahora tenemos sólo media hora para almorzar—¡imagínese!°

---

prácticamente *practically*   la costumbre *custom*   acabar *to run out, end, finish*
¡imagínese! *Just imagine!*

---

1. En el Perú, ¿dónde se cierran las tiendas al mediodía? ¿Dónde no se cierran? 2. ¿Por qué se cambió el sistema en las grandes ciudades?   3. Según Patricia, ¿qué va a pasar si no conservamos el petróleo?   4. ¿Cree usted que el nuevo sistema será bueno para el país?

A. The pronoun **se** followed by a verb in the third person singular is a construction frequently used when it is not important to express or identify the "doer" of an action. This use of **se** is often translated in English with *one, people, we, you,* or a passive construction. It is known as the impersonal **se.**

Se sabe que no hay muchos trabajos para arqueólogos ahora.	*It's known (Everybody knows, It's common knowledge) that there aren't many jobs for archeologists now.*
¿Es cierto que ya no se duerme la siesta? Sí, eso no se hace mucho hoy en día.	*Is it true they (people) don't take a midday nap anymore? Yes, that's not done much these days.*
Se cree que el poder de los antiguos sacerdotes de los incas era muy grande.	*It is believed (People believe) that the power of the ancient priests of the Incas was very great.*
Se dice que José consiguió un buen puesto en el gobierno. Podría ser.	*People say that José got a good job in the government. It could be.*

B. When there is a grammatical subject, **se** is followed by a verb in the third person singular or plural, agreeing with the subject.

Se habla español allí.	*Spanish is spoken there.*
Se hablan varias lenguas allí.	*Several languages are spoken there.*
Se vendían periódicos allí.	*Newspapers used to be sold there.*
¿Se permite fumar aquí? ¿Le molestaría a alguien?	*Is it OK (permitted) to smoke here? Would it bother anyone?*

This rule applies to things or infinitives.

C. The same structure is used to report unplanned events. Any person affected by the event may be mentioned with an indirect object pronoun, with additional clarification if necessary. Contrast the straightforward sentence **Paré el coche** (*I stopped the car*) with the following.

Se paró.	*It stopped.*
Se me paró el coche.	*My car stopped ("on me").*
A Ana y a Guillermo se les paró el coche.	*Ana and Guillermo's car stopped ("on them").*
A Ana y a Guillermo se les pararon los coches.	*Ana's and Guillermo's cars stopped ("on them").*

This construction is often used to put a certain polite distance between an event and the person responsible for it, or to imply that the event was an accident. Compare the following pairs of sentences.

No olvides el número de teléfono.	*Don't forget the telephone number.*
Se me olvidó el número de teléfono.	*I forgot the phone number (it slipped my memory).*
El ama de casa perdió las tarjetas de crédito.	*The housewife lost the credit cards.*
Se le perdieron las tarjetas de crédito al ama de casa.	*The housewife (unintentionally) lost the credit cards.*

Many verbs are used in this construction. **Olvidar, perder, romper, caer** (*to fall, to drop*), and **acabar** are among the most common.

Se le rompió el vaso (a él).	*The glass (in his possession) broke.*
Se me cayó.	*It dropped. (It fell while in my possession.)*
Se nos acabó el tiempo y no pudimos terminar el examen.	*We ran out of time and couldn't finish the test.*

EJERCICIOS

A. Háblame del Perú.   Susan es estudiante de intercambio (*exchange student*) en la Universidad de San Marcos. Quiere aprender algo sobre el Perú. Haga el papel de su amigo peruano Horacio y conteste las preguntas de Susan. Use **se** como en los modelos.

MODELOS   ¿Qué lenguas estudian los jóvenes aquí? (inglés y francés)
Se estudian inglés y francés.

¿Qué sistema siguen las universidades? (el sistema de semestres)
Se sigue el sistema de semestres.

1. ¿Qué clase de película ven los jóvenes? (muchas películas norteamericanas)
2. ¿Qué deporte juegan los chicos? (el fútbol)
3. ¿Qué deporte no juegan mucho? (el béisbol)

4. ¿Cuánto pagan los estudiantes por asistir a la universidad? (nada)
5. ¿Dónde compra la gente la comida? (en los mercados)
6. ¿Dónde venden papel y lápices? (en las librerías)
7. ¿Cuándo cierran las tiendas los comerciantes? (al mediodía y otra vez a las siete)

B. **¡Ya se hizo!**   Siga los modelos.

MODELOS   ¿arreglar / la computadora?
Sí, ya se arregló la computadora.

¿escribir / las cartas?
Sí, ya se escribieron las cartas.

1. ¿servir / la cena?
2. ¿hacer / la reservación?
3. ¿resolver / el problema?
4. ¿pintar / la casa?
5. ¿hacer / el reportaje?
6. ¿traducir / los libros?

C. **Otra edad, otro mundo.**   Vamos a imaginar que vivimos en otra edad o hasta en otro mundo. Todo se hace de otra forma. Mencione algunas cosas que se hacen de otra forma.

MODELOS   **Se construyen las casas en un solo día.**

Se celebran todos los cumpleaños el mismo día.

D. **La traducción.**   Traduzca al español las siguientes oraciones.

1. Spanish is spoken here.
2. You can't buy love.
3. Few large cars are sold in Peru.
4. Carlos forgot his girlfriend's telephone number.
5. We ran out of bread.
6. It is said that German is difficult.

Preguntas

1. ¿Cómo se dice *housewife* en español? ¿*travel agent*?   2. ¿Qué se necesita cuando se viaja a otro país?   3. ¿A qué hora se abren los bancos? ¿Y a qué hora se cierran?   4. ¿En qué países se juega mucho al béisbol?   5. ¿Qué lengua se habla en el Perú? ¿en Italia? ¿en el Brasil? ¿en Australia?   6. ¿Qué lenguas se enseñan en esta universidad?   7. ¿Dónde se vive muy bien? ¿Dónde se sabe divertirse? ¿Dónde se come bien?   8. ¿Se come bien en la cafetería de la universidad?   9. ¿Se puede fumar en la clase? ¿Se permite comer?   10. ¿Dónde se compran las medicinas? ¿los libros?   11. ¿Se le perdió algo recientemente? ¿Se le olvidó algo hoy?

III. Los adjetivos usados como sustantivos

Oficinas de profesionales en un edificio del centro, Lima

Dos señoras hablan por teléfono.

SEÑORA 1   Buenos días.
SEÑORA 2   Buenos días. Tengo unas preguntas sobre los formularios° que
recibí de ustedes. ¿Mando *el corto* o *el largo*° al gobierno?
¿Y qué copia les devuelvo a ustedes—*la azul* o *la amarilla*?
SEÑORA 1   ¿Cómo? No la entiendo.
SEÑORA 2   ¿No hablo con la agencia de trabajo Empleos de Hoy?
SEÑORA 1   No, esto es una oficina de abogados: Díaz, Blas, Bosco y Concha Boy.
SEÑORA 2   ¡Oh! Pues, disculpe, disculpe, disculpe, disculpe...

formularios   *forms*   el corto...largo   *the short one or the long one*

1. ¿Qué preguntas tiene la segunda señora?   2. ¿Con quién cree que está hablando?   3. ¿Con quién habla en realidad?

A. In Spanish, a noun that is modified by an adjective may be deleted unless its absence will cause confusion. The adjective that remains then functions as a noun; it keeps the same ending as if the original noun were still expressed. (In English, the noun is not just dropped, but is replaced, usually by *one* or *ones*.)

Leo la edición nueva y la vieja.　　　*I'm reading the new edition and the old one.*

B. Nouns are often deleted in Spanish when:

1. the noun is preceded by a demonstrative adjective or an article.

estos zapatos pequeños
　→ **estos pequeños**　　　*these small ones*
la mano derecha
　→ **la derecha**　　　*the right one*

Un becomes **uno** before an adjective used as a noun.

un coche viejo
　→ **uno viejo**　　　*an old one*

2. the adjective is an adjective of nationality or a descriptive adjective expressing color, size, height, and so forth.

La francesa es programadora de computadoras.　*The French woman is a computer programmer.*
Me gusta el vino tinto, pero prefiero el blanco.　*I like red wine, but I prefer white.*

C. Nouns can also be dropped from phrases.

Leo la edición de la mañana y la de la tarde.　*I read the morning edition and the afternoon one.*
Arreglaron mi coche y el de mi hermana.　*They fixed my car and my sister's.*

EJERCICIOS

Es tu cumpleaños, Anita.　¿Qué quieres hacer? Haga el papel de Anita y conteste las preguntas de su mamá.

MODELO　¿Prefieres el vestido verde o el vestido amarillo?
　　　Prefiero el verde.

1. ¿Vas a comprar los zapatos blancos o los zapatos negros?
2. ¿Quieres comer en el restaurante italiano o en el restaurante francés?
3. ¿Te gustaría un vino tinto o un vino blanco?
4. ¿Deseas una fiesta grande o una fiesta pequeña?

Preguntas

1. ¿Qué tipo de música prefiere usted: la clásica, la popular, la folklórica...?
2. ¿Qué autos le gustan más a usted: los norteamericanos, los alemanes, los japoneses (*Japanese*)...?　3. ¿Qué color prefiere: el rojo, el amarillo, el azul...?
4. ¿Con qué mano escribe usted: con la izquierda o con la derecha?

IV. El futuro y el condicional perfectos

La Plaza de las
Armas, Lima

La novia de Manuel va a Lima en un viaje de negocios.

MANUEL   ¿Crees que Amelia ya *habrá llegado* a Lima?
GUSTAVO Lo dudo, Manuel. Te *habría llamado* desde allí, ¿no?
MANUEL   Tienes razón. Me *habría llamado* desde el aeropuerto.
GUSTAVO No te preocupes. Para el próximo sábado ya *habrá vuelto* y la
         tendrás contigo otra vez.

---

1. ¿Adónde va la novia de Manuel? ¿Por qué?   2. ¿Cree Gustavo que Amelia ya
habrá llegado? ¿Por qué sí o por qué no?   3. ¿Para cuándo habrá vuelto Amelia?

A. The future perfect tense is formed with the future tense of the auxiliary verb
haber plus a past participle.

habré	habremos	
habrás	habréis	+ *past participle*
habrá	habrán	

It expresses a future action with a past perspective—that is, an action that will
have taken place (or may have taken place) by some future time. It can also
express probability, an action that must have or might have taken place.

Habré terminado los estudios para el año 1992.	*I will have finished my studies by the year 1992.*
Para el mes próximo habrás conseguido un puesto como ingeniero.	*By next month you will (probably) have gotten a job as an engineer.*
Habrán recibido la carta.	*They must have received the letter.*

B. The conditional perfect tense is formed with the conditional of **haber** plus a past participle.

habría	habríamos	
habrías	habríais	+ *past participle*
habría	habrían	

It often corresponds to the English *would have* plus past participle.

Habríamos llamado a los bomberos. ¿Qué habrían hecho ustedes?	*We would have called the fire department (fire fighters). What would you have done?*

It is also used to express the probability that a past action happened prior to another point in the past.

El hombre de negocios habría pensado en abrir otro restaurante en Machu Picchu.	*The businessman had probably thought about opening another restaurant in Machu Picchu.*

You don't need to use these tenses actively now, but the exercises that follow will help you learn to recognize and understand them.

EJERCICIOS

A. La respuesta (*response*) apropiada. ¿Cuál es la respuesta apropiada para cada pregunta?

1. ¿Habría comido Juan antes de venir?
   a. Sí, habré comido antes.
   b. Sí, habría comido antes.
   c. Sí, habríamos comido antes.
2. ¿Qué habrías hecho tú?
   a. Habrán llamado a la policía.
   b. Habría llamado a la policía.
   c. Habrás llamado a la policía.
3. ¿Qué habrá hecho el presidente ayer?
   a. Habrá hablado en el Congreso.
   b. Habrán hablado en el Congreso.
   c. Habría hablado en el Congreso.
4. ¿Qué coche habrían comprado ustedes?
   a. Habría comprado el rojo.
   b. Habríamos comprado el rojo.
   c. Habremos comprado el rojo.

B. Traducción. Traduzca al inglés las siguientes oraciones.

1. —¿Qué habrás hecho para el año 2000?
   —Habré terminado mis estudios para médica y me habré casado con Felipe.
2. —¿Qué habremos hecho en clase para la semana que viene?
   —Habremos terminado este capítulo y habremos empezado el capítulo 19.
3. —Mis notas del año pasado fueron excelentes.
   —Tus padres se habrán puesto muy contentos.
4. —Ayer fuimos a un concierto y conocimos a uno de los músicos.
   —Habrá sido muy interesante hablar con él.
5. —Para mañana habremos ido a Machu Picchu.
   —Y habremos visto las ruinas incas allí.
6. —¿Habrías podido entender una película en español el año pasado?
   —No, pero ahora podría hacerlo.

CUZCO: LA ANTIGUA CAPITAL DE LOS INCAS

La fortaleza de Sacsahuamán, cerca de Cuzco, Perú

Unos amigos de Lima cenan en casa de los Menéndez en el Cuzco.[1]

LUISA	¿Qué les parece el Cuzco?
ANDRÉS	Es maravilloso. La catedral, las iglesias, los museos... ¡es el sueño° de los arqueólogos!
BLANCA	Acabamos de ver las ruinas incas en Sacsahuamán.[2] ¡Qué buena profesión tienes, Luisa!
MARÍA ELENA	Hablando de profesiones, ¿estás contenta con la decisión que tomaste° de estudiar para arqueóloga? ¿Qué otra carrera te habría gustado seguir?
LUISA	No sé. Tal vez me habría gustado ser médica. Hay tanta ne-cesidad de médicos aquí. Y tú, ¿qué habrías sido?
MARÍA ELENA	Enfermera o tal vez dentista... El cuidado de la salud es muy importante y, como ustedes saben, aquí falta personal médico°.
LUISA	Andrés, deja que te sirva un poco de este plato tan delicioso.
ANDRÉS	Gracias, Luisa, pero hablando de la salud, no me des ese trozo° grande... Estoy a dieta. Dame el pequeño.
LUISA	María Elena, ¿por qué no viniste a mi conferencia sobre el Cuzco de la época de Pizarro?[3]
MARÍA ELENA	Porque mientras tú hablabas de ese tema° tan interesante, yo estaba volviendo de Machu Picchu en el tren.[4]
LUISA	Ah, sí, se me había olvidado.
BLANCA	Ahora que hemos hablado de lo que habríamos sido, ¿por qué no hablamos de lo que habremos hecho en cinco años?
ANDRÉS	Muy bien, empieza tú.

Se oye un ruido° muy grande en la cocina°.

ROBERTO	*(desde la cocina)* ¡Ayyy!
ANDRÉS	Roberto, ¿qué estás haciendo? ¿Qué pasa?
ROBERTO	Nada. Se me cayó el pollo.
BLANCA	Para entonces habré hecho los planos° para muchos edificios.
LUISA	Pues, para ese año ya habré terminado mi estudio del imperio° inca.
ROBERTO	*(entrando con el pollo)* Yo habré llegado a ser° jefe de todos los programadores del departamento... ¡y habré aprendido a cocinar!

sueño *dream*   la... tomaste *the decision you made*   personal médico *medical personnel*
el trozo *slice*   el tema *topic*   ruido *noise*   cocina *kitchen*   planos *plans*   imperio *empire*   llegado a ser *become*

PREGUNTAS

1. ¿Cuál es la profesión de Luisa? ¿Qué otra carrera le habría gustado seguir?
2. ¿Qué le habría gustado ser a María Elena?   3. ¿Sobre qué tema habló Luisa recientemente?   4. ¿Qué le pasa a Roberto?   5. ¿Qué piensa hacer Blanca para 1995? ¿y Luisa? ¿y Roberto? ¿y usted?

NOTAS CULTURALES

1. **Cuzco,** capital of the far-reaching Inca empire, dates from the eleventh century. The Inca empire was highly advanced, particularly in the fields of engineering, botany, and the arts. The Incas built a very extensive system of roads and were master stonecutters.

2. **Sacsahuamán** is an impressive fortress with three gateways and the remains of three towers; it sits on a hill overlooking Cuzco. The Incas built massive walls from huge polygonal blocks so precisely shaped and chiseled that no mortar was necessary. Stones with as many as twelve sides fit so perfectly together that a razor blade cannot be inserted between them. It is amazing that the Incas, who like other American Indians did not have the benefit of the wheel, were able to transport these stones over long distances. The rocks used in constructing **Sacsahuamán** weigh up to 300 tons.

3. The Inca empire had been weakened by civil war when first challenged in 1532 by a band of 200 Spaniards led by Francisco Pizarro. With treachery, daring, 27 horses, and firearms, the Spaniards quickly toppled the empire's ruling structure and sacked its treasuries. Civil wars among the conquerors followed; in the chaos, much of the Incan civilization was swept away.

4. Machu Picchu is a remote fortress city of the Incas, located on a mountain peak rising out of the jungles near Cuzco. It cannot be seen from the Urubamba river valley below and remained unknown to the Spaniards and the outside world until 1911, when an Indian boy showed it to the American archeologist Hiram Bingham. Temples, stairways, walls, and houses—many carved into the solid rock of the mountain—still stand, offering a unique glimpse into the life of the ancient Incas.

Funciones y *actividades*

In this chapter, you have seen examples of some important language functions, or uses. Here is a summary and some additional information about these functions of language.

EXPRESSING DOUBT

You don't know how to respond to someone because you simply don't know something.

No sé.	I don't know.
No se sabe.	No one knows. (literally, "It's not known.")
¿Quién sabe?	Who knows?
¿Qué sé yo?	What do I know? (informal)
No estoy seguro(-a).	I'm not sure.
No tengo la menor idea.	I don't have the slightest idea.
No me acuerdo.	I don't remember.
Se me olvidó.	I forget.

You have a response, but you are doubtful about it.

No estoy seguro(-a) que (+ *subj*)...	I'm not sure that . . .
Es posible (probable) que (+ *subj*)...	It's possible (probable) that . . .
Puede (Podría) ser.	It could be.
Tal vez... , Quizá(s)...(+ *subj* or *ind*)	Perhaps . . .
Que yo sepa... (+ *ind*)	As far as I know . . .
Creo que sí (no).	I believe so (not).
Creo que (+ *ind*)... , No creo que (+ *subj*)...	I believe that . . . , I don't believe that . . .
Pienso que sí (no).	I think so. (I don't think so.)
Pienso que (+ *ind*)... , No pienso que (+ *subj*)...	I think that . . . , I don't think that . . .
Es dudoso.	It's doubtful.
Lo dudo.	I doubt it.
Tengo mis dudas.	I have my doubts.

ASKING FOR PERMISSION

¿Me permite (+ *inf*)... ?	May I . . . ? (Will you allow me to . . . ?)
¿Se permite (+ *inf*)... ? ¿Se debe (+ *inf*)... ?	May one (we, I) . . . ? Should one (we, I) . . . ?
¿Se puede (+ *inf*)... ?	Can one (we, I) . . . ?
¿Está bien que (+ *subj*)... ?	Is it OK to . . . ?
¿Le molestaría que... (+ *subj*)?	Would it bother you if . . . ?

GRANTING OR DENYING PERMISSION

Sí, está bien que (+ *subj*)...	*Yes, it's OK to . . .*
Sí, estoy seguro(-a) que puede(s)...	*Yes, I'm sure you can . . .*
No me molestaría.	*It wouldn't bother me.*
No, no está bien que (+ *subj*)...	*No, it's not OK to . . .*
No, está prohibido que (+ *subj*)...	*No, it's prohibited to . . .*
Se prohíbe (+ *inf*)...	*It's prohibited (forbidden) to . . .*
No se permite (+ *inf*)...	*It's not permitted to . . .*
Eso no se hace.	*That's not done (allowed).*
No nos dejan...	*They don't allow us to . . .*
¡Ni hablar!	*Don't even mention it!*

Ahora haga las siguientes actividades, usando las expresiones que acaba de aprender.

A. Dudas. Juanita tiene muchas ideas extrañas sobre cómo se debe encontrar trabajo. Exprese sus dudas cuando ella le dice las siguientes cosas. Use tantas expresiones de duda como le sea posible.

MODELO   Es bueno llegar media hora temprano a una entrevista de empleo.
No estoy seguro(-a) de que sea bueno llegar tan temprano.

1. La mejor forma de encontrar trabajo es caminar por las calles y mirar los letreros *(signs)* en las ventanas.
2. Otra buena forma de encontrar trabajo es entrar en una oficina y hablar con la primera persona con quien se encuentre allí.
3. No es importante saber mucho sobre la compañía donde uno tiene una entrevista.
4. La primera pregunta al futuro jefe debe ser «¿Cuánto paga este trabajo?»
5. Cuando se habla de los empleos pasados, está bien exagerar sobre la experiencia que uno ya tiene.

B. Rafael tiene un jefe muy estricto. Cuando Rafael le pide las siguientes cosas, su jefe le dice que no. Con un(a) compañero(-a), hagan los papeles de Rafael y su jefe, el señor Blanco. Sigan el modelo. Usen tantas expresiones para pedir permiso como les sea posible.

MODELO   fumar aquí en la oficina (no me gusta que...)
¿Está bien que fume aquí en la oficina?
No, no me gusta que fume aquí en la oficina.

1. tomar tres semanas de vacaciones en julio (le pido que no...)
2. salir temprano mañana (no quiero que...)
3. pasar tres horas en el almuerzo del jueves (no está bien que...)
4. dejar este trabajo para la semana que viene (insisto en que no...)
5. llevar el auto de la compañía a la casa (se prohíbe)
6. cambiar el horario para llegar a las diez y salir a las cinco

C. ¿Qué están diciendo las siguientes personas? Use tantas expresiones para pedir, dar y negar (*deny*) permiso como le sea posible. Si quiere, use algunas de estas palabras: **cerrar, prestar su lápiz, pescar, abrir, fumar, sentarme aquí, sacar una foto, entrar.**

MODELO ¿Se puede sentar aquí?

MODELO

1.

2.

3.

4.

5.

6.

VOCABULARIO ACTIVO

Cognados

la agencia	el, la inca	el programador, la programadora
la edición	el petróleo	la siesta
la experiencia	peruano	el sistema
imaginar	la profesión	

Verbos

acabar	*to end, finish, run out*
caer	*to fall; to drop*
conseguir	*to obtain, get*
dejar	*to let, allow*

Profesiones y oficios

el abogado, la abogada	*lawyer*
el ama de casa (*f*)	*housewife*
el arqueólogo, la arqueóloga	*archeologist*
el bombero, la bombera	*fire fighter*
la carrera	*career*
el, la comerciante	*business person*
la compañía	*company*
el consejero, la consejera	*counselor*
el cura	*priest*
el hombre (la mujer) de negocios	*businessperson*
el jefe, la jefa	*boss*
el ingeniero, la ingeniera	*engineer*
el médico, la médica	*doctor*
el mesero, la mesera	*waiter, waitress*
el oficio	*job, trade*
el peluquero, la peluquera	*barber, beautician*
el sacerdote	*priest*

Otras palabras y frases

antiguo	*old, ancient; former*
el gobierno	*government*
la lengua	*language*
la peluquería	*barbershop, beauty parlor*
próximo	*next*
tinto	*red (wine)*

Expresiones útiles

Es dudoso.	*It's doubtful.*
Eso no se hace.	*That's not done (allowed).*
¿Le molestaría que... ?	*Would it bother you if . . . ?*
¡Ni hablar!	*Don't even mention it!*
No tengo la menor idea.	*I don't have the slightest idea.*
Puede (Podría) ser.	*It could be.*
Que yo sepa... (+ *ind*)	*As far as I know . . .*
Tengo mis dudas.	*I have my doubts.*

LECTURA IX

Hispanoamérica en el siglo veinte

Para comprender la situación actual° de Hispanoamérica, hay que tener en cuenta° que el vínculo° permanente que une° los países hispanos está más en su pasado común como colonias españolas que en los acontecimientos que ocurrieron después en cada una de estas naciones independientes. El imperio° español de las Américas—el imperio más grande de la historia— duró aproximadamente 350 años, desde 1492 hasta mediados° del siglo diecinueve. Simón Bolívar, el gran Libertador, después de echar° al último ejército español del continente suramericano, trató con poco éxito° de unificar los nuevos países bajo un gobierno federal.

Cuando los españoles se retiraron° del continente americano, dejaron como herencia° su idioma°, su cultura, su música y algunas instituciones sociopolíticas, pero no dejaron bases firmes para la democracia. Por todas partes° comenzaron luchas° internas, muchas veces originadas en los intereses de grupos particulares más que en el interés general. El caudillo, cabecilla de gente armada que imponía su voluntad,° era el seguro candidato a la presidencia de su país. Después vinieron los dictadores. Todos podemos nombrar a algunos de ellos: Rafael Trujillo de República Dominicana, «Tacho» Somoza de Nicaragua, Alfredo Stroessner de Paraguay y Augusto Pinochet de Chile. Actualmente, los dictadores o los caudillos más o menos encubiertos° están aliados° con el ejército; ellos usan esta institución del estado para imponer sus órdenes°.

current
tener... take into account/link / unites

empire
the middle
throwing out
success

withdrew
legacy/language

Por... Everywhere/struggles
cabecilla... the ringleader of an armed group that imposed his will
covered up, behind the scenes/allied

orders

Escena de la campaña electoral de Carlos Salinas de Gortari, candidato del Partido Revolucionario Institucional, 1987

Después de una revolución que duró unos diez años—entre 1910 y 1920—y muchas luchas internas, México es hoy día° una democracia. Los presidentes gobiernan° por un período de seis años y no pueden ser reelegidos°. Sin embargo°, un solo partido° domina el país y hay, aparentemente, mucha corrupción en el gobierno.

En 1938 el presidente Lázaro Cárdenas nacionalizó las compañías extranjeras° de petróleo. Los mexicanos consideran que esa fecha es el aniversario de la independencia económica de su país. PEMEX (Petróleos Mexicanos) tuvo gran éxito en los años 70. Sin embargo, debido a° la mala administración y a una crisis petrolera mundial,° la economía mexicana sufrió° mucho y hoy su deuda externa° es enorme.

hoy... today, nowadays
govern/reelected
Sin... However /
party

foreign

debido.. due to

worldwide/suffered *deuda...*
foreign debt

El presidente de
Costa Rica, Óscar
Arias Sánchez,
aceptando el Premio
Nóbel de la Paz, 1987

Desde hace unos años, en Centroamérica hay grandes problemas políticos y económicos. En El Salvador la guerra civil continúa, con un costo tremendo de vida humana. En Nicaragua, un grupo llamado los «sandinistas» derrocó° la dictadura de «Tacho» Somoza en 1979 y estableció un gobierno socialista. Pero desde un principio° Estados Unidos se opuso a° ese gobierno; apoyó a los «contras», grupo de gente que trata de derrocar a los sandinistas. En este momento es imposible predecir° qué pasará en Nicaragua o en El Salvador porque la situación cambia de un día a otro.

Los gobiernos de Guatemala, Panamá y Honduras son democracias nominales, que a veces funcionan como verdaderas democracias y otras veces no. En cambio°, el gobierno de Costa Rica es muy estable y democrático. Costa Rica tiene una asamblea° legislativa que es elegida° por el pueblo cada cuatro años. En 1987 el presidente de Costa Rica, Óscar Arias Sánchez, recibió el Premio Nóbel por sus esfuerzos° en llegar a un acuerdo pacífico° en Centroamérica. Según Arias, sólo habrá paz allí cuando todas las fuerzas° militares extranjeras se retiren del área. En Costa Rica no hay ejército; la Guardia Nacional funciona como un cuerpo de policía civil. Aunque algunos costarricenses piensan que esa institución es insuficiente para cuidar° las fronteras°, otros temen la presencia militar en su democracia. En Honduras,

debt

overthrew

desde... from
the very beginning/*se...*
opposed
to predict

En... On the
other hand
assembly/
elected

efforts/*acuerdo..*
peace agreement
forces, powers

guard

borders

Un desfile a favor del presidente de la Argentina, Raúl Alfonsín

donde la fuerza militar ha aumentado mucho en los años 80, también han aumentado drásticamente las violaciones a los derechos humanos.

Los cinco países andinos°—Venezuela, Colombia, Ecuador, Perú y Bolivia— tienen gobiernos democráticos, pero no son completamente estables debido a los grandes problemas económicos de la región. Como en Centroamérica, hay grupos de guerrilleros que quieren cambiar las estructuras básicas de sus países y darle más poder a la gente necesitada°. En Colombia y Perú especialmente ha habido mucha actividad guerrillera. Venezuela tiene el gobierno más estable de la región, pero también tiene problemas económicos.

En el Cono Sur°, hay graves problemas en Chile y Paraguay, ambos° países gobernados por dictadores crueles. En Chile, el general Augusto Pinochet no permite que haya libertad de prensa° ni oposición política. La misma situación existe en Paraguay, donde Alfredo Stroessner gobierna desde hace más de treinta años. Pero en Uruguay las cosas han cambiado. En 1984 los uruguayos derrocaron una dictadura militar y eligieron como presidente a Julio María Sanguinetti, volviendo así a su larga tradición democrática. Y un año antes, en 1983, Argentina también derrocó su gobierno militar y eligió a Raúl Alfonsín como presidente. Los argentinos tratan así de volver a la democracia después de 47 años de luchas, golpes de estado°, dictaduras militares y una situación económica desastrosa. Desgraciadamente°, Alfonsín no ha podido mejorar° la economía de Argentina ni resolver el problema de la deuda externa. En 1987 los peronistas (seguidores° del general Juan Perón, presidente argentino entre 1946 y 1955 y otra vez entre 1973 y 1974) nuevamente° empezaban a ganar popularidad.

No hay mucha esperanza° que se realice° pronto el sueño de Bolívar: la unificación de toda Hispanoamérica. Sin embargo, en los años 80 existe cierto optimismo. A pesar de una pésima° situación económica (con una tasa° de inflación muy alta y serios problemas con la deuda externa), parece que Latinoamérica sigue buscando el camino° hacia la democracia total, tanto política como económica y social.

Andean

needy, underprivileged

Cono... Southern Cone (of South America)/both
press

golpes... coups d'état
Unfortunately
improve
followers
once again

hope/*se...* will be realized

A... In spite of a
terrible/rate

road, way

¿Verdadero or falso?

1. El imperio romano fue el más grande de la historia; duró 350 años.
2. Un caudillo siempre representaba los intereses del pueblo en general, no de grupos particulares.
3. «Tacho» Somoza fue un gran presidente de Nicaragua, elegido por su pueblo democráticamente.
4. PEMEX quiere decir Petróleos Mexicanos.
5. Los países andinos son Perú, Colombia, Venezuela, Panamá y Costa Rica.
6. Los peronistas son los seguidores de Juan Perón.

PREGUNTAS

1. ¿Qué hay que tener en cuenta para comprender la situación actual de Hispanoamérica?   2. ¿Cuál fue el sueño de Simón Bolívar? ¿Se realizó ese sueño?   3. ¿Qué dejaron los españoles cuando se retiraron del continente americano?   4. ¿Puede nombrar a algunos dictadores hispanoamericanos de este siglo?   5. ¿Qué ocurrió en México entre 1910 y 1920? ¿y en 1938?   6. ¿En qué países centroamericanos hay mucha violencia hoy día?   7. ¿Quiénes son los sandinistas? ¿Qué gobierno derrocaron?   8. ¿Cómo es el gobierno de Costa Rica? Según Óscar Arias, ¿qué es necesario para que haya paz en Centroamérica?   9. ¿Por qué hay mucha actividad guerrillera en Colombia y en Perú?   10. ¿Cuáles son los países del Cono Sur? ¿Cuáles tienen dictaduras? ¿y cuáles no?   11. ¿Qué pasó en Uruguay en 1984? ¿y en Argentina en 1983?

Casas fuera de Cuenca,
Ecuador

EN CASA

Vocabulario. In this chapter you will talk about housing.

Gramática. You will discuss and use:
1. Additional uses of the definite article
2. Omission of the indefinite article
3. The neuter article **lo**
4. The passive voice (*for recognition only*)

Cultura. The dialogues take place in Ecuador.

Funciones

- Adding information
- Changing the subject
- Expressing empathy

¿DÓNDE VIVE USTED?

1. el edificio de apartamentos
2. la casa
3. el jardín
4. el garaje

Los cuartos *(rooms)* de un apartamento

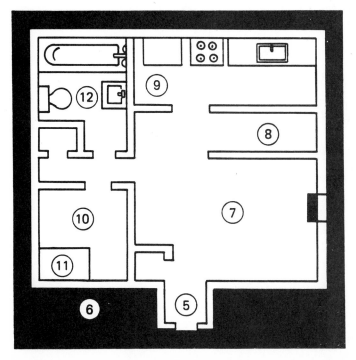

5. la entrada
6. el pasillo
7. la sala (de estar)
8. el comedor
9. la cocina
10. el dormitorio, la alcoba
11. el ropero
12. el cuarto de baño, el baño

El baño y la cocina

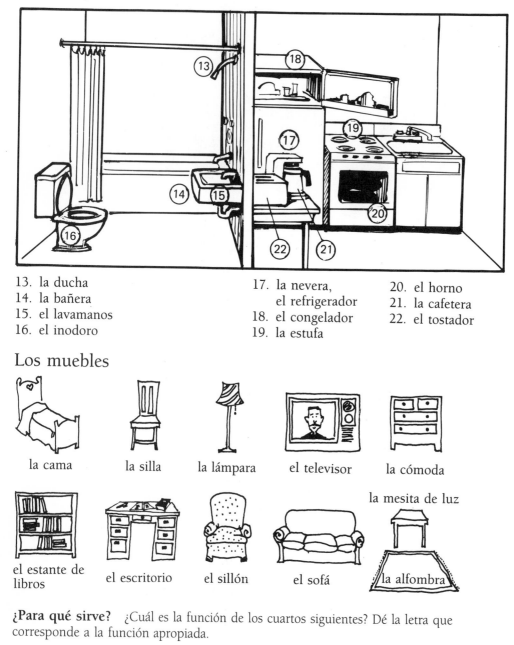

13. la ducha
14. la bañera
15. el lavamanos
16. el inodoro

17. la nevera,
    el refrigerador
18. el congelador
19. la estufa

20. el horno
21. la cafetera
22. el tostador

Los muebles

la cama

la silla

la lámpara

el televisor

la cómoda

el estante de libros

el escritorio

el sillón

el sofá

la mesita de luz

la alfombra

¿Para qué sirve? ¿Cuál es la función de los cuartos siguientes? Dé la letra que corresponde a la función apropiada.

1. el dormitorio
2. el comedor
3. la cocina
4. la sala
5. el baño

a. cocinar
b. dormir
c. bañarse, lavarse
d. comer
e. mirar televisión, leer

En construcción.   Usted está construyendo una casa. Escoja las cosas apropiadas para cada cuarto.

1. En la sala de estar hay (el tostador, la mesita de luz, la cómoda, el sillón, el sofá).
2. En el cuarto de baño hay (la ducha, el refrigerador, la bañera, el lavamanos, el tostador).
3. En la cocina hay (la lámpara, la estufa, el horno, el congelador, la cama).
4. En el dormitorio hay (el inodoro, la cama, la cómoda, la ducha, la estufa).

Preguntas

1. Usted acaba de comprar la casa y los muebles que vemos en estas dos páginas. ¿Dónde pondría usted el sofá? ¿la cama? ¿el sillón? ¿la mesita de luz? ¿el televisor? ¿el estante de libros? ¿el escritorio?   2. ¿Qué muebles pondría usted en el comedor? ¿en la sala?   3. ¿Qué muebles no usaría usted en el dormitorio? 4. ¿Adónde iría usted para tomar sol? ¿para jugar a los naipes? ¿para preparar la comida?   5. ¿Dónde pondría usted el auto? ¿el tostador? ¿y la cafetera? 6. Describa la casa de sus padres. ¿Qué muebles hay en la sala? ¿en el comedor? ¿en los dormitorios? ¿Cuántos dormitorios hay? ¿y baños? ¿Tiene jardín la casa? ¿y patio? ¿y garage?

I. Usos adicionales del artículo definido

Una casa en
construcción

En casa de Josefina y Ramón, en Quito

JOSEFINA ¿Qué tal tu insomnio, mi amor? ¿Te sigue doliendo *la cabeza?°*

RAMÓN Sí, bastante. Esta mañana fui a la médica. Me dio unas píldoras. ¡Tuve que esperar casi una hora! Por suerte° hay sillas cómodas en la sala de espera...° Después, por la tarde, fui al doctor Sabelotodo, el experto en *las* causas psicológicas del insomnio.

JOSEFINA ¿Y qué te dijo él?

RAMÓN Pues... que a menos que agrandemos° la casa...

JOSEFINA Hablando de casas, ¿sabes quién fue el primer presidente que vivió en la Casa Blanca?

RAMÓN ¡No cambies de tema!° El doctor Sabelotodo me dijo que en mi caso *los* dolores de cabeza y *la* tensión probablemente están relacionados con el arreglo° de la casa... Necesito un lugar tranquilo para descansar y meditar... porque, según él, *la* tensión es la causa principal del insomnio. Además, me dijo que sería ideal tener una bicicleta de ejercicios.

JOSEFINA Esa idea sí me parece razonable. ¡Y qué coincidencia! La semana próxima hay una gran oferta en «La casa de *las* bicicletas». Tienen muy buenas bicicletas de ejercicios y las venden a 10.000 sucres *el* par°. ¡Deberíamos comprar dos! A propósito,° ¿cómo recomienda el doctor Sabelotodo que paguemos la construcción de ese cuarto adicional?

RAMÓN Pues...según el doctor Sabelotodo, su hermano acaba de comprar una compañía de construcción... .

¿Te sigue... ? *Does your head still hurt?*   Por suerte *Luckily*   sala de espera *waiting room*   agrandemos *we enlarge*   ¡No ...tema! *Don't change the subject!*   arreglo *fixing*   el par *a pair*   A propósito *By the way*

---

1. ¿Qué problema tiene Ramón?   2. ¿En qué es experto el doctor Sabelotodo? 3. ¿Por qué recomienda él que agranden la casa?   4. Según él, ¿cuál es la causa principal del insomnio?   5. A Josefina, ¿qué idea del doctor le parece razonable? 6. En su casa, ¿hay algún lugar tranquilo para descansar? ¿para hacer ejercicios físicos? ¿para leer? ¿para estudiar?   7. Sus padres, ¿han agrandado alguna vez su casa? ¿Sabe usted si piensan agrandarla? Según usted, ¿necesitan algún cuarto adicional? ¿otro baño? ¿una sala más grande?

Spanish and English differ in minor ways in their use of the definite article. Several of these differences have already been noted, such as the use of the article with titles (**la doctora Arias...** Chapter 1), with certain country names (**el Ecuador...** Chapter 2), and with dates and days of the week (**el lunes...** Chapter 4). Here are several other ways that Spanish speakers use the definite article.

A. With parts of the body, personal effects, and articles of clothing, when it is clear who the possessor is. The possessive adjective is not used in these instances.

La médica se lava las manos en el lavamanos.	The doctor washes her hands in the sink.
Ricardo se quitó el abrigo en el pasillo.	Ricardo took off his coat in the hall.

B. Before a noun used in a general sense as representative of its class or type. The noun can be singular or plural, concrete or abstract.

Me gustan más las casas viejas que las modernas.	I like old houses better than modern ones.
La tensión es la causa principal del insomnio.	Tension is the main cause of insomnia.

But when the reference is to only part of the general class or type, the definite article is not used. Compare the following sentences.

Las sillas importadas cuestan más.	Imported chairs cost more.
Venden sillas importadas en esa mueblería.	They sell imported chairs in that furniture store.

C. With names of languages or fields of study, except after **en** and after **hablar, escribir, enseñar, estudiar, aprender,** and **leer,** when it is usually omitted.

Aprendo japonés. El japonés es una lengua muy difícil.	I'm learning Japanese. Japanese is a very difficult language.
Me gustan las ciencias en general.	I like sciences in general.
¿Cómo se dice «buen provecho» en francés? «Bon appétit.»	How do you say "Enjoy the meal" in French? «Bon appétit.»

D. For rates and prices.

Compré un vino excelente a 2.000 sucres el litro.*	I bought an excellent wine for 2,000 sucres a liter.
¿Ese queso cuesta 1.000 sucres el kilo?—No tengo la menor idea.	Does that cheese cost 1,000 sucres a kilo?—I don't have the slightest idea.

E. Before each noun in a series.

No funcionan ni la ducha, ni el inodoro, ni el grifo del lavamanos. ¡Y éste es un baño nuevo!	Neither the shower, nor the toilet, nor the faucet of the sink is working. And this is a new bathroom!

F. With the preposition **a** + *a time expression* to mean *per.*

Pagamos el alquiler una vez al mes y los impuestos federales una vez al año.	We pay the rent once per month and federal taxes once per year.

*In September, 1988, the exchange rate was 525 **sucres** per dollar.

EJERCICIOS

A. ¿Qué se puso Gloria?   Gloria estaba preparándose para salir… Le llevó tiempo terminar de vestirse porque había dejado la ropa por toda la casa. Diga qué ropa se puso y dónde.

> **MODELO**   blusa blanca / el dormitorio de sus padres
> **Se puso la blusa blanca en el dormitorio de sus padres**.

1. la falda nueva / el dormitorio de su hermana
2. las medias / el baño
3. el suéter / la sala
4. el impermeable / el comedor
5. las botas de lluvia / el garaje

B. Los gustos de Luisa (*Luisa's tastes*).   Luisa le describe a su novio Raúl las cosas que a ella no le gustan. Haga el papel de Luisa y describa sus gustos siguiendo el modelo.

> **MODELO**   casas viejas
> **No me gustan las casas viejas**.

1. roperos pequeños
2. alfombra violeta de la mamá de Raúl
3. hornos sin luz
4. cafeteras automáticas
5. lámparas de Raúl
6. inodoros que no funcionan bien
7. cocinas que no son modernas
8. comedor de la abuela de Raúl
9. lavamanos blancos

C. Completar las frases.   Complete las frases que siguen, usando el artículo definido cuando sea necesario.

1. Teresa abre _____ ojos.
2. Horacio lleva el pasaporte en _____ mano.
3. Miguel se ponía _____ abrigo en la sala.
4. Ana se quitó _____ zapatos en la cocina.
5. Me dolía _____ cabeza cuando escuchaba esa música.
6. « _____ tiempo es oro.»
7. A Jaime no le gustan _____ apartamentos pequeños.
8. Compré un buen vino chileno a 400 sucres _____ litro.
9. _____ español es una lengua muy práctica.
10. ¿Habla usted _____ alemán?
11. Aquí venden las manzanas a 100 sucres _____ kilo.

Preguntas

1. ¿Qué clase de comida le gusta más? ¿Y qué clase de comida le gusta menos?
2. Según su opinión, ¿cuáles son las lenguas más importantes? ¿Por qué?
3. Cuando usted se despierta por la mañana, ¿abre los ojos fácilmente o con mucha dificultad?   4. Cuando está nervioso(-a), ¿le duele la cabeza? ¿y el estómago? ¿y la espalda? ¿Qué toma o hace usted entonces?   5. Cuando camina o corre mucho, ¿le duelen los pies? ¿y las piernas? ¿y el cuello?   6. En estos días, ¿cuánto cuesta la gasolina? ¿Y cuánto cuestan las naranjas?   7. ¿Qué ropa se pone usted cuando

hace frío? ¿cuando hace calor? ¿cuando llueve?   8. ¿Le interesa el arte? ¿la política? ¿la literatura?   9. ¿Le gustaría agrandar su casa? ¿Qué cuartos adicionales le gustaría tener? ¿Por qué o para qué?

II. La supresión del artículo indefinido

Un almacén ecuatoriano

En casa de la familia Ruiz

ELENA   Carmen, ven acá.

CARMEN   Sí, mamá. ¿Qué quieres?

ELENA   ¿Me haces *otro* favor? Ve a la panadería y cómprame *media* docena° de huevos. Voy a hacer unas galletitas.

CARMEN   Sí, mamá, voy en seguida°. Me gustaría ver a Ricardo. ¿Sabías que está trabajando en la panadería?

ELENA   ¿Ricardo...panadero°? ¿No me habías dicho que iba a *ser abogado*?

CARMEN   Sí, ¡y va a ser el mejor abogado de Quito! Sólo dije que trabaja en la panadería; no que era *panadero*. El dinero que gana le sirve para pagar el alquiler del apartamento en que vive...

ELENA   ...y para comprarle regalos a *cierta*° muchacha que conozco, ¿no?

---

media docena *half a dozen*   en seguida *right away*   panadero *baker*   cierta *a certain*

---

1. ¿Qué favor le pide Elena a Carmen?   2. ¿A quién quiere ver Carmen en la panadería?   3. ¿Cuándo trabaja Ricardo en la panadería?   4. ¿Dónde vive Ricardo?   5. ¿Va usted a veces a una panadería? ¿Qué compra?   7. ¿Hay algún(a) panadero(-a) en su familia? ¿entre sus amigos? ¿los amigos de sus padres? ¿sus vecinos (*neighbors*)?

Spanish speakers omit the indefinite article in many situations where English speakers use *a* or *an*.

A. Remember that following the verb **ser,** the indefinite article is omitted before an unmodified noun that indicates profession, religion, nationality, or political affiliation.

Juan es {
atleta.
católico.
socialista.
ecuatoriano.
}

Juan is {
an athlete.
a Catholic.
a socialist.
en Ecuadoran.
}

Es un {
buen atleta.
católico devoto.
socialista práctico.
ecuatoriano patriótico.
}

He is a {
good athlete.
devout Catholic.
practical socialist.
patriotic Ecuadoran.
}

B. The indefinite article is not used before words such as **medio, otro,** and **cierto.** The latter agree in gender and number with the nouns they modify.

Hay media docena de huevos en el refrigerador.	There are half a dozen eggs in the refrigerator.
Claudia compró otra mesita de luz.	Claudia bought another end table.
Cierto poeta dijo eso.	A certain poet said that.

C. The indefinite article is usually omitted after **de** meaning *as,* and in negative expressions with **tener.**

Raúl trabaja de agente de viajes.	Raúl works as a travel agent.
Ellos no tienen auto.	They don't have a car.

D. The indefinite article is also omitted in exclamations using **¡Qué...!** + *noun.*

¡Qué casa más linda!	What a pretty house!
¡Qué estufa más moderna!	What a modern stove!
¡Qué lástima!	What a shame!

EJERCICIOS

A. ¿Qué, quiénes son? Haga oraciones usando las siguientes palabras. Siga el modelo, haciendo los cambios que sean necesarios.

MODELO   esa señora / argentino   **Esa señora es argentina.**

1. mis amigos / protestante
2. Juan y José / pintor
3. Ana / doctor
4. nosotros / socialista
5. los Pérez / cubano
6. tú / norteamericano
7. Miriam / judío
8. Jorge Andrade / poeta

B. Asociaciones. ¿Qué profesiones, intereses políticos y nacionalidades asocia usted con las personas abajo *(below)* mencionadas?

> **MODELO** Karl Marx **Karl Marx fue escritor, filósofo, comunista, y alemán.**

1. Pablo Picasso
2. el Rey Juan Carlos
3. Albert Einstein
4. Miguel de Cervantes
5. Gabriela Mistral
6. Pablo Neruda
7. Teresa de Jesús
8. El Greco
9. Sor Juana Inés de la Cruz
10. Pancho Villa

C. Cualidades y características. Ahora diga usted una característica o cualidad de las personas mencionadas en el ejercicio B.

> **MODELO** Pablo Picasso **Pablo Picasso fue un pintor famoso.**

Preguntas

1. ¿Qué profesión tiene su padre? ¿su madre? ¿Qué profesión quiere tener usted?
2. ¿Es usted demócrata? ¿republicano(-a)? ¿independiente? ¿y sus padres?
3. ¿Puede usted nombrar *(name)* a un(a) socialista o comunista fanático(-a)? ¿a un(a) católico(-a) devoto(-a)? ¿a un(a) protestante famoso(-a)? ¿a un(a) judío(-a) intelectual? ¿a un futbolista latinoamericano? ¿a un(a) atleta muy rico (-a)? 4. ¿Cuánto cuesta media docena de galletitas en la panadería de su ciudad? ¿Y cuánto cuesta media docena de huevos? 5. ¿Ha trabajado usted alguna vez de panadero(-a)? ¿de pintor(a)?

III. El artículo neutro *lo*

Cotopaxi, volcán de los Andes del Ecuador

Los señores Fuentes buscan un nuevo sofá en una pequeña mueblería.

SRA. FUENTES	No es exactamente *lo* que teníamos en mente° pero sí es un sofá lindo.
VENDEDOR	Sí, señora, y es de muy buena calidad°.
SR. FUENTES	Pero...*lo* malo de este sofá es el color.
SRA. FUENTES	Por el contrario,° querido° ...Para mí, *lo* bueno de este mueble es que hace juego con la alfombra y el sillón que tenemos.
SR. FUENTES	¡Pero son horribles! Creo que *lo* peor de nuestros muebles y de esa alfombra...¡es el color!
SRA. FUENTES	Pues...querido, el verde es mi color favorito y *lo* bueno del verde es...
VENDEDOR	¿Querrían ver muebles de otros colores? También renovamos° muebles. Es fácil cambiar el color de un sillón, *lo* que aparentemente le gustaría muchísimo al señor... Y además vendemos alfombras de buena calidad y de muchos colores. En esta mueblería hacemos todo *lo* posible para dar gusto° a los clientes.
SRA. FUENTES	¡Y también todo *lo* posible para que gasten todo *lo* que tienen!

---

teníamos en mente   *we had in mind*   calidad   *quality*   Por el contrario   *On the contrary*
querido   *dear*   renovamos   *we renovate*   dar gusto   *to please*

---

1. ¿Qué es lo malo del sofá, según el señor Fuentes?   2. ¿Qué es lo bueno del sofá, según la señora Fuentes?   3. ¿Cuál es el color favorito de ella?   4. ¿Venden alfombras en la mueblería?   5. ¿Le gusta a usted ir de compras en una mueblería? ¿Por qué?   6. ¿Hay algún color que le guste especialmente para los muebles de su cuarto? ¿y algún color que no le guste?   7. ¿Hacen juego los muebles de su cuarto en la residencia universitaria? ¿en su apartamento o casa?

A. The neuter article **lo** can be used with the masculine form of an adjective to express an abstract quality or idea.

Lo bueno de vivir aquí es la seguridad.	The good part about living here is the security.
Haremos lo posible.	We'll do what's possible (whatever we can).

If the adjective phrase refers to a specific person or thing whose gender is known, **el, la, los,** or **las** must be used instead of **lo.**

Este apartamento es el más grande del edificio.	This apartment is the largest in the building.
El más chiquito está en la planta baja.	The smallest is on the ground floor.

B. **Lo** can replace an adjective or refer to a whole idea previously stated.

¿Es demasiado cara la casa? Sí, lo es.	Is the house too expensive? Yes, it is.

¿Eres dueño de casa? No, no lo
 soy. Soy estudiante.

*Are you a homeowner? No, I'm not.
 I'm a student.*

c. **Lo que** can be used to express something imprecise or to sum up a preceding idea, but it must precede a conjugated verb.

Nuestra vecina pudo arreglar el grifo,
 lo que nos alegró mucho.

*Our neighbor was able to fix the
 faucet, which pleased us a lot.*

EJERCICIOS

A. Lo bueno y lo malo. Diga lo que es bueno y lo que es malo para cada una de las siguientes cosas. Siga el modelo.

> **MODELO** el verano **Lo bueno del verano es el calor.**
> **Lo malo del verano son los insectos.**

1. la casa o el apartamento de usted
2. los apartamentos de su ciudad
3. el estilo de las casas de su ciudad
4. el cuarto de baño de su residencia universitaria o de su casa o apartamento
5. las calles viejas
6. la arquitectura de su ciudad
7. el clima de su ciudad
8. las habitaciones de su residencia universitaria o de su casa o apartamento
9. la clase de español
10. los muebles de su cuarto

B. ¿Le gusta o no le gusta? Exprese su opinión sobre las siguientes personas y cosas.

> **MODELO** hacer / el presidente
> **(No) me gusta lo que hace el presidente.**

1. pasar / en el mundo
2. yo / ver / en la televisión
3. comprarme / mi novio(-a)
4. servirse / en la cafetería
5. enseñar / los profesores
6. yo / leer / en el periódico

C. Traducción. Exprese en español.

1. The good part about living in the city is that there are many cultural activities.
2. The bad thing about driving in the city is the traffic.
3. The best part about my house is the large living room.
4. Our friend is able to fix the television set, which pleases us very much.
5. What I want is for you to sit down on the sofa and enjoy yourself at the party.

Preguntas

1. ¿Qué es lo más interesante de la vida universitaria? ¿lo más aburrido? ¿lo más divertido? 2. ¿Qué es lo mejor de su vida? ¿y lo peor? 3. ¿Qué es lo que más

le gusta a usted de su familia? ¿y de su casa?   4. ¿Qué es lo que le gusta del presidente? ¿Qué es lo que no le gusta de él?   5. ¿Qué es lo interesante de esta ciudad? ¿y de la ciudad donde usted vive?   6. ¿Qué es lo mejor de la ciudad? ¿lo peor?   7. ¿Qué es lo mejor de la vida en el campo? ¿lo peor?   8. ¿Sabe usted lo que está pasando en Nicaragua? ¿en el Ecuador? ¿en este país? ¿en esta universidad?

IV. La voz pasiva

La Catedral de Quito en la Plaza de la Independencia

Querida Inés:

Desde hace dos días estoy aquí en Quito, la capital del Ecuador. Creo que me quedaré unos diez días más antes de volver a casa. Esta capital histórica y bonita *fue fundada*° en 1534. Hay jardines y pequeñas plazas por todas partes. La ciudad tiene magníficos edificios que *fueron construidos* por los españoles en el siglo XVI. Ahora tiene más de un millón de habitantes°. Hoy visité la Catedral donde está enterrado° Antonio José de Sucre, el héroe nacional de este país. También fui al Palacio Nacional. Hace varios siglos que ese palacio es el centro del gobierno ecuatoriano. Mañana iré a la Universidad Central que tiene muchos edificios modernos. Esa Universidad Central tiene sus orígenes en un seminario° que *fue fundado* en 1594. También visitaré el monumento que marca la línea ecuatorial. ¡Allí es posible tener un pie en el hemisferio norte y otro en el sur...!* ¿Qué te parece? ¡Todo esto es de lo más fascinante°!

Bueno..., como te darás cuenta,° ¡me encanta Ecuador! Te llamaré en cuanto llegue a Boston, ¿OK?

Cariños,°
Eugenia

*See Cultural note 1, page 495.

fue fundada *was founded*   habitantes *inhabitants*   está enterrado *is buried*
seminario *seminary*   de...fascinante *most fascinating*   te darás cuenta *you probably can*
tell   Cariños *Affectionately*

¿Verdadero o falso?

1. La ciudad de Quito fue fundada en 1534.
2. Antonio José de Sucre fue un conquistador español.
3. La Universidad Central tiene muchos edificios de estilo colonial.
4. En Ecuador, hay un monumento que marca la línea ecuatorial.
5. Eugenia volverá a Boston el año que viene.

A. In Spanish, as well as in English, sentences can be in either the active or the passive voice. In an active construction, the subject performs the action of the verb. In a passive construction, the subject is acted upon. Compare the following sentences. The subjects are shown in bold type.

Active voice:

Los incas construyeron la ciudad de Cuzco.	*The Incas built the city of Cuzco.*
(Ellos) hicieron esos muebles en México.	*They made those pieces of furniture in Mexico.*

Passive voice:

La ciudad de Cuzco fue construida por los incas.	*The city of Cuzco was built by the Incas.*
Esos muebles fueron hechos en México.	*Those pieces of furniture were made in Mexico.*

B. The passive voice in Spanish consists of a form of **ser** plus a past participle. The past participle behaves like an adjective, changing its ending to agree in gender and number with the subject. When the agent (the "doer" of the action) is mentioned, it is generally introduced by the preposition **por.**

subject	+	**ser**	+	*past participle*	+	**por**	+	*agent*
La ciudad		fue		construida		por		los incas.

Las papas fueron descubiertas en América.	*Potatoes were discovered in America.*
A propósito, ¿sabías que los muros fueron pintados por los chicos?	*By the way, did you know that the walls were painted by the boys?*
La novela *Nada* fue escrita por Carmen Laforet.	*The novel* Nada *was written by Carmen Laforet.*

C. To express the state or condition resulting from an action, a form of **estar** is used; the past participle functions as an adjective, changing its ending to agree in gender and number with the subject. No agent is ever expressed. (This structure contrasts with the passive voice, which focuses on the action itself.) Study the following pairs of sentences.

La casa fue renovada por mi primo.	*The house was renovated by my cousin.*
La casa está renovada.	*The house is renovated.*
El garaje fue construido por un vecino que es carpintero.	*The garage was built by a neighbor who is a carpenter.*
El garaje ya está construido.	*The garage is already built.*

D. The passive voice is used less frequently in Spanish than in English. When no agent is expressed, **se** plus a verb in the third person is generally used instead. The verb is singular or plural to agree with its grammatical subject.

Se habla español.	*Spanish is spoken.*
Se necesita carpintero.	*A carpenter is needed.*
Se necesitan muchos materiales para reparar la casa.	*Many materials are needed to repair the house.*

You don't need to use the passive voice now, but the following exercises will help you learn to recognize and understand it.

EJERCICIOS

A. Infórmese sobre Ecuador. Escoja la forma apropiada del verbo para completar la frase.

1. La línea ecuatorial _____ por algunos científicos franceses en 1735.
   a. estuvo marcada   b. fue marcada
2. El Ecuador _____ al noroeste del Perú y al sur de Colombia.
   a. fue situado   b. está situado
3. Las regiones de Ecuador y Perú _____ por Francisco Pizarro.
   a. fueron conquistadas   b. estuvieron conquistadas
4. El rey inca Atahualpa y muchos otros indios _____ por los españoles.
   a. estuvieron matados   b. fueron matados
5. Las Islas Galápagos, al oeste del Ecuador, _____ por Charles Darwin en 1835.
   a. fueron visitadas   b. estuvieron visitadas
6. La ciudad de Guayaquil _____ en la costa del Ecuador.
   a. está situada   b. fue situada
7. Muchos objetos de arte indio _____ en Ecuador.
   a. están hechos   b. son hechos

B. ¿Por quién? Diga quién (o quiénes) hizo (hicieron) las acciones descritas en las siguientes frases.

MODELO La mesa fue reparada por el carpintero. **El carpintero**

1. El poema fue escrito por Jorge Andrade, un famoso poeta ecuatoriano.
2. Los edificios fueron renovados por un grupo de hombres norteamericanos.
3. Yo fui invitada a una fiesta por mi amiga que tiene una casa nueva.
4. La puerta rota del garaje fue abierta por un muchacho fuerte.
5. Muchas iglesias de Quito fueron construidas por los españoles en el siglo XVI.

C. Dicho de otra manera. Para cambiar las frases de la forma pasiva (en bastardilla) a la construcción con *se*, marque con un círculo la letra del verbo apropiado.

MODELO Hoy día muchas novelas en español *son traducidas* al inglés.
  Hoy día _____ al inglés muchas novelas en español.
  a. se traduce
  ⓑ. se traducen
  c. se tradujeron

1. La vista desde el balcón siempre *ha sido muy admirada.*
   a. se ha admirado mucho   b. se admiran mucho   c. será muy admirada
2. Ese museo *será visitado* todos los días.
   a. se había visitado   b. se visitará   c. se visita
3. Aquellos edificios *fueron construidos* antes de 1850.
   a. se construyeron   b. se construían   c. se construyen
4. Los muebles *serían comprados* en Ecuador.
   a. se comprarán   b. se han comprado   c. se comprarían
5. Esas casas *fueron vendidas* el año pasado.
   a. se vendieron   b. se venderán   c. se venderían

D. ¿Cuál es la mejor traducción? Escoja *a* o *b* para indicar la mejor traducción de las frases en bastardilla que siguen.

1. Large closets *are being built* in the new houses.
   a. están construidos   b. se construyen
2. The entry to our apartment building *will be renovated* next year.
   a. se renovará   b. estará renovada
3. The coffeepot *was broken* by one of the neighbor's children.
   a. estuvo rota   b. fue rota
4. The freezer *is repaired* now, but it wasn't working for two days.
   a. es reparado   b. está reparado
5. *Was* the oven *opened* by someone a few minutes ago?
   a. fue abierto   b. estuvo abierto
6. Those houses *will be enlarged* by January.
   a. estarán agrandadas   b. se agrandarán

QUITO: LA CIUDAD DE LA ETERNA PRIMAVERA

Una linda plaza colonial en Quito

En el restaurante del Hotel Colón, en Quito

LAURA Así que piensan mudarse a Quito.[1] ¡Deben estar muy contentos! Pero, ¿cuándo... ?

PEDRO Pues, nos gustaría estar aquí para Año Nuevo. Yo me jubilo° el mes próximo, ¡por fin! Por ahora, buscamos casa... Lo malo es la inseguridad de no saber dónde vamos a vivir.

LUIS Realmente lo que me sorprende es que ya puedas jubilarte. ¿No eres muy joven para eso? Tienes un aspecto bastante juvenil° y cierto aire de juventud° y energía...

ESTELA «Las apariencias engañan».° ¡Ya hace treinta años que Pedro trabaja para la misma compañía! Para nosotros, lo difícil será dejar Guayaquil[2] después de vivir tantos años allá. La compañía fue fundada por amigos del padre de Pedro, ¿lo sabían?

LUIS No lo sabíamos... Pero lo lindo, lo positivo, lo interesante de la vida en Quito es que aquí siempre hace un tiempo magnífico, ¿no?

LAURA Así es. Por algo llaman a Quito «la ciudad de la eterna primavera», ¿no? Estoy segura de que la vida aquí les gustará muchísimo. Lo bueno de vivir en la capital es que hay muchas actividades culturales, ¡y la ciudad ha sido construida con jardines y pequeñas plazas encantadoras°! Será un cambio muy beneficioso°.

PEDRO Eso espero. El ambiente° será bastante diferente al que estamos acostumbrados. Muchos edificios de Guayaquil fueron elevados° en los últimos diez años. Parece que se construyen nuevos edificios cada semana. Lo peor de la vida allá es el tráfico, ...y además hace bastante calor.

LAURA Cambiando de tema, ¿arreglaron lo de la habitación que no les gustaba?

PEDRO No. Pedí una habitación doble, con dos camas, pero no me la pudieron dar.

LAURA ¿Y por qué no se quedan con nosotros?

LUIS ¡Buena idea! Tenemos un dormitorio para huéspedes°, con baño, dos camas y una sala pequeña con sofá y sillones.

ESTELA   Es que no nos gustaría molestar...

LAURA   ¡Por favor! Esa habitación les va a gustar y la pueden usar por el tiempo que quieran. ¿Aceptan?

PEDRO   Bueno, si no les causaremos problemas. Estela, ¿qué opinas?

ESTELA   ¡Por supuesto que sí! Y un millón de gracias. Sé que con ustedes estaremos cien veces° mejor que en el hotel.

---

me jubilo *I'm retiring*   juvenil *youthful*   juventud *youth*   «Las apariencias engañan» *Appearances are deceiving*   encantadoras *enchanting*   un cambio muy beneficioso *a very beneficial change*   ambiente *environment*   fueron elevados *were built, "put up"* huéspedes *guests*   cien veces *one hundred times*

¿Cuál es la respuesta correcta?

1. ¿Cuándo se jubila Pedro?
   a. el año próximo   b. el mes próximo
2. ¿Qué es lo malo de mudarse?
   a. la inseguridad   b. la contaminación
3. ¿Cuántos años hace que Pedro trabaja para la misma compañía?
   a. 20 años   b. 30 años
4. ¿Qué es lo bueno de vivir en la capital?
   a. Siempre hace un tiempo magnífico allá.   b. La capital está situada cerca del océano.
5. ¿Qué es lo peor de la vida en Guayaquil?
   a. los edificios nuevos   b. el tráfico
6. ¿Por qué no les gusta la habitación en el hotel a Pedro y a Estela?
   a. No tiene vista del mar.   b. No es una habitación doble.
7. Describa el dormitorio para huéspedes que tienen Laura y Luis.
   a. Tiene baño y una sala pequeña.   b. Tiene dos baños y dos camas.

NOTAS CULTURALES

1. Quito, the capital city of Ecuador (elevation 9,500 feet), has been aptly called "a great outdoor museum" because of its numerous buildings in the ornate Spanish colonial style. The city was founded in 1534 on the site of the capital city of the pre-Inca kingdom of the Scyris, which had fallen to the Incas shortly before the arrival of the Spaniards. There is little seasonal variation of temperature, because the city is so close to the equator. In fact, the monument marking the equator is located about 15 miles north of Quito. There visitors enjoy crossing the equator several times and standing with one foot in the Southern Hemisphere and the other in the Northern.

2. Guayaquil and Quito strongly dominate the life of Ecuador. Quito, the government center, located high in the Andes, has a cool climate and outstanding colonial architecture. Guayaquil, with a tropical climate, is a fast-growing modern port and the banking center of the country. Over 85 percent of Ecuador's trade passes through Guayaquil.

Funciones y actividades

In this chapter, you have seen examples of some important language functions, or uses. Here is a summary and some additional information about these functions of language.

ADDING INFORMATION

Además...	*In addition (Furthermore)*	También...	*Also . . .*

CHANGING THE SUBJECT

A propósito...	*By the way . . .*
Cambiando de tema...	*To change the subject . . .*
En cambio...	*On the other hand . . .*
Entre paréntesis...	*Incidentally . . . (By the way . . .)*
Por el contrario...	*On the contrary . . .*
Sin embargo...	*However . . .*

EXPRESSING EMPATHY

One of the most common language functions is expressing empathy, indicating that you understand what someone is feeling or thinking. Here are some ways to express empathy.

¡Estará(s) muy contento(-a)!	*You must be very happy!*
Debe(s) estar muy desilusionado(-a) (muy contento (-a)).	*You must be very disappointed (happy).*
Se (Te) sentirá(s) muy orgulloso(-a).	*You must feel very proud.*

You might review the expressions of emotion from the **Vocabulario activo** of Chapter 16 for other words used in expressing empathy.

Ahora haga las siguientes actividades, usando las expresiones que acaba de aprender.

A. Además...　¿Cuánto recuerda usted de lo que ha aprendido en este libro? Trabaje con un(a) compañero(-a) de clase. Uno(-a) de ustedes lee la información que sigue. El otro (La otra) da más información. Forme una frase con **además**.

> **MODELO**　El Museo del Prado está en Madrid. Allí se ven muchísimos cuadros famosos.
> **Además es posible ver *Las Meninas*, uno de los cuadros más famosos del mundo. Fue pintado por Diego Velázquez.**

1. La famosa Pirámide del Sol está cerca de la Ciudad de México. Ningún europeo la había visto hasta el siglo XVI.

2. Un acueducto impresionante está en Segovia. Todavía se lo usa para llevar agua a la ciudad.

3. Una novela muy importante se publicó en 1605. El título completo es *El ingenioso hidalgo Don Quijote de la Mancha.*

4. La famosa mezquita de Córdoba está en el sur de España. Se lo construyó en el siglo VIII.

5. Se baila la sardana en Cataluña. Es un baile folklórico.

6. Los payadores (*folksingers*) de la Argentina y del Uruguay cantan melodías tristes.

B. Cambiando de tema. Trabaje con un(a) compañero(-a) de clase. Hagan los papeles de Ramón y Cecilia. Ellos van a comprar una nueva casa. Cecilia quiere decorar la casa con muebles antiguos de estilo colonial, pero Ramón prefiere el estilo moderno. Cecilia describe los muebles que prefiere, y Ramón trata de hablar de otra cosa.

C. Reacciones. Dé una reacción para cada una de las siguientes situaciones. Use la forma de **tú**.

MODELO La esposa de un amigo está en el hospital ahora mismo. Va a tener un bebé. Su amigo lo (la) llama del hospital para decirle las noticias.
¡Tú **estarás muy nervioso!**

1. Una amiga acaba de comprar una casa nueva y muy linda.

2. Juan y Gloria van a casarse pero acaban de pelearse (*to quarrel*). Gloria le cuenta a usted todo lo malo de su novio.

3. El tío Eugenio acaba de encontrar un lindo apartamento en el centro de la ciudad. Le cuenta a usted todo lo bueno del apartamento.

4. Es posible que el esposo de una amiga pierda su trabajo. Ella llega para decírselo a usted.

5. Un amigo le dice a usted que su hija recibió una beca (*scholarship*) para asistir a una universidad excelente.

6. Su amiga está preparándose para los exámenes. Hace dos semanas que ella estudia más de doce horas por día. Lo (La) llama por teléfono y le cuenta todo.

VOCABULARIO ACTIVO

Cognados

adicional	la construcción	importado	republicano
católico	demócrata	el insomnio	socialista
la causa	devoto	protestante	la tensión
comunista	ecuatoriano	razonable	tranquilo

Verbos

agrandar	to enlarge
funcionar	to work (an appliance or machine)
renovar	to renovate
reparar	to repair

En casa

la alfombra	carpet, rug
la bañera	bathtub
la cafetera	coffeepot
la cama	bed
la cocina	kitchen
el comedor	dining room
la cómoda	bureau, dresser
el congelador	freezer
el cuarto	room
el cuarto de baño, el baño	bathroom
el dormitorio, la alcoba	bedroom
la ducha	shower
el estante de libros	bookshelf
la estufa	stove
el garaje	garage
el horno	oven
el inodoro	toilet
el jardín	garden
la lámpara	lamp
el lavamanos	sink
la mesita de luz	end, side table
el mueble	piece of furniture
los muebles	(pieces of) furniture
el refrigerador	refrigerator
el ropero	closet
la sala (de estar)	living room
el sillón	armchair
el tostador	toaster

Otras expresiones y frases

cambiar de tema	to change the subject
el carpintero	carpenter
la docena	dozen
judío	Jewish
cierto	certain; a certain
medio	half
el panadero	baker

Expresiones útiles

A propósito...	By the way . . .
Cambiando de tema...	To change the subject . . .
¡Debe(n) estar muy contento(s)!	You must be very happy!
Por el contrario...	On the contrary . . .

Vista parcial de la
Universidad de
Santo Domingo

CAPÍTULO
VEINTE

COMUNICACIÓN Y
RELACIONES HUMANAS

Vocabulario.   In this chapter you will practice
words and phrases that show consideration and
politeness.

Gramática.   You will learn to read and recognize:

1. The present perfect and the past perfect
   subjunctive
2. Sequence of tenses with the subjunctive
3. Idiomatic constructions that express *to become,
   to get* . . .

Cultura.   The dialogues take place in the
Dominican Republic.

LOS SALUDOS (*GREETINGS*)

Formal

Buenos días / Buenas tardes / Buenas noches, don Enrique. ¿Cómo está?

Informal

Hola, Enrique. ¡Tanto tiempo! ¿Qué tal? / ¿Cómo te va?

Las Presentaciones (*Introductions*)

—Le presento a la doctora Gutiérrez.

—Mucho gusto en conocerla.
—Igualmente / El gusto es mío.

—Éste es mi amigo José. / Quiero que conozcas a mi amigo José.
—Hola, ¿qué tal?
—Encantada. / Mucho gusto.

Las despedidas

Ha sido un gran placer verla / conocerla. Encantado de verla.

Hasta la próxima. (*Until next time.*)

Saludos a tus padres.

Saludos y despedidas por carta

Estimado(-a) señor(a/ita): Distinguido(-a) señor(a/ita): Muy señor mío:

Cordialmente, Atentamente / Respetuosamente,

Querido(-a)...: Hola,...:

Cariñosamente, (*Affectionately,*) Un abrazo de Luisa

Y PARA FELICITAR (CONGRATULATE)

Felicitaciones!

¡Felicitaciones!

Disculparse... (*to apologize*)

Con permiso.

Perdón.

Brindar...y desear lo mejor...

¡Salud!
¡Buen provecho!
(*Enjoy your meal!*)

Expresar sorpresa...

¡Caramba! (*Good grief!*)
¡Dios mío!

Expresar compasión...

Lo siento.

Agradecer... (*to thank*)

Gracias.
(Estoy) muy agradecido(-a).
Le agradezco mucho.

El qué dirán. Mire los dibujos y decida cuál sería una reacción apropiada para cada situación.

MODELO

Hasta la próxima.

1

2

3

4

5

6

Situaciones ¿Qué diría la gente en las siguientes situaciones?

MODELO Una persona quiere brindar. Levanta la copa y dice algo.
ⓐ. ¡Salud!
b. ¡Qué lástima!

1. Un(a) amigo(-a) le ofrece algo de comer pero usted no tiene hambre.
   a. Igualmente.
   b. Gracias.
2. Su padre le da un regalo elegante a su mamá por su cumpleaños.
   a. ¡Muchísimas gracias!
   b. ¡Buen provecho!
3. Una amiga le dice que se va a casar pronto.
   a. ¡Felicitaciones!
   b. Con permiso.
4. Usted va a un funeral y le dice algo a la madre o al padre de la persona muerta.
   a. Perdón.
   b. Lo siento mucho.

I. El presente perfecto y el pluscuamperfecto del subjuntivo

El Alcázar, construído (entre 1510 y 1520) para residencia de la familia de Diego Colón, hijo de Cristóbal Colón

La oficina de una abogada en Santo Domingo

CATALINA Pareces muy cansada, Marisa. Espero que no *hayas tenido* demasiado trabajo últimamente.

MARISA ¡Ay, señora! ¡Usted no *hubiera hecho* ese viaje la semana pasada... !

CATALINA ¿Por qué dices eso, Marisa... ?

MARISA ¡Es que aquí hubo tanto trabajo! Yo tuve que trabajar todas las noches.

CATALINA ¿Todas las noches... ? Lo siento mucho. Ojalá no *hayas faltado* a clases por culpa mía.°

MARISA No, eso no. Pero si usted *hubiera estado* aquí, yo no *habría tenido* tantos problemas en mi clase de ciencias de computación...

CATALINA Perdóname, Marisa.

MARISA La semana que viene tengo exámenes. ¿Me permitiría un día libre°?

CATALINA ¡Cómo no! Lo tienes muy merecido.°

Ojalá...mía *I hope you didn't miss class because of me.*   libre *off*   Lo...merecido *You deserve it very much.*

¿Verdadero o falso?

1. Marisa está muy cansada.   2. Si no hubiera sido por el viaje de Catalina, Marisa no habría tenido tantos problemas en una de sus clases.   3. Marisa faltó a clases por culpa de Catalina.   4. Marisa sigue un curso de literatura.   5. Catalina le dice a Marisa que puede tener una semana libre.

A. The present perfect subjunctive is formed with the present subjunctive of **haber (haya, hayas, haya, hayamos, hayáis, hayan)** plus a past participle.

Espero que ya hayas pagado la cuenta.   *I hope you have already paid the bill.*

B. The present perfect subjunctive is used when:

1. The verb in the main clause is in the present or future tense. (Less frequently, the present perfect subjunctive is used when the main verb is a command.)
2. The subjunctive is required in the dependent clause; and
3. The dependent verb describes either of the following:
a. An action that is to happen before the action described by the main verb.

Iremos a Santiago sólo después de que hayamos vendido la casa.	*We'll go to Santiago only after we have sold the house.*
Devuélvemela cuando hayas terminado de leerla.	*Return it to me when you have finished reading it.*

b. A past action or condition. It may still be going on at the time of the main verb, or the speaker may be focusing on the consequences of its being complete at the time of the main verb.

Sentimos que ella haya estado enferma.	*We're sorry she has been sick.*
Espero que ya hayan visitado Puerto Plata.	*I hope you've already visited Puerto Plata.*

4. The present perfect subjunctive may also be used after **ojalá** and expressions like **tal vez** to describe earlier actions.

Ojalá que el agente haya mandado los boletos.	*Let's hope the agent has sent the tickets.*
Tal vez él ya la haya visto.	*Perhaps he has already seen her.*

Compare the following sentences:

Espero que te paguen el sueldo.	*I hope they pay you your salary.*
Espero que te hayan pagado el sueldo.	*I hope they've paid you your salary.*

C. The past perfect subjunctive is formed with the past subjunctive of **haber (hubiera, hubieras, hubiera, hubiéramos, hubierais, hubieran)** plus the past participle.

Esperaba que ya hubieras pagado la cuenta.	*I was hoping that you had already paid the check.*

D. The past perfect subjunctive is used when:

1. The verb in the main clause is past (imperfect, preterit, or conditional);
2. The past subjunctive form is required in the dependent clause; and
3. The action described by the verb in the dependent clause took place before the action described by the verb in the main clause.

Osvaldo negó que te hubiera pagado.	Osvaldo denied that he had paid you.
No creían que hubiéramos estudiado para músicos.	They didn't believe that we had studied to be musicians.

But if the dependent verb refers to a simultaneous or future action or condition, the past subjunctive is used. Compare the following sentences:

Ella dudaba que tuvieras tiempo.	She doubted that you had time.
Ella dudaba que hubieras tenido tiempo.	She doubted that you had had time.

E. The pluperfect subjunctive is also used with the conditional perfect in contrary to fact *if* clauses that refer to the past.

Si hubiéramos tenido más dinero, habríamos renovado la casa.	If we had had more money, we would have renovated the house.

EJERCICIOS

A. Noticias de San Juan, Puerto Rico. La señora Torres recibió una carta de unos amigos que están viviendo en San Juan. Le cuenta las noticias a su esposo y él hace comentarios. Haga el papel del señor Torres, escogiendo la respuesta apropiada para completar las oraciones.

MODELO   Clara dice que allá llovió durante una semana.
Siento mucho que allá _____ durante una semana.
a. llovió
ⓑ. haya llovido
c. ha llovido

1. Carlos ganó la lotería.
Me alegro que él _____ la lotería.
a. haya ganado   b. ganó   c. gane
2. Clara y su esposo fueron de vacaciones a Ponce.
¡Es estupendo que ellos _____ de vacaciones allá!
a. fueron   b. han ido   c. hayan ido
3. Elena pasó una semana con ellos en San Juan.
¿Estás contenta que ella _____ toda una semana con ellos?
a. pasó   b. haya pasado   c. pase
4. Los tres vieron más de veinte iglesias coloniales.
Dudo que ellos _____ tantas iglesias en una semana.
a. hayan visto   b. vean   c. habían visto
5. Comieron en restaurantes muy lindos.
Es bueno que _____ en restaurantes lindos.
a. han comido   b. hayan comido   c. comieron
6. Yo también quiero ir a Puerto Rico.
Me gusta que tú también _____ a Puerto Rico.
a. hayas querido ir   b. quieras ir   c. quieres ir

B. Pensamientos nostálgicos.   Patricia es de Santo Domingo pero ahora vive en los Estados Unidos. Piensa en su familia y en los amigos que dejó en República Dominicana. Escoja la respuesta de la columna B que más lógicamente expresa los pensamientos de ella.

A	**B**
1. Es posible que Rosita	si hubiera ganado la lotería
2. Es una lástima que tío Ernesto	haya hecho el viaje que quería hacer
3. Mis padres me habrían ayudado	no haya podido venir a visitarme aquí
4. Espero que mi primo	si hubieran querido que me quedara en
5. Raúl ya habría dejado de	República Dominicana
trabajar	ya se haya casado

C. ¡Qué suerte!   Roberto acaba de regresar al pueblo donde había nacido. Está charlando con un amigo y se alegra de oír las noticias. Haga el papel de Roberto y escoja la expresión más apropiada para expresar su alegría.

MODELO   Nuestros mejores amigos se casaron.
Me alegro de que ellos _____ .
a. se casaron.
ⓑ. se hayan casado.
c. se hubieran casado.

1. Antonio es jefe de una agencia importante.
   ¡Qué bueno que Antonio _____ !
   a. fuera jefe de esa agencia
   b. es jefe de esa agencia
   c. sea jefe de esa agencia
2. Los Fuentes compraron una casa más grande.
   ¡Qué suerte que los Fuentes _____ !
   a. hayan comprado una casa más grande
   b. compraron una casa muy grande
   c. hubieran comprado una casa más grande
3. Elena nos trajo muchísimos recuerdos de su viaje a España.
   ¡Es estupendo que _____ tantos recuerdos de su viaje a España!
   a. les traiga
   b. les haya traído
   c. les trae
4. El año pasado fui a muchas fiestas con mis amigos.
   ¿Insistieron tus amigos en que _____ con ellos?
   a. vayas a muchas fiestas
   b. fueras a muchas fiestas
   c. vas a muchas fiestas
5. Mis abuelos todavía viven en la misma casa.
   Es increíble que tus abuelos todavía _____ .
   a. viven en la misma casa
   b. hayan vivido en la misma casa
   c. vivan en la misma casa

D. Sueños. Enrique quiere cambiar su estilo de vida. Escoja el verbo apropiado para completar sus pensamientos.

MODELO ... , yo habría sido rico.
    a. Si compro menos discos
    b. Si no gastara tanto en jeans
    ⓒ. Si hubiera ahorrado más

1. _____ , habría sido una persona más interesante.
    a. Si hubiera viajado más
    b. Si viajara más
    c. Si viajo más
2. _____ , sería más feliz.
    a. Si hubiera encontrado una novia simpática
    b. Si encontrara una novia simpática
    c. Si encuentro una novia simpática
3. _____ , habría sabido hablar portugués.
    a. Si naciera en Brasil
    b. Si hubiera nacido en Brasil
    c. Si mi madre fuera brasileña
4. _____ , les compraría una linda casa a cada uno de ellos.
    a. Si tengo muchos hijos
    b. Si tuviera muchos hijos
    c. Si hubiera tenido muchos hijos
5. _____ , podría tener una buena profesión.
    a. Si estudiara más
    b. Si estudio más
    c. Si hubiera estudiado más

II. La sucesión de tiempos con el subjuntivo

Monumento a Cristóbal Colón y vista parcial de la catedral dominicana, primera catedral de América (construída entre 1514 y 1540)

En el correo

EMPLEADO   Buenas tardes, señor. Perdone que lo *haya hecho* esperar. ¿En qué puedo servirle?

SEÑOR   Quiero mandar esta carta certificada a los Estados Unidos.

EMPLEADO   ¿Por avión?

SEÑOR   Sí, por favor. Quiero que *llegue* lo más pronto posible. El próximo lunes es el cumpleaños de mi hija. Sería una lástima que no *llegara* a tiempo.

EMPLEADO   Pues, si usted quiere que su hija la *reciba* pronto, sería mejor que la *mandara* expreso. Las cartas certificadas a Estados Unidos tardan° unos diez días.

SEÑOR   No creí que *tardaran* tanto. Entonces la mandaré expreso para que *llegue* más rápido.

EMPLEADO   Muy bien. ¿Algo más, señor?

SEÑOR   Sí, un amigo me ha pedido que le *compre* estampillas° y aerogramas.

EMPLEADO   Estampillas, aerogramas y tarjetas postales° pueden comprarse en el mostrador° de enfrente.

SEÑOR   Muchas gracias, señor.

---

tardan   *take (a period of time)*   estampillas   *stamps*   tarjetas postales   *postcards*
el mostrador   *the counter*

¿Verdadero o falso?

1. Al llegar al correo, el señor quiere mandar una carta certificada.   2. Quiere que la carta vaya por avión.   3. El cumpleaños de su hija es el próximo viernes.
4. El señor decide mandar la carta expreso.   5. Un amigo le había pedido al señor que le comprara tarjetas postales.

When a verb in the subjunctive is required in the dependent clause, its tense usually follows logically from the tense of the verb in the main clause.

A. A dependent clause usually takes the present or present perfect subjunctive when the verb in the main clause is:

1. In the present.

Ramón quiere que vayamos con él a Puerto Plata.	*Ramón wants us to go with him to Puerto Plata.*
¿Dudas que la carta llegue pronto?	*Do you doubt that the letter will arrive soon?*

2. In the present perfect.

La profesora les ha pedido a los estudiantes que preparen esos ejercicios.	*The professor has asked the students to prepare those exercises.*

3. In the future.

Saldremos para San Cristóbal después que llegue Pablo.	*We'll leave for San Cristóbal after Pablo arrives.*
Hablaré con alguien que haya viajado por el canal de Panamá.	*I'll talk to someone who has traveled through the Panama Canal.*

4. A command.

Perdone que lo haya hecho esperar.	*Excuse me for having made you wait.*
Lee la carta tan pronto como la recibas.	*Read the letter as soon as you receive it.*

In general, a compound tense is used in Spanish in the same way that it is used in English. For instance, if you want to say *I am happy that they are winning,* you would say in Spanish **Me alegro de que ganen.** If you want to say *I am happy that they have won,* you would say **Me alegro de que hayan ganado.**

B. A dependent clause usually takes a verb in the imperfect or past perfect subjunctive when the verb in the main clause is:

1. In the preterit.

¿No me pediste que te comprara un recuerdo de Santo Domingo?	*Didn't you ask me to buy you a souvenir from Santo Domingo?*

2. In the imperfect.

El señor quería que el regalo de cumpleaños llegara lo más pronto posible.	*The man wanted the birthday present to arrive as soon as possible.*
No sabíamos que hubiera existido un pueblo indio en ese lugar.	*We didn't know an Indian town had existed in that place.*

3. In the past perfect.

La madre de José había insistido en que se disculpara.	*José's mother had insisted that he apologize.*

4. In the conditional.

Me sorprendería que no tuvieran razón.	*It would surprise me if they were wrong.*

EJERCICIOS

A. La respuesta más lógica. Complete las frases escogiendo una cláusula de la columna B para cada cláusula de la columna A.

A	B
1. Espero que...	a. tu amiga te ayudara, ¿no?
2. Ella quería que...	b. ella no haya recibido tu carta
3. Deseabas que...	c. ellos me habrían ayudado, ¿no?
4. Dudan que...	d. tú no hayas hecho eso
5. Es verdad que...	e. ustedes compraran más regalos para la familia
6. Tenemos miedo de que...	f. los López no venden la casa
7. Si hubieran podido...	g. Paco y Gabriela vengan a la fiesta esta noche.

B. Una breve charla. Escoja la forma correcta del verbo para completar la conversación que sigue.

ANA   No puedo asistir a la reunión a menos que los niños
(1) _____ quedarse con los vecinos. Les pediré que me
(2) _____ ese favor tan pronto como (3) _____ .

GLORIA   Estoy segura que ellos (4) _____ a ayudarte en eso. ¡Tus hijos son buenísimos! Llámame cuando (5) _____ salir.

ANA   De acuerdo. Te llamaré antes de que (6) _____ a los niños a casa de los vecinos.

1. a. pueden   b. puedan   c. pudieran
2. a. hagan   b. hacen   c. hicieran
3. a. llegaran   b. llegan   c. lleguen
4. a. vayan   b. van   c. fueran
5. a. quisieras   b. quieras   c. quieres
6. a. lleva   b. lleve   c. llevara

C. La sociedad colonial. Escoja de la lista de abajo (below) la forma verbal correcta para completar el siguiente párrafo.

a. protestaran   c. trabajaran   e. sería   g. se construirían
b. habría   d. pudiera   f. viviéramos   h. empezaran

Si nosotros (1) _____ en un lugar como la Española (antiguo nombre de República Dominicana) durante los siglos de la Colonia, la sociedad sería muy diferente. (2) _____ edificios nuevos de estilo colonial todos los días y muchas personas viajarían por barco para descubrir tierras desconocidas (unknown lands). Pero la sociedad (3) _____ casi feudal; (4) _____ cuatro grupos de personas: indios, mestizos, criollos, y españoles. Sería necesario que los indios (5) _____ duro (hard) para los españoles y los criollos. Si (6) _____ probablemente los jefes los matarían. Los españoles tendrían todo el poder. Por eso, era inevitable que los criollos (7) _____ los movimientos de independencia.

A mí no me gustaría vivir en una sociedad de esa clase con tantas injusticias. Y usted, si (8) _____ escoger, ¿preferiría ser español(a) del siglo dieciséis o norteamericano(-a) de este siglo?

III. Modos de decir *to get, to become*

Una estudiante de
medicina

En el apartamento de Sebastián y Ángela

SEBASTIÁN   ¿Por qué no te sientas? *Te vas a cansar.* Siempre *me pongo* nervioso cuando estudias de pie°.

ÁNGELA   ¿Que tú *te pones* nervioso?° ¿Y cómo me siento yo? Tengo un examen oral a las tres y *se me hace* tarde°.

SEBASTIÁN   Querida, no sé cómo *te vas a hacer* médica° si *te vuelves* loca° cada vez que tienes que pasar un examen oral.

ÁNGELA   Es que todos nos preocupamos por las preguntas del doctor Solís. *Se hacen* cada vez más difíciles...°

SEBASTIÁN   Mira, Ángela... te conozco bien. ¡Vas a *llegar a ser°* la mejor médica de Santo Domingo!

---

de pie *standing up*   ¿Que...nervioso? *You're saying you get nervous?*   se me hace
tarde *It's getting late for me*   te vas...médica *you're going to become a doctor*   te vuelves
loca *you go crazy*   Se hacen cada vez más difíciles *They're getting more and more difficult*
llegar a ser *to become*

¿Verdadero o falso?

1. Sebastián se pone nervioso cuando Ángela se sienta a estudiar.
2. Ángela tiene un examen oral a las tres.
3. Ángela quiere hacerse abogada.
4. El doctor Solís hace preguntas fáciles.
5. Sebastián duda que Ángela vaya a salir bien en el examen.

A. Some Spanish verbs when used reflexively express meanings translated by English *to get* or *to become.* Below are a few.

casarse	*to get married*	enfermarse	*to get sick*
cansarse	*to get tired*	entristecerse (zc)	*to become sad*

Raquel se casa en junio.	*Raquel is getting married in June.*
Los viejos se cansan fácilmente.	*Old people get tired easily.*
El (La) profesor(a) nunca se enferma.	*The professor never gets sick.*
Me entristezco en las bodas.	*I become sad at weddings.*

B. Several Spanish verbs may be used in special situations to express ideas translated by English *to get* or *to become.* These verbs are: **ponerse, volverse, hacerse,** and **llegar a ser.**

1. Ponerse used with an adjective describes a change in condition or state that usually does not last long. It often describes changes in emotions.

En las fiestas Miguel se pone contento, pero Juan se pone nervioso.	*Miguel becomes happy at parties, but Juan gets nervous.*

2. Volverse is also used with adjectives, but to describe a long-lasting change. It is often used in the expression **volverse loco.**

La pobre mujer se volvió loca.	*The poor woman became ("went") crazy.*
Después de ganar todo ese dinero, el se volvió egoísta.	*After earning all that money, he became selfish.*

3. Hacerse is used with nouns or adjectives to describe a change in profession or status that comes about by the person's own effort. **Hacerse** emphasizes the process of becoming and not the result. It is also used with the progress of time, and to express *to become* in the sense of *to turn into.*

Eugenio estudió mucho y se hizo profesor.	*Eugenio studied a lot and became a professor.*
Se (me, nos) hace tarde.	*It's getting late (for me, for us).*
El agua se hace vapor.	*The water is turning into steam.*

4. Llegar a ser is also used with professions and status, but it usually indicates either that there was a long process involved, or that the change came about because of outside factors. In contrast to **hacerse, llegar a ser** emphasizes the result and not the process.

Finalmente llegó a ser gobernador.	*He finally became governor.*
Era socialista pero después de ganar «el gordo» en la lotería, llegó a ser conservador.	*He was a socialist, but after winning the grand prize in the lottery, he became a conservative.*

EJERCICIOS

A. La vida interesante de Esteban. Escoja la expresión apropiada para completar la descripción de la vida de Esteban.

1. La vida de Esteban _____ cada día más interesante.
   a. se hace
   b. llega a ser
2. No, no _____ nervioso cuando hace sus tareas.
   a. se vuelve
   b. se pone
3. Siempre _____ feliz cuando piensa en los estudios.
   a. se pone
   b. se hace
4. Sus amigos creen que _____ loco.
   a. se está haciendo
   b. se está volviendo
5. Quiere _____ ingeniero y tiene suficiente tiempo para estudiar.
   a. llegar a ser
   b. ponerse
   ...porque ¡Esteban sólo tiene doce años... !

B. Las aspiraciones de Mariana. Mariana describe lo que quiere hacer en el futuro. Escoja los verbos apropiados para completar el párrafo que sigue.

a. me pongo   d. se harán
b. hacerse   e. me estoy volviendo
c. llegar a ser   f. me pondré

Algún día, yo querría (1) _____ profesora de química. Me gustan mucho las ciencias y me encantan mis clases. Los otros estudiantes dicen que los exámenes (2) _____ cada vez más difíciles, pero realmente lo dudo. Cuando trabajo en el laboratorio siempre (3) _____ nerviosa al principio, pero sé que después de unas horas (4) _____ feliz. A veces no quiero dejar el laboratorio y mis amigas dicen que (5) _____ loca. Yo les explico que uno debe estudiar y trabajar mucho para (6) _____ profesora. Es el precio que debo pagar para hacer que mi sueño se haga realidad.

C. Traducción. Lea las siguientes frases. ¿Qué verbo—**ponerse, hacerse, llegar a ser** o **volverse**—usaría usted para traducir al español las palabras en bastardilla? Vea las respuestas correctas abajo.

1. I always *get* nervous before exams.
2. Elena is studying very hard in order to *become* a lawyer.
3. *It's getting* later and later.
4. After a sudden rise in his popularity, he *became* president.
5. The poor man has so many problems. I'm afraid *he's becoming* crazy.
6. It's very hot today. The ice cream *is turning into* a liquid.*

---

*1. ponerse 2. hacerse 3. hacerse 4. llegar a ser 5. volverse 6. hacerse

LA QUE SE VA, LOS QUE SE QUEDAN

Torre del Homenaje, primera fortaleza de piedra (*stone*) del Nuevo Mundo

Brenda, especialista y consejera° norteamericana en ciencias de computación, está trabajando en Santo Domingo para una compañía dominicana.[1]

BRENDA   ¡Gracias por traerme los programas tan pronto! Tengo mucho que hacer porque la oficina de Miami me ha pedido que vuelva la semana que viene.

JOSÉ   ¡No me digas que ya vas a volver a tu país! Creo que te sientes muy cómoda aquí, ¡como si fueras realmente dominicana!, ¿no?

BRENDA   Tienes razón, José. Me encanta tu país. Aquí el clima es fantástico[2] y me parece fascinante poder visitar tantos monumentos históricos.[3] Yo preferiría que ellos no me hubieran llamado todavía, pero...así es la vida.

JOSÉ   Entre paréntesis,° ¿te he presentado a mi amigo, Juan?

JUAN   Mucho gusto en conocerla, Brenda. ¿Dice José que usted va a volver a los Estados Unidos? ¡Pero yo acabo de conocerla!

BRENDA   Sí, la compañía de Miami quiere que yo pase unas semanas de entrenamiento° allá antes de partir° para Ecuador... donde voy a ayudar con la instalación de otro centro de computación. ¡Mi vida se hace cada día más interesante! ¡Me encanta viajar!

JOSÉ   Pues...¡Felicitaciones! Tú llegarás a ser la experta en ciencias de computación más popular de toda Hispanoamérica...

BRENDA   José, te agradezco pero exageras un poco...

JUAN   Pero...sabes una cosa... ¡Nosotros también tenemos una oficina en Quito! ¿Por qué no vamos a tomar una copa y a brindar por el nuevo puesto° de Brenda? Podríamos hacer planes para reunirnos en Quito...si ella nos enviara su nueva dirección...

BRENDA   ¡Claro que sí! Sólo les pido que me den unos quince minutos para terminar este proyecto... y después, ¡salimos para brindar por el futuro!

---

consejera *consultant*   Entre paréntesis *By the way* (literally, "in parentheses")
entrenamiento *training* . partir *leaving*   puesto *position*

¿Verdadero o falso?

1. Brenda es especialista en ciencias naturales.
2. La oficina principal de ella está en Los Ángeles.
3. José es amigo de Brenda.
4. Juan ya conoce a Brenda desde hace mucho tiempo.
5. Brenda irá al Ecuador dentro de unos meses.
6. Allí ella ayudará con la instalación de un centro de computación.
7. Los amigos quieren brindar por el nuevo puesto de Brenda.
8. Brenda quiere salir inmediatamente.

NOTAS CULTURALES

1. The Dominican Republic (**República Dominicana**) occupies about two-thirds of the island Hispaniola (**La Española**) located between Cuba and Puerto Rico. Its capital, Santo Domingo, was the first permanent European city established in the New World. Its residents are called **capitaleños.** Two other important cities are Santiago and San Cristóbal. The country is now experiencing some stability and progress after years of dictatorship and U.S. occupation.

2. The tropical climate of this island nation makes it popular with tourists. Puerto Plata is an especially beautiful tourist site. The national mean temperature is 77°F (25°C). The temperature rarely goes above 90°F (32°C) and even in the mountains, where cooler weather is experienced, the overall mean is about 69°F (21°C).

3. The first church built by the Spaniards in the New World is located in Santo Domingo and is claimed to contain the remains of **Cristóbal Colón.** Also in Santo Domingo are two other important remains from Colonial times: the **Alcázar,** built between 1510 and 1520 as the family residence of **Diego Colón,** son of **Cristóbal Colón;** and the **Torre del Homenaje,** first stone fortress in the New World. The university, now the **Universidad Autónoma de Santo Domingo (UASD),** is the oldest in the Americas, founded in 1538.

VOCABULARIO ACTIVO

Cognados

la comunicación   el futuro   nervioso

Verbos

hacerse   *to become, turn into*
llegar a ser   *to become*
volverse   *to become*
   volverse loco   *to go crazy*

Comunicación y relaciones humanas

brindar   *to toast*
¡Buen provecho!   *Cheers!*
¡Felicitaciones!   *Congratulations!*
¡Salud!   *Cheers!*
sentir(lo)   *to feel sorry*

APÉNDICE I

División en sílabas

Spanish words of more than one syllable always have a syllable that is accentuated, or spoken more forcefully than the others. Here is how to recognize the syllables in Spanish words.

A. Every Spanish syllable contains only one vowel, diphthong, or triphthong. Diphthongs and triphthongs are not divided, but two strong vowels are.

cre-o   le-al   a-diós   lim-piáis

B. A single consonant (including **ch** and **ll**) between two vowels begins a new syllable.

co-mo   mu-cho   fe-li-ci-da-des
a-pe-lli-do   gra-cias   Te-re-sa

C. When two consonants occur between vowels, they are usually divided.

ex-ce-len-te   cua-der-no   Ca-li-for-nia
es-pa-ñol   u-ni-ver-si-dad   Jor-ge

D. However, most consonants, when followed by **l** or **r,** form a cluster with the **l** or **r.** Such clusters are not divided.

ha-blar   es-cri-to-rio
in-glés   pi-za-rra

Acentuación y el uso del tilde *(accent mark)*

A few short rules describe the way most Spanish words are accentuated, or stressed.

A. Most words ending in a vowel, **-n,** or **-s** are stressed on the next-to-last syllable.

cla-ses   **co**-mo   re-**pi**-tan   his-**to**-ria   **bue**-nos   e-le-**fan**-te

B. Most words ending in a consonant other than **-n** or **-s** are stressed on the last syllable.

es-pa-**ñol**   fa-**vor**   a-**rroz**   se-**ñor**   us-**ted**   pre-li-mi-**nar**

C. Words that are stressed in any other way carry a written accent on the vowel of the syllable that is stressed.

ca-**fé**   a-**quí**   Gon-**zá**-lez   in-**glés**   **lá**-piz   a-**diós**

D. Written accent marks are also used to mark the difference between pairs of words with the same spelling, and also on all question words.

el *the*   él *he*   si *if*   sí *yes*   como *as*   ¿cómo? *how*

APÉNDICE II

El uso de las letras mayúsculas

Capital letters are used in Spanish, as in English, to begin proper names and for the first word in a sentence. But Spanish does not use capital letters in the following cases:
Words used to address someone (except abbreviations).

Perdón, profesor(a).	*Excuse me, Professor.*
Perdón, señorita.	*Excuse me, Miss.*
Perdón, señor Robles.	*Excuse me, Mr. Robles.*
Perdón, Sr. Robles.	

Book titles—except for the first letter and proper names.

¿Habla español?	*Do you speak Spanish?*
La muerte de Artemio Cruz	*The Death of Artemio Cruz*
Cien años de soledad	*One Hundred Years of Solitude*

The names of languages.

el español	*Spanish*
el inglés	*English*

Nouns and adjectives of nationality.

los mexicanos	*the Mexicans*
la bandera argentina	*the Argentine flag*

Days, months, and seasons of the year.

lunes	*Monday*
julio	*July*
primavera	*Spring*

VERBOS

REGULAR VERBS—SIMPLE TENSES

INDICATIVE

	PRESENT	IMPERFECT	PRETERIT	FUTURE	CONDITIONAL
hablar	hablo	hablaba	hablé	hablaré	hablaría
hablando	hablas	hablabas	hablaste	hablarás	hablarías
hablado	habla	hablaba	habló	hablará	hablaría
	hablamos	hablábamos	hablamos	hablaremos	hablaríamos
	habláis	hablabais	hablasteis	hablaréis	hablaríais
	hablan	hablaban	hablaron	hablarán	hablarían
comer	como	comía	comí	comeré	comería
comiendo	comes	comías	comiste	comerás	comerías
comido	come	comía	comió	comerá	comería
	comemos	comíamos	comimos	comeremos	comeríamos
	coméis	comíais	comisteis	comeréis	comeríais
	comen	comían	comieron	comerán	comerían
vivir	vivo	vivía	viví	viviré	viviría
viviendo	vives	vivías	viviste	vivirás	vivirías
vivido	vive	vivía	vivió	vivirá	viviría
	vivimos	vivíamos	vivimos	viviremos	viviríamos
	vivís	vivíais	vivisteis	viviréis	viviríais
	viven	vivían	vivieron	vívirán	vivirían

REGULAR VERBS—PERFECT TENSES

INDICATIVE

PRESENT PERFECT		PAST PERFECT		FUTURE PERFECT		CONDITIONAL PERFECT	
he		había		habré		habría	
has		habías		habrás		habrías	
ha	hablado	había	hablado	habrá	hablado	habría	hablado
hemos	comido	habíamos	comido	habremos	comido	habríamos	comido
habéis	vivido	habíais	vivido	habréis	vivido	habríais	vivido
han		habían		habrán		habrían	

REGULAR VERBS—PROGRESSIVE TENSES

INDICATIVE

PRESENT		IMPERFECT	
estoy		estaba	
estás		estabas	
está	hablando	estaba	hablando
estamos	comiendo	estábamos	comiendo
estáis	viviendo	estabais	viviendo
están		estaban	

REGULAR VERBS—SIMPLE TENSES

SUBJUNCTIVE

PRESENT	IMPERFECT	COMMANDS
hable	hablara (-se)	—
hables	hablaras (-ses)	habla (no hables)
hable	hablara (-se)	hable
hablemos	habláramos (-semos)	hablemos
habléis	hablarais (-seis)	hablad (no habléis)
hablen	hablaran (-sen)	hablen
coma	comiera (-se)	—
comas	comieras (-ses)	come (no comas)
coma	comiera (-se)	coma
comamos	comiéramos (-semos)	comamos
comáis	comierais (-seis)	comed (no comáis)
coman	comieran (-sen)	coman
viva	viviera (-se)	—
vivas	vivieras (-ses)	vive (no vivas)
viva	viviera (-se)	viva
vivamos	viviéramos (-semos)	vivamos
viváis	vivierais (-seis)	vivid (no viváis)
vivan	vivieran (-sen)	vivan

REGULAR VERBS—PERFECT TENSES

SUBJUNCTIVE

PRESENT PERFECT		PAST PERFECT	
haya		hubiera (-se)	
hayas		hubieras (-ses)	
haya	hablado	hubiera (-se)	hablado
hayamos	comido	hubiéramos (-semos)	comido
hayáis	vivido	hubierais (-seis)	vivido
hayan		hubieran (-sen)	

STEM-CHANGING, SPELLING-CHANGING, AND IRREGULAR VERBS

These charts contain the principal irregular verbs from the text plus model verbs showing standard patterns of stem and spelling changes. The verbs are numbered for easy reference to the Spanish-English vocabulary. Forms containing an irregularity are printed in **bold type**. In the text, verb changes are in parentheses. These verbs show the patterns signaled.

STEM-CHANGING VERBS

i,i	pedir	24	ue	jugar	21
ie	pensar	25	ue	volver	43
ie	perder	26	ue,u	dormir	13
ie,i	sentir	35	y	construir	7
ú	continuar	9	y	creer	10
ue	contar	8			

SPELLING-CHANGING VERBS

c	empezar	14	j	escoger	15
i,g	seguir	34	qu	buscar	3
gu	pagar	23	z	vencer	40
í	esquiar	16	zc,j	conducir	5
í	prohibir	29	zc	conocer	6

INFINITIVE PRESENT PARTICIPLE PAST PARTICIPLE	**INDICATIVE**				
	PRESENT	IMPERFECT	PRETERIT	FUTURE	CONDITIONAL
1. **andar** andando andado	ando andas anda andamos andáis andan	andaba andabas andaba andábamos andabais andaban	**anduve** **anduviste** **anduvo** **anduvimos** **anduvisteis** **anduvieron**	andaré andarás andará andaremos andaréis andarán	andaría andarías andaría andaríamos andaríais andarían
2. **avergonzar** avergonzando avergonzado	**avergüenzo** **avergüenzas** **avergüenza** avergonzamos avergonzáis **avergüenzan**	avergonzaba avergonzabas avergonzaba avergonzábamos avergonzabais avergonzaban	**avergoncé** avergonzaste avergonzó avergonzamos avergonzasteis avergonzaron	avergonzaré avergonzarás avergonzará avergonzaremos avergonzaréis avergonzarán	avergonzaría avergonzarías avergonzaría avergonzaríamos avergonzaríais avergonzarían

This verb combines the changes illustrated in charts 8 and 14; **g** also changes to **gü** before **e**.

	PRESENT	IMPERFECT	PRETERIT	FUTURE	CONDITIONAL
3. **buscar (qu)** buscando buscado	busco buscas busca buscamos buscáis buscan	buscaba buscabas buscaba buscábamos buscabais buscaban	**busqué** buscaste buscó buscamos buscasteis buscaron	buscaré buscarás buscará buscaremos buscaréis buscarán	buscaría buscarías buscaría buscaríamos buscaríais buscarían

In verbs ending in **-car** the **c** changes to **qu** before **e**: **ataqué, busqué, critiqué, provoqué, toqué.**

	PRESENT	IMPERFECT	PRETERIT	FUTURE	CONDITIONAL
4. **caer** **cayendo** **caído**	**caigo** caes cae caemos caéis caen	caía caías caía caíamos caíais caían	caí **caíste** cayó **caímos** **caísteis** **cayeron**	caeré caerás caerá caeremos caeréis caerán	caería caerías caería caeríamos caeríais caerían
5. **conducir (j,zc)** conduciendo conducido	**conduzco** conduces conduce conducimos conducís conducen	conducía conducías conducía conducíamos conducíais conducían	**conduje** **condujiste** **condujo** **condujimos** **condujisteis** **condujeron**	conduciré conducirás conducirá conduciremos conduciréis conducirán	conduciría conducirías conduciría conduciríamos conduciríais conducirían

In verbs ending in **-ducir**, the **c** changes to **zc** before **a** or **o**: **conduzco, traduzca.** In the preterit they follow pattern 12.

	PRESENT	IMPERFECT	PRETERIT	FUTURE	CONDITIONAL
6. **conocer (zc)** conociendo conocido	**conozco** conoces conoce conocemos conocéis conocen	conocía conocías conocía conocíamos conocíais conocían	conocí conociste conoció conocimos conocisteis conocieron	conoceré conocerás conocerá conoceremos conoceréis conocerán	conocería conocerías conocería conoceríamos conoceríais conocerían

In verbs ending in a *vowel* + **-cer** or **-cir**, the **c** changes to **zc** before **a** or **o**: **agradezca, conozca, parezca, ofrezca.**

SUBJUNCTIVE

PRESENT	IMPERFECT	COMMANDS
ande	anduviera (-se)	—
andes	anduvieras (-ses)	anda (no andes)
ande	anduviera (-se)	ande
andemos	anduviéramos (´-semos)	andemos
andéis	anduviérais (-seis)	andad (no andéis)
anden	anduvieran (-sen)	anden
avergüence	avergonzara (-se)	—
avergüences	avergonzaras (-ses)	avergüenza (no avergüences)
avergüence	avergonzara (-se)	avergüenza
avergoncemos	avergonzáramos (´-semos)	avergoncemos
avergoncéis	avergonzarais (-seis)	avergonzad (no avergoncéis)
avergüencen	avergonzaran (-sen)	avergüencen
busque	buscara (-se)	—
busques	buscaras (-ses)	busca (no busques)
busque	buscara (-se)	busque
busquemos	buscáramos (´-semos)	busquemos
busquéis	buscarais (-seis)	buscad (no busquéis)
busquen	buscaran (-sen)	busquen
caiga	cayera (-se)	—
caigas	cayeras (-ses)	cae (no caigas)
caiga	cayera (-se)	caiga
caigamos	cayéramos (´-semos)	caigamos
caigáis	cayerais (-seis)	caed (no caigáis)
caigan	cayeran (-sen)	caigan
conduzca	condujera (-se)	—
conduzcas	condujeras (-ses)	conduce (no conduzcas)
conduzca	condujera (-se)	conduzca
conduzcamos	condujéramos (´-semos)	conduzcamos
conduzcáis	condujerais (-seis)	conducid (no conduzcáis)
conduzcan	condujeran (-sen)	conduzcan
conozca	conociera (-se)	—
conozcas	conocieras (-ses)	conoce (no conozcas)
conozca	conociera (-se)	conozca
conozcamos	conociéramos (´-semos)	conozcamos
conozcáis	conocierais (-seis)	conoced (no conozcáis)
conozcan	conocieran (-sen)	conozcan

INFINITIVE	INDICATIVE				
PRESENT PARTICIPLE					
PAST PARTICIPLE	PRESENT	IMPERFECT	PRETERIT	FUTURE	CONDITIONAL
7. construir (y)	construyo	construía	construí	construiré	construiría
construyendo	construyes	construías	construiste	construirás	construirías
construido	construye	construía	construyó	construirá	construiría
	construimos	construíamos	construimos	construiremos	construiríamos
	construís	construíais	construisteis	construiréis	construiríais
	construyen	construían	construyeron	construirán	construirían

In **construir** and **destruir**, a y is inserted before any ending that does not begin with i: **construyo, destruyo**, etc. An i changes to **y** between two vowels: **construyó, destruyó**.

8. contar (ue)	cuento	contaba	conté	contaré	contaría
contando	cuentas	contabas	contaste	contarás	contarías
contado	cuenta	contaba	contó	contará	contaría
	contamos	contábamos	contamos	contaremos	contaríamos
	contáis	contabais	contasteis	contaréis	contaríais
	cuentan	contaban	contaron	contarán	contarían

Numerous -ar verbs change their stem vowel from o to **ue** in the shoe-pattern forms of the present indicative and present subjunctive and in the affirmative **tú** command.

9. continuar (ú)	continúo	continuaba	continué	continuaré	continuaría
continuando	continúas	continuabas	continuaste	continuarás	continuarías
continuado	continúa	continuaba	continuó	continuará	continuaría
	continuamos	continuábamos	continuamos	continuaremos	continuaríamos
	continuáis	continuabais	continuasteis	continuaréis	continuaríais
	continúan	continuaban	continuaron	continuarán	continuarían

In verbs ending in -uar, the u changes to **ú** in the shoe-pattern forms of the present indicative and present subjunctive and in the affirmative **tú** command.

10. creer (y)	creo	creía	creí	creeré	creería
creyendo	crees	creías	creíste	creerás	creerías
creído	cree	creía	creyó	creerá	creería
	creemos	creíamos	creímos	creeremos	creeríamos
	creéis	creíais	creísteis	creeréis	creeríais
	creen	creían	creyeron	creerán	creerían

In verbs ending in -eer, the i changes to y between vowels. The stressed i of an ending takes a written accent: **creído**.

11. dar	doy	daba	di	daré	daría
dando	das	dabas	diste	darás	darías
dado	da	daba	dio	dará	daría
	damos	dábamos	dimos	daremos	daríamos
	dais	dabais	disteis	daréis	daríais
	dan	daban	dieron	darán	darían

SUBJUNCTIVE

PRESENT	IMPERFECT	COMMANDS
construya	construyera (-se)	—
construyas	construyeras (-ses)	construye (no construyas)
construya	construyera (-se)	construya
construyamos	construyéramos (´-semos)	construyamos
construyáis	construyerais (-seis)	construid (no construyáis)
construyan	construyeran (-sen)	construyan

cuente	contara (-se)	—
cuentes	contaras (-ses)	cuenta (no cuentes)
cuente	contara (-se)	cuente
contemos	contáramos (´-semos)	contemos
contéis	contarais (-seis)	contad (no contéis)
cuenten	contaran (-sen)	cuenten

continúe	continuara (-se)	—
continúes	continuaras (-ses)	continúa (no continúes)
continúe	continuara (-se)	continúe
continuemos	continuáramos (´-semos)	continuemos
continuéis	continuarais (-seis)	continuad (no continuéis)
continúen	continuaran (-sen)	continúen

crea	creyera (-se)	—
creas	creyeras (-ses)	cree (no creas)
crea	creyera (-se)	crea
creamos	creyéramos (´-semos)	creamos
creáis	creyerais (-seis)	creed (no creáis)
crean	creyeran (-sen)	crean

dé	diera (-se)	—
des	dieras (-ses)	da (no des)
dé	diera (-se)	dé
demos	diéramos (´-semos)	demos
deis	dierais (-seis)	dad (no deis)
den	dieran (-sen)	den

INFINITIVE PRESENT PARTICIPLE PAST PARTICIPLE	INDICATIVE				
	PRESENT	IMPERFECT	PRETERIT	FUTURE	CONDITIONAL
12. decir diciendo dicho	digo dices dice decimos decís dicen	decía decías decía decíamos decíais decían	dije dijiste dijo dijimos dijisteis dijeron	diré dirás dirá diremos diréis dirán	diría dirías diría diríamos diríais dirían
13. dormir (ue,u) durmiendo dormido	duermo duermes duerme dormimos dormís duermen	dormía dormías dormía dormíamos dormíais dormían	dormí dormiste durmió dormimos dormisteis durmieron	dormiré dormirás dormirá dormiremos dormiréis dormirán	dormiría dormirías dormiría dormiríamos dormiríais dormirían

Selected -ir verbs change their stem vowel from o to **ue** in the shoe-pattern forms of the present indicative and present subjunctive and in the affirmative **tú** command. They show an additional stem-vowel change of o to **u** in the **nosotros** and **vosotros** forms of the present subjunctive, the **usted** and **ustedes** forms of the preterit, all forms of the imperfect subjunctive, and the present participle.

14. empezar (c) empezando empezado	empiezo empiezas empieza empezamos empezáis empiezan	empezaba empezabas empezaba empezábamos empezabais empezaban	empecé empezaste empezó empezamos empezasteis empezaron	empezaré empezarás empezará empezaremos empezaréis empezarán	empezaría empezarías empezaría empezaríamos empezaríais empezarían

In verbs ending in -zar, the z changes to c before an **e**: almorcé, comencé, empecé. (Empezar also follows stem-change pattern 25.)

15. escoger (j) cogiendo cogido	escojo escoges escoge escogemos escogéis escogen	escogía escogías escogía escogíamos escogíais escogían	escogí escogiste escogió escogimos escogisteis escogieron	escogeré escogerás escogerá escogeremos escogeréis escogerán	escogería escogerías escogería escogeríamos escogeríais escogerían

In verbs ending in -ger or gir, the g changes to j before **a** or **o**: escoja, proteja, corrija.

16. esquiar (í) esquiando esquiado	esquío esquías esquía esquiamos esquiáis esquían	esquiaba esquiabas esquiaba esquiábamos esquiabais esquiaban	esquié esquiaste esquió esquiamos esquiasteis esquiaron	esquiaré esquiarás esquiará esquiaremos esquiaréis esquiarán	esquiaría esquiarías esquiaría esquiaríamos esquiaríais esquiarían

Two other verbs conjugated like **esquiar** are **enviar** and **variar**; the i changes to **í** in the shoe-pattern forms of the present indicative and present subjunctive and in the affirmative **tú** command.

SUBJUNCTIVE

PRESENT	IMPERFECT	COMMANDS
diga	dijera (-se)	—
digas	dijeras (-ses)	di (no digas)
diga	dijera (-se)	diga
digamos	dijéramos (´-semos)	digamos
digáis	dijerais (-seis)	decid (no digáis)
digan	dijeran (-sen)	digan
duerma	durmiera (-se)	—
duermas	durmieras (-ses)	duerme (no duermas)
duerma	durmiera (-se)	duerma
durmamos	durmiéramos (´-semos)	durmamos
durmáis	durmierais (-seis)	dormid (no durmáis)
duerman	durmieran (-sen)	duerman
empiece	empezara (-se)	—
empieces	empezaras (-ses)	empieza (no empieces)
empiece	empezara (-se)	empiece
empecemos	empezáramos (´-semos)	empecemos
empecéis	empezarais (-seis)	empezad (no empecéis)
empiecen	empezaran (-sen)	empiecen
escoja	escogiera (-se)	—
escojas	escogieras (-ses)	escoge (no escojas)
escoja	escogiera (-se)	escoja
escojamos	escogiéramos (´-semos)	escojamos
escojáis	escogierais (-seis)	escoged (no escojáis)
escojan	escogieran (-sen)	escojan
esquíe	esquiara (-se)	—
esquíes	esquiaras (-ses)	esquía (no esquíes)
esquíe	esquiara (-se)	esquíe
esquiemos	esquiáramos (´-semos)	esquiemos
esquiéis	esquiarais (-seis)	esquiad (no esquiéis)
esquíen	esquiaran (-sen)	esquíen

INFINITIVE PRESENT PARTICIPLE PAST PARTICIPLE	**INDICATIVE**				
	PRESENT	IMPERFECT	PRETERIT	FUTURE	CONDITIONAL
17. estar estando estado	estoy estás está estamos estáis están	estaba estabas estaba estábamos estabais estaban	estuve estuviste estuvo estuvimos estuvisteis estuvieron	estaré estarás estará estaremos estaréis estarán	estaría estarías estaría estaríamos estaríais estarían
18. haber habiendo habido	he has ha hemos habéis han	había habías había habíamos habíais habían	hube hubiste hubo hubimos hubisteis hubieron	habré habrás habrá habremos habréis habrán	habría habrías habría habríamos habríais habrían
19. hacer haciendo **hecho**	hago haces hace hacemos hacéis hacen	hacía hacías hacía hacíamos hacíais hacían	hice hiciste hizo hicimos hicisteis hicieron	haré harás hará haremos haréis harán	haría harías haría haríamos haríais harían
20. ir yendo ido	voy vas va vamos vais van	iba ibas iba íbamos ibais iban	fui fuiste fue fuimos fuisteis fueron	iré irás irá iremos iréis irán	iría irías iría iríamos iríais irían
21. jugar (ue) jugando jugado	juego juegas juega jugamos jugáis juegan	jugaba jugabas jugaba jugábamos jugábais jugaban	jugué jugaste jugó jugamos jugasteis jugaron	jugaré jugarás jugará jugaremos jugaréis jugarán	jugaría jugarías jugaría jugaríamos jugaríais jugarían

The verb **jugar** changes its stem vowel from **u** to **ue** in the shoe-pattern forms of the present indicative and present subjunctive and in the affirmative **tú** command. (**Jugar** also follows spelling change pattern 23.)

22. oír **oyendo** **oído**	oigo oyes oye oímos oís oyen	oía oías oía oíamos oíais oían	oí **oíste** **oyó** oímos **oísteis** **oyeron**	oiré oirás oirá oiremos oiréis oirán	oiría oirías oiría oiríamos oiríais oirían

SUBJUNCTIVE

PRESENT	IMPERFECT	COMMANDS
esté	estuviera (-se)	—
estés	estuvieras (-ses)	está (no estés)
esté	estuviera (-se)	esté
estemos	estuviéramos (-semos)	estemos
estéis	estuvierais (-seis)	estad (no estéis)
estén	estuvieran (-sen)	estén
haya	hubiera (-se)	—
hayas	hubieras (-ses)	he (no hayas)
haya	hubiera (-se)	haya
hayamos	hubiéramos (-semos)	hayamos
hayáis	hubierais (-seis)	habed (no hayáis)
hayan	hubieran (-sen)	hayan
haga	hiciera (-se)	—
hagas	hicieras (-ses)	haz (no hagas)
haga	hiciera (-se)	haga
hagamos	hiciéramos (-semos)	hagamos
hagáis	hicierais (-seis)	haced (no hagáis)
hagan	hicieran (-sen)	hagan
vaya	fuera (-se)	—
vayas	fueras (-ses)	vé (no vayas)
vaya	fuera (-se)	vaya
vayamos	fuéramos (-semos)	vayamos
vayáis	fuerais (-seis)	id (no vayáis)
vayan	fueran (-sen)	vayan
juegue	jugara (-se)	—
juegues	jugaras (-ses)	juega (no juegues)
juegue	jugara (-se)	juegue
juguemos	jugáramos (-semos)	juguemos
juguéis	jugarais (-seis)	jugad (no juguéis)
jueguen	jugaran (-sen)	jueguen
oiga	oyera (-se)	—
oigas	oyeras (-ses)	oye (no oigas)
oiga	oyera (-se)	oiga
oigamos	oyéramos (-semos)	oigamos
oigáis	oyerais (-seis)	oíd (no oigáis)
oigan	oyeran (-sen)	oigan

INFINITIVE PRESENT PARTICIPLE PAST PARTICIPLE	**INDICATIVE**				
	PRESENT	IMPERFECT	PRETERIT	FUTURE	CONDITIONAL
23. **pagar (gu)** pagando pagado	pago pagas paga pagamos pagáis pagan	pagaba pagabas pagaba pagábamos pagabais pagaban	**pagué** pagaste pagó pagamos pagasteis pagaron	pagaré pagarás pagará pagaremos pagaréis pagarán	pagaría pagarías pagaría pagaríamos pagaríais pagarían

In verbs ending in -gar, the g changes to **gu** before an **e**: **llegué, pagué.**

| 24. **pedir (i,i)** **pidiendo** pedido | **pido** **pides** **pide** pedimos pedís **piden** | pedía pedías pedía pedíamos pedíais pedían | pedí pediste **pidió** pedimos pedisteis **pidieron** | pediré pedirás pedirá pediremos pediréis pedirán | pediría pedirías pediría pediríamos pediríais pedirían |

Selected -ir verbs change their stem vowel from **e** to **i** in the shoe-pattern forms of the present indicative and present subjunctive and in the affirmative **tú** command. They show an additional stem-vowel change of **e** to **i** in the **nosotros** and **vosotros** forms of the present subjunctive, the **usted** and **ustedes** forms of the preterit, all forms of the imperfect subjunctive, and the present participle.

| 25. **pensar (ie)** pensando pensado | **pienso** **piensas** **piensa** pensamos pensáis **piensan** | pensaba pensabas pensaba pensábamos pensabais pensaban | pensé pensaste pensó pensamos pensasteis pensaron | pensaré pensarás pensará pensaremos pensaréis pensarán | pensaría pensarías pensaría pensaríamos pensaríais pensarían |

Numerous -ar verbs change their stem vowel from **e** to **ie** in the shoe-pattern forms of the present indicative and present subjunctive and in the affirmative **tú** command.

| 26. **perder (ie)** perdiendo perdido | **pierdo** **pierdes** **pierde** perdemos perdéis **pierden** | perdía perdías perdía perdíamos perdíais perdían | perdí perdiste perdió perdimos perdisteis perdieron | perderé perderás perderá perderemos perderéis perderán | perdería perderías perdería perderíamos perderíais perderían |

Numerous -er and -ir verbs change their stem vowel from **e** to **ie** in the shoe-pattern forms of the present indicative and present subjunctive and in the affirmative **tú** command.

| 27. **poder** **pudiendo** podido | **puedo** **puedes** **puede** podemos podéis **pueden** | podía podías podía podíamos podíais podían | **pude** **pudiste** **pudo** **pudimos** **pudisteis** **pudieron** | podré podrás podrá podremos podréis podrán | podría podrías podría podríamos podríais podrían |

SUBJUNCTIVE

PRESENT	IMPERFECT	COMMANDS
pague	pagara (-se)	—
pagues	pagaras (-ses)	paga (no pagues)
pague	pagara (-se)	pague
paguemos	pagáramos (´-semos)	paguemos
paguéis	pagarais (-seis)	pagad (no paguéis)
paguen	pagaran (-sen)	paguen
pida	pidiera (-se)	—
pidas	pidieras (-ses)	pide (no pidas)
pida	pidiera (-se)	pida
pidamos	pidiéramos (´-semos)	pidamos
pidáis	pidierais (-seis)	pedid (no pidáis)
pidan	pidieran (-sen)	pidan
piense	pensara (-se)	—
pienses	pensaras (-ses)	piensa (no pienses)
piense	pensara (-se)	piense
pensemos	pensáramos (´-semos)	pensemos
penséis	pensarais (-seis)	pensad (no penséis)
piensen	pensaran (-sen)	piensen
pierda	perdiera (-se)	—
pierdas	perdieras (-ses)	pierde (no pierdas)
pierda	perdiera (-se)	pierda
perdamos	perdiéramos (´-semos)	perdamos
perdáis	perdierais (-seis)	perded (no perdáis)
pierdan	perdieran (-sen)	pierdan
pueda	pudiera (-se)	
puedas	pudieras (-ses)	
pueda	pudiera (-se)	
podamos	pudiéramos (´-semos)	
podáis	pudierais (-seis)	
puedan	pudieran (-sen)	

INFINITIVE PRESENT PARTICIPLE PAST PARTICIPLE	INDICATIVE				
	PRESENT	IMPERFECT	PRETERIT	FUTURE	CONDITIONAL
28. **poner** poniendo **puesto**	**pongo** pones pone ponemos ponéis ponen	ponía ponías ponía poníamos poníais ponían	**puse** pusiste **puso** pusimos pusisteis pusieron	**pondré** pondrás pondrá pondremos pondréis pondrán	**pondría** pondrías pondría pondríamos pondríais pondrían
29. **prohibir (í)** prohibiendo prohibido	**prohíbo** **prohíbes** **prohíbe** prohibimos prohibís **prohíben**	prohibía prohibías prohibía prohibíamos prohibíais prohibían	prohibí prohibiste prohibió prohibimos prohibisteis prohibieron	prohibiré prohibirás prohibirá prohibiremos prohibiréis prohibirán	prohibiría prohibirías prohibiría prohibiríamos prohibiríais prohibirían

In verbs with the stem root **ahi**, **ahu**, **ehi**, **ehu**, and **ohi**, the i when stressed is written **í**.

30. **querer** queriendo querido	**quiero** **quieres** **quiere** queremos queréis **quieren**	quería querías quería queríamos queríais querían	**quise** quisiste **quiso** quisimos quisisteis quisieron	**querré** **querrás** **querrá** querremos querréis **querrán**	**querría** **querrías** **querría** querríamos querríais **querrían**
31. **reír** **riendo** **reído**	**río** **ríes** **ríe** **reímos** reís **ríen**	reía reías reía reíamos reíais reían	reí **reíste** rió **reímos** **reísteis** rieron	reiré reirás reirá reiremos reiréis reirán	reiría reirías reiría reiríamos reiríais reirían
32. **saber** sabiendo sabido	**sé** sabes sabe sabemos sabéis saben	sabía sabías sabía sabíamos sabíais sabían	**supe** **supiste** **supo** **supimos** **supisteis** **supieron**	**sabré** **sabrás** **sabrá** sabremos sabréis sabrán	**sabría** **sabrías** **sabría** sabríamos sabríais sabrían
33. **salir** saliendo salido	**salgo** sales sale salimos salís salen	salía salías salía salíamos salíais salían	salí saliste salió salimos salisteis salieron	**saldré** **saldrás** **saldrá** **saldremos** **saldréis** **saldrán**	**saldría** **saldrías** **saldría** **saldríamos** **saldríais** **saldrían**

SUBJUNCTIVE

PRESENT	IMPERFECT	COMMANDS
ponga	pusiera (-se)	—
pongas	pusieras (-ses)	pon (no pongas)
ponga	pusiera (-se)	ponga
pongamos	pusiéramos (-semos)	pongamos
pongáis	pusierais (-seis)	poned (no pongáis)
pongan	pusieran (-sen)	pongan
prohíba	prohibiera (-se)	—
prohíbas	prohibieras (-ses)	prohíbe (no prohíbas)
prohíba	prohibiera (-se)	prohíba
prohibamos	prohibiéramos (-semos)	prohibamos
prohibáis	prohibierais (-seis)	prohibed (no prohibáis)
prohíban	prohibieran (-sen)	prohíban
quiera	quisiera (-se)	—
quieras	quisieras (-ses)	quiere (no quieras)
quiera	quisiera (-se)	quiera
queramos	quisiéramos (-semos)	queramos
queráis	quisierais (-seis)	quered (no queráis)
quieran	quisieran (-sen)	quieran
ría	riera (-se)	—
rías	rieras (-ses)	ríe (no rías)
ría	riera (-se)	ría
riamos	riéramos (-semos)	riamos
riáis	rierais (-seis)	reíd (no riáis)
rían	rieran (-sen)	rían
sepa	supiera (-se)	—
sepas	supieras (-ses)	sabe (no sepas)
sepa	supiera (-se)	sepa
sepamos	supiéramos (-semos)	sepamos
sepáis	supierais (-seis)	sabed (no sepáis)
sepan	supieran (-sen)	sepan
salga	saliera (-se)	—
salgas	salieras (-ses)	sal (no salgas)
salga	saliera (-se)	salga
salgamos	saliéramos (-semos)	salgamos
salgáis	salierais (-seis)	salid (no salgáis)
salgan	salieran (-sen)	salgan

INFINITIVE PRESENT PARTICIPLE PAST PARTICIPLE	**INDICATIVE**				
	PRESENT	IMPERFECT	PRETERIT	FUTURE	CONDITIONAL
34. **seguir (i,g)** **siguiendo** seguido	**sigo** **sigues** **sigue** seguimos seguís **siguen**	seguía seguías seguía seguíamos seguíais seguían	seguí seguiste **siguió** seguimos seguisteis **siguieron**	seguiré seguirás seguirá seguiremos seguiréis seguirán	seguiría seguirías seguiría seguiríamos seguiríais seguirían

In verbs ending in **-guir**, the **gu** changes to **g** before **a** and **o**: **sigo, siga**. (**Seguir** also follows stem-change pattern 24.)

35. **sentir (ie,i)** **sintiendo** sentido	**siento** **sientes** **siente** sentimos sentís **sienten**	sentía sentías sentía sentíamos sentíais sentían	sentí sentiste **sintió** sentimos sentisteis **sintieron**	sentiré sentirás sentirá sentiremos sentiréis sentirán	sentiría sentirías sentiría sentiríamos sentiríais sentirían

Certain **-ir** verbs change their stem vowel from **e** to **ie** in the shoe-pattern forms of the present indicative and present subjunctive and in the affirmative **tú** command. They show an additional stem-vowel change of **e** to **i** in the **nosotros** and **vosotros** forms of the present subjunctive, the **usted** and **ustedes** forms of the preterit, all forms of the imperfect subjunctive, and the present participle.

36. **ser** siendo sido	soy eres es somos sois son	era eras era éramos erais eran	fui fuiste fue fuimos fuisteis fueron	seré serás será seremos seréis serán	sería serías sería seríamos seríais serían
37. **tener** teniendo tenido	**tengo** **tienes** **tiene** tenemos tenéis **tienen**	tenía tenías tenía teníamos teníais tenían	**tuve** **tuviste** **tuvo** **tuvimos** **tuvisteis** **tuvieron**	**tendré** **tendrás** **tendrá** **tendremos** **tendréis** **tendrán**	**tendría** **tendrías** **tendría** **tendríamos** **tendríais** **tendrían**
38. **traer** **trayendo** **traído**	**traigo** traes trae traemos traéis traen	traía traías traía traíamos traíais traían	**traje** **trajiste** **trajo** **trajimos** **trajisteis** **trajeron**	traeré traerás traerá traeremos traeréis traerán	traería traerías traería traeríamos traeríais traerían
39. **valer** valiendo valido	**valgo** vales vale valemos valéis valen	valía valías valía valíamos valíais valían	valí valiste valió valimos valisteis valieron	**valdré** **valdrás** **valdrá** **valdremos** **valdréis** **valdrán**	**valdría** **valdrías** **valdría** **valdríamos** **valdríais** **valdrían**

SUBJUNCTIVE

PRESENT	IMPERFECT	COMMANDS
siga	siguiera (-se)	—
sigas	siguieras (-ses)	sigue (no sigas)
siga	siguiera (-se)	siga
sigamos	siguiéramos (-semos)	sigamos
sigáis	siguierais (-seis)	seguid (no sigáis)
sigan	siguieran (-sen)	sigan
sienta	sintiera (-se)	—
sientas	sintieras (-ses)	siente (no sientas)
sienta	sintiera (-se)	sienta
sintamos	sintiéramos (-semos)	sintamos
sintáis	sintierais (-seis)	sentid (no sintáis)
sientan	sintieran (-sen)	sientan
sea	fuera (-se)	—
seas	fueras (-ses)	sé (no seas)
sea	fuera (-se)	sea
seamos	fuéramos (-semos)	seamos
seáis	fuerais (-seis)	sed (no seáis)
sean	fueran (-sen)	sean
tenga	tuviera (-se)	—
tengas	tuvieras (-ses)	ten (no tengas)
tenga	tuviera (-se)	tenga
tengamos	tuviéramos (-semos)	tengamos
tengáis	tuvierais (-seis)	tened (no tengáis)
tengan	tuvieran (-sen)	tengan
traiga	trajera (-se)	—
traigas	trajeras (-ses)	trae (no traigas)
traiga	trajera (-se)	traiga
traigamos	trajéramos (-semos)	traigamos
traigáis	trajerais (-seis)	traed (no traigáis)
traigan	trajeran (-sen)	traigan
valga	valiera (-se)	—
valgas	valieras (-ses)	val (no valgas)
valga	valiera (-se)	valga
valgamos	valiéramos (-semos)	valgamos
valgáis	valierais (-seis)	valed (no valgáis)
valgan	valieran (-sen)	valgan

INFINITIVE PRESENT PARTICIPLE PAST PARTICIPLE	INDICATIVE				
	PRESENT	**IMPERFECT**	**PRETERIT**	**FUTURE**	**CONDITIONAL**
40. **vencer** (z) venciendo vencido	**venzo** vences vence vencemos vencéis vencen	vencía vencías vencía vencíamos vencíais vencían	vencí venciste venció vencimos vencisteis vencieron	venceré vencerás vencerá venceremos venceréis vencerán	vencería vencerías vencería venceríamos venceríais vencerían

In verbs ending in *consonant* + **cer** or **-cir**, the **c** changes to **z** before **a** or **o**.

| 41. **venir** **viniendo** venido | **vengo** **vienes** **viene** venimos venís **vienen** | venía venías venía veníamos veníais venían | **vine** **viniste** **vino** **vinimos** **vinisteis** **vinieron** | **vendré** **vendrás** **vendrá** **vendremos** **vendréis** **vendrán** | **vendría** **vendrías** **vendría** **vendríamos** **vendríais** **vendrían** |

| 42. **ver** viendo **visto** | **veo** ves ve vemos veis ven | **veía** **veías** **veía** **veíamos** **veíais** **veían** | **vi** viste **vio** vimos visteis vieron | veré verás verá veremos veréis verán | vería verías vería veríamos veríais verían |

| 43. **volver** (ue) volviendo **vuelto** | **vuelvo** **vuelves** **vuelve** volvemos volvéis **vuelven** | volvía volvías volvía volvíamos volvíais volvían | volví volviste volvió volvimos volvisteis volvieron | volveré volverás volverá volveremos volveréis volverán | volvería volverías volvería volveríamos volveríais volverían |

Numerous **-er** and **-ir** verbs change their stem vowel from **o** to **ue** in the shoe-pattern forms of the present indicative and present subjunctive and in the affirmative **tú** command.

SUBJUNCTIVE

PRESENT	IMPERFECT	COMMANDS
venza	venciera (-se)	—
venzas	vencieras (-ses)	vence (no venzas)
venza	venciera (-se)	venza
venzamos	venciéramos (´-semos)	venzamos
venzáis	vencierais (-seis)	venced (no venzáis)
venzan	vencieran (-sen)	venzan
venga	viniera (-se)	—
vengas	vinieras (-ses)	ven (no vengas)
venga	viniera (-se)	venga
vengamos	viniéramos (´-semos)	vengamos
vengáis	vinierais (-seis)	venid (no vengáis)
vengan	vinieran (-sen)	vengan
vea	viera (-se)	—
veas	vieras (-ses)	ve (no veas)
vea	viera (-se)	vea
veamos	viéramos (´-semos)	veamos
veáis	vierais (-seis)	ved (no veáis)
vean	vieran (-sen)	vean
vuelva	volviera (-se)	—
vuelvas	volvieras (-ses)	vuelve (no vuelvas)
vuelva	volviera (-se)	vuelva
volvamos	volviéramos (´-semos)	volvamos
volváis	volvierais (-seis)	volved (no volváis)
vuelvan	volvieran (-sen)	vuelvan

GLOSSARY OF GRAMMATICAL TERMS

As you learn Spanish, you may come across grammatical terms in English with which you are not familiar. The following glossary is a reference list of grammatical terms and definitions with examples. You will find that these terms are used in the grammatical explanations of this book. If the terms are unfamiliar to you, it will be helpful to refer to this list.

adjective   a word used to modify, qualify, define, or specify a noun or noun equivalent (*intricate* design, *volcanic* ash, *medical* examination)
A **demonstrative adjective** designates or points out a specific item. (*this* area)
A **descriptive adjective** provides description. (*narrow* street)
An **interrogative adjective** asks or questions. (*Which* page?)
A **possessive adjective** indicates possession. (*our* house)
A **predicate adjective** forms part of the predicate, complements a verb phrase. (His chances are *excellent.*)
In Spanish, the adjective form must agree with or show the same gender and number as the noun it modifies.
See **clause, adjective.**

adverb   a word used to qualify or modify a verb, adjective, another adverb, or some other modifying phrase or clause (soared *gracefully, very* sad)
See **clause, adverbial.**

agreement   the accordance of forms between subject and verb, in terms of person and number
In Spanish, the form of the adjective must also conform in gender and number with the modified noun or noun equivalent.

antecedent   the noun or noun equivalent referred to by a pronoun (The *book* is interesting, but *it* is difficult to read.)

article   a determining or nondetermining word used before a noun
A **definite article** limits, defines, or specifies. (*the* village)
An **indefinite article** refers to a nonspecific member of a group or class. (*a* village, *an* arrangement)
In Spanish, the article takes different forms to indicate the gender and number of a noun.

auxiliary   a verb or verb form used with other verbs to construct certain tenses, voices, or moods (He *is* leaving. She *has* arrived. You *must* listen.)

clause   a group of words consisting of a subject and a predicate and functioning as part of a complex or compound sentence rather than as a complete sentence.
An **adjective clause** functions as an adjective. (The ad calls for someone *who can speak Spanish*)
An **adverbial clause** functions as an adverb. (*Clearly aware of what he was saying,* he answered our question.)
A **dependent clause** modifies and is dependent upon another clause. (*Since the rain has stopped,* we can have a picnic.)
A **main clause** is capable of standing independently as a complete sentence. (If all goes well, *the plane will depart in twenty minutes.*)
A **noun clause** functions as subject or object. (I think *the traffic will be heavy.*)

cognate a word having a common root or being of the same or similar origin and meaning as a word in another language (*university* and *universidad*)

command See **mood (imperative)**.

comparative level of comparison used to show an increase or decrease of quantity or quality or to compare or show inequality between two items (*higher* prices, the *more* beautiful of the two mirrors, *less* diligently, *better* than)

comparison the forms an adjective or adverb takes to express change in the quantity or quality of an item or the relation, equal or unequal, between items

conditional a verb construction used in a contrary-to-fact statement consisting of a condition or an *if* clause and a conclusion (If you had told me you were sick, *I would have offered* to help.)
See **mood (subjunctive)**.

conjugation the set of forms a verb takes to indicate changes of person, number, tense, mood, and voice

conjunction a word used to link or connect sentences or parts of sentences

contraction an abbreviated or shortened form of a word or word group (*can't, we'll*)

diminutive a form of a word, usually a suffix added to the original word, used to indicate a smaller or younger version or variety and often expressive of endearment (duck*ling*, pup*py*, novel*lette*)

diphthong in speech, two vowel sounds changing from one to the other within one syllable (s*oi*l, b*oy*)

gender the class of a word by sex, either biological or linguistic. In English, almost all nouns are classified as masculine, feminine, or neuter according to the biological sex of the thing named; in Spanish, however, a word is classified as feminine or masculine (there is no neuter classification) on the basis of grammatical form or spelling.

idiom an expression that is grammatically or semantically unique to a particular language (*I caught a cold. Happy birthday.*) It must be learned as a unit because its meaning cannot be derived from knowing its parts.

imperative See **mood**.

indicative See **mood**.

infinitive the basic form of the verb, and the one listed in dictionaries, with no indication of person or number; it is often used in verb constructions and as a verbal noun, usually with "to" in English or with "-ar," "-er" or "-ir" in Spanish.

inversion See **word order (inverted)**.

mood the form and construction a verb assumes to express the manner in which the action or state takes place.
The **imperative mood** is used to express commands. (*Walk* to the park with me.)
The **indicative mood**, the form most frequently used, is usually expressive of certainty and fact. (My neighbor *walks* to the park every afternoon.)
The **subjunctive mood** is used in expressions of possibility, doubt, or hypothetical situations. (If I *were* thin, I'd be happier.)

noun   word that names something and usually functions as a subject or an object (*lady, country, family*)
See **clause, noun.**

number   the form a word or phrase assumes to indicate singular or plural (*light/lights, mouse/mice, he has/they have*)
A **cardinal number** is used in counting or expressing quantity. (*one, twenty-three, 6,825*)
An **ordinal number** refers to sequence. (*second, fifteenth, thirty-first*)

object   a noun or noun equivalent
A **direct object** receives the action of the verb. (The boy caught a *fish.*)
An **indirect object** is affected by the action of the verb. (Please do *me* a favor.)
A **prepositional object** completes the relationship expressed by the preposition. (The cup is on the *table.*)

participle   a verb form used as an adjective or adverb and in forming tenses
A **past participle** relates to the past or a perfect tense and takes the appropriate ending. (*written* proof, the door has been *locked*)
A **present participle** assumes the progressive "-ing" ending in English. (*protesting* loudly; will be *seeing*)
In Spanish, a participle used as an adjective or in an adjectival phrase must agree in gender and number with the modified noun or noun equivalent.

passive   See **voice (passive).**

person   designated by the personal pronoun and/or by the verb form
first person the speaker or writer (*I, we*)
second person the person(s) addressed (*you*)
In Spanish, there are two forms of address: the familiar and the polite.
third person the person(s) or thing(s) spoken about (*she, he, it, they*)

phrase   a word group that forms a unit of expression, often named after the part of speech it contains or forms
A **prepositional phrase** contains a preposition. (*in the room, between the window and the door*)

predicate   the verb or that portion of a statement that contains the verb and gives information about the subject (He *laughed.* My brother *commutes to the university by train.*)

prefix   a letter or letter group added at the beginning of a word to alter the meaning (*non*committal, *re*discover)

preposition   a connecting word used to indicate a spatial, temporal, causal, affective, directional, or some other relation between a noun or pronoun and the sentence or a portion of it (We waited *for* six hours. The article was written *by* a famous journalist.)

pronoun   a word used in place of a noun
A **demonstrative pronoun** refers to something previously mentioned in context. (If you need hiking boots, I recommend *these.*)
An **indefinite pronoun** denotes a nonspecific class or item. (*Nothing* has changed.)
An **interrogative pronoun** asks about a person or thing. (*Whose* is this?)
An **object pronoun** functions as a direct, an indirect, or a prepositional object. (Three persons saw *her.* Write *me* a letter. The flowers are for *you.*)

A **possessive pronoun** indicates possession. (The blue car is *ours*.)

A **reciprocal pronoun** refers to two or more persons or things equally involved. (María and Juan saw *each other* today.)

A **reflexive pronoun** refers back to the subject. (They introduced *themselves*.)

A **subject pronoun** functions as the subject of a clause or sentence. (*He* departed a while ago.)

reciprocal construction See **pronoun (reciprocal)**.

reflexive construction See **pronoun (reflexive)**.

sentence a word group, or even a single word, that forms a meaningful complete expression

A **declarative sentence** states something and is followed by a period. (*The museum contains many fine examples of folk art.*)

An **exclamatory sentence** exhibits force or passion and is followed by an exclamation point. (*I want to be left alone!*)

An **interrogative sentence** asks a question and is followed by a question mark. (*Who are you?*)

subject a noun or noun equivalent acting as the agent of the action or the person, place, thing, or abstraction spoken about (*The fishermen* drew in their nets. *The nets* were filled with the day's catch.)

suffix a letter or letter group added to the end of a word to alter the meaning or function (like*ness*, transport*ation*, joy*ous*, love*ly*)

superlative level of comparison used to express the highest or lowest level or to indicate the highest or lowest relation in comparing more than two items (*highest* prices, the *most* beautiful, *least* diligently)

The **absolute superlative** expresses a very high level without reference to comparison. (the *very beautiful* mirror, *most diligent*, *extremely well*)

tense the form a verb takes to express the time of the action, state, or condition in relation to the time of speaking or writing

The **future tense** relates something that has not yet occurred. (It *will* exist. We *will* learn.)

The **future perfect tense** relates something that has not yet occurred but will have taken place and be complete by some future time. (It *will have* existed. We *will have* learned.)

The **past tense** relates to something that occurred in the past, distinguished as **preterit** (It *existed*. We *learned*.) and **imperfect** (It *was* existing. We *were learning*.)

The **past perfect tense** relates to an occurrence that began and ended before or by a past event or time spoken or written of. (It *had existed*. We *had learned*.)

The **present tense** relates to now, the time of speaking or writing, or to a general, timeless fact. (It *exists*. We *learn*. Fish *swim*.)

The **present perfect tense** relates to an occurrence that began at some point in the past but was finished by the time of speaking or writing. (It *has existed*. We *have learned*.)

The **progressive tense** relates an action that is, was, or will be in progress or continuance. (It *is* happening. It *was happening*. It *will be happening*.)

triphthong in speech, three vowel sounds changing from one to another within one syllable (*wire, hour*)

verb a word that expresses action or a state or condition (*walk, be, feel*)

A **spelling-changing verb** undergoes spelling changes in conjugation (infinitive: *buy*; past indicative: *bought*)

A **stem-changing verb** undergoes a stem-vowel change in conjugation (infinitive: *draw*; past indicative: *drew*)

voice the form a verb takes to indicate the relation between the expressed action or state and the subject

The **active voice** indicates that the subject is the agent of the action (The child *sleeps*. The professor *lectures*.)

The **passive voice** indicates that the subject does not initiate the action but that the action is directed toward the subject. (I *was contacted* by my attorney. The road *got slippery* from the rain. He *became* tired.)

word order the sequence of words in a clause or sentence

In **inverted word order**, an element other than the subject appears first. (*If the weather permits*, we plan to vacation in the country. *Please* be on time. *Have* you met my parents?)

In **normal word order**, the subject comes first, followed by the predicate. (*The people celebrated the holiday*.)

VOCABULARIO ESPAÑOL-INGLÉS

This vocabulary includes contextual meanings of all active vocabulary and idiomatic expressions as well as most passive words not otherwise glossed where they appear in the text. It excludes most cardinal numbers; diminutives; superlatives ending in **-ísimo**; most adverbs ending in **-mente**; most proper names and most conjugated verb forms. The entries are arranged according to the Spanish alphabet; that is, words beginning with **ch, ll,** and **ñ** are found listed separately after all words beginning with **c, l,** and **n**, respectively. In the same way, words containing **ch, ll,** and **ñ** are placed alphabetically after words containing, **c, l,** and **n**, respectively. A number following a word or phrase indicates the chapter of its first appearance. **CP** refers to the **Capítulo preliminar** and **L1** to **L9** refer to the nine interchapter **lecturas**. A number in parentheses after a verb entry refers to one of the numbered verb paradigms in **Verbos**, the verb charts on pages 522-538. Stem and spelling changes are also given in parentheses after a verb entry.

The following abbreviations are used:

adj	adjective	*p*	plural
adv	adverb	*pp*	past participle
contr	contraction	*prep*	preposition
dir obj	direct object	*pres*	present
f	feminine	*pres p*	present participle
fam	familiar	*pret*	preterit
imp	imperfect	*pron*	pronoun
indic	indicative	*recip*	reciprocal
indir obj	indirect object	*refl*	reflexive
inf	infinitive	*rel pron*	relative pronoun
m	masculine	*subj*	subject
n	noun	*subjunc*	subjunctive
obj of prep	object of preposition		

A

a to **1**; **a menos que** unless **16**; **a pie** on foot **12**; **A propósito...** By the way . . . **19**; **A ver.** Let's see. **8**; **¿A qué hora?** At what time? **5**; **¿a quién?** whom? **2**

el **abogado,** la **abogada** lawyer **18**

abrazar (c/14) to hug, embrace **15**

el **abrazo** hug **15**

el **abrigo** overcoat **8**

abril April **4**

abrir to open **2**

abstracto abstract **13**

absurdo: ¡Qué absurdo! How absurd! **14**

la **abuela** grandmother **1**

el **abuelo** grandfather **1**

aburrido (*with* **estar**) bored; (*with* **ser**) boring **2**

aburrirse to be (get) bored **16**

acabar to end, finish, run out **18**; **acabar de** (+ *inf*) to have just (*done something*) **16**

el **accidente** accident **9**

acerca de concerning, about **6**

acompañado de accompanied by **L4**

acompañar to accompany **8**

aconsejar: Le (Te) aconsejo que

(+ *subjunc*) . . . I advise you to . . . **16**

el **acontecimiento** event, happening **11**

acordarse (ue/8) (de) to remember **10**; **No me acuerdo.** I don't remember. **18**

acostarse (ue/8) to go to bed **8**

acostumbrarse to get used to **8**

el **acto** act (*in a play*) **13**

el **actor** actor **13**

la **actriz** actress **13**

actual current, present **L4**

actualmente at present **L8**

el **acuerdo**: el **acuerdo pacífico** peace agreement **L9**; **Estoy de acuerdo.** I agree. **14**; **No, no estoy de acuerdo.** No, I don't agree. **14**

además (de) besides, in addition to **L7**, **19**

adicional additional **19**

Adiós. Good-bye. **CP**

admirar to admire **11**

¿adónde? (to) where? **2**

el **adorno** decoration, ornament **14**

la **aduana** customs, customs house **12**

el **aeropuerto** airport **1**

el **aficionado**, la **aficionada** fan, enthusiast **9**

la **agencia** agency **18**; la **agencia de trabajo** employment agency **18**; la **agencia de viajes** travel agency **2**

el, la **agente** agent **1**; el, la **agente de aduana** customs agent **12**; el, la **agente de viajes** travel agent **18**

agosto August **4**

agradable pleasant, nice **2**

agradecer (zc/6) to thank **20**

agradecido thankful, grateful **4**; **Muy agradecido.** (I'm) very grateful. **4**

agrandar to enlarge **19**

el **agua** *f* water **5**; el **agua mineral** mineral water **6**

ahora now **1**; **ahora mismo** right now **3**

ahorrar to save (*time, money*) **17**

el **aire** air **5**

aislar (í/16) to isolate **L8**

al (*contr of* **a** + **el**) to the **1**; **al** (+ *inf*) on, upon (+ *pres p*) **16**; **Al contrario...** On the contrary . . . **14**

el **alba** *f* dawn **13**

la **alcoba** bedroom **19**

alegrarse to be (get) happy **16**

alegre happy **16**

alegremente happily **14**

la **alegría** happiness **16**

alemán German **2**

la **alfarería** pottery; potter shop **17**

la **alfombra** carpet, rug **19**

algo something **14**

alguien someone, anyone **14**

algún, alguno(-a, -os, -as) some, any **L5**, **14**

aliado allied **L9**

allí (*or* **allá**) there **1**

el **alma** *f* soul **12**

el **almacén** grocery store **17**

el **almirante** admiral **L8**

almorzar (ue,c/8,14) to eat lunch **6**

el **almuerzo** lunch (*main meal in most Hispanic countries*) **6**

el **alquiler** rent **17**

alto high; tall **2**

el **ama de casa** *f* housewife **18**

amable kind, nice, pleasant **2**; **Usted es (Tú eres) muy amable.** You're very kind. **4**

el, la **amante** lover **16**

amarillo yellow **8**

ambos both **L8**

amenazar (c/14) to threaten **L8**

el **americano**, la **americana** American **5**

el **amigo**, la **amiga** friend **CP**

el **amor** love **15**

anaranjado orange **8**

andar (1) to walk; to run (*as a watch, car*) **5**; **andar en bicicleta** to ride a bicycle **12**

andino Andean **L9**

anglosajón Anglo-Saxon **L3**

el **anillo** ring **15**

el **aniversario** anniversary **14**

anoche last night **8**

ansioso anxious **16**

anterior earlier **L3**

antes (de) before **6**; **antes (de) que** before **16**

antiguo old, ancient **L1**, **10**; (*before noun*) former **18**

la **antología** anthology **13**

la **antropología** anthropology **3**

la **anulación matrimonial** marriage annulment **15**

anunciar to announce **11**

el **anuncio** announcement **11**

el **año** year **3**; el **año pasado** last year **8**; el **Año Nuevo** New Year's Day **14**; los **años 70** the seventies **L9**

apagar (gu/23) to turn off, extinguish **11**

el **apartamento** apartment **2**

el **apellido** surname **5**

apoyar to support **L8**

el **apoyo** support **L8**

aprender to learn **2**

aquel, aquella *adj* that **3**

aquél, aquélla *pron* that (one) **3**

aquello *neuter pron* that **3**

aquellos, aquellas *adj* that **3**

aquéllos, aquéllas *pron* those **3**

aquí (*or* **acá**) here **CP**

el **árbol** tree **14**

argentino Argentine **1**

el **arma** *f* arm, weapon **11**

el **arpa** *f* harp **L4**

la **arqueología** archeology **3**

el **arqueólogo**, la **arqueóloga** archeologist **18**

la **arquitectura** architecture **3**

arreglarse to work out, turn out all right **14**

el **arroz** rice **6**

el **arte** *f* art **13**

la **artesanía** craft work **17**

el **artesano**, la **artesana** artisan **17**

el, la **artista** artist **1**

la **asamblea** assembly **L9**

así thus **L7**; **Así así.** So-so. **CP**; **así que** so **9**; **Sí, así es.** Yes, that's so **14**; **Así pienso.** That's how I think. **14**

asistir a to attend **3**

la **aspirina** aspirin **3**

asustado scared, frightened, startled **16**

asustar to scare, to frighten **16**

asustarse to be (get) scared, frightened **16**

atacar (**qu/3**) to attack **11**

el, la **atleta** athlete **10**

el **atletismo** athletics **9**

aumentar to increase, to go up **17**

el **aumento** increase, raise **11** el **aumento de sueldo** raise in salary **11**

aún still, yet **10**

aunque although **16**

el **auto** automobile **CP**

el **autobús** bus **5**

el **autor**, la **autora** author **13**

el **autostop** hitchhiking **12**; **hacer autostop** to hitchhike **12**

la **avenida** avenue **2**

avergonzado embarrassed, ashamed **16**

avergonzarse (**üe,c/2**) to be (get) embarrassed, ashamed **16**

el **avión** airplane **1**

ay: ¡Ay, Dios mío! Oh, my goodness! **5**

ayer yesterday **8**

la **ayuda** help **7**

ayudar to help **5**

azteca Aztec **3**

el **azúcar** sugar **6**

azul blue **L2, 8**

B

bailar to dance **1**

el **bailarín**, la **bailarina** dancer **7**

el **baile** dance **7**

bajar to go down, decrease **11**; **bajar (de)** to get off, descend **8**

bajo short (*person*) **3**

el **balcón** balcony **14**

el **ballet** ballet **13**

el **banco** bank **5**

la **bandera** flag **8**

bañarse to bathe **8**

el **baño** bathroom **19**

barato cheap, inexpensive **17**

barbaridad: ¡Qué barbaridad! Good grief! **5**

el **barco** boat, ship **12**

el **barrio** neighborhood **5**

el **básquetbol** basketball **9**

bastante *adj* enough **5**; *adv* quite, rather, fairly **5**

la **basura** garbage, trash **5**

el **bebé** baby **10**

beber to drink **3**

la **bebida** drink, beverage **6**

el **béisbol** baseball **9**

besar to kiss **15**

el **beso** kiss **15**

la **biblioteca** library **2**

la **bicicleta** bicycle **4**

bien well, OK **CP**; **¡Qué bien!** Good! (How nice!) **9**

el **bien** good **L7**

Bienvenido. Welcome **11**

la **biología** biology **3**

el **bistec** steak **6**

el **bizcocho** cookie, biscuit **17**

blanco white **8**

la **blusa** blouse **8**

la **boca** mouth **10**

la **boda** wedding **15**

la **boina** beret **8**

el **boleto** ticket (*for an event or transportation*) **7**

el **bolívar** *monetary unit of Venezuela* **17**

el **bolso** handbag, purse **8**

el **bombero**, la **bombera** fire fighter **18**

bonito pretty **2**

la **bota** boot **8**

la **boutique** boutique **17**

el **brazo** arm **10**

brindar to toast **20**

broma: ¡Pero lo dices en broma! But you're kidding! **10**; **¿Habla(s) en broma?** Are you joking? **10**

bueno (*shortened form,* **buen**) good **2**; **¡Buena**

lección! That's a (good) lesson for you! 5; **Buena pregunta.** Good question. 8; **Buenas noches.** Good evening. *(after sunset)* **CP; Buenas tardes.** Good afternoon. *(until about sunset)* **CP; Bueno.** Good; OK; Well . . . 1; **Bueno, nos vemos.** We'll be seeing each other. 1; **Buenos días.** Good morning. Hello. **CP; ¡Buen provecho!** Good appetite!, Enjoy your meal! 6

buscar (qu/3) to look for 1

C

el, la **cabecilla** ringleader, rebel leader **L9**

el **cabello** hair 10

la **cabeza** head 10

cabo: Al fin y al cabo... In the end . . . To make a long story short . . . 17

cada each, every 11; **cada vez más** more and more **L8**

la **cadera** hip 10

caer (4) to fall; to drop 18

el **café** cafe 1; coffee 6

la **cafetera** coffeepot 19

la **cafetería** cafeteria 2

la **caja** cashier's office; cash register 12

el **cajero,** la **cajera** cashier 12

los **calcetines** socks 8

el **calendario** calendar 3

la **calidad** quality 17

caliente hot *(not used for weather or people)* 4

calmarse to calm down 16

los **calzoncillos** underpants 8

la **calle** street 2

la **cama** bed 19

la **cámara** camera 1

la **camarera** waitress 6

el **camarero** waiter 6

cambiar to change 5; to exchange 10; **cambiar de tema** to change the subject 19

cambio: Pero en cambio... But on the other hand . . . 14

caminar to walk 8

el **camino** road, way **L5**

la **camisa** shirt 8

la **camiseta** undershirt 8

el **campamento** camp 4; **ir de campamento** to go camping 4

el **campeón,** la **campeona** champion 9

el **campo** country *(as opposed to city)* 4

el **canal** channel 11

la **canción** song 7

la **cancha** court; *(sport)* field *(e.g.,* **cancha de fútbol)** 9

el **candelabro** candelabrum, menorah 14

cansado tired 16

cansarse to be (get) tired 16

el, la **cantante** singer 13

cantar to sing 7

la **capital** capital (city) **CP**

el **capítulo** chapter **CP**

la **cápsula** capsule 10

la **cara** face 10

¡Caramba! Good grief! 5

el **Caribe** Caribbean **L1**

cariñosamente affectionately 20

la **carne** meat 6

caro expensive 3

el **carpintero,** la **carpintera** carpenter 19

la **carrera** career 18

la **carta** letter 2; las **cartas** playing cards 7

el **cartaginés,** la **cartaginesa** Carthaginian **L5**

la **casa** house, home **CP**

casado married 15

el **casamiento** marriage; wedding 15

casarse (con) to get married (to) 8

casi almost **L2,** 9

las **castañuelas** castanets **L4**

el **catalán,** la **catalana** Catalan, of Catalonia **L2**

el **catarro** cold 10; **tener catarro** to have a cold 10

la **catedral** cathedral 2

católico Catholic 19

la **causa** cause 19

la **celebración** celebration 14

celebrar to celebrate 11

celoso jealous 7; **ponerse celoso** to become jealous 15

la **cena** supper 6

cenar to have dinner 8

la **censura** censorship **L8**

el **centro** downtown; center 2

la **cerámica** ceramics, pottery 12

cerca (de) near (to), nearby 1

el **cerdo** pork 6; **chuleta de cerdo** pork chop 6

el **cereal** cereal, grain 6

cerrar (ie/25) to close 5

la **cerveza** beer 6

cien(to) one hundred 3

la **ciencia** science 3; las **ciencias de computación** computer science 3; las **ciencias naturales** natural science 3; las **ciencias políticas** political science 3; las **ciencias sociales** social science 3

costar (ue/8) to cost **6**

el **costo** cost **17**; el **costo de (la) vida** cost of living **11**

creer (que) (y/10) to believe, think (that) **2**; **Creo que** (+ *indic*) . . . I believe that . . . **15**; **Creo que sí (no).** I believe so (not). **18**; **No creo que** (+ *subjunc*) . . . I don't believe that . . . **18**; **¡No lo puedo creer!** I can't believe it! **10**; **¡Ya lo creo!** I believe it! **14**

el **crimen** crime **5**

el, la **criminal** criminal **5**

la **cruz** cross **11**; la **Cruz Roja** Red Cross **11**

cruzar (c/14) to cross, go across **L1, 3**

el **cuaderno** notebook, workbook **CP**

la **cuadra** block **12**

el **cuadro** painting, picture **12**

¿cuál(es)? which? which ones? **2**; **¿Cuál es el número de teléfono?** What is the telephone number? **3**

cualquier any **L7**

cuando when **2**

¿cuándo? when? **2**

cuanto: en cuanto a with regard to **L8**

¿cuánto(-a, -os, -as)? how much? how many? **2**; **¿Cuánto cuesta(n)?** How much does it (do they) cost? **3**; **¡Cuánto me alegro!** How happy I am! **9**

cuarto fourth **2**

el **cuarto** room **19**; el **cuarto de baño** bathroom **19**

cubano-americano Cuban-American **9**

cubrir to cover **12**

la **cuchara** spoon **6**

el **cuchillo** knife **6**

el **cuello** neck **10**

la **cuenta** check, bill **6**; **La cuenta, por favor.** The check, please. **6**; **A fin de cuentas...** After all . . . , All things considered **17**

el, la **cuentista** short story writer **13**

el **cuento** short story, tale **13**

la **cuerda** string **L4**

el **cuerpo** body **10**

la **cueva** cave **L5**

Cuidado. Watch out., Be careful. **4**

cuidar (a) to take care (of) **17**

culpa: Tiene(s) la culpa., Es su (tu) culpa. It's your fault **5**

la **cumbia** *Latin American dance* **7**

el **cumpleaños** birthday **4**

cumplir to carry out, to fulfill **15**

la **cuñada** sister-in-law **1**

el **cuñado** brother-in-law **1**

el **cura** priest **18**

curarse to be cured, get well **10**

el **curso** course **6**

Ch

la **chaqueta** jacket **8**

el **charango** *guitar made from an armadillo shell* **L4**

¡Chau! Bye!, So long! **1**

el **cheque: cheque de viajero** traveler's check **12**

la **chica** girl **2**

el **chico** boy **2**

el **chile** chili, pepper **6**

chileno Chilean **4**

el **chiste** joke **16**

el **chocolate** chocolate **6**

D

la **dama** lady **13**

dar (11) to give **7**; **dar un paseo** to take a walk, go for a stroll **7**; **darle hambre (sed, sueño)** to make (someone) hungry (thirsty, sleepy) **7**; **darle las gracias** (to thank (someone) **7**; **darle rabia (a alguien)** to make (someone) angry **16**; **darle risa (a alguien)** to make (someone) laugh **16**; **darle vergüenza (a alguien)** to make (someone) ashamed **16**

de of; from; about; made of **15**; **¿De acuerdo?** OK?, Do you agree? **1**; **¿de dónde?** from where? **2**; **de habla hispana** Spanish-speaking **L3**; **de la mañana** A.M. **5**; **de la noche** P.M. (*after sunset*) **5**; **de la tarde** P.M. (*noon to sunset*) **5**; **De nada.** You are welcome., It's nothing. **4**; **¿De qué color es...?** What color is . . . ? **8**; **¿de quién?** whose? **2**; **¿De veras?** Really? **10**; **de vez en cuando** from time to time **4**; **el, la de** that of **L6**

debajo (de) under **6**

deber to owe **17**; **deber** (+ *inf*) ought to, should, must (do something) **2**; **¡Debe(n) estar muy**

contento(s)! You must be very happy! 19; **Eso debe ser terrible.** That must be terrible 5; **¿Se debe (+ inf.)...?** Should one (we, I) . . . ? 18

debido a due to **L9**

decidir to decide 8

décimo tenth 2

decir (12) to say, tell 6; **¿Cómo se dice...?** How do you say . . . ? 1

el **dedo** finger 10; el **dedo del pie** toe 10

dejar to leave (something behind) 8; to let, allow 18; **dejar de** to stop **L8**

del (contr of **de** + **el**) from the; of the 1

delante de in front of **L4**

delgado slim 6

delicioso delicious 2

demasiado too much 8; **Es demasiado...** It's too . . . 17; **¡Esto (Eso) es demasiado!** This (That) is too much 9

demócrata democratic 19

dentro (de) inside, within 2

depender: Depende de... It depends on . . . 8

el, la **dependiente** salesclerk; shop assistant; clerk 17

deprimido depressed 16

deprimirse to be (get) depressed 16

derecho adj right 10; straight ahead (for directions) 12; **a la derecha** on, to the right 2

el **derecho** right 11; los **derechos humanos** human rights 11

derrocar (qu/3) to overthrow **L9**

el **desayuno** breakfast 6

descansar to rest 10

el **descendiente** descendant **L3**

descortés impolite 2

describir to describe 2

descubrir to discover 2

desde from (a certain time); since 6; **desde un principio** from the very beginning **L9**

desear to want, wish 1; **¿Qué desea(n) pedir?** What do you wish (would you like) to order? 6

el **desempleo** unemployment 5

el **desfile** parade 14

desgraciadamente unfortunately **L8**

la **desilusión** disappointment **L4**

desilusionado disappointed 16

despacio: Más despacio, por favor. Slower, please 3

la **despedida** farewell, leave-taking 16

despertarse (ie/25) to wake up 8

después (de) after; later, afterwards, then 5; **Después...** Then . . . 11; **Después de pasar...** After passing . . . 12; **después (de) que** after 16; **Después de todo...** After all . . . 17; **¿Y después?** And then what? 11; **¿Y qué pasó después?** And then what happened? 11

destruir (y/7) to destroy 10

el **detalle** detail 9

el, la **detective** detective 16

detener (37) to arrest **L8**

detrás (de) behind 6

la **deuda** debt **L9**; **deuda externa** foreign debt **L9**

devolver (ue/43) to return, to take back 12

devoto devout 19

el **día** day **CP**; el **Día de Acción de Gracias** (U.S.) Thanksgiving 14; **Día de la Madre** Mother's Day 14; el **Día de los Muertos** Day of the Dead 14; el **Día de (los) Reyes** Epiphany 14; el **Día de los Trabajadores** Labor Day 14; el **día feriado** holiday 14

el **diablo** devil **L7**

el **diagnóstico** diagnosis 10

diariamente daily 14

diciembre December 4

la **dictadura** dictatorship **L8**

los **dientes** teeth 10

la **dieta** diet 6; **estar a dieta** to be on a diet 6

diferente different 14

difícil difficult 2

difícilmente with difficulty 14

el **dinero** money 5

el **Dios** God 4; **¡Ay, Dios mío!** Oh, my goodness! 5; **Gracias a Dios.** Thank God., Thank goodness 9

directamente directly 14

el **director,** la **directora** director 13

el **disco** record (music) 17

la **discoteca** disco, discotheque 7

la **discriminación** discrimination 5

disculpar to forgive 16; **Discúlpeme.** Excuse me., I'm sorry. 16

disculparse to apologize, to excuse oneself **20**

la **diversión** diversion, pastime **7**

divertido amusing, funny **9**

divertirse (ie,i/35) to have a good time; to enjoy oneself **8**

divorciarse to (get a) divorce **15**

el **divorcio** divorce **15**

doblar to turn **8**; **Doble a la izquierda (derecha).** Turn left (right). **12**

la **docena** dozen **19**

el **doctor,** la **doctora** doctor **CP**

el **dólar** dollar **3**

doler (ue/43) to hurt **10**; **Me duele el pie.** My foot hurts. **10**

el **dolor** pain **10**; el **dolor de cabeza** headache **3**; el **dolor de estómago** stomachache **3**

el **domingo** Sunday **4**

don *title of respect used before a man's first name* **11**

donde where **2**

¿dónde? where? **1**

doña *title of respect used before woman's first name* **11**

dormir (ue,u/13) to sleep **6**

dormirse (ue, u/13) to fall asleep **8**

el **dormitorio** bedroom **19**

el **drama** drama, play **13**

la **ducha** shower **19**

la **duda** doubt **18**; **No hay duda de que** (+ *indic*) There's no doubt that . . . **15**

dudar to doubt **14**

dudoso: Es dudoso. It's doubtful. **18**

el **dulce** candy **14**; los **dulces** sweets, candies **14**

durante during **6**

durar to last **L5, 15**

E

e and (*replaces* y *before words beginning* i- *or* hi-) **17**

echar to throw out **L9**

económico economic **11**

ecuatoriano Ecuadorian **19**

la **edición** edition **18**

el **edificio** building **3**

el **ejemplo** example **CP**; **por ejemplo** for example **CP**

el **ejercicio** exercise **CP**

el **ejército** army **11**

el the **1**

él he **CP**; **él** *obj of prep* him **6**

la **elección** election **11**

el **elefante** elephant **8**

elegante elegant **2**

elegido elected **L9**

ella she **CP**; **ella** *obj of prep* them **6**

ellos, ellas they **CP**; *obj of prep* them **6**

embargo: sin embargo nevertheless, however **L8, 19**

la **emoción** emotion **16**

emocionante exciting **9**

la **empanada** a type of meat pastry **10**

empeorar to worsen **L8**

empezar (ie,c/25,14) to begin, start **5**

el **empleado,** la **empleada** employee **17**

el **empleo** job, employment **5**

empujar to push **16**

en in, on; at **CP**; **En cambio...** On the other hand . . . **14**; **en casa** at home **CP**; **en caso (de) que** in case **16**; **en cuanto** as soon as **16**; **en general** in general **1**; **en punto** on the dot **5**; **En resumen...** In summary . . . , In conclusion . . . **17**; **¿En serio?** Really? **11**

enamorarse (de) to fall in love (with) **15**

encabezar (c/14) to head **L8**

Encantado. I am delighted **CP**

encantar to delight **6**; **Me encanta(n)...** I love . . . **6**

la **enchilada** enchilada **6**

encontrar (ue/8) to find **L2, 6**

encontrarse (ue/8) con to meet (up with); to run into **12**

encubierto covered up, behind the scenes **L9**

el **enemigo,** la **enemiga** enemy **L6**

enero January **4**

enfadarse to get angry **8**

enfermarse to get sick **10**

la **enfermedad** sickness, illness **10**

el **enfermero,** la **enfermera** nurse **10**

enfermo sick **1**

enfrente de in front of, opposite **2**

enojado angry **16**

enojarse to get angry **8**

la **ensalada** salad **6**

el, la **ensayista** essayist **13**

el **ensayo** essay **13**

enseñar to teach; to show **1**

entender (ie/26) to understand **5**

enterarse (de) to find out (about) **9**

entonces then; well **5**

la **entrada** ticket (*for an event*) **7**; entrance, entryway **19**

entrar (en) to enter, come *or* go in **5**

entre between **6**; **Entre paréntesis...** Incidentally . . . , By the way . . . **19**

entregarse (gu/23) to surrender **L8**

entristecerse (zc/6) to become sad **20**

enviar (í/16) to send **12**

la **época** time, era, epoch **11**

el **equipaje** baggage, luggage **12**

el **equipo** team **9**

escaparse to escape **L3**

la **escena** scene **13**

el **escocés**, la **escocesa** Scot **L2**

escoger (j/15) to choose **13**

escribir to write **2**

el **escritor**, la **escritora** writer **13**

el **escritorio** desk **CP**

la **escritura** writing **L6**

escuchar to listen (to) **7**

la **escuela** school **2**

el **escultor**, la **escultora** sculptor **13**

la **escultura** sculpture **13**

ese, esa *adj* that **3**

ése, ésa *pron* that (one) **3**

el **esfuerzo** effort **L9**

eso *neuter pron* that **3**; **Eso debe ser terrible.** That must be terrible. **5**; **Eso es.** That's it. **14**; **¡Eso es demasiado!** That is too much! **9**; **¡Eso es terrible (aburrido)!** That's terrible (boring)! **17**

Eso no se hace. That's not done (allowed). **18**

esos, esas *adj* those **3**

ésos, ésas *pron* those **3**

la **espalda** *n* back **10**

el **español** Spanish (*language*) **CP**

especial special **CP**

especialmente specially, especially **14**

el **espectador**, la **espectadora** spectator **9**

la **esperanza** hope **L9**

esperar to hope, to want (for) **4**; **Es de esperar.** It's to be expected. **5**; **¡Espere(n)!** Wait! **4**

la **esposa** wife **1**

el **esposo** husband **1**

el **esquí** ski **9**

el **esquiador**, la **esquiadora** skier **9**

esquiar (í/16) to ski **4**

la **esquina** corner **12**

establecer (zc/6) to establish **L8**

la **estación** season **4**; station **8**

el **estadio** stadium **3**

el **estado** state **L6**

los **Estados Unidos** United States **1**

estante: el **estante de libros** bookshelf **19**

estar (17) to be **CP**; **estar bien (mal, así así)** to be well (unwell, so-so) **CP**; **estar de acuerdo (con)** to agree, to be in agreement (with) **2**; **estar de buen humor** to be in a good mood **13**; **estar de vacaciones** to be on vacation **2**; **estar enamorado (de)** to be in love (with) **15**; **Está al lado de...** It's next

to . . . **12**; **Está al norte (sur, este, oeste) de...** It's north (south, east, west) of . . . **2**; **Está bien.** It's OK. **16**; **¿Está bien que** (+ *subjunc*) ...? Is it OK to . . . ? **18**; **Está en el centro.** It's downtown. **12**; **Está en la esquina de...** It's on the corner of . . . **12**; **Estoy de acuerdo.** I agree. **14**; **Estoy seguro que** (+ *indic*)... I'm sure that . . . **15**

el **este** east **1**

este, esta *adj* this **3**

éste, ésta *pron* this (one) **3**

el **estilo** style **2**

estimado dear (*in a formal letter heading*) **20**

esto *neuter pron* this **3**; **¡Esto es increíble!** This is incredible! **10**

el **estómago** stomach **10**

estos, estas *adj* these **3**

éstos, éstas *pron* these **3**

el, la **estudiante** student **CP**

estudiar to study **1**

el **estudio** study **3**

la **estufa** stove **19**

estupendo great, wonderful **3**

eterno eternal **15**

exacto exact; exactly **14**

el **examen** test, exam **3**

excelente excellent **CP**

excepto except **6**

el **exilado**, la **exilada** exile **L3**

la **experiencia** experience **18**

el **experto**, la **experta** expert **11**

explicar (qu/3) to explain **L2**

el **explorador**, la
exploradora explorer
11

la **exposición** exhibit,
exhibition **13**

extra extra **6**

extranjero foreign **L8**

extremadamente
extremely **14**

F

fabuloso fabulous **17**

fácil easy **2**

fácilmente easily **14**

la **falda** skirt **8**

falso false **CP**

la **falta** lack **15**

faltar to be missing *or*
lacking **6**; **Nos
falta(n)...** We need . . .
6

la **familia** family **CP**

famoso famous **10**

fantástico fantastic **12**

la **farmacia** pharmacy **1**

fascinante fascinating **9**

el **favor** favor **6**; **Por favor.**
Please. **CP**

favorito favorite **4**

febrero February **4**

la **fecha** date (*day of year*) **4**

¡Felicitaciones!
Congratulations! **CP**

felicitar to congratulate
20

feliz happy **2**; **Feliz fin
de semana.** Have a
good weekend. **1**

el **fenicio**, la **fenicia**
Phoenician **L5**

el **ferrocarril** railway **12**

la **fiebre** fever **10**

fiel faithful **7**

la **fiesta** party; holiday;
celebration **7**; la **fiesta
de Janucá** Chanukah
14

la **filosofía** philosophy **2**

el **fin** end **7**; **A fin de
cuentas...** After all
. . . , All things
considered . . . **17**; **Al
fin y al cabo...** In the
end . . . , To make a
long story short . . .
17; **el fin de semana**
weekend **7**; **¡Por fin!**
Finally! **9**

la **física** physics **3**

el **flan** flan (*a type of
caramel custard*) **6**

la **flauta** flute **L4**

la **flor** flower **14**

florecer (zc/6) to flourish
L5

la **fortaleza** fortress **L6**

la **fortuna** fortune **17**

la **foto** photo, photograph **7**

el **francés** French (*language*)
7

francés *adj* French **7**

el, la **franquista** supporter of
Franco **L8**

la **frazada** blanket **17**

fresco cool; fresh **4**

el **frijol** bean, kidney bean **6**

la **frontera** border **L9**

el **frontón** jai alai court;
wall **9**

frustrado frustrated **16**

frustrarse to be (get)
frustrated **16**

la **fruta** fruit **6**

el **fuego**: los **fuegos
artificiales** fireworks
L7

fuerte strong **10**

la **fuerza** force, power **L9**

fumar to smoke **15**

la **función** show,
performance; function
13

funcionar work (*an
appliance or machine*)
19; **Esto (Eso) no
funciona.** This (That)
doesn't work. **17**

furioso furious **16**

el **fútbol** soccer **9**; el **fútbol
americano** football **9**

el, la **futbolista** football player
9

el **futuro** future **20**

G

las **gafas** (*eye*) glasses, **8**; las
gafas de sol sunglasses
8

la **galería** gallery **13**

el **gallego**, la **gallega**
Galician **L2**

la **galleta** cracker **17**

ganar to earn; to win **3**

el **garaje** garage **19**

la **garganta** throat **10**

la **gasolina** gasoline **11**

gastar to spend; to waste
17

generalmente generally
14

generoso generous **7**

la **gente** people **L1, 4**

el **gitano** gypsy **L4**

gobernar (ie/25) to
govern **L9**

el **gobierno** government **18**

el **golf** golf **9**

el **golpe**: el **golpe de estado**
coup d'état **L8**

gracias. thanks., thank
you. **CP**; **Gracias a
Dios.** Thank God.,
Thank goodness. **9**;
Mil gracias. Thank
you very much. **4**

la **graduación** graduation **14**

grande large; great **2**

grave serious **L8**

el **griego**, la **griega** Greek
L5

la **gripe** flu **10**; **tener (la)
gripe** to have the flu
10

gris gray **8**

gritar to shout **14**

los **guantes** gloves **8**

la **guerra** war **L3, 11**

el **guerrillero**, la **guerrillera** guerrilla (*warrior*) 11

el, la **guía** guide (*person*); la **guía turística** tourist guide (*book*) 8

la **guitarra** guitar 7

el **guitarrón** *large Andean guitar* L4

gustar to be pleasing; to like 6; ¿**Le (te) gustaría ir a... (conmigo)?** Would you like to go to . . . (with me)? 13; **Me gusta(n)...** I like . . . 6; **Me gustaría** (+ *inf*) . . . I would like (+ *inf*) . . . 17; (**No) me gusta... porque...** I (don't) like . . . because . . . 17

el **gusto: El gusto es mío.** The pleasure is mine. **CP**

H

haber (18) (+ *pp*) to have (+ *pp*), 12; **hay** (*impersonal*) there is, are **CP** (*see* **hay**)

la **habitación** room 12

el, la **habitante** inhabitant L3

hablar to talk; to speak 1; ¡**Ni hablar!** Don't even mention it! 18

hacer (19) to do; to make 4; **Eso no se hace.** That's not done (allowed). 18; **hace... que** (+ *pres*) something has been -ing for . . . 12; **hace... que** (+ *pret or imp*) ago 12; **hacer buen (mal) tiempo** to be good (bad) weather 4; **hacer calor (frío, fresco, viento, sol)** to be hot (cold, cool,

windy, sunny) 4; **hacer la maleta** to pack one's suitcase 4; **hacer un viaje** to take a trip 4; **hacía... que** (+ *imp*) something had been -ing for . . . 12; ¿**Me hace el favor de** (+ *inf*)...**?** Will you do me the favor of . . . ? 7

hacerse (19) to become, turn into 20

hacia toward 6

la **hacienda** estate L6

hallar to find L1

el **hambre** *f* hunger 5

la **hamburguesa** hamburger 6

hasta until 6; **Hasta la próxima.** Until next time. 20; **Hasta luego.** See you later. **CP**; **Hasta mañana.** See you tomorrow 1; **Hasta pronto.** See you soon. 1; **hasta que** until 16

hay there is, there are (*see* **haber**) **CP**; **hay que** it is necessary, one must (+ *inf*) 10; **No hay de qué.** It's nothing. You're welcome. 16; **No hay duda de que** (+ *indic*) . . . There's no doubt that . . . 15; **No hay ninguna posibilidad de que** (+ *subjunc*) . . . There's no possibility that . . . 15; **No hay (ningún) problema.** There's no problem. 16; **No hay pena.** No need to be embarrassed. 16

el **hecho** fact, act L8

el **helado** ice cream 6

la **herencia** heritage, legacy L2

la **hermana** sister 1

el **hermano** brother 1

la **hija** daughter 1

el **hijo** son 1

hispano Hispanic 2

la **historia** history 3; story 6

Hola. Hello, Hi. **CP**; **Hola. ¿Quién habla?** Hello. Who is this? 1

el **hombre** man 1

el **hombro** shoulder 10

la **honra** honor L7

la **hora** hour 5; **No veo la hora de** (+ *inf*) I can't wait (+ *inf*) 13

el **horario** schedule, timetable 12

el **horno** oven 19

horrible horrible **CP**

el **hospital** hospital **CP**

el **hotel** hotel 1

el **hotelero**, la **hotelera** hotel manager 12

hoy today 1; **hoy día** today, nowadays L9

la **huelga** strike 5

el **huevo** egg 6

I

el **ibero**, la **ibera** Iberian L5

ida: de ida y vuelta round-trip 12

la **idea** idea 5

idealista idealist 2

el **idioma** language L9

la **inglesia** church 10

igualmente likewise **CP**

la **imaginación** imagination **CP**

imaginar imagine 18

el **imperio** empire L6

el **impermeable** raincoat 8

importado imported 19

la **importancia** importance 3

importante important 2

importar to matter; to be important 6; **No importa.** It doesn't matter. 16

imposible impossible **4**
impresionante impressive **L6**
el, la inca Inca **18**
el incendio fire **11**
la independencia independence **4**
indígena Indian, native, indigenous **L4**
indocumentado undocumented **L3**
la inflación inflation **5**
la información information **1**
la ingeniería engineering **3**
el ingeniero, la ingeniera engineer **18**
el inglés English **CP**
iniciar to begin **L8**
inmediatamente immediately **14**
el, la inmigrante immigrant **4**
el inodoro toilet **19**
insistir (en) to insist (on) **14**
insociable unsociable **2**
el insomnio insomnia **19**
el instructor, la instructora instructor **13**
inteligente intelligent **2**
intentar to attempt **L8**
interesante interesting **2**
interesar to interest **6**; Me interesa(n)... I'm interested in . . . **6**
el invasor, la invasora invader **L5**
el inventario inventory **17**
el invierno winter **4**
invitar to invite **6**
la inyección injection, shot **10**
ir (20) to go **4**; ir de campamento to go camping **4**; ir de compras to go shopping **4**; ir de vacaciones to go on vacation **4**; ¡Qué va! Oh, come on! **14**;

Vaya derecho. Go straight ahead. **12**; Voy a... I'm going to . . . **15**
el irlandés, la irlandesa Irish **L2**
irse (20) to leave, go away **8**
la isla island **L1, 12**
italiano Italian **1**
izquierdo *adj* left **10**; a la izquierda on, to the left **2**

J

el jai alai jai alai **9**
jamás never, not ever **14**
el jamón ham **6**
el jarabe (de tos) (cough) syrup **10**
el jardín (*flower*) garden **19**
el jardinero, la jardinera gardener **18**
los jeans jeans **8**
el, la jefe boss; chief **L6, 18**
joven young **2**
el joven young man, youth **L4**
la joven young woman, young lady **L4**
judío Jewish **19**
el juego game **7**; hager juego con to match, to go with **17**
el jueves Thursday **4**
el jugador, la jugadora player **9**
jugar (ue/21) to play (*game, sport*), **6**; jugar a las cartas to play cards **7**
el juglar minstrel **L4**
el jugo juice **6**
julio July **4**
junio June **4**
juntos together **10**
el kilo kilogram **17**

L

la the **1**; *dir obj* you, her, it **4**
el laboratorio laboratory **CP**
el lado side **1**; al lado (de) next (to), beside **1**
el lago lake **L6**
la lámpara lamp **19**
la lana wool **8**
el lápiz pencil **CP**
largo long **8**
las the *pl* **1**
la lástima pity **5**; ¡Qué lástima! What a shame (pity)! **5**
el lavamanos sink **19**
lavarse to wash (oneself) **8**
le *indir obj* (to, for) you, him, her, it **5**
la lección lesson **4**
la leche milk **6**
la lechuga lettuce **6**
leer (y/10) to read **2**
la legumbre vegetable **6**
lejos (de) far (from) **1**
la lengua language **18**
les *indir obj* (to, for) you, them **5**
la letra letter (*of alphabet*) **CP**; lyrics **L4**; las letras letters, writing **13**
levantarse to get up **8**
la ley law **L5**
la librería bookstore **2**
el libro book **CP**
el, la líder leader **11**
lindo pretty **2**
la liquidación sale **17**
el líquido liquid **10**
listo ready **13**; ¡Listo! I'm ready (to go)! **13**
la literatura literature **3**
lo *dir obj* you, him, it **4**; *neuter article* the **19**; lo (+ *adj*) the (*adj*) thing, part **19**; lo que which; that which,

what **19**; **lo que es hoy** what is today **L6**
local local **17**
loco crazy **7**
los the *pl*, **1**; *dir obj* you, them **4**
la **lucha** struggle **L9**
luchar to struggle **L8**
luego then **L1**; **Hasta luego.** See you later. **CP**
el **lugar** place **5**
la **luna: luna de miel** honeymoon **15**
el **lunes** Monday **4**
la **luz** light **9**

Ll

llamar to call **1**
llamarse to be named, called **8**; **¿Cómo se llama usted?** What is your name? **CP**; **Me llamo...** My name is . . . **CP**
la **llave** key **15**
la **llegada** arrival **12**
llegar (gu/23) to arrive **11**; **llegar a ser** to become **20**; **llegar tarde** to be late, arrive late **5**
llevar to carry; to take (along) **1**; to wear **8**; to take (*a period of time*) **12**; **llevar a** to lead to **L6**
llevarse (bien) to get along (well) **15**
llorar to cry **16**
llover (ue/43) to rain **6**; **Llueve.** It's raining. **4**
la **lluvia** rain **4**

M

la **madre** mother **1**
el **maíz** corn **6**

mal *adv* badly **CP**
el **mal** evil **L7**
la **maleta** suitcase **4**
malo (*shortened form* **mal**) bad **2**
la **mamá** mom, mamma **1**
mandar to send **5**; to order, to command **13**; **¿Mande?** What? (*Mexico*) **3**
manejar to drive **16**
manera: ¡De ninguna manera! No way! **14**
la **manifestación** demonstration **11**
la **mano** hand **10**; **en manos de** in the possession of **L6**
mantenerse (37) to sustain oneself, to remain **L8**
la **mantequilla** butter **6**
el **manto** mantle **L7**
la **manzana** apple **6**
mañana tomorrow **1**; la **mañana** morning **5**; **Hasta mañana.** See you tomorrow. **1**
el **mapa** map **1**
el **mar** sea **4**
el **maratón** marathon **9**
maravilloso marvelous, wonderful **7**
mareado dizzy **10**
el **mareo** dizziness, nausea, motion sickness **10**; **darle (a uno) mareos** to give (someone) motion sickness, make someone nauseous **10**
marrón brown **8**
el **martes** Tuesday **4**
marzo March **4**
más plus; more **2**; **más... que** more . . . than **10**; **más de** (+ *number*) more than **7**; **Más despacio, por favor.** More slowly, please. **3**; **más pequeño** smaller **10**; **más grande** bigger

10; **el, la más pequeño(-a)** smallest **10**; **el, la más grande** biggest **10**
la **máscara** mask **L7**
las **matemáticas** mathematics **3**
el **matrimonio** matrimony **15**; **el matrimonio civil** civil marrige **15**
mayo May **4**
mayor greater; larger; older; greatest; largest; oldest **10**; **el, la mayor** oldest **10**
mayoría: la gran mayoría the great majority **L3**
me *dir obj* me **4**; *indir obj* (to, for) me **5**; *refl pron* myself **8**
media; media hora half an hour **5**; **la una y media** 1:30 **5**
mediados: hasta mediados del siglo until about the middle of the century **L9**
la **medianoche** midnight **12**
las **medias** stockings **8**
el **medicamento** medication, medicine **10**
la **medicina** medicine **3**
el **médico**, la **médica** doctor **18**
medio half **19**
el **mediodía** noon **12**
mejor better; best **L3, 10**; **el, la mejor** best **10**; **Es mejor que usted (tú)** (+ *subjunc*) . . . It's better for you to . . . **16**
mejorar to improve **L8**
menor smaller; lesser; younger; smallest; least; youngest **10**; **el, la menor** youngest **10**; **No tengo la menor idea.** I don't have the slightest idea. **18**

menos less 3; **menos...
que** less . . . than 10
mentir (ie,i/35) to lie 5
el **mercado** market 10
el **mes** month 4; **el mes
que viene** next month
7
la **mesa** table CP
la **mesera** waitress 18
el **mesero** waiter 18
la **meseta** plateau L1
la **mesita de luz** end, side
table 19
mestizo of mixed
ancestry L2
el **metro** subway 5
mexicano Mexican 2
la **mezcla** mixture L2
mezclarse to mix, to
intermarry L5
la **mezquita** mosque L5
mí *obj of prep* me, myself
6
mi(s) my 5
mientras while 11;
mientras (que) while
16
el **miércoles** Wednesday 4
mil thousand 3; **Mil
gracias.** Thank you
very much. 4
militar *adj* military L3
los **militares** the military L8
la **milla** mile 9
el **millón** million 3
millonario millionaire 17
mineral mineral 6
la **minoría** minority 5
mío, mía, míos, mías
my, of mine 15
mirar to look (at); to
watch 1
mismo same 11
misterioso mysterious 12
el **modelo** model, example
CP; el, la **modelo**
model (*person*) 13
moderno modern 3
molestar to bother,
annoy 6; **¿Le
molestaría que...**

(+ *subjunc*)? Would it
bother you if . . . ? 18
el **momento** moment 3
monótono monotonous
15
la **montaña** mountain L1
el **monumento** monument
10
morir(se) (ue,u/13) to
die 9
mostrar (ue/8) to show 6
la **muchacha** girl 2
el **muchacho** boy 2
mucho *adj* much 1;
many, a lot of 2; *adv*
very much 4; **Muchas
gracias.** Thank you
very much. 4; **Mucho
gusto.** Glad to meet
you. CP
mudarse to move (*change
residence*) 8
el **mueble** piece of furniture
19; los **muebles**
furniture 19
la **mueblería** furniture store
17
la **muerte** death L8
la **mujer** woman 1
mundial worldwide L9
el **mundo** world L1, 4;
todo el mundo
everyone, everybody 4
el **mural** mural 3
el **museo** museum 1
la **música** music 3
el, la **músico** musician 13
el **musulmán** Moslem L5
muy very CP; **Muy
agradecido.** Much
obliged., I'm very
grateful. 4; **Muy bien.**
Very well CP

N

nacer (zc/6) to be born 8
la **nación** nation 11; las
Naciones Unidas
United Nations 11

la **nacionalidad** nationality
5
nada nothing, not
anything 14; **De nada.**
You're welcome., It's
nothing. CP
el **nadador,** la **nadadora**
swimmer 9
nadar to swim 7
nadie no one, not anyone
14
los **naipes** (*playing*) cards 7
la **naranja** orange 6
la **nariz** nose 10
la **natación** swimming 9
naturalmente naturally,
sure, of course 14
la **Navidad** Christmas 14
necesario necessary 10;
Es necesario It is
necessary (+ *inf*) 10
necesitado needy,
underprivileged L9
necesitar to need 1
negocios: el **hombre** (la
mujer) de negocios
businessperson 18
negro black L2, 8
nervioso nervous 20
nevar (ie/25) to snow 5;
Nieva. It's snowing. 4
la **nevera** refrigerator 19
¡Ni hablar! Don't even
mention it! 14; **ni:
ni... ni** neither . . . nor
14; **¡Ni por todo el
dinero del mundo!**
Not for all the money
in the word! 14; **ni
siquiera** not even 14
la **niebla** fog 4; **Hay niebla.**
It's foggy. 4
la **nieta** granddaughter 1
el **nieto** grandson 1
la **nieve** snow 4
**ningún, ninguno(-a, -os,
-as)** none, not any, no,
neither (of them) 14
la **niña** girl, child 1
el **niño** boy, child 1

no no; not **CP**; **¿No?**
Right? True? **1**; **No
hay de qué.** You're
welcome. It's nothing.
11

la **noche** night, evening
(*after sunset*) **5**; la
Noche del Grito Night
of the Cry (*Mexico*) **L7**

nombrar to name **L8**

el **nombre** name **5**

nordeste northeast **L2**

el **norte** north **1**

norteamericano North
American **2**

nos *dir obj* us **4**; *indir obj*
(to, for) us **5**; *refl pron*
ourselves **8**; *recip* each
other, one another **8**

nosotros, nosotras we
CP; *obj of prep* us,
ourselves **6**

la **noticia** (*piece of*) news **9**;
las **noticias** news **10**

el **noticiero** news program
11

la **novela** novel **8**

noveno ninth **2**

la **novia** girlfriend **15**

el **noviazgo** engagement,
courtship **15**

noviembre November **4**

el **novio** boyfriend **15**

la **nube** cloud **4**; **Hay
nubes.** It's cloudy. **4**

nublado cloudy **4**; **estar
nublado** to be cloudy
4

nuestro(s), nuestra(s)
our, (of) ours **5**

nuevamente once again
L9

nuevo new **5**

la **nuez** nut **6**

el **número** number **CP**

nunca never, not ever **14**

O

o or **1**; **o... o** either . . .
or **14**

la **obra** work, artistic work
7; la **obra de teatro**
play **7**; la **obra
maestra** masterpiece
13

el **obrero**, la **obrera** worker
11

el **océano** ocean **8**

octavo eighth **2**

octubre October **CP**

ocurrir to happen, occur
11

el **oeste** west **1**

ofender to offend **16**

ofenderse to be (get)
offended; to take
offense **16**

la **oferta** sale, (special) offer
17

la **oficina** office **5**; la **oficina
de correos** post office
2

el **oficio** job, trade **18**

ofrecer (zc/6) to offer **7**

oír (22) to hear **6**

ojalá (que) I (we, let's)
hope (that); hopefully
13

el **ojo** eye **L2, 10**

la **ola** wave **L3**

olvidar to forget **7**; **Se
me olvidó.** I forgot. **18**

la **ópera** opera **13**

oponerse (28) to oppose
L9

la **oportunidad** opportunity
5

optimista optimistic **2**

el **orden** *n* order **L9**

la **oreja** (*outer*) ear **10**

la **organización** organization
17

orgulloso proud **L2, 16**

el **oro** gold **7**

la **orquesta** orchestra **13**

os *dir obj* you **4**; *indir obj*
(to, for) you **5**; *refl
pron* yourselves **8**

oscuro dark **L2, 8**

el **otoño** fall, autumn **4**

otro other, another **4**;
otra vez again **6**; **Otro
día tal vez...** Another
day perhaps . . . **13**

P

la **paciencia** patience **5**

el **padre** father **1**; los
padres parents; fathers
1

pagar (gu/23) to pay **8**

la **página** page **CP**

el **país** country, nation **L1,
4**

la **palabra** word **6**

el **pan** bread **6**

la **panadería** bakery **10**

el **panadero**, la **panadera**
baker **19**

los **pantalones** pants **8**

el **pañuelo** scarf **8**; el
pañuelo de seda silk
scarf **8**

el **papá** dad, papa **1**

el **Papa** Pope **11**

la **papa** potato **6**

el **papel** paper **CP**; role **L4**;
hacer un papel to play
a role **13**

para for, to, in order to
3; **para que** so that **16**

el **paraguas** umbrella **8**

el **paraíso** paradise, heaven,
4

parar to stop **8**

parecer (zc/6) to seem,
appear **7**; **¿Qué le (te)
parece si vamos a...?**
How do you feel about
going to . . . ? **13**

parecido similar **L9**

la **pared** wall **CP**

la **pareja** couple **10**

el, la **pariente** relative **1**

el **parque** park **L1, 5**; el
parque de diversiones
amusement park **8**; el
parque zoológico zoo
8

la **parte** part **10**; la **mayor
parte** majority **L2**; **Por**

otra parte... On the other hand . . . **19**

el **partido** match, game **9**; (*political*) party **L9**; el **partido de fútbol** soccer game **3**

el **pasado** past **6**; last **8**

el **pasaje** ticket **12**

el **pasajero**, la **pasajera** passenger **12**

el **pasaporte** passport **CP**

pasar to pass; to spend (time) **1**; to happen, occur **11**

el **pasatiempo** pastime **7**

las **Pascuas** Easter **L7**

pasear to take a walk **12**

el **paseo** walk, stroll; ride, short trip **7**

el **pasillo** corridor **19**

el **pastel** pastry, cake **6**

la **pastilla** tablet **10**

el **patinador**, la **patinadora** skater **9**

el **patinaje** skating **9**

patinar to skate **9**

el **patrón**, la **patrona** master, boss **14**

el **pavo** turkey **14**

el **payador**, la **payadora** Gaucho singer **L4**

el **pecho** chest **10**

pedir (i,i/24) to ask for, order **6**

pelear to fight **13**

la **película** movie, film **5**

peligroso dangerous **L8**

el **pelo** hair **L2, 10**

la **pelota** ball **9**

la **peluquería** barbershop, beauty parlor **18**

el **peluquero**, la **peluquera** barber, beautician **18**

la **península** peninsula **12**

pensar (ie/25) to think **5**; **pensar** (+ *inf*) to intend, plan (*to do something*) **5**; **pensar de** to think of, have an opinion of **5**; **pensar en** to think of, think

about **5**; **Pienso que** (+ *indic*) . . . I think that . . . **15**; **No pienso que** (+ *subjunc*)... I don't think that . . . **18**; **Pienso que sí (no).** I think so. (I don't think so.) **18**

la **pensión** boardinghouse **12**

peor worse; worst **10**; el, la **peor** worst **10**

pequeño small **2**

perder (ie/26) to lose **5**; **perder el tiempo** to waste time **5**

perdido lost **2**

Perdón. Pardon me. **CP**; **¿Perdón?** Pardon me? **3**

perdonar to forgive **16**; **Perdóneme. (Perdóname.)** Forgive me. (*also*: Excuse me., I am sorry.) **16**

perfectamente perfectly **14**

el **periódico** newspaper **10**

permanecer (zc/6) to remain **L6**

el **permiso: Con permiso.** Excuse me. **CP**

permitir to allow, to permit **13**; **¿Me permite** (+ *inf*)...? May I. . . ? (Will you allow me to. . . ? **18**; **No se permite** (+ *inf*)... It's not permitted to . . . **18**; **¿Se permite** (+ *inf*)...? May one (we, I). . . ? **18**

pero but **1 ¡Pero lo dices en broma!** But you're joking! **10**; **¡Pero no hablas en serio!** But you're not serious! **10**

la **persecución** persecution **L3**

la **persona** person **1**

el **personaje** character (*in a play*) **13**; el **personaje principal** main character, protagonist **13**

peruano Peruvian **18**

pesar: a pesar de in spite of **L9**

la **pesca** fishing **9**

el **pescado** fish **6**; jerk (*slang*)**7**

el **pescador**, la **pescadora** fisherman **9**

pescar (qu/3) to fish **7**

la **peseta** *monetary unit of Spain* **CP**

pésima terrible **L9**

pesimista pessimistic **2**

el **peso** *monetary unit of Mexico* **3**

el **petróleo** petroleum, oil **18**

el, la **pianista** pianist **13**

el **piano** piano **7**

picante hot, spicy **6**

el **pie** foot **10**

la **piel** skin **L2**

la **pierna** leg **10**

el **pijama** pajama **8**

la **píldora** pill **10**

la **pimienta** pepper **6**

la **piña** pineapple **6**

la **piñata** *suspended crock or animal-shaped balloon filled with candy (Mexico)* **14**

pintar to paint **7**

el **pintor**, la **pintora** painter **13**

la **pintura** painting; paint **L5, 13**

la **pirámide** pyramid **3**

la **piscina** swimming pool **9**

el **piso** floor **2**

la **pista** track **9**

la **pizarra** chalkboard **CP**

el **placer** pleasure **20**

el **plan** plan **3**

planear to plan **15**

el **plátano** banana; plaintain **6**

el **platillo** saucer 6
platino platinum 15
el **plato** plate; dish 6; el
plato principal main
dish 6
la **playa** beach 3
la **plaza** plaza, square 1
la **pluma** pen CP
la **población** population L2
pobre poor 5;
¡Pobrecito! Poor thing!
5
la **pobreza** povery 5
poco little; *pl* few, 5;
poco a poco little by
little L6
el **poder** power L5
poder (27) to be able,
can 6; **¿Me podría dar
(pasar,** *etc.***)... por
favor?** Could you give
(pass, *etc.*) me . . . ,
please? 7 **¿Me puede
(** + *inf***)...?** Can you
. . . for me? 7; **No
puede ser.** It can't be.
10; **¿Nos puede
traer...?** Can you bring
us . . . ? 6; **Puede
(Podría) ser.** It could
be. 18; **¿Puedo
ayudarlo(-a)?** Can I
help you? 7; **¿Se
puede (** + *inf***)...?** Can
one (we, I) . . . ? 18
poderoso powerful L5
el **poema** poem 13
la **poesía** poetry 7
el, la **poeta** poet 11
el **policía,** la **mujer policía**
police officer 5
la **policía** police force 5
el, la **político** politician 11
el **pollo** chicken 6
el **poncho** poncho 17
poner (28) to put; to
place 7; to turn on; to
light 11
ponerse (28) to put on
8; **ponerse (** + *adj***)** to
become (+ *adj*) 16

popular popular 13
por for, by, through 6;
per 10; **¿por qué?**
why? 2; **Por cierto
(** + *indic***)...** Certainly
. . . 15; **¡Por Dios!**
Good Lord! 10; **por
ejemplo** for example
CP; **Por el contrario...**
On the contrary . . .
19; **Por eso...** for that
reason, that's why 10;
por favor please CP;
por fin finally 9; **por
la mañana** in the
morning 5; **por la
noche** in the evening
(night) 5; **por la tarde**
in the afternoon 5; **por
lo tanto** therefore 15;
por otra parte on the
other hand 10; **por
supuesto** of course 10;
por todas partes
everywhere L9
porque because 2
posible possible 4; **Es
posible que (** +
*subjunc***)...** It's possible
that . . . 18
el **postre** dessert 6
practicar (qu/3) to
practice 9
práctico practical 2
el **precio** price 2; el **precio
fijo** fixed price 17; el
precio rebajado
reduced price 17
preciso necessary 10; **es
preciso (** + *inf***)** it is
necessary (+ *inf*) 10
predecir (12) to predict
L8
preferir (ie, i/35) to
prefer 5
la **pregunta** question CP
preguntar to ask 1
prender to turn on; to
light; to grasp 11
la **prensa** press L8

preocuparse (por) to
worry (about) 8
la **presentación**
introduction 20
**presentar: Quiero
presentarle(-te) a...** I
want to introduce you
to . . . (*or* I want to
introduce . . . to you)
13
el **presidente,** la **presidenta**
president 1
prestar to lend 17
la **primavera** spring 4
primero (*shortened form***
primer)** first 2
el **primo,** la **prima** cousin 1
principal principal, main
6
**probable: Es probable
que (** + *subjunc***)...** It's
probable that . . .) 18;
Es probable que sí.
Probably so 14
probablemente probably
14
el **problema** problem 1; **No
hay (ningún)
problema.** There's no
problem. 16
la **procesión** procession 14
producir (zc, j/5) to
produce 9
la **profesión** profession 18
el **profesor,** la **profesora**
professor CP
el **programa** program 3; el
programa documental
documentary program
11
el **programador,** la
**programadora (de
computadoras)**
(computer)
programmer 18
programar to program 7
progresar to progress 3
prohibir (í/29) to forbid,
prohibit 13; **Se
prohibe (** + *inf***)...** It's

prohibited (forbidden) to . . . **18**

la **promesa** promise **15**

prometer to promise **10**

la **prometida** fiancée **15**

el **prometido** fiancé **15**

pronto soon **1**; **Hasta pronto.** See you soon. **1**

propio own **L6**

propósito: A propósito de... Regarding . . . **19**; **A propósito...** By the way . . . **19**

próspero prosperous **L3**

protestante Protestant **19**

protestar to protest **11**

el **provecho: ¡Buen provecho!** Enjoy the meal! **6**

próximo next **18**

la **psicología** psychology **3**

público adj public **11**

el **público** public **13**

el **pueblo** town; people **L1**, **11**

el **puente** bridge **L5**

la **puerta** door **CP**

el **puerto** port; harbor **12**

puertorriqueño Puerto Rican **5**

Pues,... Well, . . . **2**

el **puesto** position, job **5**

el **pulgar** thumb **10**

el **punto** point **L8**

la **puntualidad** punctuality **12**

puro pure **17**

Q

que than **10**; rel pron that, which, who, whom **11**; **Que yo sepa...** (+ indic) As far as I know . . . **18**; **Es que...** The thing is that . . . **8**; **¿qué?** what? **1**; **¿De qué es?** What is it made of? **8**; **¿Para qué sirve?** What do you

use it for? **8**; **¿Qué desean pedir?** What do you wish (would you like) to order? **6**; **¿Qué es esto?** What is this? **CP**; **¿Qué espera(s)?** What do you expect? **5**; **¿Qué hay de nuevo?** What's new? **11**; **¿Qué hora es?** What time is it? **5**; **¿Qué importancia tiene eso?** What's so important about that? **5**; **¿Qué le (te) parece si vamos a...?** How do you feel about going to . . . ? **13**; **¿Qué nos recomienda?** What do you recommend to us? **6**; **¿Qué sé yo?** What do I know? (informal) **18**; **¿Qué tal?** How are you doing? How is it going? **CP**; **¿Qué tiempo hace?** What's the weather like? **4**; **¡Qué absurdo!** How absurd! **14**; **¡Qué alegría!** How wonderful! **9**; **¡Qué alivio!** What a relief! **9**; **¡Qué amable!** How nice! **9**; **¡Qué barbaridad!** Good grief!, How terrible! **5**; **¡Qué bien!** Good!, How nice! **9**; **¡Qué buen tiempo!** What nice weather! **4**; **¡Qué buena idea!** What a good idea! **13**; **¡Qué calor (frío, etc.)!** How hot (cold, etc.) it is! **4**; **¡Qué coincidencia!** What a coincidence! **4**; **¡Qué horror!** How horrible! **5**; **¡Qué increíble!** How amazing! **9**; **¡Qué insolencia!** What

nerve (insolence)! **7**; **¡Qué lástima!** What a shame (pity)! **5**; **¡Qué lindo (amable, etc.)!** How pretty (kind, etc.)! **9**; **¡Qué mala suerte!** What bad luck! **5**; **¡Qué ridículo!** How ridiculous! **10**; **¡Qué sorpresa!** What a surprise! **9**; **¡Qué suerte!** How lucky! **2**; **¡Qué tontería!** What nonsense! **14**; **¡Qué va!** Oh, come on! **10**; **¿Y qué?** So what? **5**

quedar to remain **L8**

quedarse to remain, to stay **8**

quejarse (de) to complain (about) **8**

querer (30) to want; to love, like **5**; **¿Quiere(s) ir a...?** Do you want to go to . . . ? **13**; **Quiero que conozcas a...** I want you to meet . . . **13**

querido dear (in an informal letter heading) **20**

el **queso** cheese **6**

quien rel pron who, whom **11**

¿quién(es)? who? **2**

la **química** chemistry **3**

quinto fifth **2**

quitarse to take off (clothing) **8**

quizá(s) perhaps **5**; **Quizá(s)** (+ subjunc or indic) Perhaps . . . **15**

R

la **rabia** anger, rage **16**; **darle rabia (a alguien)** to make (someone) angry **16**

la **radio** radio **4**

la **raqueta** racket 9
la **raza** race L2
razonable reasonable 19
el **realismo** realism 13
realista realistic 2
realizarse (c/14) to be realized, to come about L6
realmente really 4
rebajado reduced; marked down; on sale 17
rebajar to reduce; to mark down 17
la **recepción** reception desk 12
la **receta** prescription 10
recibir to receive 2
el **recién casado,** la **recién casada** newlywed 15
recientemente recently 9
recomendar (ie/25) to recommend 5; ¿**Qué nos recomienda?** What do you recommend to us? 6; **Recomiendo que usted (tú)** (+ *subjunc*)... I recommend that you ... 16
reconocer (zc/6) to recognize, to admit 17
la **reconquista** reconquest L5
recordar (ue/8) to remember 6; **Eso me recuerda...** That reminds me of ... 11; **Siempre recuerdo...** I('ll) always remember ... 11
el **recuerdo** souvenir; remembrance 10
la **red** net 9
reelegir (i,i, j/24,15) to reelect L9
reflejar to reflect L4
el **refresco** soft drink; refreshment 3

el **refrigerador** refrigerator 19
el **regalo** gift 1
regatear to bargain (*over prices*) 17
el **régimen** regime L3
la **región** region 11
regresar to return, go back 1
las **regulaciones** regulations 12
la **reina** the queen 13
el **reino** kingdom L5
reír(se) (31) to laugh 16
religioso religious 14
relleno stuffed 6
el **reloj** watch; clock 5
renovar (ue/8) to renovate 19
reparar to repair 19
repetir (i,i/24) to repeat 6
el **reportaje** report 11
el **reportero,** la **reportera** reporter 4
republicano republican 19
las **reservaciones** reservations 12
resfriado: estar resfriado to have a cold 10
el **resfrío** cold 10; **tener un resfrío** to have a cold 10
resolver (ue/43) to solve 12
responder to answer, respond 2
responsable responsible 2
el **restaurante** restaurant CP
resultado: Como resultado... As a result ... 15
resumen: En resumen... In summary ... 17
retirarse to withdraw L9
el **retrato** portrait 13
la **reunión** meeting 11
reunirse to get together L7

revisar to check, examine 12
la **revista** magazine 11
el **rey** the king 13; los **(tres) Reyes Magos** (Three) Wise Men 14
rico rich L4, 17
ridículo: ¡Qué ridículo! How ridiculous! 14
el **río** river L3
la **risa** laughter 16; **darle risa (a alguien)** to make (someone) laugh 16
el **robo** theft 5
la **rodilla** knee 10
rogar (ue,gu/8,23) to beg, to ask 14
rojo red 8
romántico romantic 13
romper to break 12
la **ropa** clothes, clothing 8; la **ropa interior** underwear 8
el **ropero** closet 19
rubio blond L2
las **ruinas** ruins 12
la **rutina** routine 8

S

el **sábado** Saturday 4
saber (32) to know (*facts, information*); to learn, to find out 7; **saber** (+ *inf*) to know how (*to do something*) 7; **No se sabe.** No one knows 18; **Que yo sepa...** As far as I know ... 18; **¿Y sabe(s) qué?** And do you know what? 11
el **sabio,** la **sabia** learned person L5
sacar (qu/3) to take out; to get 13; **sacar fotos** to take pictures 7
el **sacerdote** priest 18
el **saco** jacket, coat 8

la **sal** salt **6**
la **sala**: la **sala de clase** classroom **CP**; la **sala de estar** living room **19**
la **salida** departure; exit **12**
salir (33) to go out, leave; to come out **7**
la **salud** health **10**; ¡**Salud!** Cheers!, Gesundheit!, To your health! **11**; **Salud y plata y un(a) novio(-a) de yapa.** Health, money (silver), and a sweetheart besides. **13**; **Salud, amor y pesetas y el tiempo para gozarlos (gastarlos).** Health, love, and money, and the time to enjoy (spend) them. **13**
saludar(se) to greet (each other) **15**
el **saludo** greeting **20**
las **sandalias** sandals **8**
el **sandwich** sandwich **2**
la **sangre** blood **L2**
el **santo**, la **santa** saint **14**
se *indir obj* (to) him, her, it, you, them **18**; *impersonal subj pron* one, people, they **18**; *refl pron* himself, herself, itself, yourself, yourselves, themselves **8**; *recip* each other, one another **8**
seco dry **4**
el **secretario**, la **secretaria (bilingüe)** (bilingual) secretary **12**
el **seguidor**, la **seguidora** follower **L9**
seguir (i,g/34) to follow **6**; **seguir un curso** to take a course **6**; **Siga adelante (derecho).** Keep going straight. **12**; **Siga por la calle...** Follow . . . street **12**

según according to **6**; **Según (Ana, José,** *etc.*) According to (Ana, José, *etc.*) **2**
segundo second **2**
Seguramente Surely, Probably **15**
seguro sure, certain **L9**; **Seguro.** Certainly., Sure., Of Course., Naturally. **14**; **Estoy seguro que** (+ *indic*)... I'm sure that . . . **15**; **No estoy seguro que** (+ *subjunc*)... I'm not sure that . . . **18**
la **semana** week **1**; la **semana que viene** next week **7**; la **semana pasada** last week **8**
el **semestre** semester **3**
el **senador**, la **senadora** senator **11**
el **señor** man, gentleman, Mr., sir **CP**
sensible sensitive **2**
sentarse (ie/25) to sit down **8**
el **sentimiento** feeling **16**
sentir (ie,i/35) to feel; to be sorry **5**; **sentir(lo)** to feel sorry **20**; **Lo siento (mucho).** I'm (very) sorry. **16**; **Siento mucho que** (+ *subjunc*)... I'm very sorry that . . . **16**
sentirse (+ *adj or adv*) to feel (+ *adj or adv*) **16**
la **señora** woman, lady, Mrs., ma'am **CP**
los **señores** Mr. and Mrs. **1**
la **señorita** young lady, Miss **CP**
la **separación provisional** trial separation **15**
separar to separate **L2**
septiembre September **4**
séptimo seventh **2**

ser (36) to be **1**; **Es demasiado...** It's too . . . **17**; **Es dudoso.** It's doubtful. **18**; **Es poco probable que** (+ *subjunc*)... It's unlikely that . . . **15**; **Es posible que** (+ *subjunc*)... It's possible that . . . **15**; **Es probable que** (+ *subjunc*)... It's probable that . . . **15**; **Es verdad (indudable,** *etc.*) **que** (+ *indic*) It's true (certain, *etc.*) that . . . **15**; **Eso es.** That's it. **14**; **Será que...** It must be that . . . **15**; **Sería que...** It must have been that . . .**15**
serio: ¿**En serio?** Really? **11**
la **servilleta** napkin **6**
servir (i,i/24) to serve **6**; ¿**En qué puedo servirle?** How can I help you? **7**; **Esto (Eso) no sirve.** This (That) doesn't work. **17**
sexto sixth **2**
si if **5**; whether **17**
sí yes **CP**; **Sí, es verdad.** Yes, it's true. **14**; **Sí, tiene(s) razón.** Yes, you're right. **14**; ¡**Sí, qué buena idea!** Yes, what a good idea! **13**
el **SIDA** AIDS **11**
siempre always **4**
la **siesta** siesta, nap **18**
el **siglo** century **2**
la **silla** chair **CP**
el **sillón** armchair **19**
simpático nice **2**
sin without **5**; **sin casa** homeless **11**; **sin embargo** nevertheless, however **L6, 19**; **sin que** without **16**

la **sinagoga** synagogue **15**
el **síntoma** symptom **10**
el **sistema** system **18**
el **sitio** place, spot, site **12**
situar (ú/9) to situate, locate **12**
sobre on, about **5**; over, on, upon **6**
sobrevivir to survive, remain **10**
la **sobrina** niece **1**
el **sobrino** nephew **1**
sociable sociable **2**
socialista socialist **19**
la **sociología** sociology **3**
el **sofá** sofa **17**
el **sol** sun; **hacer sol** to be sunny **4**
sólo *adv* only **4**
soltero single **15**
el **sombrero** hat **8**
soñar (ue/8) (con) to dream (about) **6**
la **sopa** soup **6**
sorprender to surprise **14**
la **sorpresa** surprise **20**
el **sostén** brassiere **8**
su(s) your, his, her, their, its, one's **5**
subir to climb, go up, rise **10**; **subir (a)** to go up; to get into **8**
suceder to happen, occur **11**
la **suegra** mother-in-law **1**
el **suegro** father-in-law **1**
el **sueldo** salary **11**
el **sueño** dream **L6**
la **suerte: ¡Qué suerte!** How lucky! **2**; **¡Qué mala suerte!** What bad luck! **5**
el **suéter** sweater **8**
sufrir to suffer **L9**
la **superpoblación** overpopulation **11**
supuesto: Por supuesto. Certainly., Of Course. **14**
el **sur** south **1**
suroeste southwest **L3**

suyo, suya, suyos, suyas his, of his; her, of hers; your, of yours; their, of theirs; **15**

T

tal such **L8**; **tal vez** perhaps, maybe **13**; **Tal vez** (+ *subjunc or indic*) Perhaps . . . **15**
tamaño: ¿De qué tamaño es? What size is it? **8**
también also **1**
tampoco not either, neither **14**
tan so; as **10**; **tan... como** as . . . as **10**; **tan pronto como** as soon as **16**
el **tango** tango **7**
tanto(-a, -os, -as) so much **10**; **tanto como** as much as **10**; **Por lo tanto...** Therefore . . . **15**
el **tapiz** tapestry **17**
tarde late **5**
la **tarde** afternoon, evening (*before sunset*) **5**
la **tarjeta** card, greeting card **14**; la **tarjeta de crédito** credit card **12**
la **taza** cup **6**
te *dir obj* you **4**; *indir obj* (to, for) you **5**; *refl pron* yourself **8**
el **té** tea, **6**
el **teatro** theater **1**
el **teléfono** telephone **1**
la **televisión** television **CP**
el **televisor** television set **4**
el **tema** theme, subject **L4**; **Cambiando de tema...** To change the subject . . . **19**
temer to fear **14**
temprano early **5**
el **tenedor** fork **6**
tener (37) to have **3**; **tener... años** to be . . .

years old **3**; **tener calor** to be hot **3**; **tener celos (de)** to be jealous (of) **15**; **tener cuidado** to be careful **3**; **tener dolor de cabeza** to have a headache **3**; **tener dolor de estómago** to have a stomachache **3**; **tener en cuenta** to take into account **L9**; **tener éxito** to be successful **3**; **tener fiebre** to have a fever **3**; **tener frío** to be cold **3**; **tener ganas de** (+ *inf*) to want to, feel like (*doing something*) **3**; **tener hambre** to be hungry **3**; **tener lugar** to take place **L8**; **tener miedo** to be afraid **3**; **tener prisa** to be in a hurry **3**; **tener que** (+ *inf*) to have to . . . **3**; **tener razón** to be right **3**; **tener sed** to be thirsty **3**; **tener sueño** to be sleepy **3**; **tener suerte** to be lucky **3**; **tener tos** to have a cough **10**; **tener una cita** to have a date; to have an appointment **15**; **Tengo mis dudas.** I have my doubts. **18**; **Tiene(s) la culpa.** It's your fault. **5**; **Sí, tiene(s) razón.** Yes, you're right. **14**
el **tenis** tennis **6**
la **tensión** tension **19**
tercero (*shortened form* **tercer**) third **2**
terminar to finish, end **11**
el **termómetro** thermometer **10**

el **terremoto** earthquake **11**
terrible terrible **4**
el **territorio** territory **L3**
ti *obj of prep* you, yourself **6**
la **tía** aunt **1**
el **tiempo** time **3**; weather **4**
la **tienda** store, shop **5**
la **tierra** land, country **L1**
tinto red *(wine)* **18**
el **tío** uncle **1**
típico typical **2**
la **tiza** chalk **CP**
tocar (qu/3) to touch; to play *(musical instrument)* **7**
todavía still; yet **12**
todo (a) whole, (an) entire **3**
tolerar to tolerate **15**
tomar to take; to drink **1**; **tomar sol** to sunbathe **12**
el **tomate** tomato **6**
tontería: ¡Qué tontería! What nonsense! **14**
el **torero**, la **torera** bullfighter **9**
el **toro** bull **9**
la **torta** cake **6**
la **tos** cough **10**
el **tostador** toaster **19**
total: Total que... So . . . **17**
totalmente totally **14**
trabajador hardworking **2**; el **Día de los Trabajadores** Labor Day **14**
trabajar to work **1**
el **trabajo** work, job **5**; la **agencia de trabajo** employment agency **18**
tradicional traditional **14**
la **traducción** translation **1**
traducir (zc, j/5) to translate **7**
traer (38) to bring **7**
el **tráfico** traffic **5**

el **traje** suit; outfit **8**; el **traje de baño** bathing suit **8**
tranquilo tranquil, calm, quiet **19**
tratar (de) to try (to) **16**
el **tren** train **4**
triste sad **2**
tropical tropical **4**
tú *subj* you *fam* **CP**
tu(s) your **5**
el, la **turista** tourist **1**
tuyo, tuya, tuyos, tuyas your, of yours **15**

U

u or *(replaces* **o** *before words beginning* **o-** *or* **ho-)** **17**
últimamente recently **12**
último latest, most recent, final **7**
un, una a, an; one **CP**
el **único** the only one **L4**
unificar (qu/3) to unify **L9**
unir to unite **L9**
la **universidad** university **CP**
universitario *adj* university **3**
unos, unas some, a few **1**
la **uña** fingernail **10**
urbano urban **5**
usar to use **10**
usted *subj* you *formal* **CP**; *obj of prep* you **6**
ustedes *subj* you *formal pl* **CP**; *obj of prep* you **6**
la **uva** grape **8**

V

las **vacaciones** vacation **1**
valer (39) to be worth **13**; **valer la pena** to be worth it **13**

el **valor** value, price **6**
variar (í/16) to vary **L2**
varios various; several **5**
el **vasco**, la **vasca** Basque **L2**
el **vaso** *(drinking)* glass **6**
el **vecino**, la **vecina** neighbor **17**
vencer (z/40) to defeat **9**
el **vendedor**, la **vendedora** salesperson **10**
vender to sell **2**
la **venganza** revenge **16**
venir (41) to come **5**
la **venta** sale, selling **17**; **en venta** on sale **17**
la **ventana** window **CP**
ver (42) to see **7**; **A ver.** Let's see. **8**; **Bueno, nos vemos.** We'll be seeing each other. **1**; **No veo la hora de** (+ *inf*) I can't wait (+ *inf*) **13**
el **verano** summer **4**
la **verdad** truth **1**; **¿Verdad?** Right? True? **1**; **Sí, es verdad.** Yes, it's (that's) true **14**
verdaderamente truly, really **14**
verdadero true **CP**
verde green **8**
la **verdura** green vegetable **6**
la **vergüenza** shame **16**; **darle vergüenza (a alguien)** to make (someone) ashamed **16**
el **vestido** dress **8**
vestirse (i,i/24) to get dressed **8**; **vestirse de** to dress as **L7**
vez: cada vez más more and more **L8**
viajar to travel **1**
el **viaje** trip **1**; la **agencia de viajes** travel agency **18**
el **viajero**, la **viajera** traveler **12**
la **vida** life **2**
viejo old **2**

el **viento** wind **4**
el **viernes** Friday **4**
el **vínculo** link **L9**
el **vino** wine **6**
  violeta purple **8**
el **violín** violin **7**
la **visita** visit **7**; **estar de visita** to be visiting **7**
  visitar to visit **1**
la **vitamina** vitamin **10**
  vivir to live **2**
el **vólibol** volleyball **9**
  volver (ue/43) to return, go back **6**

volverse (ue/43) to become **20**; **volverse loco** to go crazy **20**
vosotros, vosotras *subj* you (*fam pl*) **CP**; *obj of prep* you, yourselves **6**
la **voz** voice **L4**
vuestro(s), vuestra(s) your, (of) yours **5**

Y

y and **CP**; **¿Y qué?** So what? **5**

ya already **6**; **ya no** no longer, not . . . any longer **6**; **¡Ya lo creo!** I believe it! **14**
yanqui Yankee **12**
yo I **CP**

Z

la **zapatería** shoe store **10**
el **zapato** shoe **8**; los **zapatos de tenis** tennis shoes **8**

ENGLISH-SPANISH VOCABULARY

A number in parentheses after a verb entry refers to one of the numbered verb paradigms in **Verbos**, the verb charts on pages 522–538. Stem and spelling changes are also given in parentheses after a verb entry.

The following abbreviations are used:

- adj   adjective
- adv   adverb
- conj   conjunction
- dir obj   direct object
- f   feminine
- imp   imperfect
- indir obj   indirect object
- inf   infinitive
- m   masculine
- obj of prep   object of preposition

- poss adj   possessive adjective
- pp   past participle
- prep   preposition
- pres   present
- pres p   present participle
- pret   preterit
- refl   reflexive
- rel pron   relative pronoun
- subj   subject
- v   verb

A

a, an un, una
able: be able poder (27)
about de, acerca de, sobre
abstract abstracto
accident el accidente
accompany acompañar; **accompanied by** acompañado de
according to según
across: go across cruzar (c/14)
act el hecho; el acto (*in a play*)
actor el actor
actress la actriz
additional adicional; **in addition (to)** . . . además (de)...
admiral el almirante
admire admirar
admit reconocer (zc/6)
advice los consejos; **piece of advice** el consejo
affectionately cariñosamente
afraid: be afraid tener miedo
after *adv* después; *conj* después (de) que; *prep* después de; **after all** a fin de cuentas, después de todo

afternoon la tarde; **in the afternoon** por la tarde
afterwards después
again otra vez; **once again** nuevamente
against contra
agency la agencia
agent el, la agente
ago hace... que + (*pret or imperf*)
agree estar de acuerdo
AIDS el SIDA
air el aire
airplane el avión
airport el aeropuerto
allied aliado
allow dejar, permitir
almost casi
already ya
also también
although aunque
always siempre
A.M. de la mañana
American el americano, la americana
amusing divertido
ancient antiguo
and y; (*before* i- *or* hi-) e
Andean andino

anger la rabia, el enojo
Anglo-Saxon anglosajón
angry enojado; **get angry** enojarse, enfadarse; **make (someone) angry** darle rabia (a alguien)
anniversary el aniversario
announce anunciar
announcement el anuncio
annoy molestar
another otro
answer contestar, responder
anthology la antología
anthropology la antropología
anxious ansioso
any algún, alguno (-a, -os, -as); cualquier(a); **not any** ningún, ninguno (-a)
anyone alguien; cualquiera
apartment el apartamento
apologize disculparse
appear parecer (zc/6)
apple la manzana
appointment la cita; **have an appointment** tener una cita
April abril
archeologist el arqueólogo, la arqueóloga
archeology la arqueología

architecture la arquitectura
Argentine argentino
arm el brazo
armchair el sillón
arms las armas
army el ejército
arrest detener (37)
arrival la llegada
arrive llegar (gu/23)
art el arte *f;* **the arts** las artes
artisan el artesano, la artesana
artist el, la artista
as como; **as . . . as** tan... como; **as much as** tanto como; **as soon as** en cuanto, tan pronto como
ashamed avergonzado; **be (get) ashamed** avergonzarse (üe,c/2, 14); **make (someone) ashamed** darle vergüenza (a alguien)
ask preguntar; rogar (ue, gu/8, 23); **ask for** pedir (i,i/24)
asleep: fall asleep dormirse (ue,u/13)
aspirin la aspirina
assembly la asamblea
at en; **at home** en casa
athlete el, la atleta
athletics el atletismo
attack atacar (qu/3)
attempt intentar
attend asistir a
August agosto
aunt la tía
author el autor, la autora
automobile el auto
autumn el otoño
avenue la avenida
Aztec azteca

B

baby el bebé
back la espalda
bad malo *(shortened form* mal)
badly mal
baggage el equipaje
baker el panadero, la panadera
bakery la panadería

balcony el balcón
ball *(sports)* la pelota
ballet el ballet
banana el plátano, la banana
bank el banco
barber el peluquero, la peluquera
barbershop la peluquería
bargain *(over prices)* regatear
baseball el béisbol
basketball el básquetbol
Basque vasco
bathe bañarse
bathing suit el traje de baño
bathroom el baño, el cuarto de baño
bathtub la bañera
be estar (17); ser (36); *(impersonal)* haber (18); **be in a good mood** estar de buen humor; **be in agreement (with)** estar de acuerdo; **be in love (with)** estar enamorado (de); **be missing** *or* **lacking** faltar; **be on vacation** estar de vacaciones
beach la playa
bean el frijol
beautician el peluquero, la peluquera
beauty parlor la peluquería
because porque
become *(through conscious effort)* hacerse (19), llegar (gu/23) a ser; *(temporarily)* ponerse (28); *(relatively permanently)* volverse (ue/43)
bed la cama
bedroom el dormitorio, la alcoba
beer la cerveza
before *adv conj* antes (de) que; *prep (time)* antes de
beg rogar (ue,gu/8,23)
begin comenzar, empezar (ie,c/25,14), iniciar
behind detrás (de)
believe creer (y/10)
belt el cinturón
beret la boina

beside al lado (de)
besides además de
best mejor; el, la mejor
better mejor
between entre
beverage la bebida
bicycle la bicicleta
big grande *(shortened form* gran)
bigger más grande
biggest el, la más grande
bilingual bilingüe
bill la cuenta
biology la biología
birthday el cumpleaños
biscuit el bizcocho
black negro
blanket la frazada, la manta
block la cuadra
blond rubio
blood la sangre
blouse la blusa
blue azul
boardinghouse la pensión
boat el barco
body el cuerpo
book el libro
bookshelf el estante de libros
bookstore la librería
boot la bota
border la frontera
bored aburrido; **be (get) bored** aburrirse
boring aburrido
born: be born nacer (zc/6)
boss el, la jefe
both ambos
bother molestar
boutique la boutique
boy el chico, el muchacho, el niño
boyfriend el novio
brassiere el sostén
bread el pan
break romper
breakfast el desayuno
bridge el puente
bring traer (38)
brother el hermano
brother-in-law el cuñado
brown marrón

build construir (y/7)
building el edificio
bull el toro
bullfight la corrida de toros
bullfighter el torero, la torera
bureau la cómoda; el buró, el escritorio
bus el autobús; (*South America*) el ómnibus, el colectivo; (*Caribbean*) la guagua
businessperson el, la comerciante; el hombre (la mujer) de negocios
but pero
butter la mantequilla
buy comprar
by por; **by the way** a propósito
Bye! ¡Chau!

C

cafe el café
cafeteria la cafetería
cake el pastel, la torta
calendar el calendario
call llamar
calm down calmarse
camera la cámara
camp el campamento; **go camping** ir de campamento
can *v* poder (27)
candelabrum el candelabro
candy el dulce, los dulces
capital (*city*) la capital
capsule la cápsula
car el coche, el auto
card la tarjeta; **credit card** la tarjeta de crédito; **playing cards** las cartas, los naipes
care: take care (of) cuidar (a)
career la carrera
careful: be careful tener cuidado
Caribbean el Caribe
carpenter el carpintero, la carpintera
carpet la alfombra
carry llevar; **carry out** cumplir
Carthaginian el cartaginés, la cartaginesa

cashier el cajero, la cajera; **cashier's office** la caja
cash register la caja
castanets las castañuelas
Catalan el catalán, la catalana
cathedral la catedral
Catholic católico
cause *n* la causa
cave la cueva
celebrate celebrar
celebration la celebración, la fiesta
censorship la censura
center el centro
century el siglo
ceramics la cerámica
cereal el cereal
certain cierto, indudable, seguro
Certainly. Claro., Cómo no., Por supuesto.; Por cierto.
chair la silla
chalk la tiza
chalkboard la pizarra
champion el campeón, la campeona
change cambiar; **change the subject** cambiar de tema
channel el canal
Chanukah la fiesta de Janucá
chapter el capítulo
character (*in a play*) el personaje
cheap (*price*) barato
check *n* (*restaurant*) la cuenta; (*bank*) el cheque; *v* revisar; **traveler's check** el cheque de viajero
Cheers! ¡Salud!
cheese el queso
chemistry la química
chest el pecho
chicken el pollo
chief el jefe, la jefa
child el niño, la niña
Chilean chileno
chili el chile
chocolate el chocolate
choose escoger (j/15)
Christmas la Navidad
church la iglesia

citizen el ciudadano, la ciudadana
city la ciudad
civilization la civilización
class la clase
classic clásico
classroom la (sala de) clase
clearly claramente
clerk el, la dependiente
client el, la cliente
climate el clima
climb subir
cloak el manto
clock el reloj
close cerrar (ie/25)
closet el ropero
clothing la ropa
cloud la nube
cloudy nublado
club el club
coast la costa
coat el saco; el abrigo
coffee el café
coffeepot la cafetera
coincidence la coincidencia
cold *n* el catarro, el resfrío; **be cold** (*weather*) hacer frío; **be (feel) cold** tener frío; **have a cold** tener catarro, estar resfriado, tener un resfrío
colonial colonial
colonist el colonizador, la colonizadora
Colombian colombiano
come venir (41); **come about** realizarse (c/14); **come out** salir (33)
comfortable cómodo
command mandar
communication la comunicación
communist comunista
company la compañía
complain quejarse (de)
composer el compositor, la compositora
composition la composición
comprehend comprender
computer la computadora; **computer science** las ciencias de computación

concerning acerca de
concert el concierto
conference la conferencia
congratulate felicitar
Congratulations! ¡Felicitaciones!
congress el congreso
conquer conquistar
consequence: As a consequence . . . Como consecuencia...
construct construir (y/7)
construction la construcción
consult consultar
contemporary contemporáneo
contented contento
continue continuar (ú/9)
contrary: On the contrary Al contrario, Por el contrario
conversation la conversación
cook v cocinar
cookie el bizcocho
cool fresco; **be cool** (weather) hacer fresco
corn el maíz
corner la esquina
correct adj correcto
correctly correctamente
corridor el pasillo
cosmetics los cosméticos
cost n el costo; v costar (ue/8); **cost of living** el costo de (la) vida
cough n la tos; **have a cough** tener tos
counselor el consejero, la consejera
count contar (ue/8); **count on** contar con
country (nation) el país, la tierra; (countryside) el campo
coup d'état el golpe de estado
couple la pareja
course el curso; **of course** por supuesto, claro
court (sports) la cancha; (jai alai) el frontón
courtship el noviazgo
cousin el primo, la prima
cover v cubrir; **covered up** encubierto, cubierto

cracker la galleta
craft work la artesanía
crazy loco
crime el crimen
criminal el, la criminal
cross n la cruz; v cruzar (c/14)
cry llorar
Cuban-American cubano-americano
cup la taza
current adj actual
custard: caramel custard el flan
customs agent el, la agente de aduana
customs, customs house la aduana

D

dad el papá
daily diariamente
dame la dama
dance n el baile; v bailar
dancer el bailarín, la bailarina
dangerous peligroso
dark oscuro
date (day of year) la fecha; **have a date** tener una cita
daughter la hija
dawn el alba f
day el día; **Day of the Dead** el Día de los Muertos
dear (formal letter) estimado; (informal letter) querido
death la muerte
debt: foreign debt la deuda externa
December diciembre
decide decidir
decoration el adorno
decrease bajar
defeat vencer (z/40)
delicious delicioso
delight encantar
delighted encantado
democratic demócrata; democrático
demonstration la manifestación
departure la salida

depend: It depends on . . . Depende de...
depressed deprimido; **be (get) depressed)** deprimirse
descend bajar (de)
descendant el descendiente
describe describir
desk el escritorio
dessert el postre
destroy destruir (y/7)
detail el detalle
detective el, la detective
devil el diablo
devout devoto
diagnosis el diagnóstico
dictatorship la dictadura
die morir(se) (ue,u/13)
diet la dieta; **be on a diet** estar a dieta
different diferente
difficult difícil; **with difficulty** difícilmente
dining room el comedor
dinner la cena; **have dinner** cenar
directly directamente
director el director, la directora
disappointed desilusionado
disappointment la desilusión
disco, discotheque la discoteca
discover descubrir
discrimination la discriminación
dish el plato; **main dish** el plato principal
diversion la diversión
divorce el divorcio; **get a divorce** divorciarse
dizziness el mareo
dizzy mareado
do hacer (19)
doctor el doctor, la doctora; el médico, la médica
dollar el dólar
door la puerta
dot: on the dot en punto
doubt n la duda; v dudar
doubtful dudoso
downtown el centro
dozen la docena
drama el drama

dream *n* el sueño **dream (about)** soñar (ue/8) (con)

dress *n* el vestido; **dress as** vestirse de; **get dressed** vestirse (i,i/24)

dresser la cómoda

drink *n* la bebida; *v* beber, tomar

drive conducir (zc,j/5), manejar

drop caer (4)

dry seco

due to debido a

during durante

E

each cada; **each other** nos, os, se; el uno (la una, etc.) al otro (a la otra, etc.)

ear *(outer)* la oreja

earlier anterior, previo

early temprano

earn ganar

earthquake el terremoto

easily fácilmente

east el este

Easter la(s) Pascua(s)

easy fácil

eat comer; **eat lunch** almorzar (ue,c/8,14)

economic económico

Ecuadorian ecuatoriano

edition la edición

effort el esfuerzo

egg el huevo

eighth octavo

either . . . or o... o

elected elegido

election la elección

elegant elegante

elephant el elefante

embarrassed avergonzado; **be (get) embarrassed** avergonzarse (üe,c/2)

embrace abrazar (c/14)

emotion la emoción

empire el imperio

employee el empleado, la empleada

employment el empleo; **employment agency** la agencia de trabajo

enchilada la enchilada

end *v* acabar, terminar; **in the end** al fin y al cabo, al final

enemy el enemigo, la enemiga

engagement el noviazgo

engineer el ingeniero, la ingeniera

engineering la ingeniería

English *(language)* el inglés; *adj* inglés

enjoy (oneself) divertirse (ie,i/35); **Enjoy your meal!** ¡Buen provecho!

enlarge agrandar

enough bastante

ensemble el conjunto

enter entrar (en)

enthusiast el aficionado, la aficionada

entire: (an) entire todo

entrance, entryway la entrada

Epiphany el Día de (los) Reyes

epoch la época

escape escaparse

especially especialmente

essay el ensayo

essayist el, la ensayista

establish establecer (zc/6)

estate la hacienda

eternal eterno

evening *(before sunset)* la tarde; *(after sunset)* la noche; **in the evening** por la tarde (noche)

event el acontecimiento

every cada

everybody todo el mundo

everywhere por todas partes

evil el mal

exactly exacto, exactamente

exam el examen

examine revisar, examinar

example el ejemplo; el modelo; **for example** por ejemplo

excellent excelente

except excepto

exchange cambiar

exciting emocionante

excuse oneself disculparse; **Excuse me.** *(for past action)* Perdón., Discúlpeme.; *(for future action)* Con permiso.

exercise *n* el ejercicio; *v* hacer ejercicios

exhibit, exhibition la exposición

exile el exilado

exit la salida

expensive caro

experience la experiencia

expert el experto, la experta

explain explicar (qu/3)

explorer el explorador, la exploradora

extinguish apagar (gu/23)

extra extra

extremely extremadamente

eye el ojo

F

fabulous fabuloso

face la cara

fact el hecho

fairly bastante

faithful fiel

fall *n* el otoño; *v* caer (4); **fall asleep** dormirse (ue,u/13); **fall in love (with)** enamorarse (de)

false falso

family la familia

famous famoso

fan el aficionado, la aficionada

fantastic fantástico

far (from) lejos (de)

farewell la despedida

fascinating fascinante

father el padre

father-in-law el suegro

fault la culpa

favor el favor

favorite favorito

fear *v* temer

February febrero

feel sentir (ie,i/35); *(physical or mental state)* sentirse; **feel like (doing something)** tener ganas (de + *inf*)

feeling el sentimiento

fever la fiebre; **have a fever** tener fiebre

few pocos; **a few** unos, unas

fiancé el prometido

fiancée la prometida

field *(sports)* la cancha

fifth quinto

fight pelear

film la película

final final; último

finally por fin, finalmente

find hallar, encontrar (ue/8); **find out (about)** enterarse (de); saber (32) *pret*

finger el dedo

fingernail la uña

finish acabar; terminar

fire el incendio; el fuego

fire fighter el bombero, la bombera

fireworks los fuegos artificiales

first primero *(shortened form* primer*)*

fish *n* el pescado; *v* pescar (qu/3)

fisherman el pescador, la pescadora

fishing la pesca

fixed fijo

flag la bandera

floor el piso

flourish florecer (zc/6)

flower la flor

flu la gripe

flute la flauta

fog la niebla

follow seguir (i,g/34)

follower el seguidor, la seguidora

food la comida

foot el pie; **on foot** a pie

football el fútbol americano; **football player** el, la futbolista

for para; por; **for example** por ejemplo; **something had**

been -ing for . . . hacía... que + *imp*; **something has been -ing for . . .** hace... que + *pres*

forbid prohibir (í/29)

force la fuerza

foreign extranjero

forget olvidar

forgive disculpar, perdonar

fork el tenedor

former antiguo; primero, anterior

fortress la fortaleza

fortune la fortuna

fourth cuarto

freezer el congelador

French *(language)* el francés; *adj* francés

fresh fresco

Friday el viernes

friend el amigo, la amiga

frighten asustar

frightened asustado; **be (get) frightened** asustarse

from de; **from** *(a certain time)* desde; **from the** del *(contraction of* de + el*)*; **from the very beginning** desde un principio

front: in front of enfrente de; delante de

fruit la fruta

frustrated frustrado; **be (get) frustrated** frustrarse

fulfill cumplir

function la función

funny divertido

furious furioso

furniture los muebles; **piece of furniture** el mueble

future el futuro

G

Galician *(language)* el gallego; *adj* gallego

gallery la galería

game el juego; *(sports)* el partido; **soccer game** el partido de fútbol

garage el garaje

garbage la basura

garden *(flower)* el jardín; *(vegetable)* la huerta

gardener el jardinero, la jardinera

gasoline la gasolina

generally generalmente

generous generoso

gentleman el señor

German *(language)* el alemán; *adj* alemán

Gesundheit! ¡Salud!

get conseguir (i,g/34), sacar (qu/3); **get along (well)** llevarse (bien); **get into** subir (a); **get off** bajar (de); **get together** reunirse; **get up** levantarse; **get used to** acostumbrarse

gift el regalo

girl la chica, la muchacha, la niña

girlfriend la novia

give dar (11)

glass *(drinking glass)* el vaso; *(wineglass)* la copa

glasses las gafas, los lentes, los anteojos

gloves los guantes

go ir (20); **go away** irse (20); **go back** regresar, volver (ue/43); **go camping** ir de campamento; **go crazy** volverse loco; **go down** bajar; **go for a stroll** dar un paseo; **go on vacation** ir de vacaciones; **go out** salir (33); **go shopping** ir de compras; **go to bed** acostarse (ue/8); **go up** *(increase)* aumentar; **go up** *(climb)* subir; **go with** *(match)* hacer juego con

God (el) Dios; **Thank God.** Gracias a Dios.

gold el oro

golf el golf

good *adj.* bueno *(shortened form* buen*)*; *n* el bien **Good!** ¡Qué bien!; **Good afternoon.** *(until sunset)* Buenas tardes.;

Good appetite! ¡Buen provecho!; **Good-bye.** Adiós. **Good grief!** ¡Caramba!; **Good morning.** Buenos días.; **Good night.** Buenas noches.

govern gobernar (ie/25)

government el gobierno

graduation la graduación

grain el cereal

granddaughter la nieta

grandfather el abuelo

grandmother la abuela

grandson el nieto

grape la uva

grasp prender

grateful agradecido

gray gris

great (*big*) grande; (*wonderful*) estupendo; **the great majority** la gran mayoría

Greek (*language*) el griego; *adj* griego

green verde

greet (each other) saludar(se)

greeting el saludo

guard cuidar

guerrilla fighter el guerrillero, la guerrillera

guide: tourist guide (*book*) la guía turística; (*person*) el, la guía de turismo

guitar la guitarra

gypsy el gitano, la gitana

H

hair el pelo; el cabello

half medio

ham el jamón

hamburger la hamburguesa

hand la mano; **on the other hand** por otra parte

handbag el bolso

happen ocurrir, pasar, suceder

happening el acontecimiento

happily alegremente

happiness la felicidad; la alegría

happy alegre, feliz, contento; **be (get) happy** alegrarse

harbor el puerto

hardworking trabajador

harp el arpa *f*

hat el sombrero

have tener (37); **have + *pp*** haber (18); **+ *pp*; have a cold** tener catarro, tener un resfrío; **have a good time** divertirse (ie,i/35); **have an opinion of** pensar de; **have just (done something)** acabar de + *inf*

he él

head *n* la cabeza; *v* encabezar (c/14)

headache el dolor de cabeza; **have a headache** tener dolor de cabeza

health la salud

hear oír (22), entender (ie/26)

heart el corazón

heaven el paraíso

Hello. Hola.

help *n* la ayuda; *v* ayudar

her *dir obj* la; *indir obj* le, se; *obj of prep* ella; *poss adj* su, suyo

here aquí, acá

heritage la herencia

hers *poss pron* el suyo, la suya, los suyos, las suyas

herself *refl* se

Hi. Hola.

high alto

him *dir obj* lo; *indir obj* le, se; *obj of prep* él

himself *refl* se

hip la cadera

his *poss adj* su, suyo; *poss pron* el suyo, la suya, los suyos, las suyas

Hispanic hispano

history la historia

hitchhike hacer autostop

hitchhiking el autostop

holiday el día feriado, la fiesta

home la casa

homeless sin casa

honeymoon la luna de miel

honor la honra

hope *n* la esperanza; *v* esperar; **I (we, let's) hope (that)** ojalá (que)

hopefully ojalá (que)

horrible horrible

hospital el hospital

hot (*temperature*) caliente; (*food*) picante; **be hot** (*weather*) hacer calor; (*people*) tener calor

hotel el hotel; **hotel manager** el hotelero, la hotelera

hour la hora; **half an hour** media hora

house la casa

housewife el ama de casa *f*

how cómo; **how?** ¿cómo?; **how much?, how many?** ¿cuánto (-a, -os, -as)?; **How are things?** ¿Qué tal?

however sin embargo

hug *n* el abrazo; *v* abrazar (c/14)

hundred cien(to)

hunger el hambre; **be hungry** tener hambre

hurry: be in a hurry tener prisa

hurt *v* doler (ue/43); **My foot hurts.** Me duele el pie.

husband el esposo

I

I yo

Iberian *adj* ibero

ice cream el helado

idea la idea

idealist idealista

if si

illness la enfermedad

imagination la imaginación

imagine imaginar

immediately inmediatamente

immigrant el, la inmigrante

impolite descortés

importance la importancia

important importante; **be important (to someone)** importar (a alguien)
imported importado
impossible imposible
impressive impresionante
improve mejorar
in en; **in case** en caso (de) que; **in front of** delante de; **in order to** para; **in the afternoon** por la tarde; **in the evening (night)** por la noche; **in the morning** por la mañana
Inca el, la inca
increase *n* el aumento; *v* aumentar
independence la independencia
Indian *adj* indígena, indio
indigenous indígena, nativo
inexpensive barato
inflation la inflación
information la información
inhabitant el, la habitante
injection la inyección
inside dentro (de)
insist (on) insistir (en)
insomnia el insomnio
instructor el instructor, la instructora
intelligent inteligente
intend (to do something) pensar (+ *inf*)
interest *v* interesar
interesting interesante
introduce presentar
introduction la presentación
invader el invasor, la invasora
inventory el inventario
invite invitar
Irish *adj* irlandés; **Irishman** el irlandés; **Irishwoman** la irlandesa
island la isla
isolate aislar (í/16)
it *dir obj* lo, la; *indir obj* le, se; *obj of prep* él, ella, ello
Italian (*language*) el italiano; *adj* italiano
its *poss adj* su, suyo; *poss pron* el suyo

itself *refl* se

J

jacket la chaqueta, el saco
jai alai el jai alai
January enero
jealous celoso; **be jealous (of)** tener celos (de)
jeans los jeans
Jewish judío
job el trabajo, el empleo, el puesto
jogging *n* el correr
joke *n* el chiste
juice el jugo
July julio
June junio
just: have just (done something) acabar de + *inf*

K

key la llave
kilogram el kilo
kind *adj* amable
king el rey
kingdom el reino
kiss *n* el beso; *v* besar
kitchen la cocina
knee la rodilla
knife el cuchillo
know (*facts, information*) saber (32); (*person, place, subject matter*) conocer (zc/6); **know how** (*to do something*) saber (+ *inf*); **well known** muy conocido
knowledge el conocimiento

L

Labor Day el Día de los Trabajadores
laboratory el laboratorio
lack *n* la falta; **to be lacking** faltar
lady la dama, la señora

lake el lago
lamp la lámpara
land la tierra
language la lengua, el idioma
large grande (*shortened form* gran)
last *adj* pasado; *v* durar; **last night** anoche; **last week** la semana pasada; **last year** el año pasado
late tarde
later más tarde; después; **See you later.** Hasta luego.
latest último
laugh *v* reír, reírse (31)
laughter la risa
law la ley
lawyer el abogado, la abogada
lead to llevar a
leader el, la líder; **rebel leader** la cabecilla
learn aprender; saber (32) *pret*
leave *v* salir (33); irse (20); **leave behind** dejar; **leave-taking** la despedida
left *adj* izquierdo; **on, to the left** a la izquierda
leg la pierna
legacy la herencia
legume la legumbre
lend prestar
less menos; **less . . . than** menos... que
lesson la lección
let dejar, permitir
letter (*note*) la carta; (*alphabet*) la letra
lettuce la lechuga
library la biblioteca
lie *v* mentir (ie,i/35)
life la vida
light *adj* claro; *n* la luz; *v* prender
like *prep* como; *v* querer (30), gustar; **I like . . .** Me gusta...
likewise igualmente
link el vínculo
liquid el líquido
liquidation la liquidación
listen (to) escuchar
literature la literatura

little *adj* pequeño; poco; *adv* poco; **a little** un poco; **little by little** poco a poco
live vivir
living room la sala (de estar)
local local
locate situar (ú/9)
long largo
look (at) mirar; **look for** buscar (qu/3)
lose perder (ie/26)
lost perdido
lot: a lot *adv* mucho; **a lot of** *adj* mucho
love *n* el amor; *v* querer (30); **I love . . .** *(thing)* Me encanta(n)...
lover el, la amante
lucky: be lucky tener suerte
luggage el equipaje
lunch el almuerzo; **eat lunch** almorzar (ue,c/8,14)
lyrics la letra

M

magazine la revista
main principal
majority la mayoría; la mayor parte
make hacer (19); **made of** de; **make (someone) angry, ashamed, hungry, laugh, thirsty, sleepy** darle rabia, vergüenza, hambre, risa, sed, sueño (a alguien);
mamma la mamá
man el hombre, el señor
many muchos; **as, so many** tantos; **how many?** ¿cuántos?; **too many** demasiados
map el mapa
marathon el maratón
March marzo
mark down *(price)* rebajar; **marked down** rebajado
market el mercado
marriage el casamiento

marriage annulment la anulación matrimonial
married casado; **get married (to)** casarse (con)
marvelous maravilloso
mask la máscara
masterpiece la obra maestra
match *n (sports)* el partido; *v* hacer juego con
mathematics las matemáticas
matrimony el matrimonio
matter *v* importar
May mayo
maybe tal vez, quizás
me *dir, indir obj* me; *obj of prep* mí; **with me** conmigo
meal la comida
meat la carne
medication el medicamento
medicine la medicina
meet conocer (zc/6); **meet up with** encontrarse con
meeting la reunión
Mexican *adj* mexicano
middle: in the middle of the century a mediados de(l) siglo
midnight la medianoche
mile la milla
military *adj* militar; **the military** los militares
milk la leche
million el millón
millionaire el millonario, la millonaria
mine *poss pron* el mío, la mía, los míos, las mías
mineral *adj* mineral; **mineral water** el agua mineral
minority la minoría
minstrel el juglar
Miss la señorita
mix *v* mezclar(se)
mixed: of mixed ancestry mestizo
mixture la mezcla
model el modelo; *(person)* el, la modelo
modern moderno
mom la mamá

moment el momento
Monday el lunes
money el dinero
monotonous monótono
month el mes
monument el monumento
more más; **more . . . than** más... que; **more than** más de (+ *number*); **more and more** cada vez más
morning la mañana; **in the morning** por la mañana
Moslem el musulmán, la musulmana
mosque la mezquita
mother la madre; **Mother's Day** el Día de la Madre
mother-in-law la suegra
mountain la montaña
mouth la boca
move *(change residence)* mudarse
movie la película; **movies** el cine; **movie theater** el cine
Mr. el señor
Mr. and Mrs. los señores
Mrs. la señora
much *adj, adv* mucho
mural el mural
museum el museo
music la música
musician el, la músico
must (+ *inf*) deber (+ *inf*), hay que (+ *inf*)
my *poss adj* mi, mío
myself *refl* me
mysterious misterioso

N

name *n* el nombre; *v* nombrar; **be named** llamarse
nap la siesta
napkin la servilleta
nation la nación; el país
nationality la nacionalidad
native indígena, nativo
natural sciences las ciencias naturales

naturally naturalmente;
   Naturally. Claro.,
   Naturalmente.
nausea la náusea; los mareos
near (to) nearby cerca (de)
necessary necesario, preciso; **it
   is necessary (to do
   something)** es necesario, es
   preciso, hay que (+ *inf*)
neck el cuello
need necesitar
needy necesitado
neighbor el vecino, la vecina
neighborhood el barrio
neither tampoco; **neither (of
   them)** ningún, ninguno;
   neither . . . nor ni... ni
nephew el sobrino
nervous nervioso
net la red
never jamás, nunca
nevertheless sin embargo
new nuevo; **New Year's Day** el
   Año Nuevo
newlywed el recién casado, la
   recién casada
news las noticias; **news
   program** el noticiero; **piece
   of news** la noticia
newspaper el periódico
next próximo; **next (to)** al lado
   (de); **next week (month)** la
   semana (el mes) que viene,
   la semana (el mes)
   próxima(-o)
nice agradable, amable,
   simpático
niece la sobrina
night la noche; **Night of the
   Cry** (*Mexico*) la Noche del
   Grito
ninth noveno
no no; ningún, ninguno; **no
   longer** ya no, no... más; **no
   one** nadie
none ningún, ninguno
noon el mediodía
north el norte; **North
   American** *adj*
   norteamericano

northeast el nordeste, el
   noreste
nose la nariz
not no; **not any** ningún,
   ninguno; **not anyone** nadie;
   not either tampoco; **not
   even** ni siquiera; **not ever**
   jamás, nunca
notebook el cuaderno
nothing nada
novel la novela
November noviembre
now ahora
nowadays hoy día
number el número
nurse el enfermero, la
   enfermera
nut la nuez

O

obtain conseguir (i,g/34)
occur ocurrir, pasar, suceder
ocean el océano
October octubre
of de; **of the** del (*contraction of*
   de + el)
offend ofender; **be (get)
   offended** ofenderse
offer ofrecer (zc/6); **special
   offer** la oferta; la ganga
office la oficina
oil el petróleo; el aceite
OK bien; bueno; de acuerdo
old viejo, antiguo
older mayor
oldest mayor; el, la mayor
on en; sobre; **on** (+ *pres p*) al
   (+ *inf*)
one un, una; (*impersonal pron*)
   se; **one another** nos, se;
   one's su(s)
only *adv* sólo, solamente; **the
   only one** el único
open abrir
opera la ópera
opportunity la oportunidad
oppose oponerse (28) (a)
opposite enfrente de
optimistic optimista

or o, (*before* o- *or* ho-) u
orange *n* la naranja; *adj*
   anaranjado
orchestra la orquesta
order *n* el orden; *v* mandar,
   pedir (i,i/24)
organization la organización
ornament el adorno
other otro
ought to (do something) deber
   (+ *inf*)
our *poss adj* nuestro
ours el nuestro, la nuestra, los
   nuestros, las nuestras
ourselves *refl* nos
outfit el traje
oven el horno
over sobre
overcoat el abrigo
overpopulation la
   superpoblación
overthrow derrocar (qu/3)
owe deber
own *adj* propio

P

pack one's suitcase hacer la
   maleta
page la página
pain el dolor
paint *n* la pintura; *v* pintar
painter el pintor, la pintora
painting la pintura, el cuadro
pajama el pijama
pants los pantalones
papa el papá
paper el papel
parade el desfile
paradise el paraíso
Pardon me. Perdón.,
   Perdóneme.
parents los padres
park el parque; **amusement
   park** el parque de
   diversiones
part la parte; **the** (*adj*) **part** lo
   (+ *adj*)
party la fiesta; (*political*) el
   partido

pass (*time*) pasar
passenger el pasajero, la pasajera
passport el pasaporte
past el pasado
pastime el pasatiempo, la diversión
pastry el pastel
patience la paciencia
patron el patrón, la patrona
pay pagar (gu/23)
peace; peace agreement el acuerdo de paz; **peace treaty** el tratado de paz
pen la pluma; **ballpoint pen** la birome, el bolígrafo
pencil el lápiz
peninsula la península
people la gente, el pueblo; *impersonal pron* se
pepper (*spice*) la pimienta; (*hot*) el chile
per por
perfectly perfectamente
performance la función
perhaps quizá(s), tal vez
period (*time*) la época; el período
permit permitir
persecution la persecución
person la persona
Peruvian peruano
pessimistic pesimista
petroleum el petróleo
pharmacy la farmacia
philosophy la filosofía
Phoenician el fenicio, la fenicia
photo, photograph la foto
physics la física
pianist el, la pianista
piano el piano
pill la píldora
pineapple la piña
place *n* el lugar, el sitio; *v* poner (28)
plan *n* el plan; *v* planear; **plan (to do something)** pensar (+ *inf*)
plantain el plátano
plate el plato
plateau la meseta

platinum el platino
play *n* el drama, la obra de teatro; *v* (*game, sport*)jugar (ue/21); (*musical instrument*) tocar (qu/3); **play a role** hacer un papel
player el jugador, la jugadora
plaza la plaza
pleasant agradable, amable
please por favor; **be pleasing** gustar
pleasure el placer; **The pleasure is mine.** El gusto es mío.
plus más
P.M. (*noon to sunset*) de la tarde; (*after sunset*) de la noche
poem el poema
poet el, la poeta
poetry la poesía
point el punto
police force la policía
police officer el policía, la mujer policía
polite cortés
political science las ciencias políticas
politician el, la político
pollution la contaminación
poncho el poncho
pool (*swimming*) la piscina
poor pobre; **Poor thing!** ¡Pobrecito!
Pope el Papa
popular popular
population la población
pork el cerdo; **pork chop** la chuleta de cerdo
port el puerto
portrait el retrato
position (*job*) el puesto
possession: in the possession of en manos de
possible posible
post office la oficina de correos, el correo
potato la papa
pottery la alfarería, la cerámica; **potter shop** la alfarería
poverty la pobreza
power la fuerza; el poder

powerful poderoso
practical práctico
practice practicar (qu/3)
predict predecir (12)
prefer preferir (ie,i/35)
prescription la receta
present actual; **at present** actualmente, en la actualidad
preserve conservar
president el presidente, la presidenta
press la prensa
pretty bonito, lindo
price el precio, el valor
priest el sacerdote, el cura *m*
principal principal
probable probable
probably probablemente, seguramente
problem el problema
procession la procesión
produce producir (zc, j/5)
profession la profesión
professor el profesor, la profesora
program *n* el programa; *v* programar
programmer (*computer*) el programador, la programadora
progress progresar
prohibit prohibir (í/29)
promise *n* la promesa; *v* prometer
prosperous próspero
protagonist el, la protagonista; el personaje principal
protest protestar
Protestant protestante
proud orgulloso
provided that con tal (de) que
psychology la psicología
public *adj* público; *n* el público
Puerto Rican *adj* puertorriqueño
punctuality la puntualidad
pure puro
purple violeta
purse el bolso
push empujar

put poner (28); **put on** ponerse
   (28)
pyramid la pirámide

Q

quality la calidad
queen la reina
question la pregunta
quite bastante; muy

R

race la raza
racket la raqueta
radio la radio
rage la rabia
railway el ferrocarril
rain n la lluvia; v llover (ue/43)
raincoat el impermeable
raise n (salary) el aumento
rather adv más bien; bastante
read leer (y/10)
ready: **I'm ready.** Estoy
   listo(-a).
realism el realismo
realistic realista
realized: **be realized** realizarse
   (c/14)
really realmente;
   verdaderamente; **Really?** ¿De
   veras?, ¿En serio?
reasonable razonable
receive recibir
recently recientemente,
   últimamente
reception desk la recepción
recognize reconocer (zc/6)
recommend recomendar (ie/25)
reconquest la reconquista
record n (music) el disco
red rojo; (wine) tinto; **Red
   Cross** la Cruz Roja
reduce rebajar; **reduced**
   rebajado
reelect reelegir (i,i, j/24,15)
reflect reflejar
refreshment el refresco
refrigerator el refrigerador, la
   nevera, la heladera

regarding en cuanto a; a
   propósito de
regime el régimen
region la región
regulations las regulaciones
relative el pariente
religious religioso
remain permanecer (zc/6),
   quedarse
remember acordarse (ue/8)
   (de), recordar (ue/8)
remembrance el recuerdo
renovate renovar (ue/8)
rent n el alquiler; v alquilar
repair reparar, arreglar
repeat repetir (i,i/24)
report el reportaje
reporter el reportero, la
   reportera
Republican republicano
reservation la reservación
respond responder
responsible responsable
rest v descansar
restaurant el restaurante
result el resultado; **As a
   result. . .** Como resultado...
return regresar, volver (ue/43);
   (bring back) devolver (ue/43)
revenge la venganza
rice el arroz
rich rico
ride n el paseo; **ride a bicycle**
   andar en bicicleta
right adj derecho; correcto; n el
   derecho; **be right** tener
   razón; **human rights** los
   derechos humanos; **on, to
   the right** a la derecha;
   Right? ¿No?, ¿Verdad?
ring n el anillo
ringleader el, la cabecilla
rise subir
river el río
road el camino
role el papel; **play a role** hacer
   un papel
romantic romántico
room el cuarto
roommate el compañero, la
   compañera de cuarto

round-trip de ida y vuelta
routine la rutina
rug la alfombra
ruin n la ruina
run correr; (as a watch, car)
   andar (1); **run into**
   encontrarse con; **run out**
   acabar
runner el corredor, la corredora
running n el correr

S

sad triste; **become sad**
   entristecerse (zc/6)
saint el santo, la santa
salad la ensalada
salary el sueldo
sale la oferta; la venta; **for sale**
   en venta; **on sale** en oferta,
   en liquidación, rebajado
salesclerk el, la dependiente
salesperson el vendedor, la
   vendedora
salt la sal
same mismo
sandals las sandalias
sandwich el sandwich
Saturday el sábado
saucer el platillo
save (time, money) ahorrar
say decir (12)
scare asustar
scared asustado; **be (get)
   scared** asustarse
scarf el pañuelo
scene la escena
schedule n el horario
school la escuela
science la ciencia; **computer
   science** las ciencias de
   computación; **natural
   science** las ciencias
   naturales; **political science**
   las ciencias políticas; **social
   science** las ciencias sociales
Scot el escocés, la escocesa
sculptor el escultor, la
   escultora
sculpture la escultura

sea el mar
season la estación
second segundo
secretary el secretario, la secretaria
see ver (42)
seem parecer (zc/6)
sell vender
semester el semestre
senator el senador, la senadora
send enviar (í/16), mandar
sensitive sensible
separate separar
separation: trial separation la separación provisional
September septiembre, setiembre
serious grave
serve servir (i,i/24)
seventh séptimo
several varios
shame la vergüenza; **What a shame!** ¡Qué lástima!; ¡Qué vergüenza!
she ella
ship el barco
shirt la camisa
shoe el zapato; **shoe store** la zapatería
shop n la tienda
shopping compras; **to go shopping** ir de compras
short bajo; **short story** el cuento
shot la inyección
should (+ inf) deber (+ inf)
shoulder el hombro
shout v gritar
show n la función; v enseñar, mostrar (ue/8)
shower la ducha
sick enfermo; **get sick** enfermarse
sickness la enfermedad; **motion sickness** los mareos
siesta la siesta
silk la seda
similar parecido, similar
since desde
sing cantar
singer el, la cantante

single soltero
sink el lavamanos
Sir Señor
sister la hermana
sister-in-law la cuñada
sit (down) sentarse (ie/25)
site el sitio
situate situar (ú/9)
sixth sexto
skate v patinar
skater el patinador, la patinadora
skating n el patinaje
ski n el esquí; v esquiar (í/16)
skier el esquiador, la esquiadora
skiing n el esquí
skin la piel
skirt la falda, (South America) la pollera
sleep dormir (ue,u/13); **be sleepy** tener sueño
slim delgado
slip la combinación
slower: Slower, please. Más despacio, por favor.
small pequeño
smaller menor, más pequeño
smallest menor; el, la más pequeño(-a)
smoke v fumar
snow n la nieve; v nevar (ie/25)
so adv tan; así que; **So. . .** Total que...; **so much** tanto(-a, -os, -as); **so-so** así así, más o menos; **so that** para que
soccer el fútbol
sociable sociable
social science las ciencias sociales
socialist socialista
sociology la sociología
socks los calcetines
soda el refresco
sofa el sofá
soft drink el refresco
solve resolver (ue/43)
some algún, alguno(-a, -os, -as); unos(-as)
someone alguien

something algo
son el hijo
song la canción
soon pronto
sorry: be sorry sentir (ie,i/35); **I'm sorry.** Discúlpeme., Perdón.; **I'm (very) sorry.** Lo siento (mucho).
soul el alma f
soup la sopa
south el sur
southwest el suroeste
souvenir el recuerdo
Spanish (language) el español; **Spanish-speaking** de habla hispana
speak hablar
special especial
specially especialmente
spectator el espectador, la espectadora
spend gastar; (time) pasar
spicy picante
spite: in spite of a pesar de
spoon la cuchara
sport el deporte
spot el sitio
spring la primavera
square la plaza
stadium el estadio
start empezar (ie,c/25,14)
startled asustado
state el estado
station la estación
stay quedarse
steak el bistec
still aún, todavía
stockings las medias
stomach el estómago; **have a stomachache** tener dolor de estómago
stop dejar de; parar
store la tienda; **furniture store** la mueblería; **grocery store** el almacén; **shoe store** la zapatería
story la historia; **short story** el cuento
stove la estufa
street la calle

strike *n* la huelga
string la cuerda
stroll *n* el paseo
strong fuerte
struggle *n* la lucha; *v* luchar
student el, la estudiante
study *n* el estudio; *v* estudiar
stuffed relleno
style el estilo
subject el tema
subway el metro
successful: be successful tener éxito
such tal
suffer sufrir
sugar el azúcar
suit el traje
suitcase la maleta
summary: in summary en resumen
summer el verano
sun el sol
sunbathe tomar sol
Sunday el domingo
sunglasses las gafas de sol
sunny: be sunny hacer sol
supper la cena
support *n* el apoyo; *v* apoyar
sure seguro; **Sure!** ¡Cómo no!; **Sure.** Claro., Por supuesto.
Surely Seguramente (+ *indic*)
surname el apellido
surprise *n* la sorpresa; *v* sorprender
surrender entregarse (gu/23)
survive sobrevivir
sustain oneself mantenerse (37)
sweater el suéter
sweets los dulces
swim nadar
swimmer el nadador, la nadadora
swimming *n* la natación; **swimming pool** la piscina
symptom el síntoma
synagogue la sinagoga
syrup: (cough) syrup el jarabe (de tos)
system el sistema

T

table la mesa; **end table** la mesita de luz
tablet la pastilla
take tomar; *(a period of time)* llevar; *(along)* llevar; **take a course** seguir un curso; **take a trip** hacer un viaje; **take a walk** pasear; **take back** devolver (ue/43); **take into account** tener en cuenta; **take off** *(clothing)* quitarse; **take out** sacar (qu/3); **take pictures** sacar fotos; **take place** tener lugar
tale el cuento
talk hablar
tall alto
tango el tango
tapestry el tapiz
tea el té
teach enseñar
team el equipo
teeth los dientes
telephone el teléfono
television la televisión; **television set** el televisor
tell decir (12); *(a story)* contar (ue/8)
tennis el tenis; **tennis shoes** los zapatos de tenis
tension la tensión
tenth décimo
terrible terrible, pésimo
territory el territorio
test la prueba, el examen
than que
thank agradecer (zc/6), dar(le) las gracias; **Thank God.** Gracias a Dios.
thankful agradecido
Thanks. Gracias.
Thanksgiving el Día de Acción de Gracias *(U.S.)*
that *adj* ese, esa; aquel, aquella; *conj* que; *rel pron* que **that (one)** *pron* ése, ésa; eso; aquél, aquélla; aquello; **that of** el, la de; **that which** lo que

the el, la, los, las; **the seventies** los (años) 70
theater el teatro
theft el robo
their *poss adj* su; suyo
theirs *poss pron* el suyo, la suya, los suyos, las suyas
them *dir obj* los, las; *indir obj* les, se; *obj of prep* ellos, ellas
theme el tema
themselves *refl* se
then entonces, luego; después; **Then . . .** Después..., Entonces...
there allí, allá; **there is, there are** hay
therefore por lo tanto
thermometer el termómetro
these *adj* estos(-as); *pron* éstos(-as)
they ellos, ellas; *impersonal pron* se
thing la cosa; **the (adj) thing** lo (+ *adj*)
think pensar (ie/25); *(believe)* creer (y/10); **think about** pensar en; **think of** pensar de; **I (don't) think so.** Pienso que sí (no).; **I think that . . .** Pienso que (+ *indic*)...
third tercer, tercero
thirsty: be thirsty tener sed
this *adj* este, esta; **this (one)** *pron* éste, ésta; esto
those *adj* esos, esas, aquellos, aquellas; *pron* ésos, ésas, aquéllos, aquéllas
thousand mil
threaten amenazar (c/14)
throat la garganta
through por, a través de
throw out echar
thumb el pulgar
Thursday el jueves
thus así
ticket *(for an event)* el boleto, la entrada; *(for transportation)* el boleto, el pasaje
tie la corbata

time (*abstract*) el tiempo; (*specific*) la hora, la vez; **from time to time** de vez en cuando
timetable el horario
tired cansado; **be (get) tired** cansarse
to a; (*in order to*) para; **to the** al (*contraction of* a + el)
toast *v* brindar
toaster el tostador
today hoy
toe el dedo del pie
together juntos
toilet el inodoro; (*bathroom*) el baño
tolerate tolerar
tomato el tomate
tomorrow mañana
too también; **too much** demasiado
totally totalmente
touch tocar (qu/3)
tourist el, la turista
toward hacia
town el pueblo
track la pista
trade el oficio
traditional tradicional
traffic el tráfico
train el tren
tranquil tranquilo
translate traducir (zc,j/5)
translation la traducción
trash la basura
travel *v* viajar; **travel agency** la agencia de viajes; **travel agent** el, la agente de viajes
traveler el viajero, la viajera
tree el árbol
trip el viaje
tropical tropical
true verdadero; **True?** ¿Verdad?, ¿No?
truly verdaderamente
truth la verdad
try (to) tratar (de)
Tuesday el martes
turkey el pavo
turn *v* doblar; **turn into** hacerse (19); **turn off** apagar
(gu/23); **turn on** prender; **turn out all right** arreglarse
typical típico

U

umbrella el paraguas (*pl* los paraguas)
uncle el tío
under debajo (de)
underpants los calzoncillos
underprivileged necesitado
undershirt la camiseta, la camisilla
understand comprender, entender (ie/26)
underwear la ropa interior
undocumented indocumentado
unemployment el desempleo
unfortunately desgraciadamente, por desgracia, desafortunadamente
unify unificar (qu/3)
unite unir
United Nations las Naciones Unidas
United States los Estados Unidos
university *adj* universitario; *n* la universidad
unless a menos que
unlikely poco probable, improbable
unsociable insociable
until hasta (que)
unwell mal
upon sobre; **upon** (+ *pres p*) al (+ *inf*)
urban urbano
us *dir obj* nos; *indir obj* nos; *obj of prep* nosotros, nosotras
use *v* usar

V

vacation las vacaciones; **be on vacation** estar de vacaciones; **go on vacation** ir de vacaciones

value el valor
various varios
vary variar (í/16)
vegetable la legumbre; **green vegetables** las verduras
very muy
violin el violín
visit *n* la visita; *v* visitar; **be visiting** estar de visita
vitamin la vitamina
voice la voz
volleyball el vólibol

W

wait (for) esperar
waiter el mesero, el camarero
waitress la mesera, la camarera
wake up despertarse (ie/25)
walk *n* el paseo; *v* andar (1), caminar; **take a walk** dar un paseo
wall la pared
want desear, querer (30); **want to (do something)** tener ganas de (+ *inf*)
war la guerra
wash (*oneself*) lavarse
waste gastar; **waste time** perder el tiempo
watch *n* el reloj; *v* mirar, observar; **Watch out.** Cuidado.
water el agua *f*
wave *n* la ola
way el camino
we nosotros, nosotras
weapon el arma *f*
wear (*clothes*) llevar
weather el tiempo; **be good (bad) weather** (hacer buen (mal) tiempo
wedding la boda, el casamiento
Wednesday el miércoles
week la semana
weekend el fin de semana
welcome *v* dar la bienvenida; **Welcome.** Bienvenido.; **You are welcome.** De nada., No hay de qué.

well *adj, adv* bien; *interjection* pues, bueno; **get well** curarse

west el oeste

what *real pron* lo que; **what?** ¿qué?, ¿cuál?; **What a . . . !** ¡Qué...!; **What a shame.** ¡Qué lástima!; **What color is it?** ¿De qué color es?; **What (did you say)?** ¿Cómo?, *(Mexico)* ¿Mande?; **what is today** lo que es hoy; **What is your name?** ¿Cómo se (te) llama(s)?; **What's going on?** ¿Qué pasa?; **What's new?** ¿Qué hay de nuevo?; **What's the weather like?** ¿Qué tiempo hace?; **What time is it?** ¿Qué hora es?

when cuando; **when?** ¿cuándo?

where donde; **where?** ¿dónde?; **(to) where?** ¿adónde?

whether si

which *rel pron* que; **which?** ¿cuál(es)?, ¿qué?; **that which** lo que

while mientras (que)

white blanco

who *rel pron* que, quien; **who?** ¿quién (es)?

whole entero, todo

whom *rel pron* que, quien; **whom?** ¿a (de) quién?

whose *rel pron* cuyo, de quien; **whose?** ¿de quién?

why? ¿por qué?

wife la esposa

win ganar

wind el viento

windy: be windy hacer viento

window la ventana

wine el vino; **red wine** vino tinto

winter el invierno

wise: wise person el sabio, la sabia; **the Three Wise Men** los (tres) Reyes Magos

wish *v* desear, querer (30)

with con

withdraw retirarse

within dentro (de)

without *conj* sin que; *prep* sin

woman la mujer, la señora

wonderful maravilloso, estupendo

wool la lana

word la palabra

work *n* el trabajo; *(artistic)* la obra; *v* trabajar; *(an appliance or machine)* funcionar; **work as** trabajar de

workbook el cuaderno (de ejercicios)

worker el obrero, la obrera

world el mundo

worldwide mundial

worry preocuparse (por)

worse peor

worst peor; el, la peor

worsen empeorar

worth: be worth valer (39); **be worth it** valer la pena

write escribir

writer el escritor, la escritora; **short-story writer** el, la cuentista

writing la escritura; las letras

Y

Yankee yanqui

year el año; **be . . . years old** tener... años

yellow amarillo

yes sí

yesterday ayer

yet aún, todavía

you *subj* tú, vosotros(-as), usted(es) (Ud., Uds.); *obj of prep* ti, vosotros(-as), usted(es); *dir obj* te, os, lo, la, los, las; *indir obj* te, os, le, les, se; **with you** contigo, con vosotros(-as), con usted(es)

young joven; **younger** menor; **youngest** menor; el, la menor; **young man** el joven; **young woman** la joven

your *poss adj* tu, de ti, tuyo; vuestro, de vosotros; su, de usted, suyo

yours *poss pron* el tuyo, la tuya, los tuyos, las tuyas; el suyo, la suya, los suyos, las suyas; el vuestro, la vuestra, los vuestros, las vuestras

yourself, yourselves *refl* te, os, se

youth la juventud

Z

zoo el (parque) zoológico

INDEX OF GRAMMAR AND FUNCTIONS

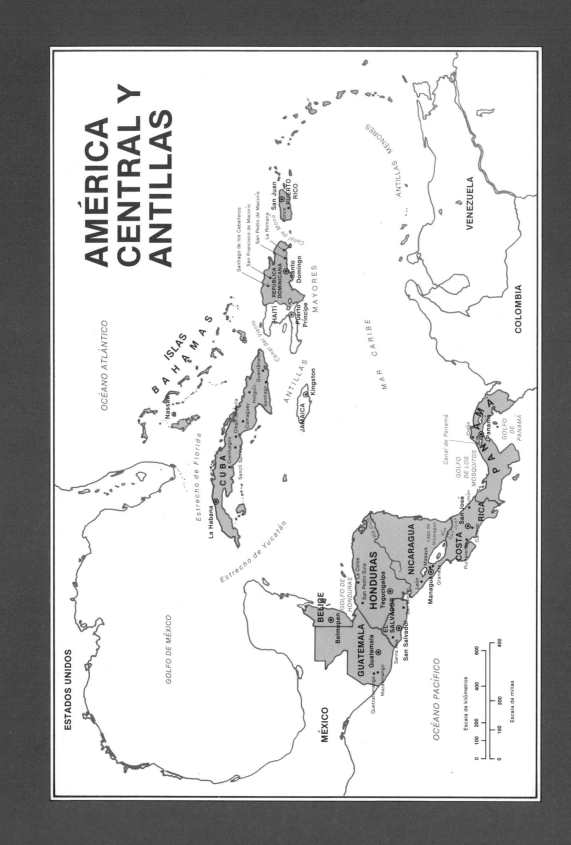

AMÉRICA CENTRAL Y ANTILLAS

ESTADOS UNIDOS

MÉXICO

GOLFO DE MÉXICO

OCÉANO ATLÁNTICO

ISLAS BAHAMAS

Nassau

Estrecho de Florida

CUBA

La Habana

Cienfuegos

Sancti Spíritus

Santiago

Camagüey

Holguín

Ciego de Ávila

Guantánamo

Canal del Viento

Estrecho de Yucatán

MAR CARIBE

ANTILLAS

JAMAICA

Kingston

HAITÍ

Puerto Príncipe

REPÚBLICA DOMINICANA

Santiago de los Caballeros

San Francisco de Macorís

San Pedro de Macorís

Santo Domingo

La Romana

Canal de la Mona

Ponce

San Juan

PUERTO RICO

MAYORES

ANTILLAS MENORES

VENEZUELA

COLOMBIA

BELICE

Belmopan

GOLFO DE HONDURAS

GUATEMALA

Guatemala

Quetzaltenango

Mazatenango

Santa Ana

EL SALVADOR

San Salvador

HONDURAS

San Pedro Sula

La Ceiba

Tegucigalpa

León

Managua

Masaya

Granada

NICARAGUA

Lago de Nicaragua

COSTA RICA

San José

Limón

Puntarenas

GOLFO DE LOS MOSQUITOS

PANAMÁ

Colón

Canal de Panamá

Panamá

GOLFO DE PANAMÁ

OCÉANO PACÍFICO

Escala de kilómetros

0   100   200   400   600

Escala de millas

0   100   200   400